Less managing. More teaching. Greater learning.

INSTRUCTORS...

Would you like your **students** to show up for class **more prepared**?
(Let's face it, class is much more fun if everyone is engaged and prepared…)

Want an **easy way to assign** homework online and track student **progress**?
(Less time grading means more time teaching…)

Want an **instant view** of student or class performance?
(No more wondering if students understand…)

Need to **collect data and generate reports** required for administration or accreditation?
(Say goodbye to manually tracking student learning outcomes…)

Want to **record and post your lectures** for students to view online?
(The more students can see, hear, and experience class resources, the better they learn…)

With **McGraw-Hill's Connect,**®

INSTRUCTORS GET:

- Simple **assignment management**, allowing you to spend more time teaching.
- **Auto-graded** assignments, quizzes, and tests.
- **Detailed visual reporting** where student and section results can be viewed and analyzed.
- Sophisticated **online testing** capability.
- A **filtering and reporting** function that allows you to easily assign and report on materials that are correlated to learning objectives and Bloom's taxonomy.
- An easy-to-use **lecture capture** tool.
- The option to **upload course documents** for student access.

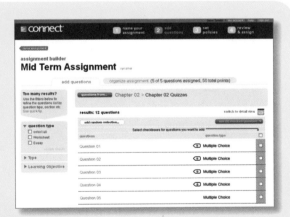

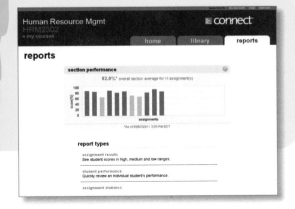

FIFTH CANADIAN EDITION

Advertising & Promotion

An Integrated Marketing Communications Perspective

GEORGE E. BELCH
San Diego State University

MICHAEL A. BELCH
San Diego State University

MICHAEL A. GUOLLA
University of Ottawa

McGraw-Hill Education | McGraw-Hill Ryerson

Dedicated to my wonderful family, Teresa, Louise, Daniel, and Nicholas.

McGraw-Hill
Ryerson

Advertising & Promotion:
An Integrated Marketing Communications Perspective
Fifth Canadian Edition

ISBN-13: 978-0-07-089130-2
ISBN-10: 0-07-089130-3

1 2 3 4 5 6 7 8 9 10   TCP   1 9 8 7 6 5 4

Printed and bound in Canada.

Care has been taken to trace ownership of copyright material contained in this text; however, the publisher will welcome any information that enables them to rectify any reference or credit for subsequent editions.

Director of Product Management: Rhondda McNabb
Group Product Manager: Leanna MacLean
Executive Marketing Manager: Joy Armitage Taylor
Product Developer: Amy Rydzanicz
Senior Product Team Associate: Stephanie Giles
Product Team Associate: Amelia Chester
Supervising Editor: Jessica Barnoski
Photo/Permissions Researcher: Tracy Leonard
Copy Editor: Kelli Howey
Proofreader: Cat Haggert
Plant Production Coordinator: Scott Morrison
Manufacturing Production Coordinator: Lena Keating
Cover Design: Mark Cruxton
Cover Images: Street scene: © imagebroker.net_SuperStock (RM); Man: mattjeacock_iStock (RF)
Interior Design: Mark Cruxton
Page Layout: Christopher Hudson
Printer: Transcontinental Printing Group

Library and Archives Canada Cataloguing in Publication

Belch, George E. (George Edward), 1951–, author
    Advertising & promotion : an integrated marketing communications perspective / George E. Belch, Michael A. Belch, Michael A. Guolla. — Fifth Canadian edition.

Includes bibliographical references and index.
ISBN 978-0-07-089130-2

    1. Advertising—Textbooks. 2. Sales promotion—Textbooks. 3. Communication in marketing—Textbooks. I. Belch, Michael A., author II. Guolla, Michael Angelo, author III. Title. IV. Title: Advertising and promotion.

HF5823.B38 2014   659.1   C2013-906008-1

Brief Contents

Contents

Preface

ADVERTISING AND PROMOTION

Advertising and other forms of promotion influence people even though they might not admit it or realize it. Organizations in both the private and public sectors frequently demonstrate that communicating effectively and efficiently with their target audiences is critical to their success. Advertising and other types of promotional messages known as marketing communication are used to sell goods and services, promote causes and individuals, and influence attitudes and behaviour to resolve societal problems. In fact, it would be impossible to find an organization that does not communicate externally to its constituents to achieve its mandate, and marketing communication usually plays a critical role in achieving objectives consistent with what an organization intends to accomplish.

In today's complex world, an organization communicating effectively—the right message to the right audience at the right time—is a critical and difficult task for promotional planners to achieve efficiently. A marketer's audiences are current customers, potential customers, and external stakeholders; all require a customized message to be accepted. The message design is informational and/or transformational and usually communicated with creativity to convince the audiences. And there are myriad media for message delivery—broadcast (TV networks, specialty TV, radio), print (newspaper, magazines), out-of-home (outdoor, transit, place-based), and Internet (websites, content publishers, social media)—that are strengthened with sales promotions, events, sponsorships, and public relations.

Moreover, the Internet's interactive characteristics strengthen (and possibly weaken) an organization's image or reputation due to consumers' brand-related online activities. Watching brand-related videos, reading brand-related information on social networking sites, commenting on brand-related blogs or uploading brand-related pictures/images potentially influences an organization's audiences. These activities are prompted directly by a brand's communication, and are also a manifestation of attitudes established over time yet initiated by motives we are only beginning to uncover as marketers. In either case, promotional planners must take an even broader and more encompassing view of marketing communication if they are to be successful in their decision making.

This text introduces students to advertising and promotion with an integrated marketing communications (IMC) perspective. IMC calls for a "big picture" approach to planning promotion programs and coordinating the communication tools described above to positively enhance a brand. To make effective promotional decisions, a promotional planner must decide how the IMC tools will work individually and collectively so that the organization can achieve its goals efficiently.

FIFTH CANADIAN EDITION ADVANTAGES

This fifth Canadian edition accomplishes the task of showing students how to plan and construct an IMC plan better than any other product on the market. Its numerous advantages include:

- **IMC Perspective**—Advertising and promotion is approached with an integrated marketing communications perspective to attain communication and behavioural objectives for multiple target audiences. The importance of specific communication objectives for each target audience and the importance of unique messages that resonate for each target audience are developed throughout. This approach shows promotional planners how to establish a unique brand position for each target audience while maintaining the overall market position of the brand.
- **Canadian Practice**—Canadian ads and uniquely Canadian examples are featured to give a comprehensive look at the most innovative marketing communications occurring in our country. The text has approximately 450 references from sources such as *Marketing Magazine, Strategy,* the *National Post, The Globe and Mail,* and others to illustrate uniquely Canadian stories so that future promotional planners can see what successful marketing communication looks like. The 50 new perspectives and vignettes are additional stories representing another 150 articles.
- **Canadian Data**—Statistical information presented in tables, charts, and figures appears throughout the text. There are about 230 figures, of which a substantial portion describe the Canadian marketing communication environment. Much of these data occur in the media chapters, the most thorough coverage of media by anyone's standards.
- **Decision Oriented**—Chapter 1 summarizes a planning framework and identifies the content of an IMC plan. This framework is followed closely throughout the text as major parts are organized and given a title that corresponds to the steps in the IMC plan. A distinction is made between the type of decisions that an advertiser makes versus the information used to formulate the decision. This approach makes it easier for students to understand the key decisions that need to be made for a successful IMC plan.

- **Internet Focus**—Internet media and tools occur throughout the text where they appear most relevant. The majority of the opening vignettes and chapter perspectives highlight the use of websites or other digital tools. A balance between Internet media and other media reinforces the importance of IMC decision making.
- **Social Media Planning**—Internet media coverage is expanded considerably in Chapter 17 with the inclusion of a major section on social media. An application of how it can be used as "owned, paid, earned media" to achieve a brand's objectives is developed and the scope of social media is shown with its numerous media classes and vehicles.
- **Current Theory**—Extensive updating of academic references from the *Journal of Advertising* and the *Journal of Advertising Research* and others occurred independently by the Canadian author over the past three editions. The text references about 350 journal articles to give students a resource for further understanding of how marketing communication works and to demonstrate that the material presented is credible.
- **Visual Balance**—The number of Figures and Exhibits grows with each edition. It now stands at just over 500 visuals, up from just over 400 in the fourth edition and up from just over 300 in the first edition. As part of this process, paragraphs have been carefully edited and less necessary text has been withdrawn or concisely summarized.

ORGANIZATION OF THIS TEXT

The fifth Canadian edition is divided into five parts. In Part 1, "Understanding Integrated Marketing Communications," we provide background in the areas of IMC planning, consumer behaviour, and communication. Chapter 1 provides an overview of advertising and promotion and an IMC planning model shows the steps in the promotional planning process. This model provides a framework for developing the IMC program and is followed throughout the text. In Chapter 2, we describe the role of ad agencies and other firms that deliver promotional services. Chapter 3 explains how managers use an understanding of buyer behaviour to develop effective communication that is directed to specific target audiences. Chapter 4 examines communication models of how consumers respond to advertising messages and other forms of marketing communication.

In Part 2, "Articulate the Message," we consider how firms develop objectives for their IMC programs and how to translate those objectives into meaningful messages. Chapter 5 stresses the importance of knowing what to expect from advertising and promotion, the different types of communication and behavioural objectives, characteristics of good objectives, and problems in setting objectives.

Chapter 6 explores various ways advertisers try to position their brands through effective communication. Chapter 7 discusses the planning and development of the creative strategy and advertising campaign. In Chapter 8 we turn our attention to ways to execute the creative strategy and some criteria for evaluating creative work. Chapter 9 discusses how to measure the effectiveness of promotional messages from an IMC program, including methods for pretesting and posttesting advertising messages and campaigns.

For Part 3, "Deliver the Message," we explore how to direct the message through media to the target audience in Chapters 10 through 13. Chapter 10 introduces the key principles of media planning and strategy, and examines how a media plan is developed for all IMC tools. We have also included into this chapter methods for determining and allocating the promotional budget across all IMC tools. Chapter 11 discusses the strengths and limitations of broadcast media, as well as issues regarding the purchase of radio and TV time and audience measurement. Chapter 12 considers the same issues for the print media (magazines and newspapers). Chapter 13 examines the role of out-of-home and support media.

In Part 4, "Strengthen the Message," we examine other promotional tools with a continued IMC emphasis. Chapter 14 covers sales promotion, including both consumer promotions and programs targeted to the trade (retailers, wholesalers, and other intermediaries). Chapter 15 reviews the role of public relations in IMC. Chapter 16 looks at direct marketing and the importance of databases that allow companies to communicate directly with target audiences through various media. Chapter 17 describes how Internet media deliver promotional messages and how social media is an important part of an IMC plan.

The text concludes with Part 5, "Advertising and Society," and contains Chapter 18, which discusses the regulatory, social, ethical, and economic issues for advertising and promotion.

CHAPTER FEATURES

The following features in each chapter enhance students' understanding of the material as well as their reading enjoyment.

Learning Objectives

Learning Objectives are provided at the beginning of each chapter to identify the major areas and points covered in the chapter and guide the learning effort. The objectives are tagged throughout the chapter and summarized at the conclusion of each chapter.

LEARNING OBJECTIVES

 Describe the importance of marketing communication within the marketing mix.

Chapter Opening Vignettes

Each chapter begins with a new vignette that describes an exciting example of the effective use of integrated marketing communications by a company or ad agency, bringing current industry issues into focus as they pertain to the chapter.

IMC Planning

Each chapter includes an IMC Planning section illustrating how chapter content relates to integrated marketing communication. It provides guidance on how a manager can use the conceptual material to make better practical decisions.

IMC and Technology Perspectives

These boxed items feature descriptions of interesting issues related to the chapter material or the practical application of integrated marketing communication. NEW IMC Technology Perspectives focus on how changes and/or advances in various areas are impacting the field of integrated marketing communication.

Learning Objectives Summaries

These synopses provide a quick review of the key topics covered and serve to illustrate how the learning objectives have been achieved.

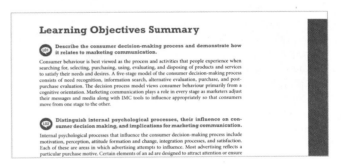

Review and Applied Questions

Questions at the end of each chapter give students an opportunity to test their understanding of the material. These questions can also serve as a basis for class discussion or assignments. NEW Applied Questions provide students with the opportunity to apply what they have learned within the chapter. Each numbered review and applied question corresponds to the numbered learning objective of the chapter.

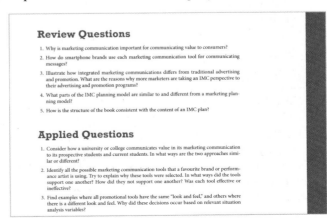

SUPPORT MATERIAL

With this support package, you and your students receive everything from the basic supplements to the latest in educational technologies. Check it out for yourself.

Mc Graw Hill Education connect®

McGraw-Hill Connect™ is a web-based assignment and assessment platform that gives students the means to better connect with their coursework, with their instructors, and with the important concepts that they will need to know for success now and in the future.

With Connect, instructors can deliver assignments, quizzes, and tests online. Instructors can edit existing questions and author entirely new problems. Track individual student performance—by question, assignment, or in relation to the class overall—with detailed grade reports. Integrate grade reports easily with Learning Management Systems (LMS).

By choosing Connect, instructors are providing their students with a powerful tool for improving academic performance and truly mastering course material. Connect allows students to practise important skills at their own pace and on their own schedule. Importantly, students' assessment results and instructors' feedback are all saved online—so students can continually review their progress and plot their course to success.

Connect also provides 24/7 online access to an eBook—an online edition of the text—to aid them in successfully completing their work, wherever and whenever they choose.

Key Features

Simple Assignment Management

With Connect, creating assignments is easier than ever, so you can spend more time teaching and less time managing.

- Create and deliver assignments easily with selectable questions and testbank material to assign online.
- Streamline lesson planning, student progress reporting, and assignment grading to make classroom management more efficient than ever.
- Go paperless with the eBook and online submission and grading of student assignments.

Smart Grading

When it comes to studying, time is precious. Connect helps students learn more efficiently by providing feedback and practice material when they need it, where they need it.

- Automatically score assignments, giving students immediate feedback on their work and side-by-side comparisons with correct answers.

- Access and review each response, manually change grades, or leave comments for students to review.
- Reinforce classroom concepts with practice tests and instant quizzes.

Instructor Library

The Connect Instructor Library is your course creation hub. It provides all the critical resources you'll need to build your course, just how you want to teach it.

- Assign eBook readings and draw from a rich collection of textbook-specific assignments.
- Access instructor resources, including ready-made PowerPoint presentations and media to use in your lectures.
- View assignments and resources created for past sections.
- Post your own resources for students to use.

eBook

Connect reinvents the textbook learning experience for the modern student. Every Connect subject area is seamlessly integrated with Connect eBooks, which are designed to keep students focused on the concepts key to their success.

- Provide students with a Connect eBook, allowing for anytime, anywhere access to the textbook.
- Pinpoint and connect key concepts in a snap using the powerful eBook search engine.
- Manage notes, highlights, and bookmarks in one place for simple, comprehensive review.

The following tools are available on Connect to support instructors:

- **Instructor's Manual.** The Instructor's Manual includes Chapter Overviews, Learning Objectives, Chapter and Lecture Outlines, Teaching Suggestions, Answers to Review and Applied Questions, and Additional Discussion Questions and Answers (not shown in text).
- **PowerPoint® Presentation and Digital Assets.** These incorporate a high-quality photo and art program, including figure slides, product shots, and advertisements.
- **Computerized Test Bank.** This test bank contains over 3,000 questions categorized by topic and level of learning (definitional, conceptual, or application). The instructor-friendly format allows easy selection of questions from any part of the text, boxed materials, and cases. The program allows you to select any of the questions, make changes if desired, or add new questions—and quickly print out a finished set customized to your course.
- **Video Case Studies.** A unique series of contemporary advertising cases is available on Connect.

SUPERIOR LEARNING SOLUTIONS AND SUPPORT

The McGraw-Hill Ryerson team is ready to help you assess and integrate any of our products, technology, and services into your course for optimal teaching and learning performance. Whether it's helping your students improve their grades or putting your entire course online, the McGraw-Hill Ryerson team is here to help you do it. Contact your Learning Solutions Consultant today to learn how to maximize all of McGraw-Hill Ryerson's resources!

For more information on the latest technology and Learning Solutions offered by McGraw-Hill Ryerson and its partners, please visit us online: **www.mcgrawhill.ca/he/solutions**.

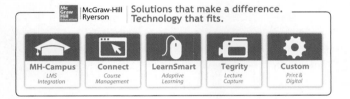

ACKNOWLEDGEMENTS

Many colleagues provided detailed and thoughtful reviews that helped immensely. I would like to thank the following reviewers who provided valuable feedback to guide the content of the fifth Canadian edition: Tom Arhontoudis, *George Brown College*; Mary-Ann Cipriano, *Concordia University*; Mary-Sharon Dellar, *McGill University*; Sameer Deshpande, *University of Lethbridge*; Ian Fisher, *Sheridan Institute of Technology*; Susan Graham, *University of Prince Edward Island*; Judith Nash, *Southern Alberta Institute of Technology*; Beth Pett, *Niagara College*; and Lillian Tepera, *Georgian College*. It is impossible to make everyone happy, but I assure you that I thoughtfully read all the suggestions many times to figure out how to make the book better within the time allotted.

I would like to recognize the cooperation I received from people in the business, advertising, and media communities. The fifth Canadian edition contains additional ads, illustrations, charts, and tables published by advertisers and/or their agencies, trade sources, and other advertising and industry organizations. Many individuals provided materials and gave permission to use them. A special thanks to all of you for helping us teach students with up-to-date examples and information. A marketing book cannot exist without the assistance of marketing people!

A successful book like this happens because of the publisher's exceptional work. Talented individuals at McGraw-Hill Ryerson who contributed to this project over the past 18 months make the final product look fantastic. My group product manager, Leanna MacLean, encouraged a complete revision with an emphasis to make it more visually appealing. A special thanks goes to Amy Rydzanicz, my product developer, for her tremendous effort and high expectations to stay on schedule and to produce a meticulously prepared manuscript. I want to acknowledge the outstanding work of Tracy Leonard for obtaining permissions for the Canadian content that appears throughout the book. I'd also like to recognize Kelli Howey for her splendid copy editing skills that improved the text. I appreciate the observational proficiency of Cat Haggert during the final stage as she proofread every page. Thank you to Jessica Barnoski for managing the production process. Thanks also to other members of the production team for their hard work on this edition.

I have taught many students IMC over the years; it has been gratifying to see former students enjoy my teaching and use the knowledge attained. So many students from the Telfer School of Management of the University of Ottawa achieved great marketing success and I hope that learning how to make effective promotion decisions proved useful in their career. To my current students, I hope you enjoy reading the book, and achieve great success after graduating like your predecessors. To students beyond my classroom, I wish you success as well after reading this material, and please thank your professor for selecting this book as it demonstrates their great insight!

On a personal note, my children, Louise, Daniel, and Nicholas, have been supportive during the time-consuming and involving process of finding, researching, writing, editing, organizing the material for this text. All my love and gratitude goes to my wife, Teresa, since I disappeared to my offices for hours on end to produce this fifth edition.

Michael Guolla

ABOUT THE AUTHOR

Michael Guolla is an assistant professor at the Telfer School of Management of the University of Ottawa. He completed his Ph.D. in Business Administration with a concentration in Marketing at the Stephen M. Ross School of Business of the University of Michigan (Ann Arbor) and received his Honours in Business Administration from the Richard Ivey School of Business at the University of Western Ontario. Dr. Guolla has published articles in academic journals, proceedings of scholarly conferences, and management journals.

Integrated Marketing Communications

1

LEARNING OBJECTIVES

LO1 Describe the importance of marketing communication within the marketing mix.

LO2 Identify the tools of the promotional mix—advertising, sales promotion, public relations, direct marketing, Internet marketing, and personal selling—and summarize their purpose.

LO3 Illustrate the concept of integrated marketing communications (IMC) by distinguishing its evolution, renewed perspective, and importance.

LO4 Explain the IMC planning process model and express the steps in developing a marketing communications program.

LO5 Identify how the IMC planning process is continued throughout all chapters.

McDonald's Canada Answers to Consumers

Faced with many food myths that had dogged the largest quick service restaurant for many years, McDonald's Canada launched its "Our Food. Your Questions" digital marketing communications program to clearly and honestly articulate how its food is made and presented. The premise hinged on simply answering consumer questions, like "What is in the sauce that is in the Big Mac?" "Is your beef actually 100 percent pure beef or is that just the name of the company?" and "Does your Egg McMuffin use real eggs?"

Consumers asked their questions at Mcdonalds.ca/Your-Questions when also logged into their Facebook or Twitter account. Visitors viewed the profiles of the questioners to ascertain the credibility of the source and observed real people, not advertising personnel! A 10-person response team trained for two weeks to be ready to address concerns and the expected misconceptions that many skeptics believed.

In the spring, a preliminary YouTube clip directed consumers to the website to ask a question. Initial communication of the answers posted on YouTube occurred in the summer with a TV commercial, wild postings, video projections on buildings, and transit dominations in key markets. By the end of 2012, the chain had answered 19,000 questions. Visitors to the website stayed an average of 4.5 minutes and read 12 questions.

McDonald's Canada answered all questions and addressed some of them with a video posted on the company's YouTube channel. The basic production by employees of the food suppliers provided an open approach that appeared very believable for almost anyone. One of the most watched (8,000,000 by year-end) videos featured Hope Bagozzi, who took consumers through an astonishing journey that explained why a hamburger looked different in ads versus what consumers saw when they opened the packaging in the restaurant.

The impetus for the communication occurred when brainstorming ideas for using QR codes as a way of informing consumers about the food quality. Eventually agency and marketing personnel hit upon the idea of honest communication with the question and answer format.

According to a senior marking manager for McDonald's Canada, "Canadians were talking about our brand perhaps not in a factual manner and we wanted to get into that social environment with our facts and our story and change those perceptions that Canadians have about our brand." The food quality message and focus on other unique attributes appeared as a strong area to concentrate on as McDonald's Canada faced pressure from high-end burger shops and the development of breakfast menu items in other restaurants such as Tim Hortons.

Many are interested in the success of this campaign. Social media users south of the border commented on the campaign significantly, thereby increasing international curiosity. Other global McDonald's operations are looking at this marketing program to see if it can be implemented in their countries. With the growth of cheaper digital media, many are looking toward substituted investments rather than more expensive TV expenditures.

McDonald's Canada succeeded in other areas beyond this program, with solid communication of its many new product launches such as fruit smoothies, grilled chicken wraps, and the McCafé brand of coffee and espresso-based beverages. McCafé became one of the largest launches in the company's history with TV, radio, out-of-home, digital, social media, and periodic sampling promotions. With all of these accomplishments, it is no wonder that *Marketing Magazine* recognized McDonald's Canada as Marketer of the Year for 2012!

Sources: Alicia Androich, "Why McDonald's Bare-Bones Marketing Approach Works," *Marketing Magazine,* October 1, 2012; Kristin Laird, "2012 Marketers of the Year Shortlist: McDonald's Canada," *Marketing Magazine,* November 20, 2012; Kristin Laird, "Marketer of the Year 2012," *Marketing Magazine,* January 23, 2013; Susan Krashinsky, "From Twitter to TV, McDonald's Offers Answers," *The Globe and Mail,* October 2, 2012.

Questions:
1. Why would consumers accept this approach for communicating food quality?
2. Do the results highlighted indicate a successful or unsuccessful campaign?

As the opening vignette illustrates, companies use advertising, websites, direct marketing, sales promotion, public relations, and social media to communicate something about their products, prices, or availability. In fact, finding the right combination of marketing communication tools is a critical decision for small and large firms, private and public organizations, and those that market goods, services, or ideas. In response, many companies use *integrated marketing communications* to link or connect their promotional tools and communicate with their current and prospective customers. Companies develop their marketing communication plans such that each promotional tool retains its unique communication effect and that the combination of promotional tools contributes to the overall communication effect of the brand or organization.

This opening chapter sets the direction for the entire book as it highlights the marketing context for advertising and promotion. First, it describes the importance of marketing communication. It then briefly defines the different promotional or marketing communication tools available for marketers. Next, it illustrates the idea of integrated marketing communications and indicates why it is so important. Finally, it explains the content of an integrated marketing communications (IMC) plan as a way of orienting the perspective and organization of this text.

(LO1) Marketing Communication

In this opening section we describe the importance of marketing communication within an organization's overall marketing effort. We begin by reviewing the definition of marketing to understand the importance of marketing communication to deliver value to consumers. We then explore examples of the content of marketing communication plans to illustrate their many different purposes.

Exhibit 1-1   This Patak's ad attempts to show and explain how consumers would enjoy the taste.

MARKETING

Historically, the American Marketing Association (AMA), the organization that represents marketing professionals in the United States and Canada, defined marketing as *the process of planning and executing the conception, pricing, promotion, and distribution of ideas, goods, and services to create exchanges that satisfy individual and organizational objectives.*[1] This definition focused on **exchange** as a central concept in marketing and the use of key marketing activities to create and sustain relationships with customers.[2] For exchange to occur there must be two or more parties with something of value to one another, a desire and ability to give up that something to the other party, and a way to *communicate* with each other. Marketing communication plays an important role in the exchange process by informing consumers of an organization's product and convincing them of its ability to satisfy their needs or wants. Exhibit 1-1 conveys how the Patak's Taste of India brand provides satisfaction.

The marketing function in an organization facilitates the exchange process by examining the needs and wants of consumers, developing a product or service that satisfies these needs, offering it at a certain price, making it available at a particular place or through a channel of distribution, and developing a program of promotion or marketing communication. These four Ps—product, price, place (distribution), and promotion (marketing communication)—are elements of the **marketing mix**. The main purpose of the marketing

Product Decisions	Price Decisions	Distribution Decisions
Product Type	Price Level	Channel Type
Features or Attributes/Benefits	Price Policy	Channel Policy
Corporate Name/Identification	Discount	Type of Intermediary or Reseller
Brand Name/Identification	Allowance	Type of Location/Store
Package Design	Flexibility	Service Level

Figure   1-1

Examples of typical marketing decisions

function is to combine these four elements into a marketing program that facilitates the potential for exchange with consumers in the marketplace. The remainder of this section describes how the marketing mix decisions of product, price, and distribution (Figure 1-1) are often the primary content of marketing communication messages.

COMMUNICATING PRODUCT

Each of the product facets listed in Figure 1-1 can be the focus of marketing communication. This section shows how marketing messages can communicate the value of the product type, the importance of salient attributes or benefits, and the identity of the brand or organization, in order to assist with brand equity development.

Product Value   An organization exists because it offers a product to consumers, generally in exchange for money. This offering may come in the form of a physical good (such as a soft drink, pair of jeans, or car), a service (banking, air travel, or legal assistance), a cause (United Way, March of Dimes), an idea (don't drink and drive), or even a person (political candidate). The product is anything that can be marketed and that, when consumed or supported, gives satisfaction to the individual. And these different product types are not always independent. When eating at a restaurant, consumers enjoy the food itself but also value the service of not having to prepare the meal, or the opportunity to eat food they may not have the culinary skill to make. Thus, whatever the product type, marketing communication attempts to show how consumers can receive value through the product offering.

Product Attributes/Benefits   Every product has fairly obvious features or attributes that characterize what it is. A chocolate bar can have varying types of chocolate (e.g., milk, dark) and different kinds of ingredients (e.g., nuts, wafers). Thus, marketing communication can take the simple role of identifying the ingredients or composition of a good. For example, ads for Rice Krispies cereal reminded consumers that each "krisp" contained a single grain of rice, while ads for Shreddies cereal highlighted its unique diamond shape. Notice how the ESQ ad in Exhibit 1-2 highlights attributes of the watch regarding the watch face and functions. Moreover, organizations often use marketing communication to educate consumers on how the services are delivered. For instance, WestJet ads demonstrate the personal attentiveness the airline's staff provide to customers, while Keg Steakhouse ads focus on the ambiance of the restaurant as well as the food.

Consumers typically view a product as a bundle of benefits signifying what the attributes can do. Benefits can be functional (the performance of the product), experiential (what it feels like to use the product), and/or psychological (self-esteem or status that result from owning a particular brand). Advertising and other marketing communication

Exhibit 1-2   Quality attributes are identified for the ESQ watch.

tools draw attention toward these benefits. Managers often have to decide which benefits to emphasize or how to portray the benefits in a message, and the best way to deliver that message. BMW's latest advertising emphasizes the joy of driving a BMW vehicle (i.e., experiential benefit) by showing an "expression of joy." One print ad did not show the product, but rather depicted the car's tire marks in colour as if they were painted upon a canvas.[3]

Product symbolism refers to what a product or brand means to consumers and what they experience in purchasing and using it.[4] For products with strong symbolic features, the social meaning of the experiential or psychological benefits may be more important than functional utility.[5] For example, designer clothing such as Versace, Gucci, and Prada is often purchased on the basis of its symbolic meaning. Marketing communication plays an important role in developing and maintaining the symbolism of these brands (Exhibit 1-3).

Brand Identity   A brand or corporate name and its identification through its logo, symbol, or trademark represent critical product decisions. Marketers use brand names that can communicate product concepts clearly, such as Air Canada (airlines) and Seadoo (water craft). The importance of selecting an appropriate visual representation of the brand is clear by noticing the symbol of any automobile brand or company. One primary purpose of marketing communication is to present the brand and its identification in favourable locations, situations, or time frames that allow consumers to think or feel more positively toward the brand. The identification of a logo in an ad is critical, as evidenced by a legal challenge Molson-Coors filed against Labatt in which the company suggested the stylized mountaintop shown in a Kokanee ad appeared too similar to the logo used by Coors Light.[6]

Brand identification and the symbolism of the brand are often reinforced by the tagline or slogan appearing in any form of marketing communication. IKEA's latest slogan encapsulates the essence of the brand magnificently with "Any space can be beautiful." Some executives suggest that the tagline is still very relevant since it "communicates a brand position or brand benefit." For example, Swiss Chalet returned to a previously successful tagline, "Always so good for so little," after making many changes the past few years. Harvey's has reminded us often over the years of the beauty of its hamburgers. Firms that offer many types of goods and services use an audio logo as one way of connecting brand messages across multiple media and IMC tools, much like a visual logo. For example, the Rogers audio logo can be heard for many of its services, including wireless and cable. Continuity and consistency in the promotional message across IMC tools—television, radio, wireless, interactive displays, Internet, podcasts—makes simple reminders of brand identification a key part of the brand experience.[7]

Packaging provides functional benefits such as economy, protection, and storage, which can be the main purpose of a marketing communication message. However, since the package is associated so closely with the brand by giving it a distinctive look, its symbolism and identity often become the focal point of a marketing communication message. For example, the main point of an ad can be to show the packaging of the product, since this influences consumer choice as in the case of perfume (Exhibit 1-4). Other characteristics of packaging, like it being fully biodegradable, are a concern for marketers and have become the focal message for marketing communication.[8]

Exhibit 1-3   This ad for Joe's Jeans conveys symbolic meaning through the use of sexuality.

Brand Equity Finally, the culmination of marketing communication messages of product value, product attributes/benefits, and brand identification assists in creating and maintaining brand equity. **Brand equity** is an intangible asset of added value or goodwill that results from the favourable image, impressions of differentiation, and/or strength of consumer attachment to a company name, brand name, or trademark.[9] Brand equity allows a brand to earn greater sales volume and/or higher margins than it could without the name, providing the company with a competitive advantage (Exhibit 1-5). Conceptually, IMC planning and resulting decisions are expected to strongly generate brand equity.[10] Figure 1-2 highlights the top 10 most valuable Canadian brands as determined by Brand Finance, while Figure 1-3 identifies the best Canadian brands as compiled by Interbrand.[11] From a related point of view, Ipsos Reid undertook research to uncover the most influential brand in Canada. President's Choice attained the highest rank at number three with consumers saying the brand is relevant (38%), dependable (53%), and likable in social media (24%).[12]

COMMUNICATING PRICE

The price refers to what the consumer must give up to purchase a product. Price is usually expressed in dollar amount exchanged for an item; however, the true cost of a product to the consumer includes time, mental activity, and behavioural effort.[13] Price planning involves decisions concerning the level, policy, adjustments through discounts or allowances, and flexibility when facing competition. Moreover, it also signals the economic cost to consumers for all product benefits combined. Communicating price information is so critical that the federal government regulated airlines to advertise their full price that would include all fees and taxes.[14]

Marketing communication plays a role in reinforcing a consumer's belief that the product's benefit or quality accurately reflects the price. One historical study regarding price, product quality, and advertising expenditures concluded that pricing and advertising strategies go

Exhibit 1-4 Showing packaging is often a focus of ads.

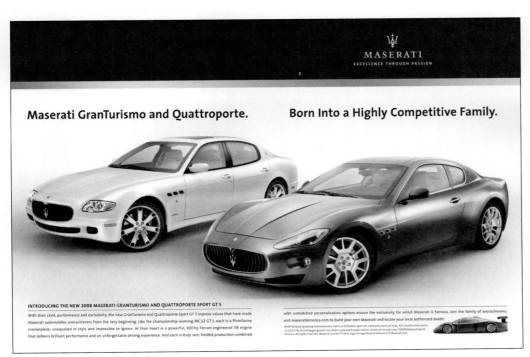

Exhibit 1-5 This Maserati ad contributes to its brand equity.

Figure 1-2

The top 10 most valuable Canadian brands

Rank 2012	Brand	Parent Company
1	RBC	Royal Bank of Canada
2	TD	TD Bank Financial Group
3	Scotiabank	Bank of Nova Scotia
4	BMO	Bank Of Montreal
5	Bell	BCE Inc.
6	Enbridge	Enbridge Inc.
7	CIBC	Canadian Imperial Bank Of Commerce
8	Bombardier	Bombardier Inc.
9	Rogers	Rogers Communications
10	BlackBerry	Research In Motion

Source: Brand Finance PLC 2013.

together. High relative ad expenditures should accompany premium prices, and low relative ad expenditures should be tailored to low prices.[15]

Price is often a key message conveyed. For example, car dealerships focus on price and discounts and allowances offered in many aspects of their marketing communication. Internet ads focus on price or offers that attempt to influence consumer price beliefs. The information on websites offering deals is predominantly price related (e.g., redtag.ca). A main purpose of the Rogers ad in Exhibit 1-6 is to communicate the price of the phone. Research concludes that price comparison advertising plays a key role in consumers' reference price for products when determining the value of a product. Other research finds that communicating price information is critical for influencing consumers who are in the process of deciding to buy a product.[16]

Figure 1-3

Best Canadian Brands

1	TD
2	Thomson Reuters
3	RBC Financial Group
4	Blackberry
5	Scotiabank
6	Tim Hortons
7	Lululemon
8	Shoppers Drug Mart
9	Bell
10	Rogers

Source: http://www.interbrand.com/en/Interbrand-offices/Interbrand-Toronto/Best-Canadian-Brands-2012.aspxf.

Exhibit 1-6   Some ads feature price information to support the quality claim.

COMMUNICATING DISTRIBUTION

Marketing channels, the "place" element of the marketing mix, are "sets of interdependent organizations involved in the process of making a product or service available for use or consumption."[17] Most consumer product companies distribute through **indirect channels**, usually using a network of wholesalers and/or retailers. A company can choose not to use any channel intermediaries and sell to its customers through **direct channels** such as the Internet.

In either case, marketing communication often provides information as to where a product can be purchased. For example, since most sporting goods companies have different quality and price levels, they might be inclined to communicate which brands and models are at different types of retailers. Alternatively, different kinds or levels of service might be available in various locations of the distribution network and this could be the focus of marketing communication. For instance, particular locations for cosmetics products offer customized beautifying services, while others can be close to self-serve. Extensive marketing communication occurs in order to direct consumers to organizational websites for online purchases.

The Promotional Mix

Promotion is the coordination of all seller-initiated efforts to set up channels of information and persuasion to sell goods and services or promote an idea.[18] While implicit communication occurs through the other elements of the marketing mix, most of an organization's communication with the marketplace occurs as part of a carefully planned and controlled promotional program. The tools an organization uses in a promotional program are referred to as the **promotional mix** (Figure 1-4). While either term is suitable, promotion or marketing communication, many marketers use the latter since the tools are often connected. For example, a television commercial can direct viewers to a website. Or a brand may use the same type of message in its radio and print ads. We now define of each of the tools and summarize their purpose.

ADVERTISING

Advertising is defined as any paid form of nonpersonal communication about an organization, product, service, or idea by an identified sponsor.[19] The *paid* aspect of this definition reflects the fact that the space or time for an advertising message generally must be bought. An occasional exception to this is the public service announcement (PSA), whose advertising space or time is donated by the media.

The *nonpersonal* component means advertising involves mass media (e.g., TV, radio, magazines, newspapers) that can transmit a message to large groups of individuals, often at the same time. The nonpersonal nature of advertising means there is generally no opportunity for immediate feedback from the message recipient (except in direct-response advertising). Therefore, before the message is sent, the advertiser must consider how the audience will interpret and respond to it.

Canadian advertisers spend more than $14 billion annually to reach their audiences, and there are several reasons why advertising is such an important part of many marketers' promotional mixes.

The Promotional Mix

| Advertising | Direct marketing | Internet marketing | Sales promotion | Public relations | Personal selling |

Figure 1-4

Tools of the promotional mix

Cost-Efficient   Advertising can be a very cost-efficient method for communicating with large audiences. For example, during a television season, prime-time network television reached 85 percent of Canadians on a daily basis. The most-watched TV show each week attracts an audience of about 3 million English-speaking viewers. The average top-10 show audience is about 2.4 million viewers, while the average audience for the top 11 to 20 shows is about 1.7 million viewers.[20] One study quotes media experts who estimate the cost per thousand reached at $25 for a top 10 show and $20 for a top 11–20 show. To reach an audience for Canadian-produced television shows costs $16 per thousand; specialty channel audiences cost $8 per thousand.[21]

Cost-Effective   Assuming that a majority of the viewers actually watched a TV ad, paid attention during the airing, and remember something about the message, then advertising can be seen as a very cost-effective form of marketing communication for many brands. In general, advertising can be a cost-effective method for allowing potential customers to know something about a brand and have a positive attitude toward the brand prior to, during, or after purchasing a product.

Brand Effects   Advertising is also a valuable tool for building company or brand equity as it is a powerful way to provide consumers with information as well as to influence their attitudes. Advertising can be used to create favourable and unique images and associations for a brand, which can be very important for companies selling products or services that are difficult to differentiate on the basis of functional attributes. Brand image and brand reputation play an important role in the purchase of many goods and services, and advertising remains a recommended approach to build a brand.[22]

Brand Interaction   Increasingly, advertising in media such as television, print, and outdoor is employed to encourage consumers to interact with the brand online. For example, a Broil King campaign created the fictitious journalist Rob Liking, who interviewed people grilling on their barbeques. Executives identified research showing that consumers researched their purchase online prior to a store visit, thus leading to a primary objective of influencing consumers' behaviour in the form of visiting the company's website.[23]

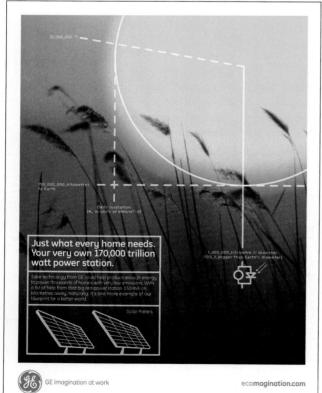

Flexible Tool   Advertising is a flexible tool that can be used for many industries (e.g., cars or soft drinks), market situations (e.g., new product launch or market development for established product), channel members (e.g., consumers or retailers), and target audiences (e.g., new customers or loyal customers). For example, the new campaign for American Express tries to attract customers of other credit cards with its message, "Impossible? Nah. Does that sound like the service you get from your card?"[24]

Multiple Domains   Different types of advertising occur in many domains. Canadian marketers of goods and services advertise to consumer markets with national or regional brand messages, and in some cases with messages to particular international consumer markets. Alternatively, local retailers and other goods and services providers use advertising for many communication purposes in order to achieve sales objectives. Also, industry associations, like the Dairy Farmers of Canada, advertise extensively to consumer markets as do all levels of government and non-governmental organizations like Canadian Blood Services. Shoppers Drug Mart used advertising to celebrate its fiftieth anniversary with its largest media buy ever to support all of its marketing communication.[25]

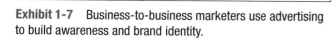

Exhibit 1-7   Business-to-business marketers use advertising to build awareness and brand identity.

Business-to-business advertising is directed to those who buy or influence the purchase of goods or services for their organization. Exhibit 1-7 shows an example of how General Electric communicates to other organizations that it competes in the solar energy market. Professional advertising directed to those with specific designations is found in many industries such as health, management, government, and technology. Finally, advertising directed to channel members like wholesalers, distributors, and retailers is found in all industry sectors around the world.

SALES PROMOTION

Sales promotion is defined as marketing activities that provide extra value or incentives to the sales force, distributors, or the ultimate consumer and can influence their behaviour to stimulate sales. Sales promotion is generally broken into two major categories: consumer-oriented and trade-oriented activities.

Consumer sales promotion is targeted to the ultimate user of a product or service and includes tools like coupons, samples, premiums, rebates, contests, events, and point-of-purchase materials. These promotional tools encourage consumers to make an immediate purchase, participate in a brand activity by attending the Red Bull Crashed Ice competition in Quebec City, or be more involved with the organization's marketing communication by uploading a video to a social media site celebrating one's consumption of a brand. Exhibit 1-8 is an example of a coupon offer within an ad that encourages parents to switch to a healthier snack for their children. Shoppers Drug Mart celebrated its anniversary with a contest offering 50 grand prizes and attracted more than 900,000 entrants.

Trade sales promotion is targeted toward marketing intermediaries such as wholesalers, distributors, and retailers. Promotional and merchandising allowances, price deals, sales contests, and trade shows are examples of the promotional tools used to encourage the trade to stock and promote a company's products. Some trade promotions benefit consumers since they receive information contained in display or receive discounted prices that are passed along to them from the retailer. Retail personnel at Shoppers Drug Mart liked the specialized point-of-purchase material so much they avoided dismantling it even after the party was over.

PUBLIC RELATIONS

Public relations (PR) occurs when an organization systematically plans and distributes information in an attempt to control and manage its image. **Public relations** is defined as "the management function which evaluates public attitudes, identifies the policies and procedures of an individual or organization with the public interest, and executes a program of action to earn public understanding and acceptance."[26] Public relations uses a variety of tools—including special publications, participation in community activities, fundraising, sponsorship of special events, and public affairs activities—to enhance an organization's image. Many organizations make PR an integral part of their predetermined marketing and promotional strategies. Exhibit 1-9 shows how sponsorship activities are part of a PR strategy. PR is now recognized as a communications tool that uses and supports advertising and sales promotion.[27] For example, Cisco and the CBC, two key drivers of the "One Million Acts of Green" program, recruited Tim Hortons to their cause through the promotion of a 10-cent discount for each hot drink purchased and consumed with a reusable travel mug.[28] Shoppers Drug Mart sponsored the Toronto

Exhibit 1-8 Dole combines its sales promotion with its advertising.

Exhibit 1-9   Jackson-Triggs supports the Toronto International Film Festival, which gives the brand added prestige.

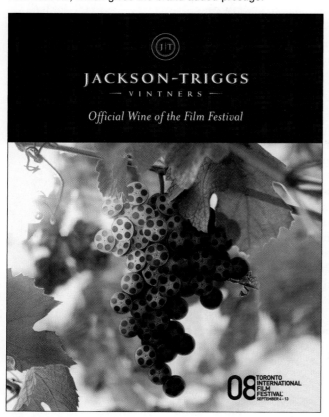

International Film Festival and featured its imagery with the red carpet entry of the celebrities.

Publicity refers to nonpersonal communications regarding an organization, product, service, or idea not directly paid for or run under identified sponsorship. The message reaches the public in the form of a news story, editorial, or announcement. Like advertising, publicity involves nonpersonal communication to a mass audience, but unlike advertising, publicity is not directly paid for by the organization. The organization encourages the media to cover or run a favourable story by using tools like news releases, press conferences, feature articles, and audio-visual media.

An advantage of publicity over other forms of promotion is its credibility. Consumers generally tend to be less skeptical toward favourable information about a product or service when it comes from a source they perceive as unbiased. For example, the success (or failure) of a new movie is often determined by the reviews it receives from film critics, who are viewed by many moviegoers as objective evaluators. Another advantage of publicity is its low cost, since the company is not paying for time or space in a mass medium. While an organization may incur costs in developing publicity items or maintaining a staff to do so, these expenses will be far less than those for the other promotional programs.

DIRECT MARKETING

Direct marketing occurs when organizations communicate directly with target audiences to generate a response and/or a transaction. Direct marketing includes telemarketing and call centres, direct mail, mail-order catalogues, and direct-response ads in broadcast and print media. Traditionally, direct marketing has not been considered a part of the promotional mix since it had distinct objectives, strategies, and tactics. However, we view direct marketing as an important component of a firm's marketing communication program since it is connected to many other communication tools. Extensive direct marketing activities also occur with the administration of loyalty programs designed to keep in touch with frequent purchasing customers. Shoppers Drug Mart revamped its Optimum points program while celebrating its fiftieth anniversary, which translated into a 20 percent growth in its membership.

Direct-marketing tools are used by companies that distribute their products to consumers directly and by companies that distribute their products through traditional distribution channels or their own sales force. In order to communicate directly, companies develop and maintain databases containing contact information (e.g., address, phone number, e-mail) of present and prospective customers. They use telemarketing to call customers directly and attempt to sell products and services or qualify them as sales leads. Call centres are used to respond to customer inquiries or concerns. Marketers also send out direct-mail pieces ranging from simple letters and flyers to detailed brochures, catalogues, and DVDs to give potential customers information about their products or services. Direct-marketing techniques are also used to distribute product samples and other promotional items. In addition, marketers use **direct-response advertising**, whereby a product is promoted through an ad (e.g., television or print) that encourages the consumer to purchase directly from the manufacturer (Exhibit 1-10).

INTERNET MARKETING

We are currently experiencing a dynamic change in marketing through interactive media, delivered via the Internet. **Interactive media** allow for a back-and-forth flow of information whereby users can participate in and modify the form and content of the information they receive instantly. Unlike traditional forms of marketing communication such as advertising, which are one-way in nature, these new media allow users to perform a variety of functions such as receiving and altering information and images, making inquiries, responding to questions, and, of course, making purchases. Shoppers Drug Mart attracted many new fans in social media and further developed its online luxury boutique Murale.

Many websites provide current and potential customers with information about the company's activities and products. Other firms develop websites

Exhibit 1-10 Under Armour uses direct-response advertising to promote its products.

to entertain or communicate more emotionally with their clientele. In fact, as part of a complete IMC program that included advertising, sales promotion, events, and public relations, BMW's Smart Car used Internet media with a dedicated microsite, a customized Facebook page, and YouTube to demonstrate the car's big interior despite it being small on the outside.[29]

As this example illustrates, the Internet is a medium that can be used to execute all the elements of the promotional mix. In addition to advertising on the Web, marketers offer sales promotion incentives such as coupons, contests, and sweepstakes online, and they use the Internet to conduct direct marketing, personal selling, and public relations activities more effectively and efficiently. For example, Exhibit 1-11 shows how consumers can interact with the Naked Juice brand on the Internet.

Social media avenues like Facebook and YouTube are ways for marketers to reach consumers with print and video ads, respectively. Each also allows brands to establish groups (Facebook) or channels (YouTube) for all kinds of marketing communication activities such as simple ads and sophisticated sales promotions. With imagination and creativity, all aspects of marketing communication are adapted in these new opportunities. Moreover, the interactive features of new media allow for extended communication among members, thereby providing a powerful means of additional communication.

Access to websites, social media, and other interactive experiences and their resulting marketing communication sponsorship (i.e., ads) has been made easier and more prevalent with the development of wireless mobile media devices. In essence, these smart portable devices and their accompanying applications are opening the door for marketers to adapt and invent ways of implementing marketing communication. For example, while walking down the street a person could receive a message with an incentive to turn back and eat at a restaurant he just passed by.

PERSONAL SELLING

The final promotional mix element is **personal selling**, a form of person-to-person communication in which a seller assists and/or persuades prospective buyers to purchase the company's product or service or to act on an idea. Personal selling involves direct contact between buyer and seller, either face-to-face or through telecommunications. This interaction gives the marketer communication flexibility; the seller can see or hear the potential buyer's reactions and tailor the message to their specific needs or situation. We do not cover personal selling in this book as many decisions pertaining to this topic are the responsibility of a sales manager.

PARTICIPANTS IN THE PROMOTIONAL PROCESS

Thus far we have identified the major promotional tools that marketers use. To understand the context in which promotional decisions are made, we identify the participants of the

Exhibit 1-11 Naked Juice used a creative Facebook application to promote its new recyclable bottle.

Figure   1-5   Participants in the promotional process

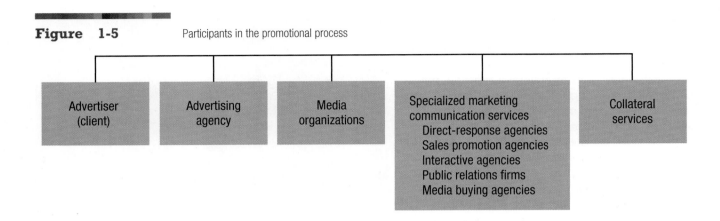

promotional process (Figure 1-5). Overall, there are five major groups: advertisers, advertising agencies, media organizations, specialized marketing communication services, and collateral services. Each group has specific roles in the promotional process.

Advertisers have the products, services, or causes to be marketed, and they provide the funds that pay for advertising and promotions. Advertisers assume major responsibility for developing the marketing program and making the final decisions regarding the advertising and promotional program. An organization may perform most of these efforts itself, either through its own advertising department or by setting up an in-house agency.

Advertising agencies are outside firms that specialize in the creation, production, and/or placement of promotional messages. An agency may also provide other services like research to facilitate the promotional process. Advertisers are referred to as **clients** if they retain the services of advertising agencies. Many large advertisers retain the services of a number of agencies, particularly when they have multiple products. Often, an ad agency will act as a partner with an advertiser and assume more responsibility for developing the marketing and promotional programs.

Media organizations provide information or entertainment to their subscribers, viewers, or readers. From the perspective of the promotional planner, media provides an environment for the firm to deliver its marketing communication message. The media must have editorial or program content that attracts consumers so advertisers and their agencies will want to buy time or space with them. While the media perform many other functions that help advertisers understand their markets and their customers, a medium's primary objective is to sell itself as a way for companies to effectively reach their target audiences with their messages (Exhibit 1-12). Media companies in Canada have grown significantly over the past decade through acquisition of different formats, thus allowing considerable integration options for advertisers. For example, Rogers offers customers virtually all media opportunities and its staff has a strong integration orientation when selling packages to its clients.[30]

Specialized marketing communication services include direct marketing agencies, sales promotion agencies, interactive agencies, public relations firms, and media buying agencies. These organizations provide services in their areas of expertise. A direct-response agency develops and implements direct-marketing programs, while sales promotion agencies develop contests and sweepstakes, premium offers, or sampling programs. Interactive agencies develop websites, social

Exhibit 1-12 *National Geographic* promotes its value to advertisers.

media activities, or other types of Internet ads. Public relations firms generate and manage publicity for a company and its products and services as well as to focus on its relationships with its relevant publics. Media buying agencies work with clients and the media organizations for optimal placement of advertiser's messages.

Collateral services include marketing research companies, package design firms, consultants, photographers, printers, video production houses, and event marketing services. These individuals and companies perform specialized functions the other participants (advertisers, agencies, media organizations, and specialized marketing communication services) use in planning and executing the IMC plan.

(L03) Integrated Marketing Communications

Most large companies understand that the wide range of promotional tools must be coordinated to communicate effectively and present a consistent image to target audiences. In turn, even smaller-scale marketers have followed suit and are moving to a more comprehensive perspective of marketing communication. We now illustrate the topic of integrated marketing communications by distinguishing its evolution, renewed perspective, and importance.

THE EVOLUTION OF IMC

During the 1980s, many companies moved toward integrated marketing communications (IMC) as the need for strategic planning and integration of their promotional tools intensified. Marketers subsequently asked their agencies to coordinate the use of more promotional tools rather than rely primarily on media advertising. Companies also looked beyond traditional advertising agencies and employed other promotional specialists to develop and implement other components within their promotional plans. At this point in time, a task force from the American Association of Advertising Agencies defined integrated marketing communications as:

> a concept of marketing communications planning that recognizes the added value of a comprehensive plan that evaluates the strategic roles of a variety of communication disciplines—for example, general advertising, direct response, sales promotion, and public relations—and combines these disciplines to provide clarity, consistency, and maximum communications impact.[31]

In the 1990s, companies saw IMC as a way to coordinate and manage their marketing communication programs to ensure customers received a consistent message. IMC represented an improvement over the traditional method of treating the promotional tools as virtually separate activities as all agencies contributed to the IMC planning for their clients.[32] IMC became one of the "new-generation" marketing approaches used by companies to better focus their efforts in acquiring, retaining, and developing relationships with customers and other stakeholders.[33] With this change, IMC faced criticism that it primarily relied on the tactical coordination of communication tools with the goal of making them look and sound alike.[34] Others criticized it as an "inside-out" marketing approach that simply bundled promotional mix elements together so they have one look and speak with one voice.[35] As IMC evolved, both academics as well as practitioners suggested a renewed perspective that viewed the discipline from a strategic perspective. IMC Perspective 1-1 describes how successful marketers are making IMC decisions.

A RENEWED PERSPECTIVE OF IMC

A renewed understanding of IMC viewed it as a business process that identifies the most appropriate and effective methods for communicating and building relationships as shown in the following definition:

> Integrated marketing communication is a strategic business process used to plan, develop, execute and evaluate coordinated, measurable, persuasive brand communications programs over time with

IMC PERSPECTIVE 1-1

Winning Marketers Profiled by *Strategy*

Strategy recognized its marketers of the year by identifying four outstanding individuals: Duncan Fulton of Sport Chek, Mary De Paoli of Sun Life, Marie-Josée Lamothe of L'Oréal, and Sandra Sanderson of Shoppers Drug Mart; this is a story of their success for would-be marketers to follow in their footsteps.

Duncan Fulton is the chief marketing officer with Forzani Group Limited (FGL), operator of Sport Chek and many other sports retail banners. Working with its agency of record, Sid Lee, Fulton's effort redefined the Sport Chek brand as it devoted 25 percent of its budget to building the brand. Research indicated that the product-specific communication no longer resonated with a younger consumer who spent considerable time online, so the advertising went in a new direction. With the "Your Better Starts Here" campaign featuring Sidney Crosby, the TV spots and out-of-home ads in and near gyms showed the determination of the NHL star as he worked out while on the road to recover from an injury. The campaign also included extensive digital messages featuring Blue Jay Brett Lawrie on YouTube and Twitter. For follow-up and tracking of the improved brand, FGL moved toward extensive analytics to assess brand success and estimate marketing return on investment. In the future, Fulton plans for Sport Chek to provide the most digital store experience in Canada, with video kiosks that display messages from suppliers and the brand itself.

Mary De Paoli is the chief marketing officer at Sun Life, one of three major insurance firms competing against Manulife and Great-West Life. Under her leadership, the lifestyle-themed marketing communication oriented the brand with a more humanized approach for selling insurance. A website (brighterlife.ca) allowed consumers to be part of a network that interacted to understand financial issues by asking and answering questions. Visitors arrived at the site from ads on news sites, social media, and search engines. The site garnered many awards and influenced the development of similar sites in other countries. Unexpectedly and proudly, Sun Life became an exporter of creative ideas and strategic innovations in the insurance industry. Significant investment and development with sponsorship of the Canadian Football League provided additional awareness and a source of leads for selling more products. A marketing partnership with Nestlé offered an opportunity of greater exposure for Sun Life while displayed with the consumer goods in the presentation of a contest.

Marie-Josée Lamothe is the chief marketing officer of L'Oréal, Canada's leading beauty brand with 31 different skincare, makeup, and hair brands and an estimated one-third of the beauty industry. L'Oréal's strategic direction focused on "digitize everything," with presence in all facets of the electronic universe. Combined with innovation toward community-building campaigns, high-profile sponsorships, and a unique partnership with Rogers, L'Oréal increased its market share considerably. Digitally, the international fashion brand established a Canadian-specific Facebook page for more than 20 brands and attained a fan base of more than 1.5 million. In particular, the brand L'Oréal Paris offered extensive on-location video of its sponsorship of the Toronto International Film Festival (TIFF) and Toronto Fashion Week through its social media page. With Rogers, L'Oréal sponsored the Web series *Canada's Best Beauty Talent,* a competition for Canada's leading stylists and beauticians with five of its brands.

Sandra Sanderson is the senior vice president marketing for Shoppers Drug Mart. This number-one pharma-retailer celebrated its 50th anniversary throughout 2012 with a giant "Fabulous 50" campaign. The autumn leg of the campaign centred on the "red gift box" messaging and imagery and emphasized health, beauty, and convenience in all marketing communication and in-store decorations. The celebration continued with extensive contests that attained over 900,000 entries for prizes like cars and trips. This theme ran in tandem with a partnership with TIFF and *ET Canada* for on-air coverage that resulted in over 250 million impressions and 71,000 new Facebook fans.

Sources: Grant Surridge, "MOY: Duncan Fulton Retells Sport Chek's Story," *Strategy,* December 7, 2012; Grant Surridge, "MOY: There's Something About Mary De Paoli," *Strategy,* December 7, 2012; Megan Haynes, "MOY: Marie-Josée Lamothe's Digital Domination," *Strategy,* December 7, 2012; Megan Haynes, "MOY: Sandra Sanderson Keeps Shoppers Fabulous," *Strategy,* December 7, 2012; Jennifer Horn, "MOY: David Grisim's Golden Year," *Strategy,* December 7, 2012.

Question:

1. Explain why one of the four marketers was most successful.

consumers, customers, prospects, employees, associates and other targeted relevant external and internal audiences. The goal is to generate both short-term financial returns and build long-term brand and shareholder value.[36]

IMC is now seen as an ongoing strategic business process rather than just tactical integration of communication activities. It also recognizes that there are a number of relevant audiences that require specific communication programs. Finally, this definition reflects the increasing emphasis placed on the demand for accountability and measurement of the *outcomes* of marketing communication programs as well as marketing in general. A renewed perspective suggests that IMC has four general characteristics[37]:

1. Unified communication for consistent message and image.
2. Differentiated communication to multiple customer groups.
3. Database-centred communication for tangible results.
4. Relationships fostering communication with existing customers.

Many companies are realizing that communicating effectively with customers and other stakeholders involves more than just the tactical use of the traditional marketing communication tools. These firms, along with many advertising agencies, are embracing IMC and incorporating it into their marketing and business practices. In fact, it is hypothesized that IMC is now critically connected to a firm's market and brand orientation.[38] Research reports higher use of IMC leading to higher levels of sales, market share, and profits.[39] Academics and practitioners have questioned whether IMC is just another "management fashion" whose influence will be transitory.[40] Critics of IMC argue that it merely reinvents and renames existing ideas and concepts and that it questions its significance for marketing and advertising thought and practice.[41]

Despite these concerns, one major marketing organization significantly moved toward IMC. Procter & Gamble (P&G) overhauled its marketing and organizational operations, which had enormous implications for how P&G makes its promotional decisions with an IMC perspective. The change originated when managers decided to focus on when the consumer chooses to buy and use the product as the central driver for all decisions. Marketers in Canada work on multi-functional teams to customize worldwide product launches for local success. This has resulted in P&G Canada typically using the original TV creative, but augmenting the campaign with more targeted IMC tools. From an agency perspective, P&G partnered with diverse types of agencies and employed multiple parties to execute new brand initiatives. Furthermore, P&G expected strategic communication planning from its agencies, which were immersed in their client's newfound customer-centric direction. Innovative communication practices resulted from these internal and external developments. The Canadian campaign for Cover Girl Outlast Lipstick featured motion-sensitive ads in bars and restaurants in Toronto. Old Spice dance events, known as "Red Zone after hours," occurred at Canadian bars and included an online contest, out-of-home media, and a televised competition.[42]

While the debate over the value and relevance of IMC is likely to continue, proponents of the concept far outnumber the critics as IMC is proving to be a permanent change that offers significant value to marketers.[43] We will now discuss reasons regarding the importance of IMC.

IMPORTANCE OF IMC

A successful IMC program requires that a firm find the right combination of promotional tools, define their role and the extent to which they can or should be used, and coordinate their use. This perspective becomes important for the organization because of the many audiences it communicates with, the vast number of messages consumers receive from many brands, the emergence of strong marketing relationships, consumer adoption of technology and media, and improved managerial planning.

Audience Contacts   Marketers use the promotional mix elements to communicate with current and/or prospective customers as well as other relevant audiences such as employees, suppliers, community, and government. Companies take an *audience contact* perspective whereby they consider all the potential ways of reaching their target audience and presenting the message of the company or brand in a favourable manner. In terms of customers, for example, marketers identify how their loyal buyers interact with a company or brand. This contact can range from seeing or hearing an ad to actually using or experiencing a brand at a company-sponsored event. Moreover, this idea can be extended to non-customers and all other potential audiences the company or brand may choose to target its marketing communication.

Figure 1-6 shows how target audiences can come into contact with a company or brand. Marketers must determine how valuable each contact tool is for communicating with their target audience and how they can be combined to form an effective IMC program. This is generally done by starting with the target audience and determining which IMC tools will be most effective in reaching, informing, and persuading them and ultimately influencing their behaviour. Nissan took a multiple audience approach with its advertising. To address the problem of the brand languishing in the Quebec market, Nissan launched the "Gros Bon Sens" (Big Common Sense) campaign to counter the belief that Nissan sold more expensive cars. This message fit well with the Quebec market since consumers purchase a higher percentage of small, less expensive cars. The Gros Bons Sens concept manifested with an approachable, everyday kind of guy who represented the average consumer Nissan targeted. In the TV ads the character advised Nissan engineers and design personnel on how to improve their car initially, and then moved on to other aspects of buying and enjoying a Nissan Sentra and Versa. In other parts of Canada, Nissan highlighted the enjoyment consumers experience with their vehicles with the message, "Best part of your day." Ads showed people struggling with day-to-day activities only to find their day brighten once they began to use or drive their Rogue, Versa, or Sentra. Consumers found comfort, convenience, and excitement depending upon the situation represented.[44]

Consumer's Point of View   It is important for marketers to keep concepts distinct to communicate with colleagues within the organization or other organizations when making decisions. For example, when planning a sales promotion, it is useful to refer to it as a sales promotion so that everyone involved can discuss its merits appropriately and allocate the sales promotion expenditure within the correct budget. What is the right sales promotion (e.g., coupon versus bonus pack)? Is the incentive strong enough to encourage the target audience to switch to our brand? Consumers, on the other hand, receive many exposures from many different brands, each using many different promotional tools. In fact, consumers receive so many exposures that they have the habit of often referring to any promotional tool as "advertising."

Figure   1-6   IMC audience contact tools

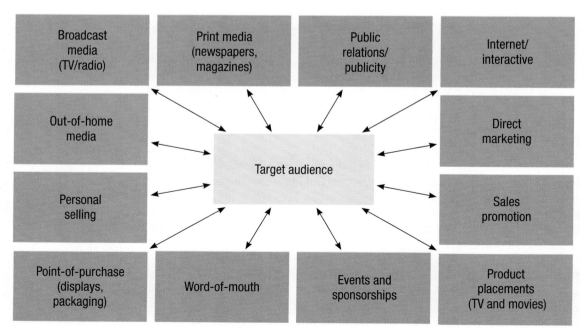

Given this situation, the need for planning with an IMC perspective becomes imperative. All the elements of the promotional campaign have to be carefully linked so that the message is clear and the brand is represented well as seen in this example.

The "Become a Doritos Guru" contest, promoted on TV, social media, MuchMusic, and Doritos packaging, invited Canadians to develop their own vision of the brand with the chance to receive a financial prize of $25,000 and 1 percent of sales, see the ad on national TV, and experience the thrill of having their ad disseminated throughout the digital world. Doritos worked with a variety of marketing communication agencies including BBDO Toronto (creative), Capital C (packaging and point-of-purchase display), Proximity (digital media), Fleishman-Hillard (public relations), and OMD Canada (media placement). Together, these experts conceived a concept where contestants would post their entry to DoritosGuru.ca, Facebook, or YouTube, allowing viewers to vote on the one they liked best to identify the five semi-finalists. The contest obtained 30,000 Facebook fans, 1.5 million visitors to the YouTube channel, 2,100 video submissions (surpassing the number received in a similar campaign conducted in the United States a year previously), and 589,000 votes. A judging panel selected as the winner a team headed by Ryan Coopersmith, which branded the new chip "Scream Cheese." The ad showed a number of people screaming while doing everyday activities (e.g., work, movie, dinnertime), and ended with "What are you screaming about?" Coopersmith's team planned to use the winnings to finance their own feature film.[45]

Relationship Marketing Many marketers seek more than a one-time exchange or transaction with customers and concentrate on developing and sustaining *relationships* with their customers. This has led to a new emphasis on **relationship marketing**, which involves creating, maintaining, and enhancing long-term relationships with individual customers as well as other stakeholders for mutual benefit.[46] The banking industry has been very successful with building relationships; the extensive personal and financial information banks have access to allows them to offer products and services in a timely manner as people's financial needs change. This is enhanced through services provided by financial advisers and wealth managers.

This relationship focus is generally more profitable since it is often more cost-effective to retain customers than to acquire new ones. Furthermore, these retained customers tend to buy more products or expand their purchases to other products that an organization offers. Marketers are giving more strategic importance in their plans to the *lifetime value* of a customer because studies have shown that reducing customer defections by just 5 percent can increase future profit by as much as 30 to 90 percent.[47] The AMA adopted a revised and more strategic definition of **marketing**, which is as follows:

> Marketing is an organizational function and a set of processes for creating, communicating and delivering value to customers and for managing customer relationships in ways that benefit the organization and its stakeholders.[48]

In order to facilitate the relationship, companies build databases containing customer names; geographic, demographic, and psychographic profiles; purchase patterns; media preferences; credit ratings; and other characteristics. Marketers use this information to target consumers through a variety of IMC tools thereby enhancing the relationship. With so many tools, and since their customers are involved so closely with the firm, the need for consistency and coordination becomes even more critical.[49]

Consumer Adoption of Technology and Media The expanded use of integrated marketing communications is more critical due to consumer adoption of technology and media. For example, technology has vastly expanded the number of channels available to viewers. As a result, audiences are more fragmented and television advertising reaches smaller and more selective audiences. This requires brands to ensure their messages are attended to in other media or other IMC tools. Thus, the more selective television ad might direct the viewer to seek out the brand's website for a coupon or sample, or to read about its charitable sponsorship activities. TV ads also direct viewers to the brand's social media like Facebook for similar reasons with the goal of encouraging them to become "fans."

Online services provide information and entertainment as well as the opportunity to shop for and order a vast array of products. Marketers are responding by developing websites where they

Exhibit 1-13   Maple Lodge reassures consumers about the safety of its meat products with its new symbol.

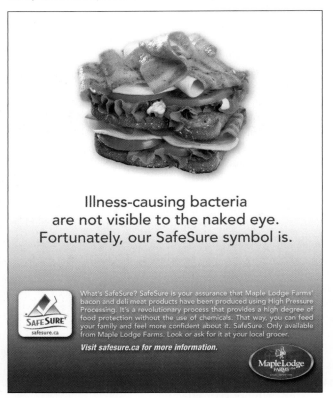

Illness-causing bacteria
are not visible to the naked eye.
Fortunately, our SafeSure symbol is.

What's SafeSure? SafeSure is your assurance that Maple Lodge Farms' bacon and deli meat products have been produced using High Pressure Processing. It's a revolutionary process that provides a high degree of food protection without the use of chemicals. That way, you can feed your family and feel more confident about it. SafeSure. Only available from Maple Lodge Farms. Look or ask for it at your local grocer.

Visit safesure.ca for more information.

can advertise their products and services interactively as well as transact sales. New applications for advertising on the Internet are invented each year, allowing marketers greater opportunity to reach particular audiences. For instance, brands have initiated "sponsored groups" on Facebook where consumers can join and receive brand messages and promotional offerings like contests and samples. Toyota created the F1 Canada group and offered desktop wallpapers and ringtones for its 3,000 members. Other applications included targeted banner ads based on consumer profile variables like demographics, psychographics, and media consumption preferences. Telus experimented with a virtual-reality world that 120,000 of its 1.2 million customers experienced; word of the new venture spread through blogs and newspaper articles. With essentially no monetary investment in the venture, the media exposure Telus received helped convey it as a technologically advanced company. More importantly, Telus ultimately planned promotions to customers based on the behaviours exemplified in the simulated game.[50]

Planning Efficiency and Effectiveness   A final reason for IMC importance is that marketers understand the value of strategically integrating the communication functions rather than having them operate autonomously. By coordinating their marketing communications efforts, companies can avoid duplication, take advantage of synergy among promotional tools, and develop more efficient and effective marketing communications programs. Advocates of IMC argue that it is one of the easiest ways for a company to maximize the return on its investment in marketing and promotion.[51] Empirical research supports this contention as strong IMC performance leads to stronger market performance.[52] Exhibit 1-13 shows a marketing effort where planning is paramount. Much of Shoppers Drug Mart's success in their "Fabulous 50" campaign hinged on a dedicated 30-person cross-functional team in charge of the IMC plan who ensured consistency across all audience contact points.

(L04) Integrated Marketing Communications Planning

In developing an IMC strategy, a company combines the promotional mix elements to produce an effective program for marketing communication. **IMC planning** involves the process of conceiving, executing, evaluating, and controlling the use of promotional mix elements to communicate effectively with target audiences. The marketer decides which promotional tools to use and how to combine them to achieve IMC objectives. Furthermore, the marketer decides on the role and function of the specific elements of the promotional mix, develops strategies for each element, and implements the plan. The resulting **IMC plan** provides the framework for developing, implementing, and controlling the organization's IMC program. A model of the IMC planning process is shown in Figure 1-7. The remainder of this chapter explains the model and expresses the steps in developing a marketing communications program. IMC Perspective 1-2 shows these ideas in action with Maple Leaf Foods.

REVIEW THE MARKETING PLAN

Before developing an IMC plan, promotional planners must understand where the company (or the brand) has been, its current position in the market, where it intends to go, and how

Figure   1-7   An integrated marketing communications planning model (continues on next page)

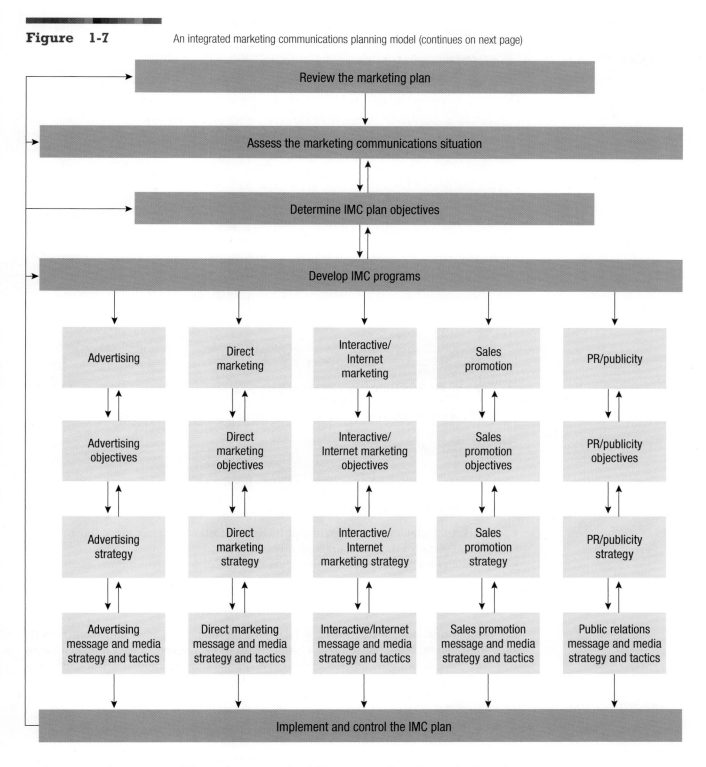

it plans to get there. Most of this information should be contained in the **marketing plan**, a written document that describes the overall marketing strategy and programs developed for an organization, a particular product line, or a brand. Marketing plans can take several forms but generally include five basic parts:

- A detailed situation analysis that consists of an internal marketing review and an external analysis of the market, company, consumer, competition, and macro-environment.
- Specific marketing objectives that provide direction, a time frame for marketing activities, and a mechanism for measuring performance.

Figure 1-7 (concluded)

An integrated marketing communications planning model

Review the Marketing Plan
Focus on market, company, consumer, competitive, and environmental information
Examine marketing objectives, strategy, and programs
Understand role of promotion within marketing plan

Assess the Marketing Communications Situation
Internal analysis
    Relative strengths and weaknesses of products/services
    Previous promotional programs
    Brand image
    Promotional organization and capabilities
External analysis
    Customer behaviour analysis
    Competitive analysis
    Environmental analysis

Determine IMC Plan Objectives
Establish IMC communication objectives
Establish IMC behavioural objectives

Develop IMC Programs
For advertising, sales promotion, public relations, direct marketing, and Internet marketing:
    Set specific communication and behavioural objectives for each IMC tool
    Determine budget requirements
    Develop relevant message strategy and tactics
    Select suitable media strategy and tactics
Investigate integration options across all five programs

Implement and Control the IMC Plan
Design all promotional materials internally or with agencies and buy media space/time
Measure promotional program results/effectiveness and make adjustments

- A marketing strategy and program that includes selection of target market(s) and decisions and plans for the four marketing mix elements.
- A program for implementing the marketing strategy, including determining specific tasks to be performed and responsibilities.
- A process for monitoring and evaluating performance and providing feedback to permit proper control and allow for strategic or tactical revisions.

The promotional plan is developed similarly to the marketing plan and often uses its detailed information. However, some IMC strategy decisions require more comprehensive or specific information, or more detailed analysis and specific consideration of existing information, therefore requiring a situation analysis for marketing communication.

ASSESS THE MARKETING COMMUNICATIONS SITUATION

In the IMC program, the situation analysis focuses on relevant internal and external factors for developing a promotional strategy much like the marketing situation analysis.

Internal Analysis The internal analysis assesses four relevant areas: product, previous promotional programs, firm or brand image, and organizational capabilities (Figure 1-8).

The internal analysis assesses the relative strengths and limitations of the product; the product's unique selling points, attributes, or benefits; and its packaging, price, and design. This information is important to the creative personnel who must develop the brand's advertising message and communicate aspects of the brand.

IMC PERSPECTIVE **1-2**

Suppers Ready with Maple Leaf Foods

Maple Leaf Foods (MLF) energized its marketing in 2011 and won *Marketing Magazine*'s Marketer of the Year with product innovation and creative marketing communication to win back consumer confidence after the tragic deaths of 22 people who had consumed their goods in 2008. Chief Marketing Officer Stephen Graham led five business units—Canada Bread, Maple Leaf Consumer Foods, Tenderflake, Olivieri, and New York Bakery Company—and encouraged interaction across the divisions so that learning of best practices developed throughout all marketing activities. Furthermore, consumer research indicated they looked for new and fresh ideas from food producers.

After the product recall that cost about $70 million and a brand reputation rank that dropped from 21 to 86, the food giant recognized the need for considerable change. With its competitor McCain Foods starting up the "It's All Good" initiative in 2010, MLF certainly felt the pressure to rejuvenate its marketing. The new direction started with healthier and more convenient products across many product categories with brands like Schneiders, Dempster's, and Prime and communicated across a number of media and IMC tools, which moved MLF to a rank of 56 for reputation in 2011. Extensive redesign of all websites and the development of YouTube and Twitter channels for most brands propelled MLF as a true innovator in the world of marketing communications.

MFL revamped Schneiders Country Naturals to include only natural ingredients written on the front of the package to be easily read by consumers. The launch TV ad highlighted the wholesome ingredients and the opening song, Buffalo Springfield's "For What It's Worth" (rerecorded) played in the background with the words "there's something happening here," which signalled significant change for MLF. Combined with sampling and a Facebook event that awarded money to a community so it could transform a public space into the ultimate picnic location, the brand put forth its straightforward and simple personality.

Dempster's bread is baked fresh and delivered daily by Canada Bakery, and MLF altered the packaging to show its freshness and communicate its natural ingredients. Communication support featured TV and print ads to go along with a new consumer website, social media messages on Facebook, and blogger relations. Later, Dempster's showed Sidney Crosby in point-of-sale displays and a TV ad that linked his preparation for a game with the effort devoted by the brand to deliver outstanding bread. A contest and online game found at the Facebook page supported these initiatives, all of which were well received by consumers and channel partners.

Prime chicken's advertising moved from a focus on its attributes (i.e., 100 percent all-vegetable grain-fed poultry) to how the convenience of the brand can bring families together to create lasting memories with vignettes of families enjoying their dinner together. MLF intended for consumers to connect with the brand on an emotional level by highlighting the enjoyment people have with food at dinner time as they connect with one another.

Sources: Kristin Laird, "All the Right Moves," *Marketing Magazine,* January 16, 2012; Kristin Laird, "Maple Leaf Foods," *Marketing Magazine,* November 28, 2011; Kristin Laird, "Dinner Time Is Prime Time for Maple Leaf Foods," *Marketing Magazine,* June 16, 2011; Kristin Laird, "Maple Leaf Joins the Natural Ingredient Movement with Country Naturals," *Marketing Magazine,* May 2, 2012.

Question:
1. Why would digital communication tools be a useful source of information for food consumers?

Since the firm is planning a new promotional plan, it is imperative that a review of previous promotional objectives, budgets, strategies, and tactics of all elements should occur to understand the strengths and limitations. Furthermore, if the firm has utilized marketing research to track the results of previous programs, this information needs to be examined closely. This step helps determine what promotional decisions should be retained, revised, or withdrawn.

The strengths and limitations of the firm or the brand from an image perspective will have a significant impact on the way it can advertise and promote itself as well as its products and services. Companies or brands that are new to the market or those for whom perceptions are

Figure   1-8   Areas covered in the situation analysis

Internal Factors	External Factors
Assessment of firm's promotional capabilities	**Customer behaviour analysis**
Organization of promotional department	Who buys our product or service?
Capability to develop and execute promotional programs	Who makes the decision to buy the product?
Role and function of all agencies	Who influences the decision to buy the product?
	How is the purchase decision made? Who assumes what role?
Assessment of firm's previous promotional programs	What does the customer buy? What needs must be satisfied?
Promotional objectives	Why do customers buy a particular brand?
Promotional budgets and allocations	Where do they go or look to buy the product or service?
Promotional mix strategies and programs	When do they buy? Any seasonality factors?
Results of promotional programs	What social, lifestyle, or demographic factors influence the purchase decision?
Assessment of firm or brand image	
What are customers' attitudes toward our product/service?	**Competitive analysis**
	Who are our direct and indirect competitors?
Assessment product/service strengths and weaknesses	What key benefits and positioning are used by our competitors?
What are its key attributes and benefits?	What is our position relative to the competition?
Does it have any unique selling points?	How big are competitors' promotion budgets?
Are the package and label consistent with the brand image?	What promotion strategies are competitors using?
	Environmental analysis
	What current trends or developments affect the promotional program?

negative may have to concentrate on their images. Firms with a strong image need to understand how to maintain their image.

For example, Starbucks has an outstanding image that is a result of the quality of its coffee and other products as well as its reputation as a socially responsible company. The company is recognized as a good citizen in its dealings with communities, employees, suppliers, and the environment. Starbucks understands that being identified as a socially responsible company is an important part of its success, which guides the selection of its promotional decisions. For example, Starbucks publishes a Corporate Social Responsibility Annual Report each year that describes the company's social, environmental, and economic effects in the communities it serves (Exhibit 1-14).

Reviewing the capabilities of the firm and its ability to develop and implement a successful promotional program, and the organization of the promotional department, the analysis may indicate the firm is not fully capable of planning and implementing the promotional program. If this is the case, it would be wise to look for assistance from an advertising agency or other promotional facilitator. If the organization is already using an ad agency, the focus will be on the quality of the agency's work and the results achieved by past and/or current campaigns.

External Analysis   The **external analysis** focuses on factors such as characteristics of the firm's customers, market segments, competitors, and environment, as shown in Figure 1-8. A detailed consideration of customers' characteristics (e.g., demographics, psychographics) and buying patterns, their decision processes, and factors influencing their purchase decisions are all relevant for promotional planners to make effective decisions. Often, marketing research studies are needed to answer these questions. A key element of the external analysis is an assessment of the market. The attractiveness of different market segments must be evaluated and the segments to target identified. Exhibit 1-15 shows ads from a campaign for Tourism Kelowna, where a good consumer understanding is important.

The external phase of the promotional program situation analysis also includes an in-depth examination of both direct and indirect competitors. Focus is on the firm's primary competitors: their specific strengths and limitations; their segmentation, targeting, and positioning strategies; and the promotional strategies they employ. The size and allocation of their promotional budgets, their media strategies, and the messages they are sending to the marketplace should all be considered.

DETERMINE IMC PLAN OBJECTIVES

An important part of this stage of the promotional planning process is establishing relevant and appropriate objectives. In this text, we stress the importance of distinguishing among different types of objectives that are generally decided during the planning of different strategies.

Marketing objectives refer to what is to be accomplished by the overall marketing program. They are often stated in terms of sales, market share, or profitability and are determined when the marketing plan is constructed. Precise definition of marketing objectives is important to give guidance on what is to be accomplished in the marketing communication plan. With the re-launch of Tourism BC, the government looked to increase tourism revenue by 5 percent over a five-year time period.[53]

Exhibit 1-14   Starbucks has a very strong brand image and reputation as a socially responsible company.

Communication objectives refer to what the firm seeks to accomplish with its IMC program. They are often stated in terms of the nature of the message to be communicated or what specific communication effects are to be achieved, such as awareness. The promotional planner must think about the process consumers will go through in responding to marketing communications. Tourism BC needed to improve its image as visits declined while tourism gained in other provinces. **Behavioural objectives** in terms of trial purchase or repeat purchase, among others, may be defined along with the communication objectives. Tourism BC sought to increase the number of visitors from Ontario, presumably many for the first time, to achieve impressive revenue growth. Communication and behavioural objectives should be the guiding force for the IMC strategy and for each promotional tool.

Exhibit 1-15   Tourism Kelowna's ads have visuals that encourage visits from across Canada.

While determining these objectives, two questions are asked to tentatively set the budget: What will the promotional program cost? and How will these monies be allocated? Ideally, the amount a firm spends on promotion should be determined by what must be accomplished to achieve communication and behavioural objectives. Tourism BC decided to spend $52 million for 2012 down from the $65 million it spent in 2009.

DEVELOP IMC PROGRAMS

As Figure 1-7 shows, each promotional mix element has its own set of objectives, overall strategy, message and media strategy and tactics, and a budget. For example, the advertising program will have its own set of objectives, usually involving the communication of a message or appeal to a target audience. A budget will be determined, providing the advertising manager and the agency with an idea of how much money is available for developing the ad campaign and purchasing media to disseminate the ad message.

Two important aspects of the advertising program are development of the message and the media strategy. Message development, often referred to as *creative strategy*, involves determining the basic message the advertiser wishes to convey to the target audience. This process, along with the ads that result, is to many students the most fascinating aspect of promotion. The Heart & Stroke ad shown in Exhibit 1-16 conveys an important message regarding the value of the Health Check logo.

Media strategy involves determining which communication channels will be used to deliver the advertising message to the target audience. Decisions must be made regarding which types of media will be used (e.g., newspapers, magazines, radio, TV, billboards) as well as specific media selections (e.g., a particular magazine or TV program). This task requires careful evaluation of the media options' strengths and limitations, costs, and ability to deliver the message effectively to the target audiences.

A similar process and set of decisions occur for ALL other elements of the IMC program as objectives are set, an overall strategy is developed, and message and media strategies are determined. If a firm decides to include a sales promotion, it might decide to use a specific message and media strategy and tactics to communicate information about the sales promotion, in addition to whatever advertising decisions that have been recommended.

Furthermore, if a firm considers using multiple tools for its complete plan it must decide which ones best fit together to solve a particular marketing communication problem. For example, Hellmann's mayonnaise communicated its natural ingredients of eggs, oil, and vinegar to challenge consumers' attitude that the product contained unhealthy contents. The campaign evolved over three years with multiple IMC tools and media resulting in substantial improvement in brand measures and profitability (Figure 1-9).[54] Finally, an IMC plan might evolve from an initial plan from one tool used, especially advertising. For example, Visa's "Win what you buy" sales promotion built upon the same message of "disappearing debt" conveyed in the television and print ads.[55]

IMPLEMENT AND CONTROL THE IMC PLAN

Once the message and media strategies have been determined for each tool, steps must be taken to implement

Exhibit 1-16   The Heart & Stroke Foundation logo is a sign of healthy food choices.

Budget:	$3 million to $4 million
Time Frame:	January 2007 to December 2009
Target:	Women 18–50
Strategic Message:	Real Food Movement
Annual Messages:	Eat Real. Eat Local (2009), Evergreen Partnership (2008), Urban Gardens (2007)
Events	Community Gardens
Advertising Media:	Television, Newspaper, Magazines
Sales Promotion:	Coupon, Contest, In-store display, Gifts/Premiums, Discounts
Internet:	Garden widget, forums, eatrealeatlocal.ca, mini-documentary, digital influencers, e-mail,
Public Relations	News coverage with Canadian Living and CanWest media partnerships

Figure 1-9

Hellman's Mayonnaise

them. Most large companies hire advertising agencies to plan and produce their messages and to evaluate and purchase the media that will carry their ads. However, most agencies work very closely with their clients as they develop the ads and select media, because it is the advertiser that ultimately approves (and pays for) the creative work and media plan. While the marketer's advertising agencies may be used to perform other IMC functions, they may also hire other communication specialists.

It is important to determine how well the promotional program is meeting communication and behavioural objectives and helping the firm accomplish its overall marketing objectives. The promotional planner wants to know not only how well the promotional program is doing but also why. For example, problems with the advertising program may lie in the nature of the message or in a media plan that does not reach the target audience effectively. The manager must know the reasons for the results in order to take the right steps to correct the program.

This final stage of the process is designed to provide managers with continual feedback concerning the effectiveness of the promotional program, which in turn can be used as input into the planning process. As Figure 1-7 shows, information on the results achieved by the promotional program is used in subsequent promotional planning and strategy development.

(L05) IMC Planning: Organization of Text

This book provides a thorough understanding of advertising and other elements of a firm's promotional mix and shows how they are combined to form a comprehensive marketing communications program with an IMC planning perspective. To implement this idea, we conclude each chapter of the book with an IMC planning section. Its purpose is to relate the chapter material to the content of an IMC plan and illustrate how to make IMC decisions. The final section of this chapter establishes this approach by illustrating how the entire book is organized around the IMC planning perspective. The book is organized around five major parts to facilitate this goal.

UNDERSTANDING INTEGRATED MARKETING COMMUNICATION

Part I comprises four chapters that define the topic of the book and provide the context for marketing communication decisions. This initial chapter introduces the IMC tools and how they relate to marketing. The chapter also gives a brief description of IMC and the content of a promotional plan.

We discuss how advertisers work with ad agencies and other firms that provide marketing and promotional services in Chapter 2. Agencies are an important part of the IMC planning process as they assist in the decision making with promotional planners and execute many of the decisions by creating promotional messages.

To plan, develop, and implement an effective IMC program, those involved must understand consumer behaviour and the communications process. We focus on consumer behaviour and the target audience decision, and summarize many communication response models in Chapters 3 and 4, respectively. Combined, these two chapters establish a conceptual foundation for developing the subsequent decisions of an IMC plan.

ARTICULATE THE MESSAGE

Part II concerns a number of decisions that firms make to put together a persuasive marketing communication message and comprises five chapters. The ideas developed here are applicable for advertising and all other IMC tools. Sales promotion offers include a brand message, as do public relations activities. All brand-initiated communication in Internet media provides a clear message about the brand.

Chapter 5 explains how to set IMC objectives to achieve the desired effects. A general model is explained for setting behavioural and communication objectives that are universally applicable to all IMC tools.

Chapter 6 reviews the important decisions to construct a brand positioning strategy. This is the heart of marketing communication, where decisions regarding how brands compete with marketing communication messages are determined.

The most exciting aspects of IMC are presented in Chapters 7 and 8, where we illustrate creative strategy and creative tactics decisions that are reflected in the vibrant and exciting ads we all experience in every part of our daily living. Creative illustration of a brand is the pinnacle task of creative specialists and their work is central for building a brand.

Chapter 9 examines how to measure promotional message effectiveness. The research ideas presented in this chapter also set the stage for understanding how to assess the effects of all IMC tools found in later chapters.

DELIVER THE MESSAGE

Part III comprises four chapters and explores the key media strategy, media tactics decisions, and budgeting for IMC, along with the use of six different media.

Chapter 10 provides the technical information for media planning. Media planning is an important advertising decision and this information is also used to plan media for the implementation of other IMC tools. Scheduling and determining how many consumers should receive a message and how often is critical with Internet media like all other media. Similarly, the timing and media presentation of promotional offers assist in the success of their execution. The chapter also explores how to construct a budget and allocate the budget for advertising and all IMC tools.

Chapters 11, 12, and 13 describe the use and strengths and limitations of media choices that have been historically labelled as *mass media* (i.e., television, radio, magazines, newspapers, out-of-home, and support). Once again, background on these topics is useful for implementing advertising and for using these media in executing other IMC tools. Much of these mass media are used to direct consumers to different aspects of Internet media. There are QR codes on outdoor ads. TV and radio messages say "Facebook us" to carry on further communication. These media are also used for presentation of community activities designed to "give back" and foster goodwill among citizens.

STRENGTHEN THE MESSAGE

Our interest turns to the other areas of the promotional mix—sales promotion, public relations, direct marketing, and Internet marketing—in Part IV, "Strengthen the Message." Each tool is explored in its own chapter and related to communication objectives as done in Part III.

Chapter 14 investigates consumer and trade sales promotions that are often combined with advertising to influence behaviourally and from a communication standpoint. A multitude of options are available for planners to both stimulate sales and enhance brand equity.

Chapter 15 presents the topic of public relations and related topics of publicity through media and corporate advertising. Using other tools or building a corporate brand through IMC are important topics to fully understand how to put together a complete IMC plan.

Chapter 16 covers direct marketing and direct-response media used to communicate to this particular IMC tool. Improved technology allows brands to communicate to individuals and vice versa. Methods for advertising and promoting directly are described in this chapter.

Chapter 17 examines the considerable options for interactive communication via the Internet. While continued growth makes this a challenge to remain current, the available options and how brands are built with electronic communication are developed to fulfill the need for a comprehensive IMC plan.

ADVERTISING AND SOCIETY

Part V concludes the book with one chapter that examines advertising regulation and the ethical, social, and economic effects of an organization's advertising and promotional program. Advertising is a very public and controversial part of any organization's activities and this chapter explores the complexities of these points. Each topic is relevant at varying points of the earlier chapters and may be read when desired.

Learning Objectives Summary

 Describe the importance of marketing communication within the marketing mix.

Marketing combines the four controllable elements, known as the marketing mix, into a comprehensive program that facilitates exchange with a group of customers. The elements of the marketing mix are the product, price, place (distribution), and promotion (market communication). Advertising and other forms of promotion are an integral part of the marketing process in most organizations since these tools communicate the value consumers receive within the exchange. Marketing communication conveys many aspects of the product including attributes, benefits, symbolic meaning, and brand identity with the hopes of building brand equity. Providing price and distribution information are two other important roles of marketing communication so that value is perceived by both customers and non-customers.

 Identify the tools of the promotional mix—advertising, sales promotion, public relations, direct marketing, Internet marketing, and personal selling—and summarize their purpose.

Promotion is accomplished through a promotional mix that includes advertising, sales promotion, public relations, direct marketing, Internet marketing, and personal selling. The inherent advantages and disadvantages of each of these promotional mix elements influence the roles they play in the overall marketing program. In developing the promotional program, the manager must decide which tools to use and how to combine them to achieve the organization's objectives. Many organizations assist promotional managers in developing or implementing their plans including advertising agencies, media organizations, and specialized communication services firms like direct-response agencies, sales promotion agencies, interactive agencies, and public relations firms.

 Illustrate the concept of integrated marketing communications (IMC) by distinguishing its evolution, renewed perspective, and importance.

Historically, companies used mass-media advertising extensively in their promotional plans. Eventually, companies linked their promotional tools to achieve a more efficient and effective communication program. Managers referred to this practice as integrated marketing communications (IMC). Today, IMC is viewed as a strategic and comprehensive planning perspective for all facets of an organization's marketing communication.

An IMC perspective is an important direction for decision making for a number of reasons. Most organizations need to communicate with multiple target audiences requiring decisions on the consistency or uniqueness of messages to each member. When planning for IMC, managers have to consider how each promotional tool will communicate the brand effectively depending on who is receiving the brand message. The emergence of IMC has become even more important for organizations that communicate with messages to current customers and with other messages to prospective customers.

An IMC perspective also starts with the consumer's point of view in that much marketing communication is perceived as being very similar to or at least labelled as advertising. Moreover, an IMC perspective for promotional planning has become critical as audiences receive messages from competing brands across different IMC tools.

A movement toward building long-term relationships through strategies like relationship marketing has altered the communication perspective of many promotional planners. Customized communication to individual customers via extensive databases to enhance the lifetime value of customers makes IMC more critical.

Increased consumer adoption of technology and media allows marketers far-reaching avenues for communication that makes paramount the need to consider each tool's effects. Finally, the advantages of taking an IMC perspective are increasingly viewed as being a very effective way of planning for promotion that can lead to greater efficiencies.

 Explain the IMC planning process model and express the steps in developing a marketing communications program.

IMC management involves coordinating the promotional mix elements to develop an integrated program of effective marketing communication. The model of the IMC planning process in Figure 1-7 contains a number of steps: a review of the marketing plan; a marketing communication situation analysis; determining IMC plan objectives; development of IMC programs; and implementation and control of the overall program. This model is consistent with the more general marketing planning model, but is more specific to the context of marketing communication. It shows that individual marketing communication tools can be recommended to achieve multiple objectives so that the completely coordinated or integrated plan can build brand equity across multiple target audiences.

Identify how the IMC planning process is continued throughout all chapters.

The IMC planning process is an important perspective that is continually reinforced in every chapter. All chapter material for the rest of the book is presented with an approach to assist in decision making for every step.

Key Terms

Review key terms and definitions on Connect.

Review Questions

1. Why is marketing communication important for communicating value to consumers?

2. How do smartphone brands use each marketing communication tool for communicating messages?

3. Illustrate how integrated marketing communications differs from traditional advertising and promotion. What are the reasons why more marketers are taking an IMC perspective to their advertising and promotion programs?

4. What parts of the IMC planning model are similar to and different from a marketing planning model?

5. How is the structure of the book consistent with the content of an IMC plan?

Applied Questions

1. Consider how a university or college communicates value in its marketing communication to its prospective students and current students. In what ways are the two approaches similar or different?

2. Identify all the possible marketing communication tools that a favourite brand or performance artist is using. Try to explain why these tools were selected. In what ways did the tools support one another? How did they not support one another? Was each tool effective or ineffective?

3. Find examples where all promotional tools have the same "look and feel," and others where there is a different look and feel. Why did these decisions occur based on relevant situation analysis variables?

4. Why is it important for those who work in the field of advertising and promotion to understand and appreciate all IMC tools, not just the area in which they specialize?

5. How does one of your favourite brands link or integrate its different IMC communication tools? Is it done effectively?

GO ONLINE

For more information on the resources available from McGraw-Hill Ryerson, go to www.mcgrawhill.ca/he/solutions.

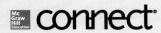

Organizing for IMC: Role of Agencies

CHAPTER TWO

2

LEARNING OBJECTIVES

LO1 Identify the role of the advertising agency and the services it provides.

LO2 Describe methods for compensating and evaluating advertising agencies.

LO3 Contrast the role and functions of specialized marketing communication organizations.

LO4 Evaluate the perspectives on the use of integrated services across agencies or within one agency, and agency–client responsibilities and partnerships.

Independent Sid Lee Shoots for the Big Time

For three years in a row, in 2009, 2010, and 2011, *Marketing Magazine* named Sid Lee Agency of the Year. According to the editors, while other agencies might feel a little jealous, the independent agency founded in Montreal even received private kudos from its competitors' presidents! Originally named Diesel, Sid Lee is an anagram of that name to distinguish it from the stylish fashion producer. From its humble beginnings 16 years ago when the first owners had no advertising agency experience, Sid Lee ramped up to 600 employees and four more offices located in Toronto, Amsterdam, Paris, and Austin.

A Canadian advertising agency expanding to the international stage is almost unheard of historically, but Sid Lee proved it can be done—and what a client list with its current achievements. Adidas recognized the talent and hired the agency on as the leader for its worldwide marketing communication. One development featured a mobile app where a shoe photo would direct the user to the closest store with the product available. Sid Lee achieved another success by landing the Dell account despite 40 other agencies pitching for the work. According to senior partner Bertrand Cesvet, both the German and American firms admired Sid Lee for truly understanding European and American consumers and marketing in these countries.

And the admiration continued; Sport Chek's CMO Duncan Fulton liked that Sid Lee immediately took a strategic approach to solving his brand's marketing communication issues by asking about growth, brand, and business objectives. Together, Sport Chek and Sid Lee planned to completely alter the shopping experience for sporting goods consumers with extensive digital content throughout the store and fresher brand concepts and images.

Cirque de Soleil hired on with Sid Lee more than a decade ago and the innovative agency handled all decisions for some of Cirque's new shows, from brand identification to positioning to key messaging. The relationship blossomed so much that Cirque became a minor owner among 25 owners including Sid Lee's management staff. With Cirque's worldwide distribution and exposure, Sid Lee looked to leverage that experience for greater steps abroad.

Across numerous other clients—like Videotron, Red Bull, and MGM Grand Hotel—Sid Lee married its skill in branding and marketing communication to its understanding of the customer experience to redesign facilities so that they fit with the overall strategy and what the agency created from a messaging standpoint. Additional high-profile clients have included Fatboy, Vitamin Water, Dom Perignon, and IMAX.

Senior management at Sid Lee attributed their success to the informal work culture, with relaxed dress and no hierarchy. A professional and organizational development program launched recently showed new employees the Sid Lee way of doing business. Expansion to Jimmy Lee, a production outfit, and Quick Lee, a social intranet that allows creative specialists to connect, are other innovations that keep the agency on a solid path of good service, management, and creativity.

Sources: David Brown, "Sid Lee," *Marketing Magazine,* December 12, 2011; David Brown, "Sid Lee vs. The World," *Marketing Magazine,* January 16, 2012; Bertrand Marotte, "Sid Lee's Texas Office Builds on its Global Ambitions," *The Globe and Mail,* May 5, 2011; Nicholas Van Praet, "Status Quo Sucks for Petite Sid Lee," *National Post,* February 24, 2012.

Question:

1. As the owner of Sid Lee, would you sell the agency to a major super agency or retain your independence?

Developing and implementing an IMC program is usually a complex process involving the efforts of individuals from the marketing firm, the advertising agency, and often other types of agencies. Strong relationships with these agencies are important as their expertise in creative planning, media placement, new digital executions, and other activities contributes to successful brand development. Alternatively, brands also work with a full-service marketing communication agency capable of providing all services. This chapter explores how these agencies function for those who may want to work in the marketing communication agency industry.

This chapter first identifies the characteristics of a full-service agency and its client relationship. It then describes how agencies are compensated and evaluated. Next, the chapter contrasts the role of specialized marketing communication organizations such as creative boutiques, media buying services, direct-response, sales promotion and interactive agencies, and public relations firms. These organizations are increasingly involved in IMC planning and some are owned by large agencies which they work with considerably. Finally, the chapter evaluates whether marketers are best served by using the integrated services of one large agency or the separate services of multiple marketing communication specialists.

(L01) Advertising Agencies

Many different types of advertising agencies make the selection a unique decision for each advertiser. In this section we provide a general overview of advertising agencies; we review the agency decision, highlight the agency industry, and describe the activities of a full-service agency.

ADVERTISING AGENCY DECISION

Marketing organizations have a fundamental choice of whether a firm will have its own in-house agency or whether it will employ an external advertising agency. We now briefly discuss the relative merits and concerns of both options.

In-House Agency   An **in-house agency** is an advertising agency that is set up, owned, and operated by the advertiser. Some in-house agencies are essentially advertising departments, but in other companies they are given a separate identity and are responsible for the expenditure of large sums of advertising dollars. Research finds that about half of all companies use an in-house agency and that the likelihood of this occurring decreases with larger advertising budgets but increases with advertising intensity (i.e., advertising/sales ratio), technological intensity, and for creative industries.[1] Many companies use in-house agencies exclusively; others combine in-house efforts with those of outside agencies. For example, Target has an internal creative department that handles the design of its weekly circulars, direct-mail pieces, in-store displays, promotions, and other marketing materials. However, the retailer uses outside agencies to develop most of its branding and image-oriented ads and for specific TV and print assignments.[2] Joe Fresh, a key brand for Loblaw, moved its creativity in-house from an agency to get "our staff thinking about our brand" as it opened up stores in the United States. Coincidentally, that staff of 14 includes a couple of creatives from Target.[3]

A major reason for using an in-house agency is to reduce advertising and promotion costs. Companies with very large advertising budgets pay a substantial amount to outside agencies. An in-house agency can also provide related work—such as sales presentations and sales force materials, package design, and public relations—at a lower cost than outside agencies. A study by M. Louise Ripley found that creative and media services were the most likely functions to be performed outside, while merchandising and sales promotion were the most likely to be performed in-house.[4]

A study by Forrester Research concluded that in-house agencies are preferred because they provide stronger connection to senior managers and stability for the marketing communication function.[5] They found that nearly 60 percent of in-house agencies report directly to the company's CEO or chief marketing officer (CMO). Furthermore, external agencies yielded much higher turnover levels, which can take a toll on the client–agency relationship.

Time savings, bad experiences with outside agencies, and the increased knowledge and understanding of the market that come from working on advertising and promotion for the product or service day by day also support in-house agency use. Companies can also maintain tighter control over the process and more easily coordinate promotions with the firm's overall marketing program.[6]

A limitation of an in-house agency is that personnel may grow stale while working on the same product line in comparison to an outside agency where creative specialists design campaigns for a variety of products. Furthermore, changes in an in-house agency could be slow or disruptive compared to the flexibility of hiring a new outside agency.

Advertising Agency Many major companies use an advertising agency to assist them in developing, preparing, and executing their promotional programs. An ad agency is a service organization that specializes in planning and executing advertising programs for its clients. Probably the main reason why outside agencies are used is that they provide the client with the services of highly skilled specialists. An advertising agency's staff may include artists, writers, media analysts, researchers, and others with specific skills, knowledge, and experience who can help market the client's products or services. Many agencies specialize in a particular type of business and use their knowledge of the industry to assist their clients. For example, Mentus Inc. is an agency that specializes in the high-technology, e-commerce, and bioscience industries (Exhibit 2-1).

An outside agency's objective viewpoint of the market and the client's business is not subject to internal company policies, biases, or other limitations. The agency can draw on the broad range of experience it has gained while working on a diverse set of marketing problems for assorted clients. For example, an ad agency handling a travel-related account may employ individuals with travel-related industry experience (e.g., airlines, cruise ships, travel agencies, hotels). This industry knowledge may be combined with experience of having previously worked on the advertising account of one of the client's competitors.

The Institute of Communications and Advertising offers a comprehensive document that acts as a guide for selecting the most appropriate agency. Using a "best practices" approach, the steps in the search process are carefully diagrammed and explained so that both clients and agencies could benefit. If all the steps are adhered, selecting the right agency could range from 8 to 16 weeks. In the end, the client and agency form a partnership where the responsibilities of each are recorded and agreed upon with the intention of a positive working relationship.

ADVERTISING AGENCY INDUSTRY

The Canadian advertising agency industry is similar to that in other countries—there is a combination of small and mid-sized domestic firms and large international organizations with domestic service providers. The strong presence of international ad agencies in Canada reflects a global trend of large agencies merged with or acquired by other agencies and support organizations. These **superagencies** now provide clients with integrated marketing communications services worldwide. Many mid-size agencies were acquired by or forged alliances with larger agencies because clients wanted an agency with international marketing communication capabilities, and their alignment with larger organizations permitted access to a network of agencies around the world. Currently, most major agencies offer specialized services in areas of interactive communications, direct marketing, and sales promotion so that they can offer their clients an ever-broader range of

Exhibit 2-1 Mentus specializes in creating ads for bioscience companies.

Exhibit 2-2   TAG Heuer uses a global campaign featuring different celebrity ambassadors for various countries.

IMC services.[7] In fact, a larger multiservice firm is a **marketing communication agency**, making the term "advertising agency" somewhat obsolete for these situations. Global advertising campaigns are facilitated by using larger international agencies (Exhibit 2-2).

Figure 2-1 summarizes the "agency family tree" produced by *Marketing Magazine*.[8] The tree identifies all the major players on the Canadian advertising scene. (Note that the original tree spanned eight pages; we retained the scope of the diagram and acknowledge missing information or lack of detail to fit this broad array of information in a single table.) The idea of the super-agency is readily observed—we see two major Canadian firms, Vision 7 International and MDC, along with their full agency and other businesses that cater to all marketing communication services. As expected, two major players exist based in New York, Omnicom and Interpublic; each one includes famous advertising agencies recognized for their creative talent.

Canadian affiliates of these large agencies are responsible for country-based marketing communication activities that are part of the worldwide campaigns. For example, BBDO Proximity of Toronto developed an Internet application to promote the Gillette Fusion brand in Canada (Exhibit 2-3). Additionally, the table includes two major European conglomerates that own established American advertising greats like Ogilvy & Mather, JWT, and Leo Burnett. IMC Perspective 2-1 highlights the accomplishments of Canadian agencies.

Two agencies with strong Canadian roots developed internationally. Over the past decade, Taxi won about 1,200 national and international awards and *Strategy* named them agency of the year five times. Taxi expanded to the United States and Europe and the prestigious One Club recognized it as one of the top advertising agencies in the world. Acquired by WPP, the agency continues to set new standards of excellence for its clients like Mini. Sid Lee expanded to the United States and Europe as well and developed an international presence for Adidas in 100 countries with its

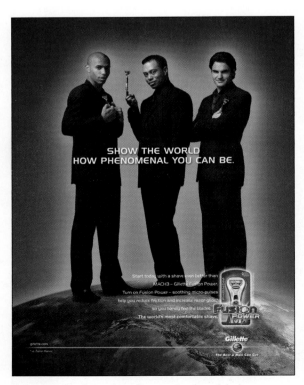

Exhibit 2-3   Agencies often customize global campaigns for local markets.

Figure   2-1   A summary of the "agency family tree" produced by *Marketing Magazine*

	Advertising or Full Service	Public Relations	Digital and Direct	Sales Promotion	Media Buying	Design	Other
Vision 7 International (Quebec City)	Cossette	Citizen Optimum	Dare Rocket XL	Elvis	Cossette Jungle	Identica	Koo Creative Impact Research
MDC (Toronto)	Capital G CPG KBS+P	Veritas	Henderson Bas Kenna	6 Degrees		Bruce Mau Ombrand	Bryan Mills Northstar
OmniComm (New York)	DDB BBDO DAS	DDB PR Porter Novelli Ketchum FleishmanHillard	Tribal DDB Rapp Radar DDB Proximity		OMG	Karacters Nolin CDM	Kidthink Shopper DDB TBWA Radiate MarketStar IMS
Interpublic (New York)	MacLaren McCann Lowe Draft FCB CMG		MRM Rivet GolinHarris	Momentum Segal	Media Brands	Brandid Future Brands	McGill Octagon
WPP (London)	Grey Ogilvy & Mather JWT Young & Rubicam Taxi	Hill & Knowlton Res Publica	Group M OgilvyOne Wunderman	OgilvyAction	GroupM	JWT Sauce Sudler	Kantar Redworks Ethos JWT
Publicis (Paris)	Publicis Leo Burnett Saatchi & Saatchi	Starcom	Rosetta		Starcom		MSL Zenith

ambitious digital delivery.[9] Individual Canadians who achieved success are also in demand internationally, finding top-level positions paying seven figures.[10]

Many small and mid-sized agencies handle local and regional work throughout Canada. *Marketing Magazine* featured up-and-coming new agencies in western Canada like Giant Ant Media (Creative Agency/Production Studio) with MEC as a key client, FCV (Interactive Agency) with Telus, Nike, and Scotiabank as key clients, and Smak (Experiential/Media Agency) with Future Shop as a key client.[11] Across the country, these independent agencies offer opportunity for students to get their "foot in the door" to pursue a career in the advertising industry. One smaller agency, Acart in Ottawa, continues to outbid other more dominant players as it secures many government advertising assignments.[12] And in the oldest city in North America, Target of St. John's continues to innovate as it listens to the "beat of a different drum" while enjoying the view of the Atlantic Ocean. Check out its creative "Weiner News Network" on YouTube![13]

FULL-SERVICE AGENCY

The services offered and functions performed vary depending upon the size of the agency. A **full-service agency** offers its clients a complete range of marketing, communication, and promotion services including planning, performing research, creating the message of the ad campaign, producing the advertising, and selecting media. A full-service agency may also offer nonadvertising services, such as strategic market planning, sales promotions, direct marketing,

IMC PERSPECTIVE 2-1

Agency of the Year for DDB—Again!

Strategy magazine named DDB its Agency of the Year for 2009 and 2010, a deserving honour when one looks at the awards it received and the creativity of its work. In Subaru, DDB scored with its spots for the Outback and Forester brands. One spot begins as an infomercial for the ubiquitous Snuggie (a blanket with sleeves); after 11 seconds, the scene quickly changes via a crowbar prying the ad away from the screen, revealing an intervening man who is outdoors with his Outback. The super suggests, "Maybe you should get out more" to its target—owners of small SUVs who live in cities and appreciate the outdoors. DDB saw that Subaru, with only 2 percent market share, needed a surprise in its message and the approach certainly worked, with a 200 percent sales increase. For the Forester, DDB featured "sexy" sumo wrestlers in a campaign that won the "Best of the Best" award and numerous other gold awards from the Canadian Marketing Association. This sporting imagery improved sales by more than 100 percent.

For the BC Dairy Foundation, DDM invented a number of quirky scenarios reflecting competitive situations that teens experience in life. Each concluded with the vanquished participant saying "Must drink more milk," implying that milk would give more energy and reverse the outcome. With the goal of increasing consumption among teens who understood the health benefits of milk, the campaign proved successful with a 3 percent growth in volume. Moreover, spillover to user-generated executions on YouTube enabled milk to take a central role in teen life once again.

"Locals know" became the theme for a campaign for the Canadian Tourism Commission to increase the amount of domestic travel—in other words, to encourage Canadians to visit Canada instead of international destinations. DDB put together the message and visuals to show the country's unique and exotic places that only "locals" know about. A number of print images and TV ads asked, "Where is this?"

in reference to unexpected Canadian geography such as sand dunes, a volcano, and tropical blue water. Viewers went to the website to find out the answer, upload vacation pictures, or talk about different locations. Forbes cited the campaign as one of the top 10 in the world, 450,000 visited the website, and follow-up research found 22 percent booked a domestic trip in response to the ads. The social media continued as an emphasis with renewed effort for enhanced creativity.

DDB achieved success for Knorr Sidekicks with a salt shaker that comes to life, but is heart-broken when finding out that salt is significantly reduced in the new dishes. Dejected, "Salty" found a new life in a series of Web videos showing what the character tried to do in life resulting in a few humorous escapades.

The growth of DDB in Canada prompted the agency of the Omnicom group to partner with a local agency in Montreal to establish credibility in order to serve the Quebec market. Local clients retained the services of Bleublancrouge and now obtained the opportunity to work with the national and international talent of the larger organizations.

Sources: Susan Krashinsky, "DDB Partners with Montreal's Bleublancrouge," *The Globe and Mail,* July 26, 2012; Emily Wexler, "Seizing Emotions," *Strategy,* February 1, 2011; Carey Toane, "AOY Gold: DDB Rules the Roost," *Strategy,* November 2009; Kristin Laird, "Subaru Pulls Off Snuggie Ad for Outback Spot," *Marketing Magazine,* November 17, 2009; Jeromy Lloyd, "Subaru's Sumo Take Top Prize at CMAS," *Marketing Magazine,* November 30, 2009.

Question:

1. In what way is each of the campaigns creative?

interactive services, public relations and publicity, and package design. The full-service agency has departments led by a director that provide the activities needed to perform the advertising functions and serve the client, as shown in Figure 2-2. In this section we summarize these main characteristics.

Account/Client Services Account services, or client services, is the link between the ad agency and its clients. Depending on the size of the client and its advertising budget, one or more account executives serve as liaison. The **account executive** is responsible for understanding the advertiser's marketing and promotions needs and interpreting them to agency

Figure 2-2 Full-service agency organizational chart

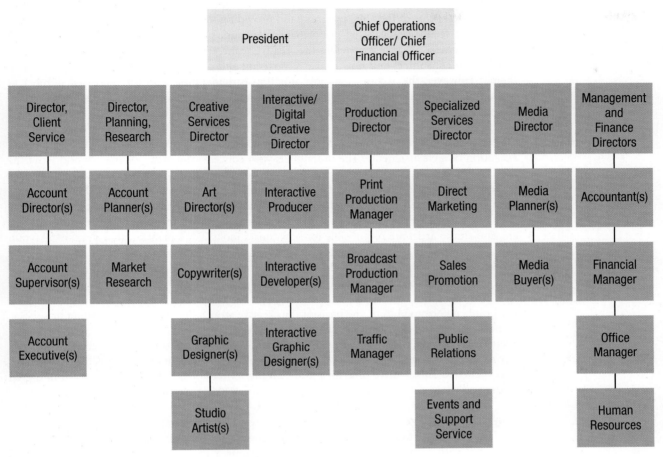

personnel. He or she coordinates agency efforts in planning, creating, and producing ads. The account executive also presents agency recommendations and obtains client approval. As the focal point of agency–client relationships, the account executive must know a great deal about the client's business and be able to communicate this to specialists in the agency working on the account. The ideal account executive has a strong marketing background as well as a thorough understanding of all phases of the advertising process.

Planning/Research Services Most full-service agencies maintain a research department whose function is to gather, analyze, and interpret information as input for advertising decisions. Both primary research—where a study is designed, executed, and interpreted by the research department—or secondary (previously published) sources of information are relied upon. The research department also acquires studies conducted by independent syndicated research firms or consultants, interprets the findings, and disseminates the information to agency personnel working on that account. The research department may also design and conduct research to pretest the effectiveness of advertising the agency is considering. For example, copy testing is conducted to determine how messages developed by the creative specialists are likely to be interpreted by the receiving audience.

Research services may be augmented with services performed by account planners, who gather relevant information that can be used to develop the creative strategy and other aspects of the IMC campaign. Account planners work with the client and other agency personnel including the account executives, creative team members, media specialists, and research department personnel to collect information to better understand the client's target audience and the best ways to communicate with them. They gather and organize information about consumers, competitors, and the market to prepare the **creative brief**, which is a document that the agency's creative department uses to guide the development of advertising ideas and concepts.

Account planners may also be involved in assessing consumers' reactions to the advertising and other elements of the IMC program and providing the creative staff and other agency personnel with feedback regarding performance. Account planning is a very important function in many agencies because it provides the creative team, and other agency personnel, with more insight into consumers and how to use advertising and other IMC tools to communicate with them.[14] However, the account planning function is demanding with the increased number of marketing communication channels. Account planners interact with individuals from all marketing communication disciplines and require expertise in each area.

Creative Services   The creative services department is responsible for the creation and execution of advertisements. The individuals who conceive the ideas for the ads and write the headlines, subheads, and body copy (the words constituting the message) are known as **copywriters**. They may also be involved in determining the message appeal and/or theme of the ad campaign and often prepare a rough initial visual layout of the print ad or television commercial.

While copywriters are responsible for what the message says, the art director, graphic designers, and studio artist are responsible for how the ad looks. For a print ad, they prepare a **layout**, which is drawing that shows what the ad will look like and from which the final artwork will be produced. For a TV commercial, the layout is known as a **storyboard**, a sequence of frames or panels that depict the commercial in still form.

Members of the creative department work together to develop ads that will communicate the key points determined to be the basis of the creative strategy for the client's product or service. Writers and artists generally work under the direction of the agency's creative director, who oversees all the advertising produced by the organization. The director sets the creative philosophy of the department and may even become directly involved in creating ads for the agency's largest clients. The creative director's job is all the more demanding with the growth of digital media and client demands to be part of the decision making earlier in the creative process.[15]

Digital Creative Services   Digital creative shares similarity with established creative departments with respect to copywriters and specialists with graphics skills. However, other personnel with computer technology skills are required for programming various interactive features of creative ads found in Internet media vehicles. Moreover, this newer genre of creativity includes an interactive producer to oversee all operations and to coordinate with creative work done in mass media. In order to grow this side of the business, full-service agencies purchase small or mid-sized independent interactive agencies.[16]

Production Services   The ad is turned over to the production department once the copy, layout, illustrations, and mechanical specifications are completed and approved. Most agencies do not actually produce finished ads; they hire printers, engravers, photographers, typographers, and other suppliers. For broadcast production, the storyboard must be turned into a finished commercial. The production department may supervise the casting of people to appear in the ad, the setting for the scenes, and choose an independent production studio. The department may hire an outside director to turn the creative concept into a commercial. Specialists from all departments and client representatives may all participate in production decisions, particularly when large sums of money are involved.

Creating an advertisement often involves many people and takes several months. In large agencies with many clients, coordinating the creative and production processes is a major task. A **traffic department**, or traffic manager, coordinates all phases of production to see that the ads are completed on time and that all deadlines for submitting the ads to the media are met. The traffic department can be in production or may be a separate department or located in other service departments.

Media Services   The media department of an agency analyzes, selects, and contracts for space or time in the media that will be used to deliver the client's advertising message. The media department is expected to develop a media plan that will reach the target audience and effectively communicate the message. Since most of the client's ad budget is spent on media time and/or space, this department must develop a plan that both communicates with the right audience and is cost-effective and cost-efficient.

Media specialists must know what audiences the media reach, their rates, and how well they match the client's target audience. The media department reviews information on demographics, magazine and newspaper readership, radio listenership, and consumers' TV and Internet viewing patterns to develop an effective media plan. The media buyer implements the media plan by purchasing the actual time and space. The media department is an important part of the agency business as many large advertisers consolidate their media buying with one or a few agencies to improve media efficiency. An agency's strategic ability to negotiate prices and effectively use the vast array of media vehicles available is as important as its ability to create ads. Many full-service agencies see value in offering this service since media companies are competing against agencies by offering creative services. For example, *Metro* newspaper has a creative department that helps advertisers, like an agency does, to put together a print campaign.[17]

Specialized Services   Large, full-service agencies offer additional marketing services to their clients to assist in other promotional areas. An agency may have a sales promotion department, or merchandising department, that specializes in developing contests, premiums, promotions, point-of-sale materials, and other sales materials. It may have direct-marketing specialists and package designers, as well as a PR/publicity department. Many agencies have developed interactive media departments to create websites or develop social media and e-mail campaigns for their clients. This media growth initiated the opportunity for creative expression of brands and required agencies to organize additional creative departments. In a completely new direction, Rethink and Sid Lee moved toward design services. Rethink involved themselves tremendously with the new look in Freshco grocery stores. Sid Lee opened up its own architecture services as part of its design offering so that a consistent look is presented from both the retail and marketing communication perspectives.[18]

Organizational Structure   To provide superior service for its accounts, agencies use the **group system**, in which individuals from each department work together in groups to service particular accounts. In contrast to the **departmental system** we have been discussing thus far, each group is headed by an account executive or supervisor and includes media planners and buyers; a creative team, which includes copywriters, art directors, artists, and production personnel; and one or more account executives. The group may also include individuals from other departments such as marketing research, direct marketing, or sales promotion. The size and composition of the group varies depending on the client's billings and the importance of the account to the agency. For very important accounts, the group members may be assigned exclusively to one client. A group system is preferred because employees become very knowledgeable about the client's business and there is continuity in servicing the account.

(L02) Agency Compensation and Evaluation

Agencies use a variety of compensation methods depending on the type and amount of service they provide to their clients. We review a number of methods, because there is no one method of compensation to which everyone subscribes. We also examine the related topic of performance evaluation and explore reasons why clients switch agencies.

COMMISSIONS FROM MEDIA

The historical method of compensating agencies is through a **commission system**, where the agency receives a specified commission (usually 15 percent) from the media on any advertising time or space it purchases for its client. This system provides a simple method of determining payments, as shown in the following example.

Assume an agency prepares a full-page magazine ad and arranges to place the ad on the back cover of a magazine at a cost of $100,000. The agency places the order for the space and delivers the ad to the magazine. Once the ad is run, the magazine will bill the agency for $100,000, less the 15 percent ($15,000) commission. The media will also offer a 2 percent cash discount for early payment, which the agency may pass along to the client. The agency will bill the client $100,000 less the 2 percent cash discount on the net amount, or a total of $98,300, as shown in Figure 2-3. The $15,000 commission represents the agency's compensation for its services.

The commission system has been quite controversial despite its prevalent use for decades. Critics argue that it encourages agencies to recommend high-priced media to increase their commission level. Another concern regarding the commission system is that it ties agency compensation to media costs, allowing the agency to be disproportionately rewarded. Critics have argued that it provides an incentive for agencies to recommend mass-media advertising when other forms of communication such as direct marketing or public relations might do a better job.[19]

Defenders of the commission system argue that it is easy to administer and it keeps the emphasis in agency competition on non-price factors like advertising quality. Proponents argue that agency services are proportional to the size of the commission, since more time and effort are devoted to the large accounts that generate high revenue for the agency. They also say the system is more flexible than it appears because agencies often perform other services for large clients at no extra charge, justifying such actions by the large commission they receive.

A study of agency compensation conducted by the Association of Canadian Advertisers (ACA) indicates that agency compensation based on the traditional 15 percent commission is becoming rare.[20] The survey found that the commission model was one of many approaches used and that no one model stood out as being the very best. Instead, advertisers use a **negotiated commission** system where commissions average 8 to 10 percent and are based on a sliding scale that becomes lower as clients' media expenditures increase. Agencies rely less on media commissions for their income as their clients expand their integrated marketing communications programs to include other forms of promotion and cut back on mass-media advertising. As the percentage of agency income from media commissions declines a greater percentage is coming through other methods such as fees and performance incentives.

FEE ARRANGEMENT

There are two types of fee arrangement systems. In the straight or **fixed-fee method**, the agency charges a monthly fee for all of its services and credits to the client any media commissions earned. Agency and client agree on the specific work to be done and the amount the agency will be paid for it. Sometimes agencies are compensated through a **fee–commission combination**, in which the media commissions received by the agency are credited against the fee. If the commissions are less than the agreed-on fee, the client must make up the difference. If the agency does much work for the client in noncommissionable media, the fee may be charged over and above the commissions received.

Both types of fee arrangements require that the agency carefully assess its costs of serving the client for the specified period, or for the project, plus its desired profit margin. To avoid any later

Figure   2-3

Example of commission system payment

Media Bills Agency		Agency Bills Advertiser	
Costs for magazine space	$100,000	Costs for magazine space	$100,000
Less 15% commission	−15,000	Less 2% cash discount	−1,700
Cost of media space	$ 85,000	Advertiser pays agency	$ 98,300
Less 2% cash discount	−1,700		
Agency pays media	$ 83,300	Agency income	$ 15,000

disagreement, a fee arrangement should specify exactly what services the agency is expected to perform for the client. An interview of four agency executives suggests that the fee arrangement is becoming the more accepted method of compensation in Canada.[21]

COST-PLUS AGREEMENT

Under a **cost-plus system**, the client agrees to pay the agency a fee based on the costs of its work plus an agreed-on profit margin (often a percentage of total costs). This system requires that the agency keep detailed records of the costs it incurs in working on the client's account. Direct costs (personnel time and out-of-pocket expenses) plus an allocation for overhead and a markup for profits determines the amount the agency bills the client. An agency can add a markup of percentage charges to various services the agency purchases from outside providers (e.g., market research, artwork, printing, photography).

Fee agreements and cost-plus systems are commonly used in conjunction with a commission system. The fee-based system can be advantageous to both the client and the agency, depending on the size of the client, advertising budget, media used, and services required. Many clients prefer fee or cost-plus systems because they receive a detailed breakdown of where and how their advertising and promotion dollars are being spent. However, these arrangements can be challenging for the agency, as they require careful cost accounting and may be difficult to estimate when bidding for an advertiser's business. Agencies are also reluctant to let clients see their internal cost figures.

INCENTIVE-BASED COMPENSATION

Clients expect accountability from their agencies and link agency compensation to performance through an **incentive-based system**. The idea is that the agency's ultimate compensation level will depend on how well it meets predetermined performance goals. In Canada, the Performance by Results (PBR) system, initiated by the Institute of Communications and Advertising, highlights the importance of clearly identifying the objectives of the promotional plan and measuring the performance of the plan based on these objectives. PBR defines an advertising remuneration process where the basic advertising agency fee is adjusted by a reward based on the degree of achieving mutually agreed upon objectives between the client and the agency. Overall, the remuneration is a part of a system of linking performance, its measurement, and reward within the client–agency relationship. The benefits of the PBR system are:

Greater efficiency and accountability	Stronger mutual understanding
Achievement of cost efficiencies	Improved retention of creative talent
Higher productivity	Increased agency strategic input
Fewer barriers of self-interest	Improved client–agency communication

Three general groups of performance measures are critical in the PBR system: overall business performance, marketing communication effectiveness, and agency process evaluation. Business measures include sales, market share, profitability, and margins. Marketing communication effectiveness measures include brand awareness, brand image ratings, and likability of advertising. This group also includes four objectives that are more behavioural: intent to purchase, trial, repeat purchase, and brand loyalty. The final group concerns the services the agency provides and its overall management process.

The PBR system claims that there is no standard formula in applying these measures. The relative importance of each measure needs to be investigated for each brand and its marketing situation. Furthermore, the measures should take into account the role of promotion in the marketing mix and how promotion contributes to business results for the brand and within the product category or industry. In addition, the PBR system provides the following suggestions. Objectives can be short term and long term. An appropriate number of objectives should be used to focus the organization. The objectives should be consistent with other performance measures used in the organization. Objectives should be periodically re-evaluated by the client and the agency. Although these recommendations may be intuitive, the Canadian PBR is the most thorough published examination of the PBR system in the world. Another remarkable achievement for our marketing communication industry![22]

Data show that about one-third of all Canadian marketers compensated their agencies with a form of payment by results. However, this overall figure varies depending upon the size of the communications budget. A total of 58 percent of firms spending more than $100 million use incentives, compared to only 18 percent of firms spending less than $15 million. Moreover, about two-thirds of clients compensating their agencies in this manner report improved performance. Larger firms, like Unilever, for example, employ this compensation method for all of their service agencies including sales promotion and public relations.[23]

EVALUATION OF AGENCIES

Regular reviews of the agency's performance are necessary. The agency evaluation process usually involves two types of assessments, one financial and operational and the other more qualitative. The **financial audit** focuses on how the agency conducts its business. It is designed to verify costs and expenses, the number of personnel hours charged to an account, and payments to media and outside suppliers. The **qualitative audit** focuses on the agency's efforts in planning, developing, and implementing the client's advertising programs and considers the results achieved.

The agency evaluation can be done on a subjective, informal basis, particularly in smaller companies where ad budgets are low or advertising is not seen as the most critical factor in the firm's marketing performance. Companies have developed formal, systematic evaluation systems, particularly when budgets are large and the advertising function receives much emphasis. As advertising costs continue to rise, the top management of these companies wants to be sure money is being spent efficiently and effectively.

As part of its mandate as an industry resource, the Institute of Communications and Advertising provides a Guide to Best Practice that includes information to facilitate agency evaluation (the Guide and PBR information identified earlier in the chapter are available at www.icacanada.ca). The document provides guidelines on the client–agency relationship and includes many forms that can be used as a basis for evaluating an agency in all areas of performance such as account management, creative, planning and research, production, media planning and buying, budget and financial, agency management, direct marketing, interactive marketing, and public relations.

One example of a formal agency evaluation system is that used by Whirlpool, which markets a variety of consumer products. Whirlpool management meets once a year with the company's agencies to review their performance. Whirlpool managers complete an advertising agency performance evaluation, part of which is shown in Figure 2-4. These reports are compiled and reviewed with the agency at each annual meeting. Whirlpool's evaluation process covers six areas of performance. The company and the agency develop an action plan to correct areas of deficiency.

REASONS FOR AGENCIES LOSING CLIENTS

The evaluation process described above provides valuable feedback to both the agency and the client, such as indicating changes that need to be made by the agency and/or the client to improve performance and make the relationship more productive. Many agencies have had very long-lasting relationships with their clients; however, long-term relationships are less common.

Agency-of-record (AOR) is the term used to describe those situations where a client works with a primary agency for a number of years. It is the very foundation on which the advertising agency business exists—a service provider whose foremost interest is in building the client's brand. In some instances, the AOR will subcontract work to other specialized agencies; however, the AOR will have considerable responsibility given its designation with the client. A trend is that advertisers do not have a specific AOR, but work with different agencies at once, or in succession, depending upon their communication needs. In essence, agencies perform project-like work for a client by developing a short campaign or performing creative work only. For

Figure 2-4 Whirlpool's ad agency performance evaluation

CREATIVE SERVICES						
Always	**Often**	**Occasionally**	**Seldom**	**Never**	**NA**	**Marks Scored**
4	**3**	**2**	**1**	**0**		

1. Agency produces fresh ideas and original approaches
2. Agency accurately interprets facts, strategies and objectives into usable advertisements and plans
3. Creative group is knowledgeable about company's products, markets and strategies
4. Creative group is concerned with good advertising communications and develops campaigns and ads that exhibit this concern
5. Creative group produces on time
6. Creative group performs well under pressure
7. Creative group operates in a businesslike manner to control production costs and other creative charges
8. Agency presentations are well organized with sufficient examples of proposed executions
9. Creative group participates in major campaign presentations
10. Agency presents ideas and executions not requested but felt to be good opportunities
11. Agency willingly accepts ideas generated by other locations/agency offices vs. being over-protective of its own creative product
12. Other areas not mentioned
13. Agency demonstrates commitment to client's business
14. Agency creative proposals are relevant and properly fulfill creative brief

Value—(marks)

	Rating:			
	Excellent	90–100%	Total marks scored	
	Good	80–89%		
	Average	70–79%	Total possible marks	
	Fair	60–69%		
	Poor	below 60%	Score	

ACCOUNT REPRESENTATION & SERVICE						
Always	**Often**	**Occasionally**	**Seldom**	**Never**	**NA**	**Marks Scored**
4	**3**	**2**	**1**	**0**		

1. Account representatives act with personal initiative
2. Account representatives anticipate needs in advance of direction by client (ie: are proactive)
3. Account group takes direction well
4. Agency is able to demonstrate results of programs implemented
5. Account representatives function strategically rather than as creative advisors only
6. Account representatives are knowledgeable about competitive programs and share this information along with their recommendations in a timely manner
7. Account representatives respond to client requests in a timely fashion
8. Account group operates in a businesslike manner to control costs
9. Agency recommendations are founded on sound reasoning and supported factually, and appropriately fit within budget constraints
10. Agency is able to advise the client on trends and developments in technology
11. Account representatives demonstrate a high degree of professionalism in both written and oral communication
12. Agency presents ideas and executions not requested by felt to be good opportunities
13. Agency makes reasoned recommendations on allocation of budgets
14. Agency demonstrates commitment to client's business
15. There is a positive social relationship between client and agency

Value—(marks)

	Rating:			
	Excellent	90–100%	Total marks scored	
	Good	80–89%		
	Average	70–79%	Total possible marks	
	Fair	60–69%		
	Poor	below 60%	Score	

example, a client can contract the creative work to an agency but rely on its own market research resources. Advertisers believe they are saving money, finding the best ideas for an assignment, and putting pressure on agencies to perform. Critics believe this allows marketing investments to gravitate away from advertising and limit brand development, minimizes consistency across multiple campaigns, or constrains creativity to position the brand effectively.[24]

While the debate continues, many Canadian campaigns such as Coors, Shoppers Drug Mart, Mr. Sub, Budget, Apple, and WestJet are the result of project work. In certain cases, the brand had an AOR status but the client decided to use a smaller or different agency for a particular assignment. Advertisers cite the need to remain flexible and the desire to test out new agencies for future relationships. In fact, a considerable amount of the project work went to smaller independent agencies or creative boutiques, which opens the possibility for future longer-term relationships.[25]

Figure 2-5 summarizes reasons why clients switch agencies.[26] If the agency recognizes these warning signs, it can adapt to make sure the client is satisfied. Some of the situations discussed here are unavoidable, and others are beyond the agency's control. One study reports that a decline of market share in the immediate two quarters precedes an agency firing.[27] So despite doing everything in its power, an agency could feel the brunt of weak performance in other marketing mix variables of the client's brand. Losing a major client can have a disastrous effect on a smaller agency, such that it could in fact go under as many of the staff leave for greener pastures. However, in the case of Grip Limited, the loss of Bell—accounting for one-quarter of revenue—allowed the upstart agency established with the help of Labatt to forge on and reinvent itself with a stronger focus toward interactive media and a more diversified client base.[28]

Figure   2-5

Common reasons for agencies to lose clients

Performance Quality	Client dissatisfied with advertising and/or service.
Declining Sales	Advertising is blamed when client's sales decline.
Communication	Poor working relationship with weak personal communication.
Demands	Client expects service beyond compensation paid.
Conflict	A lack of rapport among those working together.
Conflicts of Interest	Change in either business creates unworkable situation.
Conflicting View	Disagreement with level or method of compensation.
Size Change	Agency or client outgrows one another.
Strategy Change	Client strategy change requires new agency.
Personnel Change	New personnel prefer to work with established colleagues.
Policy Change	Either party evaluates the importance of the relationship.

Specialized Services

Many companies assign the development and implementation of their promotional programs to an advertising agency. But several other types of organizations provide specialized services that complement the efforts of ad agencies. Creative boutiques, media buying services, sales promotion agencies, public relations firms, direct-response agencies, and interactive agencies are important to marketers in developing and executing IMC programs. One survey found that PR firms and digital agencies posed as the strongest threat to supplanting full-service agencies.[29] Let us examine the functions these specialized marketing communication organizations perform.

CREATIVE BOUTIQUES

A **creative boutique** is an agency that provides only creative services. These specialized agencies have creative personnel but do not have media, research, or account planning capabilities. Creative boutiques have developed in response to companies' desires to use only the creative services of an outside agency while managing the other functions internally. While most creative boutiques work directly for companies, full-service agencies often subcontract work to creative boutiques when they are very busy or want to avoid adding full-time employees to their payrolls. Many creative boutiques have been formed by members of the creative departments of full-service agencies who leave the firm and take with them clients who want to retain their creative talents. Exhibit 2-4 highlights an example of Canada's most successful creative boutiques.

One area where Canadian agencies have worked with specialized creative firms is in the development of messages targeted to specific ethnic markets. It is very expensive and difficult for large agencies to be set up for each ethnic community that it may try to reach in a campaign, so they rely on specialists who have the expertise. With tremendous growth

How would they get by without you?

BCAA Life Insurance is one of the most important purchases you can make when it comes to securing your family's financial future. Whether you're a new parent or a first time homeowner, BCAA has a plan that's right for you and your family. Call toll-free 1-800-663-1956 or 604-268-5555 to speak with a Life Insurance advisor.

Exhibit 2-4   An example of Rethink's creative talent.

in the numbers of Chinese immigrants in Toronto and Vancouver, firms such as Ford have used tailored messages and ethnic media to influence the attitudes of this target audience, which has very different beliefs than other consumers because of its heritage. Ford could not succeed in establishing a unique brand position with this target audience without the assistance of those more familiar with it. One trade-off that advertisers need in order to make this work is to put the media savings from lower-cost publications or TV programming into the production of appropriate creative messages.[30]

MEDIA BUYING SERVICES

Media buying services are independent companies that specialize in the buying of media, particularly radio and television time. The task of purchasing advertising media has grown more complex as specialized media proliferate, so media buying services have found a niche by specializing in the analysis and purchase of advertising time and space. Agencies and clients usually develop their own media strategies and hire the buying service to execute them. Media buying services do help advertisers plan their media strategies. Because media buying services purchase such large amounts of time and space, they receive large discounts and can save the small agency or client money on media purchases. IMC Perspective 2-2 describes a prominent Canadian media agency.

Media buying services have been experiencing strong growth as clients seek alternatives to full-service agency relationships. Many companies have been unbundling agency services and consolidating media buying to get more clout from their advertising budgets. As noted earlier, many of the major agencies have formed independent media services companies that handle the media planning and buying for their clients and also offer their services separately to companies interested in a more specialized or consolidated approach to media planning, research, and/or buying. The rise of the independent media-buying services, operating outside the structure of the traditional ad agency media department, and the divestment of these departments from the agency system are two of the most significant developments that have occurred in the advertising industry. Exhibit 2-5 shows how Initiative, which is one of the largest media specialist companies, promotes its services.

SALES PROMOTION AGENCIES

Developing and managing sales promotion programs such as contests, sweepstakes, refunds and rebates, premium and incentive offers, and sampling programs is a complex task. Most companies use a **sales promotion agency** to develop and administer these programs. Some large ad agencies have created their own sales promotion department or acquired a sales promotion firm (refer to Figure 2-1). However, most sales promotion agencies are independent companies that specialize in providing the services needed to plan, develop, and execute a variety of sales promotion programs.

Sales promotion agencies often work in conjunction with the client's advertising and/or direct-response agencies to coordinate their efforts with the advertising and direct-marketing programs. Services provided by large sales promotion agencies include promotional planning, creative, research, tie-in coordination, fulfillment, premium design and manufacturing, catalogue production, and contest/sweepstakes management. Many sales promotion agencies are also developing direct/database marketing to expand their integrated marketing services capabilities. Sales promotion agencies are generally compensated on a fee basis.

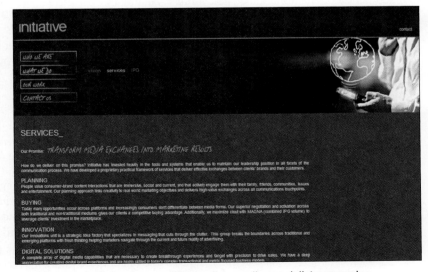

Exhibit 2-5 Initiative is one of the leading media specialist companies.

MediaCom's Innovative Recommendations Take Hold

Strategy magazine recognized MediaCom as Media Agency of the Year for its creative use of media and important organizational design changes. Innovative use of media and leading-edge development of new technology puts the agency on firm footing for the future.

MediaCom arranged exclusive "fashion authority" sponsorship of the MuchMusic Video Awards (MMVAs) for Swedish retailer H&M. It created a page on the MMVAs microsite for fashion news and H&M ads. Additional promotional elements included a contest where entrants uploaded their personal fashion via video and encouraged social media contacts for votes, an in-store music event, and extensive on-air ads. Impressive results followed, with 67 percent more viewers, 125 percent more microsite visits, and a jump in social media following.

For the retailer HomeSense, MediaCom coordinated access to famous set designs of popular TV shows (e.g., *Grey's Anatomy*) and produced ads featuring the sets to encourage Web visits. Once there, respondents experienced an explanation of the characters' home-styling tastes with a reference to HomeSense, which could provide that style for up to a 60 percent discount. A contest motivated visits with the prize of a Hollywood studio tour, spending money, and a gift card. Full-page ads in *The Globe and Mail* style section complemented the effort, which garnered 40,000 unique visits.

Hockey Night in Canada playoff games proved to be a viable medium that MediaCom recommended for Maytag to reach families. As a nontraditional advertiser the agency negotiated a favourable rate for the use of the popular sports icon's logo in a TV spot that showed the cleaning ability and toughness of the Maxima washing machine, which could handle a whole hockey team's jerseys. The playoffs reached the highest viewership ever with a strong skew to women and growth of 112 percent.

When taking over, MediaCom's CEO emphasized the importance of a consumer-centric way of thinking for planning media for the agency's clients. As part of this, digital leaders reported directly to strategy leaders which fostered stronger integration of IMC decision making. Furthermore, communications planning, research, and business sciences personnel remained in close contact with offices nearby to one another. An overall culture change pervaded the organization as the agency delivered strong results in key performance indicators for all clients.

As part of this improved service level, MediaCom looked to innovate with extensive placement of TV-like video messages in many out-of-home locations, and anticipated placement of additional ads in the future addressable TV. As well, MediaCom began to investigate the dissemination of Passive Audio Fingerprinting technology to deliver ads to mobile devices when signals are picked up from media exposure from a CTV broadcast; the agency worked with Bell to develop the technology.

Sources: Jonathan Paul, "MAOY Gold: MediaCom's Innovation Evolution," *Strategy,* November 10, 2011; Chris Powell, "Bell, MediaCom Take Optimistic But Cautious Approach with New Multi-Screen Tech," *Marketing Magazine,* August, 24, 2012; Alicia Androich, "Neale Named Managing Partner at MediaCom Canada," *Marketing Magazine,* January 12, 2012.

Question:

1. Explain why a media agency is so critical for advertising.

PUBLIC RELATIONS FIRMS

Large companies use both an advertising agency and a PR firm. The **public relations firm** develops and implements programs to manage the organization's publicity, image, and affairs with consumers and other relevant publics, including employees, suppliers, shareholders, government, labour groups, citizen action groups, and the general public. The PR firm analyzes the relationships between the client and these diffuse publics, determines how the client's policies and actions relate to and affect these publics, develops PR strategies and programs, implements these programs using public relations tools, and evaluates their effectiveness.

The activities of a public relations firm include planning the PR strategy and program, generating publicity, conducting lobbying and public affairs efforts, becoming involved in community activities and events, preparing news releases and other communications, conducting research, promoting and managing special events, and managing crises. As companies adopt an IMC approach to promotional planning, they are coordinating their PR activities with advertising and other promotional areas. Many companies are integrating public relations and publicity into the marketing communications mix to increase message credibility and save media costs.[31]

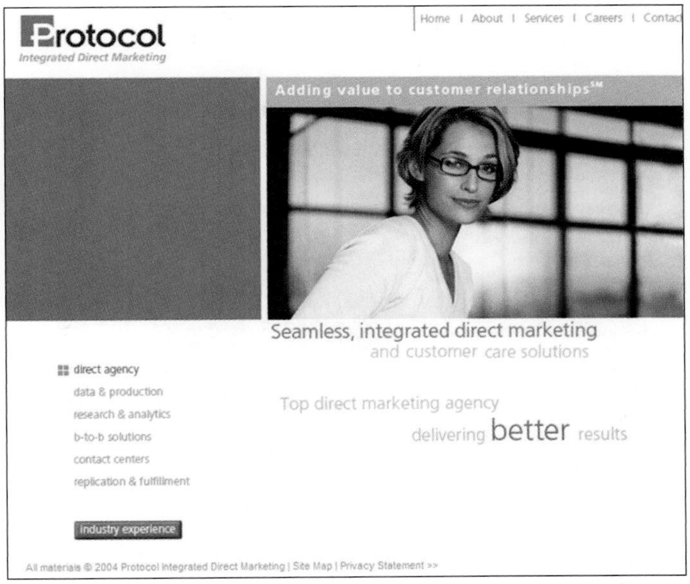

Exhibit 2-6   Protocol promotes its direct-marketing services.

DIRECT-RESPONSE AGENCIES

Direct marketing is where companies communicate with consumers through telemarketing, direct mail, television, the Internet, and other forms of direct-response advertising. As this industry has grown, numerous direct-response agencies have evolved that offer companies their specialized skills in both consumer and business markets. Many of the top direct-marketing agencies are subsidiaries of large agency holding companies (refer to Figure 2-1). However, there are also a number of independent direct-marketing agencies including those that serve large companies as well as smaller agencies that handle the needs of local companies (Exhibit 2-6).

Direct-response agencies provide a variety of services, including database management, direct mail, research, media services, and creative and production capabilities. A typical direct-response agency is divided into three main departments: account management, creative, and media. Agencies can also have a department whose function is to develop and manage databases for their clients. Database development and management is an important service as many companies use database marketing to pinpoint new customers and build relationships and loyalty among existing customers. The account managers work with their clients to plan direct-marketing programs and determine their role in the overall integrated marketing communications process. The creative department consists of copywriters, artists, and producers and is responsible for developing the direct-response message. The media department is concerned with its placement in the most appropriate direct-response media.

INTERACTIVE AGENCIES

Many marketers are using **interactive agencies** that specialize in the development and strategic use of interactive marketing tools such as websites for the Internet, banner ads, text messages, search engines, social media applications, e-mail campaigns, and kiosks. The development of successful interactive marketing programs requires expertise in technology and areas such as creative website design, database marketing, digital media, and customer relationship management. Many traditional advertising agencies have established interactive capabilities, ranging from a few specialists within the agency to an entire interactive division (refer to Figure 2-1).

While many agencies have developed or are developing interactive capabilities, a number of marketers are turning to more specialized interactive agencies to develop websites and interactive media. They feel these companies have more expertise in designing and developing websites as well as managing and supporting them. Interactive agencies range from smaller companies that specialize in website design and creation to full-service interactive agencies that provide all the elements needed for a successful Internet/interactive marketing program. These services include strategic consulting regarding the use of the Internet and online branding, technical knowledge, systems integration, and the development of electronic commerce capabilities. For

Exhibit 2-7 Agency.com developed online promotions for British Airways.

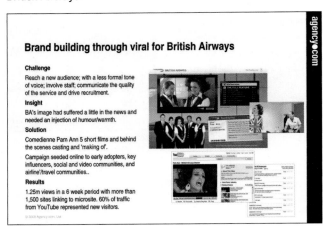

example, Agency.com developed the website and online promotions that support the global brand positioning strategy for British Airways (Exhibit 2-7).

(LO4) IMC Planning: Agency Relationships

Currently, marketers can choose from a variety of organizations to assist them in planning, developing, and implementing an integrated marketing communications program. Companies must decide whether to use specialized organizations for each marketing communications function or consolidate them with a large advertising agency that offers all of these services. In this final section, we discuss whether an advertiser would want to use an integrated services agency, assess the agency–client responsibilities for IMC, and summarize the current situation regarding the agency–client relationship in the context of an IMC environment.

INTEGRATED IMC SERVICES

Historically, marketing communication services were run as separate profit centres with each motivated to push its own expertise and pursue its own goals rather than develop truly integrated marketing programs. For example, creative specialists resisted becoming involved in sales promotion or direct marketing and preferred to concentrate on developing magazine ads or television commercials rather than designing coupons or direct-mail pieces. While agencies transitioned to full-service providers, proponents of the "one-stop shop" contend that these past problems are resolved and the individuals in the agencies and subsidiaries are working together.

Integrated services offer clients three benefits. First, clients maintain control of the entire promotional process and achieve greater synergy among each of the communications program elements. Second, it is more convenient for the client to coordinate all of its marketing efforts—media advertising, direct mail, special events, sales promotions, and public relations—through one agency. Finally, an agency with integrated marketing capabilities can create a single image for the client's brand and address everyone, from wholesalers to consumers, with one voice.

Concern regarding an advertising agency offering full services is the opinion that it is neither sufficiently staffed to ensure complete integration, nor fully cognizant of multiple target audiences. Advertising agency personnel are trained in particular aspects of the process and are less inclined to consider many marketing variables in their decisions. Furthermore, they tend to consider only the end user or consumer rather than all the parties in the marketing process who are connected to the results of the communications plan. It is recommended that marketers ensure the agencies consider the needs of all (e.g., customer service staff, sales representatives, distributors, and retailers) in their communication plans.[32]

A study by Forrester Research notes that major agencies continue to bundle traditional and nontraditional services together and position themselves as being able to offer all of them. However, the more likely scenario is that marketers will have a number of agencies from different areas working on their business and they must decide who is going to be in charge of managing and coordinating the IMC program.[33] Experimentation along these lines occurs on the agency side with a virtual ad agency that links creative specialists from many locations to produce work for a variety of clients. Giant Hydra and Cloud are two examples of "agencies" that have started to create uncertainty in the industry.[34]

AGENCY–CLIENT RESPONSIBILITY

Surveys of advertisers and agency executives have shown that both groups believe integrated marketing communication is important to their organizations' success. However, marketers and agency executives have very different opinions regarding who should be in charge of the integrated marketing communications process. Many advertisers prefer to set strategy for and coordinate their own IMC campaigns, but most agency executives see this as their domain.[35]

While agency executives believe their shops are capable of handling the elements an integrated campaign requires, marketers historically preferred to allocate creative services to their advertising agency and use specialized service agencies or in-house departments for other IMC tools.[36] Another study of advertising and marketing communication executives of global companies and agency executives found that "the traditional, static model of a single ad agency or a fixed roster of agencies working on a brand is being supplanted by an open-source model for some marketers. Under this model, marketers hire numerous marketing partners—sometimes on a project basis—to leverage their special talents and expertise as needed." The report notes that clients will increasingly be relegating their lead agencies to be brand stewards and coordinators of a network of specialists in different IMC areas.[37]

On the one hand, agencies still view themselves as strategic and executional partners and are offering their clients a full line of services (e.g., interactive and multimedia advertising, database management, direct marketing, public relations, and sales promotion). On the other hand, marketers still want to set the strategy for their IMC campaigns and seek specialized expertise, more quality and creativity, and greater control and cost efficiency by using multiple providers. Steven Center, the chief marketing officer for Honda of America, takes a position that is probably shared by most top marketing executives. He notes that "Agencies are exposed to much more than us, and they have to bring in raw ideas, market reconnaissance, and intelligence. But they will not tell us how to organize our company to accomplish our marketing mission. That responsibility should always fall entirely with the owner of the brand."[38]

AGENCY–CLIENT PARTNERSHIP

In a series of interviews, executives from major Canadian marketers answered questions surrounding agency–client relations. Are agencies meeting clients' needs? What can marketers do to forge stronger relations with agency partners?[39] Agencies are performing very well, but there is room for improvement, as shown in Figure 2-6. Marketers believe they can help agencies by being better clients through good personnel, clear decision making, sufficient budgets and lead times, and solid market research. In addition, clients should provide clear direction of their needs at the start of the creative process and involve the agency completely. This also includes sharing sensitive and confidential information so the agency understands the client's business, marketing, and market positioning objectives. In the end, the agency and client must be viewed as one team, not two organizations.

These and other findings emerged from a survey of agencies and clients conducted in both Canada and the United States. In partnership, *Marketing Magazine* and *Brandweek* administered more than 10,000 addressed e-mail questionnaires (Figure 2-7). In addition, clients valued creativity, strategic insights, and excellence in execution fairly equally, but believed agencies performed poorly in multidisciplined thinking (31 percent), strategic depth (30 percent), creative breadth (26 percent), and resource availability (26 percent).[40]

Performance Trend	Concern for Improvement
Growth in IMC integration	Bias to a particular IMC tool
Improved creative planning	Full accountability of performance
Breadth in services offered	Unclear client benefit
Communication effects measurement	Need for ROI measurement
Fantastic creative ideas	Desire for more strategic thinking

Figure 2-6

Client's assessment of agency performance

Figure 2-7

Perspectives on partnership

Client's Partnership View	Agency Partnership View
45% maintain a primary agency relationship	50% focus on multiple IMC tools, 50% on one IMC tool
Prefer project work or multiple specialty agencies	AOR and project work split evenly
Advertising agency use (79%)	One or two primary clients
Specialty agency use (50% avg)	60% of client relationships longer than three years

In conclusion, there is divergence of views on the agency–client partnership. A different belief regarding performance-based remuneration is a challenge for agreement. Long-term relationships appear to be more difficult to maintain. The degree to which claimed and actual integration across disciplines occurs is at odds. The ability of agencies to deliver independent marketing ideas and focus on ROI may be a limitation that clients will desire improvement with increased frequency. Despite these concerns, both sides know and understand their dependence on one another for success.

Learning Objectives Summary

 Identify the role of the advertising agency and the services it provides.

The development, execution, and administration of an advertising and promotion program involve the efforts of many individuals, both within the company and outside it. Firms have to decide whether they will hire an external advertising agency or use an in-house service to create their ads and purchase media. In-house agencies, while offering the advantages of cost savings, control, and increased coordination, have the disadvantage of less experience and flexibility. Many firms use advertising agencies to help develop and execute their programs. These firms offer the client a full range of services (including creative, account, marketing, and financial and management services). A full-service agency provides the services of highly skilled individuals and the objectivity to resolve the client's communication issues.

 Describe methods for compensating and evaluating advertising agencies.

Historically, clients compensated agencies through commission systems based on media sales, and fee- and cost-based systems. Increased emphasis on agency accountability has given rise to incentive-based compensation systems that tie agency compensation to performance measures such as sales and market share. Other more comprehensive measures include achievement of marketing communication objectives and how the agency operates and delivers services. Agencies are evaluated on both financial and qualitative measures that are formal in certain situations and less formal in others. Upon evaluation, a client may no longer require the service of agency for a number of performance related issues. Some clients retain the services of an agency for a relatively long period of time and retain the status of "agency of record."

 Contrast the role and functions of specialized marketing communication organizations.

In addition to using ad agencies, marketers use the services of other marketing communication specialists including creative boutiques and media buying services, direct marketing agencies, sales promotion agencies, public relations firms, and interactive agencies. Contracting out work to a specialized agency can enhance the creativity of the overall IMC plan with experts from specific fields. Moreover, while it may be more costly or time-consuming working with other specialists, these organizations may reach the target audience more precisely, thus yielding a favourable ROI. A marketer must decide whether to use a different specialist for each promotional function or to have all of its integrated marketing communications done by an advertising agency that offers all of these services under one roof. This latter idea allows an account team to know and control all aspects of the communication.

 Evaluate the perspectives on the use of integrated services across agencies or within one agency, and agency–client responsibilities and partnerships.

Studies have found that most marketers believe it is their responsibility, not the ad agency's, to set strategy for and coordinate IMC campaigns. The lack of a broad perspective and specialized skills in non-advertising areas is seen as the major barrier to agencies' increased involvement in integrated marketing communications, and individual perspectives of clients and agencies will continue to adapt as the growth of IMC evolves.

Key Terms   **connect**

Review key terms and definitions on Connect.

Review Questions

1. How are the characteristics of a full-service agency contrasted with the characteristics of specialized marketing communication agencies?

2. Why is compensating with the performance by results approach optimal in comparison with other methods?

3. What are the similar and dissimilar functions of each of the specialized marketing communication agencies?

4. What are the issues of using one full-service agency versus multiple specialized agencies?

Applied Questions

1. The chapter distinguished between full-service and specialized agencies. Using Figure 2-1 as a guide for different agency names based in Canada, examine the websites of different full-service marketing communication agencies. Identify which type of services each type offers. Using the websites as the main source of information, which agency would be best suited to be hired?

2. Which type of compensation system that an agency faced most often from its clients is an environment where a young advertising graduate would most like to work?

3. Again, using Figure 2-1 as a guide for different agency names based in Canada, examine the websites of different specialized marketing communication agencies. Identify which type of services each type offers. Using the websites as the main source of information, which agency would be best suited to be hired?

4. Given the evaluation of different agencies in the above questions, which approach is recommended for smartphone brands? for breakfast cereal brands? for energy drink brands?

GO ONLINE

For more information on the resources available from McGraw-Hill Ryerson, go to www.mcgrawhill.ca/he/solutions.

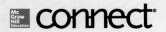

Consumer Behaviour and Target Audience Decisions

3

LEARNING OBJECTIVES

LO1 Describe the consumer decision-making process and demonstrate how it relates to marketing communication.

LO2 Distinguish internal psychological processes, their influence on consumer decision making, and implications for marketing communication.

LO3 Contrast how the consumer decision-making process varies for different types of purchases and the effects on marketing communication.

LO4 Compare the similarities and differences of target market and target audience.

LO5 Identify the options for making a target audience decision for marketing communication.

LO6 Express why a profile of the target audience is important for message, media, and IMC tool decisions.

Consumer Insight for IMC Decisions

Marketing communication planners are constantly interested in research to help guide their promotional decisions, and younger consumers are often their focus. *Marketing Magazine* and research firm Studentawards Inc. surveyed 1,195 young consumers aged 16–24 and found many are saving for tuition (78%) and travel (39%), pay for their cell phone (48%), have a credit card (53%), work part-time or seasonally (53%) with an hourly wage of $10–$15, and are most influenced by TV (24%) and price promotions (37%). While other responses naturally occurred, these percentages profile the "average" young adult still in school or transitioning to adulthood.

Similarly, *Strategy* and research firm DECODE surveyed and interviewed a similar number of young adults aged 15–35 for insights on their consumer behaviour. Young consumers are seemingly online at all times, but on a weekly basis the numbers are social networks (68%), SMS texting (46%), e-mail (48%), and Twitter (8%). Clearly Facebook is the winner; consumers will bring information from this vehicle to other media vehicles. The researchers concluded that aspects of social media in fact precluded social interaction, and that the active participation of Twitter required too much effort for many to desire to be involved.

Variation exists in social media across many uses: listening/reading/looking (86%), creating (76%), commenting (63%), and sharing (48%). While these statistics look impressive, half are not sharing at all and not all those who are creating are commenting (and vice versa), resulting in less participation with social media than expected. Beyond the "bandwagon" of brands using social media, one expert suggests that influential members who are active within the social network could be an avenue for targeting. DECODE research suggests that about one-third of young adults are active-participant-worthy of finding for developing marketing communication programs.

These numbers are reinforced by verbal elaborations by social media users. For example, they commonly have 500 contacts on Facebook but consider only 15 to 25 percent to be true friends, where they interact on a more personal level. With respect to branded Facebook pages, consumers responded with mixed feelings and thoughts of enjoyment and trepidation, believing that the social medium's purpose was not advertising. The younger consumers could also not see the use or value of Twitter except for following one or two vehicles that were definitely not brands looking to advertise to consumers.

Furthermore, young consumers found great difficulty in recalling any brands advertising on Facebook or Twitter; however, they unanimously identified the Doritos social media advertising over the past few years that requested user-generated content as entry criteria for a contest. Doritos understood that added effort on the part of consumers to generate content excluded many consumers and made its current requirement a 200-word advertising pitch—a much reduced effort compared to the previous campaign's video production. A balance of fun and social interaction is also seen with the Canada's Wonderland Facebook page, the fifth-largest branded page after BlackBerry, Tim Hortons, Budweiser, and Telus. Much of its activities revolve around providing entertaining pieces of information about the popular amusement park that are fit for its most loyal customers.

Sources: Emily Wexler, "Teens Log In," *Strategy,* April 1, 2011; Emily Wexler, "Decoding Digital Friends," *Strategy,* April 1, 2011; Emily Wexler, "Social Studies," *Strategy,* April 1, 2011; Doug Picklyk, "What (and Where) Are Canadian Students Buying?" *Marketing Magazine,* March 12, 2012.

Questions:

1. How does such varied creativity help Kraft?
2. Would it be possible for Kraft to have a similar creative message for all of its products?

The opening vignette reveals that effective marketing communication programs require knowledge of consumer behaviour. The resulting insight helps marketers to see how to encourage consumers to buy a product, what to emphasize in communication to specific audiences, whom to target the marketing communication toward, and which types of IMC tools might be used. It is beyond the scope of this text to examine consumer behaviour in depth. However, promotional planners need an understanding of consumer decision making, factors that influence it, and how this knowledge assists in developing promotional strategies and programs.

This chapter describes the consumer decision-making process to demonstrate how marketers use this information for marketing communication decisions. In doing so, it distinguishes relevant psychological processes for each stage. Next, the chapter contrasts how the process varies for different types of consumer decision making. It then identifies the target audience options for marketing communication plans, and expresses the importance of identifying a detailed profile of the target audience.

Consumer Decision-Making Process

Consumer behaviour is the process and activities people experience when searching for, selecting, purchasing, using, evaluating, and disposing of products and services so as to satisfy their needs and desires. The conceptual model in Figure 3-1 is a framework for understanding the consumer decision-making process. It views the consumer as a problem solver and information processor who evaluates alternative brands and determines the degree to which they might satisfy needs or purchase motives, which is a form of cognitive learning.[1] Other perspectives exist; however, this model is widely accepted and managerially useful. We will describe what occurs at each of the five stages and demonstrate how advertising and promotion can be used to influence decision making. We also distinguish internal psychological processes that are prevalent at each stage, their influence on consumer decision making, and implications for marketing communication.

LO1   NEED RECOGNITION

The first stage in the consumer decision-making process is **need recognition**, which occurs when the consumer perceives a need and becomes motivated to enter a decision-making process to resolve the felt need. Marketers are required to know the specific needs consumers are attempting to satisfy and how they translate into purchase criteria since it allows them to accurately portray the need in promotional messages or place messages in an appropriate location.

Need recognition is caused by a difference between the consumer's *ideal state* and *actual state*. A discrepancy exists between what the consumer desires the situation to be like and what the situation is really like. A goal exists for the consumer, and this goal may be the attainment of a more positive situation from a neutral state. Or, the goal could be a shift from a negative situation, and the consumer wishes to be at a neutral state. A **want** has been defined as a felt

Figure   3-1   A basic model of consumer decision making

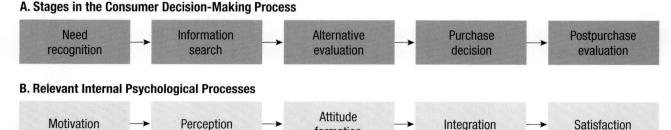

A. Stages in the Consumer Decision-Making Process

| Need recognition | → | Information search | → | Alternative evaluation | → | Purchase decision | → | Postpurchase evaluation |

B. Relevant Internal Psychological Processes

| Motivation | → | Perception | → | Attitude formation | → | Integration | → | Satisfaction |

need that is shaped by a person's knowledge, culture, and personality.[2] Many advertised products satisfy consumer wants rather than their basic needs. Notice how the ad shown in Exhibit 3-1 associates its clothing product to those who desire the atmosphere of the beach.

The sources of need recognition can be internal or external, may be very simple or very complex, and arise from changes in the consumer's current and/or desired state. Advertising (i.e., external) may be used to help consumers crystalize their dissatisfaction with a currently used product. For example, the Oral B ad shown in Exhibit 3-2 helps users realize that its toothbrushes are superior. New needs arise quite simply with changes in one's financial situation, employment status, or lifestyle. For example, graduates from college or university may need a wardrobe change when starting a new professional career. Finally, the Moen ad shown in Exhibit 3-3 explains the product's improved features which highlight the desired state one may have when remodelling their home.

 ## CONSUMER MOTIVATION

The way a consumer perceives a purchase situation and becomes driven to resolve it will influence the remainder of the decision process. For example, one consumer may perceive the need to purchase a new watch from a functional perspective and focus on reliable, low-priced alternatives. Another consumer may see the purchase of a watch as part of their fashion wardrobe and accessories and focus on the design and image. To better understand the reasons underlying consumer purchases, marketers extensively consider **motives**—that is, those factors that compel a consumer to take a particular action.

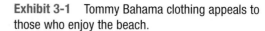
Exhibit 3-1   Tommy Bahama clothing appeals to those who enjoy the beach.

Exhibit 3-2   Oral B identifies reasons why consumers might be dissatisfied with their current toothbrushes in this ad.

Exhibit 3-3   Moen highlights the design features of its new faucets.

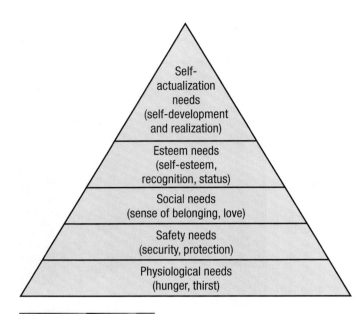

Figure   3-2

Maslow's hierarchy of needs

One approach for understanding consumer motivations is based on the classic theory of human motivation popularized by psychologist Abraham Maslow.[3] His **hierarchy of needs** theory postulates five levels of human needs, arranged in a hierarchy based on their importance. As shown in Figure 3-2, the five needs are (1) *physiological*—the basic level of primary needs for things required to sustain life, such as food, shelter, clothing, and sex; (2) *safety*—the need for security and safety from physical harm; (3) *social/love and belonging*—the desire to have satisfying relationships with others and feel a sense of love, affection, belonging, and acceptance; (4) *esteem*—the need to feel a sense of accomplishment and gain recognition, status, and respect from others; and (5) *self-actualization*—the need for self-fulfillment and a desire to realize one's own potential. For example, Columbia Sportswear Company focuses on the importance of personal protection when marketing its clothing and equipment (Exhibit 3-4).

Maslow's needs hierarchy offers a framework for marketers to use in determining what needs their products and services satisfy. Advertising campaigns can be designed to show how a brand fulfills these needs for one or multiple segments of consumers. For example, a young single person may be attempting to satisfy social or self-esteem needs in purchasing a car, while a family with children will focus more on safety needs. The Porsche ad in Exhibit 3-5 appears to address self-actualization. We will revisit the importance and an alternate view of motivation for marketing communication purposes in Chapter 6 when we present the topic of positioning.

Exhibit 3-4   Columbia shows the importance of the protection features of its outerwear.

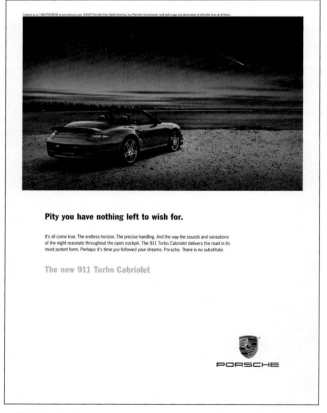

Exhibit 3-5   Porsche uses an appeal to self-actualization.

INFORMATION SEARCH

The second stage in the consumer decision-making process is *information search*. Once consumers perceive a need that can be satisfied by the purchase of a product, they begin to search for information needed to make a purchase decision. The initial search effort often consists of an attempt to scan information stored in memory to recall past experiences and/or knowledge regarding purchase alternatives.[4] This information retrieval is referred to as **internal search**. For many routine, repetitive purchases, previously acquired information that is stored in memory (such as past performance or outcomes from using a brand) is sufficient for comparing alternatives and making a choice.

If the internal search does not yield enough information, the consumer will seek additional information by an **external search**. External sources of information include:

- *Personal sources* (e.g., friends, relatives, or co-workers, face-to-face or via social media)
- *Marketer-controlled sources* (e.g., advertising, salespeople, displays, Internet)
- *Public sources* (e.g., articles in print media, reports on TV, Internet discussion boards)
- *Personal experience* (e.g., past use, actually handling, examining or testing the product)

Determining how much and which sources of external information to use involves several factors, including the importance of the purchase decision, the effort needed to acquire information, the amount of relevant past experience, the degree of perceived risk associated with the purchase, and the time available. For example, the selection of a movie to see on a Friday night might entail simply talking to a friend (digitally or in person), checking the movie guide in the newspaper, or using a mobile app. A more complex purchase such as a new car might use a number of information sources—perhaps a review of *Road & Track, Motor Trend,* or *Consumer Reports*; discussion with family members and friends; and test-driving of cars. At this point in the purchase decision, the information-providing aspects of advertising are extremely important.

The Internet influences consumers' external search patterns significantly for many products. For the travel industry, 60 percent indicated in 2006 that the Internet is very or extremely important for making travel plans, compared to one-third in 2002. TNS Canadian Facts research also noted that website satisfaction reached 36 percent, compared with 27 percent previously. The type of information sought involved significant moves from simple things like researching the weather or the destination to more complex comparisons of travel costs and accommodations.[5] The growth of mobile devices allows consumers to search for any information at any time while shopping; 21 percent of all Canadians use a smartphone. While this is lower than other countries, and Canadians are reluctant to spend more for their devices, clearly consumers are relying on the mobile tools for product information purposes.[6]

PERCEPTION

Knowledge of how consumers acquire and use information from external sources is important in formulating communication strategies. Message and media decisions are dependent on (1) how consumers sense external information, (2) how they attend to different sources of information, (3) how this information is interpreted and given meaning, and (4) how the information is retained. These four processes are all part of **perception**, the process by which an individual receives, attends to, interprets, and stores information to create a meaningful picture of the world.[7] Perception depends on internal factors such as a person's beliefs, experiences, needs, moods, and expectations. The perceptual process is also influenced by the characteristics of a stimulus (such as its size, colour, and intensity) and the context in which it is seen or heard. Selectivity occurs throughout the four stages of the consumer's perceptual process. Perception may be viewed as a filtering process in which internal and external factors influence what is received and how it is processed and interpreted. The sheer number and complexity of the marketing stimuli a person is exposed to in any given day requires that this filtering occur. **Selective perception** may occur within all four stages of the perceptual process, as shown in Figure 3-3.

Sensation Sensation is the immediate, direct response of the senses (taste, smell, sight, touch, and hearing) to a stimulus such as an ad, package, brand name, point-of-purchase display,

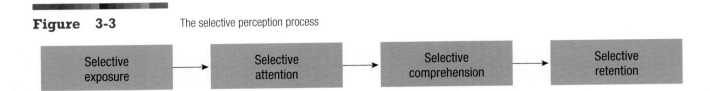

Figure   3-3   The selective perception process

| Selective exposure | → | Selective attention | → | Selective comprehension | → | Selective retention |

or mobile alert. Perception uses these senses to create a representation of the stimulus. Marketers plan certain marketing stimuli to achieve consumers' physiological reactions. For example, the visual elements of an ad must be designed so that consumers sense their existence. This is one reason why many TV ads start with a particular sound effect or visual movement. The ping of an e-mail message from a favourite brand of shoes is also now used for sensation purposes.

Marketers try to increase the level of sensory input so that their advertising messages will get noticed. For example, marketers of colognes and perfumes often use strong visuals as well as scent strips to appeal to multiple senses and attract the attention of magazine readers. **Selective exposure** occurs as consumers choose whether or not to make themselves available to information. For example, a viewer of a television show may change channels or leave the room during commercial breaks. A non-user of perfume might decide to not open the scented strip to sample the aroma. Or, the smartphone user can decide to simply delete an unwanted e-mail message from an unfamiliar brand.

Selecting Information   An individual's perceptual processes usually focus on elements of the environment that are relevant to his or her needs and tune out irrelevant stimuli. In a marketing communication context, two people may perceive the same stimuli (e.g., Intenet banner ad, sample offer) in very different ways because they select and attend to messages differently. Determinants of whether marketing communication stimuli will be attended to and how they will be interpreted include internal psychological factors such as the consumer's personality, needs, motives, expectations, and experiences.

Selective attention occurs when the consumer chooses to focus attention on certain stimuli while excluding others. One study of selective attention estimates the typical consumer is exposed to nearly 1,500 ads per day yet perceives only 76 of these messages.[8] Other estimates range as high as 3,000 exposures per day. This means advertisers must make considerable effort to get their messages noticed. Advertisers often use the creative aspects of their ads to gain consumers' attention. For example, advertisers set their ads off from others by showing their products with vibrant colours (Exhibit 3-6). Marketers also place ads in certain times or locations so that consumers will notice them more easily. For example, a consumer may pay more attention to a commercial that is heard while alone at home than to one heard in the presence of friends, at work, or anywhere distractions may be present. If advertisers can isolate a particular time when the listener is likely to be attentive, they will probably earn his or her undivided attention.

Interpreting the Information   Once a consumer selects and attends to a stimulus, the perceptual process focuses on organizing, categorizing, and interpreting the incoming information. This stage of the perceptual process is very individualized and is influenced by internal psychological factors. The interpretation and meaning an individual assigns to an incoming stimulus also depend in part on the nature of the stimulus. For example, many ads are objective, and their message is clear and straightforward. Other ads are more ambiguous, and their meaning is strongly influenced by the consumer's individual interpretation.

Even if the consumer does notice the advertiser's message, there is no guarantee it will be interpreted in the intended manner. Consumers may have **selective comprehension**, interpreting information on the basis of their own attitudes, beliefs, motives, and experiences. They often

Exhibit 3-6 Tropicana uses colour to focus attention on orange juice.

interpret information in a manner that supports their own position. For example, an ad that disparages a consumer's favourite brand may be seen as biased or untruthful, and its claims may not be accepted.

Retaining the Information   The final stage of the perceptual process involves the storage of the information in short-term or long-term memory. Consumers may make mental notes or focus on part of an advertising message to ensure that they will not forget, thus permitting easy retrieval during the information search stage. **Selective retention** means consumers do not remember all the information they see, hear, or read even after attending to and comprehending it. Advertisers attempt to make sure information will be retained in the consumer's memory so that it will be available when it is time to make a purchase. **Mnemonics** such as symbols, rhymes, associations, and images that assist in the learning and memory process are helpful. Energizer put pictures of its pink bunny on packages to remind consumers at the point of purchase of its creative advertising.

ALTERNATIVE EVALUATION

After acquiring information, the consumer moves to the **alternative evaluation** stage, where he or she compares the brands identified as being capable of satisfying the needs or motives that initiated the decision process. The brands identified as purchase options are referred to as the consumer's *evoked set*.

The evoked set is generally only a subset of all the brands of which the consumer is aware. The consumer reduces the number of brands to be reviewed during the alternative evaluation stage to a manageable level. The exact size of the evoked set varies from one consumer to another and depends on such factors as the importance of the purchase and the amount of time and energy the consumer wants to spend comparing alternatives.

The goal of most advertising and promotional strategies is to increase the likelihood that a brand will be included in the consumer's evoked set and considered during alternative evaluation. Marketers of strong or existing brands use advertising as a reminder to maintain *awareness* among consumers so that their brands are part of the evoked set of their target audiences. The Olay ad in Exhibit 3-7 is an example of a brand with this objective. Marketers of new brands or those with a low market share need to gain awareness among consumers and break into their evoked sets.

Once consumers have identified an evoked set and have a list of alternatives, they evaluate the brands by comparing the choice alternatives on specific and important criteria. **Evaluative criteria** are the attributes of a product that are used to compare different alternatives which can be objective or subjective. For example, in buying an automobile, consumers use objective attributes such as price, warranty, and fuel economy as well as subjective attributes such as image or styling.

Products are *bundles of attributes* and consumers also tend to think about products or services in terms of their consequences or *bundles of benefits*. Consequences are specific events or outcomes that consumers experience when they purchase and/or consume a product.[9] **Functional benefits** are concrete outcomes of product usage that are tangible and directly related to product performance. The taste of a soft drink or a potato chip, the acceleration of a car, and the clarity of a fax transmission are examples of functional consequences. **Experiential benefits** are related to how a product makes the consumer feel while consuming the product. These emotions can be feelings of happiness or joy, for example, as seen by car ads illustrating consumers enjoying the drive in a particular brand. **Psychological benefits** can refer to the status a consumer encounters when associated with a brand.

Marketers distinguish between product attributes and benefits, because the importance and meaning consumers assign to an attribute are usually determined by its consequences for them. Moreover,

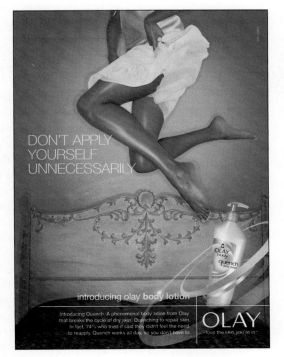

Exhibit 3-7   Olay's ads help contribute to high levels of awareness.

Exhibit 3-8 Cashmere's campaign conveys the softness of its product.

Nothing feels like Cashmere

advertisers communicate the link between a particular attribute and a benefit to enhance consumers' understanding. For example, the Cashmere ad in Exhibit 3-8 focuses on the extraordinary softness of its tissue. Product attributes and the benefits consumers think they will experience from a brand are very important, for they are often the basis on which consumers form attitudes and decide among their choice alternatives.

ATTITUDES

Attitudes are learned predispositions to respond to an object and represent one of the most heavily studied concepts in consumer behaviour.[10] Other perspectives view attitudes as a summary construct that represents an individual's overall feelings toward or evaluation of an object.[11] Consumers hold attitudes toward a variety of objects that are important to marketers, including individuals (endorsers like Sidney Crosby), brands (Cheerios), companies (Microsoft), product categories (beef, pork, tuna), retail stores (Hudson's Bay, Sears), or even advertisements.

Attitudes are important to marketers because they theoretically summarize a consumer's evaluation of an object (or brand or company) and represent positive or negative feelings and behavioural tendencies. Marketers' keen interest in attitudes is based on the assumption that they are related to consumers' purchase behaviour. Considerable evidence supports the basic assumption of a relationship between attitudes and behaviour.[12] The attitude–behaviour link does not always hold since other factors can affect behaviour.[13]

Advertising and promotion are used to create favourable attitudes toward new products/services or brands, reinforce existing favourable attitudes, and/or change negative attitudes. Technology Perspective 3-1 illustrates how advertising influences attitudes.

PURCHASE DECISION

At some point in the buying process, the consumer must stop searching for and evaluating information about alternative brands in the evoked set and make a *purchase decision*. As an outcome of the alternative evaluation stage, the consumer may develop a **purchase intention** or predisposition to buy a certain brand. Purchase intentions are generally based on a matching of purchase motives with attributes or characteristics of brands under consideration. Their formation involves many of the personal subprocesses discussed in this chapter, including motivation, perception, and attitude formation.

A purchase decision is not the same as an actual purchase. Once a consumer chooses which brand to buy, he or she must still implement the decision and make the actual purchase. Additional decisions may be needed, such as when to buy, where to buy, and how much money to spend. Often, there is a time delay between the formation of a purchase intention or decision and the actual purchase, particularly for highly involved and complex purchases such as automobiles, personal computers, and consumer durables.

For nondurable products such as consumer packaged goods, the time between the decision and the actual purchase may be short as it occurs while in the store or while planning at home. Before leaving home, the consumer may make a shopping list that includes specific brand names because the consumer has developed **brand loyalty**—a preference for a particular brand that results in its repeated purchase. In this situation, marketers strive to maintain brand loyalty with reminder advertising to keep their brand names in front of consumers, prominent shelf positions

IMC TECHNOLOGY PERSPECTIVE 3-1

Digitally Adapting Consumers

SHOP LIKE IT'S THE FUTURE

Like in past decades, digital technology continues to evolve with fantastic marketing communication opportunities to influence consumer behaviour. The presentation of information in retail settings is transforming the way they gather information and compare brands while shopping for a multitude of products. As the technology appears to be helpful and enjoyable for consumers, some are concerned that the value-added characteristics have the potential to overwhelm the retail experience and make it less convenient and more time consuming.

Adidas implemented a touch-screen interface where consumers can view all of its 8,000-plus shoes. Facial recognition technology customizes the display for male or females allowing consumers a 3-D view of their options. Links to social media provide access to what others thought or felt about the particular model. And if consumers find something they like, the whole system facilitates the transaction much like shopping online at home.

Wind Mobile implemented Microsoft's Surface technology with touch-screen features so that consumers can look through the details of its devices and service plans. Each unit amounted to $15,000, with newer versions pegged at half that cost, paving the way for much more efficient and wider distribution in the coming few years. Wall-mounted screens summarize consumer comments, reinforcing its "Power of Conversation" positioning.

Videotron, a Quebec telecommunications brand, installed a sound-proof booth with an 85-inch HD screen and extensive multi-touch flat-screen countertops in its main downtown Montreal location. Similar units faced the exterior to interact with passersby and entice them into the store. Bell introduced similar interactive technology as part of its rebranding and delivery of comprehensive product and service information.

Beyond touch screens, marketing communication planners are building their databases resulting from technology that tracks consumer behaviour farther than just what they are looking at. A direct link from American Express to its customers allows the brand to observe individual spending patterns and customize its communications when offering its many exclusive features to different types of cardholders. MasterCard did not have such a link; having to go through banks as an intermediary in Canada, it recently developed a program to more directly communicate via a website registration so that it could build competitive programs in same market as American Express.

Marketing communication got significantly more convenient for consumers with the development of near field communication (NFC), where a digital wallet will permit instantaneous transactions to facilitate purchase and exchange of information. With smartphone penetration hitting over 50 percent for those in the 18 to 24 age range, future shopping behaviour appears very technologically driven.

Sources: Michelle Warren, "How Will Google Wallet Change Your Job?" *Marketing Magazine,* June 13, 2011; Simon Houpt, "Gathering Reams of Customer Data? Priceless," *The Globe and Mail,* November 4, 2011; Jonathan Paul, "Digital Hits the Aisles," *Strategy,* March 1, 2011.

Question:

1. How does in-store communication with digital technology change consumer behaviour?

---

and displays in stores, and periodic promotions to deter consumers from switching brands. Competitors also use many techniques to encourage consumers to try their brands and disrupt the loyalty of non-customers. In sum, marketers in many different product categories must continually battle to maintain their loyal consumers while replacing those who switch brands.

INTEGRATION PROCESSES

A key part of the purchase decision stage is the way consumers combine information about the characteristics of brands. **Integration processes** are the way product knowledge, meanings, and beliefs are combined to evaluate two or more alternatives.[14] Analysis of the integration process

Exhibit 3-9   Market leaders such as Levis can appeal to consumer affect.

LIVE UNBUTTONED. LEVIS 501

focuses on the different types of *decision rules* or strategies consumers use to decide among purchase alternatives.

Consumers often make purchase selections by using formal integration strategies or decision rules that require examination and comparison of alternatives on specific attributes. This process involves a very deliberate evaluation of the alternatives, attribute by attribute. When consumers apply such formal decision rules, marketers need to know which attributes are being considered so as to provide the information the consumers require.

Sometimes consumers make their purchase decisions using more simplified decision rules known as **heuristics**. Heuristics are easy to use and are highly adaptive to specific environmental situations (such as a retail store).[15] For familiar products that are purchased frequently, consumers may use price-based heuristics (buy the least expensive brand) or promotion-based heuristics (choose the brand for a price reduction through a coupon, rebate, or special deal).

One type of heuristic is the **affect referral decision rule**,[16] in which consumers make a selection on the basis of an overall impression or summary evaluation of the alternatives under consideration. This decision rule suggests that consumers have affective impressions of brands stored in memory that can be accessed at the time of purchase. Marketers selling familiar and popular brands may appeal to an affect referral rule by stressing overall affective feelings or impressions about their products. Market leaders, whose products enjoy strong overall brand images, often use ads that promote the brand as the best overall (Exhibit 3-9).

POSTPURCHASE EVALUATION

The consumer decision process does not end with the purchase. After consumption, the consumer assesses the level of performance of the product or service. The postpurchase evaluation process is important because the feedback acquired from actual use of a product will influence the likelihood of future purchases. Positive performance means the brand is retained in the evoked set and increases the likelihood it will be purchased again. Unfavourable outcomes may lead the consumer to form negative attitudes toward the brand, lessening the likelihood it will be purchased again or even eliminating it from the consumer's evoked set.

Consumers explore a number of activities during the postpurchase evaluation process. They may seek out reassurance and opinions from others to confirm the wisdom of their purchase decision, lower their attitudes or opinions of the unchosen alternative, deny or distort any information that does not support the choice they made, or look for information that does support their choice. An important source of supportive information is advertising; consumers tend to be more attentive to advertising for the brand they have chosen.[17] Thus, it may be important for companies to advertise to reinforce consumer decisions to purchase their brands.

SATISFACTION

The most significant psychological concept during the postpurchase evaluation process is satisfaction. A leading expert in satisfaction research defined **satisfaction** as a judgment that consumers make with respect to the pleasurable level of consumption-related fulfillment.[18] The notion of fulfillment implies that a consumer's goal has been achieved (i.e., needs met), and that the fulfillment is "judged with reference to a standard." Thus, consumers make a comparison between the consumption outcome and another referent.

Consumers can make many comparisons. One is to compare the level of product performance to the expectations of the product that consumers had prior to purchase. Satisfaction can occur when the consumer's expectations are either met or exceeded, whereas dissatisfaction results when performance is below expectations. Consumers can also compare the product performance to an absolute standard of quality to perceive satisfaction or dissatisfaction.

Another aspect of satisfaction is **cognitive dissonance**, a feeling of psychological tension or postpurchase doubt that a consumer experiences after making a difficult purchase choice. Dissonance is more likely to occur in important decisions where the consumer must choose among close alternatives (especially if the unchosen alternative has unique or desirable features that the selected alternative does not have).

Marketers must recognize the importance of the postpurchase evaluation stage. Dissatisfied consumers not only are unlikely to repurchase the marketer's product but also may spread negative word-of-mouth information that deters others from purchasing the product or service. The best guarantee of favourable postpurchase evaluations is to provide consumers with a quality product or service that always meets their expectations. Marketers must be sure their advertising and other forms of promotion do not create unreasonable expectations their products cannot meet.

Marketers understand that postpurchase communication is important. Companies send follow-up letters or emails and brochures to reassure buyers and reinforce the wisdom of their decision. Companies use toll-free numbers, websites, and social media to allow for consumer feedback. Marketers also offer liberal return and refund policies and extended warranties and guarantees to ensure customer satisfaction.

(L03) Variations in Consumer Decision Making

We have reviewed the consumer decision-making process with respect to individual purchases. However, variations in this process arise depending upon the type of purchase and whether the individual is making the decision with other people. We now contrast these two variations in the consumer decision-making process and the effects on marketing communication.

TYPES OF DECISION MAKING

The general model of consumer decision making is a useful description; however, consumers do not always experience all five steps of the purchase decision process or proceed in the sequence presented. They may minimize or even skip one or more stages if they have previous experience in purchasing the product or service or if the decision is of low personal, social, or economic significance. To develop effective promotional decisions, marketers need to understand the type of problem-solving processes their target consumers use to make purchase decisions.[19]

Many purchase decisions consumers make are based on a habit known as **routine problem solving** or routine response behaviour. For many low-priced, frequently purchased products, the decision process consists of little more than recognizing the need, performing a quick internal search, and making the purchase. The consumer spends little or no effort with external search or alternative evaluation.

Marketers of products characterized by a routine response purchase process want consumers to follow a routine choice process and continue to purchase their products. These marketers use relevant IMC tools to maintain high levels of brand awareness and positive brand attitude. Alternatively, marketers of new brands or those with a low market share face a different challenge. They must find ways to disrupt consumers' routine choice processes and get them to consider their brand by using IMC tools that encourage consumers to reconsider their habit or routine choice and switch brands. The Sun-Rype ad in Exhibit 3-10 tries this approach.

A more complicated decision-making process occurs when consumers have limited experience in purchasing a particular product or service and little or no knowledge of the brands available and/or the criteria to use in making a purchase decision. Consumers learn what attributes or criteria should be used in making a purchase decision and how the alternatives perform

Exhibit 3-10   The visual in Sun-Rype's ad invites consumers to reconsider their beverage choice.

Exhibit 3-11   A reference group is shown in the images of this website message.

on these dimensions. For products or services characterized by **limited problem solving** or **extended problem solving**, marketers should make information available that will help consumers make a decision. Advertising that provides consumers with detailed information about a brand and how it can satisfy their purchase motives and goals is important. Marketers may also want to give consumers information through other ways (e.g., displays, brochures, websites).

GROUP DECISION MAKING

A group is defined as "two or more individuals who share a set of norms, values, or beliefs and have certain implicitly or explicitly defined relationships to one another such that their behavior is interdependent."[20] Groups are one of the primary factors influencing learning and socialization, and group situations constitute many of our purchase decisions. For example, a woman's purchase of a dress for a party might be influenced by the type of party and who is attending.

A **reference group** is "a group whose presumed perspectives or values are being used by an individual as the basis for his or her judgments, opinions, and actions." Consumers use reference groups as a guide to specific behaviours, even when the groups are not present.[21] In the party example, peers—although not present—provided a standard of dress that referred the woman to her clothing selection. Likewise, friends, family, and co-workers, or even a group to which she aspires, may serve as referents, and consumption patterns will typically conform to the expectations of the groups that are most important to her.

Marketers use reference group influences in developing advertisements and promotional strategies. The images in Exhibit 3-11 are an example of an *aspirational* reference group (to which we might like to belong). Marketers also use *disassociative* groups (to which we do not wish to belong), such as in ads related to drinking and driving.

Furthermore, the group may be involved more directly than just as a referent. Family members serve as referents to each other, or are involved in the purchase decision process—acting as an individual buying unit. As shown in Figure 3-4, family members can assume a variety of roles in the decision-making process.[22] There can be group interaction at every stage of the consumer decision-making process since members take on many roles throughout the process. The ad in Exhibit 3-12 is directed to a particular role, the purchaser rather than the consumer.

Each role has implications for marketers. First, the advertiser must determine who is responsible for the roles in the decision-making process so that messages can be targeted at that person (or those people) and placed in the most appropriate and effective media. Second, understanding the decision-making process and the use of information by

The initiator. The person responsible for initiating the purchase decision process; for example, the mother who determines she needs a new car.

The information provider. The individual responsible for gathering information to be used in making the decision; for example, the teenage car buff who knows where to find product information in specific magazines or collects it from dealers.

The influencer. The person who exerts influence as to what criteria will be used in the selection process. All members of the family may be involved. The mother may have her criteria, whereas others may each have their own input.

The decision maker(s). That person(s) who actually makes the decision. In our example, it may be the mother alone or in combination with another family member.

The purchasing agent. That individual who performs the physical act of making the purchase. In the case of a car, a couple may decide to choose it together and sign the purchase agreement.

The consumer. The actual user of the product. In the case of a family car, all family members are consumers. For a private car, only the mother might be the consumer.

Figure 3-4

Roles in the family decision-making process

individual family members is critical to the design of messages and choice of promotional program elements. In general, to create an effective promotional program, a marketer must have an overall understanding of how the decision process works and the role that each group member plays.

(L04) Target Audience Decision

We reviewed the consumer decision-making process since marketers need to understand the behaviour they are trying to influence through their promotional plans. Marketers also try to understand consumers as much as possible since an IMC plan, IMC program (e.g., advertising campaign), or ad is directed to a target audience or multiple target audiences, which is usually a primary decision prior to other communication decisions. The target audience decision is derived from the segmentation and target market decisions of the marketing plan. In this section, we therefore review the marketing planning process to understand the context of promotional planning. Next, we summarize approaches for market segmentation and identify how it is used for target market selection. Finally, we explore how these marketing decisions provide direction for identifying options for the target audience decision.

MARKETING PLANNING PROCESS

The process of developing and implementing marketing and promotion decisions is summarized in Figure 3-5. The target market is an important focus of the firm's marketing effort, and specific sales, market share, and profitability objectives are set according to where the company wants to be and what it hopes to accomplish in this market. The method by which marketers do this involves three basic steps: segment the market, select a target market, and determine the market positioning strategy. The selection of the target market (or markets) in which the firm will compete has direct implications for its advertising and promotional efforts. Specific communication objectives are derived and the promotional mix strategies are developed to achieve these objectives. Thus, different objectives may be established, different budgets may be used, and the promotional mix strategies may vary, depending on the market selected.

Exhibit 3-12 Ads for Kinder Surprise target the purchaser.

Figure   3-5   Marketing and promotions process model

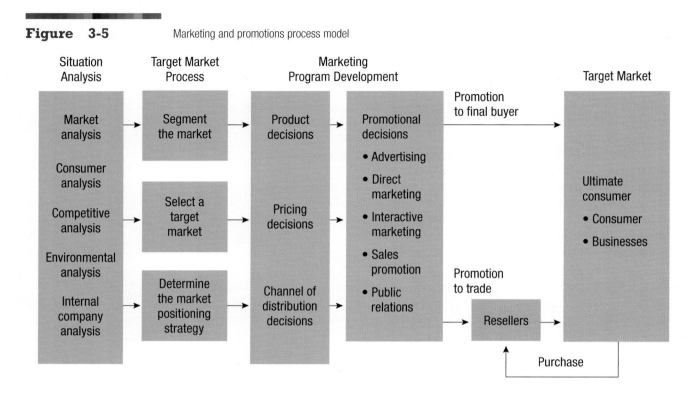

As we introduced this section, we used the terms target market and target audience. We concur with the perspective that suggests promotional planners should make a careful distinction between these concepts since an advertising plan or IMC plan is one part of the overall marketing plan.[23] The **target market** is the group of consumers toward which an overall marketing program is directed. The **target audience** is a group of consumers toward which the advertising campaign, for example, is directed. Conceptually, these targets are interdependent but their distinction allows promotional planners the ability to make more effective communication decisions with enhanced precision.

The difference between target audience and target market can be seen when firms develop selective promotional programs beyond their normal target market. For example, tea represents the fourth most consumed drink after coffee, milk, and tap water. With many types of tea and different kinds of tea drinkers, tea brands need to approach specific audiences with their communication efforts. The health benefits perceived with tea have attracted many young Canadian consumers toward specialty teas. In particular, sales for green, red, and white teas rose substantially in 2006; however, herbal and black tea dropped slightly. Although the main tea consumer is women over 40, according to Twinings tea, the well-established brand developed its latest campaign toward newer consumers (i.e., younger) with a strong emphasis to teach the less experienced more about tea. Its communication consisted of door-hangers and samples to specific locations and displays for select retailers.[24]

The difference between target audience and target market can also be seen when firms develop promotional programs that fit with an established target market that has a new cohort of consumers every couple of years. This occurs with products like Pogo (a wiener covered with a bread substance on a stick), which has a clear demographic target market of teenage boys. Yet these boys grow older, so every few years there is a whole new group of teenage boys that Pogo directs marketing communication toward, and is therefore a new target audience (i.e., unaware, or unfamiliar with the brand experience). A fun marketing venture included Pogothons, street events, short flash TV ads of eight seconds, stickers delivered in skateboard parks, and so on, all with the intention to encourage website visits so that the new users—a new audience—could relate to the brand.[25] IMC Perspective 3-1 shows the target audience of the advertising for a few popular brands.

Targeting with Advertising

Reaching multicultural groups of consumers is an ever-present issue for all marketers to evaluate. Some marketers target with specific marketing strategies or communication strategies; others do not see cultural or ethnic targeting as a requirement for successful implementation. In the opinion of experts, marketers have not fully realized the potential as they have not considered the decision with sufficient depth.

With Chinese (381,000) the largest group in Vancouver, South Asian (684,000) the largest group in Toronto, and Black consumers from African or Caribbean cultures the largest group in Montreal (169,000), it is no wonder marketers would carefully consider their communication plans. In fact, within Canada's three largest cities, these three groups represent a total of about 2.5 million consumers. These numbers are fuelled by immigration over the past two decades and second-generation individuals whose parents moved to Canada in the previous two decades.

Recently, Nissan devoted a sizable portion of its advertising budget to South Asians when its agency discovered that a car purchase represented an important first step for this group when arriving in Canada. The message concentrated on the in-vehicle technology and all-wheel-drive systems and reached consumers via TV, digital media, and social media to ensure strong top-of-mind awareness.

Clorox sponsored Carnival China 2012 as part of its new approach to multicultural marketing communication. After extensive demographic and psychographic research on Chinese and South Asian consumers, the large packaged goods manufacturer looked to build long-term plans to fully develop these growing consumer markets.

The media landscape continues to evolve, allowing marketers to effectively reach these consumer groups. Global News offers its programs in additional languages, as does Multimedia Nova Corporation. To support the credibility of these media to advertisers, the audiences for these new vehicles are audited to ensure sufficient numbers for advertisers to be willing to invest their budgets.

Rogers has historically split its advertising resources across "mainstream" and "multicultural" media; however, it considered greater collaboration or integration as the notion of groups of different cultures appeared less relevant. Echoing this idea is Western Union, which viewed all its activities as completely integrated across all cultures and seemed to be a reflection of the diversity in its marketing staff.

Print Measurement Bureau and other data contrasted these points of view as the statistics showed Black consumers spending more on phone plans and beauty and personal care products, and being associated with faith-based organizations at higher levels. A factor complicating the development of specific advertising messages for this consumer group rested on the point that many Black consumers speak English, thereby limiting the perceived need for media organizations to create unique vehicles for customized reach. Additionally, experts believe that in reality a number of different Black consumer groups exist, rather than simply one. For example, they cite differences among those from the Caribbean, from Africa, and those who have historical ties to Canada spanning three or four generations. This is especially relevant in a Tim Hortons ad where a man welcomed his wife at the airport—with a coffee, naturally, and warm clothes contained in a plastic straw bag from his original African home.

Marketers witnessed a similar issue regarding multiple groups within a larger segment in the differences among Hong Kong Chinese who speak Cantonese, Mainland Chinese who speak Mandarin, Taiwanese who speak a dialect of Mandarin, and Canadian-born Chinese who are more likely to speak English first. And while tendencies for buying certain goods do exist among Chinese consumers, considerable variance remained within groups.

Sources: Jeromy Lloyd, "The Incredible Rise of the Ethnic Consumer," *Marketing Magazine,* March 28, 2011; Jeromy Lloyd, "Bet on Black," *Marketing Magazine,* March 28, 2011; Jeromy Lloyd, "Five Opportunities in the Black Consumer Market," *Marketing Magazine,* March 28, 2011; Doug Picklyk, "The Multicultural Mix of Urban Canada," *Marketing Magazine,* March 12, 2012; Chris Daniels, "The Visible Majority," *Marketing Magazine,* March 12, 2012.

Question:

1. How many variables should a promotional planner consider when segmenting and profiling a target audience?

MARKET SEGMENTATION

To identify a target market, the marketer identifies the specific needs of groups of people (or segments), selects one or more of these segments as a target, and develops marketing programs directed to each. This approach has found increased applicability in marketing for a number of reasons, including changes in the market (consumers are more diverse in their needs, attitudes, and lifestyles); increased use of segmentation by competitors; and the fact that more managers are trained in segmentation and realize the advantages associated with this strategy. The remainder of this section discusses different ways to segment the market (Figure 3-6). Marketers may

Figure   3-6   Examples of market segmentation variables

Main Dimension	Segmentation Variables	Typical Breakdowns
Geographic	Region	West, Central, East
	City size	Under 10,000; 10,000–24,999; 25,000–49,999; 50,000–99,999; 100,000–249,999; 250,000–499,999; 500,000–999,999; 1,000,000 or more
	Metropolitan area	Census Metropolitan Area (CMA); etc.
	Density	Urban; suburban; small town; rural
Demographic	Gender	Male; female
	Age	Under 6 yrs; 6–11 yrs; 12–17 yrs; 18–24 yrs; 25–34 yrs; 35–44 yrs; 45–54 yrs; 55–64 yrs; 65–74 yrs; 75 yrs plus
	Race	Asian; Black; Hispanic; Indian; White/Caucasian; etc.
	Life stage	Infant; preschool; child; youth; collegiate; adult; senior
	Birth era	Baby boomer (1949–1964); Generation X (1965–1976); baby boomlet/Generation Y (1977–present)
	Household size	1; 2; 3–4; 5 or more
	Residence tenure	Own home; rent home
	Marital status	Never married; married; separated; divorced; widowed
Socioeconomic	Income	<$15,000; $15,000–$24,999; $25,000–$34,999; $35,000–$49,999; $50,000–$74,999; $75,000+
	Education	Some high school or less; high school graduate; some college or university; university/college graduate; etc.
	Occupation	Managerial and professional specialty; technical, sales, and administrative support; service; farming, forestry, and fishing; etc.
Psychographic	Values	Actualizers; fulfilleds; achievers; experiencers; believers; strivers; makers; strugglers
	Lifestyle	Activities, interests, opinions
	Personality	Gregarious; compulsive; introverted; aggressive; ambitious; etc.
	Culture	Ethnic; social
	Social class	Low middle class; upper middle class; etc
Behaviour	Brand Loyalty	Completely loyal; partially loyal; not loyal
	User status	Nonuser; ex-user; first-time user; regular user
	Usage rate	Light user; medium user; heavy user
	Situation	Usage situation; purchase situation
	Benefits sought	Quality; service; price/value; convenience; prestige

use one of the segmentation variables or a combination of approaches for both marketing and marketing communication decisions.

Geographic Segmentation   In the **geographic segmentation** approach, markets are divided into different geographic units. These units may include nations, provinces, states, counties, or even neighbourhoods. Consumers often have different buying habits depending on where they reside. To address this, advertisers use different IMC tools or advertising messages. Internet display ads are delivered geographically since the technology senses the location of the user. Out-of-home messaging relies extensively on geographic placements. Often times, brands face different penetration levels across markets and alter their sales promotions accordingly to stimulate trial purchases.

Demographic Segmentation   Dividing the market on the basis of demographic variables such as gender, age, marital status, household size, and socioeconomic variables like income, education, and occupation is called **demographic segmentation**. For example, the Alberta Securities Commission targeted young adults aged 24–35 who had very little knowledge of investing and had a perceived need for financial advice as indicated by market research. Print and radio ads directed interested consumers to an education link on the Commission's website. A second phase of the advertising message featured links on Web portals that also highlighted a contest.[26] While a demographic is a common method of segmenting markets, it is important to recognize that other factors may be the underlying basis for homogeneity and/or consumer behaviour. The astute marketer will identify additional approaches for segmenting and will recognize the limitations of demographics.

Psychographic Segmentation   Dividing the market on the basis of values and lifestyle, personality, culture, and social class is referred to as **psychographic segmentation**. Each of these variables can be the basis for segmentation.

Values and Lifestyle   The determination of lifestyles is usually based on an analysis of the activities, interests, and opinions (AIOs) of consumers that are obtained via surveys. These lifestyles are then correlated with the consumers' product, brand, and/or media usage. Lifestyle may be the best discriminator between use and nonuse for many goods or services. Harley-Davidson motorcycles demonstrated this with a campaign that showed its customer base consists of virtually every conceivable variable. Its Facebook page boasts over three million fans, many of whom are younger and not the stereotypical boomer reliving his or her glory. The main discerning characteristic is the lifestyle of enjoying motorcycle riding.[27] As another example, notice how the ad for Maybelline in Exhibit 3-13 reflects the life of the target audience member. Taken from another perspective, our activities, interests, and opinions are reflective of our individual values. We highlight two major approaches that have developed these forms of segmentation with proprietary research methods.

Psychographic segmentation occurred with the advent of the values and lifestyles (VALS) program now offered by Strategic Business Insights. Developed in the late 1970s and refined a decade later, VALS is a method for applying segmentation based on values. The underlying premise of VALS is that psychological traits and demographics are better predictors of behaviour than demographics alone. The VALS approach combines an estimate of the resources the consumer can draw on (education, income, health, energy level, self-confidence, and degree of consumerism) along with their motivation. They use this to identify eight different types of

Exhibit 3-13   The target audience's lifestyle is reflected in this Maybelline ad.

people to understand their consumption behaviour. This U.S. invention is now adapted to other cultures such as Japan, the United Kingdom, and Latin America.

PRIZM$_{NE}$, developed by Claritas, is another American lifestyle segmentation approach that has been adapted for the Canadian market through the two divisions of the research firm Environics (Research Group & Analytics). PRIZM C2 associates the lifestyle questions asked on the survey with demographic data from the federal government's Census. The analysis provides 66 different lifestyle segments and 18 social groups based on whether the respondent is a pre-boomer, boomer, or post-boomer. PRIZM C2 claims that the segmentation system is useful for communication decisions like target audience profiling and media planning, and for many other marketing strategy decisions for virtually all industries. The data from the different lifestyle segments can also be aligned with other data sources such as media consumption and geography to allow more precise targeting for marketing decisions.

Personality   Borrowing from psychological theory, we are interested in consumers' personality traits—the relatively enduring characteristics of one's personality that lead people to respond in a reasonably consistent manner. Characteristics like social orientation (introvert versus extrovert), innovativeness (degree a person likes to try new things), materialism (emphasis placed on product ownership), and self-consciousness (projection of personal image to others) are examples of personality traits used to describe a group of consumers more precisely.[28]

Culture   The broadest and most abstract of the external factors that influence consumer behaviour is **culture**, or the complexity of learned meanings, values, norms, and customs shared by members of a society. Cultural norms and values offer direction and guidance to members of a society in all aspects of their lives, including their consumption behaviour. Marketers must also be aware of changes that may be occurring in a particular culture since it could be the basis for effective segmentation.

While marketers recognize that culture exerts a demonstrable influence on consumers, they often find it difficult to respond to cultural differences in different markets. The subtleties of unique cultures are often difficult to understand and appreciate, but marketers must understand the cultural context in which consumer purchase decisions are made and adapt their advertising and promotional programs accordingly. For example, Bell Mobility rang in the Chinese New Year with an advertising and promotion campaign directed to Asian customers in Western Canada, the first of many specific communication efforts to appeal to a large group of potential customers. To resonate with the people of this culture more significantly, Bell Mobility introduced new creative messages to celebrate the Year of the Monkey. It also edited existing television ads to include scenes reflecting Asian lifestyles more accurately while also translating ads into Cantonese and Mandarin.[29]

Within a given culture are generally found smaller groups or segments whose beliefs, values, norms, and patterns of behaviour set them apart from the larger cultural mainstream. These **subcultures** may be based on age, geographic, religious, racial, and/or ethnic differences. A number of subcultures exist within Canada. These racial/ethnic subcultures are important to marketers because of their size, growth, purchasing power, and distinct purchasing patterns. Other types of subcultures are also targeted through promotional communication. For example, many major brands including Honda Civic, Adidas Canada, and Athletes World target those within the hip-hop culture. The firms have included the hip-hop culture in their television ads and marketing events.[30]

Social Class   Virtually all societies exhibit a form of stratification whereby individuals can be assigned to a specific social category on the basis of criteria important to members of that society. **Social class** refers to relatively homogeneous divisions in a society into which people sharing similar lifestyles, values, norms, interests, and behaviours can be grouped. While a number of methods for determining social class exist, class structures in Canada are usually based on occupational status, educational attainment, and income. For example, sociologists generally agree there are three broad levels of social classes in North America: the upper (14 percent), middle (70 percent), and lower (16 percent) classes.[31]

Social class is an important concept to marketers, since consumers within each social stratum often have similar values, lifestyles, and buying behaviour. Thus, the social class groups provide a natural basis for market segmentation. Consumers in the different social classes differ in the degree to which they use products and services and in their leisure activities, shopping patterns, and media habits. Marketers respond to these differences through their products and service offerings, the media strategies they use to reach different social classes, and the types of advertising messages they develop. The ad in Exhibit 3-14 shows how a product attempts to appeal to the upper classes in both copy and illustration. With smaller Canadian households (2.5 persons) and rising disposable household income, marketers of premium products find that the middle-class consumers behave as upper-class consumers for selective purchases. A sizable group of middle-class consumers who cannot afford premium or luxury goods for all their purchases are "trading up" for items such as clothing, home furnishings, or alcohol.[32]

Behaviouristic Segmentation   Dividing consumers into groups according to different actions is known as **behaviouristic segmentation**. These actions are measurable and generally observable from a research standpoint. The consumer behaviour that is most critical includes brand loyalty, user status, usage rate, situation, and benefits sought.

Loyalty   The degree of loyalty to the brand is a variable used considerably in marketing as programs are developed to retain current customers or attract consumers who purchase other brands. Loyalty status is often combined with demographic and/or psychographic criteria to develop profiles of audiences for specific communication. We will have more to say on this idea, because it is a critical variable in designing promotional messages. Its importance is easily seen; current brand users obviously are aware of the brand and have considerably stronger product knowledge, and they have some regular or irregular interaction with the brand. For example, loyal users of Nike shoes might be more likely to look at the Nike website to see the latest brands.

User Status   In the case of usage, the marketer assumes that non-purchasers of a brand or product who have the same characteristics as purchasers hold greater potential for adoption than nonusers with different characteristics. A profile (demographic or psychographic) of the user is developed, which serves as the basis for promotional strategies designed to attract new users. For example, teenagers share certain similarities in their consumption behaviours. Those who do not currently own, say, an iPod are more likely to be potential buyers than people in other age groups. In this case, the new users may view this purchase decision as a new experience requiring comparison shopping with limited problem-solving activities and are therefore more involved while reading ads or looking at websites or talking to friends online.

Usage Rate   Another factor related to the previous two concerns how much of a product category is consumed. Most product categories and most consumers can be classified along the lines of light, medium, or heavy usage. With these groups in mind, and demographic or psychographic variables, advertisers can direct messages more appropriately. For example, men tend to consume fewer cosmetic products than women (yes, men's skin care is a big business), so ads can be designed to move the many light users to more medium users.

Situation   Another way of viewing behaviouristic segmentation is to examine the situation in which consumers plan to use the product or brand since it directly affects their perceptions, preferences, and purchasing behaviours.[33] Two types of **situations** may be relevant: the specific usage situation and the purchase situation. *Usage situation* refers to the circumstance in which the product will be used. For example, purchases made for private consumption may be thought of differently from those that will be obvious to the public. Furthermore, purchases made for oneself versus for others as gifts offer another way to view consumer markets. The *purchase situation* more directly involves the environment operating at the time of the purchase. Time constraints, store environments, and other factors guide consumers' behaviour, which opens the door for inventive ways of segmenting the market.

Benefit Segmentation   In purchasing products, consumers are generally trying to satisfy specific needs and/or wants. They are looking for products that provide specific benefits to satisfy these

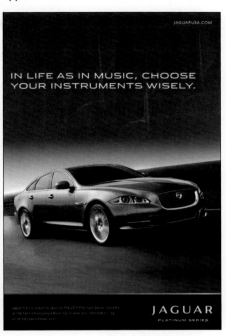

Exhibit 3-14   This Jaguar appeals to the upper class.

Exhibit 3-15   NY Fries reminds consumers of the benefit of authentic potato flavour.

needs. The grouping of consumers on the basis of attributes sought in a product is known as **benefit segmentation** and is widely used. Consider the purchase of a wristwatch. While someone might buy a watch for particular benefits such as accuracy, water resistance, or stylishness, others may seek a different set of benefits. Watches are commonly given as gifts for birthdays, Christmas, and graduation. Certainly the same benefits are considered in the purchase of a gift, but the benefits the purchaser derives are different from those the user will obtain. Ads that portray watches as good gifts stress different criteria to consider in the purchase decision. Another example of benefit segmentation can be seen in the ads for NY Fries, where potato flavour and taste are important (Exhibit 3-15).

TARGET MARKET SELECTION

As we have seen, a number of alternative segmentation approaches may be used. Each time a specific segment is identified, additional information is gathered to help the marketer understand this group. For example, once a specific segment is identified on the basis of benefits sought, the marketer will examine lifestyle characteristics and demographics to help characterize this group and to further its understanding of this market. Behaviouristic segmentation criteria will also be examined. In the purchase of ski boots, for example, specific benefits may be sought—flexibility or stiffness—depending on the type of skiing the buyer does. All this information will be combined to provide a complete profile of the skier.

Promotional planners will refer to the segmentation approach used in the marketing plan. The market segmentation may be based on demographics, so the target market could be men ages 18–24 or women ages 25–44. And it may be incumbent upon the promotional planner to perform additional research to develop a more complete profile. Alternatively, the market segmentation used in the marketing plan could employ one variable as a starting point and offer additional variables to further define the target market, as seen in the ski boots example. Mark's Work Wearhouse entered the market of premium women's wear with its Ispiri brand; the new brand, aimed at working mothers between 30 and 40, is a step up from its Denver Hayes line introduced a decade ago and a step down from high-end designer clothes.[34]

The promotional planner must consider whether the target segment is substantial enough to support individualized strategies. Can it be reached with a communications program? For example, Chapter 10 identifies instances where no media can be used to reach targeted groups. Or the promotions manager may identify a number of segments but be unable to develop the required programs to reach them. For example, the firm may have insufficient funds to develop the required advertising campaign. The more marketers segment the market, the more precise is their understanding of it. But the more the market becomes divided, the fewer consumers are in each segment. Thus, a key decision involves how far one should go in the segmentation process. Another issue arises as to which segmentation variable is used first and which others are used as additional profile variables. The answer to this question is the art of marketing: the insight promotional planners see in the information to understand their target market and target audience options.

(L05) Target Audience Options

We turn to the Rossiter and Percy (R&P) perspective of identifying and selecting the target audience for promotional communication.[35] R&P state that the primary and most logical factor for initially defining a target audience is the current behaviour of consumers. This factor is critical since it is the individual decision of each customer to purchase a brand that dictates a firm's total sales. Furthermore, this behaviour is a manifestation of a consumer's attitude toward the brand. Thus, in setting the direction for any IMC plan or component of an IMC plan (i.e., advertising), the manager must have a clear idea if the target audience is a customer (comprised of brand-loyal customers or favourable brand switchers) or a non-customer (comprised of new category users, other brand switchers, or other brand loyal consumers). We now develop each of these options for making the target audience decision for all marketing communication tool decisions.

Brand-Loyal Customers   Promotional planners have the opportunity to direct marketing communication to **brand-loyal customers** who regularly buy their firm's products. For example, The Movie Network ran an eight-week television, radio, and outdoor campaign that was entirely devoted to its current subscribers base.[36] Marketing strategies (i.e., relationship marketing, discussed in Chapter 1) and communication strategies regularly focus on a firm's current customers to ensure that customers maintain their current purchasing and consumption behaviour. As we noted in Chapter 1, it is generally very profitable to maintain a stable core of current customers. From a communication standpoint, it suggests that we do not have to advertise as often or we do not have to have as many sales promotions. Part of the success with Tide is a stable group of loyal customers to whom the brand often advertises (Exhibit 3-16). However, we still see campaigns directed toward current loyal customers.

Toyota demonstrated the importance of communicating to customers in the wake of its difficulties by having mass media messages, online video messages, specialized communications on safety, and a feel-good ad of customers enjoying the Corolla for decades.[37] While BlackBerry has had ups and downs over time, it recognized the importance of communicating to its current customer base to stay loyal and not defect to other brands.[38] To put this idea into another context we highlight the fact that one-third of all Canadians do not drink beer at all, and that 74 percent of all Canadian beer drinkers claim they are loyal to their favourite beer.[39] This raises the question as to whether beer company ads should target their loyal customers and ensure future purchases by strengthening the loyalty with relevant messages, or target the remaining customers who claim they are not loyal to a specific beer.

Favourable Brand Switchers   The second customer group highlighted by R&P are **favourable brand switchers**. These customers buy the promotional planner's brand but also buy other brands within a given relevant time period for the product category. For certain product categories, consumers habitually purchase from a few favourites or those brands within their evoked set. These types of purchases may occur for many reasons. Consumers often face different purchase situations (e.g., own purchase versus gift). Sometimes certain moods influence brand choice. Whatever the motivation or external influencing factor, consumers adjust their purchases accordingly. While a promotional planner would undoubtedly strive to have all customers be truly loyal, favourable brand switchers are an important source of purchases and are loyal to a degree. For these reasons, marketers would like to communicate directly with these consumers so that their brand remains in the evoked set. For example, the Gain ad in Exhibit 3-17 emphasizes its pleasant aroma to switch consumers back to the brand for their next purchase.

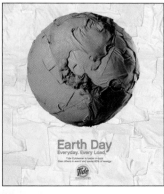

Exhibit 3-16   Tide often directs ads to its loyal customers.

Exhibit 3-17   Gain tries to sway consumers back to the brand by reminding them of the scent.

The importance of varying degrees of loyalty within a brand's customer base is a key topic. In a study of the cola market, the authors provide a decision-making framework for measuring varying degrees of customer loyalty and link these customers to varying levels of ROI. The conclusions suggest that customer groups with different loyalty levels are predicated upon their beliefs toward the brand on the more salient attributes.[40]

Returning to our beer example, it turns out that Canadian beer drinkers may not be strongly aligned to one beer, as 30 to 40 percent will switch brands if a promotional offer coincides with an advertising message.[41] In reality, it appears many Canadian beer drinkers are loyal to their favourite beer to a degree, but they will also include it along with other brands. This implies that a brand manager for beer (e.g., Molson Canadian) is faced with the task of communicating to favourable brand switchers, a group of consumers who are habitually buying their brand and a few others (e.g., Labatt Blue). In turn, another brand manager (e.g., Labatt Blue) could be faced with the same task of communicating to favourable brand switchers who consume an entirely different group of beer brands (e.g., Lakeport, Steamwhistle).

New Category Users   Consumers that are not purchasing within the promotional planner's product category are within the non-customer group and are known as **new category users**. Exhibit 3-18 shows an ad for a product for people looking for a product to assist them to stop smoking. Oftentimes, new category users arise due to changes in one's life. For example, after graduating from college or university many young adults begin to enter numerous categories partly because they have the income but also because they are at a stage of their life when new or latent needs emerge. Advertisers attempt to court this target audience since many of these consumers are potentially ready to make a purchase. Later on in life consumers face different needs and move into a product category. Marketers believe that steady communication may entice these customers to their brand when the time comes for these consumers to actually purchase. Capital One, a financial services organization, attracted as new customers new Canadians (i.e., recent immigrants) who had not fully developed their credit history and who had minimal or no purchases with respect to banking products and services. To attract those who did not have a credit card Capital One used "take-one" pads on signage of street cars that passed through Chinatown in Toronto, pre-movie ads shown before Bollywood films, and point-of-purchase ads in ethnic grocery stores.[42]

New category users also appear when brands try to attract new customers who might not perceive the product category as relevant for fulfilling their needs. Most people have entertainment needs that can be satisfied in many ways (e.g., dancing at club, watching a movie at theatre). Young people typically do not see the arts, such as ballet, as potentially fulfilling their entertainment needs, so the National Ballet of Canada faced an interesting communication challenge to attract new young consumers to its production of *The Seagull*. The solution involved distributing an actual origami gull—5,000 of them, in fact—in Toronto bars, restaurants, and coffee shops. The unfolded gull displayed a flyer with key information and an opportunity to win tickets to the production.[43]

Other Brand Switchers   Another type of consumer that is in the non-customer group are **other brand switchers**. They are like the switchers in the customer group in that they purchase a few different brands within a category. However, from a promotional planner's perspective, they are fundamentally different because they are not purchasing their brand. This is a challenging target audience, as the brand needs to break into consumers' evoked set and within the brands that these consumers are currently purchasing. It's a formidable task, but still the focus of a considerable amount of advertising and promotion. (Exhibit 3-19 is an ad to attract drinkers of other brands of beer.)

For example, Coffee Crisp started advertising on television after a 10-year hiatus. As the brand manager noted, "Because Coffee Crisp hasn't been advertised for so many years, we haven't brought in a new generation of Coffee Crisp consumers." Naturally, many young consumers were eating

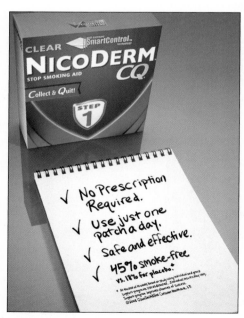

Exhibit 3-18   Nicoderm offers to help those who want to stop smoking

other brands of chocolate bars, so Coffee Crisp faced the challenge of appealing to these other brand switchers with a taste alternative. Research showed that Coffee Crisp "owned" the coffee association in the chocolate bar market, and with a generation of young coffee drinkers that frequent cafés the brand had a good opportunity to improve sales with its new ads. In fact, the room for growth is impressive—the famous bar, which once was ranked number one or two in Canada, had fallen to number five with a lack of advertising for so many years.[44]

The Gap targeted "millennials" with online videos of the denim design team living and working in Los Angeles with "street feel" imagery. While this initially appears to be demographic targeting, in fact it is closer to behavioural as the fashionable brand that peaked in the 1990s looked to attract consumers who currently did not visit the store to replenish their wardrobe with the iconic brand's latest offerings.[45] Most clothing retailers try to attract non-customers to build sales and look to secondary variables like demographics to better profile the target audience, as this example suggests. Yet the strategy often is misinterpreted from the key targeting variable when news reports centre on the age factor instead of the behavioural one.

Other Brand Loyals R&P's final non-customer group for target audience selection includes **other brand loyals**. As this label implies, these consumers purchase only one other brand. It is difficult to say how much in advertising and promotion expenditure is directed to these types of consumers across many industries. Logically, it would be very difficult to break the strongly held consumer behaviours. Nevertheless, this is still a potential target to which a firm may wish to deliver advertising and promotion. The tourism ad in Exhibit 3-20 encourages travellers to consider Canada as a destination to visit.

IMC Planning: Target Audience Profile

According to R&P, after prioritizing the target audience in terms of customer groups other segmentation variables like lifestyle or demographics are used to develop a complete target audience profile. A complete profile of the target audience beyond the initial behavioural variable is necessary for direction of the remaining decisions in the promotional plan. Creative decisions involving the main message to be communicated require appropriate content so that consumers will attend to and understand the message. Effective media decisions require the promotional planner to match the consumer characteristics of the specific media with a complete target audience profile. Finally, more information about the target audience allows greater precision when assessing and choosing IMC tools to deliver the message. We now explore the planning implications of these three ideas.

PROFILE FOR MESSAGES

In later chapters we will identify different aspects of constructing the main message a promotional planner would want to develop for its advertising or sales promotion or any other IMC tool like the Internet or public relations. For the message to be completely understood, the content of the message must be consistent with the background or

Exhibit 3-19 Grolsch plays on its name to attract new customers.

Exhibit 3-20 Travel Alberta and the Canadian Tourism Commission jointly try to attract visitors to Canada.

experiences of the intended audience. For example, if the ad uses language or references to a lifestyle that is unfamiliar to the target audience, there is less likelihood of it influencing in the direction intended. Thus, a complete profile of the target audience will be useful when finalizing the body copy in a print ad or the scenes in a television commercial.

Many companies target a younger demographic. We may read in the press or in marketing trade publications that a firm is targeting an 18- to 24-year-old demographic. While this may be true, often there is an inherent behavioural variable implied. Sometimes it is more like a new category user, since young adults start to consume new categories of products as they mature. Other times, it is more like favourable brand switchers in an attempt to make these consumers exhibit stronger loyalty. Thus, a communication message has to resonate with the target audience based on their current behaviour, whether they buy the brand or not, and another variable like demographics.

One clever ad by Tide detergent illustrates this point from the other direction. The ad shows a child sitting in a highchair who has just finished eating a bowl of spaghetti. The picture clearly shows the child's face and the child is naturally very messy. The headline reads, "The day I switched to Tide," and there is no other text in the ad. It appears that this message is targeted toward other brand switchers or other brand loyals who are at a particular stage of the family life cycle. The ad represents the significant decision they undertook to finally stop consuming a current brand and move on to a presumably better brand. Had the ad shown an alternative picture, the additional profile variable would have been considerably different. For instance, the image of a young woman wearing athletic clothing who observes a stain or that the colours of her clothing are fading too quickly suggests an active lifestyle. This illustrates that any marketing segmentation variable can be used to further profile the behavioural variable.

PROFILE FOR MEDIA

Later in this text, we will also identify the different media decisions. For example, the promotional planner could select television or radio to deliver its message, or the promotional planner might consider newspapers or magazines or a multitude of other media. Each medium offers many avenues that also must be considered. For instance, would the promotional planner place the television commercial on a TSN sports event during the day, or on a CTV drama in the evening? A detailed profile of the target audience allows the message to be more precisely delivered in a medium that has a higher proportion of the target audience.

Critics contend that the advent of many different television channels leading to greater audience fragmentation has led to television being less efficient, since an advertiser is required to place a commercial on more than one station to reach a larger audience. In contrast, the detailed target audience profile for media helps a promotional planner move toward greater effectiveness. With the possibility of offering a more customized message to different audiences, promotional planners can have one type of commercial oriented toward younger non-customers on one channel and another message to older current customers on a different channel. Or, with the extensive number of new television channels in languages other than the two official languages, advertisers can provide more customized messages on the respective channels. For example, the OpenRoad Auto Group brand of car dealerships selling Toyota, Lexus, Honda, Acura, Hyundai, and Audi vehicles has successfully used different combinations of media to effectively reach the Vancouver resident with a Chinese background.[46]

Moving toward more interactive media for the purposes of building and maintaining relationships, brands could use certain kinds of media and media vehicles to communicate with different segments based on unique relationship variables that are within the firm's database.[47] This would allow more accurate exposure and more customized messages depending upon where the customer is within the relationship.

PROFILE FOR IMC TOOLS

Similarly, in a later part of the book we investigate the decisions involved for other IMC tools like sales promotion, public relations, direct marketing, and the Internet. Each of these represents additional avenues for reaching target audiences, and each represents a tool with a greater opportunity for building the brand. Like media, there is also the possibility of more closely aligning the use of a tool with a promotional planner's target audience, provided sufficient profiling is done.

Western Union created cultural events for Toronto, Vancouver, and Winnipeg residents with Filipino heritage to encourage usage when sending money to their previous country. This idea arose after research indicated an interest in entertainment, in particular performers and celebrities from the former country. Ethnically based media advertising supported this effort to convince these consumers that the brand was not an overpriced, indifferent global company.[48]

From another angle, Canadian Tire—historically geared for men—continues to evolve with a greater emphasis toward women. Altering its product offerings and store design was just one step, as it offers a substantially different set of communications directed to women with a stylish-home kind of lifestyle. Its television advertising featured creative messages more fitting for women, placed on specialty channels. Canadian Tire featured print advertising in stylish publications like *Wish, Style at Home,* and *Canadian House & Home.* Store displays appeared more inspiring and less informational, also to fit with this newfound audience.[49]

Learning Objectives Summary

 Describe the consumer decision-making process and demonstrate how it relates to marketing communication.

Consumer behaviour is best viewed as the process and activities that people experience when searching for, selecting, purchasing, using, evaluating, and disposing of products and services to satisfy their needs and desires. A five-stage model of the consumer decision-making process consists of need recognition, information search, alternative evaluation, purchase, and post-purchase evaluation. The decision process model views consumer behaviour primarily from a cognitive orientation. Marketing communication plays a role in every stage as marketers adjust their messages and media along with IMC tools to influence appropriately so that consumers move from one stage to the other.

 Distinguish internal psychological processes, their influence on consumer decision making, and implications for marketing communication.

Internal psychological processes that influence the consumer decision-making process include motivation, perception, attitude formation and change, integration processes, and satisfaction. Each of these are areas in which advertising attempts to influence. Most advertising reflects a particular purchase motive. Certain elements of an ad are designed to attract attention or ensure that the target audience retains the information or symbolic message. The body copy in a print ad, for example, can be written to influence the receiver's attitude, and allows certain ways of integrating the information. Finally, advertising is designed to suggest to consumers that they made the correct purchase so they feel satisfied.

 Contrast how the consumer decision-making process varies for different types of purchases and the effects on marketing communication.

Consumer decision making is classified along a continuum from routine problem solving to extended problem solving. Consumers generally spend more time and effort as they move from routine to extended problem solving. Different types of marketing communication are more relevant than others depending upon the type of behaviour expected. Consumer decision making moves from an individual decision to a group decision, and once again marketing communication must adjust its message, media, or IMC tool accordingly.

Compare the similarities and differences of target market and target audience.

This chapter also investigated how promotional planners make a target audience decision for any aspect of an IMC plan. To understand the context of this decision, the chapter examined the role of promotion in the overall marketing process, as shown in Figure 3-5. The process includes a situation analysis, target market process, and marketing program development all directed toward a prescribed target market.

One of the key aspects pertains to the target marketing process, which includes segmenting the market, selecting a target market, and determining the market positioning strategy, as this process gives direction to the target audience decision. Accordingly, we reviewed how marketing planners and promotional planners segment the market, and explained how each made the target market and target audience decision, respectively.

 Develop the options for making a target audience decision for marketing communication.

The chapter identified a model to profile a target audience by considering the current purchase behaviour of the target audience with respect to the promotional planner's brand as the primary segmentation variable. Promotional messages can be directed to current customers, such as brand-loyal or favourable brand switchers. Alternatively, promotional messages could be targeted to non-customers, like new category users, other brand switchers, or other brand loyals.

 Express why a profile of the target audience is important for message, media, and IMC tool decisions.

Finally, the chapter concluded by expressing how other variables more accurately profile the audience in terms of lifestyle or psychographics variables after the initial direction is finalized. This descriptive profile becomes useful for all facets of the promotional plan (i.e., message, media, IMC tools).

Key Terms

Review key terms and definitions on Connect.

Review Questions

1. What are the stages of the consumer decision-making model? Why are they important for planning marketing communication?

2. What are the primary psychological processes associated with each stage of the consumer decision-making model? How does marketing communication influence each stage?

3. How do the stages of the consumer decision-making model differ with the three types of problem solving?

4. When defining a target audience for communications, why is it a good idea to use consumer behaviour with respect to your brand as the primary variable before using other variables such as demographics or lifestyle?

5. What are the five customer groups? Explain in terms of beverage product like soft drinks or beer.

6. Why is a complete profile of a target audience important for marketing communication?

Applied Questions

1. Explain the difference among functional, experiential, and psychological benefits. Why might the messages recommended in an IMC plan for smartphones focus on each one separately or together?

2. How are ads or brand messages experienced in social media influenced by consumers' selective perception system?

3. Consider a group purchasing situation you have previously experienced, like going out for the evening. What role did each person play during prepurchase, purchase and consumption, and postpurchase?

4. In what situations is the target audience and the target market the same? In what situations is the size of the target audience larger or smaller than the target market?

5. Examine the ads in this chapter and identify the target audience the ad is directed toward using the model of five customer groups. Suggest other relevant segmentation variables to further profile the target audience. Also identify a relevant segmentation variable to pinpoint the target market.

6. Which segmentation variables are more useful or appropriate for profiling a target market for an automobile like the Mini? Similarly, which are more useful or appropriate for profiling the target audience for an automobile like the Mini?

GO ONLINE

For more information on the resources available from McGraw-Hill Ryerson, go to www.mcgrawhill.ca/he/solutions.

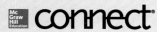

Communication Response Models

4

LEARNING OBJECTIVES

LO1 Explain the elements of the communication process and identify the role of marketing communication.

LO2 Contrast traditional communication response models and alternative response hierarchies.

LO3 Develop the response processes of receivers of marketing communication through two models of cognitive processing.

LO4 Illustrate a response model for managerial decision making.

LO5 Construct ideas on how the knowledge of response models can be used for IMC planning.

Subaru's Hot Autos

Japan-based Subaru faced tremendous competition from the likes of other Asian import car companies such as Honda, Toyota, and Hyundai in addition to Ford, GM, and Chrysler when competing in the Canadian market. The trifecta from the other side of the world regularly sold 11,000 to 16,000 units per month while the USA contingent sold 18,000 to 24,000 units per month compared to Subaru's 2,600 per month. Despite this obstacle, Subaru managed to impress with successful ads for its Outback and Forester brands in recent years. The company faced a tricky marketing communication issue as consumers more likely viewed it as a mid-sized SUV manufacturer when it planned to launch a sports coupe, BRZ, and compact utility vehicle, XV Crosstrek, with a substantially smaller budget.

The solution for the BRZ involved making it a "hot" new addition to Subaru's lineup with a super-slow-motion video showing the heat radiating off the car as it melted everything in the parking garage. It ended with customary close-up shots of its sleek styling and showcased its handling while accelerating with the joyful sounds of the engine roaring; the spot was viewed by many visitors to Subaru's YouTube channel. According to Geoff Craig of Subaru, "What drove a lot of our thinking was this car was really catching fire with the online community. People knew about the vehicle long before it was introduced to Canada, and we thought we could accelerate that momentum."

Combined with the video, Subaru ignited the front cover of *Grid,* a free Toronto city magazine, with a hologram cover that looked like a regular cover but when slightly tilted showed an image of the BRZ burning through the page. DDB assistant creative director Paul Riss explained, "It's a hot new car and we wanted each element in the integrated campaign to turn heads."

Other media included ads in national newspapers and magazines showing similar images of the BRZ burning through the pages. Online images in banner ads displayed the same burning effect digitally. A display on the streets of Montreal re-created the video effect with scorched street items like a mailbox and bike rack surrounding the BRZ. Wild postings permitted viewers to "tap or snap" with their smartphone to see a dedicated page for a full description. Craig believed that, "We need to get noticed, and to get noticed we need to be different and unique. We pride ourselves on always doing things a bit differently, but we've put work out there that hopefully makes sense to consumers."

And the target audience of young men aged 30–35 who are tech-savvy driving enthusiasts sure noticed the brand; sales reached its goal of selling all 450 of its allotted units to the Canadian market as orders piled up for 2013.

With such innovation for the BRZ, *Marketing Magazine* recognized Subaru as one of the top 10 marketers for 2012, and the company made the shortlist for marketer of the year. Subaru rounded out the BRZ effort with its largest media spend ever for the XV Crosstrek. The ads conveyed the dual city/country use of the small crossover vehicle with an actor representing both a city dweller and a rural enthusiast.

Sources: Chris Powell, "Subaru Canada Sizzles with New Campaign," *Marketing Magazine,* July 6, 2012; Jeromy Lloyd, "2012 Marketers of the Year Shortlist: Subaru," *Marketing Magazine,* November 14, 2012; Alicia Androich, "Holy Holograms! The Grid Gets Special Cover Treatment," *Marketing Magazine,* June 20, 2012.

Questions:

1. Why was the Subaru executive so concerned about the BRZ being noticed?
2. Was the approach selected a good way to get noticed for this type of car and this brand?

An organization's IMC strategy is implemented through the communication tools and messages it sends to current or prospective customers as well as other relevant publics. Organizations communicate in many ways, such as through advertisements, websites, press releases, sales promotion, and visual images. Those involved in the planning of an IMC program need to understand how consumers will perceive and interpret their messages and how these reactions will shape consumers' responses to the company and/or its product or service.

This chapter takes a historical perspective to illustrate how academics and practitioners have evolved in their thinking to understand how persuasion works in the context of marketing communication. We begin with a model to illustrate the complexity of the communication process. Next, we examine the response process of consumers that is explained by traditional models, alternative hierarchies, and cognitive processing of communication. Finally, we summarize with a framework that illustrates an IMC planning perspective.

LO1 A Model of the Communication Process

Communication has been defined as the passing of information, the exchange of ideas, or the process of establishing a commonness or oneness of thought between a sender and a receiver.[1] This definition suggests that for communication to occur, there must be common thinking between two parties and information must be passed from one person to another (or from one group to another). This section elaborates on this idea by explaining the elements of the communication process and identifying the role of marketing communication.

OVERVIEW OF THE MODEL

The communication process is often very complex. Success depends on such factors as the nature of the message, the audience's interpretation of it, and the environment in which it is received. The receiver's perception of the source and the medium used to transmit the message may also affect the ability to communicate, as do many other factors. Words, pictures, sounds, and colours may have different meanings to different audiences, and people's perceptions and interpretations of them vary. Marketers must understand the meanings that words and symbols take on and how they influence consumers' interpretation of products and messages.

Over the years, a model of the communication process has evolved, as shown in Figure 4-1.[2] Two elements represent the major participants in the communication process: the sender and the receiver. Another two are the major communication tools: message and channel. Four others are the major communication functions and processes: encoding, decoding, response, and feedback. The last element, noise, refers to any extraneous factors in the system that can interfere with the process and work against effective communication.

SOURCE/ENCODING

The sender, or **source**, of a communication is the person or organization that has information to share with another person or group of people. The source may be an individual (say, a salesperson or hired spokesperson, such as a celebrity who appears in a company's advertisements) or a nonpersonal entity (such as the brand or organization itself). Because the receiver's perceptions of the source influence how the communication is received, marketers must be careful to select a communicator the receiver believes is knowledgeable and trustworthy or with whom the receiver can identify or relate in some manner.

The communication process begins when the source selects words, symbols, pictures, and the like to represent the message that will be delivered to the receiver(s). This process, known as **encoding**, involves putting thoughts, ideas, or information into a symbolic form. The sender's goal is to encode the message in such a way that it will be understood by the receiver. This means

Figure   4-1   A model of the communication process

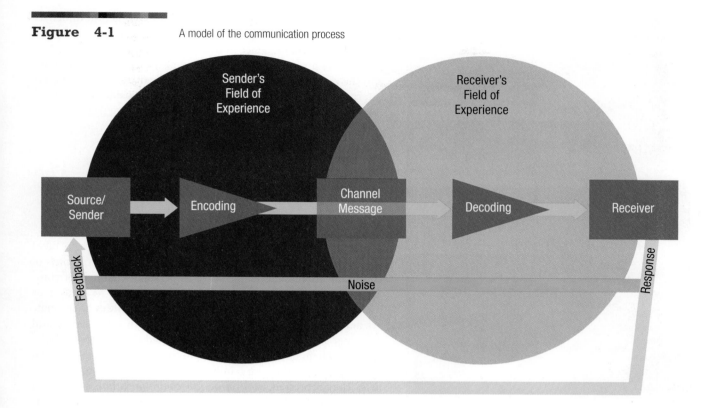

using words, signs, or symbols that are familiar to the target audience. The Nestea ad in Exhibit 4-1 is constructed to allow multiple meanings for the receiver. Many companies also have highly recognizable symbols—such as McDonald's golden arches, Nike's swoosh, or the Coca-Cola trademark. So when these symbols are shown in a message, consumers instantly understand the brand that is associated with the message.

MESSAGE

The encoding process leads to development of a **message** that contains the information or meaning the source intends to convey. The message may be verbal or nonverbal, oral or written, or symbolic. Messages are put into a transmittable form that is appropriate for the channel of communication. In advertising, this may range from simply writing words or copy that will be read as a radio message to producing an expensive television commercial.

Marketers make decisions regarding the message content, structure, and design for optimal communication. **Message content** refers to the information and/or meaning contained in the message. **Message structure** and **message design** refer to the way the message is constructed to deliver the information or intended meaning. Message decisions are covered in more detail in Chapters 7 and 8.

For many products, it is not the actual words of the message that determine its communication effectiveness but rather the impression or image the ad creates. Notice how

Exhibit 4-1   The many elements in this ad require extensive decoding by consumers.

the Coach ad shown in Exhibit 4-2 uses only a picture to deliver its message. However, the brand name and picture help communicate a feeling of eloquence and the classic design of its handbag. The meaning of products, brands, symbols to represent brands, and the story implied about the brand influences how consumers interpret messages suggesting that careful consideration of the message is a critical task for promotional planners.[3]

CHANNEL

The **channel** is how the communication travels from the source or sender to the receiver. At the broadest level, channels of communication are of two types, personal and nonpersonal.

Personal Channels   Direct interpersonal (face-to-face) contact with target individuals or groups are *personal channels* of communication. Salespeople serve as personal channels of communication when they deliver their sales message to a buyer or potential customer. With video and other capabilities of computers and the Internet, face-to-face contact with sales people and customer service personnel is now mediated through technology.

Social channels of communication such as friends, neighbours, associates, co-workers, or family members are also personal channels. They represent *word-of-mouth communication,* a powerful source of information for consumers.[4] Companies attempt to generate positive word-of-mouth for their brands. Knowing that the average consumer often listens to what others say about a brand, marketers will target specific groups of influential consumers such as trendsetters or loyal customers and use a many new techniques to enhance the effectiveness of this channel. Companies encourage consumer to communicate their brand in day-to-day living by offering incentives like free products.[5] One critic believes it is only a matter of time before brands privately remunerate regular families to talk about brands to their friends, much like in the 2009 movie *The Joneses*.[6]

Consumers communicate about brands with social media, chat sites, and so on, and use the networking features of the Internet to send ads and links to whomever they choose. While there is no face-to-face contact in many of these instances, the interactive capabilities suggest it closely resembles a personal channel. Marketers use this as an opportunity to disseminate a message through the resulting word-of-mouth communication of these newfound personal channels of communication.

Furthermore, communication in social media like Twitter shares characteristics of a social channel where brand personnel interact with loyal customers. Continued messaging among Dove and its favourite followers who happened to be influential bloggers allowed the brand to recruit these women for a day-long beauty session that resulted in them all being part of a cast of dancers in a rendition of *Singing in the Rain* to promote its Nourishing Oil Care line of shampoo shown on TV and Internet media. During their spa day, the women used social media to describe the experience for all to vicariously enjoy the moment.[7]

One study conducted on the effects of a word-of-mouth campaign for a chain store examined the characteristics of the most successful "agents" so that firms could better understand at whom they should target their marketing efforts.[8] They found that agents who were not loyal customers of the store were more effective at generating sales through word-of-mouth than were loyal customers. The explanation offered for these counterintuitive findings is that loyal customers have already told their friends and acquaintances about a product and are already generating positive word-of-mouth. Alternatively, nonloyal customers may be more responsive to marketing campaigns designed to encourage them to spread the word about a product. Other studies find that post-campaign word-of-mouth contributes to strengthening profitability through customer lifetime value calculations and that advertising does lead to a measurable link to enhanced word-of-mouth communication.[9]

Other research shows that 90 percent of conversations about products, services, and brands take place offline. Face-to-face interaction accounts for the vast majority of word-of-mouth communication (72 percent) about a brand, while phone conversations rank second (18 percent). Only 7 percent of word-of-mouth takes place through online channels such as e-mail/instant messages, blogs, and chat rooms. The research also shows that nearly half the word-of-mouth conversations included references to the IMC tools used for a brand, including print and television ads, websites, and other marketing tools such as point-of-sale displays and promotions.[10]

Finally, an investigation of a sample of 70 product launches showed that only 10 percent produced 85 percent of the word-of-mouth communication. The majority of it occurred before the launch and with a strong traditional media expenditure for distinctive brands in ubiquitous product categories.[11]

Nonpersonal Channels Methods of communication that carry a message without interpersonal contact between sender and receiver are **nonpersonal channels**. These channels are generally referred to as the **mass media** or mass communication, since the message is sent to many individuals at one time. For example, a TV commercial broadcast on a prime-time show may be seen by a two or three million people. Nonpersonal channels of communication consist of two major types, print (e.g., newspapers, magazines) and broadcast (e.g., radio and television). Specialized magazines provide a good channel for luxury products to communicate their brand (Exhibit 4-3).

The technical capabilities of the Internet allow innovative marketers to use it as a personal channel as noted above, and as a nonpersonal channel with both print and broadcast characteristics. It is a nonpersonal channel as major TV stations like CTV stream live sports broadcasts online, while CBC offers shows online that cannot fit on the regular TV schedule.[12]

The wide acceptance of the Internet can be seen in its competition with TV for audience share. For Canada's broadcasters, the Internet began as a dumping ground of sorts—a place to show old and cancelled programs and video clips, and to advertise their main network offerings. That practice has all but disappeared in the quest for eyeballs and supplementary advertising. Canada's broadcasters now view their online sites as mini-networks—places to air original content, bonus material, and special events.

Volkswagen adapted its marketing communication to many activities including a new website, new dealer websites, and exclusive ads to support online TV shows on CTV.ca to continue the "Very Volkswagen" idea. On Sympatico.ca, VW implemented mini webisodes that featured its own personnel and those from its agency in a spoof where an agency tries to develop jingles for VW with obvious difficulty (off tune, wrong message) to illustrate the humour.[13]

RECEIVER/DECODING

The **receiver** is the person(s) with whom the sender shares thoughts or information. Generally, receivers are the consumers in the target market or audience who read, hear, and/or see the marketer's message. The target audience may consist of individuals, groups, niche markets, market segments, or a general public or mass audience as discussed in the previous chapter. The ad in Exhibit 4-4 targets a small group of drivers who can afford the price of a Porsche.

Exhibit 4-3 Print channels convey a positive effect for luxury brands like Rolex.

Hopefully, you'll run into your ex.

The new Boxster is here.

Exhibit 4-4 Porsche attracts an audience from a niche market with its ads.

Exhibit 4-5   This Sen5es ad allows for many interpretations in decoding.

feed your perspective

sen5es

at the SoHo Metropolitan Hotel

Decoding is the process of transforming the sender's message back into thought. This process is heavily influenced by the receiver's frame of reference or **field of experience**, which refers to the experiences, perceptions, attitudes, and values he or she brings to the communication situation. For effective communication to occur, the message decoding process of the receiver must match the encoding of the sender. Simply put, this means the receiver understands and correctly interprets what the source is trying to communicate. Exhibit 4-5 shows an ad where many ways of decoding might occur.

As Figure 4-1 showed, the source and the receiver each have a frame of reference (the circle around each) that they bring to the communication situation. Effective communication is more likely when there is *common ground* (i.e., overlap of circles) between the two parties. The more knowledge the sender has about the receivers, the better the sender can understand their needs, empathize with them, and communicate effectively.

While this notion of common ground between sender and receiver may sound basic, it often causes great difficulty in the advertising communications process. Marketing and advertising people often have very different fields of experience from the target audience with whom they must communicate in terms of age, education, and life experiences. Advertisers invest in research to understand the frames of reference of the target audiences and pretest messages to make sure consumers understand and decode them in the manner the advertiser intended prior to the launch. IMC Perspective 4-1 exemplifies the difficulty that comes with not communicating effectively.

NOISE

Throughout the communication process, the message is subject to extraneous factors that can distort or interfere with its reception. This unplanned distortion or interference is known as **noise**. Errors or problems that occur during message encoding or distractions at the point of reception are examples of noise. Perhaps the foremost distraction is advertising clutter, whereby the receiver is confronted with many competing messages. Noise may also occur because the fields of experience of the sender and receiver don't overlap. Lack of common ground may result in improper encoding of the message—using a sign, symbol, or words that are unfamiliar or have different meaning to the receiver.

RESPONSE/FEEDBACK

The receiver's set of reactions after seeing, hearing, or reading the message is known as a **response**. Receivers' responses can range from nonobservable actions such as storing information in memory to immediate action such as visiting the brand's Facebook page after seeing an ad. Other responses can be emotional where consumers enjoy or dislike messages they receive. Furthermore, responses such as stronger awareness of the brand or attitude to the brand may occur as well. The next section investigates the responses consumers experience to marketing communication more thoroughly.

Marketers are very interested in **feedback**, that part of the receiver's response that is communicated back to the sender. Feedback closes the loop in the communication flow and lets the sender monitor how the intended message is being decoded and received. While the ultimate

IMC PERSPECTIVE 4-1

Did You Get the Message?

Whether the brand message is delivered via print, video, or audio across a multitude of avenues, the underlying challenge remains: communicating clearly and accurately so that consumers understand the message. Creative experts critiqued a series of ads to assess whether they pass this true test of advertising effectiveness.

Creative agency Rethink established an identity for Science World in Vancouver with the "We Can Explain" campaign, which illustrates enjoyable visual solutions based on scientific facts. Despite overwhelming success, it still ran into criticism with its take on how belly button lint makes great kindling. An unknowing beachgoer sitting in the sun finds smoke emitting from his tummy and scrambles to the sand to put it out, with a super claiming that Science World can explain. Cosmo Campbell, creative director for DDB Vancouver, commented, "I love this campaign—I just don't love this ad. The real problem is that the fact that is being highlighted is neither interesting nor informative." Echoing this, Fiona Birch, creative director of Tonic Global, claimed, "It is a fine line when you are trying to amaze and entertain, but still keep the ad believable." Finally, Luis Vieira suggested a website address or additional communication would have completed the well-executed story. Collectively, the creative colleagues see ample opportunity for this message to resonate better with the target audience.

CP&B ventured to compare Molson 67 Sublime with a martini and produced a sober reminder of how difficult it is to communicate a distinctive product difference creatively. Two martinis on a bar viewed the beer, with a pair of olives in each glass moving about like a pair of eyes; they faced a "martinis beware" message from the 67-calorie, lime-flavoured beer. Henry Wong, creative director of Tenzing Communications, wondered, "Are martini drinkers really concerned with the caloric count of their drink? It's the right product—just wrong positioning." Chris Hall, president of Huxley Quayle Von Bismark, remarked, "It's too rational. Good advertising also takes a creative leap and adds an emotion reason to change your mind." In closing, one professor concluded, "Comparing martinis to beer is like comparing apples to avocados. Fear not, my little martini friend, you're safe for now."

An ad intended to remind people of water safety and staying away from dams and hydro stations that was sponsored by Ontario Power Generation and the Ontario Provincial Police and developed by Rain43 received weak reception. Wong claimed, "This nicely art-directed, atmospherically shot, interestingly acted spot is a sign masquerading as an ad." Hall observed, "Ontario Power Generation looks like they wanted to do something interesting and provocative and what they got was something confusing that buries a very important message." The professor wrapped it up with, "I am unapologetic that it took me a few too many viewings to figure out or even get the basic message."

Sources: "Science Ad Sparks, But Fails to Ignite," *National Post*, October 28, 2011; "Martinis Need Not Fear 67 Sublime," *National Post,* July 8, 2011; "That's All Very Well, But What's the Message?" *National Post,* June 17, 2011.

Question:

1. Do you agree with the criticism of these ad reviewers?

---

form of feedback occurs through sales, it is often hard to show a direct relationship between marketing communication and purchase behaviour. So marketers use other methods to obtain feedback, among them customer inquiries, store visits, participation levels with promotions, and visits to websites.

Trends in brand-related consumer-generated content and digital forwarding of ads or stories about products is another instance where planners can observe feedback from their audiences. However, after a few years of running contests or promotional events with user-generated content, brands began to exert control over their messages and appeared more cautious about encouraging further content growth.[14] With Coca-Cola's sponsorship of the torch relay for the 2010 Olympics, the popular brand could gauge the success of the message that encouraged Canadians to sign up for a chance to carry the torch at icoke.ca.[15] With research-based information like this, advertisers can determine reasons for success or failure in the communication process and make adjustments.

SUMMARY OF THE MODEL

The model has stood the test of time for more than 50 years to describe how advertising communicates through traditional media. Practitioners are debating how new digital channels and social media are affecting their marketing communication decisions. They appear to conclude that despite the revolution of new communication occurring, the fundamental tenets of a consistent brand strategy and understanding how that message is delivered through the new avenues is still a critical perspective.[16]

We can still conclude that successful communication is accomplished when the marketer selects an appropriate source, develops an effective message or appeal that is encoded properly, and then selects the channels or media that will best reach the target audience so that the message can be effectively decoded and delivered. So whether we are talking about delivering a message on television or through social media, the general communication principles are important to consider for effective decisions. Since these decisions must consider how the target audience will respond to the promotional message, the remainder of this chapter examines the process by which consumers respond to marketing communication.

(L02) The Response Process

An important aspect of developing effective communication programs involves understanding the *response process* the receiver may go through in moving toward a specific behaviour and how the promotional efforts of the marketer influence consumer responses. To explain the response process we now review two types of response hierarchy models—traditional and alternative.

TRADITIONAL RESPONSE HIERARCHY MODELS

A number of models have been developed to depict the process a consumer may pass through in moving from a state of not being aware of a company, product, or brand to actual purchase behaviour. Figure 4-2 shows three response models, which are known as hierarchy models since there is a prescribed order or defined steps the receiver experiences. While these response models may appear similar, they were developed for different reasons.

Figure   4-2

Models of the response process

Stages	Models		
	AIDA model	Hierarchy of effects model	Information processing model
Cognitive stage	Attention	Awareness	Presentation
			Attention
		Knowledge	Comprehension
Affective stage	Interest	Liking	Yielding
		Preference	
	Desire	Conviction	Retention
Behavioural stage	Action	Purchase	Behaviour

The **AIDA model** was developed to represent the steps a salesperson must take a customer through in the personal selling process.[17] The salesperson must first get the customer's attention and then arouse interest in the company's product or service. Strong levels of interest should create desire to own or use the product. The action step in the AIDA model involves getting the customer to make a purchase commitment and closing the sale. When applying this idea to marketing communication, planners encourage pre-purchase consumer usage through a sampling program or allowing consumers to use a product with minimal commitment (Exhibit 4-6). Subsequent action would be a trial purchase as the consumer adopts the product. Alternatively, brands try to encourage a behaviour such as participation in a contest, like Coca-Cola did with its "Cover" promotion where music-loving youth sang a song by a favourite artist and uploaded the recording (covers.muchmusic.com) to solicit votes to win.[18]

The **hierarchy of effects model** assumes a consumer passes through a series of steps in sequential order from initial awareness of a product or service to actual purchase.[19] A basic premise is that advertising effects occur over a period of time. Marketing communication may not lead to immediate behavioural response or purchase; rather, a series of effects must occur, with each step fulfilled before the consumer can move to the next step in the hierarchy. Xbox Kinect advertised and promoted its gaming console and received tremendous participation levels at its demonstration hubs set up in a few major Canadian cities. With celebrities visiting the hubs, the events attracted many new users who eventually purchased leading to stronger trial purchases down the road.[20]

The **information processing model** of advertising effects assumes the receiver in a persuasive communication situation like advertising is an information processor or problem solver.[21] The series of steps a receiver goes through in being persuaded constitutes a response hierarchy that is similar to the hierarchy of effects sequence. However, this model includes a step not found in the other models: *retention,* or the receiver's ability to retain that portion of the comprehended information that he or she accepts as valid or relevant. This step is important since most promotional campaigns are designed not to motivate consumers to take immediate action but rather to provide information they will use later when making a purchase decision. In some ways mobile apps are helping with future purchases, for example, Cineplex's app allows consumers to see schedules, read entertainment news, view movie trailers, and obtain promotional offers.[22] While the initial loading of the app and reading about the brand online did not make an immediate sale, the app certainly facilitates future repeat purchases.

Exhibit 4-6 Sampling of disposable contact lenses encourages a trial purchase.

IMPLICATIONS OF THE TRADITIONAL HIERARCHY MODELS

Implications for the response models are grouped into the individual steps within each of the models and the consistent stages across all three models.

Individual Steps The hierarchy models of communication response are useful for promotional planners to make specific marketing communication decisions for each step. Potential buyers may be at different steps in the hierarchy, so the advertiser will face different sets of communication problems. For example, using the hierarchy of effects model, a company introducing an innovative product like the Sony Reader may use media advertising to make people aware of the product along with its features and benefits (Exhibit 4-7). Sony provides product information in its ads but also encourages consumers to visit its retail stores and website to learn more about its product. These consumers will progress through the response hierarchy and move closer to purchase than those who only see an ad since they may like or prefer the brand more with greater exposure or experience with it.

Exhibit 4-7   Advertising for innovative new products such as the Sony Reader must make consumers aware of their features and benefits.

The steps within the hierarchy models are intermediate measures of communication effectiveness that guide communication decisions. The marketer needs to know where audience members are on the response hierarchy and makes the appropriate decision. For example, research may reveal that one target segment has low awareness of the advertiser's brand and the communication task involves increasing the awareness level for the brand by increasing the number of ads. Another target segment may be aware of the brand and its attributes but has a low level of liking or brand preference requiring the advertiser to develop a message that addresses the negative feelings.

Consistent Stages   As shown in Figure 4-2, the three models presented all consistently view the response process as involving movement through a sequence of three *stages* even though the specific *steps* within a stage may be unique or defined with variation. The *cognitive stage* represents what the receiver knows or perceives about the particular product or brand. This stage includes awareness that the brand exists and knowledge, information, or comprehension about its attributes, characteristics, or benefits. The *affective stage* refers to the receiver's feelings or affect level (like or dislike) for the particular brand. This stage also includes stronger levels of affect such as desire, preference, or conviction. The *conative* or *behavioural stage* refers to the consumer's action or behaviour toward the brand such as purchase.

All models assume a similar ordering of the three stages. Cognitive development precedes affective reactions, which precede behaviour. One might assume that consumers become aware of and knowledgeable about a brand, develop feelings toward it, form a desire or preference, and then make a purchase. While this logical progression is often accurate, the response sequence does not always operate this way. Over the past few decades, considerable research in marketing, social psychology, and communications has led to questioning of the traditional cognitive → affective → behavioural sequence leading to other configurations of the response hierarchy.

ALTERNATIVE RESPONSE HIERARCHIES

Michael Ray has developed a model of information processing that identifies three alternative orderings of the three stages based on perceived product differentiation and product involvement.[23] Figure 4-3 identifies

Figure   4-3

Alternative response hierarchies

	Topical involvement	
	High	Low
High (Perceived product differentiation)	(Learning model) Cognitive → Affective → Conative	(Low-involvement model) Cognitive ↓ Conative ↓ Affective
Low	(Dissonance/attribution model) Conative → Affective → Cognitive	

the alternative response hierarchies as the standard learning, dissonance/attribution, and low-involvement models.[24]

The Standard Learning Hierarchy   In many purchase situations, the consumer will go through the response process in the sequence depicted by the traditional communication models. Ray terms this a **standard learning model**, which consists of a learn → feel → do sequence. Information and knowledge acquired or *learned* about the brands are the basis for developing affect, or *feelings,* that guide what the consumer will do (e.g., actual trial or purchase). In this hierarchy, the consumer is viewed as an active participant in the communication process who gathers information through active learning.

Ray suggests the standard learning hierarchy is likely when the consumer is highly involved in the purchase process and there is much differentiation among competing brands. High-involvement purchase decisions such as consumer durables (e.g., electronics, appliances, cars) are product categories where a standard learning hierarchy response process is likely for most consumers. Ads for these products and services are usually very detailed and provide consumers with information that can be used to evaluate brands and help them make a purchase decision (Exhibit 4-8). However, for a loyal customer who simply renews the lease of the same brand of car over a few purchases, the decisions are likely much less involving.

Exhibit 4-8   Ads for high-involvement decisions provide consumers with information to help them evaluate brands.

The Dissonance/Attribution Hierarchy   A second response hierarchy proposed by Ray involves situations where consumers first behave, then develop attitudes or feelings as a result of that behaviour, and then learn or process information that supports the behaviour. This **dissonance/attribution model**, or do → feel → learn, occurs in situations where consumers must choose between two alternatives that are similar in quality but are complex and/or may have unknown attributes. The consumer may purchase the product on the basis of a recommendation by a nonmedia source and then attempt to support the decision by developing a positive attitude toward the brand and perhaps even developing negative feelings toward the rejected alternative(s). This reduces any *postpurchase dissonance* (as discussed in Chapter 3) the consumer may experience resulting from doubt over the purchase. This is consistent with consumers' *selective perception* (as discussed in Chapter 3) where support reasons (i.e., attributions) for brand choice are relied upon. According to this model, attitudes develop *after* purchase, as does learning from the mass media. Ray suggests that in these situations the main effect of the mass media is not the promotion of original choice behaviour and attitude change but rather the reduction of dissonance by reinforcing the wisdom of the purchase or providing supportive information. For example, the ad shown in Exhibit 4-9 reinforces the consumer's decision to use a Visa credit card by providing reassurance regarding the layers of security the company provides to its cardholders.

Critical marketers resist this view of the response hierarchy because they can't accept the notion that the mass media have no effect on the consumer's initial purchase decision. But the model doesn't claim the mass media have no effect—just that their major impact occurs after the purchase has been made. Marketing communications planners must be aware of the need for advertising and promotion efforts, not just to encourage brand selection but also to reinforce choices and ensure that a purchase pattern will continue. For example,

Exhibit 4-9   This ad reinforces the wisdom of the decision to use a Visa credit card.

one study found that advertising can lessen the negative effects of an unfavourable trial experience on brand evaluations when the ad is processed before the trial. However, when a negative trial experience precedes exposure to an ad, cognitive evaluations of the ad are more negative.[25] Other research showed that advertising can affect consumers' objective sensory interpretation of their experiences with a brand and what they remember about it.[26]

The Low-Involvement Hierarchy   For the **low-involvement hierarchy**, the receiver is viewed as passing from cognition to behaviour to attitude change. This learn → do → feel sequence characterizes situations of low consumer involvement in the purchase process. This hierarchy tends to occur when involvement in the purchase decision is low, there are minimal differences among brand alternatives, and mass-media (especially broadcast) advertising is important.

The notion of a low-involvement hierarchy is based in large part on Herbert Krugman's theory explaining the effects of television advertising.[27] Krugman wanted to find out why TV advertising produced a strong effect on brand awareness and recall but little change in consumers' attitudes toward the product. He hypothesized that TV is basically a low-involvement medium and the viewer's perceptual defences are reduced or even absent during commercials. In a low-involvement situation, the consumer does not compare the message with previously acquired beliefs, needs, or past experiences. The commercial results in subtle changes in the consumer's knowledge structure, particularly with repeated exposure. This knowledge change does not result in attitude change but is related to learning something about the advertised brand, such as a brand name, ad theme, or slogan. Subsequently, the knowledge may be sufficient to trigger a purchase when the consumer enters a purchase situation. The consumer will then form an attitude toward the purchased brand as a result of experience with it.

In the low-involvement hierarchy, the advertiser understands that a passive, uninterested consumer may focus more on nonmessage elements such as music, characters, symbols, and slogans or jingles than actual message content. The advertiser might capitalize on this situation by developing a catchy jingle that is stored in the consumer's mind without any active cognitive processing and becomes salient when he or she enters the actual purchase situation.

Advertisers of low-involvement products also repeat simple product claims such as a key copy point or distinctive product benefit. One study found that under low-involvement conditions, repetition of simple product claims increased consumers' memory of and belief in those claims.[28] Advertisers of low-involvement products might find it more profitable to pursue a heavy repetition strategy than to reach larger audiences with lengthy, more detailed messages. For example, Heinz has dominated the ketchup market by repeatedly telling consumers that its brand is the thickest and richest. Heinz has used a variety of advertising campaigns over the years, but they all repeat the same basic message and focus on the consistent quality of the brand (Exhibit 4-10).

Exhibit 4-10   Advertising promoting taste quality has helped Heinz dominate the ketchup market.

No one grows Ketchup like Heinz.

IMPLICATIONS OF THE ALTERNATIVE RESPONSE MODELS

A review of the alternative response models shows that the standard learning model (i.e., traditional hierarchy model) does not always apply. The notion of a highly involved consumer who engages in active information processing and learning and acts on the basis of higher-order beliefs and a well-formed attitude may be inappropriate for particular types of purchases. Sometimes consumers make a purchase decision on the basis of general awareness resulting from repetitive exposure to advertising, and attitude development occurs after the purchase, if at all. The role of advertising and other forms of promotion may be to induce trial, so consumers can develop brand preferences primarily on the basis of their direct experience with the product. Technology Perspective 4-1 shows how receiving messages and shopping may evolve in the future with new ways to communicate.

IMC TECHNOLOGY PERSPECTIVE 4-1

A New Tech Reality for Marketers

Digital innovations and other inventions offer new avenues for promotional planners to communicate with consumers at varying stages of their decision making, offering interesting ways to consider how they will process messages and presenting unique challenges to figure out the brand effects. And with such technological change, companies are working with agencies and technology companies equally looking for insightful ways of communicating. Some of the more interesting innovations include things that look almost futuristic or like they are from science fiction movies.

Holograms are featured in events making a spectacular vision for spectators. For example, Nissan Canada reflected 3-D images over water to simulate a lake-surface car chase on Canada Day. Technology to measure brainwaves gives advertisers the ability to sense shoppers' mood (e.g., stressed or relaxed) and adjust messages accordingly. Laser-guided sound systems emit an audio message when people are within a specific distance or facing a screen.

Other proximity- and time-based means of communication occur through data from consumers' smartphones and their use of social media. Finding patterns of routine behaviour, such as buying a daily coffee at one location and time, can be an impetus for targeting people to switch with an incentive or relevant message. Application of these kinds of algorithms produced substantially accurate results. Specialized shopping apps allow consumers to receive personalized information while roaming retail aisles. One expert commented, "Whether you're letting them know about specials, or pushing through promotions tailored to them, it's an easy way of reaching consumers because they opted in at the start of their shopping journey."

Ads witnessed through special polarized glasses hit airwaves recently with Ray-Ban as one of the early leaders. Facial recognition permits advertisers to determine if the recipient is male or female, thus allowing for customizing of advertising messages. Oakley and Google invented glasses with smartphone and computer capabilities. Imaginative marketers suggest interesting uses at retail settings for additional product information or for customer service personnel, such as for bank personnel to use when meeting consumers to have their profile instantly accessible.

Individual Facebook profiles proved to be the resource to personalize the presentation of advertising messages for advertisers. An award-winning Canadian Blood Services campaign used a user's friends and family to illustrate the far-reaching effect of donating blood. Intel created the "Museum of Me," which took logged-in users through a visual experience of their life using images from their profile along with music and video.

Sources: Grant Surridge, "New Partners for a New Reality," *Strategy,* August 29, 2012; Megan Hayes, "Brand Storytelling Gets Seriously Tech-ified," *Strategy,* August 29, 2012; "Tech to Watch," *Strategy,* August 29, 2012; Emily Jackson, "Shopper Marketing Techs Up," *Strategy,* August 29, 2012.

Question:

1. How do these technological innovations affect how consumers will interpret marketing communication messages?

From a promotional planning perspective, it is important that marketers examine the communication situation for their product or service and determine which type of response process is most likely to occur. They should analyze involvement levels and product/service differentiation as well as consumers' use of information sources and their levels of experience with the product or service. Once the manager has determined which response sequence is most likely to operate, the integrated marketing communications program can be designed to influence the response process in favour of the company's product or service.

For example, Cover Girl found itself in a precarious market position as high-end labels (e.g., Lancôme, Clinique) improved their penetration. Enter the Shade Brigade, a street team that went to high-traffic areas and helped the target select the right shade for her complexion and skin tone. After the consultation, the consumer was given a coupon indicating the correct shade to facilitate her purchase at a retail location. For those not reached by the team, in-store shade selectors assisted in decision making or acted as a key selling tool for beauty consultants, such as the ones in Shoppers Drug Mart. The turnaround moved overall market share up incrementally three years in a row to reach 17 percent.[29]

(L03) Cognitive Processing of Communications

For many years, research on the previous response models centred on identifying relationships between specific controllable variables (such as source and message factors) and outcome or response variables (such as attention, comprehension, attitudes, and purchase intentions). This approach appeared limited since it did not explain what caused the reactions.[30] In response, researchers attempted to understand the nature of cognitive reactions to persuasive messages. This section reviews two widely accepted approaches for understanding consumers' cognitive processing of advertising messages.

THE COGNITIVE RESPONSE APPROACH

One widely used method for examining consumers' cognitive processing of advertising messages is assessment of their **cognitive responses**, the thoughts that occur to them while reading, viewing, and/or hearing a communication.[31] These thoughts are usually measured by having consumers write or verbally report their reactions to a message. The assumption is that these thoughts reflect the recipient's cognitive processes or reactions and shape ultimate acceptance or rejection of the message.

Both academics and advertising practitioners use the cognitive response approach. Its focus has been to determine the types of responses evoked by an advertising message and how these responses relate to attitudes toward the ad, brand attitudes, and purchase intentions. Figure 4-4 depicts the three categories of cognitive responses—product/message, source-oriented, and ad execution thoughts—and how they may relate to attitudes and intentions.

Product/Message Thoughts   The first category of thoughts comprises those directed at the product or service and/or the claims being made in the communication. Much attention has focused on two particular types of responses: counterarguments and support arguments.

Figure   4-4   A model of cognitive response

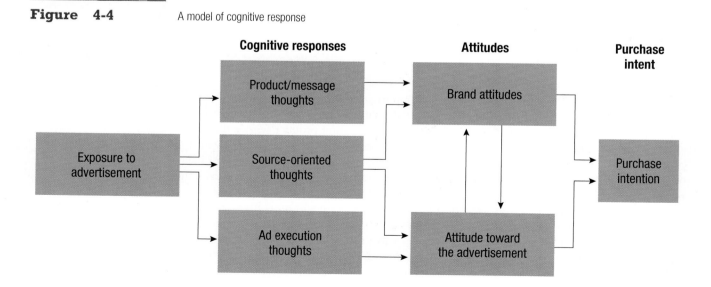

Counterarguments are thoughts the recipient has that are opposed to the position taken in the message. For example, consider the ad for Ultra Tide shown in Exhibit 4-11. A consumer may express disbelief or disapproval of a claim made in an ad—"I don't believe that any detergent could get that stain out!" Other consumers who see this ad may generate **support arguments**, or thoughts that affirm the claims made in the message—"Ultra Tide looks like a really good product—I think I'll try it."

The likelihood of counterarguing is greater when the message makes claims that oppose the receiver's beliefs. For example, a consumer viewing a commercial that attacks a favourite brand is likely to mentally, and potentially verbally, disagree. These counterarguments relate negatively to message acceptance; the more the receiver counterargues, the less likely he or she is to accept the position advocated in the message.[32] Support arguments, on the other hand, relate positively to message acceptance. Thus, the marketer should develop ads or other promotional messages that minimize counterarguing and encourage support arguments.

Source-Oriented Thoughts A second category of cognitive responses is directed at the source of the communication. One of the most important types of responses in this category is **source derogations**, or negative thoughts about the spokesperson or organization making the claims. Such thoughts generally lead to a reduction in message acceptance. If consumers find a particular spokesperson annoying or untrustworthy, they are less likely to accept what this source has to say.

Source-related thoughts are not always negative. Receivers who react favourably to the source generate favourable thoughts, or **source bolsters**. In general, most advertisers attempt to hire spokespeople their target audience likes so as to carry this effect over to the message. Considerations involved in choosing an appropriate source or spokesperson will be discussed in Chapter 7. How might consumers react to the model in Exhibit 4-12?

Ad Execution Thoughts The third category of cognitive responses shown in Figure 4-4 consists of the individual's thoughts about the ad itself. Many of the thoughts receivers have when reading or viewing an ad do not concern the product and/or message claims directly. Rather, they are affective reactions representing the consumer's feelings toward the ad.[33] These thoughts may include reactions to ad execution factors such as the creativity of the ad, the quality of the visual effects, colours, and voice tones. **Ad execution-related thoughts** can be either favourable or unfavourable.[34] They are important because of their effect on attitudes toward the advertisement as well as the brand.

Attitude to Ad Consumers' affective reactions to ads are an effect of cognitive responses, something not included in the previous models. **Attitude toward the ad** (A → ad) represents the receivers' favourable or unfavourable feelings toward the ad.[35] Advertisers are interested in consumers' reactions to the ad because they know that affective reactions are an important determinant of advertising effectiveness, since these reactions may be transferred to the brand itself or directly influence purchase intentions. One study found that people who enjoy a commercial are twice as likely as those who are neutral toward it to be convinced that the brand is the best.[36] Another study finds that those with more positive attitudes toward advertising in general result in stronger persuasion levels.[37]

Exhibit 4-11 Consumers often generate support arguments in response to ads for quality products.

Exhibit 4-12 The source in this ad could elicit both types of source thoughts.

Consumers' feelings about the ad may be just as important as their attitudes toward the brand (if not more so) in determining an ad's effectiveness.[38] The importance of affective reactions and feelings generated by the ad depend on several factors, among them the nature of the ad and the receiver's processing.[39] Many advertisers now use emotional ads designed to evoke feelings and affective reactions as the basis of their creative strategy. The success of this strategy depends in part on the consumers' involvement with the brand and their likelihood of attending to and processing the message.

THE ELABORATION LIKELIHOOD MODEL

Differences in the ways consumers process and respond to persuasive messages are shown in Figure 4-5, a simplified illustration of the **elaboration likelihood model (ELM)** of persuasion.[40] Richard Petty and John Cacioppo devised the ELM to explain the process by which persuasive communications (such as ads) lead to persuasion by influencing *attitudes*. According to this model, the attitude formation or change process depends on the amount and nature of *elaboration*, or processing, of relevant information that occurs in response to a persuasive message.

The ELM shows that elaboration likelihood is a function of two elements, motivation and ability to process the message. *Motivation* to process the message depends on such factors as involvement, personal relevance, and individuals' needs and arousal levels. *Ability* depends on the individual's knowledge, intellectual capacity, and opportunity to process the message.

High elaboration (central route to persuasion) means the receiver carefully considers, thinks, and evaluates the information or arguments contained in the message. Low elaboration (peripheral route to persuasion) occurs when the receiver does not actively process the information or think but rather infers conclusions about the position being advocated in the message on the basis of simple positive or negative cues.

Central Route   Under the **central route to persuasion**, the receiver is viewed as a very active, involved participant in the communication process who has high ability and motivation to attend, comprehend, and evaluate messages. When central processing of an advertising message occurs, the consumer pays close attention to message content and scrutinizes the message arguments. A high level of cognitive response activity or processing occurs, and the ad's ability

Figure   4-5

Simplified elaboration likelihood model of persuasion

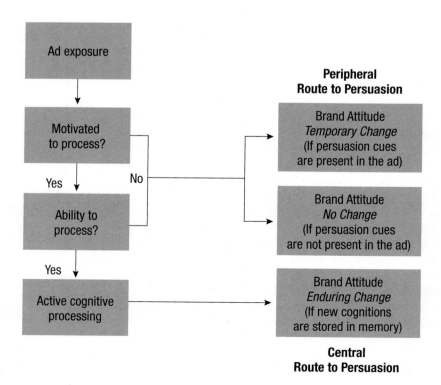

to persuade the receiver depends primarily on the receiver's evaluation of the quality of the arguments presented. Predominantly favourable cognitive responses (support arguments and source bolsters) lead to favourable changes in cognitive structure, which lead to positive attitude change, or persuasion. Conversely, if the cognitive processing is predominantly unfavourable and results in counterarguments and/or source derogations, the changes in cognitive structure are unfavourable resulting in negative attitude change. Attitude change that occurs through central processing is relatively enduring and should resist subsequent efforts to change it.

Peripheral Route   Under the **peripheral route to persuasion**, the receiver is viewed as lacking the motivation or ability to process information and is not likely to have detailed cognitive processing. Rather than evaluating the information presented in the message, the receiver relies on peripheral cues that may be incidental to the main arguments. The receiver's reaction to the message depends on how he or she evaluates these peripheral cues.

The consumer may use several types of peripheral cues or cognitive shortcuts rather than carefully evaluating the message arguments presented in an advertisement.[41] Favourable attitudes may be formed if the endorser in the ad is viewed as attractive and/or likable, or if the consumer likes certain executional aspects of the ad such as the way it is made, the music, or the imagery. Notice how the ad in Exhibit 4-13 contains positive peripheral cues contained in the excellent visual imagery. These cues might help consumers form a positive attitude toward the brand even if they do not process the message portion of the ad.

Exhibit 4-13   The colourful imagery of the spices in this ad acts as a peripheral cue.

Peripheral cues can also lead to rejection of a message. For example, ads that advocate extreme positions, use endorsers who are not well liked or have credibility problems, or are not executed well (such as low-budget ads for local retailers) may be rejected without any consideration of their information or message arguments. As shown in Figure 4-5, the ELM views attitudes resulting from peripheral processing as temporary. Therefore, favourable attitudes must be maintained by continual exposure to the peripheral cues, such as through repetitive advertising.

Explanation for ELM   One reason for explaining how the peripheral route to persuasion works lies in the idea of **classical conditioning**. Classical conditioning assumes that learning is an *associative process* with an already existing relationship between a stimulus and a response. This process is transferred to a **conditioned stimulus** that elicits a **conditioned response** resembling the original unconditioned reaction. Two factors are important for learning to occur through the associative process. The first is contiguity, which means the unconditioned stimulus and conditioned stimulus must be close in time and space. The other important principle is *repetition,* or the frequency of the association. The more often the unconditioned and conditioned stimuli occur together, the stronger the association between them will be.

Buyers can be conditioned to form favourable impressions of brands through the associative process. Advertisers strive to associate their products and services with perceptions and emotions known to evoke positive reactions from consumers. Products are promoted through image advertising, in which the brand is shown with an unconditioned stimulus that elicits pleasant feelings. When the brand is presented simultaneously with this unconditioned stimulus, the brand itself becomes a conditioned stimulus that elicits the same favourable response. The ad in Exhibit 4-14 shows an application of this strategy. Notice how this ad associates Mariah Carey's perfume with the flavour of a lollipop. Extending beyond visual elements of a message, research

Exhibit 4-14   Mariah Carey's new perfume associates the product with the sweetness of lollipops.

supports the importance of music in ads to enhance the associative process.[42]

Implications of the ELM   The ELM has important implications for marketing communication since the most effective type of message depends on the route to persuasion the target audience follows. If the involvement level of the target audience is high, the message should contain strong arguments that are difficult for the receiver to refute or counterargue. The interactive characteristics of social media suggest it is useful for influencing high-involvement audiences, as shown in Exhibit 4-15. If the involvement level of the target audience is low, peripheral cues such as music or images may be more important than detailed message arguments. Therefore, marketers of low-involvement products often rely on creative tactics that emphasize peripheral cues and use repetitive advertising to create and maintain favourable attitudes toward their brand.

An interesting test of the ELM showed that the effectiveness of a celebrity endorser in an ad depends on the receiver's involvement level.[43] When involvement was low, a celebrity endorser had a significant effect on attitudes. When the receiver's involvement was high, however, the use of a celebrity had no effect on brand attitudes; the quality of the arguments used in the ad was more important. The explanation given for these findings was that a celebrity may serve as a peripheral cue in the low-involvement situation, allowing the receiver to develop favourable attitudes based on feelings toward the source rather than engaging in extensive processing of the message. A highly involved consumer, however, experiences more detailed central processing of the message content. The quality of the message claims becomes more important than the identity of the endorser.

LO4 Response Model for Managerial Decision Making

In this section we reconcile the models presented in this chapter and illustrate a response model relevant for managerial decision making. The first section concludes that traditional communication response models based on a hierarchy or adaptation of a hierarchy are limited in their

Exhibit 4-15   The Energizer Bunny has its own Facebook page for its devoted followers.

ability to explain how advertising works. The subsequent sections summarize another part of the Rossiter and Percy perspective that is managerially oriented and will be used to set communication objectives and plan for creative messages in subsequent chapters.

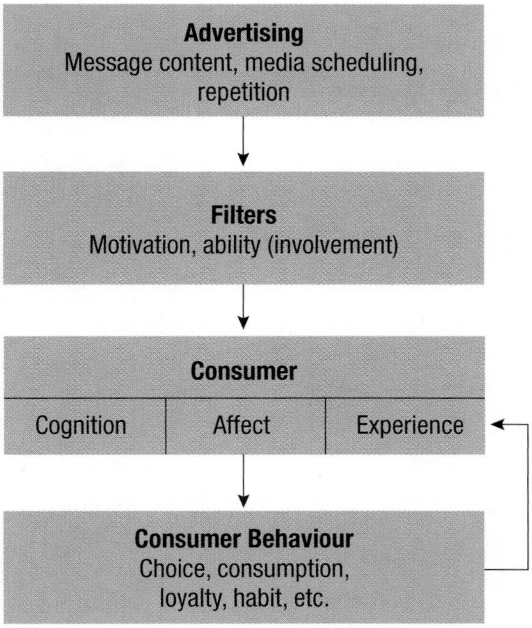

IMPORTANCE OF A MANAGERIAL MODEL

A comprehensive literature review to better understand advertising effectiveness highlights the need for a response model that assists managerial decision making.[44] The authors concluded that although hierarchy models have been actively employed for nearly 100 years, there is little support for the temporal (i.e., time-based) sequence of the hierarchy of effects and that the models exclude product category and brand experiences.

As observed in the other models, the consumers' response process includes *cognition,* the "thinking" dimension of a person's response; *affect,* the "feeling" dimension; and *experience,* which is a feedback dimension based on the outcomes of product purchase and usage. However, as Figure 4-6 shows, there is no prescribed order or hierarchy. Each response can be a result of audience's motivation and ability to process the message. Advertising, and other marketing communication, is mediated or filtered by factors that can change the individual's response. The implication is that promotional planners should focus on cognition, affect, and experience as critical responses that advertising may influence; however, they should not assume a particular sequence of response.

In contrast to the other models, the consumers' response process is significantly dependent on product category and brand experiences. They suggest that the effects of advertising should be evaluated using the cognition, affect, and experience dimensions, with intermediate variables being more important than others depending on factors such as the product category, stage of the product life cycle, target audience, and competition. Advertising and marketing communication have differing effects depending on whether the consumer currently uses the *product* or not when receiving the message. Furthermore, these differing effects also emerge when considering if a consumer currently uses the *brand* or not when receiving the message.

Figure 4-6

A framework for studying how advertising works

MANAGERIAL MODEL APPROACH

We introduced the Rossiter and Percy (R&P) perspective in Chapter 3 when identifying options for the target audience decision. This perspective suggests promotional planners initially consider the message as being directed to either customers purchasing their brand or non-customers who have not purchased their brand. This managerial view starts with the consumer and is based on the consumer's previous brand experience and degree of brand loyalty, two critical factors that influence how motivated or involved the audience would be when responding to promotional messages.[45]

A continuation of the R&P perspective is a communication response model that takes a managerial view by identifying the responses in terms of the promotional manager's brand for any type of marketing communication decision. Figure 4-7 shows the initial processing stage, which highlights the immediate responses to any advertising message while receiving the ad exposure. This implies the psychological experiences that occur in the target audience's mind while watching a television commercial, for example. Communication effects refer to the lasting brand impressions that remain with the target audience after the target audience processes the message. This implies the target audience's memory of the brand that results after watching the television commercial.

The example of processing and communication effects for a TV ad can be readily extended to all methods of marketing communication. Marketing communication professionals and researchers have called for an alternative model that accounts for consumer responses to all

Figure   4-7

Planning for processing and
communication effects

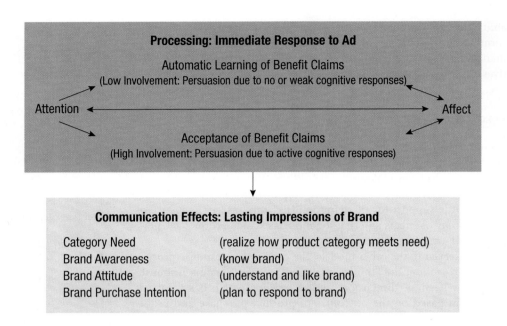

Figure   4-7

Planning for processing and
communication effects

aspects of marketing communication.[46] The decision-making orientation of this model with a focus on brand building appears to address these requests.

PROCESSING OF MESSAGES

This notion of processing is consistent with all the features of the previous models. After attending to the ad, the target audience may have low or high involvement in terms of how much thought regarding the brand's benefit claims is generated while receiving the message. For example, as the ELM indicated, highly involved target audiences are more likely to have active cognitive responses. In addition, affect, or emotional responses, will influence and be generated as a result of these cognitive responses. Furthermore, pleasant or unpleasant emotional responses may occur while attending to the execution variables (e.g., music) of the message, and positive (or negative) emotional responses may focus greater (or less) attention to the message.

The seemingly simultaneous cognitive and emotional responses occurring while attending to a message is consistent with current views of marketing communication and how the brain works in psychology.[47] Anecdotal evidence of this is seen when one considers reactions to a Super Bowl ad (e.g., TV commercial) where both thinking and feeling something about the brand occurs. Furthermore, the temporal concern of the hierarchical models is diminished by considering the processing stage prior to the communication effects stage.

From an IMC planning perspective, managers need to design brand messages with the understanding of the target audience's processing. For instance, to attract new customers, the manager may consider brand messages that will support high-involvement processing. And, as we will see in the media chapters and the chapters relating to other communication tools, the manager may consider more involving avenues for delivering the message (e.g., social media).

Alternatively, companies often have programs to both attract and retain customers. This could require promotional planners to strategically evaluate the balance of their messages. Should messages that attempt to generate high involvement be primary or secondary in the overall message strategy? Analytical questions such as this emerge by considering the processing stage as a key precursor to planning for the communication effects stage.

COMMUNICATION EFFECTS OF MESSAGES

Figure 4-7 also distinguishes the brand communication effects that are established more permanently in the target audience's memory. Overall, R&P summarize four **communication effects** for the target audience.

Category Need   *Category need* involves the target audience's perception of requiring a specific product category to satisfy a particular need. This communication effect is relevant for a number of reasons. It supports the development of primary demand of a product category independent of the particular brand, something that certain industries and brands are considerably concerned about. Product factors are evident in the alternative hierarchy model where product differentiation affected consumer responses to messages, so a product category effect is especially important in most marketing communication situations. The start of the decision-making process is need recognition, so linking a product to a particular need is an ongoing marketing communication task for most brands.

Brand Awareness   *Brand awareness* involves the target audience's ability to recognize and/or recall the brand within the product category in sufficient detail to make a purchase. This communication effect is strong form of consumer knowledge as the target audience knows extensive details about the brand to have confidence in the purchase selection. It also highlights the importance of distinguishing between knowledge that can be retrieved via brand recall and knowledge that is salient when given a prompt or cue via brand recognition.

Brand Attitude   *Brand attitude* involves the target audience's overall evaluation of the brand in relation to its ability to satisfy the reason why they want it. Brand attitude is a central communication effect where the target audience's evaluation includes both cognitive and affective components, acknowledging that each aspect is relevant for planning for all purchase situations. Other models represented the entire response process (i.e., cognition, affect, behaviour) as reflecting an attitude that occurred in various orders. This idea of brand attitude does not rely on any hierarchical order of the attitude components.

Brand Purchase Intention   Brand purchase intention involves the target audience's self-instruction to respond (shopping behaviour, purchase) to the brand. A mental activity predicated on the anticipation of participating in a behavioural action specifically directed to the brand is another indicator of the effects of marketing communication.

(L05) IMC Planning: Managerial Decision Making

We suggest a few conclusions for managers in making advertising and promotion decisions based on the models presented regarding how advertising works in terms of consumer response; after all, academics will continue this investigation while managers still need to make decisions.

First, it appears that managers should consider and plan for both the cognitive and the affective responses of the receiver when the latter is processing advertising or any promotional message. Receivers typically have both cognitive and emotional reactions to the messages they see all around them every day.

Second, managers are undoubtedly concerned with the resulting effects of the advertising or promotional message for a time period after the receiver has received and processed the message. As suggested in many of the models, managers want to know if their messages are improving awareness or attitudes.

Finally, the primary characteristic that influences communication success appears to be the receiver's previous brand experience. This implies managers should be cognizant of to whom exactly they are directing their message. As discussed in Chapter 3, the manager needs a detailed profile of the target audience to have an understanding to gauge communication success. Thus, managers require a decision framework that addresses these points.

The managerial approach suggested at the end of this chapter offers two important IMC planning considerations. One, there is an obvious and clear connection to the target audience's purchase of the promotional manager's particular brand. This is apparent with its reference to the brand in three communication effects. It is also seen in the connection to category need,

Figure   4-8

IMC Planning Matrix

	Source	Message	Channel	Receiver
Exposure				
Processing (attention and comprehension)				
Communication Effects (yielding and retention)				
Action				

which addresses the underlying reason why the target audience is motivated to buy the promotional manager's brand, and where the target audience understands the brand fits in the market in relation to other brands.

Two, the managerial model can be applied for all aspects of an IMC program as shown in Figure 4-8.[48] The managerial decisions (i.e., controllable variables), source, message, channel, and receiver (via target audience selection) are assessed in terms of resulting outcomes, exposure, processing, communication effects, and action. For example, ads with iPhone users (i.e., source) taking pictures or listening to music (i.e., message) shown on TV (i.e., channel) are directed to the target audience, who are likely to be users of iPhones. Promotional planners would undoubtedly be interested in four communication results listed for this execution. Furthermore, this logic could be extended for print ads or video-type ads placed on the Internet, either on a website or in social media.

Similarly, the same approach applies for a whole advertising campaign over time. For example, Telus ads with multiple animals (i.e., source) behaving in a way to visually convey a product (i.e., message) across multiple media (i.e., channels) are directed to the target audience, who are likely to be users of other brands (e.g., Bell, Rogers). Across all aspects of this advertising, Telus promotional planners would concern themselves with all four communication results. Furthermore, this idea can be extend to other promotional tools like Telus's public relations activities.

The final implication of this is that all elements of an entire IMC program can be planned with a matrix including any communication via the Internet and any kind of promotional event/ activity or sales promotion. Any tool for communication retains the characteristics of the communication model in Figure 4-1. One revision would be situations where a receiver encounters a brand message from another consumer in social media; however, the other consumer is the sender in this respect, and the planning retains its characteristics. However, the brand is concerned with how it influenced the consumer who is the sender of the message. This is evident in many social media contexts where the brand encourages the development of user-generated content, or other forms of marketing communication from ordinary consumers.

The R&P model and the other communication response models will be revisited in the next chapter. Promotional planners use a communication response model to determine the communication objectives for advertising and other promotional tools. It is important to base marketing communication decisions on a model and translate them into specific objectives since promotional planners need clear guidance for the remaining marketing communication decisions.

Learning Objectives Summary

 Explain the elements of the communication process and identify the role of marketing communication.

The function of all elements of the promotional mix is to communicate, so promotional planners must understand the communication process. This process can be very complex; successful marketing communication depends on a number of factors, including the nature of the message, the audience's interpretation of it, and the environment in which it is received. For effective communication to occur, the sender must encode a message in such a way that it will be decoded by the receiver in the intended manner. Feedback from the receiver helps the sender determine whether proper decoding has occurred or whether noise has interfered with the communication process.

 Contrast traditional communication response models and alternative response hierarchies.

Promotional planning begins with the receiver or target audience, as marketers must understand how the audience is likely to respond to sources of communication or types of messages. Traditional response models provide an initial understanding of this process; however, limitations of these models led to more comprehensive approaches. Alternative response hierarchies imply modification of the traditional models due to the target audience's involvement and perceived product differentiation. Different orderings of the traditional response hierarchy include the standard learning, dissonance/attribution, and low-involvement models. The alternative response hierarchy postulated different ordering of cognition, affect, and behaviour depending upon the involvement and differentiation.

 Develop the response processes of receivers of marketing communication through two models of cognitive processing.

The cognitive processing of communication revealed two models: the cognitive response approach and the elaboration likelihood model. The former examines the thoughts evoked by a message in terms of product/message thoughts, source-oriented thoughts, and ad execution thoughts and how they shape the receiver's ultimate acceptance or rejection of the communication by influencing brand attitude and attitude to the ad. The elaboration likelihood model of attitude formation and change recognizes two forms of message processing, the central and peripheral routes to persuasion, which are a function of the receiver's motivation and ability to process a message. The model postulates that each route leads to varying degrees of attitude change.

 Illustrate a response model for managerial decision making.

Theoretical research concludes that there are three critical intermediate effects between advertising and purchase: cognition, affect, and experience. Those responsible for planning the IMC program should learn as much as possible about their target audience and how it may respond to advertising and other forms of marketing communications. A managerial view of the response process provides direction for understanding how promotional planners should determine their brands' communication strategies.

 Construct ideas on how the knowledge of response models can be used for IMC planning.

A more managerially useful approach for understanding how advertising works is included in this chapter. The model suggests both cognitive and emotional processing responses are critical during the initial stages of receiving the message, and the lasting brand communication effects can be construed.

Key Terms

Review key terms and definitions on Connect.

Review Questions

1. Recall the elements of Figure 4-1 and identify them for all aspects of an IMC plan—advertising, sales promotion, direct marketing, public relations, and Internet marketing.

2. Explain why the three response models of Figure 4-2 are limited in planning for an IMC campaign.

3. Explain what is meant by a central versus peripheral route to persuasion and the factors that would determine when each might be used by consumers in response to an advertisement.

4. What are the key differences between traditional response models and the response model shown in Figure 4-7?

5. Why is it important to use a response model that is more applicable to managerial decision making?

Applied Questions

1. Consider ads found in social media like Facebook, Twitter, and YouTube and assess whether the model in Figure 4-1 is useful for explaining how marketing communication works in these digital contexts.

2. Assume that you are the marketing communications manager for a brand of paper towels. Discuss how the low-involvement hierarchy could be of value in developing an advertising and promotion strategy for this brand.

3. Select an ad that would be processed by a central route to persuasion and one where peripheral processing would occur. Show the ads to several people and ask them to write down the thoughts they have about each ad. Analyze their thoughts using the cognitive and emotional responses discussed in the chapter.

4. Find an example of a print ad and evaluate it using the response model shown in Figure 4-7. Identify the specific types of cognitive and emotional responses that the ad might elicit from consumers and discuss why they might occur.

5. Red Bull has numerous IMC activities including its TV advertising, events, and promotional activities. Check the Red Bull website and any other online material for background, and apply them to the matrix in Figure 4-8 to validate whether each activity assists in planning for an IMC.

GO ONLINE

For more information on the resources available from McGraw-Hill Ryerson, go to www.mcgrawhill.ca/he/solutions.

Objectives for the IMC Plan

5

LEARNING OBJECTIVES

LO1 Distinguish among marketing, behavioural, and communication objectives and identify the value of setting each type of objective.

LO2 Describe the historical approaches for setting communication objectives for advertising.

LO3 Evaluate the options for setting behavioural objectives and apply them when constructing a promotional plan.

LO4 Choose among the options for setting communication objectives and apply them when designing IMC recommendations.

LO5 Assemble the best combination of behavioural and communication objectives for each stage of the consumer decision-making process.

Hellmann's Gets Real

In 2007, Hellmann's mayonnaise established a plan to create a "Real Food Movement" to encourage Canadians to enjoy more real, local food. Led by its signature product with its all-natural ingredients of eggs, canola oil, and vinegar, all sourced from Canada, Hellmann's portrayed its brand as a natural part of everyone's diet. Consumer research supported the initiative in that virtually everyone believed consuming real food was important; however, only 6 percent made all their meals with real food. A senior brand manager concluded, "It's clear that Canadians care about eating food with simple ingredients, but they could use help incorporating real food into their daily lives." Everyone else understood the success when the CASSIES awarded Hellmann's the 2011 Grand Prix for best overall IMC program over the past few years.

Step one featured Urban Gardens, where 60 deserving city residents received an allotment to grow fresh fruits and vegetables. Extensive TV, newspaper, digital, direct, and in-store notification invited applicants to the program, resulting in 500 entries. Step two in 2008 extended the city gardens with a partnership with Evergreen, an organization devoted to expanding the usage of gardens in large cities. Hellmann's worked with Chef Chuck Hughes, who created real food recipes for TV ads and online videos, participated in a broadcast tour, and demonstrated how meal preparation with real food is fun and easy. Hellmann's employed similar media and increased its publicity with coverage of the campaign.

Step three moved to the "Eat Real. Eat Local" phase, where a three-minute "family dinner" video documented the state of Canada's food delivery system and emphasized the importance of following the theme of the campaign (eatrealeatlocal.ca). At this point, Hellmann's stepped up the effort as it developed news editorial pieces with Can-West News and *Canadian Living*, and increased its digital presence with stronger social media communication.

During 2011 the brand donated $100,000 in 23 areas that contributed to the movement such as school lunch programs, farmers' markets, sandwich-making competitions, and greenhouses. Impressive results emerged, with 1,300 applications and 42 million media impressions. As part of this, Hellmann's featured one notable effort with a short clip that showed the complete renovation of a school cafeteria in Alberta. The improved kitchen technology and design permitted the preparation of fresher food. Hellmann's promised a $1 donation to other food initiatives for every viewing.

Overall, business measures impressed during the six years: sales growth averaged about 7 percent per year, which culminated in a market share of nearly 50 percent, and consumer belief that Hellmann's contained real and simple ingredients doubled to nearly 50 percent of the population. To execute all these programs Hellmann's retained numerous agencies to coordinate public relations activities, digital tools, advertising, and in-store presentations, which all drove traffic to the Internet site (realfoodmovement.ca). One expert summed up the success of the work with this opinion: "The Real Food Movement wasn't the bandwagon effort we see from so many brands in the environmental CSR arena. They are participating in driving the movement by providing awareness, knowledge and money."

Sources: Kristin Laird, "Unilever Stays Real for Hellmann's," *Marketing Magazine,* April 9, 2010; Kristin Laird, "Hellmann's Trashes, Renovates School Kitchen," *Marketing Magazine,* April 25, 2012; *Strategy* Staff, "Hellmann's Grants Real Food Wishes," *Strategy,* January 28, 2013; Emily Wexler, "Hellmann's Champions Real Food Movement," *Strategy,* May 1, 2011; http://cassies.ca/content/caselibrary/winners/2011_Hellmanns.pdf.

Questions:

1. Why did Hellmann's change the focus of the message over time?
2. What behavioural and communication objectives does it appear that Hellmann's achieved?

Complex marketing situations, conflicting perspectives regarding what advertising and other promotional mix elements are expected to accomplish, and uncertainty over resources make the setting of marketing communication objectives "a job of creating order out of chaos."[1] While the task of setting objectives can be complex and difficult it must be done properly, because specific goals and objectives are the foundation on which all marketing communication decisions are made and provide a standard against which performance can be measured.

This chapter examines the purpose of objectives and the role they play in the development, implementation, and evaluation of an IMC program. First, we distinguish among marketing, behavioural, and communication objectives. Then we describe the historical approaches of setting objectives for marketing communication based on the response models discussed in Chapter 4. We then present a comprehensive managerial framework for setting behavioural and communication objectives for each element of the IMC plan and for the overall IMC plan that we refer to in the remaining parts of the book.

LO1 Objective Setting

Setting specific objectives should be an integral part of the promotional planning process. However, companies can either fail to set marketing communication objectives or set ones that are inadequate for the development of the promotional plan or measuring its effectiveness. This section discusses the value of objectives and distinguishes among marketing, behavioural, and communication objectives for optimal IMC planning.

Exhibit 5-1   The objective of this ad is to demonstrate RBC's support for a cause.

VALUE OF OBJECTIVES

Perhaps one reason why companies do not set objectives for their IMC programs is a failure to see their value. Advertising and promotional objectives are needed for reasons such as communication function, planning and decision making, and measurement and evaluation of results.

Communication Function   Specific objectives for the IMC program facilitate coordination of the groups working on the campaign. Many people are involved in the planning and development of an IMC program including client personnel and contracted agencies. The program must be coordinated within the company, inside the ad agency, and between the two. Any other parties involved, such as public relations and/or sales promotion firms, research specialists, or media buying services, must know what the company hopes to accomplish through its marketing communication program. Potential problems can be avoided if all parties have written approved objectives to guide their actions and serve as a common base for discussion. For example, the ad and RBC's involvement with the cause shown in Exhibit 5-1 was dependent upon all participants understanding RBC's objectives.

Planning and Decision Making   Specific promotional objectives guide IMC plan development. All phases of a firm's promotional strategy should be based on the established objectives, including budgeting, creative, and media decisions as well as supportive programs such as direct marketing, public relations/publicity, sales promotion, and/or reseller support. Meaningful objectives also guide decision making. Promotional planners are faced with a number of strategic and tactical options in terms of choosing creative themes, selecting media, and allocating the budget among promotional mix elements. Choices should be made based on how well a particular strategy matches the firm's promotional objectives.

Measurement and Evaluation of Results Setting specific objectives provides a benchmark against which the performance of the promotional campaign can be measured. It is extremely difficult to determine what the firm's advertising and promotion efforts accomplished without specific objectives. One characteristic of good objectives is that they are measurable; they specify a method and criteria for determining how well the promotional program is working. Most organizations are concerned about the return on promotional investment; comparing actual performance against measurable objectives determines whether the return justifies the expense. With the explosion of digital communication in marketing, established procedures for measuring its effects are still undergoing development. Marketers are still trying to estimate the most appropriate methods and are not fully tracking all digital communication in comparison to established media.[2]

MARKETING OBJECTIVES

Marketing objectives are generally stated in the firm's marketing plan and are statements of what is to be accomplished by the overall marketing program within a given time period. Marketing objectives are usually defined in terms of specific, measurable outcomes such as sales volume, market share, profit, or return on investment. Good marketing objectives are quantifiable; they delineate the target market and note the time frame for accomplishing the goal (often one year). For example, a copy-machine company may have as its marketing objective "to increase sales by 10 percent in the small-business segment of the market during the next 12 months." To be effective, objectives must also be realistic and attainable.

The selection of the type of marketing objective is a function of market conditions. A company with a very high market share may seek to increase its sales volume by stimulating growth in the product category. It might accomplish this by increasing consumption by current users or encouraging nonusers to buy the product. A firm in a fast-growing market may have market share as its marketing objective since this reflects that it is growing more quickly than its direct competitors. In mature markets with limited growth, firms tend to focus on profit as the key marketing objective. Finally, a firm that faces unique consumer preferences across various geographic markets (i.e., Ontario versus Quebec) may in fact have a unique marketing objective for each region. The marketing objective guiding the ad in Exhibit 5-2 may be to increase sales volume since the message attempts to sway user of other brands of tires to consider Michelin for its gas mileage and safety.

Once the marketing communication manager has reviewed the marketing plan, he or she should understand the objectives of the marketing program, how it intends to get there, and the role advertising and promotion will play. These marketing goals defined in terms of sales, profit, or market share increases are usually not appropriate promotional objectives. They are objectives for the entire marketing program, and achieving them depends on the proper coordination and execution of *all* marketing mix elements, not just promotion. Alternatively, many promotional planners approach promotion from a communication perspective and believe the purpose of advertising and other promotional mix elements is usually to communicate information or a selling message about a product or service. The sales objective versus the communication objective is often debated and is our next topic to explore.

SALES OBJECTIVE DEBATE

Some managers believe the only meaningful objective for their promotional program is sales, since the reason why a firm spends money on advertising and promotion is to sell its product or

Exhibit 5-2 Michelin stresses higher gas mileage, as well as safety, in their ads.

service. Promotional spending represents an investment of a firm's scarce resources that requires an economic justification like any other business decision. Managers generally compare investment options on a common financial basis, such as return on investment (ROI). Their position is that monies spent on advertising and other forms of promotion should produce measurable results, such as increasing sales or the brand's market share to assess the effectiveness of the expenditure decision.

One problem with a sales objective for promotion is that poor sales results can be due to other marketing mix variables, including product design or quality, packaging, distribution, or pricing. Advertising can make consumers aware of and interested in the brand, but it can't make them buy it, particularly if it is not readily available or is priced higher than a competing brand. Furthermore, unanticipated or uncontrollable environmental factors can devastate a firm's sales forecast even with a well communicated promotion program.

Another problem with a sales objective is that the effects of advertising often occur over an extended period. Advertising has a lagged or **carryover effect**; monies spent on advertising do not necessarily have an immediate impact on sales.[3] Advertising may create awareness, interest, and/or favourable attitudes toward a brand, but these feelings will not result in an actual purchase until the consumer enters the market for the product, which may occur later. A review of econometric studies that examined the duration of cumulative advertising effects found that for mature, frequently purchased, low-priced products, advertising's effect on sales lasts up to nine months.[4] Models have been developed to account for the carryover effect of advertising and to help determine the long-term effect of advertising on sales.[5] In the case of the Kobo eReader, early advertising may help stimulate sales for a long period of time as people consider the advantages of switching to another format.

The counterargument is that a sales objective is appropriate when these two factors are not relevant. If a marketer is certain that other marketing or environmental factors were not influencing sales and that the carryover effect was not occurring, then a sales objective could be plausible. In general, the likelihood of such conditions arising appears quite remote, which necessitates the use of behavioural and communication objectives as the primary approach for promotional planning purposes. IMC Perspective 5-1 summarizes the views of marketers as to what constitutes good advertising and how technology fits with it in the future. From these comments, it is reasonable to conclude that communication is a vital component as suggested in this debate.

BEHAVIOURAL OBJECTIVES

When a firm sets a sales growth objective (e.g., increase sales by 10 percent) for a brand, the increased sales can arise from a greater number of purchases from current customers (e.g., brand loyals). Alternatively, higher sales can be gained from new customers who are currently not buying within the product category (i.e., new category users) or those currently buying within the product category, but not the firm's brand (e.g., other brand switchers). In all cases, achieving the sales growth is possible; however, the expected behaviour is fundamentally different. In the first case, the sales growth is due to a difference in the repurchase behaviour of current customers. In the latter two cases, the sales growth is due to trial behaviour by non-customers. Figure 5-1 shows examples of how marketing objectives can be attained through variations in the target audience and type of behaviour expected. We will define the behavioural objectives more exactly in a later section. Certainly other opportunities are possible by applying the concepts depending upon conclusions from a situation analysis.

Figure 5-1

Marketing objectives, audience, and behaviour

Marketing Objective	Target Audience	Behavioural Objective
Sales volume	New category users	Category and brand trial
Market share	Other brand switchers	Brand trial (switching)
Profit	Brand loyals	Repeat purchase (amount)
Return on investment	Favourable brand switchers	Repeat purchase (rate)

Marketers' View of Advertising's Future

In a serious of interviews with the *National Post*'s Hollie Shaw, market experts from a variety of backgrounds commented on interesting trends in the world of advertising that are very much related to the topic of brands achieving communication effects with their target audience. Many begin by offering how they define good advertising.

Matthew Cammaert, president of Cheil Canada, suggested that, "Good advertising is defined by the brand's ability to play the role of storyteller, fed by core human truths or human aspiration, while the brand maintains complete transparency."

Creative director of Dory Advertising Donna McCarthy says, "A good ad is one that gets noticed, wins the argument, is liked by the target group and is remembered by the product name."

Andrew Bergstrom, VP at Cossette, believes, "Good advertising is advertising that sells. Great advertising is advertising that does that and goes beyond by creating believers in the brand's raison d'etre."

Tony Chapman, founder and chief executive of Capital C, concluded, "Head, heart, hand: It is easy to understand, it is exciting, and, from a hands point of view, it is easy to act upon."

Moving to the topic of how new technology will continue to foster and deliver good advertising, a number of the executives made varying suggestions and predictions. For example, big-name brands continue to invest in digital communication. Colin Moore, president of Starbucks Canada, claimed that the famous coffee brand attained the status of being the "number one" brand on Facebook worldwide and achieved a successful following on Twitter. Its social media connection allowed Starbucks to implement different aspects of its loyalty program, My Starbucks Rewards, such that the brand achieved results 50 percent beyond expectations as it contributed to stronger repurchase rates.

Mark Sherman, founder, owner, and executive chairman of Media Experts, summarized an important trend regarding smartphone use. Consumers update their "pocket computer" about every two years, and every year increased

their search for shopping purposes or product information, making this an opportunity most marketers need to investigate for their brand.

Related to this, Chapman envisioned the need for brands to consider customized messages in each retail location. For example, in research for vacuum cleaner brand Bissell, the agency concluded that consumers in Walmart required a different information and advertising presentation than did consumers in Loblaws. From this, Chapman concluded that the age of intelligence gathering to secure the right message and media combination is at the pinnacle of marketing communication decisions.

Cammaert echoed these thoughts and claimed that mobile is capable of doing almost anything imaginable when it comes to communication. Furthermore, he elaborated, "As your phone is with you all the time, the possibilities include shopper and location-based marketing activities, digital, social, and experiential strategies and tactics." He also sees further growth with card technology in the areas of rewards programs to enhance loyalty with customization and personalization possibilities.

Sources: Hollie Shaw, "Mix Well, Stir: Advertiser Sees Recipe for Success with TV Partner," *National Post,* August 5, 2011; Hollie Shaw, "Most Exciting Business in the World," *National Post,* November 11, 2011; Hollie Shaw, "Computers Make Production Easier," *National Post,* January 14, 2011; Hollie Shaw, "Strategic Practice," *National Post,* February 11, 2011; Hollie Shaw, "New Blonde in Town," *National Post,* February 3, 2012; Hollie Shaw, "Going Independent," *National Post,* December 11, 2011.

Questions:

1. Are the ideas expressed regarding good advertising consistent with the response models of advertising?
2. How is it possible to ensure good advertising with some of the new ideas suggested?

The distinction between repeat purchase versus trial purchase behaviour is critical as it provides direction for the communication objectives, which subsequently provide guidance for message development. For example, increasing the repeat purchasing rate of brand loyals might have a message reminding these customers of the previous enjoyable consumption experiences, while a message to encourage trial from other brand switchers might require a comparative

Exhibit 5-3 Dove encourages a trial purchase with its comparative message.

message to these non-customers showing the benefits of the competing brands. In both of these cases, the communication objective is substantially different and is entirely derived from the target audience and the behavioural objective. The ad in Exhibit 5-3 is likely directed to users of other brands of body wash and Dove is encouraging a trial purchase with its comparative message.

COMMUNICATION OBJECTIVES

Communication objectives are statements of what the IMC tools will accomplish, and are usually based on one or more of the consumer response models discussed in Chapter 4. We can speak of communication objectives on three levels depending upon the decision at hand. There are communication objectives for the overall IMC plan. We can also speak of communication objectives for individual IMC tools (i.e., advertising). Often, as was shown in Chapter 1, these communication objectives are referred to as objectives for the particular tool (i.e., advertising objectives). When working in this field, marketers may use either of these terms depending upon their background or company practices. Finally, we can also define communication objectives for individual elements of a communication tool. When we design an individual print ad, we want to make sure it achieves the communication objectives we set for it.

The Ford Escape shown in Exhibit 5-4 illustrates these three considerations. The ad for this vehicle attempts to persuade non-users of hybrid vehicles of its fuel efficiency while reinforcing that it does not give up on regular SUV performance. From an advertising campaign standpoint, the communication objective would be ensuring that an overall positive belief is established so that the target audience would visit the website or dealership. Finally, the IMC plan has other IMC tools with the objective of allowing consumers to believe that the Ford Escape SUV could fulfill all needs (safety, economy, performance).

Irrespective of whether we are speaking of communication objectives for the IMC plan, a particular tool, or a specific ad, the communication objectives should be based on the particular communication tasks required to deliver the appropriate messages to the specific target audience at a relevant point within the target audience's purchase decision-making process and consumption experience.

The promotional planner should see how integrated marketing communication fits into the marketing program and what the firm hopes to achieve through advertising and other promotional elements by reviewing the marketing plan. Managers must be able to translate a general marketing objective into a particular behavioural objective and specific communication

Exhibit 5-4 The Ford Escape Hybrid attempts to influence non-hybrid users to consider this technology and brand.

objectives. The importance of setting communication objectives for a promotional plan is seen in Dove's famous Campaign for Real Beauty. Clearly the whole IMC campaign had certain esteem objectives. The advertising contributed to these IMC objectives, but also had more specific emotional effects. Finally, the sponsorship activities achieved their own behavioural change objective.

LO2 From Communication Response Models to Communication Objectives

A number of methods have been developed for setting communication objectives for advertising, related IMC tools, and complete IMC plans. We review two approaches from a historical perspective in this section. We begin with the DAGMAR model, which established the necessity for setting advertising objectives. Next, we consider managerial applications of the hierarchy of effects model and the information processing model.

DEFINING ADVERTISING GOALS FOR MEASURED RESULTS

In 1961, Russell Colley prepared a report for the Association of National Advertisers titled Defining Advertising Goals for Measured Advertising Results—DAGMAR,[6] a model for setting advertising objectives and measuring the results of an ad campaign. The major contribution of the DAGMAR model is its conclusion that communication effects are the logical basis for advertising goals and objectives against which success or failure should be measured.

Under the DAGMAR approach, an advertising goal involves a communication task that is specific and measurable. A **communication task**, as opposed to a marketing task, can be performed by, and attributed to, advertising rather than to a combination of several marketing factors. Colley proposed that the communication task be based on a hierarchical model (similar to those in Chapter 4) of the communication process:

- *Awareness*—make consumers aware of the brand or company's existence.
- *Comprehension*—develop consumers' understanding of what the product is.
- *Conviction*—develop consumers' mental disposition to buy the product.
- *Action*—get consumers to purchase the product.

DAGMAR emphasized the value of using communication-based rather than sales-based objectives to measure advertising effectiveness and encouraged the measurement of relevant responses to assess a campaign's impact. Colley's work improved the advertising and promotional planning process by providing a better understanding of the goals and objectives toward which planners' efforts should be directed. Many promotional planners use the general idea of this model as a basis for setting objectives and assessing the effectiveness of their promotional campaigns.

A second major contribution of DAGMAR to the advertising planning process was its definition of what constitutes a good objective. Colley argued that advertising objectives should specify a target audience, be stated in terms of concrete and measurable communication tasks, indicate a benchmark starting point and the degree of change sought, and specify a time period for accomplishing the objective(s).

Target Audience

A well-defined target audience may be based on behavioural variables such as customer status (i.e., brand-loyal users), usage rate, or benefits sought as well as descriptive variables such as geography, demographics, and psychographics (on which advertising media selection decisions are based). This step is critical since the communication effect has to be interpreted from the perspective of the intended receiver as discussed in Chapter 4.

Concrete, Measurable Tasks

The communication task specified in the objective should be a precise statement of what message the advertiser wants to communicate to the target audience. During the planning process, advertisers generally produce a document to describe their basic message that should be specific and clear enough to guide the creative specialists who develop the advertising message. The objective must be measurable to determine whether the intended message has been communicated properly. Other tasks beyond a message designed to influence attitudes are also required as noted in Chapter 4.

Benchmark and Degree of Change Sought

To set objectives, one must know the target audience's present level concerning response variables (e.g., awareness) and then determine the degree to which consumers must be changed by the advertising campaign. Determining the target audience's present position regarding the response requires **benchmark measures**, often requiring a marketing research study.

Establishing benchmark measures gives the promotional planner a basis for determining what communication tasks need to be accomplished and for specifying particular objectives. For example, a preliminary study for a brand may reveal that awareness is high but consumer perceptions and attitudes are negative. The objective for the advertising campaign must then be to change the target audience's perceptions of and attitudes toward the brand. Exhibit 5-5 shows an ad for Herbal Essences that is probably attempting to establish a positive attitude toward the brand's new Hydralicious formulation.

Quantitative benchmarks to set communications goals and objectives are essential for determining campaign success as they provide the standard against which the success or failure of a campaign is measured. An ad campaign that results in a 60 percent awareness level for a brand among its target audience cannot really be judged effective unless one knows what percentage of the consumers were aware of the brand before the campaign began. A 40 percent pre-campaign awareness level would lead to a different interpretation of the campaign's success than would a 20 percent level. IMC Perspective 5-2 summarizes ideas on what marketers are doing to encourage action on the part of consumers.

Exhibit 5-5   A new Herbal Essences shampoo colourfully informs consumers of its moisturizing feature.

What Consumers Do When Shopping Around

In-store communication is paramount for many product categories because consumers make so many decisions in this location. Undoubtedly a final brand choice happens while consumers are evaluating different offerings, but size, format, and model decisions are also made with the possibility for comparisons—and, in some cases, substitute products enter the equation, especially considering the myriad options available when one is, for example, looking for a snack. While retailers and manufacturers have erected displays and other forms of communication for decades, a new era of communication has emerged with consumers' ability to use technology while shopping.

Up to one-quarter of all shoppers use their phone to research their purchases, and the number of product categories evaluated increases each year along with the functions: 89 percent for value seeking, 51 percent for shopping, 24 percent for transactions, and 82 percent for information. Many marketers evaluate their options for each of the three stages of shopping behaviour—pre-shop, shop, and post-shop.

At the pre-shop stage, marketers request customer e-mail addresses during registration processes, ask permission to send text messages, and connect with consumers via social media to deliver product information. Much of this is important for communicating to mobile devices, alerting consumers toward specific retailers. Another part of this stage is the use of technology to facilitate referrals and recommendations. Ensuring comments from past consumers in a variety of digital media is an opportunity, because consumers will rely on positive experiences expressed in locations like blogs, product review sites, and branded microsites. Search engine optimization is important at this stage; consumers will type in product categories or ideas related to the definition of their needs. Estimates of $50,000 are reasonable to get a decent search response.

While many consumers will use digital resources for research at pre-shop, a majority of the process occurs in-store, where key shopping behaviours are open for influence. Some retailers like Best Buy offer in-store apps that provide deeper and richer information than what is found online that consumers obtain prior to the shopping stage. Indigo, for example, also recommends books to its Plum Rewards members via e-mail and online ads customized for communication when a membership card is swiped at the in-store kiosk. Digital in-store media networks offer specific and detailed video messages when consumers are browsing a product category, much more involved than what is found on 30-second television ads.

Communication after buying is important for marketers as well to ensure satisfaction and repeat purchasing. Brands can use social media to receive and respond to consumer follow-up questions. Forming online communities facilitates interaction with other consumers, helping resolve any possible dissonance with the purchase. Communication from a brand might also direct consumers to bloggers who have used the product and can reassure the new customers if they have been having difficulties.

Metro grocery store is one retailer embracing new technology for promotional planning. As an Air Miles partner, Metro gathers behavioural data about what customers want, what shoppers are looking for, when they're buying, and how they're buying. Combined with data from its Internet site and social media presence, Canada's third largest retailer is poised to fully develop its IMC programs. For example, it implemented a Christmas-themed promotion where Facebook visitors received an offer for each of the 24 days leading to Christmas, thereby increasing its fan base by 40 percent. The information gleaned from these sources contributed to the execution of other promotional activities, linking Campbell soup with fresh food and Unilever with its "What's for Dinner" initiative.

Sources: Alicia Androich, "Around and Around We Go," *Marketing Magazine,* June 4, 2012; Mary Maddever, "What's Next for Shopper Marketing?" *Strategy,* October 12, 2012; Grant Surridge, "In the Aisles with Metro's Nancy Modrcin," *Strategy,* January 24, 2013.

Question:

1. Why is it important for promotional planners to consider specific communication tools at each stage of consumer decision making?

Specified Time Period   A final consideration in setting advertising objectives is specifying the time period in which they must be accomplished. Appropriate time periods can range from a few days to a year or more. Most ad campaigns specify time periods from a few months to a year, depending on the situation facing the advertiser and the type of response being sought. For example, awareness levels for a brand can be created or increased fairly quickly through an intensive media schedule of widespread, repetitive advertising to the target audience. Repositioning of a product requires a change in consumers' perceptions and takes much more time.

COMMUNICATION RESPONSE MODEL APPLICATIONS

In developing the response models, authors have suggested how it could be adopted for planning and setting communication objectives. We present an application of the hierarchy of effects model (Chapter 4) since for many years it has been used in analyzing the communication response of consumers and it has been a primary approach for setting communication objectives. We also present an application of the information processing model (Chapter 4) for measuring communication effects to illustrate the importance of feedback in the communication process.

Hierarchy of Effects Model   Figure 5-2 shows the steps in the hierarchy of effects model as the consumer moves from awareness to purchase. As consumers proceed through the steps they are not expected to buy immediately; rather, advertisers realize they must provide relevant information and create positive predispositions toward the brand before trial or repurchase behaviour will occur. Figure 5-2 also shows the types of promotion or advertising relevant to each step. The ones listed are an illustration as promotional planners will select the right tools for their brand depending on factors uncovered in the situation analysis. For example, Exhibit 5-6 shows a print ad designed to influence the target audience's behaviour by going to the website and participating in the contest.

Setting communication objectives with this model is like building a pyramid over time by first accomplishing lower-level objectives such as awareness and knowledge or comprehension.

Figure   5-2   Application of the hierarchy of effects model

Response Stages	Examples of Relevant Messages	Examples of Relevant IMC Tools
Purchase	Value or minimize perceived risk copy Importance of buying now copy	Point-of-purchase display Sales promotion incentive, loyalty program
Conviction	Closing copy Recapitulate all previous copy	Take-away brochure Specialized digital app
Preference	Comparative or argumentative copy Popularity appeal	Word-of-mouth communication Social networking brand fan (e.g., Facebook)
Liking	Imagery copy Positive emotional appeals	Visually appealing media like video or print Blog, radio jingle
Knowledge	Long copy to fully understand offering Demonstration copy	Brand's website Content community (e.g., YouTube)
Awareness	Copy to ensure consumers remember brand Brand identity imagery such as logo or jingle	Mass media and digital advertising Event marketing or sponsorship

Subsequent tasks involve moving consumers who are aware of or knowledgeable about the product or service to higher levels in the pyramid (Figure 5-3). The initial levels, at the base of the pyramid, are easier to accomplish than those toward the top, such as trial and repurchase. Thus, the percentage of prospective customers will decline at the higher pyramid levels since the communication effect will not take hold on greater numbers of consumers. Actual brand data as illustrated in the exhibit requires a tracking study, proxies based on internal records of customer interactions, or research from a syndicated supplier like Nielsen.

The communication effects pyramid guides promotional objective setting. The promotional planner determines where the target audience lies concerning the levels in the pyramid. If brand awareness and knowledge of its features and benefits are low, the communication objective should be to increase them. If these levels of the pyramid are already in place, but liking or preference is low, the advertising goal may be to change the target audience's image of the brand. As the illustrative numbers indicate, the campaign could focus on "liking" since there is a substantial drop in the number of consumers at this level from the previous level. Also, the drop-off from trial to repeat purchase suggests the marketing communication need to focus on continued buying. The varying levels of objectives could be due to many factors such as behaviour (e.g., brand loyalty segmentation) or regional differences (e.g., geographic segmentation).

Information Processing Model The information processing model may be an effective framework for setting objectives like the above model and evaluating the effects of a promotional campaign. Figure 5-4 shows the steps of the model from exposure/presentation to purchase behaviour. For example, preliminary research might suggest to promotional planners that the target audience comprehends existing aspects of the brand, but does not accept a newer brand message. Thus, an objective of the marketing communication could be to enhance acceptance.

Also shown in Figure 5-4 are examples of research that can be measured at each step. The objectives can be the basis of research to assess whether the communication effects occurred as planned. This provides the advertiser with feedback regarding the effectiveness of promotional strategies tactics designed to move the consumer to purchase.

Extensive coverage of the research methods is provided in Chapter 9 to give a general direction for advertising. This understanding is then extended to measuring the effectiveness of individual IMC tools in their respective chapters later in the book. For example, investigating message acceptance is an important criterion for all aspects of marketing communication in which there are general approaches that can be applied. However, each media and IMC tool presents its own uniqueness requiring specific investigation. The ad in

Exhibit 5-6 Guylian Belgian Chocolates encourages consumers to visit the website and win the contest.

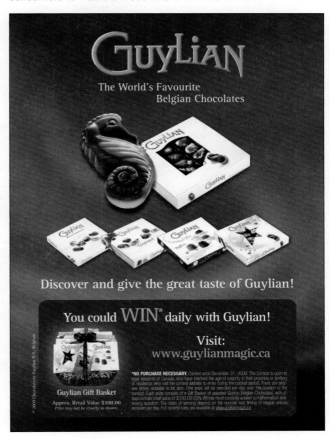

Figure 5-3

Communication effects pyramid

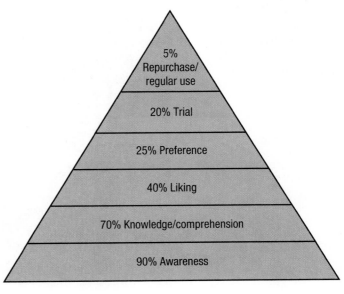

Figure   5-4

Methods of measuring
feedback in the response
process

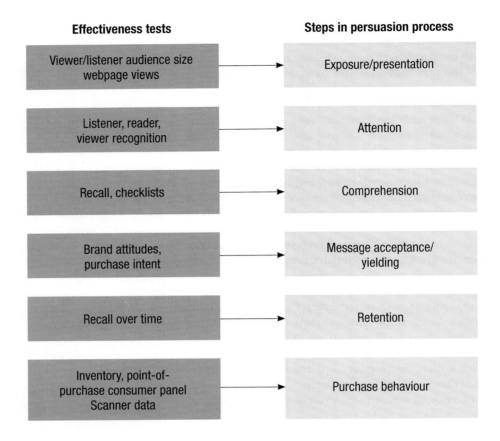

Effectiveness tests	Steps in persuasion process
Viewer/listener audience size webpage views	Exposure/presentation
Listener, reader, viewer recognition	Attention
Recall, checklists	Comprehension
Brand attitudes, purchase intent	Message acceptance/ yielding
Recall over time	Retention
Inventory, point-of-purchase consumer panel Scanner data	Purchase behaviour

Exhibit 5-7 would have multiple measures of effectiveness for the primary brand Budweiser, and each of the other brands would have its own measures as well.

Application Conclusion   Decades of research have shown that promotional planners applying communication response models to set communication objectives has been mixed. A 1969 study showed that most advertising agencies did not state appropriate objectives for determining advertising success.[7] A later study found that most advertisers did not set concrete

Exhibit 5-7   Budweiser and its partners would set objectives based on their respective position in this multi-brand promotion.

advertising objectives, specify objective tasks, measure results in terms of stages of a hierarchy of effects, or match objectives to evaluation measures.[8] Finally, another study measured the attitudes of executives with the majority saying they did not know whether their advertising was working and fewer than 10 percent saying they thought it was working well.[9]

Cleary, the evidence suggests a newer perspective with a stronger managerial point of view is warranted for enhanced adoption. We suggest the Rossiter and Percy (R&P) perspective is a worthy candidate that promotional planners should consider when setting behavioural and communication objectives.[10] We introduced their ideas in Chapter 3 when discussing the guidelines for target audience identification, selection, and profiling and in Chapter 4 when summarizing communication response models. We include the R&P perspective since it attempts to resolve the limitations of other approaches for objective setting and provides guidelines for creative tactics (i.e., Chapter 8).

The R&P perspective has three distinguishing characteristics. First, it provides guidelines for specific behavioural objectives. Many of the models say something general like purchase or behaviour, but promotional planners need to consider particular kinds of behaviour and purchase to make a connection to the marketing objectives. Second, it is consistent with the DAGMAR model by making a direct connection between the purchase decision and the communication task required for each target audience. Finally, it provides guidelines for communication objectives that are more managerially useful and that do not completely rely on a set hierarchy of effects. For example, the Air Transat ad in Exhibit 5-8 targets travellers who are likely at the need recognition stage of their decision making. Since it is a trial behaviour, the ad attempts to encourage the target audience to consider this direct option instead wasting time with connecting flights when visiting Europe.

Exhibit 5-8 This Air Transat ad encourages travellers who are non-customers to consider an alternative.

(L03) Setting Behavioural Objectives for IMC

A key part of R&P's approach is to have a clear behavioural objective for each target audience since the individual purchasing behaviour of all customers adds up to a firm's overall sales. As suggested earlier, the link between marketing objectives (i.e., sales) and communication objectives (i.e., attitude toward the brand) is behavioural objectives. Advertising and promotion can focus on influencing a particular form of behaviour based on the nature of the advertising message or IMC tool used. We now evaluate four options a manager has for setting behavioural objectives: trial purchase, repeat purchase, shopping, and repeat consumption.

TRIAL PURCHASE OBJECTIVES

A trial behaviour is one which the consumer has not previously incurred. A trial purchase objective pertaining to the target audience of a promotional planner's brand is contingent upon time, competition, and product category. We review four different trial objectives to account for these three variables.

Brand Trial A **brand trial purchase** is defined as a consumer's first purchase of a brand. For example, the purchase of most everyday products (e.g., soft drink or snack food) occurred many years ago and it is probably difficult to remember when one made their first purchase in that category or the specific brand. However, these firms continue to have a **brand trial objective** as consumers enter the market when they attain a certain age or have income (i.e., allowance

Exhibit 5-9   Huggies strives for a trial purchase of its washcloths by the consumer.

from parents). In fact, a brand trial objective is a behavioural objective for almost all firms, but it is not necessarily the primary behavioural objective for all campaigns or all communication tools. Brand trial also emerges once again for brand extensions. The message and coupon in the Huggies ad in Exhibit 5-9 suggest that brand trial is a primary objective.

Brand trial generally requires an extensive campaign. For example, with 76 percent of the Canadian coffee and baked goods market, Tim Hortons was a logical target for McDonald's to encourage coffee consumers to change their habit and try a new java with a unique brewing process. A free coffee giveaway launched the campaign, and combined with in-store communication, the company sold 1.3 million more cups of coffee. Things picked up with spectacular and very public creative executions a year later when the sample occurred once again. In Vancouver, a transit shelter filled with coffee beans slowly depleted for two weeks as a teaser for the campaign. Later, a giant coffee pot attached to a lamp post appeared as if pouring coffee into an equally huge coffee cup. Visually, the lamp post acted as the stream of coffee poured into the cup that surrounded the post on the street corner. Nationally, TV, out-of-home, radio, and online advertising during the same two-week span built momentum, so all could recall the message "Let's Start Fresh." These media highlighted the attributes of premium roast Arabica beans and full-bodied flavour.[11]

Brand Re-Trial   Alternatively, it is quite unlikely that consumers continue to purchase the same brand of soft drink as their first trial purchase. In fact, many people consume more than one brand of soft drink, and for whatever reason stop purchasing their initial brand. Many brand managers are faced with this dilemma of trying to re-capture past customers who have not purchased the brand for a period of time (e.g., perhaps a year). The manager of such a brand would like these past customers to have a new trial experience of the brand. Thus, a **brand re-trial purchase** is defined as a consumer's first purchase of a brand after a time delay. The length of the delay to focus on when setting a **brand re-trial objective** is a decision the promotion manager makes. It depends upon the purchase frequency of the product, among other factors observed from the situation analysis. Becel is in an everlasting battle with butter and periodically has a brand re-trial objective, as shown by the ad in Exhibit 5-10.

Exhibit 5-10   Becel desires brand re-trial from lapsed users who gravitated to butter for a while.

Category Trial   Now let's put the trial purchase in another perspective: consider the purchase of a smartphone, which many young adults currently own. The smartphone is a different kind of product and likely a somewhat involved purchase for many consumers. Despite this, phone companies and service providers had trial objectives as they attempted to attract consumers who did not own such technology. While this is obviously a brand trial purchase, it is also something broader. A **category trial purchase** is defined as a consumer's first purchase in a product category that the consumer has not purchased in previously. The ad in Exhibit 5-11 follows this idea as it attracts users of non-dandruff shampoo to try Head & Shoulders instead of other more dangerous ways to provide relief for one's itchy scalp. Marketers of new products, like the smartphone, have a dual challenge of attaining both **category trial objectives** and brand trial objectives.

Category trial is also possible in situations where a "purchase" does not occur. Each year, Canadian Blood Services recruits new donors, people who have never given blood. Its latest campaign tried to move the number of new donors from 85,000 to 90,000 with the message, "What if you needed blood?" The approach tried to affect the complacency people generally have with giving blood by getting them to think that at a certain point in their life they may in fact need blood and should be part of the solution.[12]

Brand Switching   A manager may plan for a brand trial or brand re-trial objective when consumers are purchasing another brand. A **brand-switching purchase** is defined as a consumer's purchase toward a brand from another competing brand. A brand-switching purchase occurs whereby the consumer makes a re-trial purchase of a brand and leaves the new favourite and returns to an old favourite. A brand-switching purchase also occurs when the consumer makes a trial purchase of a brand from a competing brand. Thus, brand trial or brand re-trial objectives are more specifically **brand-switching objectives in certain planning situations**. The Pellegrino ad in Exhibit 5-12 communicates to current bottled water users to consider a better-tasting alternative. Pepsi returned to its classic approach to switch Coca-Cola drinkers with its Taste Challenge, a taste test for consumers to demonstrate the brand they prefer while not knowing which brand is which. With a global 10 percent market share versus Coca-Cola's 25 percent, the popular idea launched nearly 40 years ago appeared as a viable alternative to stem the tide, and also keep sales afloat as soft drink consumption declined 18 percent from 2006 to 2010.[13]

REPEAT PURCHASE OBJECTIVES

In the age of relationship marketing and a focus on customer retention, this form of purchase behaviour is most critical. A **repeat purchase** is defined as a consumer's continued purchase of a brand within a specified time period. Again, the time factor for a **repeat-purchase objective** is at the discretion of the marketer, and it is contingent upon purchase frequency of the product or other factors derived from the situation analysis.

Brands can have a repeat-purchase objective for its loyal customers. Many firms communicate with these consumers to maintain their positive attitude toward the brand. For example, one might suggest that most of Coca-Cola's advertising and promotion is directed toward consumers who drink only Coca-Cola within the cola category. Direct marketing activities can have a repeat-purchasing objective in many instances as marketers will use direct mail to ensure continued buying.

Brands can have a repeat-purchase objective for customers who habitually consume two or three brands continuously (i.e., favourable brand switchers). For instance,

Exhibit 5-11   Head & Shoulders wants non-dandruff users to consider using the product.

Exhibit 5-12   Pellegrino tries to switch over users of other bottled water brands.

of 15 purchases 10 purchases might be of the brand, with the remaining five purchases spread across two other brands. While this consumer does not purchase the brand for every single occasion, the consumer is a consistent contributor to the firm's sales and a marketer would want to communicate appropriately to ensure future sales.

A repeat purchase objective pertaining to the target audience of a promotional planner's brand is contingent upon frequency (how often to purchase), amount (how much to purchase), and time (when to purchase).

Purchase Frequency   The first alternative concerns the rate, or how often to purchase the brand. This implies that a marketer may set an objective pertaining to consumers purchasing its brand every week instead of every two weeks. This example shows an option where a manager may want to *increase* the rate of purchase from a "half" product per week to "one" product per week. A second managerial option is to *maintain* the rate of purchase. While this is a more conservative objective, it is still a viable option in very competitive environments. Finally, a manager may want to *decrease* the rate of purchase. This option may be viable in unique situations of high demand or with products that have potentially negative consequences (i.e., alcohol).

Purchase Amount   The amount or how much to purchase on each occasion is the second alternative. As this alternative implies, a marketer may set an objective where consumers purchase two products per occasion versus one per occasion. As above, this option is to *increase* the amount per occasion, but a marketer could still evaluate whether to *maintain* or *decrease* the amount per occasion.

Purchase Timing   The final alternative is the timing, or when to purchase. Certain products are seasonal, have a peak in their sales, or can be easily stored. Marketers may have a behavioural objective to influence when consumers will make the purchase. For example, Wendy's restaurant advertises on television in the evening and communicates the fact that its drive-through service stays open late, thus prompting consumers to purchase at a certain time of day. Consistent with the other two alternatives, we can conceive three options: *maintain, accelerate,* and *delay.* Exhibit 5-13 encourages consumers to purchase now rather than later.

All of these objectives can be seen in the marketing activities of Cineplex, which leads its market with 66 percent. Its discounted price on Tuesdays guides purchasing timing. Its Scene Card loyalty program, where enrolled members obtain points for movie ticket purchases that can be redeemed for movies or snacks, signals a purchase frequency objective. This program provides managers with an extensive database allowing them to target messages to guide repeat patronage.[14]

Exhibit 5-13 LG encourages consumers to upgrade their appliances by focusing on product design.

SHOPPING OBJECTIVES

Often, communication is designed to encourage a consumer to progress through the decision-making process more smoothly. For example, most people find it imperative to visit a car dealership prior to buying a car. So the focus of parts of an IMC plan is to have consumers take action that will lead them one step closer to the final destination of a purchase. **Shopping behaviour** is an action consumers take that will lead to a higher probability of purchasing the brand. Many types of shopping behaviour exist, but in general most concern the consumer seeking information (e.g., visit a website) about the brand or an experience with the brand (e.g., participate in an event, watch a demonstration, consume a sample). Other terminology for this appeared historically, but a current view is to identify this as "shopper marketing" where brands foster brand experiences while consumers shop.[15]

Digital equivalents are prominent now as brands encourage website visits, interaction with other customers on Facebook, participation in Twitter, and viewing or posting of video or pictures in content communities. Accordingly, marketers can have many shopping behaviour objectives to know whether enough of the target audience is involved with the brand during the decision-making process. Firms can track the number of sales inquiries or requests for samples, or demonstrations to gauge how well it is performing for the objective. It also can track the digital exposure and participation levels as all the interaction is electronically recorded. The ad in Exhibit 5-14 directs users of two-piece hockey sticks to consider a one-piece stick made by a Canadian manufacturer.

Another aspect of shopping behaviour is that consumers seek out the opinion of their friends and family, as discussed in the word-of-mouth topic section in Chapter 4. Young people ages 18 to 24 communicate this way extensively, with virtually 100 percent telling up to four of their friends when they have a positive brand experience.[16] Thus, brands now look to achieve specific word-of-mouth objectives as part of their plans, which guides the use of experiential marketing communication or more innovative and exciting digital activities.

Exhibit 5-14 Combat directs consumers to its website and provides a QR code link.

REPEAT CONSUMPTION OBJECTIVES

Thus far we have considered repeat purchase as a behavioural objective. Related to this is repeat consumption as a behavioural objective. **Repeat consumption** is defined as the continued consumption of the brand once purchased. Marketers may have a **repeat-consumption objective** when communicating with their current customers who have previously purchased the brand and have the product at their home or work. This communication has an objective of modifying how often to consume the brand, how much to consume on each occasion, and when to consume.

To give an idea of a repeat-consumption objective in action, we will cite two common approaches. Often, food and drink products advertise certain television commercials that show consumption visuals that may prompt consumers to snack or have another beverage. Also, research suggests that for these kinds of product categories that have a well established market leader, a consumption intention is a better predictor of advertising success since goods are already in stock and a repeat purchase will not occur until the inventory is depleted.[17] Another approach is to show consumers how to enjoy the product for other uses, or in new or alternative situations. The California almonds ad in Exhibit 5-15 reinforces continued consumption by showing that the product can be taken from storage and used with vegetables for family dinner. Its health benefits are evident with the Health Check logo from the Canadian Heart & Stoke Foundation.

Milk faces a unique problem of 100 percent trial and 99 percent household penetration, yet its consumption continues to decline. The B.C. Dairy Foundation identified teens and young adults as an audience for a campaign to maintain consumption since research indicated that consumption levels dropped off during the ages of 16–23. Since many of these people still lived at home, the print and television

Exhibit 5-15 California almonds associated with a situational use to increase repeat consumption.

messages "Don't take your body for granted" and "What would life be like without a body?" tried to ensure that this age group would not stop consuming milk prior to moving out on their own. Exciting outdoor events geared toward this audience attempted to make drinking milk as "cool" as any other beverage![18] Next door, the Prairie Milk Marketing Partnership, representing the remaining western provinces, used mass, social, and location media to reach teens and increased sales by 18 percent through increased consumption once teens understood the health benefits of milk.[19]

Reducing repeat consumption is a goal in circumstances like electricity. Ads sponsored by PowerWise, the brand behind the provincial government's attempt to encourage the people of Ontario to consume less electricity, employed David Suzuki as a spokesperson. In one execution, David explains to the homeowner, Bob, that his basement beer fridge uses lots of electricity costing about $150 per year to operate. Bob quickly concludes that saving electricity means more beer and he humorously dashes throughout the house shutting off the TV, radio, and hair dryer (all, of course, while his family members are using the items). This and all other ads ended with "You Have the Power" slogan and included a visual of the website address (Powerwise.ca). A number of website video illustrations by David Suzuki clearly taught consumers how to use less electricity or showed them how to change their behaviour for less electricity consumption. The website also allowed consumers to join and submit their own electricity-saving tip, and provided extensive resources so that consumers could make necessary adaptations.

The type of purchase and consumption behaviour that firms may try to influence is quite varied. If a firm has multiple target audiences to reach, quite likely it will have to carefully specify the type of behaviour associated with each target audience so that it can develop the most appropriate message and select the most relevant IMC tool. To assist a manager in making these subsequent decisions, it is important to set clear communication objectives.

L04 Setting Communication Objectives for IMC

Earlier in this chapter we saw how communication response models help formulate communication objectives. The R&P approach is similar since it translates their perspective of communication effects into options for managers to set communication objectives. We review the options for each of the four communication objectives that promotional planners may choose from to formulate their IMC plan, which also can be applied to one target audience or multiple target audiences.

The options for communication objectives can be universally applied for (i) a specific communication like one print ad or television commercial, (ii) a specific campaign like advertising or sponsorship, and (iii) a complete IMC program that includes all promotional tools. These communication objectives retain the characteristics set forth earlier for good objective setting (i.e., a specific benchmark with the degree of change sought within a specified time period). Finally, the R&P framework is flexible enough to apply all communication objectives to each stage of the buyer decision-making process for any target audience. We now turn to summarizing the options for each communication objective.

CATEGORY NEED

Category need pertains to whether the target audience believes that purchasing within a particular product category will fulfill the consumer's need. Smartphones are a clear product where consumers are users or non-users. A phone company may try to build demand by convincing new users of the benefits of owning a smartphone versus not owning one. This type of message is likely to be different from the type of message used to convince a current user to switch to another brand when the technology improves with new features. In this example, it is a question of whether the target audience believes their communication needs would be more fulfilled with the product or without it. Exhibit 5-16 identifies how this type of watch can fulfill the need for status.

Another example of category need occurs with transportation. When thinking about buying a "car" upon graduation, a student's choice may in fact be a truck or a sports utility vehicle. In a broad sense, all vehicles can be used for transportation, but consumers have particular needs that are satisfied more easily with certain types or categories of vehicles versus others. A marketer for SUVs may try to communicate in a way so that a target audience will feel the need for an SUV more strongly than the need for a sporty sub-compact, which might be the initial category of product that young consumers would gravitate toward. In this example, it is a question of which distinct yet related category fulfills the target audience's need more completely.

With water consumption growing and soft drink consumption declining, the need for flavouring water remained since consumers often desire variety or wish to avoid blandness. This opened the door for increased demand for the "water-additive" category, and Mio entered with style to pick up an impressive share with its quirky ads.[20] Beer continues its downward spiral as per capita consumption declines, forcing beer brands to compare certain formats to wine or spirits. One Molson executive claimed that "just a beer drinker" no longer existed and the brewer needed to expand its frame of reference to include other alcohol beverages.[21]

Category Need Is Reminded   One obvious example of this is reminder advertising, where the brand is featured in the message and the need for the product is implicitly communicated or clearly illustrated. Often, the reminder option of category need is the focus of campaigns for lapsed users. For example, the ad for Dairyland Milk 2 Go products in Exhibit 5-17 reminds consumers that it is a convenient drink when away from home, like soft drinks or sports drinks.

Category Need Is Emphasized   The two examples above (that is, smartphones and vehicles) show two situations where we actively attempt to persuade the target audience to believe that the product category will fulfill a particular need. The Swiss Water Decaffeinated Coffee Company required category need as its communication objective when it faced the difficult task of explaining that its process for decaffeinating coffee used water instead of chemicals. Known as the Swiss Water Process, brand-name coffees use this approach and highlight the fact on their packages, much like the famous "Intel Inside" or the VQA designation on Canadian wines indicating an adherence to quality production. Swiss Water used the message "Decaf without the chemistry" to highlight the difference, yet not scare the target audience toward other products like decaffeinated tea.[22] Thus, a category need objective is usually imperative when competing technologies or substitute products emerge on the market thus creating two subcategories instead of one general category.

BRAND AWARENESS

Brand awareness is a universal communication objective. This means that every single point of communication should contribute to a target audience's understanding and knowledge of the brand name. This understanding and knowledge should go even further such that the target audience knows the category that the brand typically competes in when the consumer is in position to make a purchase. This stronger interpretation of awareness is important for the brand to be considered in the decision-making process. There are two types of brand awareness that we now identify. Naturally, if both forms of brand awareness are relevant, then a manager may have both as awareness objectives.

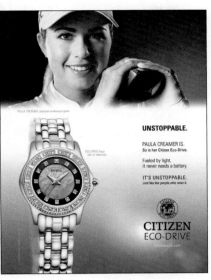

Exhibit 5-16   Professional golfer Paula Creamer endorses the features of the Citizen Eco-Drive watch.

Exhibit 5-17   This ad for Dairyland Milk 2 Go products is part of a campaign designed to increase sales and market share.

Exhibit 5-18   Nike minimized its brand identification with a small image of its famous swoosh.

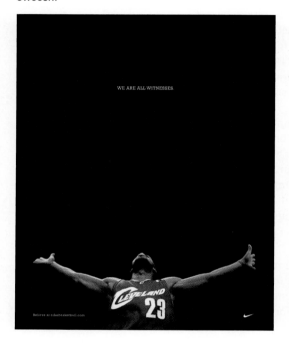

Brand Recognition   If the target audience makes a choice at the point of purchase, then simple recognition of past brand messages can be sufficient for brand consideration or purchase. The Nike ad in Exhibit 5-18 shows an example where the brand is not prominent which might reduce the brand recognition effect. However, Nike's universal recognition allows the brand to downplay its identification with a small image of the swoosh logo, and concentrate on the message and the star player to remind consumers to visit its basketball website. The "Design by Scotties" campaign raised its awareness for this often forgotten facial tissue substantially versus Kleenex over a five-year period as the message of the box being a complement to one's décor took hold.[23]

Brand Recall   If the target audience feels the need for a product but needs to remember what brands to consider away from the point of purchase, then recall becomes the focus of the campaign. Brand recall is often referred to as unaided brand awareness when measuring. McCain's "It's All Good" campaign increased recall of its brand promise for its Superfries (6% to 45%) and pizza (6% to 37%).[24]

In defining brand awareness we must be careful in distinguishing it from advertising awareness, which concerns itself with whether consumers are aware of a brand's television or print ads. While there is a logical connection between the two, they are not identical. For example, Activia established strong effects compared to industry norms of its "vitality" message for unaided advertising recall (50% vs. 18%) and aided advertising recall (60% vs. 48%) levels.[25]

Shoppers Drug Mart's marketing communication tools, loyalty program, beauty magazine, advertising, and various sales promotions reinforce this objective since brand awareness sits at 98 percent. Recall is important as consumers would often decide at home where to shop when in need of personal care, beauty, or other products that the store offers. Of course recognition is important when consumers are driving by the store and see familiar signage that prompts need recognition for shopping in the product categories offered. Thus, even when a brand attains a strong level of awareness it continues its effort to retain its strong position—such that Shoppers extended its presence with celebratory zeal with its 50th anniversary communication.[26]

BRAND ATTITUDE

Brand attitude is another universal communication objective. Like brand awareness, every aspect of a firm's IMC program or any particular element, such as a television commercial, should contribute to an aspect of the overall evaluation of the brand from the perspective of the target audience. A logical conclusion to this point is that there should be no such thing as an "awareness campaign," as every campaign should surely influence brand awareness and an aspect of brand attitude. Since brand attitude is such an important communication objective, prior understanding of the existing brand attitude is a critical guide for each option.

Establish Brand Attitude   A new target audience that has no awareness and therefore no prior attitude toward the brand generally requires extensive communication so that an attitude is created or established. The Roots ad in Exhibit 5-19

Exhibit 5-19   Roots tries to establish a clear brand attitude with this visual ad.

needs to establish a favourable brand attitude with its hand-crafted features.

Maintain Brand Attitude   Often, advertising is performed so that existing attitude levels will remain constant in order to ensure future sales. Stopping communication is one reason for declining sales that have been seen in many examples over time. In contrast, many major advertisers (e.g., Coca-Cola) consistently follow this approach to maintain sales. The Hyundai ad in Exhibit 5-20 reinforces the existing positive attitude its customers would have regarding the quality of its vehicles.

Increase Brand Attitude   Target audiences who are familiar with the brand and moderately favourable toward the brand can be influenced. For example, we can increase their brand attitude by getting the target audience to believe that the brand delivers better performance on a particular attribute or benefit. The beef ad in Exhibit 5-21 tries to increase consumers' already favourable attitude toward this source of nourishment. Looking at this from another point of view, brands that have "green" claims due to a benefit to the environment have difficulty achieving stronger brand attitudes since consumers are reluctant to pay a premium price or do not see the value to them as an individual. Research suggests that a grand "better for the environment" approach is less accepted for many mainstream consumers.[27]

Modify Brand Attitude   Similar to the previous option, if the target audience is moderately favourable we still seek to improve their attitude. However, we modify the brand attitude if no increase is possible. In this option, marketers use a different point of reference in communicating the benefits. Typically, marketers focus on a new consumer motive for purchasing the brand that the target audience will be receptive toward. The tea ad in Exhibit 5-22 attempts to influence attitudes in a new direction. Mazda presents an interesting example since its sales are considerably lower than other Japanese brands. It is now pursuing a worldwide emphasis to put the brand in a premium niche, much like BMW did as it grew from humble origins during the 1970s.[28] Its future marketing communication could likely target users of other premium brands for them to switch, or to non-premium brand users to "trade up." In either case, innovative communication will be required to modify existing attitudes.

Change Brand Attitude   Negative attitudes are difficult to influence, but particular communication situations create the challenge of changing the brand attitude for a target audience. BC Hydro faced an uphill battle illustrating a marketing communication problem that necessitated this kind of an objective. According to executives, existing consumer attitudes tended to be negative since most associated a high electrical bill when thinking of the brand. This proved to be even more difficult with bills set to rise by a third over the coming years as the utility upgraded its infrastructure. A message shift from "BC Hydro for generations" to "BC Hydro regeneration" attempted to ensure that British Columbians would feel more positive toward

Exhibit 5-20   Hyundai reminds consumers that its customers are very satisfied with vehicle quality.

Exhibit 5-21   Canadian Beef reinforces the belief that its product is a source of protein.

Exhibit 5-22   Nestea provides new reasons to consume its product.

the provincial energy provider. Interestingly, this attitude existed despite a series of positive messages for its Power Smart conservation program, which garnered 33 awards for the agencies responsible for creating positive messages to use energy wisely.[29]

BRAND PURCHASE INTENTION

There are two fairly simple options for **brand purchase intention** here:

Assume Brand Purchase Intention   In situations (i.e., low involvement) where the strength of an intention to purchase is consistent (i.e., highly correlated) with brand attitude, a marketer is not required to include this objective.

Generate Brand Purchase Intention   In contrast, managers need the target audience to have a plan to purchase a brand in situations of high involvement.

LO5   IMC Planning: Objectives for Buyer Decision Stages

In Chapter 3, we presented a model of consumer decision making that showed the stages typically experienced when making a purchase. We outlined several steps: need recognition, information search, alternative evaluation, purchase decision, and postpurchase evaluation. One important role of marketing communications is to help the target audience move through these stages. Marketers require specific communication tools and messages that will resonate with each target audience as they proceed through these stages. We assess this decision-making process for each target audience and make a conclusion as to which communication objectives are most relevant for each stage. Figure 5-5 illustrates how this works.

The analysis occurs in the first six rows, where the marketer includes the target audience information and makes a conclusion on the key communication objectives that need to be attained so that the target audience will continue to the next stage. We have addressed these ideas already. The first question (Who?) looks at the key participants in the decision. We highlighted these roles in Chapter 3. The next three questions are descriptors of where, when, and how the shopping behaviour will occur. This is based on market research, managerial experience, flashes of inspiration, and assumptions. The key point is that we need to make clear the behaviour that we are trying to influence.

After summarizing these questions, we determine which communication objectives are necessary to ensure that the consumer continues through all stages. For example, what aspect of brand attitude needs to be addressed at the need-recognition stage versus the alternative-evaluation stage? Is recall an awareness objective at the need-recognition stage and recognition an awareness objective at the purchase-decision stage? We also need to determine the most relevant behavioural objective. For example, we may wish to encourage phone enquiries at the information search stage. Or perhaps we may desire Internet visits to compare brands at the alternative evaluation stage.

Once this assessment has been done, then the marketer can outline preliminary options concerning the types of messages and communication tools that would be most useful. Returning to

Figure   5-5   Assessing the consumer decision-making process

Analysis and Conclusions	Need Recognition	Information Search	Alternative Evaluation	Purchase Decision	Postpurchase Evaluation
Who? (roles)					
Where? (location)					
When? (time, timing)					
How? (shopping behaviour)					
Why? (key motivator)					
Behavioural Objectives					
Communication Objectives					
Message Options					
Communication Tool Options					

the first question above, a marketer may decide to have a fun television commercial (e.g., communication tool option) that emphasizes the emotional attachment (e.g., brand attitude) to the product. It should be noted that when identifying options, the marketer has not fully committed or recommended that this is exactly the plan, but rather that this is the template of analysis for making the final decision.

The rest of this book focuses on how to make IMC plan decisions that are based on the target audience, behaviour objectives, and communication objectives established at the start of the plan. Chapters 6–9 focus on the message, while Chapters 10–17 focus on the communication tools. As we noted at the start of this chapter, the contents of this framework become the key criteria for making all promotional decisions and the criteria by which the results are measured. While all firms may not be able to afford comprehensive studies to assess communication effects, they would benefit from the use of the framework because it provides disciplined thinking before investing in promotion.

Learning Objectives Summary

 Distinguish among marketing, behavioural, and communication objectives and identify the value of setting each type of objective.

Objectives guide promotional program development and provide a benchmark against which performance can be measured and evaluated. Objectives also serve as a communication function for all participants in the planning process and direct all IMC program decision making.

Objectives for IMC evolve from the organization's overall marketing plan and are based on the purpose of each promotional mix element within the marketing program. Managers use sales or a related measure such as market share as the basis for setting marketing objectives. Promotional planners believe the communication role of promotional mix elements is not directly connected with sales-based objectives. They use communication-based objectives like those in the response hierarchy as the basis for setting goals. The implication of these models suggests the importance of setting specific behavioural objectives such as trial or repeat purchase and appropriate communication objectives to direct the IMC strategy so that it contributes to the attainment of marketing objectives.

 Describe the historical approaches for setting communication objectives for advertising.

Historically, considerable emphasis in setting objectives concerned traditional advertising-based views of marketing communication. This originated from an application of basic response models like DAGMAR and the hierarchy of effects. DAGMAR established the principle that objectives should specify a target audience, be stated in concrete and measurable communication tasks, indicate a benchmark starting point and the degree of change sought, and specify a time period for accomplishing the objectives. As an extension of this idea, the principles of the hierarchy of effects model, used in setting advertising objectives, could be applied to other elements in the promotional mix. The hierarchy of effects model suggested that unique promotional tools could be implemented in different stages of the response hierarchy. Managers would determine the location of a particular audience in the hierarchy and make appropriate decisions to move them closer to a trial and repeat purchase.

Adoption of communication models proved limited resulting in the need for a comprehensive managerial framework for setting behavioural and communication objectives for many IMC planning purposes, IMC plans, individual IMC tools (i.e., advertising), and specific elements (i.e., direct mail offer with coupon). Both types of objectives need to be established for any individual communication element, ranging from an activity at a sponsorship event to what is portrayed in a point-of-sale display. In short, all target audience contact points play a role in fulfilling IMC plan objectives and their expenditures can be accountable through achievement of their mandate. A complete plan requires direction through behavioural and communication objectives so that all tools and elements communicate accurately.

 Evaluate the options for setting behavioural objectives and apply them when constructing a promotional plan.

The comprehensive managerial framework identified options for behavioural objectives to guide the achievement of marketing objectives and to provide direction to form communication objectives. Behavioural objectives included brand trial, brand re-trial, brand-switching, category trial, repeat purchase, shopping behaviour, and repeat consumption. Analysis of the target audience's decision-making process assists promotional planners in determining which ones to focus on in their IMC plan for each IMC tool.

Choose among the options for setting communication objectives and apply them when designing IMC recommendations.

The comprehensive managerial framework also presented many options for setting communication objectives in terms of category need (i.e., omit, remind, emphasize), brand awareness (i.e., recognition and/or recall), brand attitude (i.e., establish, maintain, increase, modify, change), brand purchase intention (assume, generate), and brand purchase facilitation (omit, include). Similar to behavioural objectives, specific communication objectives can be attained for individual IMC tools so that the overall plan achieves each communication objective for a particular target audience. The end result provides managers with the ability to construct a multitude of IMC plans.

Assemble the best combination of behavioural and communication objectives for each stage of the consumer decision-making process.

The comprehensive managerial framework was then linked to the buyer decision-making model to show the connection between a consumer's behaviour and a particular brand's objectives. This application implies that as a consumer's decision-making progresses, managers can consider how objectives evolve at each stage in order to adjust the message, media, or IMC tool employed to communicate.

Key Terms

Review key terms and definitions on Connect.

Review Questions

1. Discuss the value of setting objectives for the integrated marketing communications program. What important functions do objectives serve?

2. What are the strengths and weaknesses of using traditional hierarchy models for setting communication objectives?

3. Some claim that promotion is all about communication, so we should focus only on communication objectives and not worry about behavioural objectives. Convince them otherwise.

4. If a firm cannot afford large market research studies to quantitatively assess whether communication objectives have been achieved, why should the firm bother setting communication objectives?

5. A firm is running a campaign with advertising, sales promotion, and public relations. Why might it have different communication objectives for each IMC tool?

Applied Questions

1. In meeting with a client for an energy drink, she informs you that the only goal of advertising and promotion is to generate sales. As an account planner for a marketing communication agency, present reasons why communication objectives must also be considered.

2. Assess what the behaviourial objectives would be for each ad in this chapter.

3. Assess what the communication objectives would be for each ad in this chapter.

4. After assessing the objectives for some of the ads of this chapter, go the brand's Internet site or social media offerings and determine if the objectives are the same or different.

GO ONLINE

For more information on the resources available from McGraw-Hill Ryerson, go to www.mcgrawhill.ca/he/solutions.

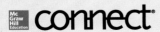

Brand Positioning Strategy Decisions

6

LEARNING OBJECTIVES

LO1 Identify the concepts of market positioning strategy and market position.

LO2 Apply the positioning concept in an advertising context by defining brand positioning strategy and brand position.

LO3 Illustrate how to formulate brand positioning strategy decisions.

LO4 Demonstrate brand repositioning strategy opportunities.

LO5 Interpret brand positioning strategy decisions in other contexts.

Barcode Coffee Maker Delivers

A brand positioning strategy evolves over time—due to a lack of success, and to a need for refinement after success. Tracking the experience of the Tassimo coffee single-serve brewing system in Canada is a fine example of where the initial introduction did not keep pace with Kraft's expectation, which prompted a new direction substantially different from the worldwide strategy. With its subsequent achievement, the brand again looked to fine-tune its progress a couple of years later.

Household penetration of single-serve coffee machines reached 70 percent in Europe but did not come close to that level in Canada as advertisers used similar ad messages focused on ease of use and consumption lifestyle. Tassimo's ads, used in all countries including Canada, emphasized the category but failed to identify its unique characteristic: the barcode ensured that the right mix of coffee and other ingredients brewed a perfect cup of java.

Enter Tassimo's "The barcode brews it better" campaign designed to increase household penetration to 10 percent, hit sales of 200,000 units, and grow coffee revenue by 60 percent (i.e., in the T-Discs units that are put into the machine). Tassimo wanted consumers to enter stores asking for "the one with the barcode" as the identification and association of that image became the key message to convey the new brand positioning strategy. The creative solution featured a "live" barcode as people dressed in white or black like a barcode chatted about the technology in a light-hearted manner.

The campaign employed multiple media: full-page ads to explain the technology and one-third-page companion ads to identify the brands of coffee in magazines during gift season; two 30-second TV and cinema ads; retail point-of-sale; newsletters delivered via email to assist lead users in word-of-mouth communication; sample units given to social media influencers who commented as they liked; and a PR event so consumers could turn in their old machines.

Sales hit 236,000, more than double the previous year, as supply could not keep up with demand and market share hit 53 percent. Coffee sales made a mark with 66 percent growth. Brand awareness numbers moved from 59 percent to 75 percent. Within Kraft Worldwide, Tassimo Canada received the award for most effective campaign! The brand continued to struggle in the United States and in most other countries.

Shortly after this success, Kraft redesigned the T-Discs packaging with a consistent brand image. Previous versions looked like the coffee brands and featured dark colours as many coffee brands did not fully differentiate on this characteristic. The new design showed lighter imagery that reinforced the distinctive shape of the T-Discs and reflected the brand personality—uncomplicated, clever, intuitive, and approachable. This design even carried over to Tim Hortons and Second Cup coffee when Tassimo expanded its lineup to include the two iconic brands.

An extension of the campaign focused on the specifics of the brewing with respect to water temperature, water amount, brew time, and the fact that Tassimo did not use powdered milk like another competitor. To emphasize the authenticity of the barcode, the message of this evolution concluded, "behind every barcode, there's a story." TV, online video, and print continued to deliver the story to new customers interested in the biggest innovation in coffee since the drip machines of 30 years ago.

Sources: Chris Powell, "Tassimo Touts Barcode Technology in New Campaign," *Marketing Magazine,* May 18, 2012; Kristin Laird, "Kraft Goes to Market with New Look for Tassimo," *Marketing Magazine,* June 10, 2011; Kristin Laird, "Tassimo Brings Timmy's Coffee Back into the Kitchen," *Marketing Magazine,* August 9, 2012; http://cassies.ca/entry/viewcase/4501.

Question:

1. Why is the focus of the positioning on the barcode so successful for this product category and brand?

As the opening vignette implies, advertising and all IMC tools that occur within a marketing strategy have a significant contribution toward the overall positioning of the product to selected target markets, or what is known as a market positioning strategy. However, advertising and each promotional activity has its own unique communication objectives to persuade a particular target audience. In this sense, we can examine how promotional tools and the whole promotional program influences the positioning of a brand to a designated target audience, or what is known as a brand positioning strategy.

Our investigation in this chapter—to understand positioning for both marketing strategy and marketing communication—is consistent with the distinction between target market and target audience (Chapter 3) and the importance of linking communication objectives and strategy with the marketing objectives and strategy (Chapter 5). First, we review market positioning strategy, define brand positioning strategy, and subsequently describe the brand positioning strategy decision process. We then define and illustrate the four decisions for developing a comprehensive brand positioning strategy. Finally, we explore opportunities for changing the brand positioning strategy, known as repositioning.

Positioning

In this section, we distinguish between positioning within the marketing strategy and positioning with marketing communication. We also highlight the difference between the decision a manager makes in terms of a positioning strategy and the resulting effects in terms of the position in which the target market or target audience perceives the firm or brand to be competing. We end the section with an overview of the decision-making process for a brand positioning strategy.

 ## MARKET POSITIONING STRATEGY

Any organization that wants to exchange its products or services in the marketplace successfully should have a **strategic marketing plan** to guide the allocation of its resources. A strategic marketing plan usually evolves from an organization's overall corporate strategy and serves as a guide for specific marketing programs and policies. In Chapter 1 we emphasized the importance of promotional planners using the marketing plan as a key information source to plan for marketing communication decisions. In particular, those creating ads should be familiar with their client's or organization's market positioning strategy since it gives direction for how a brand should be positioned in the promotional program.

Positioning has been defined as "the art and science of fitting the product or service to one or more segments of the broad market in such a way as to set it meaningfully apart from competition."[1] A **market positioning strategy** concerns the final decision of the market(s) in which firms wish to compete, combined with the specific elements of the marketing mix that are designed to fulfill the respective needs of the market(s). For example, many vehicle manufacturers now compete in the hybrid car market (Exhibit 6-1). Happy Planet drinks originally competed only in the healthy drink category, but now compete against Red Bull in the energy drink category.[2] Sobeys rejuvenated its entry to the discount grocery market by changing the name of Price Chopper to FreshCo. A redesign of the store's interior and colour scheme provides a new market positioning strategy with a strong emphasis on an improved assortment of fresh goods.[3]

Typically, firms write a market positioning strategy statement in their marketing plan to accurately communicate this decision. This statement provides direction for each of the four areas of decision within the marketing program development phase: product, price, distribution, and marketing communication. For example, different market segments in the personal computer (PC) industry include the home, education, science, and business markets. These segments can be even further divided. The business market consists of both small companies and large corporations; the education market can range from elementary schools to colleges and universities. A company that is marketing its products in the PC industry must decide in which

Exhibit 6-1   Many companies compete in the hybrid car market.

particular market segment or segments it wishes to compete. This decision depends on the amount and nature of competition the brand will face in a particular market.

While developing its market positioning strategy, the firm may consider many combinations of product attributes with varying price levels across different retail outlets. Alternatively, it could evaluate narrow product choices with very wide distribution and a mass advertising appeal. As these examples suggest, a firm considers as many feasible options as possible so that it does not miss a market opportunity. At this stage, the firm uses its market research and experience wisely to put together a "package of benefits" or "value offering" that will be acceptable to the target market selected. Porter Airlines entered the airline market as a regional alternative to Air Canada and WestJet; it serves 19 destinations versus 179 and 86 for the other two, respectively. Porter tried to distinguish itself with a premium travel experience by emphasizing its refined style of service delivery (Exhibit 6-2).

Once the marketing programs are developed and implemented, organizations may find results at, above, or below expectations. For example, sales or market share objectives may or may not be obtained. The reactions of consumers may be very close to what the firm intended, or they could be quite different. We define this consumer response to be the **market position** of a firm. This distinction signifies that it is not the current or past strategic plans of the marketing managers, but rather the intended or unintended consumer beliefs of the organization's marketing efforts.

To expand on these ideas, we will use shampoo products as an example. Shampoo is a fragmented market with over 30 brands measured by the Print Measurement Bureau (PMB). This research also reports 18 different characteristics of the product relating to the purpose of its use, like shining or thickening and anti-dandruff. The most-used brands in Canada, in order, are Head & Shoulders, Pantene Pro V, Herbal Essences, Dove, TRESemmé, and then salon-based brands. However, "other brand" is the most heavily used brand in PMB data. Ninety percent of the sample use shampoo on a weekly basis, 8 percent declined to answer the question, and 2 percent do not use shampoo.[4] We illustrate this market with a market position diagram, recognizing that alternative interpretations may be feasible (Figure 6-1). We graph two axes, cosmetic and therapeutic, with salon exclusivity and popular mainstream. The salon end-point represents brands originating from a salon or a brand extensively used by salons.

With a significant level of product category usage, it is not surprising to see that virtually every sector of this diagram would have brands competing, via brand name, ad imagery, product performance, packaging, and

porter
flying refined

Breeze into the Windy City.
Only Porter offers up to 6 daily non-stops between Toronto City Airport and Chicago's downtown Midway Airport.

Book online, call 1-888-619-8622 or contact your travel agent.

Sign up for VIPorter frequent flyer program
www.flyporter.com

Exhibit 6-2   Porter's entry to the airline market resulted in different ad campaigns.

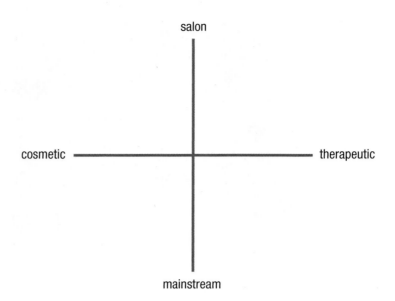

Figure 6-1

Hypothetical illustration of a market position diagram for shampoo brands

distribution location. We leave it to the reader to consider where each of the above brands may fit on these or other axes, but offer a couple of observations. Pantene Pro V implies that professionals use it with the word Pro in the brand name, and TRESemmé advertises that professional use the product as the brand moved to the consumer market after establishing itself in the business market decades ago. Head & Shoulders originally claimed itself as an anti-dandruff product but now claims benefits regarding how the shampoo makes the user's hair look and feel and has multiple formats and fragrances. Given this information, where do we think Dove and Herbal Essences would be located in this market position diagram?

The market position diagram, also known by its general term *perceptual map,* is a result of market research showing an accumulation of how all the respondents "see" the brands competing. It can also be a summary of how a manager believes consumer perceptions line up if market research is unaffordable. In conclusion, the market position diagram is entirely dependent upon clearly identifying and accurately defining the criteria for the two axes. Furthermore, multiple diagrams may be necessary if a planner desires to model three axes.

BRAND POSITIONING STRATEGY

It is tempting to believe that advertising and all other IMC tools define the market positioning strategy because all these marketing communication exposures are so publicly visible. While this may be true in certain situations, in most cases advertising and IMC campaigns typically focus on a particular message that helps consumers understand the product in comparison to other brands *within* a specific product market or category. In fact, most ads or IMC tools speak to a very specific target audience, as observed in typical marketing communication done by a bank.

A bank can have a direct-mail piece to a current customer (i.e., brand loyal) to obtain a mortgage renewal and focus the message on the ease of continuity and the good follow-up service. Or it may run a TV ad with a message of attractive interest rates and specialized options directed to customers from competing banks (i.e, favourable brand switcher). Finally, it may develop a mobile app for young adults who are beginning to buy and use new financial products and services as they mature and earn money (i.e., new category users).

These examples identify different target audiences with different competitive reference points and suggest the need to use the positioning concept appropriately in a marketing communication context that is distinct from positioning in a marketing strategy context. This notion of positioning in marketing communication is the subject of a new direction in the marketing literature,[5] and the topic to which we now turn.

Advertising practitioners consider positioning an important decision in establishing and maintaining a brand. In fact, managing a brand is so critical that the notion of branding is very topical with marketers these days; however, the original authors of the positioning concept remind us that branding cannot occur without positioning.[6] This original notion of positioning in an advertising context arose from Jack Trout and Al Ries, who distinguished between a marketer's decisions and the resulting effect in a consumer's knowledge structure.[7] Thus, in this text we use the term **brand positioning strategy** to mean the *intended* image of the product or brand relative to competing brands for a given competitive space as defined by certain product market or category characteristics.

A competitive space can be discovered with the market position diagram, as discussed previously. For example, upper left quadrant is a space where brands like Pantene Pro V and TRESemmé may be challenging for consumers, and the battle may be on more specific characteristics like we saw in the PMB data that relate to desirable hair qualities: volume, thickness, strength, smoothness, shine, and so on. The relevant dimensions of competing within a space allow managers to determine the brand positioning strategy, a key decision prior to determining the most effective selling message of advertising or other IMC tools. Exhibit 6-3 identifies a brand that competes for consumers in the specialized niche of the bottled water market.

Now consider consumer responses after being exposed to an entire IMC campaign. What do consumers feel and think about the brand after having experienced all of the messages? Do they have positive or negative feelings for the brand? What unique attributes or benefits come to mind when considering the brand? These questions pertain to the reactions consumers have to the marketing communication decisions implemented by the promotional planner. Thus, **brand position** refers to the target audience's overall assessment or image of the brand resulting from brand-related communication that tells the prospective buyer what the brand is, who it is for, and what it offers.[8]

We need to distinguish between the firm's intended brand image versus the actual brand image since both occur at different points in time and reside in different locations. The brand positioning strategy resides within the overall advertising or IMC plan, while the brand position exists within the target audience. The brand positioning strategy can be written annually or perhaps every few years depending on the company's direction. The brand position requires time, perhaps a few years, to take hold in a sufficient number of consumers before the planners will know whether the intended strategy worked. The importance of distinct vocabulary between brand positioning strategy (i.e., plan) and brand position (i.e., result) was implied by Trout and Ries many years ago and is consistent with others who have written on this topic.[9]

We now turn to our brand position diagram, where brands compete among one another more directly in a competitive space. For this we turn to the chocolate bar category. According to PMB data, this is a specific competitive space within the broader chocolate confectionary market that includes stand-up bags of wrapped chocolate, snack boxes, and bagged chocolate/candy. The broader chocolate confectionary market contains more than 100 brands, although there are duplicates with line extensions. Nevertheless, the chocolate bar category provides enough competing brands with varying characteristics such that brands manage their positioning strategy.

Exhibit 6-3 Vitaminwater competes in the enhanced water market.

Figure   6-2   Brand position by attributes—
                               illustration A

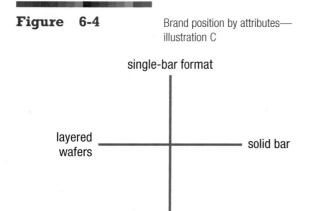

peanuts, almonds

single-bar format — unique/multi-part format

nougat, caramel

Figure   6-3   Brand position by attributes—
                               illustration B

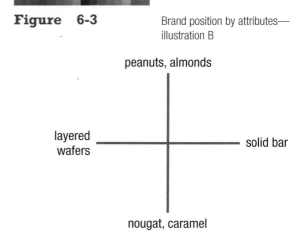

peanuts, almonds

layered wafers — solid bar

nougat, caramel

Figure   6-4   Brand position by attributes—
                               illustration C

single-bar format

layered wafers — solid bar

unique/multi-part format

Chocolate bar brands actively compete and advertise on certain **salient attributes**. For this, we suggest three possible axes: (1) single-bar format—unique/multi-part format; (2) peanuts, almonds (nut-based)—nougat, caramel; and (3) layered wafers—solid bar. While a three-dimensional brand position diagram is feasible, Figures 6-2, 6-3, and 6-4 show the individual pairs to illustrate the possibilities more easily. According to PMB, the most frequently consumed, in order, are KitKat, Coffee Crisp, Aero, Caramilk, Mars, Reese's Peanut Butter Cups, and Oh Henry!, each of which can be placed on these axes accordingly based on their attributes. We suggest that soft-centre bars like Mars and Reese's would be in the middle of the layered wafers—solid bar axis.

PMB data show that two-thirds of the sample consumed a chocolate confectionary product in the past six months and 50 percent consumed one during the past week. Clearly, a brand could consider its distinctive attributes to encourage non-users to gravitate to the product category. The attribute-based brand position diagram helps identify what the competing brands might be and gives direction on how to emphasize the distinctiveness of the attributes. For example both Reese's and Oh Henry! could target consumers who love peanuts but who do not eat chocolate bars, and specifics of the positioning are clearer if one knows which brand it is up against. Alternatively, the attribute brand position diagrams can assist the managers for the first four bars listed, since they all have a break-apart format. So if one brand tried to switch purchasers away from another brand on this feature, the approach for communicating the break-apart characteristic can be estimated more accurately. As these implications show, the brand position diagram visualizes how to consider the options for brand positioning strategy decisions, but this decision can instead be based on benefits, or a combination.

Chocolate bars also compete on certain **salient benefits**. For these, we again surmise three axes: (1) filling snack—indulgent treat; (2) individual pleasure—social sharing; and (3) pure chocolate taste—muli-flavour taste. The first axis is relatively self-explanatory as brands have competed on these aspects for decades. The individual pleasure—social dimension is relevant for the break-apart bars since the pieces can be shared, thereby signifying an interesting emotional benefit of belongingness along the lines of love for a particular consumer segment. Since one aspect of chocolate bar consumption is the flavour and sensory gratification, whether the resulting taste is mostly chocolate or a mix with others is another aspect brands may emphasize in their messages. Again, these axes are shown as three pairs in Figures 6-5, 6-6, and 6-7. Readers are encouraged to consider an alternative view and/or place the above brands accordingly to investigate the brand positioning strategy options for each brand.

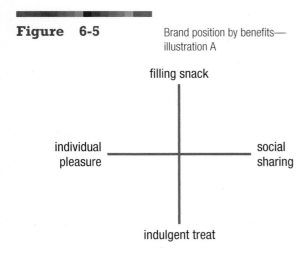

Figure   6-5   Brand position by benefits—illustration A

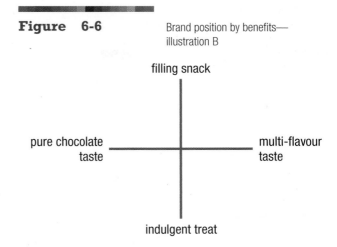

Figure   6-6   Brand position by benefits—illustration B

BRAND POSITIONING STRATEGY DECISION PROCESS

We present a five-step process for making the brand positioning strategy, adapted from other sources.[10] Chapter 1 briefly outlined this process, but here we investigate the actual steps in more detail to fully understand the brand positioning strategy decisions.

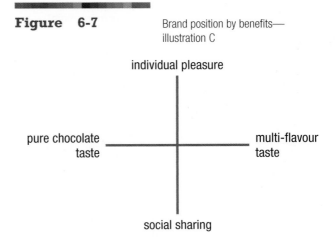

Figure   6-7   Brand position by benefits—illustration C

Develop a Market Partition   A useful approach for defining the market is to make it consistent with how consumers make a purchase decision. It is suggested that promotional planners view the market broadly as a general product category and subsequently divide the market into various sub-categories until consumers perceive brands as being relatively similar. The criteria for market partitioning include the type of product, end benefit, usage situation, and brand name. Figures 6-8 to 6-11 show a basic partition of the car market for each of these four approaches, and these simple illustrations can be expanded or altered to the decision maker's requirements. This task is important for establishing the initial parameters for identifying the most important competitors to determine a unique positioning strategy that can be communicated. A change in premium brands, otherwise known as luxury brands, is the fact that their low-end models are now priced on par with more basic brands, calling into question how marketers will plan for marketing communication with extensive overlap not previously seen in the auto market.[11]

Assess Competitors' Position   Once we define the competitors through the market partition, we then determine their respective brand positions by assessing consumers' beliefs through new or existing consumer research. Oftentimes survey research is performed to observe how consumers rate the competing brands on the relevant and important attributes and benefits that consumers use when evaluating a brand. The data from these types of surveys are used to formulate the brand position maps shown previously. Preliminary research may be necessary to identify new attributes or benefits competitors are communicating to establish their brand position. For example, cars compete on numerous attributes and benefits, and over time new product characteristics may become important and need to be added to the usual competitive profiles to accurately assess the brand positions.

Assess Brand Position   Consumer research for the promotional planner's brand is used to assess how consumers currently perceive the brand. This research would be compared with

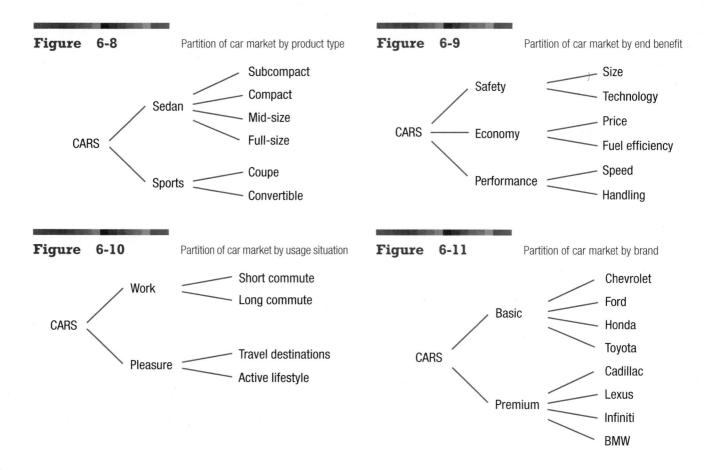

Figure   6-8   Partition of car market by product type

Figure   6-9   Partition of car market by end benefit

Figure   6-10   Partition of car market by usage situation

Figure   6-11   Partition of car market by brand

the previously determined brand positioning strategy (e.g., last year, or the prior two to four years). If current efforts are not working it may be time to consider an alternative strategy (Exhibit 6-4). Unless there is strong reason to believe a change in positioning is necessary, promotional planners are advised to maintain the current brand positioning strategy.

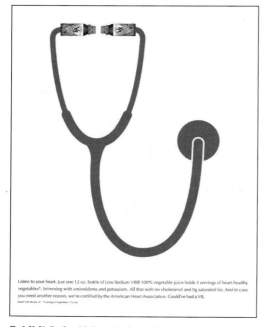

Listen to your heart. Just one 12 oz. bottle of Low Sodium V8® 100% vegetable juice holds 3 servings of heart-healthy vegetables*, brimming with antioxidants and potassium. All that with no cholesterol and 0g saturated fat. And in case you need another reason, we're certified by the American Heart Association. Could've had a V8.

©2007 CSC Brands, L.P. *3 servings of vegetables = 1½ cups.

Exhibit 6-4   V-8 revitalizes its image.

Determine Brand Positioning Strategy   Going through the first three steps should provide direction for where to establish a brand position; however, planners will often be faced with alternatives to select from. For example, Toyota previously positioned its trucks and SUVs as recreational, with messages like "I don't want to work all day," and "You belong outside." Promotional planners considered three positioning strategies along the idea of "tough" when evaluating its options for change. The first involved a "work-tough" positioning by showing the Tacoma at work on Canadian oil fields and farms. A second, "recreation-tough," would show the Tacoma engaged in off-road activities. Finally, "international-tough" intended to demonstrate the Tacoma's use throughout the world. The final choice won as the planners used live footage of Toyota trucks involved in delivering aid during international disasters to create the launch TV ad that carried the tagline "Never Quit."[12]

The remainder of this chapter presents a structure to make a well-developed brand positioning strategy decision. Managers are faced with either performing research or using subjective judgments based on experience to make the final brand positioning strategy decision among its identified alternatives. In making the decision, planners will assess whether the brand positioning strategy will be strong enough competitively and whether sufficient financial resources exist to establish the brand position over time.

Positioning for a Few Beers

For consumer products like beer, advertising and promotion play a central role in the brand positioning strategy since the product and distribution seldom or infrequently change after the product launch. In fact, many beers advertise using an authentic recipe from centuries ago! So it is no surprise to see that beers extend or revise their messages to give consumers a unique or new perspective for their brands. Molson Coors established a new positioning with its "Made From Canada" slogan. According to one executive, "The land plays a pretty significant role in all of our advertising and things that we've done." And one of those things included cause-related activities entitled "Molson Canadian Red Leaf Project," where employees and citizens planted 100,000 trees and cleaned the shorelines and urban parks in 10 communities with assistance from Tree Canada, WWF, and Evergreen. The company rewarded participants with free tickets for a concert on the event date. Summing up the experience, one remarked, "If the land is that important to Canadians and it's that important to our brand and the quality of our beer, then we should be investing in making the land better."

However, from another point of view, the project exhibited a "green" image for the brand, something that might be unexpected from a brewery. But it is a key angle for brands in many other product categories—and for Alexander Keith's, owned by competitor Labatt. A promotion encouraged purchasers to visit the Keith's Facebook page to contribute to four community green initiatives. Research indicated that consumers looked for products with a stronger commitment to the environment with less energy consumption or damage to the environment.

The other important characteristic communicated is "authenticity," exemplified with ads for Molson Export that related the story of John Molson arriving in Canada in the late 1700s to start North America's oldest brewery at the age of 22. "For a country that is so much younger than our neighbour, I think it just shows how much beer is part our culture and our history," offered the chief marketing officer for Molson Coors. While the land angle may be distinctive and unique, the authenticity attribute is associated with other brands, like Alexander Keith's. The company celebrates the originator's birthday each year by retelling the legendary story of his landing in Canada to start his brewery in 1820.

Upstart and independent Great Western Brewing Company tells of the story behind its Original 16 premium ale, where the 16 refers to the number of employees who took ownership and rescued the small plant from being closed when Molson bought the previous owner Carling O'Keefe. Sixteen video messages on the company's Internet site captured the process, from the anxiety of closure to the celebration of ownership! The agency suggested the messages conveyed that the brand was "genuine" and "authentic" and allowed people beyond Saskatchewan to understand the history of the beer. Sleeman Breweries emphasized its history right from day one, with stories of how John Sleeman reclaimed the brewery his grandfather had previously run decades ago. More recently, the brand claimed it was "notoriously good," in reference to its bootlegging history during Prohibition. Across these four brands, we see similar emphasis on the authenticity angle, yet with very different creative approaches—a key point in marketing communication, where brands may compete directly but with different imagery in the execution.

Sources: Rebecca Harris, "Molson Coors," *Marketing Magazine,* November 28, 2011, pp. 31, 36; Simon Houpt, "How Green Is Your Beer?" *The Globe and Mail,* August, 11, 2011; Simon Houpt, "How about a History Lesson with That Lager?" *The Globe and Mail,* May, 12, 2011; Richard Blackwell, "A Beer Baron's Unshakable Ties," *The Globe and Mail,* February 28, 2011, p. B13.

Questions:

1. Why are these advertising claims so important for marketing these brands of beer?

Implement Brand Positioning Strategy The content of the advertising message, its creative strategy, and creative tactics can be formulated once the brand positioning strategy is established. The implementation of other promotional communication tools also requires message and creativity development. For example, prior to launching a public relations or publicity campaign, a marketer would specify the positioning of its brand to its intended target audience before deciding upon the exact content of its message and how he or she would creatively present it. IMC Perspective 6-1 summarizes how a few beer companies implemented their brand positioning strategy.

Monitor Brand Positioning Strategy   Once a brand position has been established, we want to monitor how well it is being maintained. Tracking studies measure the image of the brand over time. Changes in consumers' perceptions can be determined, with any slippage immediately noted and reacted to. In the Toyota example, key communication effects improved substantially during the first seven months, indicating strong positioning. Brand awareness gained from 83 percent to 95 percent, advertising awareness rose from 5 percent to 19 percent, and purchase intention increased from 22 percent to 40 percent. Many consumer perception ratings rose significantly and surpassed competitors. For example, more than 70 percent of the consumers surveyed rated the Tacoma as high quality, dependable, well-built, and trusted. Sales nearly doubled in a year, with market share moving to the 14 to 16 percent range. These remarkable results occurred with Chevrolet re-branding its S-10 to Colorado and the Dodge Dakota and Ford Ranger spending more money on advertising than the Tacoma.[13]

L03 Brand Positioning Strategy Decisions

The essence of positioning the brand in the context of advertising is to clearly indicate where the brand is competing, with whom it is competing, how it is competing, and finally why consumers will purchase the brand. Each of these questions must be addressed through four decisions within the brand positioning strategy: market definition, differential advantage, target audience brand attitude, and consumer purchase motive.

MARKET DEFINITION

A primary decision for positioning is how the promotional planners define the market and where they intend for the brand to compete with its benefit claims. The market partition illustrations showed that brands compete against other brands on end benefits, brand name, usage situation, and product category. One purpose of advertising is to contribute to developing a perceived advantage over competing brands within the competitive space. Thus, each of these offer tremendous opportunity to communicate benefit claims and establish a perceived differential advantage.

Positioning by End Benefit   A common approach to positioning is setting the brand apart from competitors on the basis of its primary end benefit offered; a brand may be positioned on multiple benefits if necessary. Becel's health benefit has been portrayed in different ways over the years, and Exhibit 6-5 shows one example where its flavour is also claimed. Marketers also attempt to identify salient attributes that are important to consumers and are the basis for making a purchase decision. In this case, the positioning focuses on these specific characteristics and the benefits are not directly claimed in the message. Advertisers require good research and reasons for justifying this kind of positioning recommendation, because moving toward a specific attribute or benefit precludes messages regarding other attributes and benefits.

In all of its marketing communication, Roots Canada sticks with the singular focus of being Canadian. All imagery and messaging reflects and reinforces this key

Exhibit 6-5   Becel's health claims remain strong with product extensions.

attribute about the company. In fact, the brand takes pride in the fact that much of its products are produced in Canada, providing important support for this authentic attribute claim.[14] Alternatively, a pure benefit focus can be seen with Reebok Canada's effort as part of the global "Live with Fire" positioning. An ad with John Tavares, Matt Duchene, and Maxime Talbot promoted the new Reebok Training collection of footwear and apparel. The direction of the campaign attempted to allow consumers to experience the "passion, intent, and purpose" benefits associated with using the new product line.[15]

While we refer to either attribute or benefit positioning in this discussion, marketers will also make a direct link between a particular attribute and the derived benefit, or they may highlight the attribute and allow the target audience to interpret the benefit. Activia's marketing communication highlighted the unique probiotic culture in its yogurt and the resulting vitality that continued consumption produced with its interesting ads that featured boxed frames on people's stomachs as they danced and ate the product.[16] This approach is often done in the car market, and is how the Lexus IS F competed in performance by showing extensive visuals of the engine in many forms of digital media.[17]

Positioning by Brand Name

Marketers often use price/quality characteristics to position their brands. One way they do it is with ads that reflect the image of a high-quality brand where cost, while not irrelevant, is considered secondary to the quality benefits derived from using the brand. Premium brands positioned at the high end of the market use this approach to positioning. For example, one might speculate that much of Apple's advertising presumed a positioning by brand name.

Another way to use price/quality characteristics for positioning is to focus on the quality or value offered by the brand at a very competitive price. For example, Lands' End uses this strategy by suggesting that quality can be affordable. Remember that although price is an important consideration, the product quality must be comparable to, or even better than, competing brands for the positioning strategy to be effective. Canada Dry Ginger Ale rediscovered the importance of positioning by brand name as it reminded consumers that it contained ginger! While this obvious fact appears to not warrant advertising, the brand obtained good mileage as consumers looked at ginger as a healthy ingredient to consume in one's diet.[18] The Sobe ad in Exhibit 6-6 shows the product's positioning based on thrilling flavour.

Positioning by Usage Situation

Another way to communicate a specific image or position for a brand is to associate it with a specific use. Molson M distanced itself from mainstream beer advertising by positioning it as premium beer for a sophisticated night out.[19] While this strategy is often used to enter a market based on a particular use, it is also an effective way to expand the situational usage of a product. For example, Nutella advertised and promoted its hazelnut spread as a nutritious part of a wholesome breakfast since it contained protein. While previously viewed more as a chocolate treat, the association of breakfast provided a new usage approach for the brand.[20] Finally, empirical research suggests that marketing communication plays a strong role in consumers adopting new uses.[21] The Intuit ad in Exhibit 6-7 advertises its specific use for small business owners.

Exhibit 6-6   Sobe positions its brand as being thrillingly delicious.

Exhibit 6-7   Intuit offers products for small business usage.

Exhibit 6-8 Via competes with other forms of transportation.

Positioning by Product Category Often, the competition for a product comes from outside the product category. For example, airlines know that while they compete with other airlines, trains and buses are also viable alternatives. Via Rail has positioned itself as an alternative to airplanes, citing cost savings, enjoyment, and other advantages (Exhibit 6-8). Rather than positioning against another brand, an alternative strategy is to position the brand against another product category. V8 promotes drinking one's vegetables (Exhibit 6-9). Craft beers of Ontario made in-roads toward the higher-end spirits with their placement in the provincial alcohol retailer. Extensive messaging from the Liquor Control Board of Ontario and the Ontario Craft Brewers Association looked beyond the beer market to carve out a niche.[22]

DIFFERENTIAL ADVANTAGE

Brand benefit claims embodied in the positioning and represented in the ads contribute to the differential advantage for a brand. While it is generally expected that a brand positioning strategy should take a differential positioning approach and have a product benefit focus, we highlight situations where brands do not follow this pattern.

Differential vs. Central Positioning In the previous section, we mentioned the importance of advertising contributing to the perceived differential advantage for the brand. This is true for most brands. For example, Reitmans, a women's clothing retailer, distances itself from other high-fashion stores with its many campaigns that reinforce its positioning, "Designed for real life."[23] However, market circumstances allow brands to claim a central position within the product category. A central brand positioning strategy is possible when the brand can claim and deliver on the most salient benefits. This may be a function of the brand being the market share leader, achieving success during the growth stage of the product life cycle, or having unique brand characteristics that essentially define the category. It could be suggested that Nike takes a central position for many of its messages across several product categories, especially with its slogan Just Do It (Exhibit 6-10).

In another market context being the first brand in a product category is a good start, but research suggests it is not a guarantee; in some categories the second and third entries after the initial pioneer have also established strong positions. Yves Rocher, a pioneer in the plant-based skin-care category, lost its dominance as other brands claimed these ingredients as important in their ads (e.g., Aveeno). So the French brand ensured that its advertising, and all other marketing offers (e.g., store, spa, information lab), reflected its botanical roots to re-confirm its central position.[24] Finally, sometimes brands attempt to take a central position in a subcategory, as seen in Exhibit 6-11.

Exhibit 6-9 V8 positions itself as a drink that substitutes for vegetables.

Brand Benefit vs. User Positioning We have thus far implied that most positioning decisions involve unique and differential benefit claims that the brand can deliver. The market partition and competitive analysis gives promotional planners the opportunity to identify and determine the most important ones to claim in advertising. For example, Lay's potato chip ads extol the virtues of using 100 percent Canadian potatoes.[25] The premise of the strategy focused on getting back to the core of the product, presumably to differentiate from other snacks with less pure ingredients. The ad for Burt's Bees in Exhibit 6-12 is an example of a **brand benefit positioning** as it differentiates the lip moisturizer from other product formats.

While a brand benefit approach is useful for many product categories and brands, unique situations allow for a **user positioning**. This was the previous approach for Lay's, which challenged consumers to eat only one chip. Often, a brand is positioned by association with a particular user or group of users; an example is the DC ad shown in Exhibit 6-13. This campaign emphasizes identification or association with a specific group, in this case skateboard enthusiasts. A user positioning strategy occurs in situations where the individual is motivated for social or individual reasons, and the ads emphasize how good the consumer feels while using the brand (Exhibit 6-14). Advertising for Samsung in Canada moved from a product focus to a user focus with its "Infinite Possibilities" messages as consumers became more accustomed to accepting the Android system.[26]

Interestingly, Molson Canadian returned to ads with the "I Am Canadian" theme, signalling user positioning while at the same time maintaining its more current brand benefit positioning "Made from Canada." Executives saw it feasible to introduce a dual positioning approach since the former lingered with consumers after its previous runs from 1994 to 1998, and 2000 to 2005.[27]

CIBC emphasized a user positioning in its campaign to offer customers additional products and services with the "It's Worth a Talk" message. Each execution focuses on a key financial planning issue, like "How can I pay less tax?" and "Is there an easier way to understand my financial picture?" These kinds of questions are intended to spark interest in customers to forge a stronger relationship between themselves and CIBC's financial advisers.[28] And higher-education institutions have entered into advertising for new students each year: Brock

Exhibit 6-10 Nike likely takes a central positioning in much of its marketing communication.

Exhibit 6-11 Lipton tries to establish itself in the carbonated green tea category.

Exhibit 6-12 Positioning that focuses on the benefits.

Exhibit 6-13   DC positions by product user.

University's creative and daring visual effort, with a focus on how students can study what they desire, is again representative of a user positioning.[29] The new marketing communication for the G Series raises interesting questions regarding the first two positioning decisions, as shown in IMC Perspective 6-2.

TARGET AUDIENCE BRAND ATTITUDE

Previously in this chapter we identified the concepts of salient attributes and salient benefits. This notion is based on the idea that consumers may hold a number of different beliefs about brands in any product or service category. However, not all of these beliefs are activated in forming an attitude. Beliefs concerning specific attributes or benefits that are activated and form the basis of an attitude are referred to as **salient beliefs**. Marketers should identify these salient beliefs and understand how the saliency varies among different target audiences, over time, and across different consumption situations. Marketers can use a specific model to develop persuasive brand positioning strategies since it guides which attributes and benefits to claim in advertising.

Brand Attitude Model   Consumer researchers and marketing practitioners use multiattribute attitude models to study consumer attitudes.[30] A **multiattribute attitude model** views an attitude object, such as a product or brand, as possessing a number of attributes that provide the basis on which consumers form their attitudes. According to this model, consumers have beliefs about specific brand attributes and attach different levels of importance to these attributes. Using this approach, an attitude toward a particular brand can be represented as

$$A_B = \sum_{i=1}^{n} B_i \times E_i$$

where A_B = attitude toward a brand
  B_i = beliefs about the brand's performance on attribute i
  E_i = importance attached to attribute i
  n = number of attributes considered

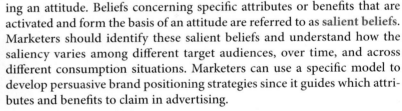

Exhibit 6-14   Positioning that focuses on the product user.

For example, a consumer may have beliefs (B_i) about various brands of toothpaste on certain attributes. One brand may be perceived as having

G Series Is Positioning in a New Direction

Launched in 1965 and rebranded to G in 2009, Gatorade has reconfigured its brand with the new G Series in the past few years. Despite holding 70 percent of the sports drink market, the brand looked to strengthen its hold with an entirely new market positioning strategy. From a product perspective, the G Series featured Prime, Perform, and Recover. Prime included carbs and B vitamins and was to be consumed prior to a workout. Perform represented the original Gatorade (or its low-calorie variant G2). Post-workout consumption included Recover, a protein- and carb-based drink. The offering also featured G Series Pro, an enriched version designed for serious athletes and sold in specialty sports stores.

The impetus for the new line resulted from research at the Gatorade Sports Science Institute that identified a need for replenishment at all three steps when consumers played sports. "What we're doing is redefining the core of what Gatorade is. Everything we do is going to be about before, during and after athletic activity; G Series is the overarching concept," asserted a lead director on the launch.

Executives saw the new G Series as moving from a hydration brand to a sports nutrition brand. Key messaging to consumers to establish the new brand position included numerous activities. First off, an event that invited 90 influencers—athletic trainers, educators, pro athletes, and nutritionists—exhibited the benefits of the product through a collection of seminars and demonstrations in a performance lab that garnered 13 million media impressions.

To follow up the event, G tracked the training of 65 athletes using the product and transformed these experiences into relevant messages for consumers when media messaging subsequently occurred. G provided the product for Hockey Canada players at different levels of competition and filmed their usage experiences. These clips became part of a YouTube presentation of testimonials. G also moved to less traditional sports, like mixed martial arts (MMA), and employed MMA fighter Georges St-Pierre as a spokesperson. While the move appeared risky at first due to the perceived violence of the sport, executives forged on with the decision when research showed its popularity over baseball.

St-Pierre is an athlete with a colourful personality and a loyal social media following; he has developed a celebrity-like persona that transcends the sport into popular culture. His sponsorship agents tested his image and found that St-Pierre rated highly on trust, sexiness, personality, and toughness—a powerful combination attractive to many advertisers including G. "Georges epitomized what the brand stood for in terms of athleticism and the heart, hustle and soul of the brand," commented one G executive.

To deliver and communicate the value of the product, G introduced a nutrition centre display in 145 Sport Chek stores. The display included the G Series and assorted sports merchandise (bottles, towels, coolers). G saw the display as a key approach for reinforcing the brand in the sports nutrition market, located right where athletes buy sports products. G trained and educated Sport Chek personnel to ensure the right message got to athletes, coaches, and other experts while they shopped.

Sources: Melinda Mattos, "Gatorade Primes for G Series," *Strategy,* March 1, 2011, p. 14; Matt Semansky, "Gatorade to Go Beyond Beverages with G Series," *Marketing Magazine,* August 18, 2010; Jonathan Paul, "Gatorade's Sport Chek Nutrition Centre Scores," *Strategy,* January 17, 2012; Susan Krashinsky, "Building a Brand When the Brand Is a Person," *The Globe and Mail,* June 2012, p. B3.

Questions:

1. Does it make sense for G to represent the brand beyond the attribute of hydration?
2. What potential risks will G encounter with this new move?

fluoride and thus preventing cavities, tasting good, and helping control tartar buildup. Another brand may not be perceived as having these attributes, but consumers may believe it performs well on other attributes such as freshening breath and whitening teeth.

To predict attitudes, one must know how much importance consumers attach to each of these attributes (E_i). For example, parents purchasing toothpaste for their children may prefer a brand that performs well on cavity prevention, a preference that leads to a more favourable attitude toward the first brand. Teenagers and young adults may prefer a brand that freshens their breath and makes their teeth white and thus prefer the second brand.

Brand Attitude Persuasion   Multiattribute models help marketers diagnose the beliefs that underlie consumers' evaluations of a brand and the importance of attributes or benefits. This analysis guides communication strategies, like maintaining attitudes of current customers or changing attitudes of non-customers. A study demonstrated that research examining attribute ratings of customers and non-customers provided important direction for improving the marketing communication strategy for a European telecommunications firm.[31] This persuasion occurs when brands claim attributes or benefits in marketing communication, which is up to the discretion of the brand's decision makers. For example, while it is popular to claim "green" or "sustainable" with a brand, not all companies decide to make the claim as part of their messaging.[32] Thus, the multiattribute model shows how marketers can persuade attitudes of target audiences regarding brand characteristics they wish to emphasize.

Influence Attribute Belief   The first strategy is to identify an attribute or benefit that is important and communicate how well the brand performs. In situations where consumers do not perceive the marketer's brand as possessing an important attribute or the belief strength is low, advertising strategies may be targeted at changing the belief rating; this approach appears to be relevant for Cashmere in Exhibit 6-15. Even when belief strength is high, advertising may be used to increase the rating of a brand on an important attribute. The Harvey's campaign for grill-cooked hamburgers illustrates this approach. Other quick-service food retailers focused on fast drive-through or convenient locations, along with enhanced menus with healthier foods. Harvey's appeared disadvantaged in comparison and faced declining sales and a reduced number of franchises. The grill attribute positioning conjured both functional benefits (e.g., fresh, natural, healthy) and emotional benefits (e.g., outdoor BBQ, male bonding). The positioning succeeded, with unaided awareness moving from 13 percent to 22 percent, key brand attitude measures improving, purchase intention rising from 21 percent to 38 percent, and negative sales growth of 3 percent reversed to positive growth of 2 percent.[33] The Molson M example cited earlier focused on the new micro-carbonation and unique colour of the beer, an interesting combination of attributes to position on.

Influence Attribute Importance   Marketers attempt to influence consumer attitudes by changing the relative importance of a particular attribute. This second strategy involves getting consumers to attach more importance to the attribute in forming their attitude toward the brand. Marketers using this strategy want to increase the importance of an attribute their particular brand has. The print ads for Jergens Ultra Care moisturizer highlight the importance to a woman of regularly applying lotion all over her body. The positioning was intended to demonstrate that moisturizing was as important as all the other beauty activities that women engage in every day. The main message suggested that women "Take care of what you wear every day" with a visual showing the lotion on a woman's body, and obviously associated a woman's skin with her wardrobe. The positioning was initiated in Quebec as the brand underachieved significantly compared to other parts of Canada. Research indicated that women from Quebec did not separate beauty and skin care from health. This insight suggested that new users could be attracted to the brand if the ads conveyed the

Exhibit 6-15   Cashmere associates its brand name with the attributes of its namesake to convey softness.

sensuality of moisturized skin. A 50 percent increase in sales in Quebec allowed the brand's positioning to be extended in English rather than continuing with the planned U.S. ads.[34]

Add New Attribute Belief The third strategy for influencing consumer attitudes is to add or emphasize a new attribute that consumers can use in evaluating a brand. Marketers do this by focusing on additional benefits or consequences associated with using the brand that have not been communicated previously. Exhibit 6-16 is an ad for Mott's Fruitsations, with enhanced nutrients for bone health. Wonder+, a line extension of the famous Wonder bread, needed to communicate that it had the same great taste as the original, but that it had the nutrition of whole wheat bread. The new brand attempted to influence lapsed users of Wonder bread due to the perception that white bread was no longer healthy. Yet at the same time, managers knew that the message had to reinforce the attitude of loyal customers. Adding the health benefit worked, with clever imagery of twins eating both types of bread and believing that they both taste the same, yet one is now whole wheat. The positioning of this advertising produced significant gains for all communication effects and sales.[35]

Influence Attribute Belief of Competitor Brand A final strategy marketers use is to change consumer beliefs about the attributes of competing brands or product categories. This strategy has become much more common with the increase in comparative advertising, where marketers compare their brands to competitors' on specific product attributes. An example of this is the comparative ad shown in Exhibit 6-17. With a stronger understanding of health, Canadian are more concerned with health and food manufacturers responded with more emphasis on the ingredients of their products in terms of natural, authentic, and real. These healthier claims spawned growth in direct comparisons on an attribute by attribute basis in many categories.[36]

A battle by telecommunications firms demonstrates how brands compete this way. Rogers asked consumers to take the "Rogers home phone challenge." Using a dual-coloured couch as a visual—red for Rogers and blue for Bell—the ads claimed price was the only difference in the services with quality being equal. Rogers entered the home phone market, a traditional Bell strength, and intended the ad as a suggestion for consumers to comparison shop. Bell shot back with the same imagery, and extended its end of the couch to defend the price claim. It also promoted its 3G network and HD channels and moved to defend its price and quality position with its own blue couch, with five blue cushions and one red cushion. The message was, "Get more than Rogers for less than Rogers." Another battle emerged in the courts when Telus sued Rogers for the latter's claims of its wireless service having "The fastest and most reliable network" and "Canada's fastest network: Two times faster than any other." A judge ordered Rogers to remove the "fastest" and "most reliable" claims on all of its marketing

Exhibit 6-16   Mott's highlights the importance of strong bones via its Fruitsations brand.

Exhibit 6-17   Kyocera tries to influence beliefs of competitor brands.

communication. As a result, Rogers discarded approximately $3 million worth of promotional material already produced and erected. Rogers switched its claim to "Canada's reliable network," dropping the word "most." At the same time, Rogers sued Bell for the latter's inaccurate claim of the "Largest, fastest and most reliable" and "The best and most powerful" network—and subsequently won.[37]

CONSUMER PURCHASE MOTIVE

Since positioning involves presenting the brand's benefit claims to a target audience, the portrayal of the benefits influences how consumers will respond to the brand's delivery and whether the target audience perceives them as important. The portrayal of benefits is reflected by the purchase motivation associated with the brand. Thus, the purchase motivation of the target audience is another important decision for the brand positioning strategy.

Importance of Purchase Motives   As we suggested with the Harvey's attribute positioning, given the content of the ad, the underlying reason for enjoying a grilled hamburger appears to be the taste sensation. However, another perspective is that it could reflect healthier eating compared to fried hamburgers, since less fat is retained in the meat and consequently less fat is consumed, so consumers can feel better about their dietary choices. This connection between the cooking attribute and healthier eating could have been communicated with subtle changes in the ads of the current campaign. Thus, the attribute positioning still requires the right kind of motivation or reason for purchase demonstrated in the ad to be completely successful.

Keep in mind that the reasons for the Harvey's hamburger purchase are quite distinct: the sensory enjoyment of the hamburger versus the individual accomplishment of eating properly. We highlight these two ideas since they are two of eight basic consumer purchase motives that are more managerially useful to guide the brand positioning strategy decision within Rossiter and Percy's framework we have discussed previously. Figure 6-12 summarizes these motives into two types consistent with psychological theory.

Informational motives are negatively based since the consumer perceives their current consumption situation as a deficit in which the purchase of the product would minimize the shortfall and bring the consumer a neutral or normal state. Exhibit 6-18 suggests an informational motive for non-users. **Transformational motives** imply consumers perceive their consumption situation as requiring improvement from a neutral state. Negative- and positive-oriented motives are consistent with psychological theories of motivation and are similar to Maslow's theory—however, there is no implied hierarchy.

Informational Motives   Problem-removal motives reflect consumption situations where consumers perceive a problem, for example dandruff, and seek a product that resolves the problem, like anti-dandruff shampoo. Many products in this category have emphasized this motive in their ads while attempting to highlight a unique attribute or benefit positioning. However, ads for Head & Shoulders currently in Canada have mentioned the problem while emphasizing how good one's hair feels after using their anti-dandruff shampoo, thus reflecting a different primary motive beyond the initial problem removal. This is the reason for connecting the purchase motive shown in the ad to the brand positioning strategy—it identifies the

Figure   6-12

Eight basic consumer purchase motives

Informational Motives	Transformational Motives
Problem removal	Sensory gratification
Problem avoidance	Intellectual stimulation or mastery
Incomplete satisfaction	Social approval
Mixed approach-avoidance	
Normal depletion	

particular way to communicate effectively with a target audience that the brand has profiled in great detail. In contrast, problem avoidance motives occur when consumers anticipate a problem if they do not take preemptive action through the purchase of a product. Insurance advertising typically addresses this as a motive as the messages show the consequences of not having coverage, or not having the right type or amount of coverage. These two examples for removal and avoidance are fairly self-evident; their application to specific brands requires unique executions so that the idea of selling the category does not dominate and the brand effects are not achieved.

Incomplete satisfaction motives are based on the consumer perceptions that they are not fully satisfied with their current brand choice and are seeking a better product. With its expanded product offerings which allowed it to compete head-on against major banks, ING moved from its old "Save Your Money" approach to "It's time to stop banking in the past" as its ads conveyed its competitors as unreceptive and not very innovative.[38] Such a message conceivably resonates with disgruntled customers of other financial institutions. Similarly, Mobilicity aggressively pointed out the shortcomings of the "Big 3" mobile providers with executions from its "Now That's Smart" positioning.[39]

Mixed approach-avoidance motives are active for consumers in purchase situations where they enjoy some elements of a product but dislike other parts and are seeking alternative solutions. Van Houtte positions its brand as being a "Master Roaster since 1919" and the Montreal-based gourmet coffee company released a series of educational videos on its blog and many social media vehicles. This historical and anthropological approach provides an air of authenticity of its beans and roasting skills thereby potentially swaying consumers who may feel that other brands have less of these important characteristics.[40] Mr. Lube advertised to owners that they did not need to bring their vehicles to dealerships for all services, suggesting that the target audience might have mixed feelings about being completely loyal to a dealership.[41]

Consumers regularly require a product because they have none on hand, and so normal depletion as a reason for purchase is an almost-everyday situation; however, it is not a viable option for a primary brand positioning strategy. A message focusing on a reminder purchase when a consumer does not have the product is featured in seasonal purchases. For example, gardening products in the spring and school supplies in the fall are two obvious ad messages we commonly see. In essence, a normal depletion motive is not a long-term strategy; however, it is useful for short-term situations and reaching particular target audiences at a particular point in time to maximize total sales during a year.

Transformational Motives As the term implies, sensory gratification motives are predicated on the product providing a positive experience via one of the five senses. The ad for Nestlé Mousse conveys the sensual enjoyment of eating this unique chocolate experience (Exhibit 6-19). Clearly, this is a valuable approach for many types of products, but it is important to focus on the right aspect with the right reference point. Newfoundland and Labrador Tourism's "Find Yourself" campaign captured the sensory

Exhibit 6-18   WD40 advertises the many uses of its product for solving problems.

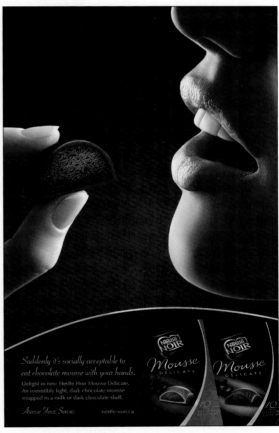

Exhibit 6-19   Nestlé conveys the sensual enjoyment of chocolate consumption.

Exhibit 6-20   Splat gives its customers a cool new look to be proud of!

experience of being in the province through an exquisite portrayal of its landscape and culture, and garnered the CASSIES Grand Prix for 2012. The breathtaking scenery and delightful storylines bring a feeling of being there instantly, providing a prototypical example of communicating transformational motives.[42]

Intellectual stimulation or mastery is an individual motive linked to an element of self-improvement through the purchase of a particular product. The marketing communication agency Sid Lee of Montreal, the global agency of record for Adidas, moved toward this motive in its messaging with the "All In" campaign. The wellness message associated with its sports gear encouraged consumers toward health, fitness, and achievement within the active sports community.[43]

Personal recognition is suggested with the social approval motive, whereby consumers are motivated to purchase certain products or brands because consumers aspire to be accepted in certain social groups; Exhibit 6-20 provides an example in the form of an unconventional hair colour. Women's fashion boutique Aritzia eschews traditional advertising, however its extensive use of public relations via influential bloggers, social media conversations, and celebrities wearing its fashions at store events all suggest a subtle connection for social approval. Its prominent placement of a flagship store on Fifth Avenue in New York City carries forth the boutique impression it strives to maintain in the market.[44]

(L04) Brand Repositioning Strategy

Developing a new brand positioning strategy for an established brand is referred to as repositioning and the reasons for the change are discovered in the situation analysis. For example, marketing objectives such as sales or share may be below forecast, or advertising claims from competitors may threaten the current strategy. Repositioning is often difficult to achieve because of ingrained consumer understanding of market structure and established brand attitudes. The options for altering the brand positioning strategy typically focus on the four topics previously defined: market definition, differential advantage, target audience, and a salient motive. Each of these is applied subsequently after identifying the communication issue for a number of recent CASSIES winners. Further details of the examples provided in this section are available at Cassies.ca.

IMPORTANCE OF REPOSITIONING

The situational analysis in terms of consumer, competition, company, market, and environment may all signal the need for a brand moving from its existing brand positioning strategy to a new one. This analysis should reveal which of these are most critical and help identify the marketing communication issue the promotional plan will address. Figure 6-13 summarizes the origin of the repositioning strategy of the CASSIES winners that we now review.

Competition   A brand's repositioning is often driven from competitive dynamics. Dove's research proved to managers that the brand appeared to be a "latecomer" to the personal care market, in which tremendous innovation had occurred in the preceding years from Procter

Figure   6-13   Critical analysis guiding repositioning decisions

Competition	Company	Consumer	Market	Environment
Dove	Canadian 67	Shreddies	Tetley Herbal Tea	Tourism
McDonald's	Cashmere	Subaru Outback	Reactine	McCain
Scotiabank	Philly Cream Cheese	Loblaw	Vespa	Hellman's

Source: Summarized from cases located on Cassies.ca

& Gamble and other entrants like Nivea, Aveeno, and Jergens. While McDonald's invented the concept of a quick-service restaurant chain offering breakfast, it faced increased competition from coffee locations now offering breakfast sandwiches (e.g., copies of the original Egg McMuffin). McDonald's weak reputation for coffee quality also made the task of encouraging consumers to consider the chain as an option for their first meal of the day even more difficult. And banks face the challenge of encouraging switching from one bank to another for increased growth, however many of the positioning strategies appear very similar and Scotiabank looked to differentiate itself with its "Richer Than You Think" campaign.

Company   Company-sourced factors can be an impetus for repositioning. While in some respects Molson introduced a new brand with Canadian 67, it replaced the previous Canadian Light and required the "re-launched" brand to develop a unique positioning distinctive from the popular Coors Light. Kruger Products (formerly Scott Paper) faced a difficult repositioning task when its licence from Kimberly-Clark ran out for the use of the highly successful Cottonelle brand in the bathroom tissue category. This looked even more challenging in the face of competition from Royale and Charmin, not to mention the expected "introduction" of Cottonelle after Kruger had put both the Cashmere and Cottonelle brand name on the package and ads for a period of time before the expiration. Philly Cream Cheese dominated the cream cheese market and its sales penetration for breakfast consumption had peaked with no room for growth, so the brand's repositioning strategy moved toward showing consumers how to use the product in cooking everyday meals for dinner.

Consumer   Brands like Shreddies, Subaru, and Loblaws all saw declines in sales as consumers appeared to no longer gravitate to them. Shreddies experienced a 2 percent per annum decline for over 15 years without any advertising support prior to its award-winning Diamond Shreddies campaign that showed the "new" product by simply rotating the "old" product 45 degrees. Subaru Outback sales declined by over 50 percent during a seven-year time period; it repositioned the brand with its ad suggesting that consumers deserve to be outdoors more. For a period of time, Loblaws declined steadily and research indicated that consumers seemed to be "living in the past" with the brand which culminated in corporate losses. To reverse the decline, it rejuvenated the well-known President's Choice brand featuring president Galen Weston as the spokesperson, much like the strategy of 25 years ago when then-president David Nichol established the brand.

Market   Tetley saw a substantial decline in the herbal tea market at 2 percent per year with the growth of other types of tea when it repositioned by associating its flavours to different moods a consumer may have prior to consumption, thereby offering the perfect solution. Reactine needed to reposition its brand as the market shifted to increased use of other product formats. Vespa needed to encourage consumers in Canada to accept the idea of buying a scooter for travel as done in Europe; in short, its repositioning had to delve into developing the market further.

Environment   The Canadian Tourism Commission and Newfoundland & Labrador Tourism both faced potential further declines in travel to Canada (from other countries) and to the province (from other provinces) during the recession and slow economic growth that

Exhibit 6-21   Hellmann's sponsored local gardens to support its Real Food Movement.

followed, which necessitated new positioning strategies. Both McCain and Hellmann's moved in a direction of health and natural food in their repositioning as consumer trends in living within a healthier lifestyle took hold.

MARKET DEFINITION

Markets are partitioned by end benefit, brand name, usage situation, and product category. One possibility for repositioning is that the brand defines its market within a new partition or reconstructs the partition favourably through its messaging so that consumers understand how brands are competing in an entirely different manner. We look at an example for each option derived from Figure 6-13.

End Benefit   Both McCain and Hellmann's defined the market by end benefit. Since each sold a variety of product categories under these umbrella brand names, the latter two market definitions are unlikely candidates (usage situation, product category). With the increased health requirements in food on the part of consumers, the healthy positioning that both brands adhered to suggests this as the most reasonable instead of brand name. Health is a broad enough end benefit that permitted the positioning to be creatively executed in many ways over time. Hellmann's "Real Food Movement" embodied the health benefit through the consumption of healthy food (Exhibit 6-21) with Hellmann's products; a key aspect of all their products. "It's All Good" by McCain signalled the brand's emphasis on authentic and natural ingredients in all of its food products.

Brand Name   Cashmere's dilemma of repositioning its product with a new brand name suggests it defined the marketing along this partition. The initial communication traced the evolution of the name change from Cottonelle to Cashmere (Exhibit 6-22). Subsequent ads connected the brand name of Cashmere to what cashmere material feels like. Maintaining the brand name forefront in the positioning proved successful since the brand retained it strength when others may have faltered. In fact, the "new" Cashmere retained its leadership position after a few years and withstood the market entrance of the "new Cottonelle."

Usage Situation   Philadelphia cream cheese continued with the same angel imagery that had established the brand for many years; however, the repositioning that occurred in a new campaign clearly addressed the idea of situational usage by educating consumers on how to cook with the product, notably for making dinner. Previous TV ads introduced the angel's good-looking sidekick Albert, and in these new executions he taught the angel how to cook with *Philly*. In the end the angel giggles as she says, "Albert cooks with *Philly* a lot. Now I can enjoy *Philly*—and Albert—more often!"

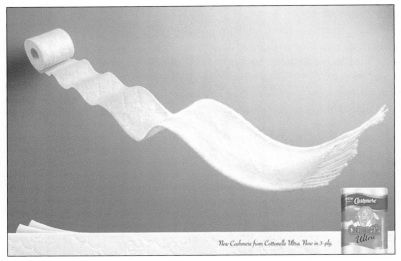

New Cashmere from Cottonelle Ultra. Now in 3-ply.

Exhibit 6-22   Cashmere highlighted its brand name for many years during the brand name transition.

Product Category   Molson 67 encouraged those drinking other alcohol, wine, and mixed drinks to switch to the brand due to its much lower calories. The brand clearly positioned itself against another category with ads that showed how small other drinks would be if they had 67 calories (Exhibit 6-23). This is much different than the positioning of other light beers and the previous Canadian Light positioning that emphasized to current beer drinkers the benefits of drinking a light beer over regular beer. However, the "guyet" ads signal another repositioning that changes the market definition.

Exhibit 6-23 Drinks with 67 calories would be considerably smaller, unlike Canadian 67 beer.

DIFFERENTIAL ADVANTAGE

One possibility for repositioning is to move from differential to central or vice versa, or to move from a product focus to a user focus or vice versa. Most often brands look for a differential element of the brand to claim in its messaging to carve out its initial positioning, and it is extremely difficult and rare to reposition centrally; nevertheless, it remains an option. It is much more common for brands to examine options on the product/user focus. We look at an example for each option derived from Figure 6-13.

Differential   McDonald's altered its coffee and used this as a springboard for repositioning its advertising for eating breakfast at the restaurant to those in the habit of eating at other quick-service outlets, notably Tim Hortons, which commanded a strong market share. McDonald's emphasized that it made each Egg McMuffin with one whole Grade A egg to defend its core business. It also claimed superior coffee since the beverage represented the number one drink purchased outside the home. Combined with eggs at number two, the pairing of both for morning consumption proved to be a key way of communicating its differential advantage. McDonald's used creative ads like the one in Exhibit 6-24 to defend its breakfast market.

Central   While Dove appeared to be a late entrant in the personal care market, the repositioning of the brand with its Campaign for Real Beauty attempted to define the market along the lines of "cosmetic beauty" and "real beauty," in which the brand would take a central position within the latter definition. Although alternate interpretations may be considered, the public relations and consumer reaction to the campaign indicate it changed the face of the market dramatically and unexpectedly. Continued messaging like the new beauty sketches likely supports this contention (Exhibit 6-25).

Brand Benefit Positioning   Shreddies demonstrated the ultimate in product focus positioning, capturing imaginations with a new angle on the historical brand. Kraft presented the legendary square turned 45 degrees so that it became a diamond—and, voila, launched the "new" Diamond Shreddies cereal. While some loved the concept—Shreddies also received the Grand Clio award—others felt the campaign's humour was too far-fetched and insulted consumers'

Exhibit 6-24   Steaming cups of coffee appeared in public to entice consumers to McDonald's.

Exhibit 6-25 Dove's ads contrast how women view themselves with how others view them.

intelligence. In either case, the objective of getting people to talk about a brand after it had been on the market for so many years was met.

User Positioning   Subaru extolled viewers of its ad to get out more often with its unusual approach of peeling the TV screen back with a crowbar. Follow-up print ads reminded consumers of the unique TV ad with the icon at the top of the page, as seen in Exhibit 6-26. An interactive website helped consumers plan their itinerary outdoors to support this user positioning.

NEW TARGET AUDIENCE

As we saw in Chapter 3, organizations target advertising messages to both customers, such as brand loyals and favourable brand switchers, and to non-customers, such as new category users, other brand switchers, and other brand loyals. We now illustrate various repositioning strategies for each of these target audiences.

Brand-Loyal Customers   The research uncovered by Shreddies indicated that a substantial number of consumers retained strong attitudinal loyalty to the brand; however, this no longer translated into behavioural loyalty, which caused the significant sales decline. Findings also supported the idea of positioning to show the brand in a new light without actually making any changes whatsoever.

Exhibit 6-26   Subaru Outback ads surprisingly showed viewers that life outdoors was better than sitting at home.

Favourable Brand Switcher Customers   Shopping for groceries and other household items leaves consumers with ample opportunity to make purchases at retail locations. For many brands in various retail categories, a fair amount of advertising dollars are directed to these kinds of customers; this proved to be a key part of the repositioning for Loblaw (Exhibit 6-27) with its President's Choice house brand. The positioning attempted to reclaim consumers who demonstrated loyalty; however, the executives felt that heightened emphasis on PC would allow it to regain a greater proportion of consumer visits when shopping for food. All ads ended with "Worth switching supermarkets for" to clearly communicate a call to action for the target audience.

Exhibit 6-27 Loblaw featured its Executive Chairman in its new positioning ads.

New Category Users   Vespa scooters (Exhibit 6-28) are a popular vehicle of choice for young adults in busy downtown cities in Europe, however the penetration is limited in Canada so the positioning for this brand had to consider giving the brand and product category a fresh view in terms of its travel merits. The imagery of the campaign provided very distinctive and cool visuals.

Other Brand Loyals   Scotiabank (Exhibit 6-29) tackled the problem of attracting non-customers after spending considerable time building loyalty among its own customers. Many consumers of other banks believed that switching banks would not be worth the effort, with an attitude that "all banks are the same." Since the four other major banks attained about 30 percent household penetration each, Scotiabank envisioned an opportunity to move beyond its level of 19 percent. Scotiabank's positioning on enhanced financial service, encapsulated by the phrase "You're richer than you think," allowed the brand to connect with consumers dissatisfied with their experiences at other banks. The ads to support this positioning clearly showed how Scotiabank would help consumers find money they did not know they had by managing their loans and financing more effectively.[45]

Other Brand Switchers   A primary target audience for promotional messages for touring or travelling to other countries or regions of a country is generally consumers who visited other places and who are looking for new adventures. Nevertheless it is a challenge to get on the consideration list of those shopping around. Both tourism brands mentioned earlier focused their repositioning on potential customers who had travelled extensively elsewhere. The Canadian Tourism Commission targeted Canadians who typically planned to travel abroad but liked to travel to unique locations so the Locals Know campaign revealed a side of Canada travel not previously evaluated (Exhibit 6-30). Similarly, for Newfoundland & Labrador the target attracted those who valued the idea of going in a new direction different from their past experiences.

Exhibit 6-28 Vespa ads portrayed its distinctive steering and mirrors as a person's head.

Exhibit 6-29   Scotiabank's messages suggested to non-brand users they meet with the bank's personnel.

PURCHASE MOTIVATION

A brand repositioning strategy through consumer purchase motivation implies a shift from one type of motive to another. The most significant shift would be moving from an informational motive to a transformational motive or vice versa. We present two examples to show successful repositioning through a new consumer purchase motivation.

Problem–Solution   Reactine's repositioning changed its motive considerably. Past approaches showed ways in which an allergy sufferer's distress and discomfort with symptoms did not accurately coincide with actual experience. Ads portrayed potential Reactine users in a humorous light without a clear rationale or reason for consumers to use the product category or brand (Exhibit 6-31). The repositioning took the problem more seriously and demonstrated the brand solving the problem in a favourable way.

Sensory Gratification   Tetley conveyed the consumption experience of drinking its herbal tea visually by connecting the mood of the consumer with the colour of the tea in an innovative use of social media (Exhibit 6-32). With the advertising visuals, the senses of consumption clearly portrayed the brand in a new light within the

Exhibit 6-30   Canadian Tourism Commission's "Locals Know" campaign reminded Canadians to visit Canada.

Exhibit 6-31   Reactine's ads addressed the problem of allergies and offered the product as a solution.

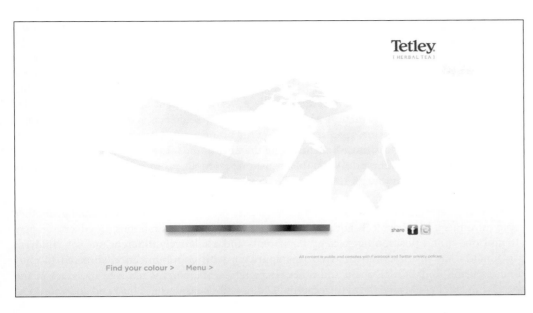

Find your colour >   Menu >

Exhibit 6-32   Tetley's Herbal Tea campaign used colour to signify the emotion and sensory experience of drinking Tetley tea.

product category. Positionings of competitors lack the sensory experience, opening the door for a successful repositioning for Tetley.

(L05) IMC Planning: Brand Positioning Extensions

From an IMC planning perspective we can extend or adapt the concepts encompassing the brand positioning strategy decisions in three directions: multiple target audiences, buyer decision stages, and corporate brands. The idea is to work with the general model for the positioning decisions and modify it for different parts of the IMC plan.

MULTIPLE TARGET AUDIENCES

Throughout this chapter we have examined the brand positioning strategy for a single target audience of end users. Many organizations target multiple audiences for their marketing communication for many reasons. For example, in Chapter 3 we outlined different customer and non-customer groups; brands in fact do have the opportunity to invest in marketing communication devoted to each group. This raises the question as to whether the brand should develop exactly the same positioning strategy for each target audience, or whether variation should exist. The new marketing strategy by Mark's has led to new target audiences for marketing communication (Exhibit 6-33). And, if variation is necessary, what aspects of the brand positioning strategy need to be customized? A number of the examples in Chapter 3 implied this issue; however, after describing positioning strategy, we need to return to the opportunity for promotional planners to fully consider their options.

Exhibit 6-33   Mark's revised its audiences while updating its marketing strategy.

Although promotional planners could consider customizing all four brand positioning strategy decisions, the first two, market definition and differential advantage, would likely remain relatively constant across customer and non-customer groups. The specific messages to influence brand attitude and the purchase motive communicated offer greater opportunity for getting the right message at the right time. One IMC tool to execute this customized brand positioning strategy is the Internet. For example, automobile advertisers might consider consumers who visit websites to gather information while searching for a vehicle as more likely to be brand switchers, and will include messages that position the brand against its strongest competitor on specific benefits and portray those benefits along the lines of the target audience having dissatisfaction with their current brand. While this is just one example, promotional planners can look at all advertising options and all IMC tools for opportunities to deliver a more specific message to a particular target audience that reinforces a particular brand positioning strategy.

Another interpretation for multiple target audiences involves group decision making, another topic introduced in Chapter 3. For example, in traditional family situations an advertiser may attempt one brand positioning strategy for parents and a relatively different one for children. McDonald's has historically employed this approach with communication directed to children featuring Ronald McDonald and other characters, while parents received messages of the special time they could enjoy with their family. Additionally, considering a husband and wife scenario, automobile brands can use print ads to emphasize certain car features that appeal to men in magazines where men represent a higher proportion of the audience, and similarly for women.

BUYER DECISION STAGES

In the IMC planning section of Chapter 5 we noted that marketers could consider message and communication tool options for each stage of the consumer decision-making process. Various message options can be discerned from the brand positioning strategy decisions outlined in this chapter. First, promotional planners can decide which part of the brand positioning strategy would be most relevant or effective at each stage. Market definition and differential advantage may be more appropriate at the pre-purchase stage or need-recognition stage. For example, the marketing for the Mini in Canada used television advertising to signal that it competed against two markets: regular compact cars like Honda Civic, and other smaller sports cars like the BMW 3 Series. It also emphasized its advantage of being small in size, but not *too* small.

In contrast, Internet microsites (mini.ca/experiment, mini.ca/choice, mini.ca/family, mini.ca/date) offered positioning on specific benefits with a transformational motive for consumers actively searching for information about the new brand. In fact, the microsites facilitated customer relationships by inviting prospects to register. Mini reported an average response rate of 20 percent for each of the four sites. The brand positioning strategies along buyer decision stages also illustrated the second option. Specifically, promotional planners can use different IMC tools to communicate certain elements of the brand positioning strategy. Finally, promotional planners can use various media to convey specific attributes that are not in other media. For example, Mini used billboards to communicate its British heritage and speed, and magazines to illustrate its safety.

CORPORATE BRANDS

Thus far we have defined brand positioning strategy and illustrated examples where the brand is at the product level. For instance, our initial brand positioning strategy example involved WestJet and how its communication intended to establish an enhanced brand position among dissatisfied Air Canada customers. Corporate brands are also part of integrated marketing communications and are the focus of the public relations topics in Chapter 15. In this context, corporate brands often have varied target audiences, for example investors or members of a particular community.

Given the broader scope of the corporate brand, the initial positioning decision for market definition would concern brand name in most cases. Establishing a differential advantage from a corporate brand entails both differential and central positioning. For example, corporate brand-building activities for Honda suggest that it attempted to establish a central positioning concerning environmental responsibility. This would coincide with its marketing activities of introducing the first hybrid vehicle. Again, the organization-wide communication would imply that most corporate brand positioning would focus on brand benefit positioning over user positioning; however, "green marketing" efforts by companies suggest potential for the latter with an appropriate message that signifies altruistic feelings upon the target audience.

All marketing communication decisions are or should be designed to influence target audience attitudes, so corporate brand attitude persuasion is entirely relevant. For example, organizations often involve themselves in various sponsorship activities to signal that they are socially responsible, a key attribute to communicate to the general public or to future employees or other stakeholders. Finally, most corporate brand communication is intended along the lines of transformational motives; the clearest examples are television commercials with triumphant music and everlasting positive images.

Learning Objectives Summary

 Identify the concepts of market positioning strategy and market position.

The strategic marketing plan describes all marketing decisions including promotion and the supporting analysis and justification. It typically includes the market positioning strategy, which summarizes the markets the organization is competing in (i.e., target market) and how the marketing mix fulfills the needs of this market. The resulting consumer perception as to where the consumer believes the organization to be competing is known as the market position. Oftentimes, market research illuminates where consumers perceive an organization with respect to its competitors, which can be graphed on a market position diagram or perceptual map. Promotional planners rely on this document for all decisions including the overall IMC direction, creative strategy, and creative tactics for advertising or any other IMC tool such as sales promotion, public relations, direct, or Internet.

 Apply the positioning concept in an advertising context by defining brand positioning strategy and brand position.

For many communication problems or opportunities, promotional messages are directed to target audiences. These audiences are a subset of the target market or an entirely different group depending upon the communications situation. As discussed in Chapter 3, promotional planners require a detailed profile of the target audience with most appropriate segmentation variables, including whether the target is a customer or non-customer. Advertising or any other promotional message is guided by the brand positioning strategy that specifies how it is intended to influence its target audience with a given product category or product market. The resulting target audience perception as to what the brand offers is known as the brand position. The flexibility of influencing a target audience's brand position through many IMC tools allows promotional managers to plan for unique brand positions for multiple target audiences.

 Illustrate how to formulate brand positioning strategy decisions.

The process for developing a brand positioning strategy in the context of marketing communications is similar to developing a positioning strategy for the overall marketing. However, it differs by evaluating or integrating very micro-level aspects of consumer behaviour in its planning by closely considering the nature of the purchase decision. The direction of the decisions is much different, with the goal of finding the most appropriate message, media, or IMC tool versus determining optimal product design features.

The brand positioning strategy comprises four decisions: market definition, differential advantage, target audience brand attitude, and consumer purchase motive. The market definition decision allows the promotional planner to consider whether to define the market in which the brand is competing by benefits, brand name, usage situation, or product category. Differential advantage decisions include whether the brand takes a differential or central positioning and whether the brand focuses its positioning on its benefit claims or the user. Target audience attitude decisions consider how the message is expected to persuade existing beliefs to the desired beliefs about the brand. Finally, promotional planners decide what type of purchase motive should be associated with the brand.

LO4 **Demonstrate brand repositioning strategy opportunities.**

In some communication situations—such as new competitors, changing consumer tastes, or poor brand performance—promotion planners need to reposition their brand. The repositioning can follow the same decisions as described above, where the promotional planner can consider an alternative market definition, communicate a new differential advantage, emphasize different benefit claims, or focus on another motivational option. Promotional planners can consider altering one or all four of these decisions to achieve moderate or very significant change in the current brand position.

LO5 **Interpret brand positioning strategy decisions in other contexts.**

A brand positioning strategy can be augmented for any marketing communication purposes. Three relevant ones to consider are multiple target audiences, buyer decision stages, and corporate brand, to name a few. Organizations often face the dual task of communicating to long-time customers and newer customers, thereby requiring a more specific message for each and therefore raising the possibility of differences in the brand positioning strategy. Similarly, brands may alter their brand positioning strategy by emphasizing different benefits, for example, at varying stages of the consumer decision-making process. Finally, a corporate identity is of paramount importance and the decisions at the brand level are readily interpreted on a broader scale.

Key Terms   connect

Review key terms and definitions on Connect.

Review Questions

1. Describe how the market positioning strategy adopted for a brand would need to be supported by all other elements of the marketing mix.

2. Why is it useful to distinguish between brand positioning strategy and brand position?

3. What problems would a brand encounter if it communicated with an incorrect motive?

4. What factors would lead a marketer to the use of a repositioning strategy?

5. Why is it important to consider unique brand positioning decisions at each of the buyer decision stages? Is it feasible to implement this approach for all product categories?

Applied Questions

1. Explain how McDonald's market positioning strategy has changed with the new developments in its menu and outlets.

2. Examine the social media presence of a brand and assess whether it clearly identifies a brand positioning strategy.

3. Explain why a central positioning is feasible. Do any brands currently use this approach in their marketing communication?

4. Develop market partition diagrams for beverages. What repositioning options are available for any brand?

5. How can brand positioning decisions be applied to new category users and brand loyal users of smartphones?

GO ONLINE

For more information on the resources available from McGraw-Hill Ryerson,
go to www.mcgrawhill.ca/he/solutions.

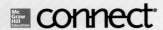

What happened to the Sunday Drive?

What happened to throwing darts at maps? Taking the back roads? Or heading off in a random direction just to see what's *out there?*

What happened to that explorer's mentality? That urge to find out what's around the next corner? What happened to giving in to a little curiosity?

Back in the 50's and 60's, families would pile into the car and just go for a drive. It was a Sunday ritual. A chance to explore the countryside or one of those small towns people usually drive past on the way to bigger towns.

Over the years, the Sunday drive has slowly become extinct. Maybe all the bumper-to-bumper traffic has made us forget what it's like to see nothing but open road out the windshield. Or maybe we just have less time. Nowadays, it's all about getting from A to B as fast as possible. But there's a lot to miss out there beyond those old, boring letters.

Hidden towns full of interesting characters. Old buildings. Swimming holes with tire swings. There's no telling what you'll come across. Maybe you'll find a lookout spot that nobody knows about. Maybe an old man running an old diner will tell you the funniest joke you've heard in a while. Who knows?

And then there are those classic roadside oddities. Diners shaped like flying saucers. Massive apples, fishing rods, and coins. Statues of lumberjacks, cowboys, and sasquatches. Houses made of bottles. Trees full of shoes. And there's nothing like stumbling across an 80-foot fiberglass dinosaur. Good times.

So if you ever find yourself at home on a Sunday, feeling a bit restless, you could always throw a dart at a map. Or set sail for the back roads. Or head off in any direction just to see where it takes you.

Destinations are overrated. Schedules are more fun to throw away than they are to follow.

And flipping a coin is a perfectly legitimate way to make a decision.

Das Auto. *See you out there.*

Creative Strategy Decisions

7

LEARNING OBJECTIVES

 Summarize the idea and importance of creativity in an advertising context.

 Describe the creative strategy planning process.

 Identify the approaches used for determining the creative theme that forms the basis of an advertising campaign.

 Summarize the different types of message appeals that advertisers use to persuade their target audience.

 Identify the source or communicator options a marketer has for a promotional message.

 Apply source and message appeal options for different ad executions.

Courage, Time, and Talk by VW

VW moved from its classic "Drivers Wanted" slogan to "Das Auto" as the German manufacturer released numerous new car models the past couple of years. And with its Canadian agency, Red Urban, the brand is moving in the right direction in Canada with a series of creative ads. During 2011, sales increased by over 40 percent, Facebook likes increased by a factor of six to 371,000, and traffic to VW.ca more than doubled.

Success occurred with a trilogy of ads for the new Golf with the theme "Drive Until." The first showed a man driving around the block a few times trying to summon the courage to propose to his girlfriend. With only the music, the song "Just Like Honey" by Scottish alt-rockers The Jesus and Mary Chain, the mood is set for a continuation of the story. The end of the ad invites VW fans to submit their idea for the next sequence.

Naturally the follow-up is a buddy road trip, which ends with the groom and three other guys arriving at the church in time with the song "Keep the Lights On" by Wave Machines.

The story wraps up with the new husband leaving his home, clearly angry, and then returning with flowers and a smile, and welcomed back by his new bride. The song "When Your Love Is Safe" by Pat Grossi plays a role in communicating the theme and emotional connection to the brand. Each ad ended appropriately—"Drive Until Courage," "Drive Until Time," and "Drive Until Talk"—to signify the storyline and add meaning to the message.

After witnessing "Courage" and "Time," one agency president felt VW re-captured the essence of the brand much like it had with the "Drivers Wanted" campaign of past years. Another critic felt VW told the story perfectly especially with the right mood of the music. It also fit well with the idea of allowing the creative to be conceived by VW fans. A third evaluator felt the storylines showed the emotional fulfillment of driving and of life's milestone moments that are intrinsically linked with travelling in one's automobile.

Similar creativity occurred with other brands. VW emphasized its German engineering for the Beetle. The campaign used billboards with augmented reality capability. After downloading an app from VW.ca, consumers could use their mobile phones when near the outdoor ad and watch a video message that appeared to arise from the billboard. For its Jetta model, VW created a 3-D ad shown in cinemas.

These Canadian ads, and two hit Super Bowl ads with a Star Wars theme showed worldwide, propelled VW back to where it once was in terms of Canadian sales. In 1999 sales hit 42,000, then plummeted to 32,000 by 2004 and surpassed the old mark when they hit 45,000. When Red Urban took over, its mandate focused on heightened emotional resonance with potential VW customers. And its first effort promoted the Golf with the suggestion "Anyone for a Sunday Drive?" Prompted by the notion that people have lost the desire to take the car out for a spin, the ads encourage consumers to visit a nearby town or the countryside—while riding in a VW, of course. The multimedia campaign (TV, newspaper, radio) also included a website (vwsundaydrive.ca) where consumers could mix music with driving scenes.

Sources: Hollie Shaw, "VW: Carmaker Pushes Its Environmental Message," *National Post,* April 15, 2011; "Facebook Fans to Drive Volkswagen Ad," *National Post,* July 22, 2011; Matt Semansky, "Volkswagen Canada," *Marketing Magazine,* November 22, 2011; press release obtained on Stockhouse. com, "Volkswagen Canada Reinvents the Sunday Drive," June 8, 2010.

Questions:

1. Why is an emotional connection to a car brand so important?
2. Why is it valuable for VW to have many different creative themes across all of its brands?

An important part of an IMC program is the advertising message, a way to tell consumers how the product can solve a problem or satisfy desires or achieve goals. Advertising messages create images or associations and establish a brand position as well as transform the experience of buying and/or using a product. Advertising messages play a leading role in the IMC program, and are crucial to the success of the brand's promotional effort. While most students may not ever design ads, everyone involved in marketing or promotion should understand the strategic decisions that underlie the development of advertising messages.

It is easy to see many ways to convey an advertising message while watching commercials on TV, seeing videos on the Internet, perusing print ads in a magazine, or witnessing advertising in out-of-home locations. Underlying these messages is a **creative strategy** that determines *what* the advertising message will communicate and **creative tactics** for *how* the message will be executed. In this chapter, we focus on three creative strategy decisions. First, we describe approaches to determine the idea of the creative theme, which provides direction for attention-getting, distinctive, and memorable messages. Second, we identify the message appeals that advertisers use to persuade consumers. Third, we focus on the key source characteristics that advertisers typically use to gain attention and alter consumers' attitudes. Prior to these decisions, we summarize the process of planning for creative strategy. We also apply these latter two points in our IMC planning perspective.

🗩 (L01) Advertising Creativity

Upon determining the direction for the communications program, the advertising agency, or the department in the organization responsible for developing ads, focuses on finding an appropriate creative approach to communicate a message that reinforces the brand positioning strategy. Good advertising creativity can often be central to determining the success of a product as it clearly contributes to a strong brand position with its intended target audience. The essence of advertising is its creativity, and we now provide a working definition and indicate its importance.

DEFINITION OF ADVERTISING CREATIVITY

For many students, as well as many advertising and marketing practitioners, the most interesting aspect of advertising is the creative side. We have all at one time or another been intrigued by an ad and admired the creative insight that went into it. A great ad is a joy to behold and an epic to create, with the cost of producing a TV commercial potentially hitting $1 million. Conceiving an ad is such an exciting and enticing activity that a contest searching for the next top ad executive is operated each year for university students by the DeGroote School of Business at McMaster University.[1] Many companies see money spent on advertising and other forms of marketing communication as good brand investment. They realize that the manner in which the advertising message is developed and executed is often critical to the success of the promotion, which in turn can influence the effectiveness of the entire marketing program. For example, BMW's creative messages over time firmly planted the idea of Ultimate Driving Experience in Canada and Ultimate Driving Machine in other countries (Exhibit 7-1).

Creativity is a commonly used term in advertising. Ads are often called creative. The people who develop ads are known as creative specialists. These specialists work for ad agencies that develop ad campaigns or for marketers that handle their own advertising without the help of an agency. Perhaps the focus on creativity occurs because many people view the specific challenge given to those who develop an advertising message as being creative. It is their job to turn all of the information regarding product features and benefits, marketing plans, consumer research, and communication objectives into a creative concept that will bring the advertising message to life. This begs the question: What is meant by *creativity* in advertising?

Advertising creativity is the ability to generate fresh, unique, and appropriate ideas that can be used as effective solutions to marketing communication issues (e.g., problem or

Exhibit 7-1 Excellent advertising helps create an image for BMW automobiles.

opportunity). To be *appropriate* and *effective,* a creative idea must be relevant to the target audience.[2] Relevance, an important characteristic of creativity, has to instantly capture the target audience's attention and generate critical brand associations through specific cognitive and emotional responses. The relevance is even more critical when an advertiser takes into account the selective attention of the target audience. Moreover, the creativity has to crystallize the brand so that it is understood by the target audience, which is also experiencing selective comprehension when faced with many competing promotional messages. Extending this further, the relevance of the creativity to the target audience is critical to establishing an important link to the brand, its benefits, and why the target audience would purchase it. In other words, relevance clearly supports the brand positioning strategy. Reinforcing this view suggests two approaches, *ad to consumer relevance* and *brand to consumer relevance.*[3] The former involves ad characteristics that are meaningful to the target audience such as the celebrity spokesperson or imagery. The latter concerns the personal interest of the product to the target audience.

Appropriate and effective creativity should offer divergence as well since the message must break through media clutter and attract the target audience's attention. Divergence is the extent to which an ad contains novel, different, or unusual characteristics.[4] Advertising creativity is divergent in terms of originality (e.g., rare or surprising ideas that are not common), flexibility (e.g., different ideas), elaboration (e.g., unexpected ideas that become intricate, complicated, or sophisticated), synthesis (e.g., normally unrelated ideas that are combined or connected), and artistic values (e.g., ideas expressed verbally or visually).

The Absolut vodka ads demonstrate the relevance and divergence notions for good creativity. The original creative strategy for Absolut vodka shows the distinctive shape of its bottle and depicts it with visual puns and witty headlines that play off the Absolut name. The agency and client customized the advertising campaign by tailoring the print ads for each magazine. The agency's creative and media departments jointly selected magazines to appeal to the readers of each publication. Its unique creativity stood the test of time for over 20 years. The working relationship of creative specialists and others demonstrated a model for working effectively. Strong results continued for many years until the brand found sales lagging a few years ago and switched direction, as shown in Exhibit 7-2. The new creative advertising relies on thought-provoking imagery using the tagline "In an Absolut World" and plays off of the brand name to illustrate an imagined world where everything is as ideal as Absolut vodka. This particular ad features New York's Times Square adorned with famous works of art rather than billboards and is designed to show media clutter as a means to share the world's artistic treasures. The creative strategy is an inspiring, humorous, and thought-provoking idea of

Exhibit 7-2   Creative advertising established Absolut vodka as an iconic brand.

Exhibit 7-3   Nintendo placed a creative ad in a women's magazine to attract new users.

what an Absolut world might look like and challenges consumers to reflect on their own visions of the world. The ultimate goal of the campaign is to maintain the brand as a cultural icon.[5]

IMPORTANCE OF ADVERTISING CREATIVITY

Perspectives on what constitutes creativity in advertising differ. At one extreme are people who argue that advertising is creative only if it sells the product. An advertising message's or campaign's impact on sales counts more than whether it is innovative. At the other end of the continuum are those who judge the creativity of an ad in terms of its artistic or aesthetic value and originality. They contend creative ads can break through the competitive clutter, grab the consumer's attention, and have a positive communication effect. Both perspectives indicate the importance of advertising creativity as it either presents a good public exposure or contributes to a brand positioning strategy and ultimately sales.

The growth of brands has highlighted the importance of advertising creativity leading to renewed investigations.[6] Surveyed executives believe creativity has improved compared to the origin of modern-day advertising during the 1960s.[7] The Leo Burnett agency and *Contagious Magazine* conduct worldwide research to uncover the success of the most creative advertising in traditional and newer evolving media, while others present new or reconfigured ideas to define creativity.[8] In general, creative advertising messages help focus the receiver's attention, allowing deeper processing and stronger recall and recognition.[9]

Perspectives on advertising creativity often diverged along marketing and artistic lines as shown in one study.[10] Product managers and account executives view ads as promotional tools whose primary purpose is to communicate favourable impressions to the marketplace. They believe a commercial should be evaluated in terms of whether it fulfills the client's marketing and communicative objectives. Alternatively, creative specialists view ads as an expression of their personal aesthetics and an opportunity to communicate their unique creative talent with the hopes of career advancement.

What constitutes creativity in advertising is probably somewhere between the two views. To break through the clutter and make an impression on the target audience an ad often must be unique and entertaining, as seen in the Nintendo ad shown in Exhibit 7-3. Research has shown that a major determinant of whether a commercial will be successful in changing brand preferences is its "likability," or the viewer's overall reaction.[11] Advertising messages that are well designed and executed and generate emotional responses can create positive feelings that are transferred to the product or service being advertised.[12] Creative specialists believe this occurs if they are given considerable latitude in developing advertising messages, but purely creative ads might fail to communicate a relevant product message. In an attempt to resolve this discussion, research findings suggest that very creative advertising messages have additional positive brand communication effects (i.e., brand quality, brand interest) beyond recall and likability.[13]

However, the issue becomes less clear as one study finds that the creative specialists themselves can disagree on the merits of creativity. A survey of art directors and copywriters finds that the former are more concerned with visual creativity while the latter more strongly believe in message delivery.[14] Finally, in the age of consumer-generated "advertising" messages, another study finds that perceptions of creativity differ among advertising professionals, students, and the general public.[15] Thus, it appears everyone must keep a balanced perspective on the creativity of advertising messages. IMC Perspective 7-1 demonstrates the importance of advertising creativity.

Finally, studies conclude that advertising creativity impacts consumers' cognitive, affective, and behavioural responses to advertising messages.[16] Novel advertising requires consumer processing time, resulting in longer exposure and greater attention. Creative ads draw more attention to the advertised brand, higher levels of recall, greater motivation to process the information, and deeper levels of processing.[17] Creative advertising positively impacts emotional reactions including attitudes and purchase intentions.[18] Divergence is a particularly important component of advertising creativity; however, clients often favour relevance over divergence as they want their agencies to create ads that communicate pertinent information such as specific product features and benefits. Researchers suggest that clients should be less resistant to divergent approaches and note that there is a fundamental need for divergent thinkers in the ad development process.[19] Considering that most advertising messages are seen and/or heard in a very cluttered media environment where marketers must compete for the attention of consumers, it is important that brand managers accept ads that are novel and divergent as well as relevant and meaningful.

(L02) **Planning Creative Strategy**

Creative specialists must take all the research, creative briefs, strategy statements, communications objectives, and other input and transform them into an advertising message. Their job is to write copy, design layouts and illustrations, or produce commercials that effectively communicate the central theme on which the campaign is based. Rather than simply stating the features or benefits of a product or service, they must put the advertising message into a form that will engage the audience's interest and make the ads memorable.[20] In this section, we describe the creative challenge, illustrate the creative process, summarize the job of an account planner, identify forms of research for creative decision making, and summarize the end results—the creative brief and advertising campaign—when planning for creative promotional communication.

CREATIVE CHALLENGE

The job of the creative team is challenging because every marketing situation is different and each campaign or advertisement may require a different creative approach. Numerous guidelines have been developed for creating effective advertising.[21] Creative people follow proven formulas when creating ads because clients can feel uncomfortable with advertising that is too different. Bill Tragos, former chair of TBWA, says, "Very few clients realize that the reason that their work is so bad is that they are the ones who commandeered it and directed it to be that way. I think that at least 50 percent of an agency's successful work resides in the client."[22] Decades later, empirical research supports this practitioner's point of view.[23]

Many creative people say it is important for clients to take risks if they want breakthrough advertising that gets noticed. One client taking a risk is Marriott International, as observed in the advertising for its Residence Inn chain. A highly evocative campaign showcases Residence

IMC PERSPECTIVE 7-1

TELUS's Nurturing Ads

What's up with all the animals on TV, online, on billboards, and in so many advertising spaces? Despite the frenzy, Telus leads the way with its distinct approach of introducing a new cast of characters with each new season, campaign, or new product. And in some cases, the more memorable—and, dare we say, famous—ones reappear to star once again or come together en masse all in one ad.

Nature became the canvas for TELUS (named Clearnet at the time) when advertising agency TAXI was inspired by a film in the late 1990s that used macro photography to capture the almost human like characteristics of insects. The simplicity of the storytelling in the film demonstrated that nature could be used as a unique brand platform to deliver the proposition of "the future is friendly." Set to a white background with emotive music, the nature and critters help make the brand feel friendly, likeable, and approachable.

For a few years, we saw exotic birds (e.g., macaws), other insects, colourful frogs, and lizards—until TELUS took over, and began with a "disco duck" to celebrate the millennium and then moved on to penguins, monkeys, pot-bellied pigs, iguanas, bunnies, meerkats, hedgehogs, fish, and back to exotic birds (flamingos, peacocks) once again. A VP for TELUS commented, "Nature has universal appeal. You can talk to any age from 7 to 77. And it allows you to do metaphors."

Pygmy goats danced to the hit "Jump Around" and a couple of other songs in more recent incarnations to market Web-enabled phones and services, but the reprised Hazina the hippo represented the biggest hit for 2009. Initially introduced during Christmas 2005, Hazina made another appearance four years later, and in early 2009 she and her bunny friend moved about the screen symbolizing the size and speed of TELUS's network. "We thought we would continue with the hippo because of consumer likeability but we wanted to add the speed factor," commented a TELUS VP. In another execution, Hazina's mother and brother frolicked in water—with the picture actually in a handset to give the screen a life-like feel.

According to experts, the characteristics associated with animals through stories (e.g., the cunning fox) act as a quick and simple reference that transfers to the advertised product. Furthermore, the feeling associated with the animal may also transfer to the product, so if someone likes Hazina they are more likely to feel positivity toward TELUS.

TELUS embarked on a tremendous addition beyond its traditional imagery of critters. An emphasis on customer care, evolved from a previous "We Hear You" message that reinforced the "putting customers first" strategy, now embraced a new level of commitment for service. And these ads featured real people, a significant divergence from past ads. The TV ads contained the usual irreverent TELUS humour, but with a storyline that did not include the established imagery throughout, but added at the end.

TELUS also established a YouTube channel that contained all of its ads, and from here we witnessed a new emphasis on using people once again, this time actual TELUS employees, in the promotion of the Samsung Galaxy phone. In the longer videos, the messages demonstrate the expertise of the service personnel who also happen to own the Galaxy phone. According to the Director of Marketing for TELUS, "People are accustomed to seeing TELUS using critters on a white background with cool music. The YouTube page allows the company to explain products beyond the 30-second TV ad format."

As part of its launch of Optik TV, TELUS established a service personnel character who confidently installs equipment and services. In one episode, he hooked up the technology in a typical household, and in another, he managed to impress Mr. Spock of *Star Trek* fame, Leonard Nemoy, who ended the ad with his trademark statement, "Fascinating."

Sources: Simon Houpt, "How Nature Can Nurture Our Brand Appreciation," *The Globe and Mail,* October 2, 2009, p. B5; Kristin Laird, "TELUS Sponsoring Cheap Tuesdays at Cineplex," *Marketing Magazine,* September 10, 2009; Kristin Laird, "Hippos Make TELUS Big and Fast," *Marketing Magazine,* March 5, 2009; Matt Semansky, "TELUS Enters the Branded YouTube Galaxy, *Marketing Magazine,* March 13, 2012; Eve Lazarus, "Telus Tunes In to Customer Care with New Campaign," *Marketing Magazine,* September 4, 2012; http://www.youtube.com/user/telus.

Question

1. Does the evolution of TELUS's creative theme make sense based on its past success?

Inn's new "Innfusion" décor, which redefines the extended-stay experience with distinctive zones that meet the living needs of the extended-stay guest—cooking, dining, working, relaxing, and sleeping. The ads use theatrical performers to show guests how to master—not just survive—a long trip. In one spot showcasing Residence's in-room grocery service, a performer flips upside down, lands on the kitchen counter, and balances an apple on her toes (Exhibit 7-4). In other ads a trapeze artist glides across the chain's newly designed rooms, a plate spinner twirls four plates to highlight the full kitchen in each unit, and a fire breather/juggler performs at an outdoor fire pit to showcase the new look of Residence properties. The television spots are part of an integrated campaign that includes print and online components such as a website that showed a virtual tour of the new Residence Inn designs.[24]

One agency that has been successful in getting its clients to take risks is Rethink, best known for its excellent creative work for Playland, Science World, A&W, and Solo Mobile. The agency's founders believe a key element in its success has been a steadfast belief in taking risks when most agencies and their clients have been retrenching and becoming more conservative. The agency can develop great advertising partly because its clients are willing to take risks and agree with the agency's approach of listening to their client and arriving at a creative solution for their marketing communication problem or opportunity.

Not all agree that advertising has to be risky to be effective, however. Many marketing managers are more comfortable with advertising that simply communicates product or service features and benefits and gives the consumer a reason to buy. They see their ad campaigns as multimillion-dollar investments whose goal is to sell the product rather than finance the whims of their agency's creative staff. They argue that creative people occasionally lose sight of advertising's bottom line: Does it sell?

Exhibit 7-4 Residence Inn takes a very creative approach with its ads.

CREATIVE PROCESS

Creativity in advertising can be viewed as a process, and creative success is most likely when an organized approach is followed. One of the most popular approaches to creativity in advertising was developed by James Webb Young, a former creative vice president at the J. Walter Thompson agency. Young said, "The production of ideas is just as definite a process as the production of Fords; the production of ideas, too, runs an assembly line; in this production the mind follows an operative technique which can be learned and controlled; and that its effective use is just as much a matter of practice in the technique as in the effective use of any tool."[25] Working from a sociological view, Young's process of creativity follows a four-stage approach:

- *Preparation.* Read background information regarding the problem.
- *Incubation.* Get away and let ideas develop.
- *Illumination.* See the light or solution.
- *Verification.* Refine the idea and see if it is an appropriate solution.

Models of the creative process such as Young's are valuable to those working in the creative area of advertising, since they offer an organized way to approach an advertising problem. These models do not say much about how this information will be synthesized and used by the creative specialist because this part of the process is unique to the individual. An investigation along these lines reveals four individual factors: orientation toward the creative work, approach to the communication problems, mindscribing (i.e., free-flow thinking), and heuristics (i.e., quick creative decision rules).[26] A study of advertising copywriters found that they work without guidance from any formal theories of communication. However, those interviewed claimed to use similar informal, implicit theories that guide them in creating ads. These theories are based on finding ways to break through the ad clutter, open the consciousness of consumers, and connect with them to deliver the message.

However, advertising creativity is not the exclusive domain of creative specialists, as creative thinking occurs from everyone involved when planning creative strategy. Agency people, such as account executives, media planners, researchers, and account planners, as well as those on the client side, such as marketing and brand managers, must all seek creative solutions to problems encountered in planning, developing, and executing an advertising campaign.[27] It is also important that those working on the client side do not create a relationship with their agencies that inhibits the creative processes required to produce good advertising. Highly skilled creative specialists aspire to work with open-minded clients who are receptive to new ideas, and they note that some of the best creative work developed by agencies does not get used because clients are resistant to taking creative risks unless they are under pressure to perform. Advertising agencies, as well as other IMC specialist organizations, thrive on creativity as it is at the heart of what they do and they must design an environment that fosters the development of creative thinking and creative advertising. Clients must also understand the differences between the perspectives of the creative personnel and marketing and product managers. While the client has ultimate approval of the advertising, the opinions of creative specialists must be respected when advertising ideas and content are evaluated.[28]

ACCOUNT PLANNING

To facilitate the creative process many agencies use **account planning**, which involves conducting research and gathering all relevant information about a client's product or service, brand, and consumers in the target audience. Jon Steel, a former vice president and director of account planning, has written an excellent book on the process titled *Truth, Lies and Advertising: The Art of Account Planning*.[29] He notes that the account planner's job is to provide the key decision makers with all the information they require to make an intelligent decision. According to Steel, "Planners may have to work very hard to influence the way that the advertising turns out, carefully laying out a strategic foundation with the client, handing over tidbits of information to creative people when, in their judgment, that information will have the greatest impact, giving feedback on ideas, and hopefully adding ideas of their own."

Account planning plays an important role during creative strategy development by driving the process from the customers' point of view. Planners will work with the client as well as other agency personnel, such as the creative team and media specialists. They discuss how the knowledge and information they have gathered can be used in the development of the creative strategy as well as other aspects of the advertising campaign. Account planners are usually responsible for all the research (both qualitative and quantitative) conducted during the creative strategy development process. In the following section we examine how research and information can provide input to the creative process of advertising.

RESEARCH IN THE CREATIVE PROCESS

The creative specialist first learns as much as possible about the product, the target audience, the competition, and any other relevant **research**. Much of this information would come from the marketing plan and advertising plan developed by the client. Alternatively, good clients will give proper direction for their agency by constructing a client brief that recapitulates their internal documents and adds additional information that would give the creative specialist an idea as to the direction of the brand positioning strategy. The Institute of Communications and Advertising produces a best practices document that shows brand managers how to construct a client brief that serves the needs of both parties, thus encouraging more creative marketing communication.

From this, the creative specialist can acquire additional background information in numerous ways:

- Read anything related to the product or market.
- Talk to people (e.g., marketing personnel, designers, engineers, consumers).
- Visit stores and malls.
- Use the product or service and become familiar with it.
- Work in and learn about the business.[30]

Creative people use both general and product-specific preplanning input. **General preplanning input** can include books, periodicals, trade publications, scholarly journals, pictures, and clipping services, which gather and organize magazine and newspaper articles on the product, the market, and the competition, including the latter's ads. Another useful general preplanning input concerns market trends and developments. Information is available from a variety of sources, including local, provincial, and federal governments, secondary research suppliers, and industry trade associations, as well as advertising and media organizations that publish research reports and newsletters. Those involved in developing creative strategy can also gather relevant and timely information by reading Canadian publications like *Marketing Magazine* or *Strategy*, and American publications like *Adweek* and *Advertising Age*.

In addition to getting general background research, creative people receive **product/service-specific preplanning input**. This information generally comes in the form of specific studies conducted on the product/service and/or the target audience. Quantitative consumer research includes attitude studies, market structure, and positioning studies such as perceptual mapping and psychographic or lifestyle profiles. As noted in Chapter 3, agencies or affiliated research companies conduct psychographic studies annually and construct detailed psychographic or lifestyle profiles of product or service users. Dove conducted one of the more significant research studies prior to launching the "Campaign for Real Beauty." The research involved numerous personal interviews and sampled women from many countries regarding their attitudes toward beauty with a survey methodology.

Qualitative research is used to gain insight into the underlying causes of consumer behaviour. Methods employed include in-depth interviews, projective techniques, association tests, and focus groups in which consumers are encouraged to bring out associations related to products and brands (see Figure 7-1). This research is often referred to as motivation research.

In-depth interviews

Face-to-face situations in which an interviewer asks a consumer to talk freely in an unstructured interview using specific questions designed to obtain insights into his or her motives, ideas, or opinions.

Projective techniques

Efforts designed to gain insights into consumers' values, motives, attitudes, or needs that are difficult to express or identify by having them project these internal states upon some external object.

Association tests

A technique in which an individual is asked to respond with the first thing that comes to mind when he or she is presented with a stimulus; the stimulus may be a word, picture, ad, and so on.

Focus groups

A small number of people with similar backgrounds and/or interests who are brought together to discuss a particular product, idea, or issue.

Figure 7-1

Qualitative marketing research methods employed to obtain consumer insight

In general, motivation research is considered important in assessing how and why consumers buy. Focus groups and in-depth interviews are valuable methods for gaining insights into consumers' feelings, and projective techniques are often the only way to get around stereotypical or socially desirable responses. Since motivation research studies typically use a low number of participants, a limitation is that findings are not generalizable to the whole population and may be discovering idiosyncrasies of a few individuals. Still, it is difficult to ignore motivation research since the resulting consumer insight inspires advertising messages aimed at buyers' deeply rooted feelings, hopes, aspirations, and fears.

Focus groups are a prevalent research tool of the four methods at this stage of the creative process. **Focus groups** are a research method whereby consumers (usually 10 to 12 people) from the target audience are led through a discussion regarding a particular topic. Focus groups give insight as to why and how consumers use a product, what is important to them in choosing a particular brand, what they like and don't like about products, and any special needs they might have that aren't being satisfied. A focus group session might also include a discussion of types of ad appeals to use or evaluate the advertising. Focus group interviews bring the creative people and others involved in creative strategy development into contact with the customers. Listening to a focus group gives copywriters, art directors, and other creative specialists a better sense of who the target audience is, what the audience is like, and to whom the creatives need to write, design, or direct in creating an advertising message.

Toward the end of the creative process, members of the target audience may be asked to evaluate rough creative layouts and to indicate what meaning they get from the ad, what they think of its execution, or how the ad makes them feel. The creative team can gain insight into how a TV commercial might communicate its message by having members of the target audience evaluate the ad in storyboard form. A **storyboard** is a series of drawings used to present the visual plan or layout of a proposed commercial. It contains a series of sketches of key frames or scenes along with the copy or audio portion for each scene (Exhibit 7-5).

Exhibit 7-5 Marketers can gain insight into consumers' reactions to a commercial by showing them a storyboard.

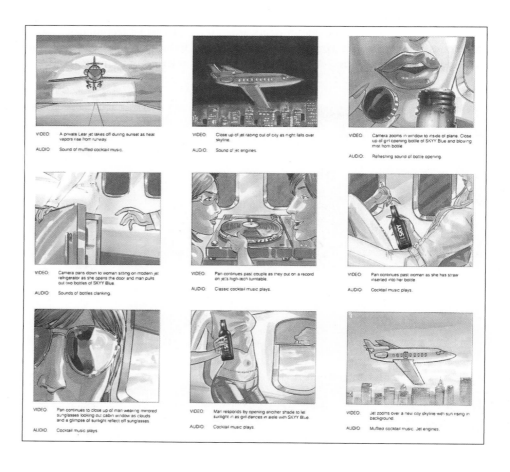

1. Basic problem or opportunity the advertising must address
2. Target audience(s) and behaviour objective(s)
3. Communication objectives
4. Brand positioning strategy statement
5. Creative strategy (creative theme, message appeal, source characteristic)
6. Supporting information and requirements

Figure 7-2

Creative brief outline

Evaluating a commercial in storyboard form can be difficult because storyboards are too abstract for many consumers to understand. To make the creative layout more realistic and easier to evaluate, the agency may produce an **animatic,** a videotape of the storyboard along with an audio soundtrack. Storyboards and animatics are useful for research purposes as well as for presenting the creative idea to other agency personnel or to the client for discussion and approval. At this stage of the process, the creative team is attempting to find the best creative strategy before moving ahead with the actual production of the ad. The process may conclude with more formal, extensive pretesting of the ad before a final decision is made. Pretesting and related procedures are examined in detail in Chapter 9.

CREATIVE BRIEF

The end result of the creative process is the written document referred to as the creative brief. It specifies the basic elements of the creative strategy and other relevant information. The **creative brief** may have other names depending upon the agency, such as creative platform, creative blueprint, creative contract, or copy platform. Essentially, it is a plan that summarizes the entire creative approach that is agreed upon by the creative team and the marketing managers. Figure 7-2 shows a sample creative brief outline. Just as there are different names for the creative brief, there are variations in the outline and format used and in the level of detail included. The creative brief for the Tacori ad in Exhibit 7-6 called for a strategy of positioning the 18K925 brand as the ultimate expression of passion, with modern, accessible style and lasting quality.

The first three sections of the creative brief are derived from the marketing plan and prior communication between the creative specialists and brand managers. The planning framework of this text, shown in Chapter 1, also supports all sections of this creative brief illustration. Chapter 1 highlighted the importance of the marketing plan for promotional planning, which should provide sufficient background on the nature of the communication problem or opportunity. Chapter 3 described important aspects of consumer behaviour along with options for target audience selection and guidelines for a target audience profile. Combined, Chapters 4 and 5 explained the usefulness of response models and communication objectives that guide remaining decisions. The previous chapter indicated different brand positioning options that creative specialists might propose as communication solutions. The rest of this chapter describes the creative strategy decisions that the creative specialists typically recommend. Finally, creative briefs may also include supporting information and requirements that should appear in any message to ensure uniformity across the ads used in a campaign.

At times, creative specialists experience communication problems among the participants of the creative process. Part of the problem is attributed to creative personnel not actually writing a creative brief. The creative process may be initially described in a series of notes

Exhibit 7-6 Tacori's positioning called for 18K925 to be the ultimate expression of passion.

or sketches, and as it evolves through the stages of the creative process some of the original participants may not be aware of all the changes. Alternatively, the lack of full description leads to misunderstanding of how the sequence of events, for example, would occur in a television commercial. And while it is important to have a written creative brief, it should be brief enough so that all participants could read it quickly and easily and still demonstrate the creativity of the advertising. In the end we can say that the creative brief should (1) be objective, (2) have proper vocabulary, spelling, and grammar, (3) demonstrate logical thinking, (4) be both creative and brief, (5) have specific recommendations, and (6) be viewed as a firm agreement.[31]

ADVERTISING CAMPAIGN

An **advertising campaign** is a set of interrelated and coordinated marketing communication activities that centre on a single theme or idea. A campaign appears in different media and IMC tools across a specified time period. Advertising campaign plans are short-term in nature and, like marketing and IMC plans, are done on an annual basis. However, the campaign themes are usually developed with the intention of being used for a longer time period. Thus far we have referred to creativity as advertising creativity since this is the history and origin of creativity in marketing communication. But, creativity is an important facet in all aspects of promotion even if there is not accompanying advertising in the campaign. Promotional elements like sponsorship of a good cause will often have advertising supporting it. And digital communication, whether one classifies it as advertising or advertising-like, contains creativity—big time!

Multiple executions are required in order for a creative message to be considered a campaign. How many executions will depend on the creative specialists and clients before approval of a campaign occurs, but generally the creative idea driving the message needs at least three to tell the story. This notion is based on the "rule of three," where stories or jokes require three episodes for complete understanding; progression occurs as tension is created, built up, and then released with the unfolding of the message. This "rule" is more an observed pattern across many walks of life with respect to communication, rather than scientifically proven; however, it is consistent with how often a consumer needs to receive a message in media planning.

Scotiabank began its "Richer than you think" campaign in 2006, and included three phases. The first focused on getting a second opinion. The executions for this included three TV ads and two print ads, with supporting digital exposure. A later one in 2009 during the recession addressed people's financial concerns with 11 TV spots conveying a message of "making the most of what you have." A third wave occurred in 2012 when multiple messages looked at how consumers defined richness in their terms, which featured user-generated spots as part of Scotiabank's Richness Project.[32] This example demonstrates the requirement and importance of multiple executions, and also how a campaign operates over time. Once an initial successful campaign takes hold, it can move toward a series of interrelated campaigns such that the original is much more than a campaign and is elevated to strategic brand communication. Alternatively, it can take on its own momentum without much change like the Absolut campaign described earlier or the 66 executions in the Mac vs. PC campaign.[33]

(L03) Creative Theme

Determining the unifying theme around which the campaign will be built is a critical decision as it often sets the tone for other forms of marketing communication that will be used, such as sales promotion or digital applications. Furthermore, the **creative theme** should be a strong idea since it represents the central message of a marketing communication program, reflects the market positioning strategy, and directly communicates the brand positioning strategy to its intended target audience. In this section, we describe four related decisions that comprise the creative theme. First, we identify ways to determine the creative theme. Then, we present the importance of slogans to reinforce brand positioning and/or creative theme. Next, we explore the issue of consistency of the creative theme across many parts of the promotional program. We conclude by exploring the importance of unique Canadian creative advertising and its success.

ORIGIN OF CREATIVE THEME

The creative team is provided with the challenge of deciding upon the strong or "big" idea of the creative theme that attracts the consumer's attention, gets a response, and sets the advertiser's product or service apart from the competition. Well-known adman John O'Toole describes the *big idea* as "that flash of insight that synthesizes the purpose of the strategy, joins the product benefit with consumer desire in a fresh, involving way, brings the subject to life, and makes the reader or audience stop, look, and listen."[34] It is difficult to pinpoint the inspiration for a big idea or to teach advertising people how to find one. However, the following approaches can guide the creative team's search for a creative theme.

- Using a unique selling proposition.
- Creating a brand image.
- Finding the inherent drama.
- Positioning.

Unique Selling Proposition   The concept of the **unique selling proposition (USP)** was developed by Rosser Reeves, former chair of the Ted Bates agency, and is described in his influential book *Reality in Advertising*. Reeves noted three characteristics of unique selling propositions:

- Each advertisement must make a proposition to the consumer. Not just words, not just product puffery, not just show-window advertising. Each advertisement must say to each reader: "Buy this product and you will get this benefit."
- The proposition must be one that the competition either cannot or does not offer. It must be unique either in the brand or in the claim.
- The proposition must be strong enough to move the mass millions, that is, pull over new customers to your brand.[35]

Reeves said the attribute claim or benefit that forms the basis of the USP should dominate the ad and be emphasized through repetitive advertising. An example of advertising based on a USP is the campaign for Colgate Total toothpaste (Exhibit 7-7). The brand has a unique, patented formula that creates a protective barrier that fights germs for 12 hours, which helps reduce and prevent gum disease.

For Reeves's approach to work, there must be a truly unique product or service attribute, benefit, or inherent advantage that can be used in the claim. The approach may require considerable research on the product and consumers, not only to determine the USP but also to document the claim. The storyboard for Activia yogurt is an excellent example where a unique characteristic of a product is emphasized in an ad (Exhibit 7-8).

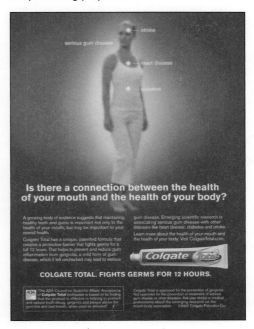

Exhibit 7-7   This Colgate Total ad uses a unique selling proposition.

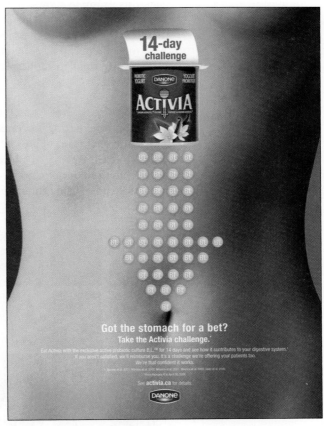

Exhibit 7-8   Activia employed a unique selling proposition in its messages.

Exhibit 7-9   Bebe uses advertising to build an image as a sexy and stylish brand.

Creating a Brand Image

In many product and service categories, competing brands are so similar that it is very difficult to communicate a unique attribute or benefit. Many of the packaged-goods products that account for most of the advertising dollars spent are difficult to differentiate on a functional or performance basis. The creative theme used to communicate these products is based on the development of a strong, memorable identity for the brand through image advertising.

David Ogilvy popularized the idea of brand image in his famous book *Confessions of an Advertising Man*. Ogilvy said that with image advertising, "every advertisement should be thought of as a contribution to the complex symbol which is the brand image." He argued that the image or personality of the brand is particularly important when brands are similar. The key to successful image advertising is developing an image that will appeal to product users. For example the Bebe ad in Exhibit 7-9 gives the fashion brand a distinctive look for its line of clothing.

Image advertising is designed to give a brand a unique association or personality, and create a certain feeling or mood that is activated when a consumer uses a particular product or service. For example, SKYY vodka ads associate the brand with cinematic-inspired cocktail moments (see Exhibit 7-10). The high-impact ads do not contain any copy but rather rely on stylish, seductive visuals that set up storylines but leave the interpretation of the actual scenarios up to the mind of the viewer. All ads feature SKYY's distinctive cobalt blue and showcase the brand as a catalyst for a great cocktail moment. As a result, SKYY achieved a deep emotional connection with the style-conscious trendsetters that the brand targets.

As this example shows, image development often occurs through literary devices such as metaphors or analogies. This involves both visual and copy elements of an ad that allow consumers to interpret the message by transferring meaning from another aspect to the brand. These metaphors can be concrete (e.g., direct, obvious) or abstract (e.g., indirect, interpretive). Selecting the right metaphor is sometimes difficult as consumers have difficulty discovering the references.[36]

Finding the Inherent Drama

Another approach to determining the creative theme is finding the inherent drama or characteristic of the product that makes the consumer purchase it. The inherent drama approach expresses the advertising philosophy of Leo Burnett, founder of the Leo Burnett Agency in Chicago. Burnett said inherent drama "is often hard to find but it is always there, and once found it is the most interesting and believable of all advertising appeals."[37] He believed advertising should be based on a foundation of consumer benefits with an emphasis

Exhibit 7-10   Advertising for SKYY vodka uses a cinematic theme to create an image for the brand.

on the dramatic element in expressing those benefits. Burnett advocated a down-home type of advertising that presents the message in a warm and realistic way.

For example, the storyboard in Exhibit 7-11 tells the tale of Salty the personified salt shaker as he realizes he is no longer wanted quite like he used to be once Knorr Sidekicks reduced the amount of sodium in its products by 25 percent. Wandering the streets with Michael Bolton's "How Am I Supposed to Live Without You" playing, Salty is inconsolable and cries salty tears. This campaign featured TV, print, wild postings, direct mail, sales promotions, banner ads, website, and tools. The drama of what happened to Salty lived on in social media as he established his own Facebook and Twitter profiles, and continued stories of what Salty did for his next career emerged with online video. While a salt shaker coming to life may not be overly realistic, the emotional connection of the story expressed a realist human condition.

Exhibit 7-11   The tragic story of Salty captured the essence of the benefit of Knorr Sidekicks.

Positioning   Since advertising helps establish or maintain the brand position, it can also be the source of the creative theme. Positioning is often the basis of a firm's creative strategy when it has multiple brands competing in the same market. For example, Procter & Gamble markets many brands of laundry detergent—and positions each one differently. Positioning is done for companies as well as for brands. For example, the ad shown in Exhibit 7-12 is part of a GE campaign that is designed to position the company as an innovator in health care.

Trout and Ries originally described positioning as the image consumers had of the brand in relation to competing brands in the product or service category, but the concept has been expanded beyond direct competitive positioning.[38] As discussed in Chapter 6, products can be positioned on the basis of end benefit, brand name, usage situation, or product category. Any of these can spark a theme that becomes the basis of the creative strategy and results in the brand's occupying a particular place in the minds of the target audience. Since brand positioning can be done on the basis of a distinctive attribute, the positioning and unique selling proposition approaches can overlap.

CAMPAIGN SLOGANS

The theme for the advertising campaign is usually expressed through a **slogan** or **tagline** that reduces the key idea into a few words or a brief statement. The advertising slogan should serve as a summation line that succinctly expresses the brand positioning strategy, as well as the message it is trying to deliver to the target audience. The slogan usually appears in every advertisement and is often used in other forms of marketing communications to serve as a reminder of, and to reinforce, the marketer's branding message.

What constitutes a good slogan? All of the following suggestions are not possible for a single slogan, but they offer guidance when

Exhibit 7-12   GE positions itself as an innovative company in health care.

making a final decision. Characteristics can pertain to the brand attitude objectives: include key benefit, differentiate the brand, evoke positive feelings, reflect brand personality, and be believable and likable. Others pertain to brand awareness objectives: be memorable, and recall brand name. Additionally, slogans are oriented strategically, to be campaign-able and competitive. Finally, aesthetics are important as slogans should be original, simple, neat/cool, and positive.[39]

Canadian advertisers continually develop slogans, and it is interesting to examine new ones to figure out whether they meet these criteria. The Kobo electronic reader displayed, "For those who love reading above all else." Autotrader turned the phrase, "The better way to buy and sell cars." Corona sipped in, "Live the finer life." Hawaiian Punch returned to Canada with "Smashingly delicious." Tassimo coffee machine frothed up, "The barcode brews it better." Contiki Tours targeted youth with two slogans, "It's time to start living" and "One life, one shot, make it count." Canadian Tire is on it fourth slogan since 2001, "Let's get started," "___ starts at Canadian Tire," "For days like today," and "Bring it on."[40]

CREATIVE THEME CONSISTENCY

Consistency in promotional creativity is generally regarded as a key success factor so that the target audience retains the brand position. We explore examples of consistency in the creative theme across time, creative execution, advertising media, promotional tools, and products. The essential point is that when the target audience is exposed to a series of messages across different contexts, the creative theme should not change such that there is a clear reinforcement of the brand positioning strategy. Deviation of the theme allows the possibility that the target audience will process the message alternatively and arrive at a different interpretation of the brand.

Consistency across Time   Advertising or communication plans are generally done on an annual basis, thus the creative theme is often short-term in nature. However, the creative themes are usually developed with the intention of being used for a longer time period. While marketers might change their campaign themes often, a successful creative theme may last for years. A consistent creative theme across time builds on the established awareness of the brand's current customers by encouraging continued processing of future advertising messages. Moreover, the familiarity of the creative theme is recognizable to a brand's non-customers when they may be entering the product category or considering switching their purchases. The ad in Exhibit 7-13 for the Honda Odyssey is consistent with other ads showing the improved features of the new model.

After its initial launch, Koodo revised its creative theme but retained many characteristics so that the campaigns appeared continuous. They retained the same "fun, quirky and colourful characters"; however, they are no longer in spandex urging consumers to lose their bloated bills from other providers. Rather, the new characters articulate clever words like, "textelation," "contractophobe," "fee-ectomy," and "bigbillification." The freshened campaign intended to keep the brand distinct from the campaign theme, as the message to consumers of other brands is to switch to this new discount provider.[41]

Consistency across Executions   As we noted above, an advertising campaign features a series of creative executions over time and it is important that marketers ensure all ads feature a similar "look and feel." Exactly what this entails is a matter of interpretation, but most advertisers and consumers would say they recognize it when they see it. For example, many would say that the creative theme for Absolut vodka is consistent in all its print ads even though we see the distinctive bottle in many different types of scenes or situations that fit with the specific target audience of each magazine the ads are placed in.

Kraft Canada has used the same creative theme of an angel consuming Philadelphia cream cheese in the clouds of heaven throughout all of its

Exhibit 7-13   Ads for the Honda Odyssey have used a similar format for many years.

television executions. This creative approach for communicating the brand's benefits has served it well as a distinctive presentation that is recognizable and consistent with positioning the brand as a tasty and healthy food product.[42]

Consistency across Media   Often a successful creative theme is one that is amenable to more than one media. For instance, the essence of creativity in a print ad is still captured in a follow-up radio ad. Or, the big idea found in a TV commercial transfers to an outdoor billboard. In both cases, the creativity of the initial media is seen in a supportive medium—one less central to the primary media, yet still important to continue exposing a similar idea to the target audience. Interestingly, this idea is difficult to convey with visual creative themes moving to radio. For a while, listeners heard a "friendly thought" from Telus that differed significantly from the nature theme portrayed in all visual media.

Consistency across Promotional Tools   Using the advertising creative theme across the various promotional tools is an issue to be resolved. The argument for the same look and feel is pervasive. For example, Telus Mobility keeps its nature theme in all of its communications—from TV ads to promotional displays to its website and finally all of its public relations and publicity. Actions such as this support the notion that the creative theme for the integrated marketing communication must support the broad market positioning and all brand positioning strategies for its many target audiences. This is also evident with Bud Light, which created the character Budd Light who appeared in all TV ads and was featured at promotional events. Representing the number-five beer in Canada, the fictional spokesperson embodies the spirit of the brand as he "Keeps the good times going." This uniquely Canadian theme works with target of fun-loving young men, yet spills over to women as well through other promotional activities like a contest to win a Caribbean cruise.[43]

Consistency across Products   The same kind of use of a consistent theme across all IMC tools is evident in RBC Financial Group's "First" campaign; the theme pervades all of RBC's tools for all its products and services. And so the campaign's consistent theme works on multiple levels. It is positioning the overall firm as an innovative and forward-looking organization, yet the campaign adapts well to a variety of purchase and consumption situations for credit or investment products that can be also adjusted depending on whether the target audience is a loyal customer or a potential one that RBC Financial Group is attempting to switch. Consistency is also evident with RBC's message of "create" and their use of the financial adviser Arbie (i.e., R.B., for Royal Bank) who appears in messages across all IMC tools and products. Arbie is especially prominent in public relations activities, like the Olympic sponsorship, and for corporate advocacy issues such as water conservation.[44] Similarly, for its consumer products Knorr has used a very similar design and colour scheme for many products advertised (Exhibit 7-14).

CANADIAN CREATIVE THEMES

We now present ideas regarding creative themes used in Canadian advertising and promotional communication. We begin with a perspective that supports the importance for unique ways of speaking to Canadian consumers. Since many brands are part of a North American or international marketing strategy, there is a tendency to standardize the

Exhibit 7-14   Colourful ads are often used in Knorr's product advertising.

message. We now highlight success stories as evidence of the importance for Canadian creativity in communication.

Importance of Canadian Creative Themes   The need for unique creative advertising can be found in the divergence of values between Canadians and Americans. Decades of consumer research by Environics researcher Michael Adams suggests that while the citizens of North America share similar aspects of society, the underlying values are quite distinct.[45] For example, in 1992, 17 percent of Canadians and 34 percent of Americans agreed that "a widely advertised product is probably a good product"; however, in 2000 the percentage for Canadians had remained unchanged while the percentage for Americans had risen to 44 percent.[46] Canadians are seen as "more inner-directed, more security-seeking, and yet are more socially liberal and tolerant of individual diversity" compared to Americans.[47]

These unique Canadian values influence the motivation for consumption—Canadians buy products for what they can do for them versus what they say about them. Canadians favour experiences over possessions and are less inclined toward conspicuous consumption. For example, Canadians are more likely to believe that a car is basic transportation versus a statement of personal style or image. Therefore, certain types of advertising messages are more palatable for Canadians since the underlying reasons for purchase are more accurately reflected in the dialogue of a commercial or the body copy of a print ad produced by Canadian advertisers. In fact, one author believes that Canada is truly in an advertising renaissance where agencies are consistently producing world-calibre creative campaigns.[48] Furthermore, the distinctiveness of Canadians derived from these data may be strong evidence for allowing Canadian managers more latitude in developing unique creative messages.[49]

Putting together a creative for Canada can be met with obstacles. Canadian managers who market U.S. brands in Canada often feel the pressure to run the same campaign in Canada that is being run in the United States. While this obviously saves on production costs of new ads, it can be more than offset with lower sales due to messages not resonating with Canadian culture. Sometimes firms need to perform specific market research to demonstrate that a unique creative is warranted for the Canadian market. For example, Maytag required an entirely different positioning and creative in Canada when American messages focused on its made-in-USA claims. The Maytag repairman ventured north to shoot new ads that played during *Hockey Night in Canada* with a usage theme for cleaning hockey equipment, among others.[50]

Successful Canadian Creative Themes   Historically and recently, insightful and innovative Canadian creative themes demonstrate effective advertising and promotional communication. We take this time to identify the Canadian organizations that recognize creative themes that have been truly outstanding. Specifically, we summarize the CASSIES, the Marketing Awards, the Bessies, and the Extra Awards. We also highlight Canada's performance at the prestigious Cannes competition held in France.

CASSIES   Awarded by the Institute of Communication and Advertising (ICA), the Association of Quebec Advertising Agencies, and Publicité Club de Montréal, this recognition is perhaps the most significant in Canada as it identifies Canadian advertising success stories. Initiated in Canada in 1993, the award is based on a similar idea started during the 1980s in the United Kingdom. Originally awarded every second year from 1993 until 2001, the CASSIES are now an annual event.

The CASSIES Award recognizes advertising and promotional campaigns that document a direct cause and effect relationship between the campaign and communication and business results. Entrants have to submit the details of their campaign in the form of a business case that summarizes the performance of the brand prior to the campaign and indicates the degree to which the performance has improved. The website, Cassies.ca, provides the complete entry requirements, identifies the winners, and contains the actual case history submitted. Newfoundland and Labrador Tourism won in 2012 when it showed spectacular and fascinating images of that province in ads across the country (Exhibit 7-15).

The world can't weigh you down
when you're standing on top of it.

Considering it took 485,000,000 years to create, it's hardly surprising what you'll find here. Not the least of which is perspective. It tends to happen when you're standing two thousand feet up, seeing things more clearly on the edge of an ancient glacier-carved fjord. A vantage point.

one would think, that could only exist for two reasons: for the view itself, and the inescapable feeling that washes over you. The feeling you get when your troubles seem less significant. And once again, anything's possible. To find your way here, call Kelly at 1-800-563-6353 or visit NewfoundlandLabrador.com

$139

Newfoundland
Labrador

WESTJET.COM

Exhibit 7-15   A breathtaking image of Gros Morne National Park captivated Canadians in this award-winning campaign.

Trade Magazines   Two awards given out annually, sponsored by different trade magazines—*Strategy* and *Marketing Magazine*—identify the top Canadian creative communication launched each year in a number of categories. For example, there is an overall winner for best multimedia campaign, a winner for best single ad and campaign across all major media, and awards for nontraditional media, point-of-purchase, and public service announcements.

Bessies   These awards are given by the Television Bureau of Canada (TVB), an organization whose members comprise television stations, networks, and specialty services. The TVB promotes the use of television as an effective medium and has an important role as an information resource for its members. The Bessies recognize the best in English TV advertising each year and have been doing so since the early 1960s, shortly after the invention of television (an equivalent award for French TV advertising is awarded at La Fête de la Pub).

Extra Awards   The Canadian Newspaper Association is similar to the TVB but for daily newspapers. Its Extra Awards recognize outstanding creative advertising in this medium by giving ads a gold, silver, bronze, or merit award in nine product categories and types of ads (i.e., local ad, local campaign, national campaign, small-space ad).

Cannes   On a global level, the Cannes Lions International Festival of Creativity is widely considered the most prestigious awards competition for advertising and all types of marketing communication. The Cannes competition receives entries from agencies around the world hoping to win Lions (the name of the award) in many categories. IMC Perspective 7-2 highlights the background of the competition and achievements of Canadian advertising at Cannes.

(LO4) Message Appeals

The **message appeal** refers to the approach used to influence consumers' attitude toward the product, service, or cause. A message appeal can also be viewed as "something that moves people, speaks to their wants or needs, and excites their interest."[51] As this suggests, the message appeal is an important creative strategy decision since it has an important role with influencing the target audience's attitude toward the brand. Hundreds of different appeals can be used as the basis for advertising messages. We summarize on five broad appeals: rational appeals, emotional appeals, fear appeals, humour appeals, and combined rational and emotional appeals. In this section, we focus on ways to use these appeals as part of a creative strategy and consider how they can be combined in developing the advertising message.

IMC PERSPECTIVE 7-2

Evolution and Canadian Winners at Cannes

Each year, the famed Cannes Lions International Festival of Creativity—which started in 1954 as the International Advertising Film Festival in Venice—recognizes the world's best advertising. Inspired by the movie industry's more famous Cannes Film Festival, the Cannes Lions is widely considered the most prestigious advertising award competition. The competition receives entries from agencies around the world hoping to win Lions in each of the major categories— film (television, cinema, and Web film ads), press and poster (print and outdoor ads), cyber advertising (online marketing and ads for websites), media planning/buying, and direct marketing. The competition recently added the Titanium Lion for innovative work across integrated media.

The annual meeting on the French Riviera is an important forum where many of the world's largest advertisers and agencies meet to discuss the future of advertising and integrated marketing communication. There are many speaking events, extensive networking opportunities, and a chance to see work from many of the competitive entries.

Much has changed over the past 20 years with a few noteworthy highlights. The year 1992 marked the first time the competition recognized media other than film by adding press and outdoor, and dropped the word film from the title. In 1998 and 1999, Cannes added cyber and media as award categories, respectively. Following this, direct marketing, radio, and promotion awards emerged in 2002, 2005, and 2006, respectively. Finally, in 2010 and 2011 public relations and advertising effectiveness were recognized as important with awards granted in those areas.

For part of this time Canada performed weakly, but that all changed in 1999 with a concerted effort to send more entries. Molson's "Rant" won Bronze Film the following year, and since then Canada has been on a roll. In 2004 VIM won Gold Film for "Prison Visitor," subsequently aired worldwide and extensively viewed on the Internet. In 2007, Dove's "Evolution" won Gold for Film and Cyber. By 2009, Canada topped 800 entries, winning Gold Outdoor for the James Ready campaign. For 2011, Canadian agencies won five Gold, three Silver, and nine Bronze Lions, with three Gold, three Silver, and 11 Bronze Lions in 2012.

Along with the opportunity to showcase talent, the growth of Cannes has made it considerably more expensive for agencies to participate. The owner of Cannes hopes to make a profit after purchasing it for more than $100 million in 2004. Furthermore, with a total of 46 advertising awards shows worldwide in a given year, the total administrative cost is substantial for agencies wishing to submit many entries to many shows to enhance their reputation. DDB employs a full-time staff to coordinate its entries for all the shows. President David Leonard commented, "Like it or not, awards are the currency by which creatives are judged by their peers. It's what makes these people famous and thus valuable." In contrast to DDB, Capital C decided to only enter Cannes (because of its new effectiveness Lions) and the CASSIES (which also recognize advertising effectiveness). Cannes requires a fee of $400 to $1,500 per entry; in 2012 Canadian entries spent a total of about $600,000.

Sources: Susan Krashinsky, "In Cannes, Ad Awards Win Critics," *The Globe and Mail,* June 15, 2012, p. B6; Jeromy Lloyd, "The Cannes Debrief," *Marketing Magazine,* August 13, 2012; "Canada Cannes Count," *Marketing Magazine,* August 13, 2012; Emily Wexler, "Canada@Cannes: A Recent History," *Strategy,* June 3, 2011; Simon Houpt, "In Sunny Riviera, Storm Clouds Gather," *The Globe and Mail,* June 24, 2011, p. B8; David Brown and Jeromy Lloyd, "The Shifting Sands of Cannes," *Marketing Magazine,* August 1, 2011.

Question:

1. Do changes to the name and focus of the Cannes awards festival make it more or less enticing for an advertising agency to enter?

RATIONAL APPEALS

Rational appeals focus on the consumer's practical, functional, or utilitarian need for the product or service and emphasize features of a product or service and/or the benefits or reasons for owning or using a particular brand. The content of these messages emphasizes facts, learning, and the logic of persuasion.[52] Rational-based appeals tend to be informative, and advertisers

Exhibit 7-16 A rational appeal is used to promote the safety features of the Acura TL.

using them generally attempt to convince consumers that their product or service has a particular attribute(s) or provides a specific benefit that satisfies their needs. Their objective is to persuade the target audience to buy the brand because it is the best available or does a better job of meeting consumers' needs. For example, the ad shown in Exhibit 7-16 uses a rational appeal to promote how the Advanced Compatibility Engineering body structure in the Acura TL automobile is an innovative safety feature. Weilbacher[53] identified several rational advertising appeals—comparative, price, news, and product/service popularity—and we add reminder appeal to this list.

Feature Appeal   Ads that use a *feature appeal* focus on the dominant traits of the product or service. These ads tend to be highly informative and present the customer with a number of important product attributes or features that will lead to favourable attitudes and can be used as the basis for a rational purchase decision. Technical and high-involvement products often use message appeal. Exhibit 7-17 shows an ad for Red Bull energy drink that focuses on the benefits of its contents.

Comparative Appeal   Ads that practise a *comparative appeal* either directly or indirectly identify competitors and compare the brands (or products) on one or more specific attributes or benefits.[54] Studies show that recall is higher for comparative than noncomparative messages, but comparative ads are generally not more effective for other response variables, such as brand attitudes or purchase intentions.[55] Advertisers must also consider how comparative messages affect credibility. Users of the brand being attacked in a comparative message may be especially skeptical about the advertiser's claims.

Comparative appeals may be particularly useful for new brands, since they allow a new market entrant to position itself directly against the more established brands and to promote its distinctive

Exhibit 7-17   Red Bull uses a feature appeal to promote its benefits to students.

advantages. Direct comparisons can help position a new brand in the evoked, or choice, set of brands the customer may be considering.

Comparative appeals are often used for brands with a small market share. They compare themselves to an established market leader in hopes of creating an association and tapping into the leader's market. Market leaders, on the other hand, often hesitate to use comparison ads, as most believe they have little to gain by featuring competitors' products in their ads.

Price Appeal   An ad with a price offer as the dominant point of the message may be known as a *price appeal*. Price appeal advertising is used most often by retailers to announce sales, special offers, or low everyday prices. Many fast-food chains have made price an important part of their marketing strategy through promotional deals and "value menus" or lower overall prices. Advertisers for vehicles and electronics use price appeals as part of their IMC strategy as well. For example, the Hewlett-Packard advertisement shown in Exhibit 7-18 promotes the affordability of the HP Officejet Pro printer for business use. The ad copy explains how it can print in colour at a cost that is up to 50 percent less per page than a laser printer and consumes less energy. The visual portion of the ad also uses vivid colours to represent the number 50 and deliver a message regarding the quality of the colour printing capabilities of the Officejet Pro.

News Appeal   When an announcement about the product, service, or company dominates the ad, advertises are using a *news appeal*. This type of appeal can be used for a new product or service or to inform consumers of significant modifications or improvements. This appeal works best when a company has important news it wants to communicate to its target market. For example, airlines sometimes use news appeals when beginning to offer service to new cities or opening new routes as a way of informing consumers as well as generating media exposure that results in publicity.

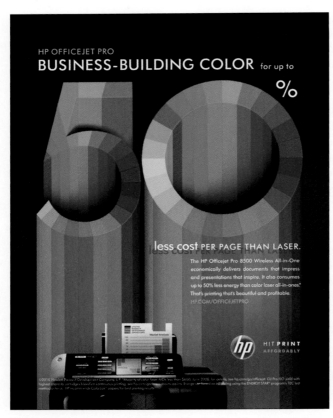

Exhibit 7-18   HP advertises the affordability of colour printing to businesses that use the Officejet Pro.

Popularity Appeal   Ads with a *popularity appeal* stress the popularity of a product or service by pointing out the number of consumers who use the brand, the number who have switched to it, the number of experts who recommend it, or its leadership position in the market. The main point of this advertising appeal is that the wide use of the brand proves its quality or value and other customers should consider using it. The ad shown in Exhibit 7-19 uses a popularity appeal by noting how TaylorMade drivers are used by more PGA Tour professionals than its leading competitors combined. Ads such as this are used to implement TaylorMade's marketing strategy, which focuses on innovation, the technological superiority of its golf equipment, and the popularity and use of its clubs by tour professionals who exert a strong influence on the purchase decisions of amateur golfers.

Reminder Appeal   When the objective of the ad is to build or maintain awareness, an advertiser might use a *reminder appeal*. Well-known brands and market leaders of frequently used products often use a reminder appeal, which is often referred to as reminder advertising (Exhibit 7-20). Products and services that have a seasonal pattern to their consumption also use reminder advertising, particularly around the appropriate period. For example, marketers of candy products often increase their media budgets and run reminder advertising around Halloween, Valentine's Day, Christmas, and Easter.

Exhibit 7-19 TaylorMade promotes the popularity of its drivers among golf professionals.

EMOTIONAL APPEALS

Emotional appeals relate to the customer's social and/or psychological needs for purchasing a product or service. Many of consumers' motives for their purchase decisions contain strong emotions, and their feelings about a brand can be more important than knowledge of its features or attributes. Many advertisers believe appeals to consumers' emotions work better at selling brands that do not differ markedly from competing brands, since rational differentiation of them is difficult.[56] The ad for Old Spice captured the emotion of consuming men's products with humour (Exhibit 7-21). Virtually every single Coca-Cola ad is dedicated to positive emotions associated with drinking the product, and when the beverage brand teamed up with Google to put digital software in dispensing machines that let consumers "buy" a Coke for someone else in the world, the joy spread exponentially.[57]

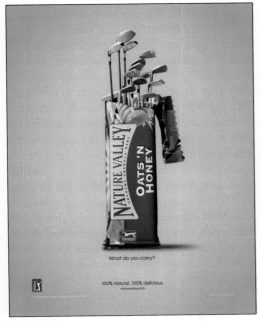

Exhibit 7-20 This ad reminds golfers to carry Nature Valley Granola Bars.

Exhibit 7-21 This Old Spice ad uses an emotional appeal.

The choice between rational or emotional appeal is a challenge and careful consideration must take place to ensure the advertising resonates with the target audience and evokes relevant processing responses connected to the purchase decision or consumption experience. Surprisingly, Google employed an emotional appeal in many ads to market its new array of products. When addressing the campaign, a Google executive even exclaimed, "It's about emotion, which is bizarre for a tech company."[58] Despite being a self-described tech company, Google's product is used and enjoyed on a daily (minute-by-minute?) basis, so how could there *not* be emotion with something involved so often in people's lives?

Hamish Pringle and Peter Field documented the effectiveness of emotion-based appeals in their book *Brand Immortality*.[59] They analyzed 880 case studies of successful advertising campaigns submitted for the United Kingdom–based Institute of Practitioners in Advertising Effectiveness Award competition over the past three decades and included campaigns from the U.K. as well as international competitions. Their analysis compared advertising campaigns that relied primarily on emotional appeals with those that used rational persuasion and information. A key finding is that advertising campaigns with purely emotional content produce nearly double the profit gains versus rational content campaigns. One reason why emotional campaigns work so well is that they reduce price sensitivity and strengthen the ability of brands to charge a price premium, which contributes to profitability.

However, emotional ads could also spur greater frequency of purchase or attract new consumers as shown by McDonald's. It changed its advertising strategy in 2003 to a common "I'm Lovin' It" theme worldwide for the very first time in its history and put an emotional emphasis into its commercials. McDonald's believes the emotional ads take advantage of the chain's unique bond with consumers, which is a significant point of differentiation in the competitive quick-service food market. The campaign helped the company achieve strong sales growth.[60] After one year of consumer research and creative brainstorming, McDonald's announced continued use of the "I'm Lovin' It" campaign. The brand intended to integrate more emotion in the executions by focusing on family bonding and fun with food as well as celebrating uniquely McDonald's moments in its ads.[61]

Kamp and MacInnis note that commercials often rely on the concept of *emotional integration,* whereby they portray the characters in the ad as experiencing an emotional benefit or outcome from using a product or service.[62] Marketers use emotional appeals in hopes that the positive feeling they evoke will transfer to the brand and/or company. Research shows that positive mood states and feelings created by advertising can have a favourable effect on consumers' evaluations of a brand.[63] Ads using lifestyle, humour, sex, and other appeals that are very entertaining, arousing, upbeat, and/or exciting can affect the emotions of consumers and put them in a favourable frame of mind. For example, Second Clothing, a Montreal-based premium denim brand, demonstrated the feeling women have when first trying on a pair of yoga jeans. With very sensual images, sexy music, and the sound of an amorous woman "cooing," one presumes the experience lives ups to the tagline "Feel Good. Real Good."[64]

Many feelings can serve as the basis for advertising appeals designed to influence consumers on an emotional level, as shown in Figure 7-3. Relying on considerable research over time, this taxonomy identifies core negative and positive emotions. Moreover, the table indicates the origin of the emotion, which demonstrates the core subjective meaning of the emotion and the action consequences of someone experiencing the emotion.[65] These additional descriptions of the emotion are important as they give direction as to the content and authenticity of the emotion for planning this emotional message appeal; advertisers that miss the mark on emotional accuracy are quickly rejected.

Each of these core emotions embodies nuances. Contentment might include things like happiness, joy, nostalgia, and sentiment. Elements of pride may be seen in recognition, status, acceptance, and approval. Other emotions appear to cross more than core emotion; for example excitement is likely part of the first four positive emotions. We now review one negative and one positive emotional appeal commonly used in message delivery.

FEAR APPEALS

Fear is an emotional response to a threat that expresses or at least implies danger. Ads sometimes use **fear appeals** to invoke this emotional response and arouse individuals to take steps

Figure   7-3   Basis for emotional appeals

Negative Emotion	Origin	Action
Anger	Offense against self	Restore justice, hold individuals responsible
Contempt	Other violates role, duty, obligation	Lower the reputation of perpetrator
Disgust	Contact with impure object or action	Push away
Embarrassment	Self has transgressed a social convention	Apologize
Envy	Other is superior to self	Reduce status of other
Fear	Imminent threat to self	Flee, reduce uncertainty
Guilt	Self has violated moral standard regarding harm	Remedy harm
Jealousy	Other threatens source of affection	Protect source of affection from others
Sadness	Irrevocable loss	Acquire new goods
Shame	Self has transgressed aspiration or ideal	Hide, avoid scrutiny

Positive Emotion	Origin	Action
Contentment	Pleasing stimulus	Savoring
Enthusiasm	Reward likely	Goal approach
Love	Perceived commitment	Affection
Sexual desire	Sexual cue or opportunity	Sexual release
Compassion	Undeserved suffering	Pro-social approach
Gratitude	Unexpected gift	Promote reciprocity
Pride	Self-relevant achievement	Status display
Awe	Self is small vs. something vast	Devotion, reverence
Interest	Novel opportunity	Exploration
Amusement	Recognize incongruity	Play
Relief	Cause of distress ends	Signal safety

Source: Dacher Keltner and Jennifer S. Lerner, "Emotion," *Handbook of Social Psychology*, ed. Susan T. Fiske, Daniel T. Gilbers, and Gardner Lindzey, 2010, John Wiley & Sons.

to remove the threat. Some, like anti-smoking ads, stress physical danger that can occur if behaviours are not altered. Others—like those for deodorant, mouthwash, or dandruff shampoos—threaten disapproval or social rejection.

Before deciding to use a fear appeal–based message strategy, the advertiser should consider how fear operates, what level to use, and how different target audiences may respond. One theory suggests that the relationship between the level of fear in a message and acceptance or persuasion is curvilinear, as shown in Figure 7-4.[66] This means that message acceptance increases as the amount of fear used rises—to a point. Beyond that point, acceptance decreases as the level of fear rises.

This relationship between fear and persuasion can be explained by the fact that fear appeals have both facilitating and inhibiting effects.[67] A low level of fear can have facilitating effects; it attracts attention and interest in the message and may motivate the receiver to act to resolve the threat. Thus, increasing the level of fear in a message from low to moderate can result in increased persuasion. High levels of fear, however, can produce inhibiting effects; the receiver may emotionally block the message by tuning it out, perceiving it selectively, or denying its arguments outright. Figure 7-4 illustrates how these two countereffects operate to produce the curvilinear relationship between fear and persuasion.

A study by Anand Keller and Block provides support for this perspective on how fear operates.[68] Their study indicated that a communication using a low level of fear may be ineffective

Figure 7-4

Relationship between fear
levels and message acceptance

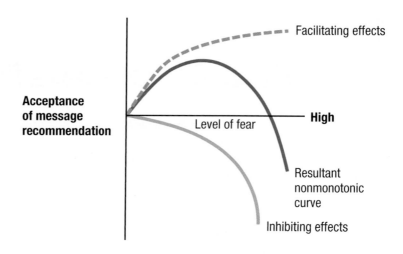

because it results in insufficient motivation to elaborate on the harmful consequences of engaging in the destructive behaviour (smoking). However, an appeal arousing high levels of fear was ineffective because it resulted in too much elaboration on the harmful consequences. This led to defensive tendencies such as message avoidance and interfered with processing of recommended solutions to the problem.

Another approach to the curvilinear explanation of fear is the protection motivation model.[69] According to this theory, four cognitive appraisal processes mediate the individual's response to the threat: appraising (1) the information available regarding the severity of the perceived threat, (2) the perceived probability that the threat will occur, (3) the perceived ability of a coping behaviour to remove the threat, and (4) the individual's perceived ability to carry out the coping behaviour. This model suggests that ads using fear appeals should give the target audience information about the severity of the threat, the probability of its occurrence, the effectiveness of a coping response, and the ease with which the response can be implemented.[70] For example, the ad shown in Exhibit 7-22 uses a mild fear appeal for Seagate Technology's Replica product designed to back up computer hard drives. The ad uses playful illustrations in a graphic style to communicate what can happen if a computer crashes and all files are lost. The ad offers a solution to the threat by showing the ease of using the Replica product and the resulting peace of mind.

In reviewing research on fear appeals, Herbert Rotfeld has argued that the studies may be confusing different types of threats and the level of potential harm portrayed in the message with fear, which is an emotional response.[71] He concludes that the relationship between the emotional responses of fear or arousal and persuasion is not curvilinear but rather is monotonic and positive, meaning that higher levels of fear do result in greater persuasion. However, Rotfeld notes that not all fear messages are equally effective, because different people fear different things. Thus they will respond differently to the same threat, so the strongest threats are not always the most persuasive. This suggests that marketers using fear appeals must

Exhibit 7-22   Seagate uses a mild fear appeal that alerts consumers to a problem and offers a solution.

consider the emotional responses generated by the message and how they will affect reactions to the message.

HUMOUR APPEALS

Humorous ads are often the best known and best remembered of all advertising messages. Humour is usually presented through radio and TV commercials as these media lend themselves to the execution of humorous messages. However, humour is occasionally used in print media as seen in the ad for car safety testing in Australia and New Zealand (Exhibit 7-23). Oftentimes humour fits with products like food, beverages, and household goods; however, advertisers are moving toward using it for personal care products that might have used a fear appeal in the past, which shows that the context and audience dictate the suitability of its use. For example, a maker for incontinence products paired up with Just for Laughs by suggesting that it was okay to laugh since their product would work. Winners of a contest would go to a Just for Laughs festival in Toronto, Montreal, or Chicago.[72]

Advertisers use **humour appeals** for many reasons. Humorous messages attract and hold consumers' attention. They enhance effectiveness by putting consumers in a positive mood, increasing their liking of the ad itself and their feeling toward the product or service. And humour can distract the receiver from counterarguing against the message.[73] Critics argue that funny ads draw people to the humorous situation but distract them from the brand and its attributes. Also, effective humour can be difficult to produce and attempts are too subtle for mass audiences. Finally, practitioners and researchers use the term humour appeal, which corresponds to amusement as the basic emotion, shown in Figure 7-3.

Clearly, there are valid reasons both for and against the use of humour in advertising. Not every product or service lends itself to a humorous approach.[74] A number of studies have found that the effectiveness of humour depends on several factors, including the type of product and audience characteristics.[75] For example, humour has been more prevalent and more effective with low-involvement, feeling products than high-involvement, thinking products.[76] An interesting study surveyed the research and creative directors of the top 150 advertising agencies.[77] They were asked to name which communications objectives are facilitated through the appropriate situational use of humour in terms of media, product, and audience factors. The general conclusions of this study are shown in Figure 7-5.

Exhibit 7-23 A clever ad shows how humour can be executed in print media.

Figure   7-5

Advertising executives'
experience with humour

Humour can:

Aid in gaining attention.

Assist with comprehension and yielding (i.e., cognitive responses).

Create a positive mood that enhances persuasion (i.e., emotional responses).

Aid name and simple copy registration (i.e., brand awareness).

Not aid persuasion in general (i.e., brand attitude), does occur.

Generally not encourage consumer action, but does occur.

Enhance persuasion to switch brands.

COMBINED RATIONAL AND EMOTIONAL APPEALS

In many advertising situations, the decision facing the creative specialist is not whether to choose an emotional or a rational appeal but rather determining how to combine the two approaches. Noted copywriters David Ogilvy and Joel Raphaelson eloquently argued many years ago that most purchases have both rational and emotional emotions associated with their use and purchase. One can experience happiness with clean clothes all due to a functional product like laundry detergent and one can find joy that accompanies the high-involvement purchase of a new car that requires careful consideration of many facts.[78] Exhibit 7-24 appeals rationally and emotionally with the text of the ad and the compelling visuals.

MasterCard's "Priceless" campaign combined rational and emotional appeals when MasterCard lagged behind Visa and American Express in third place during the late 1990s. The brand repositioning challenge looked to create an emotional bond between consumers and MasterCard while retaining the brand's functional appeal. The idea behind the campaign is that good spenders use credit cards to acquire things that are important to them and enrich their daily lives. The creative execution involved showing a shopping list of items that could be purchased for a certain dollar amount and one key item that could not and thus was deemed "Priceless." The tagline "There are some things money can't buy. For everything else there's MasterCard," positions the card as the way to pay for everything that matters. MasterCard built an entire IMC around the "Priceless" theme that includes sponsorships with Major League Baseball, the National Hockey League, and the PGA golf tour. The campaign now runs in 80 countries and has won numerous creative awards. Exhibit 7-25 shows one of the print ads from the campaign.

A unique example of combining rational and emotional appeals is the use of **teaser advertising**. Advertisers introducing a new product or new advertising campaign use teaser advertising, which is designed to build curiosity, interest, and/or excitement about a product or brand by talking about it but not actually showing it. Kia Canada's "Peer Into Your Soul" campaign launched the new urban crossover passenger car to unsuspecting TV viewers with three unbranded teaser ads over the course of three weeks. For 15 seconds, viewers watched mysterious characters staring back toward them and then saw the web address Peerintoasoul.ca—inviting enough curiosity for 180,000 visits before three branded ads for the Kia Soul appeared on TV. Picking up on the idea that people often stare into

Born Better.

Every drop of Arrowhead® 100% Mountain Spring Water comes from carefully selected mountain springs. When you start with something better, you get something better.

ARROWHEAD

Exhibit 7-24   Advertising for Arrowhead water appeals rationally and emotionally.

new cars parked on the street, Kia emulated this little nugget of consumer behaviour. The three executions spoofed different types of films. A "buddy" movie is seen in "Well," where a guy stuck in a well has his friend run for help only to get distracted by Kia's new vehicle. In a gangster style, "Mob" shows a couple of tough guys letting their hostage get away while they peer into a Soul. Finally, a horror flick emerges with "Cabin," as the intended victims awaken to find their would-be attacker fell asleep after staring at the uniquely styled car.[79]

(L05) Source Characteristics

The third creative strategy decision is the source of the message appeal. We use the term **source** to mean the person involved in communicating a marketing message, either directly or indirectly. A *direct source* is a spokesperson who delivers a message and/or demonstrates a product or service. An *indirect source* (e.g., a model) doesn't actually deliver a message but draws attention to and/or enhances the appearance of the ad. Some ads use neither a direct nor an indirect source; the source is the brand or organization with the message to communicate. Since most research focuses on individuals as a message source, our examination follows this approach. Companies carefully select individuals to deliver their advertising messages due to the costs involved and the fit with their brand positioning strategy. To understand this decision we rely on a model that identifies three basic source attributes: credibility, attractiveness, and power.[80] This section looks at the first two characteristics in the context of advertising. Source power is omitted, as compliance effect due to power is not really possible in most promotional communication.

Exhibit 7-25 MasterCard's "Priceless" campaign created an emotional bond with consumers.

SOURCE CREDIBILITY

Credibility is the extent to which the recipient sees the source as having relevant knowledge, skill, or experience and trusts the source to give unbiased, objective information implying two important dimensions to credibility, *expertise* and *trustworthiness*. A communicator seen as knowledgeable—someone with expertise—is more persuasive than one with less expertise. But the source also has to be trustworthy—honest, ethical, and believable. The influence of a knowledgeable source will be lessened if audience members think he or she is biased or has underlying personal motives for advocating a position (such as being paid to endorse a product).

One of the most reliable effects found in communications research is that expert and/or trustworthy sources are more persuasive than sources who are less expert or trustworthy.[81] Information from a credible source influences beliefs, opinions, attitudes, and/or behaviour through a process known as **internalization**, which occurs when the receiver adopts the opinion of the credible communicator since he or she believes information from this source is accurate. Once the receiver internalizes an opinion or attitude, it becomes integrated into his or her belief system and may be maintained even after the source of the message is forgotten.

Expertise Because attitudes and opinions developed through an internalization process become part of the individual's belief system, marketers want to use communicators with expertise. Spokespeople are often chosen because of their knowledge or experience with a particular product or service. Endorsements from individuals or groups recognized as experts, such as doctors or dentists, are also common in advertising (Exhibit 7-26). The importance of using expert

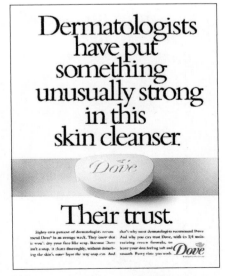

Dermatologists have put something unusually strong in this skin cleanser.

Dove

Their trust.

Exhibit 7-26 Dove promotes the fact that it is recommended by experts in skin care.

sources was shown in a study by Roobina Ohanian, who found that the perceived expertise of celebrity endorsers was more important in explaining purchase intentions than their attractiveness or trustworthiness. She suggests that celebrity spokespeople are most effective when they are knowledgeable, experienced, and qualified to talk about the product they are endorsing.[82]

Trustworthiness   While expertise is important, the target audience must also find the source (e.g., celebrities or other figures) to have a trustworthy image. For certain brands, options for selecting a trustworthy spokesperson may be limited. Alternatively, trustworthy public figures hesitate to endorse products because of the potential impact on their reputation and image.

A way of finding an appropriate trustworthy source is to use the company president or chief executive officer as a spokesperson in the firm's advertising. The use of this source is the ultimate expression of the company's commitment to quality and customer service. Research suggests the use of a company president or CEO can improve attitudes and increase the likelihood that consumers will inquire about the company's product or service.[83] Companies are likely to continue using their top executives in their advertising, particularly when they have celebrity value that helps enhance the firms' image. However, there is a risk if CEO spokespeople become very popular and get more attention than their company's product/service or advertising message. Perhaps the most prolific corporate leader acting as the advertising spokesperson is Frank D'Angelo, who promotes his beer and energy drink brands. Loblaws returned to using its president in advertising, something the retailer originated during the 1970s. Owners or presidents of medium or small sized firms and local businesses rely on this approach for source trustworthiness, as seen in Exhibit 7-27.

Limitations of Credible Sources   Several studies have shown that a high-credibility source is not always an asset, nor is a low-credibility source always a liability. High- and low-credibility sources are equally effective when they are arguing for a position opposing their own best interest.[84] A very credible source is more effective when message recipients are not in favour of the position advocated in the message.[85] However, a very credible source is less important when the audience has a neutral position, and such a source may even be less effective than a moderately credible source when the receiver's initial attitude is favourable.[86]

Another reason why a low-credibility source may be as effective as a high-credibility source is the **sleeper effect**, whereby the persuasiveness of a message increases with the passage of time. The immediate impact of a persuasive message may be inhibited because of its association with a low-credibility source. But with time, the association of the message with the source diminishes and the receiver's attention focuses more on favourable information in the message, resulting in more support arguing. However, many studies have failed to demonstrate the presence of a sleeper effect.[87] Many advertisers hesitate to count on the sleeper effect, since exposure to a credible source is a more reliable strategy.[88]

SOURCE ATTRACTIVENESS

A source characteristic frequently used by advertisers is **attractiveness**, which encompasses similarity, familiarity, and likability.[89] *Similarity* is a supposed resemblance between the source and the receiver of the message. *Likability* is an affection for the source as a result of physical appearance, behaviour, or other personal traits. Even when

Exhibit 7-27   The trustworthiness of the Chapman family is emphasized in this ad.

the sources are not famous, consumers often admire their physical appearance, talent, and/or personality. *Familiarity* refers to knowledge of the source through exposure. We describe these three characteristics and see how they operate via celebrity endorsers and decorative models in this section.

Source attractiveness leads to persuasion through a process of **identification,** whereby the receiver is motivated to seek a relationship with the source and thus adopts similar beliefs, attitudes, preferences, or behaviour. Maintaining this position depends on the source's continued support for the position as well as the receiver's continued identification with the source. If the source changes position, the receiver may also change. Unlike internalization, identification does not usually integrate information from an attractive source into the receiver's belief system. The receiver may maintain the attitudinal position or behaviour only as long as it is supported by the source or the source remains attractive. Exhibit 7-28 is an ad where source attractiveness may be working effectively.

Similarity   Research findings suggest that people are more likely to be influenced by a message coming from someone with whom they feel a sense of similarity.[90] If the communicator and receiver have similar needs, goals, interests, and lifestyles, the position advocated by the source is better understood and received. Similarity can be used to create a situation where the consumer feels empathy for the person shown in the commercial. In a slice-of-life commercial, the advertiser usually starts by presenting a predicament with the hope of getting the consumer to think, "I can see myself in that situation." This can help establish a bond of similarity between the communicator and the receiver, increasing the source's level of persuasiveness. Many companies feel that the best way to connect with consumers is by using regular-looking, everyday people with whom the average person can easily identify.

The characters for A&W have been around longer than the two guys debating whether PC or Mac is the better device, and their success may be attributed to the fact that they appear to be everyday guys (Exhibit 7-29). The A&W manager represents the typical man trying to do a good job every day, while the younger Gen-Y slacker is along to resonate with today's youth in a humorous way.[91] The men's clothing retailer Harry Rosen returned to its roots of using regular businessmen for its print ads after using more famous names the past 15 years. Moving from very familiar faces from the entertainment, sports, and business fields toward the more similar everyday manager gives a fresh look to the largely rational messages located in many newspapers.[92]

Likability   As noted in the above definition, a likable source in an ad is derived from virtually any characteristics the advertiser would like to draw attention toward in the message. Presumably, promotional planners would select a characteristic that reinforces the brand. For example, marketers of a facial skin care product would select a person who has a very good complexion so that physical characteristic would be noticed and associated with the brand name. Oftentimes beverage brands will use likable sources with personality characteristics that emerge in the story of the ad to develop the brand personality.

Advertisers often feature a physically attractive person who serves as a passive or *decorative model* rather than as an active communicator. Research suggests that physically attractive communicators generally have a positive impact and generate more favourable evaluations of both ads and products than less attractive models.[93] The gender appropriateness of the

Exhibit 7-28   The model in this Tropez ad is an example of source attractiveness.

Exhibit 7-29   This Apple ad is an example of source similarity.

Exhibit 7-30   Dove's "Campaign for Real Beauty" uses everyday women rather than supermodels in its ads.

Let's face it, firming the thighs of a size 2 supermodel is no challenge. Real women have real curves. And according to women who tried new Dove Firming, it left their skin feeling firmer in just one week. What better way to celebrate the curves you were born with? New Dove Firming. Lotion, Cream and Body Wash. For beautifully firm skin.

Exhibit 7-31   An image of an overwhelmed manager makes use of familiarity as a source characteristic.

model for the product being advertised and his or her relevance to the product are also important considerations.[94]

Some models draw attention to the ad but not to the product or message. Studies show that an attractive model facilitates recognition of the ad but does not enhance copy readership or message recall. Thus, advertisers must ensure that the consumer's attention will go beyond the model to the product and advertising message.[95] Marketers must also consider whether the use of highly attractive models might negatively impact advertising effectiveness. Studies have shown that women may experience negative feelings when comparing themselves with beautiful models used in ads and the images of physical perfection they represent.[96]

To address this, brands like Unilever's Dove developed campaigns that portray typical women and girls in their ads, in contrast to the use of supermodels or decorative models. The "Campaign for Real Beauty" (Exhibit 7-30) includes many types of ads, extensive public relations, and a website (Campaignforrealbeauty.ca) where women can discuss beauty-related issues.[97] Dove took a social advocacy approach in which it "aims to change the status quo and offer in its place a broader, healthier, more democratic view of beauty."[98] In essence, Dove relied on source similarity with the use of everyday women; however, their unexpected use in the beauty category quite possibly produced a degree of source likability due to the issues identified above. Thus, while there is often a primary source effect, a strong secondary effect may occur with creative campaigns.

Familiarity   Familiarity through exposure from another context can provide a strong source. Essentially, advertisers hope the characteristics associated with the source from which the audience knows the original context carries over to the brand. This connection is often reinforced with the creative theme of the ad, so the two strategic variables work in tandem. Without question familiarity often occurs through famous endorsers, which we discuss subsequently, but it also occurs naturally in other ways. Familiarity is used with prototypical (and sometimes stereotypical) or representative images of a familiar person or persons from a well understood context. For example the ad in Exhibit 7-31 shows the image of an overwhelmed manager who is surrounded by work. The imagery is an expected one as it uses the familiarity of what consumers would know about how a manager would look when too busy. Other times, familiarity is shown with a common situation that is known to occur within the target audience's use of the product. The ad in Exhibit 7-32 illustrates a situation and people that is familiar to many domestic households.

Celebrity Endorsers   Advertisers understand the value of using spokespeople who are admired: TV and movie stars, athletes, musicians, and other popular public figures (Exhibit 7-33). Why do companies spend huge sums to have celebrities appear in their ads and endorse their products? These celebrities are clearly very likable due to their professional achievements and anticipated physical attractiveness, and they are generally very familiar given their media exposure. Marketers expect that these celebrity characteristics draw consumer attention to

Exhibit 7-32   Levi's presents a familiar household situation of a father and son spending time together.

Exhibit 7-33   Maria Sharapova has endorsement contracts with a number of companies including Cole Haan.

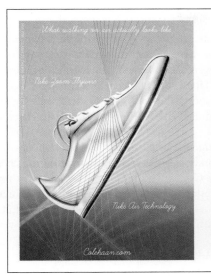 

advertising messages and favourably influence consumers' feelings, attitudes, and purchase behaviour. For example, a well-known athlete like Sidney Crosby may convince potential buyers that the product will enhance their own performance (see Exhibit 7-34).

When selecting a celebrity, marketers are encouraged to follow a clear and formal process to avoid any problems and consider the celebrity's congruence with the audience, product/service or brand, overall image, specific source characteristics, profession, popularity, availability, and cost.[99] Celebrity endorsement is also a two-way street where the endorser evaluates the brand. Steve Nash, two-time MVP of the NBA, acts a spokesperson for brands that support his charitable causes like the Steve Nash Foundation, which provides funds to children for health and education.[100] Other endorsers are quite strong in their beliefs by only endorsing products that they use or support. Four critical factors for a promotional planner include overshadowing the product, overexposure, the target audience's receptivity, and risk.

Overshadowing the Product   How will the celebrity affect the target audience's processing of the advertising message? Consumers may focus their attention on the celebrity and fail to notice the brand. Advertisers should select a celebrity spokesperson who will attract attention and enhance the brand and its message, not the celebrity. For example, Chrysler Corp. chose singer Céline Dion to appear in ads for its Pacifica sport wagon, Crossfire sports coupe, and Town & Country minivan, and also sponsored her Las Vegas show. She starred in lavish TV commercials that were part of Chrysler's "Drive & Love" campaign, designed to give Chrysler a more upscale image and achieve a premium brand positioning. However, it was believed that

Exhibit 7-34   Sidney Crosby is featured at this Gatorade promotional event.

her celebrity persona overshadowed the products and the campaign did more to sell her than the cars.[101]

Overexposure   Consumers are often skeptical of endorsements because they know the celebrities are being paid.[102] This problem is particularly pronounced when a celebrity endorses too many products or companies and becomes overexposed. Advertisers can protect themselves against overexposure with an exclusivity clause limiting the number of products a celebrity can endorse. However, such clauses are usually expensive, and most celebrities agree not to endorse similar products anyway. Many celebrities try to earn as much endorsement money as possible, yet they must be careful not to damage their credibility by endorsing too many products.

Target Audience's Receptivity   One of the most important considerations in choosing a celebrity endorser is how well the individual matches with and is received by the advertiser's target audience. Consumers who are particularly knowledgeable about a product or service or have strongly established attitudes may be less influenced by a celebrity than those with little knowledge or neutral attitudes. One study found that college-age students were more likely to have a positive attitude toward a product endorsed by a celebrity than were older consumers.[103]

Risk for Advertiser   A celebrity's behaviour may pose a risk to a company.[104] Entertainers and athletes have been involved in activities that could embarrass the companies whose products they endorsed (e.g., Tiger Woods, Michael Phelps). Marketers know celebrity endorsers can be a very expensive and high-risk strategy because what the celebrities do in their personal lives can impact their brand image. To avoid problems, companies often research a celebrity's personal life and background and include a morals clause in the contract allowing the company to terminate the endorsement if controversy arises. However, marketers should remember that adding morals clauses to their endorsement contracts only gets them out of a problem; it does not prevent it from happening.

The Meaning of Celebrity Endorsers   Advertisers must try to match the product or company's image, the characteristics of the target audience, and the personality of the celebrity.[105] An interesting perspective on celebrity endorsement was developed by Grant McCracken.[106] He argues that credibility and attractiveness don't sufficiently explain how and why celebrity endorsements work and offers a model based on meaning transfer (Figure 7-6).

According to this model, a celebrity's effectiveness as an endorser depends on the culturally acquired meanings he or she brings to the endorsement process. Each celebrity contains many

Figure   7-6   Meaning movement and the endorsement process

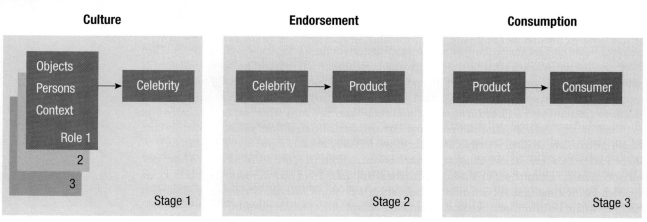

Key: ——→ = Path of meaning movement

         = Stage of meaning movement

Exhibit 7-35 Kelly Ripa helps create the impression that Electrolux appliances are designed for the "do-it-all" woman.

meanings, including status, class, gender, and age as well as personality and lifestyle. At stage 1 the characteristics associated with the celebrity from their public exposure in movies and so on extend to their persona. Celebrity endorsers bring their meanings and image into the ad and transfer them to the product they are endorsing in stage 2. In the final stage, the meanings the celebrity has given to the product are transferred to the consumer. This final stage is complicated and difficult to achieve. The way consumers take possession of the meaning the celebrity has transferred to a product is probably the least understood part of the process.

For example, Electrolux employed Kelly Ripa for its premium line of stylish, high-performance appliances in an IMC campaign that capitalizes on her image. The campaign portrays the multitalented Ripa in her busy life including scenes at work, entertaining at home, and interacting with her children (Exhibit 7-35). She is an effective endorser for the brand since she represents the quintessential do-it-all woman with an endless to-do list but who gets it all done. Electrolux delivers a brand idea that its appliances are designed to help women who are already doing amazing things in their lives to be even more amazing. To help deliver this message Electrolux shows Ripa in TV and print ads and has also created an entertaining short film for its website.

The meaning transfer model implies that marketers must first decide on the image or symbolic meanings important to the target audience and then determine which celebrity best represents the meaning or image to be projected. An advertising campaign must be designed that captures that meaning in the product and moves it to the consumer. Marketing and advertising personnel often rely on intuition in choosing celebrity endorsers for their companies or products, but companies conduct research studies to determine consumers' perceptions of celebrities' meaning. Marketers may also pretest ads to determine whether they transfer the proper meaning to the product. When celebrity endorsers are used, the marketer should track the campaign's effectiveness by assessing whether the celebrity continues to communicate the proper meaning to the target audience.

IMC Planning: Message and Source Combinations

As noted at the outset of this chapter, the creative strategy comprises decisions regarding the creative theme, message appeal, and source characteristics. In the creative theme section, we noted that promotional planners determine the degree to which there is creative consistency

Figure 7-7

Possible combinations for message and source decisions

	Rational Appeal	Emotional Appeal	Combined Appeal
Credible			
Trustworthy			
Similar			
Likable			
Familiar			

across time, executions, media, promotional tools, and products. In this IMC planning section, we present a table that allows promotional planners to consider various combinations of message and source decisions.

Figure 7-7 summarizes the possible combinations of all message and source decisions. Essentially any ad or IMC tool has one of these 15 combinations. Promotional planners can consider using certain combinations for certain parts of the IMC plan. For example, a brand may select a more credible source with a rational appeal for its print communication and possibly consider a familiar source with an emotional appeal for its television commercials. As noted in the creative consistency section, Telus has used a different message appeal and source on television and radio. Television ads feature likable critters with emotional appeals, while radio ads feature a trustworthy source with rational appeals.

While a number of combinations exist—and we have shown two examples where brands have adapted the source and message across IMC tools or media—promotional planners can certainly decide to keep the same source and message appeal for all their tools and media.

Learning Objectives Summary

 Summarize the idea and importance of creativity in an advertising context.

The creative development and execution of the advertising message are a crucial part of a firm's integrated marketing communications program. The creative specialist or team is responsible for developing an effective way to communicate the marketer's message to both customers and non-customers and reinforce the brand positioning strategy. Creativity is often difficult to articulate, but consumers and advertising people all know it when they see it. The challenge facing the writers, artists, and others who develop ads is to be creative and come up with fresh, unique, and appropriate ideas that can be used as solutions to marketing communication issues that may be problems or opportunities.

 Decribe the creative strategy planning process.

Marketers often turn to ad agencies to develop, prepare, and implement their creative strategy since these agencies are specialists in the creative function of advertising. Creativity in advertising is a process of several stages, including preparation, incubation, illumination, and verification. Various sources of information are available to help the creative specialists determine the best creative strategy. Creative strategy is guided by marketing goals and objectives and is based on a number of factors, including the basic problem the advertising must address, the target audience, behavioural and communication objectives the message seeks to accomplish, and key benefits the advertiser wants to communicate as reflected in the brand positioning strategy. These factors and the creative strategy decisions are generally stated in a copy platform, which is a work plan used to guide development of the ad campaign.

 Identify the approaches used for determining the creative theme that forms the basis of an advertising campaign.

An important part of creative strategy is determining the creative theme of the campaign. Often, a big idea strikes the creative specialist while embarking upon the creative process, which becomes the genesis of the creative theme. There are several approaches to discover this big idea, including using a unique selling proposition, creating a brand image, looking for inherent drama in the brand, and positioning. In general, the creative theme guides much of the advertising campaign or IMC program. Consistency, originality, and its ability to effectively communicate are three key strengths of a good creative. The creative theme acts as a brand story to give it uniqueness compared to competitors.

 Summarize the different types of message appeals that advertisers use to persuade their target audience.

A message appeal, the second decision of the creative strategy, is the central message used in the ad to elicit cognitive and emotional processing responses and communication effects from the target audience. A message appeal reveals the intended persuasion of the brand. Appeals can be broken into two broad groups, rational and emotional. Rational appeals focus on consumers' practical, functional, or utilitarian need for the product or service. Emotional appeals relate to social and/or psychological reasons for purchasing a product or service. Numerous types of appeals are available to advertisers within each group, and it is important for the client to clearly specify its intended message as accurately as possible.

 Identify the source or communicator options a marketer has for a promotional message.

Selection of the appropriate source or communicator to deliver a message is the third creative strategy decision. The message source is the approach to deliver the message appeal. Three important attributes are source credibility, attractiveness, and power. Marketers enhance message effectiveness by hiring communicators who are experts in a particular area and/or have a trustworthy image. The use of celebrities to deliver advertising messages has become very popular; advertisers hope they will catch the receivers' attention and influence their attitudes or behaviour through an identification process. The chapter discusses the meaning a celebrity brings to the endorsement process and the importance of matching the image of the celebrity with that of the company or brand.

 Apply source and message appeal options for different ad executions

The chapter concluded by outlining options for IMC planning by suggesting that different combinations of source and message appeal could be constructed for different media or different IMC tools. Promotional planners can apply combinations depending on the context of the media such as TV, print, or social media. Furthermore, promotional planners might consider different combinations for specific IMC tools compared to what is shown in advertising.

Key Terms ![McGraw Hill Education] connect

Review key terms and definitions on Connect.

Review Questions

1. Television commercials can use unusual creativity that has very little to do with the product being advertised. Explain why creative specialists would recommend such ads and why the brand managers would approve the production and placement.

2. Describe the types of general and product-specific preplanning input one might evaluate when assigned to work on an advertising campaign for a new brand of bottled water.

3. What is your opinion of advertising awards, such as the Cannes Lions, that are based solely on creativity? If you were a marketer looking for an agency, would you take these creative awards into consideration in your agency evaluation process? Why or why not?

4. Assume that a government agency wants to use a fear appeal to encourage college and university students not to drink and drive. Explain how fear appeals might affect persuasion and what factors should be considered in developing the ads.

5. What are source characteristics? What types are there? How do they affect processing of a message and the communication effects of the message?

6. How is it possible that an IMC program could have multiple sources for the message using both rational and emotional appeals?

Applied Questions

1. Find an example of a print ad that is very creative and an ad that is dull and boring. Select each element of the ad and figure out how it is contributing to the creativity or lack of creativity.

2. The chapter outlined a few campaigns; look on the Internet to research and figure out the most successful Canadian campaign in recent years.

3. Find an example of an ad or campaign that you think reflects one of the approaches used to develop a creative theme such as unique selling proposition, brand image, inherent drama, or positioning. Discuss how the creative theme is used in this ad or campaign.

4. Describe how a few of the negative emotions conveyed in Figure 7-3 could be used in a campaign for car insurance. Describe how a few of the positive emotions conveyed in Figure 7-3 could be used in a campaign for smartphones.

5. Find a celebrity who is currently appearing in ads for a particular company or brand and analyze and use McCracken's meaning transfer model (shown in Figure 7-7) to analyze the use of the celebrity as a spokesperson.

6. Actors portraying doctors in ads are often used for rational appeals. In what situation might it make sense to have a doctor for an emotional appeal? What type of emotional appeal would be most logical from Figure 7-3?

GO ONLINE

For more information on the resources available from McGraw-Hill Ryerson,
go to www.mcgrawhill.ca/he/solutions.

Creative Tactics Decisions

8

LEARNING OBJECTIVES

LO1 Analyze the creative execution styles that advertisers can use and the situations where they are most appropriate.

LO2 Explain different types of message structures that can be used to develop a promotional message.

LO3 Express design elements involved in the creation of print, video, and audio messages.

LO4 Apply a planning model for making creative tactics decisions.

LO5 Illustrate how clients evaluate the creative work of their agencies and discuss guidelines for the evaluation and approval process.

A Pot of Fun with the Skittles Rainbow

In 2010, Skittles candy advertising showed what would happen were someone to "touch the rainbow," with characters turning anything into Skittles by simply touching it. In 2011, Skittles wanted its consumers to actually experience touching the rainbow by placing and holding their finger on a computer screen and watching five successive online commercials where their finger had the starring role. In one scene a cat and a human-like cat licked the finger; other scenes featured a car crashing into the finger, and a woman with a Skittles face complaining about having a finger pointed at her.

Communication about the video went to bloggers and was posted on other social media. Within the time frame of the campaign, the ads garnered 6 million views, attained 11,000 fans on the candy's YouTube channel, and were featured extensively on other video outlets and social media. The campaign achieved 60 million media exposures and sales increased by 78 percent. The unique execution attained even greater stature by winning two Gold Lions at Cannes during the summer of 2011 for Film and Cyber.

Skittles adapted the execution later in the year along the lines of gift giving with a twist. Skittles started "Gif Rap the Rainbow," where consumers could go to an Internet site to send customized .gifs (graphic images that move) with holiday-themed rap songs via e-mail or social media. They could pick from different scenes, like Mrs. Claus basting a turkey with Skittles, and select their favourite song—perhaps "I Saw Mommy Dissing Santa Claus." According to the creative director, "Part of the enjoyment of things like this is the discovery of it—having it appear in your inbox as a surprise, or stumbling upon it and being able to send something customizable to a friend."

Skittles continued the concept to "Touch the Untouchable" in 2012, where people touched the screen to five new commercials online: a werewolf baby, a princess, a cyclops doctor, a tennis-playing zombie, and a sasquatch. This execution received a Bronze Lion at Cannes during the summer of 2012. Critics were less enthused about this world of strange beings and the humour associated with the brand; however, others enjoyed the random, pointless, and silly humour as an endearing way to express that the brand entertains its target audience.

The subsequent holiday season, the brand established another Internet site, CreateTheRainbow.com, where consumers could make their own wacky Skittles ad. Menu items permitted selection of five "Skittles Miracles," like a hot tub full of Skittles, various phrases, and "states of being" like happy or crying, to allow the creation of a dialogue among the characters. As in the past, Skittles communicated the short-term effort digitally via social media. Commenting on the initiative, the creative director said, "Skittles fans are creative, unique people and so we've given them the tools to be part of the brand in a way that most people never get the chance to."

Sources: Carol Neshevich, "Skittles Offers Festive 'GIF' Rapping," *Marketing Magazine*, December 15, 2011; Jeromy Lloyd and David Brown, "BBDO Lands Bronze Promo & Activation Lion," *Marketing Magazine*, June 18, 2002; Jonathan Paul, "Skittles Makes Its Rainbows Customizable for Christmas," *Marketing Magazine*, December 12, 2012; "BBDO Pushes Skittles to Top of Cheese-o-Meter," *National Post*, March 30, 2012, p. FP14; http://www.interactiveentries.com/skittlestouchcampaign.

Questions:

1. What execution style does Skittles appear to be using in these "interactive" ads?
2. Why is this execution style a good idea for a brand like Skittles?

In the previous chapter, we identified and described the three creative strategy decisions. This chapter focuses on the three main creative tactics decisions. It examines execution styles that can be used to develop the ad, the important message structure choices available, and the elements involved in the design and production of effective advertising messages. We also present a framework for guiding the creative tactics decisions. We conclude by presenting guidelines marketers can use to evaluate the creative recommendations they need to approve to effectively communicate their brand positioning strategy.

(L01) Creative Execution Style

Once the message appeal has been determined, the creative specialist or team decides the creative tactics. One critical creative tactic is the **creative execution style**, which is the way a message appeal is presented. While it is obviously important for an ad to have a meaningful message appeal to communicate to the consumer, the manner in which the ad is executed is also important. We now identify 11 commonly seen execution styles and provide examples of each. Many of these can be combined to present the message appeal.

STRAIGHT SELL

One of the most basic types of creative executions is the straight sell. This type of ad relies on a straightforward presentation of information concerning the product or service. This execution is often used with rational appeals, where the focus of the message is the product and its specific attributes and/or benefits. Straight-sell executions are commonly used in print ads. A picture of the product or service occupies part of the ad, and the factual copy takes up the rest of the space. They are also used in TV advertising, with an announcer generally delivering the sales message while the product/service is shown on the screen. Ads for high-involvement consumer products as well as industrial and other business-to-business products generally use this format. The ad for the Ford Fiesta shown in Exhibit 8-1 is an excellent example of a straight-sell execution style.

SCIENTIFIC/TECHNICAL EVIDENCE

In a variation of the straight sell, scientific or technical evidence is presented in the ad. Advertisers often cite technical information, results of scientific or laboratory studies, or endorsements by scientific bodies or agencies to support their advertising claims. The ad for Kinerase skin care treatment shown in Exhibit 8-2 uses this execution style by noting how the product has been clinically proven to reduce signs of aging.

DEMONSTRATION

Demonstration is designed to illustrate the key advantages of the product by showing it in actual use or in a staged situation. Demonstration executions can be very effective in convincing consumers of a product's utility or quality and of the benefits of owning or using the brand. TV is particularly well suited for demonstration executions, since the benefits or advantages of the product can be shown right on the screen. Although perhaps a little less dramatic than TV, demonstration ads can also work in print. The Samsung ad shown in Exhibit 8-3 uses this style to

THE FIESTA HAS ENOUGH
NEW-WORLD TECHNOLOGY
TO PUT A 50-GRAND CAR TO SHAME.

There's a lot you can get in a Fiesta. A class-exclusive 4" multifunctional LCD display* standard. A PowerShift six-speed automatic transmission** That's the kind of engineering that makes it more responsive and still keeps it fuel-efficient! The Fiesta also has available keyless entry, push-button start, voice-activated SYNC*** and even ambient lighting. All told, that's as much high-end technology as many premium cars. How's that for high tech?

IT'S A PRETTY BIG DEAL.

INTRODUCING THE NEW **FIESTA**
fordvehicles.com

Ford
Drive one.

Exhibit 8-1   Ford uses a straight-sell execution style in this ad for the new Fiesta.

demonstrate the ultra-thin feature and elegant design of its HD TV.

COMPARISON

A comparison execution style, direct, indirect, and visual, is popular among advertisers. Direct brand comparisons are the basis for advertising executions to communicate a competitive advantage or to position a new or lesser-known brand with industry leaders. For example, computer manufacturers use direct comparisons to demonstrate superior performance claims. Although previous research found little support for the effectiveness of comparative ads, one study found positive result for the situation where a challenger brand compares itself to a category leader.[1]

Exhibit 8-2 Kinerase promotes how clinical test results support the product performance claim.

One unusual indirect comparison execution style occurred with ads for the Subaru Outback that compared life outdoors with the car against life indoors with a Snuggie blanket. The ad begins as a Snuggie ad that becomes a Subaru ad after a virile man uses a crowbar to symbolically pry open the television screen so that the viewer can see the car in the wilderness. Although a tactical consideration, this element clearly reinforces the brand positioning in terms of the target, motive, and key benefits the car offers.[2] Finally, a visual comparison, instead of a brand comparison, can be used to convey particular product characteristics as seen in the colourful ad for Q HorsePower motor oil found in Exhibit 8-4.

Exhibit 8-3 This ad demonstrates the ultra-thin feature of Samsung's TV.

Exhibit 8-4 A visual comparison in this ad shows how fast the Ferrari travels with Q Horse Power brand of motor oil.

TESTIMONIAL

Many advertisers prefer to have their messages presented by way of a testimonial, where a person praises the product or service on the basis of his or her personal experience with it. Testimonial executions can have ordinary satisfied customers discuss their own experiences with the brand and the benefits of using it. This approach can be very effective when the person delivering the testimonial is someone with whom the target audience can identify or who has an interesting story to tell. The testimonial must be based on actual use of the product or service to avoid legal problems, and the spokesperson must be credible. Testimonials can be particularly effective when they come from a recognizable or popular person.

Toyota dealers in western Canada used actual customers to communicate their product's quality and dependability. Among the four spots initially produced, in one a country veterinarian drove his 13-year-old Toyota 4Runner with 742,000 km; in another, a travelling salesman complained that the odometer of his Corolla only had six digits. All ads were based on actual customer experiences, and although the campaign was a risky departure the initial results appeared promising for a regional launch prior to the spring buying season.[3]

SLICE OF LIFE

A widely used advertising format, particularly for packaged-goods products, is the slice-of-life execution. Slice-of-life executions are often criticized for being unrealistic and irritating to watch because they are often used to remind consumers of problems of a personal nature, such as dandruff, bad breath, body odour, and laundry or cleaning problems. Often these ads come across as contrived, silly, phony, or even offensive to consumers. However, many advertisers still prefer this style because they believe it is effective at presenting a situation to which most consumers can relate and at registering the product feature or benefit.

Execution is critical in using the technique effectively, as these ads are designed to be dramatizations of a supposedly real-life situation that consumers might encounter. Getting viewers to identify with the situation and/or characters depicted in the ad can be very challenging. Since the success of slice-of-life ads often depends on how well the actors execute their roles, professional actors are often used to achieve credibility and to ensure that the commercial is of high quality. Smaller companies and local advertisers often do not have ad budgets large enough to hire the talent or to pay for the production quality needed to effectively create slice-of-life spots. Thus, this execution technique is more likely to be used by companies with ad budgets that are large enough to fund the use of professional talent and production of quality commercials.

Often marketers use the slice-of-life approach since it effectively addresses a problem or issue and offers a solution. For example, Listerine used a slice-of-life commercial effectively to introduce a new Natural Citrus flavour of its popular mouthwash.[4] The spot was designed to address the problem that consumers have with the intense taste of the original flavour of the product. The spot opens with a mother returning home from the store with two surprises: Danish and Listerine. However, when her husband and two kids see the mouthwash they run and hide. The mother then tells them it is Natural Citrus Listerine, which tastes less intense. The humorous spot ends with the father coming out of a kitchen cupboard and pots and pans dangling as one of the boys climbs down from the top of the kitchen island and the voiceover says, "You can handle it. Germs can't" (see Exhibit 8-5).

ANIMATION

With animation, scenes are drawn by artists or created on the computer, and cartoons, puppets, or other types of fictional characters may be used. Cartoon animation is especially popular for commercials targeted at children for products like toys and cereal; however, we also see it elsewhere. To influence business and IT decision makers in the business market, the catchphrase "It's Everybody's Business" drove a Microsoft campaign where it claims to deliver quality information technology goods and services so that their customers' businesses can thrive. The execution for these ads featured animation of the CEOs of the Microsoft customers. With an

interview format and technological sketches to go along with the CEO images, the campaign went global with executives from many countries. In Canada, WestJet Airlines CEO Sean Durfy answered the question, "So, Durf, how do you keep the vision alive?" by talking about the company's growth through technology, highlighting the accomplishments of WestJet employees and how they rely on technology to perform their jobs.[5] In banking, RBC moved to numerous animated ads on TV and other media with its news spokesperson Arbie. The friendly financial adviser finds himself in all sorts of situations showing how helpful RBC can be for consumers who want to create various things in their lives. For adult men, the Old Spice ad in Exhibit 8-6 used animation considerably in this humorous execution.

PERSONALITY SYMBOL

Another advertising execution involves developing a central character or personality symbol that can deliver the advertising message and with which the product or service can be identified (see Exhibit 8-7). One study finds positive brand attitude effects through the use of spokes-characters.[6] Koodo's El Tabador is a new player on the scene. The Taxi 2 creative team invented him while brainstorming and ended up with the idea of a "freedom fighter" representing the little guy (e.g., consumer) who wants low prices and no contracts for the phone. According to a team member, "He is a bit of a ladies' man. He is sly and confident. We wanted him to be tough and not too cute but with a bit of self-depreciating sense of humour that would hit on the toy Barbie doll." The team pitched Telus with this one and only idea, and in the first year of ads the little guy starred in 11 executions.[7]

And it seems this industry can't get enough of personality symbols as Mobilicity entered the market with a tandem of aliens, a green male and pink female. One executive claimed that, "Aliens tend to be seen as more advanced,

Exhibit 8-6　Animation is a key part of the humour in this Old Spice ad.

Photography by Ondrea Barbe.

forward-thinking, technologically advanced and a higher life form with better decision-making skills."[8]

A personality symbol gets a change periodically; executives rebranded the iconic Ronald McDonald as "an ambassador for a balanced active lifestyle." Three versions of a TV spot called "Active Ronald, You and I" played on Teletoon and YTV in Canada, depicting Ronald changing from his clown suit into a track suit and kicking soccer balls, riding snowboards, and running and jumping his way around town.[9]

Canadian brands have been at the forefront in developing and nurturing a personality. Kool-Aid's "Face" icon and the three-dimensional Kool-Aid pitcher provide an instantly recognizable character. In fact the personality, established in Canada, has been used in campaigns in the U.S. and Mexico. Captain High Liner has been extolling the virtues of his brand of frozen fish products for decades in Canada and has a special section on the brand's website. A&W has used two types of personalities over the years, a person dressed as a bear and many family members to represent the different names of their burger products.[10]

IMAGERY

Some ads contain little or no information about the brand or company and are almost totally visual. These advertisements use imagery executions whereby the ad consists primarily of visual elements such as pictures, illustrations, and/or symbols rather than information. An imagery execution is used when the goal is to encourage consumers to associate the brand with the symbols, characters, and/or situation shown in the ad. Imagery ads are often the basis for emotional appeals that are used to advertise products or services where differentiation based on physical characteristics is difficult.

An imagery execution may be based on **usage imagery** by showing how a brand is used or performs and the situations in which it is used. For example, advertising for trucks and SUVs often shows the vehicles navigating tough terrain or in challenging situations such as towing a heavy load. The San Pellegrino ad shown in Exhibit 8-8 uses the imagery of an Italian restaurant to convey the usage of its sparkling water. This type of execution can also be based on **user imagery**, where the focus is on the type of person who uses the brand. Ads for cosmetics often use very attractive models in the hope of getting consumers to associate the model's physical attractiveness with the brand (see Exhibit 8-9). Image executions rely heavily on visual elements such as photography, colour, tonality, and design to communicate the desired image to the consumer. Marketers who rely on image executions have to be sure that the usage or user imagery with which they associate their brand evokes the right feelings and reactions from the target audience.

DRAMATIZATION

Another execution technique particularly well suited to television is dramatization, where the focus is on telling a short story with the

Consumer-Generated Executions

As an extension of the "Doritos Guru" concept described in Chapter 1, Frito Lay asked consumers to write the ending to the start of a commercial that aired during the Super Bowl on Canadian TV. The 60-second commercial showed two scientists presenting their chip creation to their queen-like "Flavour Master." Nervously awaiting the verdict between Buffalo Wings n' Ranch versus Onion Rings n' Ketchup, the men witness her decision that the weaker chip must be destroyed forever. Viewers could submit their ending at an Internet site (WriteTheEnd.ca), with seven winners from each chip moving on to be finalists.

The past two video efforts in 2009 and 2010 resulted in the average consumer being unable to submit a full video to be part of the contest, so the advertising agency saw this as an easier opportunity for all to participate. The winner received $25,000, one percent of the sales of the new flavour, and became a member of the Doritos think tank for the development of new marketing communication ideas while working with all agency personnel.

Scotiabank tried its hand with user-generated executions with a new offshoot of its highly successful ads within the "You're Richer Than You Think" campaign. In newer executions, the definition of richer moved toward how people felt rich in their lives during important life events like having a baby. With a consumer focus, the Scotiabank messages explored the meaning of moments of people's lives that matter to them. Some of these new executions used consumer-generated content across the TV ads, in branch material, and in digital ads. One such execution, entitled "Conversation," concerned the thoughts of parents of a new baby with video shots obtained from a friend of a Scotiabank employee. According to the creative director, "That's really what's at the core of this campaign is these rich moments that people are experiencing in their daily lives."

Commenting on this trend, a VP of Proximity remarked, "Years ago, big brands had policies that we couldn't take any unsolicited ideas from the public. That's been turned on its ear, and user-generated content has been embraced." In the past, many feared circumstances like Chevrolet faced a few years ago when it designed an Internet site with an ad that allowed consumers to write in their own script. Some entered negative comments suggesting the Tahoe SUV contributed to global warming as a gas-guzzling vehicle.

However, this possibility has not deterred Sport Chek, which lets consumers submit their own outdoor photos for its retail flyers distributed digitally and put in stores. And the Canadian Tourism Commission included similar video footage of visitors exploring the Canadian wilderness in its "Keep Exploring" campaign. The CTC's use of consumer-generated executions is unique in that the videos were not prompted by a contest or request, but merely submitted by enthusiastic visitors. But one thing is in fact common— all of these efforts hoped for extensive pass-along through digital avenues to enhance word-of-mouth communication.

Sources: Susan Krashinsky, "Advertising's Newest Ploy? Get Consumers to Make Your Ads," *The Globe and Mail,* February 10, 2012, p. B6; Kristin Laird, "Scotiabank Redefines Richer Campaign," *Marketing Magazine,* January 23, 2012; Kristin Laird, "Doritos Begins New Campaign with No Ending," *Marketing Magazine,* February 4, 2011.

Questions:

1. What is the motivation for consumers to participate in making an ad?
2. Are the consumers participating in the development of ads customers of the brands?

product as the star. Dramatization is akin to slice-of-life execution, but it uses more excitement and suspense in telling the story. The purpose of using drama is to draw the viewer into the action it portrays. Advocates of drama note that when it is successful, the audience becomes lost in the story and experiences the concerns and feelings of the characters.[11]

Although we typically see dramatization used in television or radio ads because they have audio capabilities, it is possible to use this execution style in print. Goodyear Tires conveyed the drama of driving in bad winter snow conditions with an effective newspaper ad that showed a

Exhibit 8-9   This Bebe ad uses an attractive model to create a favourable image for the brand.

Exhibit 8-10   Crest's dramatic claim fosters a comparison of the brand to professional whitening services.

car skidding through the weather page! Designed to evoke the worst type of January weather, the fall campaign reminded consumers about the importance of purchasing new snow tires before it was too late.[12] The ad in Exhibit 8-10 conveys a story or image of how women who are not whitening their teeth might try to mask the effect of their yellowing teeth.

HUMOUR

Like comparisons, humour was discussed in Chapter 7 as a type of message appeal, but this technique can also be used as a way of presenting other message appeals. Old Spice continued with its humorous approach by interrupting a Bounce ad; both products are Procter & Gamble brands. Former NFL player Terry Crews crashed through the wall of the home of a very surprised woman in her laundry room. He then went on about the brand's body spray.[13] A rational message appeal occurred for both brands as a simple product characteristic is communicated; however, the whole execution of the appeal is certainly funny (for most people).

Humorous executions are particularly well suited to television or radio, although print ads attempt to use this style. The Golf Pride ad in Exhibit 8-11 uses a humour execution style for a mostly rational message appeal. The snowman represents a score of 8 on a hole, which golfers want to avoid. The visual attracts the audience's attention, and the copy explains how Golf Pride can improve performance with new grips.

To understand the difference between the appeal and the execution with respect to humour, one could consider Boston Pizza's campaign with the fictitious Carl Carlson, President of the Flatties and Drummies Association, who extols about the nibs and nubs of each chicken wing. The execution style uses a personality symbol, and the delivery of the message appeal is all sardonic humour.[14]

(L02) Message Structure

Marketing communication usually consists of a number of message points that the communicator wants to convey as advertising messages have an important information provision characteristic. Extensive research has been conducted on how the structure of an advertising message can influence its persuasive effectiveness, including order of presentation, conclusion drawing, message sidedness, and verbal/visual balance. These first three message structure points mostly focus on the written words of a print message or the announcer in a video or audio message, while the last addresses the importance of visuals to deliver the message.

ORDER OF PRESENTATION

A basic consideration in the design of a persuasive message is the arguments' order of presentation. Should the most important message points be placed at the beginning of the message, in the middle, or at the end? Research on learning and memory generally indicates that items presented first and last are remembered better than those presented in the middle (see Figure 8-1).[15] This suggests that a communicator's strongest arguments should be presented early or late in the message but never in the middle.

Presenting the strongest arguments at the beginning of the message assumes a **primacy effect** is operating, whereby information presented first is most effective. Putting the strong points at the end assumes a **recency effect**, whereby the last arguments presented are most persuasive.

Whether to place the strongest selling points at the beginning or the end of the message depends on several factors. If the target audience is opposed to the communicator's position, presenting strong points first can reduce the level of counterarguing. Putting weak arguments first might lead to such a high level of counterarguing that strong arguments that followed would not be believed. Strong arguments work best at the beginning of the message if the audience is not interested in the topic, so they can arouse interest in the message. When the target audience is predisposed toward the communicator's position or is highly interested in the issue or product, strong arguments can be saved for the end of the message. This may result in a more favourable opinion as well as better retention of the information.

Exhibit 8-11   This Golf Pride ad uses a humour execution style to communicate an important product benefit.

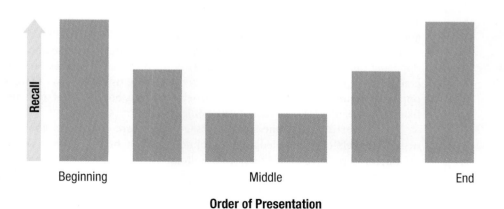

Recall

Beginning   Middle   End

Order of Presentation

Figure   8-1

Ad message recall as a function of order of presentation

The order of presentation can be critical when a long, detailed message with many arguments is being presented. For short communications, such as a 15- or 30-second TV or radio commercial, the order may be less critical. However, many product and service messages are received by consumers with low involvement and minimal interest. Thus, an advertiser may want to present the brand name and key selling points early in the message and repeat them at the end to enhance recall and retention. One study strongly concludes that the brand name should be identified at the start of a TV ad to enhance its persuasive ability.[16]

CONCLUSION DRAWING

Marketing communicators must decide whether their messages should explicitly draw a firm conclusion or allow receivers to draw their own conclusions. Research suggests that, in general, messages with explicit conclusions are more easily understood and effective in influencing attitudes. However, other studies have shown that the effectiveness of conclusion drawing may depend on the target audience, the type of issue or topic, and the nature of the situation.[17]

More highly educated people prefer to draw their own conclusions and may be annoyed at an attempt to explain the obvious or to draw an inference for them. But stating the conclusion may be necessary for a less educated audience, who may not draw any conclusion or may make an incorrect inference from the message. Marketers must also consider the audience's level of involvement in the topic. For highly personal or ego-involving issues, message recipients may want to make up their own minds and resent any attempts by the communicator to draw a conclusion. One study found that open-ended ads (without explicit conclusions) were more effective than closed-ended arguments that did include a specific conclusion—but only for involved audiences.[18]

Whether to draw a conclusion for the audience also depends on the complexity of the topic. Even a highly educated audience may need assistance if its knowledge level in a particular area is low. Does the marketer want the message to trigger immediate action or a more long-term effect? If immediate action is an objective, the message should draw a definite conclusion. When immediate impact is not the objective and repeated exposure will give the audience members opportunities to draw their own conclusions, an open-ended message may be used. Drawing a conclusion in a message may make sure the target audience gets the point the marketer intended. But many advertisers believe that letting customers draw their own conclusions reinforces the points being made in the message. The ad for Silk Soymilk in Exhibit 8-12 is a very good example of an open-ended message. The question in the headline encourages consumers to be open to the idea of drinking soymilk.

Exhibit 8-12   This Silk ad makes effective use of an open-ended approach.

MESSAGE SIDEDNESS

Another message structure decision facing the marketer involves message sidedness. A **one-sided message** mentions only positive attributes or benefits. A **two-sided message** presents both good and bad points. One-sided messages are most effective when the target audience already holds a favourable opinion about the topic. They also work better with a less educated audience.[19]

Two-sided messages are more effective when the target audience holds an opposing opinion or is highly educated. Two-sided messages may enhance the credibility of the source.[20] A better-educated audience usually knows there are opposing arguments, so a communicator who presents both sides of an issue is likely to be seen as less biased and more objective.

Most advertisers use one-sided messages. They are concerned about the negative effects of acknowledging a weakness in their brand or don't want to say anything positive about their competitors. There are exceptions, however. Occasionally, advertisers compare brands on several attributes and do not show their product as being the best on every one.

In certain situations, marketers may focus on a negative attribute as a way of enhancing overall perceptions of the product. For example, W.K. Buckley

Limited became one of the leading brands of cough syrup by using a blunt two-sided slogan: "Buckley's Mixture. It tastes awful. And it works." Ads for the brand poke fun at the cough syrup's terrible taste but also suggest that the taste is a reason why the product is effective (Exhibit 8-13). The brand moved from number 10 in the mid-80s to number one in 1992 with the launch of the message. One enjoyable copy claimed "Open wide and say @#$%&*!" In 2011, the Marketing Hall of Legends inducted Frank Buckley, the company spokesperson for many years and W.K.'s son.[21]

A special type of two-sided message is known as a **refutation**. The communicator presents both sides of an issue and then refutes the opposing viewpoint. Since this tends to "inoculate" the target audience against a competitor's counterclaims, they are more effective than one-sided messages in making consumers resistant to an opposing message.[22] Refutational messages may be useful when marketers wish to build attitudes that resist change and must defend against attacks or criticism of their products or the company. Market leaders, who are often the target of comparative messages, may find that acknowledging competitors' claims and then refuting them can help build resistant attitudes and customer loyalty.

VERBAL/VISUAL BALANCE

Thus far our discussion has focused on the information, or verbal, portion of the message. However, the nonverbal, visual elements of an ad are also very important. Many ads provide minimal amounts of information and rely on visual elements to communicate. Pictures are commonly used in advertising to convey information or reinforce copy or message claims. The ad in Exhibit 8-14 relies on the visual to communicate the nutritional value of consuming milk products.

Both the verbal and visual portions of an ad influence the way the advertising message is processed.[23] Consumers may develop images or impressions based on visual elements such as an illustration in an ad or the scenes in a TV commercial. The visual portion of an ad may reduce its persuasiveness, since the processing stimulated by the picture may be less controlled and consequently less favourable than that stimulated by words.[24]

Pictures affect the way consumers process accompanying copy. A study showed that when verbal information was low in imagery value, the use of pictures providing examples increased both immediate and delayed recall of product attributes.[25] However, when the verbal information was already high in imagery value, the addition of pictures did not increase recall. Advertisers often design ads where the visual image supports the verbal appeal to create a compelling impression in the consumer's mind.

Exhibit 8-15 is an example where the verbal message with extensive copy is paramount with supporting visual elements to enhance the emotional content of the overall ad. For very involved target audiences, such a verbal message can be quite effective for persuading consumer attitudes; however, pure text still often requires supporting visuals to heighten motivation.

Sometimes advertisers use a different approach; they design ads in which the visual portion is incongruent with or contradicts the verbal information presented. The logic behind this idea is that the use of an unexpected picture or visual image will grab consumers' attention and get them to have more effortful or elaborative processing.[26] A number of studies have shown that the use of a visual that is inconsistent with the verbal content leads to more recall and greater processing of the information presented.[27]

The "Deflate the Elephant" ads by the Liquor Control Board of Ontario designed to prevent drinking and driving used the visual of an

Exhibit 8-13 Buckley's cough syrup uses a two-sided message to promote the product's effectiveness.

Exhibit 8-14 The comparison of life with and without milk products in the visual provides a clear reason for continued consumption.

Exhibit 8-15   Extensive copy in this Lindt ad produces a mostly verbal message supported with images.

elephant appearing in social gatherings to symbolize the awkwardness people experience when they feel compelled to speak to someone who has consumed too much alcohol. While most people in the over-35 target know they should not drink and drive, once in while they slip up and drink more than planned. Their sober friends know they should speak up but suffer in a social grey zone of not knowing what to say. Hence, the elephant becomes a handy reference to give people courage and address the situation with light-hearted humour.[28]

Design Elements for IMC Tools

The design and production of advertising messages involves a number of activities, among them writing copy, developing illustrations and other visual elements of the ad, and bringing all of the pieces together to create an effective message. In this section, we examine the verbal and visual elements of an ad and discuss tactical considerations in creating print, video, and audio messages. We use general terminology of print, video, and audio as these basic design elements can be applied to any print, video, or audio media distributed through advertising or other IMC tools.

DESIGN FOR PRINT MESSAGES

The basic elements of a print message are the headline, the body copy, the visual or illustrations, and the layout. The headline and body copy are the responsibility of the copywriters; artists, often working under the direction of an art director, are responsible for the visual presentation. Art directors also work with the copywriters to develop a layout, or arrangement of the above elements. We briefly examine the three design elements and explain how they are coordinated. These elements pertain to virtually all print messages that can be found in any media.

Headlines   The headline is the words in the leading position of the ad—the words that will be read first or are positioned to draw the most attention.[29] Headlines are usually set in larger, darker type and are often set apart from the body copy or text portion of the ad to give them prominence. Most advertising people consider the headline the most important part of a print ad.

The most important function of a headline is attracting readers' attention and interesting them in the rest of the message. While the visual portion of an ad is obviously important, the headline often shoulders most of the responsibility of attracting readers' attention. Research has shown the headline is generally the first thing people look at in a print ad, followed by the illustration. Only 20 percent of readers go beyond the headline and read the body copy.[30] So in addition to attracting attention, the headline must give the reader good reason to read the copy portion of the ad, which contains more detailed and persuasive information about the product or service. To do this, the headline must put forth the main theme, appeal, or proposition of the ad in a few words. Some print ads contain little if any body copy, so the headline must work with the illustration to communicate the entire advertising message.

Headlines also perform a segmentation function by engaging the attention and interest of consumers who are most likely to buy a particular product or service (see Exhibit 8-16).

Exhibit 8-16 GE innovates with headlines by asking a question after stating a product fact.

Advertisers begin the segmentation process by choosing to advertise in certain media vehicles (e.g., fashion magazine, national newspaper, out-of-home). An effective headline goes even further in selecting good prospects for the product by addressing their specific needs, wants, or interests.

Types of Headlines   Numerous possibilities exist for headlines. The type used depends on several factors, including the creative strategy, the particular advertising situation (e.g., product type, media vehicle(s) being used, timeliness), and its relationship to other elements of the ad, such as the illustration or body copy. Headlines can be categorized as direct and indirect. **Direct headlines** are straightforward and informative in terms of the message they are presenting and the target audience they are directed toward. Common types of direct headlines include those offering a specific benefit, making a promise, or announcing a reason why the reader should be interested in the product or service.

Indirect headlines are not straightforward about identifying the product or service or getting to the point. But they are often more effective at attracting readers' attention and interest because they provoke curiosity and lure readers into the body copy to learn an answer or get an explanation. Techniques for writing indirect headlines include using questions, provocations, how-to statements, and challenges.

Indirect headlines rely on their ability to generate curiosity or intrigue so as to motivate readers to become involved with the ad and read the body copy to find out the point of the message. This can be risky if the headline is not provocative enough to get the readers' interest. Advertisers deal with this problem by using a visual appeal that helps attract attention and offers another reason for reading more of the message. For example, the ad for the Volkswagen CC shown in Exhibit 8-17 uses an indirect headline that might create curiosity among readers and encourage them to read

Exhibit 8-17   This ad uses an indirect headline and strong visual image that motivate consumers to read the copy.

further. The copy below explains how the headline refers to awards the Jetta has won and its new features like an extra-large trunk. The visual element supports the theme by highlighting the improved design.

While many ads have only one headline, it is also common to see print ads containing the main head and one or more secondary heads, or **subheads**. Subheads are usually smaller than the main headline but larger than the body copy. They may appear above or below the main headline or within the body copy. Subheads are often used to enhance the readability of the message by breaking up large amounts of body copy and highlighting key sales points.

Body Copy   The main text portion of a print ad is referred to as the **body copy** (or just *copy*). While the body copy is usually the heart of the advertising message, getting the target audience to read it is often difficult. The copywriter faces a dilemma: The body copy must be long enough to communicate the advertiser's message yet short enough to hold readers' interest.

Body copy content often flows from the points made in the headline or subheads, but the specific content depends on the type of advertising appeal and/or execution style being used. For example, straight-sell copy that presents relevant information, product features and benefits, or competitive advantages is often used with the various types of rational appeals discussed earlier in the chapter. Emotional appeals often use narrative copy that tells a story or provides an interesting account of a problem or situation involving the product. Advertising body copy can be written to go along with any message appeal or execution style. Furthermore, copywriters select body copy that is appropriate for the creative strategy (i.e., theme, message appeal, source) and supports the creative tactics like the message structure and other design elements.

An interesting example of the use of long copy occurred with Rogers (AT&T) Wireless. Borrowing from the idea that a picture is worth a thousand words, the poster ads extolled upon the attributes and benefits of picture messaging with a small photo of the product and exactly one thousand words! To garner attention and full processing of the copy, the ads involved the reader in personally relevant conversations that the target audience would be familiar with, such as a woman talking to her man-friend about which shoes to wear to her high-school reunion, and a man talking to his buddy about his golfing triumphs. The entertaining dialogue provided a quick and enjoyable read, giving the feeling that one was actually experiencing the conversation.[31]

Exhibit 8-18   The visual background of this Olay ad allows the brand to stand out and reinforce its characteristics.

Visual   The third major element of a print ad is the visual. The illustration is often a dominant part of a print ad and plays an important role in determining its effectiveness. The visual portion of an ad must attract attention, communicate an idea or image, and work in a synergistic fashion with the headline and body copy to produce an effective message. In some print ads, the visual portion of the ad is essentially the message and thus must convey a strong and meaningful image. The ad for Olay Ribbons body wash shown in Exhibit 8-18 contains important visual elements. The stunning colours of the water presumably attract the attention of women interested in such a product. In addition, the water conveys the clean and rejuvenating experience of using a body wash product. The prominent placement of the product package and ribbon signify the brand's unique characteristic and effect of the mica minerals that give a shimmering feel, which are reinforced with the shimmering light off the water.

Many decisions have to be made regarding the visual portion of the ad: what identification marks should be included (brand name, company or trade name, trademarks, logos); whether to use photos or hand-drawn or painted illustrations; what colours to use (or even perhaps black and white or just a splash of colour); and what the focus of the visual should be. Even the number of pages of visual ads is critical, as in the case of fashion products or automobiles. One study finds that advertisers should use fewer pages (e.g., 4 to 6) versus longer pages (e.g., 8 to 10) and insert the ads more frequently.[32] Exhibit 8-19 shows an ad where the visual is very important. The entire message is conveyed with the surprising image of a woman in a hazardous materials suit surrounded by second-hand smoke.

Layout While each individual element of a print ad is important, the key factor is how these elements are blended into a finished advertisement. A **layout** is the physical arrangement of the various parts of the ad, including the headline, subheads, body copy, illustrations, and any identifying marks. The layout shows where each part of the ad will be placed and gives guidelines to the people working on the ad. For example, the layout helps the copywriter determine how much space he or she has to work with and how much copy should be written. The layout can also guide the art director in determining the size and type of photos.

Many layouts are standard poster format shown in a portrait orientation, although landscape formats do occur. Sometimes there are vertical or horizontal splits, with the latter being a separation between the visual and body copy as shown in Exhibits 8-16 and 8-17. An optimal layout is an artistic expression of the brand as it achieves balance among the space, visuals, and colours. Exhibit 8-20 shows an interesting example where the creative layout raises the question as to whether the "go" is the headline or the visual of the Visa ad.

DESIGN FOR VIDEO MESSAGES

Video messages contain the elements of sight, sound, and motion that are combined to create an unlimited number of advertising appeals and executions. Video messages occur in instances beyond television, as they are seen at theatres, online, and in many place-based locations. In most of these situations, the viewer does not control the rate at which the message is presented, so there is no opportunity to review key points of interest that are not communicated clearly. However, online digital exposure and PVR technology place stronger control in the hands of viewers.

As with any form of marketing communication, a primary goal in creating a video message is to obtain and maintain a viewer's attention. This can be particularly challenging because people often view these messages while doing other things and there are multiple messages competing for viewer attention at the same time. Creating and producing a video message to overcome these obstacles is a detailed and expensive process. On a cost-per-minute basis, video messages are the most expensive production, especially for TV ads. Thus, getting the video and audio elements to work together to communicate the advertiser's message requires careful planning.

Exhibit 8-19 This ad uses a clever visual image to deliver a message about the dangers of second-hand smoke.

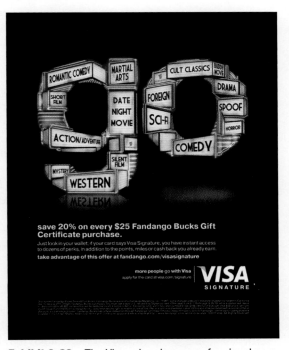

Exhibit 8-20 The Visa ad makes use of a visual as a headline to draw attention.

Video The video elements of a commercial are what the consumer sees on the screen. The visual portion generally dominates the presentation, so it must attract viewers' attention and communicate an idea, message, and/or image. A number of visual elements may have to be coordinated to produce a successful ad. Decisions have to be made regarding the product, the presenter, action sequences, demonstrations, and the like, as well as the setting(s), the talent or characters who will appear in the commercial, and such other factors as lighting, graphics, colour, and identifying symbols.

Video messages can cost a small fortune due to production personnel, equipment, location fees, video editing, sound recording and mixing, music fees, and talent. Acting talent certainly adds to the cost since good acting is an important characteristic for effective message delivery. Marketers are especially careful in selecting the presenters and actors for a video message since incorrect associations may be processed if viewers recognize the actor from another message. At the heart of the matter is that the brand creates its own identity in the message to ensure brand awareness. While there are exclusivity clauses where actors cannot be in ads for products in the same category, advertisers are concerned about overexposure of the face. However, if one looks closely, one can see many familiar ones across a spectrum of ads.[33]

For Maxwell House, Kraft stripped down the production of its TV ads and plainly showed the product, thus saving a couple hundred thousand dollars per execution. The message mentioned this, and asked where the savings should be donated. Viewers responded with ideas on the Maxwell House website, and money eventually went toward Habitat for Humanity, children's music programs, and guide dog training—certainly good deeds reinforcing the tagline, "Brew Some Good."[34] Maxwell continued with the low-cost approach with its Optimism Breaks, where consumers would upload snippets of their good behaviour directed to others with a "cup half full" outlook on life.[35]

Technology Perspective 8-1 describes new interactive TV ads that may have similar or new video features compared to existing ads. Carrying on with this idea and with the growth of consumer-generated ads, brands moved toward using reality-type filming of actual customers in purchase and consumption situations. Production costs are notably less and the reality style is fashionably accepted by viewers.[36] Kokanee's new campaign after retiring its park ranger featured a point-of-view style that followed a man's everyday activities like personal care, sports, and meeting women at a party while drinking the beer.[37]

The explosion of digital messages online produced very low-budget offerings. Surprisingly, one tactic of recording someone writing something down or while they do some simple task has taken off on the Internet. Local businesses that use TV commercials are financially restricted to very simple production methods, such as a simple customer testimonial or demonstration from the owner. With Canada's smaller population relative to the United States, by comparison it is difficult to achieve economies of scale for lavish or high-cost productions. Creative executions and the accompanying video are designed with lower costs in mind. However, quality video everywhere may emerge as digital recording technology costs become more economical in future. Despite this, Canadian-produced video ads continue to innovate, with Mini video ads as a prime example.

Audio The audio element of a video message includes voices, music, and sound effects.

Voice Voices are used in different ways. They may be heard through the direct presentation of a spokesperson or as a conversation among people appearing in the script. A common method for presenting the audio is through a **voiceover**, where the message is delivered or action on the screen is narrated or described by an announcer who is not visible. Advertisers will use a voice that works with the message and brand as the tone provides a distinctive resonance influencing emotional responses.

Music Music is also an important element that can play a variety of roles.[38] Music acts structurally in an ad, much like grammar in a sentence, and supports the time sequence, motion, repetition, brand identification, and emotion experienced. Music can be a central element as it is used to get attention, break through the advertising clutter, communicate a key selling point, establish an image or position, or add feeling.[39] Music can also create a positive mood that makes the consumer more receptive toward the advertising message.[40] Other research on consumers' cognitive and affective responses to music in advertising found that increased congruity

IMC TECHNOLOGY PERSPECTIVE 8-1

New Ways to Execute Ads

For the 2009 Super Bowl, Labatt experimented with two interactive Budweiser TV ads for the Quebec market. Labatt handles the marketing for Anheuser-Busch InBev beer products in Canada. Like most marketers, Labatt tested new technologies to find innovative ways to advertise that go beyond mass media. As one manager put it, "We're definitely trying to change our mindset to use mass TV in a more efficient and effective way. Digital extensions pick up where mass media leave off." Viewers who watched the game on RDS could use their remote to access links embedded in the ad in order to watch or bookmark a three-minute mini-documentary about the ad. Other digital connections with Super Bowl ads include online display ads, sponsorship of Super Bowl–related websites, or commercials on video hosting sites. This latest Canadian opportunity extends the exposure time, and hopefully the results.

Executed by Etc.tv, Labatt paid for the interactive ads based on the number of unique visitors, and the click-through rates were five times the average. "Given the size of the audience, given the product, we expected a lift because there are more there than just football fans, it's a cultural phenomenon," commented a VP from the agency. The link located at the bottom left corner while the Budweiser ad played attracted people to watch the extended version of the ad while the game occurred shortly thereafter. The majority of those watching viewed the extended video in HD.

Etc.tv of Montreal is a leading firm in developing interactive TV ads, and offers its service for 2 million households in Quebec with plans to develop the market throughout Canada. The Budweiser ad represented the first Super Bowl ad with a digital link to access the video-on-demand features of today's television technology. According to Etc. tv, "This is a way of reaching the right consumer at the right time with the right message, and it resonates with the digital consumer's desire to get the information they want, when they want it."

Another avenue for executing interactive ads is Microsoft's natural user-interface ads (NUads) placed on their Xbox Live network. An ad is launched by hand, voice, or controller via an ad square on the dashboard and Xbox's 360 Kinect sensor. Subway tested the new format with an ad for its Tuscan Chicken Melt sandwich. Subway provided the ad and Microsoft seamlessly incorporated the ad with the technology so it could be shown on the TV screen. The interactive results allow users to see what others are saying about the ad, while Subway can obtain instant campaign feedback. Subway interactively asked, "Where will you eat your Tuscan Chicken Melt?" with four different options for a response. Results indicated that 37 percent of the viewers explored the interactive feature, and 71 percent of those answered the poll question. One media expert commented that the 37 percent rate looked favourable compared to the 5 percent to 10 percent responses for most digital applications.

Sources: Emily Steel, "Labatt Brews Up Interactive Super Bowl Ads," *The Globe and Mail*, January 28, 2009, p. B11; Kirstin Laird, "On-Demand Bud Ads Score During Super Bowl," *Marketing Magazine,* February 4, 2009; "Interactive TV Sets Record in Super Bowl," *broadcastermagazine*, February 3, 2009; www.etc.tv; Alicia Androich, "Microsoft Releases Results For NUads Format," *Marketing Magazine,* January 8, 2013; Rebecca Harris, "Subway Tries Interactive TV with Microsoft XBOX Ad," *Marketing Magazine,* September 26, 2012.

Question:
1. When someone clicks on an interactive ad, is this experience like watching a TV ad, or like watching the brand's video message on a video-hosting website?

between the music and advertising with respect to variables such as mood, genre, score, image, and tempo contributes to the communication effectiveness of an advertisement by enhancing recall, brand attitude, affective response, and purchase intention.[41]

Well known—or reasonably well known—music is used to convey the message of the ad. For example, Delissio used the old tune "Hit the Road, Jack" to wrap up the ad for its new garlic bread pizza. After a teenager greets her date at the door, who is either Dracula or a goth, he turns into a bat and flies away once he hears about and smells the new ingredient.[42] One new trend is that music houses are placing indie music in ads, following the lead of hit TV shows like *The O.C., Grey's Anatomy,* and *Gossip Girl.* Canadian artist Emilie Mover's song "Made for Each Other" became the key song for the global campaign for Fisher-Price toys. Marketers are looking for a distinctive tone for their ad that is not associated with any other experiences to make the ad more enriching.[43]

Often music is composed specifically for a campaign. Musicians and composers participate early on in the process of developing the ad; alternatively, the creative specialists who produce the ad look for very specific types of music to support the visuals. For example, the original musical score for the Canadian launch of the Mini was written after filming the ad. The visuals and the musical request led to a very unique sound that contributed to the brand positioning strategy in such a way that people thought it was previously recorded. In fact industry experts believe that custom-written music is the best since it almost always works.[44] Finally, advertisers use **needledrop**, which refers to music that is prefabricated, multipurpose, and highly conventional, much like stock photos used in print ads.[45]

Jingle   Another memorable sound element is a **jingle**, a catchy song about a product or service that delivers the advertising theme and a simple message. For example, "Black's is photography" is a jingle that has stood the test of time. Tim Hortons moved to a new jingle, "Always fresh. Always Tim Hortons," for a while and then picked "It's time for Tim's." Swiss Chalet reverted to a previous one, "Always so good for so little," after trying four different jingles in the past 10 years.[46] Subway garnered lots of mileage with its "Five. Five. Five dollar. Five dollar foot-long." Sometimes, jingles simply identify a brand and appear at the end of the message. Jingles are often composed by companies that specialize in writing music for advertising. These jingle houses work with the creative team to determine the role music will play in the commercial and the message that needs to be communicated.

Production of Video Messages   The elements of a video message are brought together in a **script**, a written version of a message that provides a detailed description of its video and audio content. The script shows the audio elements—the copy to be spoken by voices, the music, and sound effects. The video portion of the script provides the visual plan—camera actions and angles, scenes, transitions, and other important descriptions. The script also shows how the video corresponds to the audio portion of the commercial.

Once the basic script has been conceived, the writer and art director get together to produce a **storyboard**, a series of drawings used to present the visual plan or layout. The storyboard contains still drawings of the video scenes and descriptions of the audio that accompanies each scene. Like layouts for print ads, storyboards provide those involved in the production and approval with a good approximation of what the final commercial will look like. An animatic (actual video of the storyboard along with the soundtrack) may be produced if a more finished form is needed for client presentations or pretesting. Once the storyboard or animatic is approved, it is ready to move to the production phase, which involves three stages as shown in Figure 8-2. Before the final production process begins, the client must usually review and approve the creative strategy and tactics that will be used for the advertising message.

DESIGN FOR AUDIO MESSAGES

Audio messages are mostly delivered through radio, and that is the context for most of the design guidelines; however, digital opportunities make audio messages more prevalent. For example, audio messages can be included in podcasts, and certainly any ad on the Internet (e.g., banner, pop-up) could have an audio equivalent. Imagine listening to an ad while reading the online newspaper. The key elements of an audio message are similar to the audio of video messages, so we concentrate on the verbal and sound elements.

Verbal   Historically, radio has been referred to as the theatre of the mind; the voice(s) speaking to us in these audio messages offer a description or story, like the body copy of a print ad, that allows a visual to take hold. The talking can take many forms—straight announcer, dialogue between two actors, announcer/actor, customer interview—while following any of the executional

Figure 8-2 The three phases of production for commercials

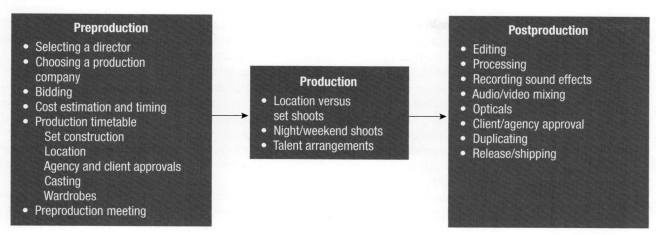

Preproduction
- Selecting a director
- Choosing a production company
- Bidding
- Cost estimation and timing
- Production timetable
  Set construction
  Location
  Agency and client approvals
  Casting
  Wardrobes
- Preproduction meeting

Production
- Location versus set shoots
- Night/weekend shoots
- Talent arrangements

Postproduction
- Editing
- Processing
- Recording sound effects
- Audio/video mixing
- Opticals
- Client/agency approval
- Duplicating
- Release/shipping

styles identified earlier in the chapter. Depending on which format is used, a script is written that will attract attention in the opening, communicate the brand's attribute or benefits, and wrap up with a close that includes a call to action, like a store visit, phone number, or website address. The dialogue of the script is critical, much like the voice-over in a video message, but the illuminating words support the theatre idea to maximize the amount of processing time of the message.

With this in mind, it is often easy to hear very silly ideas in radio ads that somehow work because of our natural curiosity to make sense of incongruence. For example, famous actor Gordon Pinsent, who has a perfect radio voice, talked about a new poutine product from NY Fries: "Only the best ingredients coming together for something so perfect, like finding the perfect pair of jeans for your kitten. Little designer ones that sit low on the hips, so that little kitten can work those little designer jeans all sassy-like.[47]

Sound Audio messages naturally rely on sound due to the lack of a visual. Brands employ unique sound effects to allow the visual to take hold in the receiver's mind. Alternatively, the unique voices of the speakers help create a personality to allow the visual to take hold even more. As seen with video messages, music becomes a key component for audio messages on a number of fronts such as attracting attention or supporting the message and reinforcing the positioning. Moreover, as seen with video messages, jingles become even more critical as they fit with the format of listening to music. Audio logos are used significantly with audio messages, and are usually the same ones. Astral Media, owner of many different radio formats, uses 11 different versions of its audio logo to fit the genre of music played on the respective station. For example, a guitar riff plays the logo on a rock station followed by the common ending "You're listening to an Astral Media radio station."[48]

L04 Frameworks for Creative Tactics

In this section, we present two planning models that guide the decision for selecting the most appropriate creative tactics. Each model builds on a perspective of the consumer response processes that we described in Chapter 4. We discuss the models from a historical perspective to explain how the current model is an improvement over the initial model.

THE FCB PLANNING MODEL

Richard Vaughn of the Foote, Cone & Belding advertising agency and his associates developed an advertising planning model by building on the alternative response hierarchy model.[49] They added the dimension of *thinking versus feeling* processing at each involvement level by bringing in theories regarding brain specialization. The right/left brain theory suggests the left side of the brain is more capable of rational, cognitive thinking, while the right side is more visual and emotional with more affective (feeling) functions. Their model, which became known as the FCB grid, delineates four primary advertising planning quadrants—informative, affective, habit formation, and self-satisfaction—along with the most appropriate variant of the alternative response hierarchies (Figure 8-3).

The informative strategy is for highly involving products where rational thinking and economic considerations prevail. The affective strategy is for highly involving/feeling purchases where advertising stresses psychological and emotional motives such as building self-esteem or enhancing one's ego or self-image. The habit formation strategy is for low-involvement/thinking products with routinized behaviour patterns. The self-satisfaction strategy is for low-involvement/feeling products where appeals to sensory pleasures and social motives are important. Vaughn acknowledges that minimal level of awareness may precede purchase of both types of low-involvement products.

The FCB grid suggested that creative specialists involved in the advertising planning process analyze consumer–product relationships and develop appropriate promotional strategies. Consumer research determined how consumers perceived products or brands on the involvement and thinking/feeling dimensions.[50] This information guided effective creative options such as using rational versus emotional appeals, increasing involvement levels, or even getting consumers to evaluate a think-type product on the basis of feelings. Although the FCB model did not explicitly give detailed suggestions for all quadrants, and its use may be limited currently, the idea of linking the target audience's response to creative tactics remains an important step in advertising theory and practice.

THE R&P PLANNING MODEL

We highlighted the Rossiter and Percy (R&P) perspective in Chapter 5 when discussing objectives for the IMC plan. Another part of their framework concerns recommendations for creative tactics so that the appropriate communication effects will occur with the target audience while they are processing the message. On the surface, their planning model appears similar to the FCB planning model as both represent consumer attitudes and explain how marketers use

Figure 8-3

The Foote, Cone, and Belding (FCB) grid

	Thinking	Feeling
High involvement	**1. Informative (thinker)** Car–house–furnishings Model: Learn–feel–do **Possible implications** Media: Long copy format Reflective vehicles Creative: Specific information Demonstration	**2. Affective (feeling)** Jewellery–cosmetics– fashion apparel Model: Feel–learn–do **Possible implications** Media: Large space Image specials Creative: Executional Impact
Low involvement	**3. Habit formation (doer)** Food–household items Model: Do–learn–feel **Possible implications** Media: Small space ads 10-second I.D.s Radio; POS Creative: Reminder	**4. Self-satisfaction (reactor)** Liquor–candy Model: Do–feel–learn **Possible implications** Media: Billboards Newspapers POS Creative: Attention

creative tactics to influence attitudes. However, we will discuss four improvements as we explain the R&P model.[51]

Brand Awareness Tactics The first improvement is that the R&P model argues that brand awareness is a necessary precursor to brand attitude. According to R&P, both brand awareness and brand attitude are universal communication objectives for all circumstances (i.e., one ad, ad campaign, IMC plan). In this view, all marketing communication should strive to achieve awareness in order to make brand attitude operational. R&P have three suggestions for awareness:

Exhibit 8-21 The Dasani ad makes use of a visual to clearly identify the brand.

- *Match* the brand stimuli and the type of response behaviour of the target audience so that understanding of the brand in a category is unambiguous.
- *Use* a unique brand execution style to connect the brand to the category.
- *Maximize* brand contact time in the exposure to reinforce name and category connection.

For awareness to be fully established, the target audience needs to understand the context (brand, behaviour, category) as this is a clue as to how or why the brand exists. If the context is not clear, then the target audience has trouble remembering the brand when it comes time to purchase. A unique execution style helps cut through the clutter. The connection to the category and sufficient exposure is required to make sure that the message is retained. For example, TV ads can sometimes show the package or brand name for too short a time for target audiences to fully grasp where the brand competes in the market.

We also noted that R&P suggest that awareness can be achieved via recognition and/or recall. R&P have two suggestions for recognition that require less media frequency as consumers need only to be familiar with the brand stimuli at the point of purchase:

- The brand package and name should have sufficient exposure in terms of time or size depending on the media.
- Category need should be mentioned or identified.

The Dasani ad in Exhibit 8-21 clearly shows the brand name with the large visual of the bottle of water. Its emergence from the plant communicates that the container is made of plant material, and is biodegradable. The could likely be reminding those who stopped consuming the bottled water due to its over reliance on the use of plastic.

Since recall is a more difficult mental task, R&P have six suggestions for this aspect of awareness. Recall also requires high levels of frequency since the brand has to be remembered prior to being at the point of purchase:

- The brand and the category need should be connected in the primary benefit claim.
- The primary benefit claim should be short to be easily understood.
- Within an exposure, the primary benefit claim should be repeated often.
- The message should have or imply a clear personal reference.
- A bizarre or unusual execution style can be used if it is consistent with the brand attitude objective.
- A jingle or similar "memory" tactic should be included.

We have many more specific recommendations for recall since it is a much more difficult mental task for consumers. Advertisers have to help their target audience know their brand prior to purchasing. The ad in Exhibit 8-22 follows many guidelines for improving recall. Thus, careful

Exhibit 8-22 Kelowna's ad uses key brand recall guidelines to encourage extended visits.

attention has to be put on all three creative tactics decisions to ensure the target audience can retrieve the brand name from long-term memory when the need to purchase a product category arises.

Brand Attitude Grid Tactics   The R&P view of consumer attitudes is also framed as a matrix, with the dimensions of involvement and motivation. For each of these dimensions, R&P argue that their view is a more accurate representation of attitude for planning purposes than the FCB model, and the use of these two concepts represents the second and third improvements.

Low-involvement decision Informational motivation	Low-involvement decision Transformational motivation
High-involvement decision Informational motivation	High-involvement decision Transformational motivation

The involvement dimension is similar to the FCB model, from low involvement to high involvement. However, R&P argue that theirs is specific to the brand as the target audience makes a purchase decision. Further, the high- and low-involvement levels are also consistent with the central and peripheral routes to persuasion. More precisely, R&P interpret involvement as the degree of risk perceived by the target audience (i.e., new category user or loyal customer) in choosing a particular brand for the next purchase occasion. One extension of this idea, not fully developed by R&P, is that the concept can extend to purchase-related behaviour that we discussed in Chapter 5. For example, how much risk does a person buying a car for the first time take in deciding to visit a particular dealer for a test drive?

The motivation dimension is a continuum from negative motive, or informational-based attitude, to positive motive, or transformational-based attitude. The historical interpretation of an informational-based attitude implies that it is based on careful reasoning that results from the cognitive responses that the target audience has while experiencing advertising messages. This purely cognitive orientation is also the foundation of the "think" dimension of the FCB model. However, R&P argue that this is too limiting as attitude is based on both cognition and affect. Accordingly, they suggest that creative tactics for this side of the matrix should account for the benefit claims (i.e., cognition) and the emotional portrayal of the motive (i.e., affect). Thus, in order for it to be an informational-based attitude, the emphasis of the benefit claim is stronger than the emotional portrayal of the negative motive.

The notion of transformational-based attitude is partly based on the idea of a transformational ad defined as, "one which associates the experience of using (consuming) the advertised brand with a unique set of psychological characteristics which would not typically be associated with the brand experience to the same degree without exposure to the advertisement."[52] This type of advertising is often used by companies in the travel industry to help consumers envision the experience or feeling they might have when they take a trip such as a cruise or visit a particular destination. Image advertising, which is designed to give a company or brand a unique association or personality, is often transformational in nature. It is designed to create a certain feeling or mood that is activated when a consumer uses a particular product or service. For example, the Lambesis agency has created a unique image for Skyy Vodka by creating ads that associate the brand with unique consumption moments (see Exhibit 8-23).

Just like the informational-based attitude is not purely cognitive, the transformational-based attitude is not purely based on emotion but includes cognitive elements. Intuitively, this makes a lot of sense as some ads with a very strong fear appeal often leave us thinking. Overall, the emphasis of the emotional portrayal is stronger than the benefit claim for transformational-based attitude. Providing information in transformational ads is part of the Fresh Air campaign for Newfoundland and Labrador. Much of the message involved breathtaking views of the landscape and a humorous way of conveying the clean air one can breathe along the coastline. Another key component included travel logistics and accommodation information.[53]

The fourth improvement of the R&P model is that its guidelines for creative tactics balance elements in the ad for cognitive and emotional responses that contribute to both aspects of brand attitude. On the emotional side, we are concerned with how the motive is portrayed or conveyed in the ad. To consider this, we have three characteristics: its authenticity, or how real it appears to the target audience; whether the target audience likes the ad; and finally, the target audience's reaction to the execution style. On the informational side, we are concerned with the brand's message with respect to the benefit claims. We also have three characteristics to consider: the number, the intensity, and the repetition of the claims.

While the guidelines for all six characteristics may be a function of all three creative tactics decisions, we can make a stronger connection for certain ones. The authenticity and whether the target audience likes the ad are typically associated with the design elements of the ad. Quite obviously, there is a direct connection between the execution style of the framework and that particular creative tactic decision discussed in this chapter. The benefit claims are mostly a function of the message structure since the latter concerns the details of explaining the product's benefits. It is also a function of the relative balance between a verbal and visual message. We now turn our attention to creative tactics recommendations for the four brand attitude cells.

Exhibit 8–23 Advertising for Skyy vodka uses an intense theme to create an image for the brand.

Low Involvement–Informational Creative Tactics   Ads designed to influence target audiences' attitudes based on low involvement–informational persuasion should have a very obvious benefit claim with an unusual execution style. New York Fries has used this idea in an ad campaign (Exhibit 8-24). Since the intention is to persuade the target audience so that they automatically learn the connection among the brand, its category, and the benefit, consumer acceptance or rejection of the message is not a factor. Further, the emotion demonstrated in the ad and whether the target audience likes the ad are not necessary as the message is intended to make a creative link among the brand, category, and benefit.

Low Involvement–Informational

Emotional portrayal of motive

Authenticity	Not necessary
Like ad	Not necessary
Execution style	Unusual, problem-solution format

Benefit claim of brand message

Number of benefits	One or two, or one clear group
Intensity of benefit claim	State extremely
Repetition of benefit claim	Few required for reminder

Exhibit 8-24   This ad contains low involvement–informational creative tactics.

Exhibit 8-25   The passion of Toronto FC fans is uniquely conveyed in this BMO sponsorship ad.

Low Involvement–Transformational Creative Tactics   Three emotional portrayal guidelines are critical for this type of attitude. These points are consistent with transformational ads described above. For example, the representation of the consumption of the brand in the drama or story of the ad must "ring true" with the target audience such that it is perceived as a very enjoyable ad. This characteristic is demonstrated in the BMO ad (Exhibit 8-25). In a low-involvement situation, benefit claims are still included but may be indirectly communicated through the story or emotion surrounding the story. Actual acceptance of the benefit claim is not a requirement; however, rejection of the overall message can lead to a reduction in the attitude of the target audience.

Low Involvement–Transformational

Emotional portrayal of motive

Authenticity	Key element and is the single benefit
Like ad	Necessary
Execution style	Unique to the brand

Benefit claim of brand message

Number of benefits	One or two, or one clear group
Intensity of benefit claim	Imply extremely by association
Repetition of benefit claim	Many exposures to buildup before trial purchase and reinforce attitude after trial

High Involvement–Informational Creative Tactics   This side of the model illustrates the importance of information as high involvement implies the requirement of considerable and accurate benefit claims. Many benefits can be claimed here but they must be organized and presented in a manner that respects the current attitude of the target audience. Since this is an informational-based attitude, the emotional portrayal is important but not the primary consideration.

Furthermore, the high-involvement characteristic means that the target audience has to accept the benefit claims. Rejection of the benefit claims may not result in any negative change in attitude if the copy respected the prior attitude of the target audience.

High Involvement–Informational

Emotional portrayal of motive

Authenticity	Key element early in product life cycle and declines as product reaches later stages
Like ad	Not necessary
Execution style	Unusual

Benefit claim of brand message

Number of benefits	Overall claim to summarize multiple (no more than seven) benefits
Intensity of benefit claim	Initial attitude is key reference point
	Very accurate claim; cannot over-claim or under-claim
	Comparative or refutation messages are strong options
Repetition of benefit claim	Many claims within an exposure

High Involvement–Transformational Creative Tactics   Persuasion through this type of attitude formation requires strong emphasis of the emotion. A positive attitude toward the ad leads to a positive brand attitude. Likewise, the target audience must truly relate to the execution style and feel like the ad supports their lifestyle. Nutella captures this point with the ad in Exhibit 8-26. The end result is that if the target audience rejects the message because the emotion is not accurate, then the persuasion will not work and may even cause significant attitude reduction. The remaining guidelines illustrate that considerable information is required similar to what is seen for the high involvement–informational attitude. Once again this implies that acceptance of the benefit claims is critical for the attitude to take hold with the target audience.

Exhibit 8-26   Nutella's ad accurately conveys the lifestyle of those consuming the product.

High Involvement–Transformational

Emotional portrayal of motive

Authenticity	Paramount; must reflect lifestyle of target audience
Like ad	Necessary
Execution style	Unique; target audience must identify with product, people, or consumption situation shown

Benefit claim of brand message

Number of benefits	Acceptable number to provide key information
Intensity of benefit claim	Very accurate claim; may over-claim but do not under-claim
Repetition of benefit claim	Many are required to support informational message

ⓁⓄ⑤ IMC Planning: Guidelines for Creative Evaluation

While the creative specialists have much responsibility for determining the message appeal and execution style to be used in a campaign, the marketer must evaluate and approve the creative approach before any ads are produced. A number of people may be involved in evaluating the creative recommendation, including the advertising or communications manager, product or brand managers, marketing director or vice president, representatives from the legal department, and even senior managers if required.

Top management is involved in selecting an ad agency and must approve the theme and creative strategy for the campaign. Evaluation and approval of individual ads proposed by the agency is often the responsibility of advertising and product managers. The account executive and a member of the creative team present the creative concept to the client's advertising and product managers for their approval before beginning production. A careful evaluation should be made before the campaign actually enters production, since this stage requires considerable time and money. Basic criteria for evaluating the creative approach focus on a number of questions requiring managerial judgment:

- *Is the creative approach consistent with the brand's marketing and advertising objectives?* Advertisers must consider whether the creative strategy and tactics recommended by the agency are consistent with the marketing strategy for the brand and the role advertising and promotion have been assigned in the overall marketing program (i.e., brand image, marketing positioning strategy).
- *Is the creative approach consistent with the communication objectives?* The creative strategy and tactics must meet the established communication objectives. Creative specialists can lose sight of what the advertising message is supposed to be and come up with an approach that fails to execute the advertising strategy. Individuals responsible for approving the ad should ask the creative specialists to explain how the creative strategy and tactics achieve the creative and communications objectives.
- *Is the creative approach appropriate for the target audience?* Careful consideration should be given to whether the creative strategy and tactics recommended will appeal to, be understood by, and communicate effectively with the target audience. This involves studying all elements of the ad and how the audience will respond to them. Advertisers do not want to approve advertising that they believe will receive a negative reaction from the target audience.
- *Does the creative approach communicate a clear and convincing message to the customer?* Most ads are supposed to communicate a message that will help sell the brand. While creativity is important in advertising, it is also important that the advertising communicate information attributes, features and benefits, and/or images that give consumers a reason to buy the brand.
- *Does the creative approach keep from overwhelming the message?* Many creative, entertaining commercials have failed to register the brand name and/or selling points effectively. With advertising clutter, it may be necessary to use a novel creative approach to gain the receiver's attention. However, the creative approach cannot inhibit or limit message delivery to the target audience.
- *Is the creative approach appropriate for the media environment in which it is likely to be seen?* Each media vehicle has its own specific climate that results from the nature of its editorial content, the type of reader or viewer it attracts, and the nature of the ads it contains. Consideration should be given to how well the ad fits into the media environment in which it will be shown.
- *Is the ad truthful and tasteful?* Marketers should consider whether an ad is truthful, as well as whether it might offend consumers. The ultimate responsibility for determining whether an ad deceives or offends the target audience lies with the client. It is the job of the advertising or brand manager to evaluate the approach against company standards. The firm's legal department may review the ad to determine whether the creative appeal, message content, or execution could cause any problems for the company.

The advertising manager, brand manager, or other personnel on the client side can use these guidelines in reviewing, evaluating, and approving the ideas offered by the creative specialists. There may be other factors specific to the firm's advertising and marketing situation. Also, there may be situations where it is acceptable to deviate from the standards the firm usually uses in judging creative output. As we shall see in the next chapter, the client may want to move beyond these subjective criteria and use more sophisticated pretesting research using quantitative and qualitative methods to determine the effectiveness of a particular approach suggested by the creative specialists.

Learning Objectives Summary

 Analyze the creative execution styles that advertisers can use and the situations where they are most appropriate.

Once the creative strategy that will guide the ad campaign has been determined, attention turns to the specific creative tactics that will enhance the cognitive and emotional processing of the message. The creative execution style is the way the advertising appeal is presented in the message and is the first of three creative tactics analyzed in this chapter. A number of common execution techniques were examined, along with considerations for their use. The most appropriate style is a matter of balancing uniqueness in the market versus effective communication to achieve the stated objectives. A number of standard approaches are available, like straight-sell, slice-of-life, testimonial, drama, humour, and imagery—all of which can be put in TV commercials, print ads, and radio spots and are now being developed for online video, banner ads, and podcast sponsorships.

 Explain different types of message structures that can be used to develop a promotional message.

The design of the advertising message is a critical part of the communication process and is the second creative tactic discussed. There are options regarding the message structure, including order of presentation of message arguments, conclusion drawing, message sidedness, refutation, and verbal versus visual traits. How these elements are constructed has important implications for enhancing the processing of the message and whether communication effects are achieved with the target audience. Message structure considerations are important for any form of delivery (i.e., video, print, audio) that may be disseminated via traditional or new media.

 Express design elements involved in the creation of print, video, and audio messages.

Attention was also given to tactical issues involved in creating print, video, and audio messages. The elements of a print ad include headlines, body copy, illustrations, and layout. We also examined the video and audio elements of video messages and considerations involved in the planning and production of commercials. Together, these showed the important design decisions that have to be made to complete the creative approach. Finally, we highlighted a couple of key factors in the development of audio messages. These design elements are relevant for producing print, video, or audio ads that can be delivered through a variety of media.

 Apply a planning model for making creative tactics decisions.

We presented a framework for creative specialists and marketers to help them make the appropriate decisions for the creative tactics. The framework uses the target audience's attitude as the key factor when deciding upon the correct execution style, message structure, and design. These three characteristics ensure that both cognitive and emotional aspects of processing and attitude formation are addressed in the receiver of the message. The model is a like a list to double check and know whether the creative execution results have characteristics that influence the target audience's attitude in the way expected.

 Illustrate how clients evaluate the creative work of their agencies and discuss guidelines for the evaluation and approval process.

Creative specialists are responsible for determining the creative strategy and tactics from the marketer's input. However, the client must review, evaluate, and approve the creative approach before any ads are produced or run. A number of criteria can be used by advertising managers, product or brand managers, and others involved in the promotional process to evaluate the advertising messages before approving final production.

Key Terms

Review key terms and definitions on Connect.

Review Questions

1. Identify the difference between a message appeal and a creative execution style. Why is it important to make this distinction?

2. What is meant by a one-sided versus two-sided message? Discuss reasons why marketers may or may not want to use a two-sided message.

3. Are headlines more important for gaining attention or reinforcing awareness?

4. What are the similarities and differences of creative tactics across the four cells of the R&P planning model?

5. Explain how the guidelines for creative evaluation can be applied to ads seen on the Internet.

Applied Questions

1. Look through ads in other chapters and figure out what execution style is used. Do the same for video ads found online.

2. What are the limitations of constructing standard print-format ads for Facebook and billboards?

3. Brands are experimenting with long-form video messages online. Using the design elements discussed in the chapter, contrast this approach with a standard 30-second TV ad. When would a brand use both within its IMC plan?

4. Find an ad for each of the four cells of the R&P framework for creative tactics. Identify the design elements that match the guidelines for each cell.

5. Apply the guidelines for creative evaluation to a campaign for Telus or Bell or Rogers, and conclude whether it passes all the criteria sufficiently.

GO ONLINE

For more information on the resources available from McGraw-Hill Ryerson,
go to www.mcgrawhill.ca/he/solutions.

Measuring the Effectiveness of the Promotional Message

CHAPTER NINE

9

LEARNING OBJECTIVES

LO1 Identify the reasons for measuring promotional program effectiveness.

LO2 Describe the measures used in assessing promotional program effectiveness.

LO3 Evaluate alternative methods for measuring promotional program effectiveness.

LO4 Appraise the requirements of proper effectiveness research.

Eye Tracking: An Old Technology Finds New IMC Applications

The usefulness of eye tracking technology for measuring advertising effectiveness is not new. Thirty years ago, advertising researchers employed this technology to determine where viewers were focusing when they looked at ads and/or TV commercials. While proven to be useful, eye tracking never went away but no one seemed to use it, which is now changing for a number of reasons. An increased emphasis on accountability and the increased pressure to determine an ad's effectiveness, improved technologies, the advent of new media, and improvements to existing media forms are reasons cited.

As a result, marketers have found a number of new applications for eye tracking, allowing the advertiser to determine what customers see and to determine the effectiveness of copy and visuals. From Web design to viewers' attention to display ads, marketers are finding eye tracking a valuable tool to enhance effectiveness. Researchers use eye movements to tell specifically where viewers are looking, to see if they are reading or scanning, and what catches their first view. They can also tell how much time viewers spend looking at a specific stimulus and the order in which they view others.

An eye tracking study asked participants to navigate Facebook, Twitter, and YouTube as they normally would. The study revealed that 65 percent of them engaged with a sponsor within 10 seconds of beginning their search, when asked to search for Pepsi on both Facebook and YouTube (Twitter was not included as it had no search tool). On Facebook, the results showed that their first attention was paid to the sponsored ads, and others were barely, if at all, viewed, while on YouTube, the top six results and the first sponsored ad got all the attention.

Another Internet study tracked how people navigate websites when looking for information. Their results indicate that to be effective an ad should be simple, with those that had only text or text and a separate image being most effective, while those that imposed text on top of images or included animation fared the worst. While the study showed that people saw 36 percent of the ads on the pages they visited, the time spent viewing them was only one-third of a second. One of the most surprising results was the fact that text-only ads scored best.

A Canadian company offers an eye-tracking device that can determine when someone looks at a billboard, where they look, and for how long, without them even knowing it—if they're within 10 metres of the billboard. It then provides Google-like metrics that greatly improve on existing methods of data collection.

In Germany, a pre- and posttest research study was designed to measure participants' perceptions and recall of ads through a virtual reality situation in which one drives a van down the street with advertisements on both sides. The eye-tracking and survey results are then combined to determine viewers' unaided/aided recall, recognition, and design aspects of the ads.

Part of the reason why eye tracking measures have not hit the mainstream is due to the high cost and obtrusiveness of the measurement equipment (participants have to wear headgear, whether in a lab setting or in the field—for example they had to walk through a department store or supermarket looking weird). There was also the question of whether the fact that the participants knew they were in a study influenced their behaviours. With advances in technology and decreases in cost—some companies now make the technology available for a rental fee—eye tracking is making a comeback.

Sources: Barbara Kiviat, "Why We Look at Some Web Ads and Not Others, www.time.com, November 8, 2009; Nathania Johnson, "Eye Tracking Study Shows Sponsored Ads Attract Social Media Searchers," July 19, 2009, blog.searchenginewatch.com; Dan Skeen, "Eye-Tracking Device Lets Billboards Know When You Look at Them," www.wired.com, June 12, 2007; G. Theuner, K. Pischke, and T. Bley, "Analysis of Advertising Effectiveness with Eye Tracking," *Proceedings of Measuring Behavior 2008*, Maastricht, The Netherlands, August 26–29, 2008, pp. 229–230.

Questions:

1. What part of advertising effectiveness does this research measure?

2. Which marketing communication decisions will most likely be tested with this kind of research?

Measuring the effectiveness of the promotional program is critical since it allows the marketing manager to assess the performance of specific program elements and provide input into the next period's situation analysis. We are concerned with evaluative research to measure the effectiveness of advertising and promotion and/or to assess various strategies and tactics before implementing them. This is not to be confused with planning research used to develop the promotional program, although the two can (and should) be used together.

In this chapter, we identify the reasons for measuring effectiveness. Next we describe key research decisions for evaluative research. Finally, we evaluate research methods and conclude with our IMC planning perspective to appraise the requirement for effectiveness research. Our primary focus is measuring the effects of advertising, because it is well established and other aspects of marketing communication have an advertisement-like message. Thus, most research techniques can be applied or have been adapted for other IMC tools. We highlight methods of measuring effectiveness for these tools in their respective chapters.

(L01) The Measuring Effectiveness Debate

Employees are generally given objectives to accomplish, and their job evaluations are based on their ability to achieve these objectives. Advertising and promotion should be held to the same standard where its performance is measured against the objectives established in the promotional plan as indicated in Chapter 5. Although this may appear logical, some consider it debatable.

REASONS FOR MEASURING EFFECTIVENESS

Assessing the effectiveness of ads both before they are implemented and after the final versions have been completed and fielded offers a number of advantages.

Avoiding Costly Mistakes Total advertising topped $14 billion in 2012, and any brand's advertising budget is often a substantial expenditure. Thus, if a program is not achieving its objectives, the marketing manager needs information to know how or where to spend money more effectively. The opportunity loss due to poor marketing communication is just as important. If the advertising and promotions program is not accomplishing its objectives, the potential gain that could result from an effective program is not realized, thereby minimizing the firm's return on its marketing investment.

Evaluating Alternative Strategies Typically, a firm has a number of strategies under consideration such as which medium should be used or whether one message is more effective than another. Or the decision may be between two promotional program elements: should money be spent on sponsorships or on advertising? Companies often test alternate versions of their advertising in different cities to determine which ad communicates most effectively. Thus, research may be designed to help the manager determine which strategy is most likely to be effective.

Increasing Advertising Efficiency The expression "can't see the forest for the trees" pertains here since advertisers get so close to the project they sometimes lose sight of their objectives. They may use technical jargon that not everyone is familiar with. Or the creative department may get too creative or too sophisticated and lose the meaning that needs to be communicated. Conducting research helps companies develop more efficient and effective communications. An increasing number of clients are demanding accountability for their promotional programs and putting more pressure on the agencies to produce.

Determining If Objectives Are Achieved In a well-designed IMC plan, specific communication objectives are established. If objectives are attained, new ones need to be established in the next planning period. An assessment of how program elements led to the attainment of the goals should take place, and/or reasons for less-than-desired achievements must be determined. Research should evaluate whether the strategy delivers the stated objectives and assess the appropriateness of the measures.[1]

REASONS FOR NOT MEASURING EFFECTIVENESS

Companies give a number of reasons for not measuring the effectiveness of advertising and promotions strategies.

Cost   A frequently cited reason for not testing is the expense; good research can be expensive in terms of both time and money. Many managers decide that time is critical and they must implement the program while the opportunity is available. Many believe the monies spent on research could be better spent on improved production of the ad, additional media buys, and the like. While the first argument may have merit, the second does not. Imagine the results of a poor campaign or the incentive program did not motivate the target audience; money would be wasted if the effects could do more harm than good. Spending more money to buy media does not remedy a poor message or substitute for an improper promotional mix.

Research Problems   A second reason cited for not measuring effectiveness is that it is difficult to isolate the effects of promotional elements. Each variable in the marketing mix affects the success of a product or service. Because it is rarely possible to measure the contribution of each marketing element directly, managers become frustrated and decide not to test at all. This argument also suffers from weak logic. While we agree that it is not always possible to determine the dollar amount of sales contributed by promotions, research can provide useful results. Communications effectiveness can be measured and may carry over to sales.

Disagreement on What to Test   The objectives sought in the promotional program may differ by industry, by stage of the product life cycle, or even for different people within the firm. The sales manager may want to see the impact of promotions on sales, top management may wish to know the impact on corporate image, and those involved in the creative process may wish to assess recall and/or recognition of the ad. Lack of agreement on what to test often results in no testing, but there is little rationale for this position. With the proper design, many or even all of the above might be measured. Since every promotional element is designed to accomplish its own objectives, research can be used to measure its effectiveness in doing so.

Objections of Creative Specialists   An age-old industry debate is that the creative department does not want its work to be tested and many agencies are reluctant to submit their work for testing. Ad agencies' creative departments argue that tests are not true measures of the creativity and effectiveness of ads: applying measures stifles their creativity, and the more creative the ad, the more likely it is to be successful. They want permission to be creative without any limiting guidelines. At the same time, the marketing manager is ultimately responsible for the success of the product or brand. Given the substantial sums being allocated to advertising and promotion, it is the manager's right, and responsibility, to know how well a specific program, or a specific ad, will perform in the market.

L02 Decisions for Measuring Effectiveness

We now describe the decisions for measuring the communication effects of advertising. This section considers what elements to evaluate, as well as when and where such evaluations should occur. We cover the issue of how to measure in the next section.

WHAT TO TEST

The focus of the testing is mostly on the creative strategy and creative tactics decisions that the advertiser makes while putting a campaign together for advertising and all IMC tools.

Creative Strategy Decisions   The primary creative strategy decision—the creative theme—can be tested. When a company decides to change its theme or is planning to launch an unusual attention-getting approach, it may want to see the reactions of the target audience prior to investing in the media placement. Similarly, different message appeals can be tested (i.e., rational versus emotional), or different versions of one appeal can be tested. Finally, another important question is whether the spokesperson being used is effective and how the target audience will respond to him or her. A product spokesperson may be an excellent source initially but, owing to a variety of reasons, may lose impact over time in terms of attractiveness or likeability. Thus, all major creative strategy decisions can be tested. IMC Perspective 9-1 summarizes research regarding emotional reactions to creative strategy decisions.

Creative Tactics Decisions   Different execution styles displayed on storyboards can be presented to members of the target audience in focus groups for their reaction. The message structure can be looked at, such as reading the body copy in an interview or another method. Specific design elements, such as the music in a television ad or the headline of a print ad, can also be the focus of research. Overall, advertisers use a variety of research methods to test essentially any creative tactic that they are unsure about or that requires confirmation.

Other Promotional Tools   Many of the other tools we will discuss in this book have an associated creative or message. Many sales promotions have a visual as well as advertising-like message that reinforces the brand position in the target audience's mind. Similarly, firms use many creative tactics to gain the attention of media personnel so that their story will be picked up by the media in order to get publicity exposure. Thus, while we have examined the creative in the context of advertising in the book, as we noted previously all the decisions are relevant in the other promotional tools, and as expected the same research is possible if the advertiser believes it necessary. We review a few specifics in each of the subsequent chapters to measure the effectiveness of other promotional tools.

Figure   9-1

Classification of testing methods

Pretests	Lab	Field
Concept	Concept tests	
Rough/copy/commercial	Rough tests	Comprehension and reaction tests
	Consumer juries	
Finished print ads	Portfolio	
	Readability	Dummy advertising vehicles
Finished TV ads	Theatre	
	Physiological	On-air

Posttests		
Finished print ads in magazines		Inquiry tests
		Recognition tests
		Recall tests
		Tracking studies
Finished TV ads on-air		Recall tests
		Comprehensive measures
		Test marketing
		Single-source
		Tracking studies

Emotionally Involved Researchers Measure Ad Effectiveness

Imagine sitting in an office wondering how consumers would react to new ads shown as storyboards developed by an advertising agency. Or perhaps consider whether the completed print ads should be placed in magazines for the next campaign. For that matter, if managers are wondering about *any* message to be delivered across any or multiple media, how or what evaluation should be implemented to ensure success? Although many standard or traditional approaches for promotional effectiveness exist, new methods continue to emerge.

One promising development is a method allowing researchers to get a better read on consumer emotions. Many approaches toward effectiveness tend to measure consumer knowledge in terms of brand recall or recognition, advertising recall or recognition, and rational thoughts connected to the brand. Typically, consumers have difficulty expressing their emotional attachment to a brand as they often convey their brand usage in relation to product attributes or benefits.

This dilemma led Ipsos-ASI to innovate with a measurement tool designed to gauge consumers' emotional reactions to an ad by asking three questions: How do you feel toward the ad? What feeling is the advertiser trying to get across? and What emotions do you associate with being a brand user? Consumers selected their emotional response from a group of facial illustrations that exhibited many emotions.

Their research also identified 12 personality traits that could be used to assess brands, such as social, outgoing, extroverted; emotional, touching, sensitive; reserved, quiet, introverted; and spontaneous, creative, impulsive. Finally, building on existing motivation research, their investigation examined 11 different motivators for purchasing a brand, such as self-sufficient, independent, autonomous; experience personal success or achievement; and pleasurable

sensuous feeling. Overall, these measures have allowed Ipsos-ASI to distinguish between categories like cars or beer, and brands such as Ford and Audi or Budweiser and Heineken.

New advances for measuring audience involvement with marketing communication messages gained ground as well. In fact, the notion of measuring involvement recently expanded to all marketing communication points beyond television. Working together, many agency and research firms explore varying approaches to understand the degree of consumer reaction to marketing messages. For example, MediaCom's new measurement tool attempts to measure the depth of involvement with the message. The Media Company's new research method looks to understand the amount of involvement of people who are actually exposed to an advertising message on television. Finally, Carat Canada's research indicated that mothers with children were less involved when receiving messages with their children versus without their children.

Sources: Paul Brent, "The New Tools of Engagement," *Marketing Magazine,* August 14, 2006; Pattie Summerfield, "Getting to Engagement," *Strategy,* June 2006; Rebecca Harris, "Measuring Emotions," *Marketing Magazine,* September 25, 2006; John Hallward, "The Creators of Motivation: Advancement in the Exploration of Emotions," *Ipsos-ASI,* June 2004.

Questions

1. Why are advertisers so concerned with measuring emotions and involvement?
2. Should promotional planners measure these two variables for other IMC tools, such as sales promotions or direct response?

WHEN TO TEST

Virtually all test measures can be classified according to when they are conducted. **Pretests** are measures taken before the campaign is implemented; **posttests** occur after the ad or commercial has been in the field. A variety of pretests and posttests are available to the marketer, each with its own methodology designed to measure an aspect of the advertising program. Figure 9-1 classifies these testing methods.

Pretesting   Pretests may occur at a number of points, from as early on as idea generation to rough execution to testing the final version before implementing it. In addition, testing could occur at more than one point in time. For example, concept testing may take place at the earliest development of the ad or commercial, when little more than an idea, basic concept, or positioning statement is under consideration. Later on in the process, layouts of the ad campaign that include headlines, body copy, and rough illustrations are tested along with storyboards and animatics for proposed TV commercials.

The methodologies employed to conduct pretests vary. In focus groups, participants freely discuss the meanings they get from the ads, consider the relative advantages of alternatives, and even suggest improvements or additional themes. In addition to or instead of the focus groups, consumers are asked to evaluate the ad on a series of rating scales. In-home interviews, mall intercept, or laboratory methods may be used to gather the data.

The advantage of pretesting is that feedback is relatively inexpensive. Any problems with the concept or the way it is to be delivered are identified before large amounts of money are spent in development. Sometimes more than one version of the ad is evaluated to determine which is most likely to be effective. Since pretesting is generally cheaper than making a mistake public without pretesting, it certainly makes sense to pretest.

The disadvantage is that mock-ups, storyboards, or animatics may not communicate nearly as effectively as the final product. The mood-enhancing and/or emotional aspects of the message are very difficult to communicate in this format. Another disadvantage is time delays. Many marketers believe being first in the market offers them a distinct advantage over competitors, so they forgo research to save time and ensure this position.

Posttesting   In contrast to pretesting, posttesting occurs after placing the marketing communication in a media like broadcast or print, or another communication tool if needed. Posttesting is designed to (1) determine if the campaign is accomplishing the objectives sought and (2) serve as input into the next period's situation analysis. A variety of posttest measures are available, most of which involve survey research methods.

WHERE TO TEST

In addition to when to test, decisions must be made as to *where*. These tests may take place in either laboratory or field settings.

Laboratory Tests   In laboratory tests, people are brought to a particular location where they are shown ads and/or commercials. The testers either ask questions about them or measure participants' responses by other methods—for example, pupil dilation, eye tracking, or galvanic skin response.

The major advantage of the lab setting is the *control* it affords the researcher. Changes in copy, illustration, formats, colours, and the like can be manipulated inexpensively and the differential impact of each assessed. This makes it much easier for the researcher to isolate the contribution of each factor.

The major disadvantage is the lack of *realism*. Perhaps the greatest effect of this lack of realism is a **testing bias**. When people are brought into a lab (even if it has been designed to look like a living room), they may scrutinize the ads much more closely than they would at home. A second problem with this lack of realism is that it cannot duplicate the natural viewing situation, complete with the distractions or comforts of home. Looking at ads in a lab setting may not be the same as viewing at home, though testing techniques have made progress in correcting this deficiency. Overall, however, the control offered by this method probably outweighs the disadvantages, which accounts for the frequent use of lab methods.

Field Tests   Field tests are tests of the ad or commercial under natural viewing situations, complete with the realism of noise, distractions, and the comforts of home. Field tests take into account the effects of repetition, program content, and even the presence of competitive messages.

The major disadvantage of field tests is the lack of control. It may be impossible to isolate causes of viewers' evaluations. If atypical events occur during the test, they may bias the results. Field tests usually take more time and money to conduct, so the results are not available to be acted on quickly. Thus, realism is gained at the expense of other important factors. It is up to the researcher to determine which trade-offs to make.

(L03) Methods of Measuring Effectiveness

Testing may occur at various points throughout the development of an ad or a campaign: (1) concept generation research, (2) rough, prefinished art, copy, and/or commercial testing, (3) finished art or commercial pretesting, and (4) market testing of ads or commercials (posttesting). In this section, we describe methods used for each of these four stages.

CONCEPT GENERATION AND TESTING

Figure 9-2 describes the process involved in advertising **concept testing**, which is conducted very early in the campaign development process to evaluate the targeted consumer's response to a potential ad or campaign, or alternative advertising strategies. Positioning statements, copy, headlines, and/or illustrations may all be under scrutiny. The material shown to the target audience may be just a headline or a rough sketch of the ad, colours, typeface, description of a storyboard, or different messages.

A commonly used method for concept testing is a focus group, which usually consists of 8 to 10 people who are within the ad's target audience. Companies have tested everything from product concepts to advertising concepts using focus groups. For most companies, the focus group is the first step in the research process. The number of focus groups used varies depending on group consensus, strength of response, and/or the degree to which participants like or dislike the concepts. In general, about 10 are usually needed to test a concept sufficiently.

Focus groups continue to be a favourite of marketers. The methodology is attractive since results are easily obtained, directly observable, and immediate. A variety of topics can be examined, and consumers are free to go into depth in any important areas. Also, focus groups don't require quantitative analysis and are more easily accepted and interpreted by managers. Weaknesses with focus groups are shown in Figure 9-3.

Another way to gather consumers' opinions of concepts is mall intercepts, where consumers in shopping malls are approached and asked to evaluate rough ads and/or copy. Rather than participating in a group discussion, individuals assess the ads via questionnaires, rating scales, and/or rankings. New technologies allow for concept testing over the Internet, where advertisers can show concepts simultaneously to consumers throughout Canada, garnering feedback and analyzing the results almost instantaneously.

Objective:	Explores consumers' responses to various ad concepts as expressed in words, pictures, or symbols.
Method:	Alternative concepts are exposed to consumers who match the characteristics of the target audience. Reactions and evaluations of each are sought through a variety of methods, including focus groups, direct questioning, and survey completion. Sample sizes vary depending on the number of concepts to be presented and the consensus of responses.
Output:	Qualitative and/or quantitative data evaluating and comparing alternative concepts.

Figure 9-2

Concept testing

Figure   9-3

Weaknesses associated with focus group research

- The results are not quantifiable.
- Sample sizes are too small to generalize to larger populations.
- Group influences may bias participants' responses.
- One or two members of the group may steer the conversation or dominate the discussion.
- Consumers become instant "experts."
- Members may not represent the target audience.
- Results may be taken to be more representative and/or definitive than they really are.

ROUGH ART, COPY, AND COMMERCIAL TESTING

Because of the high cost associated with the production of an ad or commercial, advertisers spend more on testing a rendering of the final ad at early stages. Slides of the artwork posted on a screen or animatic and photomatic **rough tests** may be used at this stage. (See Figure 9-4 for an explanation of terminology.) Because such tests can be conducted for about $5,000 to $7,000, research at this stage is becoming ever more popular.

But cost is only one factor. The test is of little value if it does not provide relevant, accurate information. Rough tests must indicate how the finished commercial would perform. Studies have demonstrated that these testing methods are reliable and the results typically correlate well with the finished ad.[2] Most of the tests conducted at the rough stage involve lab settings. Popular tests include comprehension and reaction tests and consumer juries.

Comprehension and Reaction Tests   One concern for the advertiser is whether the message conveys the meaning intended. The second concern is the reaction the ad generates. Obviously, the advertiser does not want an ad that evokes a negative reaction or offends someone. **Comprehension and reaction tests** are designed to assess these responses. Tests of comprehension and reaction employ no one standard procedure. Personal interviews, group interviews, and focus groups have all been used for this purpose, and sample sizes vary according to the needs of the client; they typically range from 50 to 200 respondents.

Consumer Juries   This method uses consumers representative of the target audiences to evaluate the probable success of an ad. **Consumer juries** rate a selection of layouts or copy

Figure   9-4

Rough testing terminology

A rough commercial is an unfinished execution that may fall into three broad categories:

Animatic Rough

Succession of drawings/cartoons

Rendered artwork

Still frames

Simulated movement: Panning/zooming of frame/rapid sequence

Photomatic Rough

Succession of photographs

Real people/scenery

Still frames

Simulated movements: Panning/zooming of frame/rapid sequence

Live-Action Rough

Live motion

Stand-in/nonunion talent

Nonunion crew

Limited props/minimal opticals

Location settings

A Finished Commercial Uses

Live motion/animation

Highly paid union talent

Full union crew

Exotic props/studio sets/special effects

Objective:	Potential viewers (consumers) are asked to evaluate ads and give their reactions to and evaluation of them. When two or more ads are tested, viewers are usually asked to rate or rank order the ads according to their preferences.
Method:	Respondents are asked to view ads and rate them according to either (1) the order of merit method or (2) the paired comparison method. In the former, the respondent is asked to view the ads, then rank them from one to n according to their perceived merit. In the latter, ads are compared only two at a time. Each ad is compared to every other ad in the group, and the winner is listed. The best ad is that which wins the most times. Consumer juries typically employ 50 to 100 participants.
Output:	An overall reaction to each ad under construction as well as a rank ordering of the ads based on the viewers' perceptions.

Figure   9-5

Consumer juries

versions presented in paste-ups on separate sheets. The objectives sought and methods employed in consumer juries are shown in Figure 9-5. While the jury method offers the advantages of control and cost effectiveness, serious flaws in the methodology limit its usefulness.

- *The consumer may become a self-appointed expert.* One jury method benefit is the objectivity and involvement that the targeted consumer can bring to the evaluation process. However, knowing they are being asked to critique ads, participants sometimes become more expert in their evaluations by paying more attention and being more critical than usual. The result may be a less than objective evaluation or an evaluation on elements other than those intended.
- *The number of ads that can be evaluated is limited.* Whether order of merit or paired comparison methods are used, the ranking procedure becomes tedious as the number of alternatives increases. Consider the ranking of 10 ads. While the top two and the bottom two may very well reveal differences, those ranked in the middle may not yield much useful information. In the paired comparison method, 15 evaluations are required for six alternatives. As the number of ads increases, the task becomes even more unmanageable.
- *A halo effect is possible.* Sometimes participants rate an ad as good (bad) on all characteristics because they like (dislike) a few and overlook specific weaknesses (strengths). This tendency, called the **halo effect**, distorts the ratings and defeats the ability to control for specific components.
- *Preferences for specific types of advertising may overshadow objectivity.* Ads that involve emotions or pictures may receive higher ratings or rankings than those employing copy, facts, and/or rational criteria. Even though the latter are often more effective in the marketplace, they may be judged less favourably by jurists who prefer emotional appeals.

Problems noted here can be remedied by the use of ratings scales instead of rankings, but ratings are not always valid either. Thus, while consumer juries have been used for years, questions of bias have led researchers to doubt their validity.

PRETESTING OF FINISHED ADS

At this stage, a finished advertisement or commercial is used; changes can still be made since it has not been presented to the market. Many researchers believe testing the ad in final form provides better information. Several test procedures are available for print and broadcast ads, including both laboratory and field methodologies. Print methods include portfolio tests, analyses of readability, and dummy advertising vehicles. Broadcast tests include theatre tests and on-air tests. Both print and broadcast may use physiological measures.

Pretesting Finished Print Messages   A number of methods for pretesting finished print ads are available. One is described in Figure 9-6. The most common of these methods are portfolio tests, readability tests, and dummy advertising vehicles.

Figure   9-6

Gallup & Robinson's Impact
System

Objective:	Understand the performance of newspaper or magazine ad executions.
Method:	Interviewers contact respondents door to door or by telephone and screen for qualification.
Output:	Scores include recall, idea communication, persuasion, brand rating, and ad liking. Diagnostics regarding ad reactions and brand attributes are reported.

Portfolio Tests   **Portfolio tests** are a laboratory methodology designed to expose a group of respondents to a portfolio consisting of both control and test ads. Respondents are then asked what information they recall from the ads. The assumption is that the ads that yield the highest recall are the most effective.

Portfolio tests compare alternative ads directly but have two weaknesses that limit their applicability. One, factors other than advertising creativity and/or presentation may affect recall. Interest in the product or product category, the fact that respondents know they are participating in a test, or interviewer instructions may account for more differences than the ad itself. Second, for certain products (those of low involvement) and brands the ability to recognize the ad when shown may be a better measure than recall.

Readability Tests   The communication efficiency of the body copy in a print ad can be tested with the **Flesch formula** to assess its readability by determining the average number of syllables per 100 words. Human interest, appeal of the material, length of sentences, and familiarity with certain words are also considered and correlated with the educational background of target audiences. Test results are compared to previously established norms for different target audiences. The test suggests that copy is best comprehended when sentences are short, words are concrete and familiar, and personal references are drawn.

This method eliminates many of the interviewee biases associated with other tests and avoids gross errors in understanding. The norms offer an attractive standard for comparison. Disadvantages are also inherent, however. The copy may become too mechanical, and direct input from the receiver is not available. Without this input, contributing elements like creativity cannot be addressed. To be effective, this test should be used only in conjunction with other pretesting methods.

Dummy Advertising Vehicles   In an improvement on the portfolio test, ads are placed in "dummy" magazines developed by an agency or research firm. The magazines contain regular editorial features of interest to the reader, as well as the test ads, and are distributed to a *random sample* of homes in predetermined geographic areas. Readers are told the magazine publisher is interested in evaluations of editorial content and asked to read the magazines as they normally would. Then they are interviewed on their reactions to both editorial content and ads. Recall, readership, and interest-generating capabilities of the ad are assessed.

The advantage of this method is that it provides a more natural setting than the portfolio test. Readership occurs in the participant's own home, the test more closely approximates a natural reading situation, and the reader may go back to the magazine, as people typically do. However, the testing effect is not eliminated, and product interest may still bias the results.

Diagnostic Measures   While all previously described methods are available, the most popular form of print ad pretesting involves a series of measures that account for the shortcomings of each of the other methods. The tests can be used for rough and/or finished ads and are most commonly conducted in the respondents' homes enabling the researcher to collect multiple measures from many samples. For example, Millward-Brown's link copy test includes measures of emotional responses to ads, assessing metrics such as enjoyment, engagement, likes, and dislikes to address overall emotional response. Ipsos-ASI's methodology also offers multiple measures, as shown in Figure 9-7.

Pretesting Finished Broadcast Ads   A variety of methods for pretesting broadcast ads are available. The most popular are theatre tests, on-air tests, and physiological measures.

Objective:	To assist advertisers in copy testing of print advertisements to determine (1) main idea communication, (2) likes and dislikes, (3) believability, (4) ad attribute ratings, (5) overall likability, and (6) brand attribute ratings.
Method:	Tests are conducted in current issues of newsstand magazines. The recall measure consists of 150 responses. Diagnostic measures range from 105 to 150 responses. Highly targeted audiences are available through a version known as the Targeted Print Test.
Output:	Standard scores and specific diagnostics.

Figure 9-7

Ipsos-ASI's Next*Print

Theatre Tests   In the past, one of the most popular laboratory methods for pretesting finished commercials was **theatre testing**. Participants are invited by telephone, mall intercepts, and/or tickets in the mail to view pilots of proposed TV programs. In some instances, the show is actually being tested, but more commonly a standard program is used so that audience responses can be compared with normative responses established by previous viewers. Sample sizes range from 250 to 600 participants. The methods of theatre testing operations vary, though all measure brand preference changes. An example of one methodology is shown in Figure 9-8.

Those opposed to theatre tests cite a number of disadvantages. First, they say the environment is too artificial and that wiring people for physiological responses takes them too far from a natural viewing situation. Second, the contrived measure of brand preference change seems too phony to believe. Critics contend that participants will see through it and make changes just because they think they are supposed to. Finally, the group effect of having others present and overtly exhibiting their reactions may influence viewers who did not have any reactions themselves.

Proponents argue that theatre tests offer distinct advantages. In addition to control, the established norms (averages of commercials' performances) indicate how one's commercial will fare against others in the same product class tested previously, and brand preference measure is supported by actual sales results.

On-Air Tests   Firms conducting theatre tests also may insert the commercials into actual TV programs in certain test markets. Typically, the commercials are in finished form. This is referred to as an on-air test and often includes single-source ad research (discussed later in this chapter). On-air pretesting of finished offers distinct advantages over lab methods and indication of the ad's success when launched due to the realistic test. Information Resources, Ipsos-ASI, MSW Group, and Nielsen are well-known providers of on-air tests.

The most commonly employed metric used in an on-air test is recall—that is, the number of persons able to recall the ad and/or its message. In an examination of real-world advertising tests, one study concludes that recall and persuasion pretests, while often employed, do not fare well in respect to reliability and/or validity. Nevertheless, most of the testing services have offered evidence of both validity and reliability for on-air pretesting of commercials. Both Ipsos-ASI and MSW Group claim their pretest and posttest results yield the same recall scores 9 out of 10 times—a strong indication of reliability and a good predictor of the effect the ad is likely to have when shown to the population as a whole. Whether the measures used are as strong an indication as the providers say still remains in question.[3]

Figure 9-8

The Ad*Vantage/ACT theatre methodology

Advertising Control for Television (ACT), a lab procedure of The MSW Group, uses about 400 respondents representing four cities. It measures initial brand preference by asking participants which brands they most recently purchased. Respondents are then divided into groups of 25 to view a 30-minute program with seven commercials inserted in the middle. Four are test commercials; the other three are control commercials with established viewing norms. After viewing the program, respondents are given a recall test of the commercials. After the recall test, a second 30-minute program is shown, with each test commercial shown again. The second measure of brand preference is taken at this time, with persuasion measured by the percentage of viewers who switched preferences from their most recently purchased brand to one shown in the test commercials.

Physiological Measures   A less common method of pretesting finished commercials involves a laboratory setting in which physiological responses are measured. These measures indicate the receiver's *involuntary* response to the ad, theoretically eliminating biases associated with the voluntary measures reviewed to this point. (Involuntary responses are those over which the individual has no control, such as heartbeat and reflexes.) Physiological measures used to test both print and broadcast ads include pupil dilation, galvanic skin response, eye tracking, and brain waves.

Pupil dilation.   Research in **pupillometrics** is designed to measure dilation and constriction of the pupils of the eyes in response to stimuli. Dilation is associated with action; constriction involves the body's conservation of energy. Pupil dilation suggests a stronger interest in (or preference for) an ad or implies arousal or attention-getting capabilities. Other attempts to determine the affective (liking or disliking) responses created by ads have met with less success. Because of high costs and methodological problems, the use of pupillometrics has waned over the past decade. But it can be useful in evaluating certain aspects of advertising.

Galvanic skin response.   Also known as **electrodermal response**, GSR measures the skin's resistance or conductance to a small amount of current passed between two electrodes. Response to a stimulus activates sweat glands, which in turn increases the conductance of the electrical current. Thus, GSR/EDR activity might reflect a reaction to advertising. A review of research in this area concluded that GSR/EDR (1) is sensitive to affective stimuli, (2) may present a picture of attention, (3) may be useful to measure long-term advertising recall, and (4) is useful in measuring ad effectiveness.[4] Another study concluded that GSR is an effective measure and is useful, yet underused, for measuring affect, or liking, for ads.[5]

Eye tracking.   A commonly employed methodology is **eye tracking** (Figure 9-9), in which viewers are asked to view an ad while a sensor aims a beam of infrared light at the eye. The beam follows the movement of the eye and shows the exact spot on which the viewer is focusing. The continuous reading of responses demonstrates which elements of the ad are attracting attention, how long the viewer is focusing on them, and the sequence in which they are being viewed. Measurement of Internet advertising has adapted many approaches and the eye-tracking has received considerable usage.

Eye tracking can identify strengths and weaknesses in an ad. For example, attractive models or background action may distract the viewer's attention away from the brand or product being advertised. The advertiser can remedy this distraction before fielding the ad. In other instances, colours or illustrations may attract attention and create viewer interest in the ad. Eye tracking research is applied to all types of traditional media, outdoor and Internet. An example of the equipment is shown in Exhibit 9-1.

Brain waves.   **Electroencephalographic (EEG) measures** can be taken from the skull to determine electrical frequencies in the brain. While EEG research attracted the interest of academic researchers, it has been much less successful in attracting the interest of practitioners, though the technology has gained in attractiveness, as shown in Technology Perspective 9-1. The electrical impulses are used in three areas of research: alpha waves, hemispheric lateralization, and indirect methods.

- **Alpha activity** refers to the degree of brain activation. People are in an alpha state when they are inactive, resting, or sleeping. The theory is that a person in an alpha state is

Figure 9-9		
Eye movement research	*Objective:*	Tracks viewers' eye movements to determine what viewers read or view in print ads and where their attention is focused in TV commercials or billboards.
	Method:	Fibre optics, digital data processing, and advanced electronics are used to follow eye movements of viewers and/or readers as they process an ad.
	Output:	Relationship among what readers see, recall, and comprehend. Scan paths on print ads, billboards, commercials, and print materials. (Can also be used to evaluate package designs.)

less likely to be processing information (recall correlates negatively with alpha levels) and that attention and processing require moving from this state. By measuring a subject's alpha level while viewing a commercial, researchers can assess the degree to which attention and processing are likely to occur.

- **Hemispheric lateralization** distinguishes between alpha activity in the left and right sides of the brain. It has been hypothesized that the right side of the brain processes visual stimuli and the left processes verbal stimuli. The right hemisphere is thought to respond more to emotional stimuli, while the left responds to logic. The right determines recognition, while the left is responsible for recall.[6] If these hypotheses are correct, advertisers could design ads to increase learning and memory by creating stimuli to appeal to each hemisphere. However, some researchers believe the brain does not function laterally, and an ad cannot be designed to appeal to one side or the other.

- **Indirect methods** use technologies originally designed for the medical field, such as positron emission tomography (PET) and functional magnetic resonance imaging (fMRI). Neuroscientists have teamed up with marketers to examine physiological reactions to ads and brands through brain scan imaging. PET tracks changes in metabolism while fMRI tracks blood flow, and both provide an indirect measure of brain activity. By monitoring the brain activity, scientists are learning how consumers make up their minds by measuring chemical activity and/or changes in the magnetic fields of the brain as well as how they react to commercials.

Exhibit 9-1   Eye-tracking services like these are now available to marketers.

MARKET TESTING OF ADS

The fact that the ad and/or campaign has been implemented does not mean there is no longer a need for testing. The pretests were conducted on smaller samples and may have questionable merit, so the marketer must find out how the ad is doing in the field. In this section, we discuss methods for posttesting an ad. Some of the tests are similar to the pretests discussed in the previous section and are provided by the same companies.

Posttests of Print Ads   A variety of print posttests are available, including inquiry tests, recognition tests, and recall tests.

Inquiry Tests   Used in both consumer and business-to-business market testing, **inquiry tests** are designed to measure advertising effectiveness on the basis of inquiries generated from ads appearing in print media. The inquiry may take the form of the number of coupons returned, phone calls generated, or direct inquiries through reader cards. Digital inquiries would include e-mails and social media communications like questions posed on Twitter or Facebook. This is a very simple measure of the ad's or medium's effectiveness; more complex methods may involve (1) running the ad in successive issues of the same medium, (2) running **split-run tests**, in which variations of the ad appear in different copies of the same newspaper or magazine, and/or (3) running the same ad in different media. Each of these methods yields information on different aspects of the strategy. The first measures the cumulative effects of the campaign; the second examines specific elements of the ad or variations on it. The final method measures the effectiveness of the medium rather than the ad itself.

While inquiry tests may yield useful information, weaknesses in this methodology limit its effectiveness. For example, inquiries may not be a true measure of the attention-getting or

Measuring Brain Waves for Ad Success

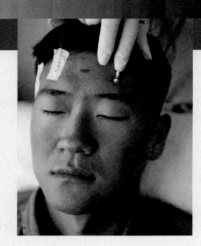

In the constant search for determining the effectiveness of advertising, marketers have turned to MRI machines and heart rate monitors along with changes in the skin and facial muscles to examine physiological responses to advertising messages. The use of neurosciences to test commercials is hailed as a major measurement breakthrough, and discounted by others as junk science.

During one Super Bowl, a company strapped caps with electrodes that were wirelessly linked to electroencephalography (EEG) machines on the heads of 20 subjects while they watched the commercials. The EEG measured and recorded brain activity in millisecond increments to 60 commercials shown on the game. After the physiological measures were taken, the group was orally tested to gauge recall of the commercials' content and brand identification, as well as their preferences for each ad. The top 10 commercials were then ranked, and interestingly, the top 10 list did not match the lists provided by pollsters and focus groups. The physiological measures provided additional insights. Sexy spots fared poorly, 60-second ads scored higher than 30-second ones, and ads with an element of surprise consistently scored high.

Nielsen, the world's leading audience measurement company, recently invested in NeuroFocus, a neuromarketing company, as Fortune 500 companies have shown increased interest in the applications of brainwave research to marketing. For example, some marketers believe that this method of testing consumer responses may be superior to focus groups since consumers are becoming predictable in their responses. Neuromarketing has been used to test differences in responses to Coke and Pepsi, men's reactions to automobiles, movie trailers, and political ads.

Others are not convinced. Professor Andrew Gelman of Columbia University contends that the reported correlations between brain activity patterns and thoughts and emotions are "too good to be true." Gelman suggests the correlations are so high that they can't be trusted. William Eddy of Carnegie Mellon agrees, noting that, "Correlations of 0.9 are unbelievable in any social science setting." While the supporters of the use of the science debate these points with blog posts and online defences, they have admitted that reported correlations are inflated.

Another nonbeliever is Professor Brian Knutson of Stanford University, who has compared the use of EEG to "standing outside a baseball stadium and listening to the crowd to figure out what happened," and neuroscientist Joshua Freedman, chief scientist at FKF Applied Research, who considers the results "worse data than you'd get by just talking to people in focus groups." But both Knutson and Freedman are optimistic that neurosciences have potential for marketing studies, Freedman arguing for the superiority of MRI over EEG. Many other neuroscientists and marketers alike are less optimistic, however, contending there have only been promises of success, and that these measures have provided few if any insights. Still others argue that studying the brain in isolation while ignoring the impact of the larger culture just doesn't make sense. Erwin Ephron, a well-respected advertising and media consultant, believes that neuroscience just doesn't go far enough in explaining consumer reactions to ads.

So what is it—a major marketing research breakthrough or just another research methodology that promises more than it delivers? Are we better off just asking people what they think about commercials or wiring them to machines to probe inside their heads? Maybe we should conduct some research.

Sources: Sharon Begley, "Of Voodoo and the Brain," www.newsweek.com, February 9, 2009; Rick Ferguson, "Neuromarketing: What the Human Brain Means to Your Campaign," www.chiefmarketer.com, October 27, 2009; Mya Frazier, "Hidden Persuasion or Junk Science?" *Advertising Age*, September 10, 2007, pp. 1, 38–39; Erwin Ephron, "The Open Mind," *Mediaweek*, February 5, 2007, p. 10; Jack Neff, "The Super Bowl Spots That Got Inside Consumers' Heads," adage.com, February 7, 2008, pp. 1–3; "Sands Research Conducts Real-Time Brain Imaging of Viewers Exposed to Super Bowl Commercials," www.reuters.com, February 11, 2008, pp. 1–3.

Question

1. Express your feelings on whether you would volunteer as a respondent to this kind of research.

Objective:	Determining recognition of print ads and comparing them to other ads of the same variety or in the same magazine.
Method:	Samples are drawn from 20 to 30 urban areas reflecting the geographic circulation of the magazine. Personal interviewers screen readers for qualifications and determine exposure and readership. Samples include a minimum of 200 males and females, as well as specific audiences where required. Participants are asked to go through the magazines, looking at the ads, and provide specific responses.
Output:	Starch Ad Readership Reports generate three recognition scores: • Noted score—the percentage of readers who remember seeing the ad. • Seen-associated score—the percentage of readers who recall seeing or reading any part of the ad identifying the product or brand. • Read-most score—the percentage of readers who report reading at least half of the copy portion of the ad.

Figure 9-10

The Starch Ad Readership Report

information-providing aspects of the ad. The reader may be attracted to an ad, read it, and even store the information but not be motivated to inquire at that particular time. Time constraints, lack of a need for the product or service at the time the ad is run, and other factors may limit the number of inquiries. But receiving a small number of inquiries doesn't mean the ad was not effective; attention, attitude change, awareness, and recall of copy points may all have been achieved. At the other extreme, a person with a particular need for the product may respond to any ad for it, regardless of specific qualities of the ad.

Major advantages of inquiry tests are that they are inexpensive to implement and they provide feedback with respect to the general effectiveness of the ad or medium used. But they are usually not very effective for comparing different versions or specific creative aspects of an ad.

Recognition Tests   A common posttest of print ads is the **recognition method**, most closely associated with Roper ASW. The *Starch Ad Readership Report* lets the advertiser assess the impact of an ad in a single issue of a magazine, over time, and/or across different magazines (see Figure 9-10). Starch claims that (1) the pulling power of the ad can be assessed through the control offered, (2) the effectiveness of competitors' ads can be compared through the norms provided, (3) alternative ad executions can be tested, and (4) readership scores are a useful indication of consumers' involvement in the ad or campaign. The theory is that a reader must read and become involved in the ad before the ad can communicate. To the degree that this readership can be shown, it is a direct indication of effectiveness. An example of a Starch scored ad is shown in Exhibit 9-2.

Many researchers have criticized the Starch recognition method (and other recognition measures) on the basis of false claiming, interviewer sensitivities, and unreliable scores:

False claiming. Research shows that in recognition tests, respondents may claim to have seen an ad when they did not. False claims may be a result of having seen similar ads elsewhere, expecting that such an ad would appear in the medium, or wanting to please the questioner. Interest in the product category also increases reporting of ad readership. Whether this false claiming is deliberate or not, it leads to an overreporting of effectiveness. On the flip side, factors such as interview fatigue may lead to an underreporting bias—that is, respondents not reporting an ad they did see.

Interviewer sensitivities. Any time research involves interviewers, there is a potential for bias. Respondents may want to impress the interviewer or fear looking unknowledgeable if they continually claim not to recognize an ad. There may

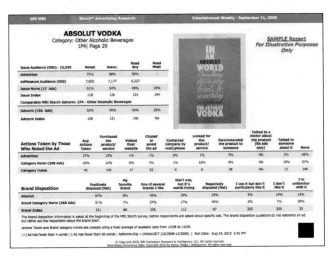

Exhibit 9-2   A Starch rating scale for an Absolut ad.

also be variances associated with interviewer instructions, recordings, and so on, regardless of the amount of training and sophistication involved.

Reliability of recognition scores. Starch admits that the reliability and validity of its readership scores increase with the number of insertions tested, which essentially means that to test just one ad on a single exposure may not produce valid or reliable results.

Recall Tests The best-known tests to measure recall of print ads are the Ipsos-ASI Next*Print test and the Gallup & Robinson Magazine Impact Research Service (MIRS) (described in Figure 9-11). These **recall tests** are similar to those discussed in the section on pretesting broadcast ads as they attempt to measure recall of specific ads.

In addition to having the same interviewer problems as recognition tests, recall tests have other disadvantages. The reader's degree of involvement with the product and/or the distinctiveness of the appeals and visuals may lead to higher-than-accurate recall scores, although in general the method may lead to lower levels of recall than actually exist (an error the advertiser would be happy with). Critics contend the test is not strong enough to reflect recall accurately, so many ads may score as less effective than they really are, and advertisers may abandon or modify them needlessly.

On the plus side, it is thought that recall tests can assess the ad's impact on memory. Proponents of recall tests say the major concern is not the results themselves but how they are interpreted. Studies have shown that the correlation between recall and recognition is very high for print ads.[7]

Posttests of Broadcast Commercials
The most common methods for posttesting broadcast commercials include a combination of day-after recall tests, persuasion measures and diagnostics, test marketing, and two types of tracking studies.

Day-After Recall (DAR) Tests The most popular method of posttesting employed in the broadcasting industry for decades was the *Burke Day-After Recall Test* (however, it no longer exists). While a number of companies offered day-after recall methodologies, the "Burke test" for all intents and purposes became the generic name attached to these tests. While popular, day-after recall tests also had problems, including limited samples, high costs, and security issues (ads shown in test markets could be seen by competitors).

Furthermore, DAR tests may favour unemotional appeals because respondents are asked to verbalize the message. Thinking messages may be easier to recall than emotional communications, so recall scores for emotional ads may be lower.[8] Other studies concluded that emotional ads may be processed differently from thinking ones, and ad agencies (e.g., Leo Burnett, BBDO) developed their own methods of determining emotional response to ads.[9]

The major advantage of day-after recall tests is that they are field tests. The natural setting is supposed to provide a more realistic response profile. These tests are also popular because they

Figure 9-11

Gallup & Robinson Magazine
Impact Research Service

Objective:	Tracking recall of advertising (and client's ads) appearing in magazines to assess performance and effectiveness.
Method:	Test magazines are placed in participants' homes and respondents are asked to read the magazine that day. A telephone interview is conducted the second day to assess recall of ads, recall of copy points, and consumers' impressions of the ads. Sample size is 150 people.
Output:	Three measurement scores are provided:

- Proven name registration—the percentage of respondents who can accurately recall the ad.
- Idea communication—the number of sales points the respondents can recall.
- Favourable buying attitude—the extent of favourable purchase reaction to the brand or corporation.

Objective:	To assist advertisers in copy testing of their commercials through multiple measures to determine (1) the potential of the commercial for impacting sales, (2) how the ad contributes to brand equity, (3) how well it is in line with existing advertising strategies and objectives, and (4) how to optimize effectiveness.
Method:	Consumers are recruited to evaluate a TV program, with ads embedded into the program as they would be on local prime-time television. Consumers view the recorded program in their homes to simulate actual field conditions. (The option to use local cable television programs with commercial inserts is also provided.)
Output:	Related recall (day-after recall) scores; persuasion scores, including brand preference shifts, purchase intent and frequency, brand equity differentiation, and relevance and communication; and reaction diagnostics to determine what viewers take away from the ad and how creative elements contribute to or distract from advertising effectiveness.

Figure   9-12

Ipsos-ASI's Next*TV

provide norms that give advertisers a standard for comparing how well their ads are performing. In addition to recall, a number of different measures of the commercial's effectiveness are now offered, including persuasive measures and diagnostics.

Comprehensive Measures   As noted in our discussion of pretesting broadcast commercials, a measure of a commercial's persuasive effectiveness is gathered and services offer additional persuasion measures, including purchase-intent and frequency-of-purchase. Copy testing firms also provide diagnostic measures. These measures are designed to garner viewers' evaluations of the ads, how clearly the creative idea is understood, and how well the proposition is communicated. Rational and emotional reactions to the ads are also examined. While each of the measures just described provides specific input into the effectiveness of a commercial, many advertisers are interested in more than just one specific input. Thus, companies provide comprehensive approaches in which each of the three measures just described (i.e., recall, persuasion, diagnostics) can be obtained through one testing program. Figure 9-12 describes one such comprehensive program, Ipsos-ASI's Next*TV test (Exhibit 9-3).

Test Marketing   Companies conduct tests designed to measure their advertising effects in specific test markets before releasing them nationally. The markets chosen are representative of the target audience. For example, a company may test its ads in London, Ontario, Peterborough, Ontario, or Winnipeg, Manitoba if the demographic and socio-economic profiles of these cities match the product's market. Many factors may be tested, including reactions to the ads (for example, alternative copy points), the effects of various budget sizes, or special offers. The ads run in finished form in the media where they might normally appear, and effectiveness is measured after the ads run.

The advantage of test marketing of ads is realism. Regular viewing environments are used and the testing effects are minimized. A high degree of control can be attained if the test is designed successfully. For example, an extensive test market study was designed and conducted by Seagram and Time Inc. over three years to measure the effects of advertising frequency on consumers' buying habits. This study demonstrated just how much could be learned from research conducted in a field setting but with experimental controls. It also showed that proper research can provide strong insights into the impact of ad campaigns. (Many advertising researchers consider this study one of the most conclusive ever conducted in the attempt to demonstrate the effects of advertising on sales.)

The Seagram study also reveals the disadvantages associated with test market measures, not the least of which are cost and time. Few firms have the luxury to spend three years and hundreds of thousands of dollars on such a test. In addition, there is always the fear that competitors may discover and intervene in the research process. Test marketing can provide

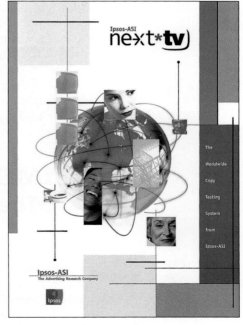

Exhibit 9-3   Ipsos-ASI offers a comprehensive testing measure.

Exhibit 9-4   Tracking studies provide useful measures.

substantial insight into the effectiveness of advertising if care is taken to minimize the negative aspects of such tests.

Single-Source Tracking Studies   More sophisticated approaches are **single-source tracking methods** that track the behaviours of consumers from the television set to the supermarket checkout counter. Participants in a designated area who agree to participate in the studies are given a card that identifies their household and gives the research company their demographics. The households are split into matched groups; one group receives an ad while the other does not, or alternate ads are sent to each. Their purchases are recorded from the bar codes of the products bought. Commercial exposures are then correlated with purchase behaviours. The single-source method can be used effectively to posttest ads, allowing for a variety of dependent measures and tracking the effects of increased ad budgets and different versions of ad copy—and even ad effects on sales.[10] After using scanner data to review the advertising/sales relationship for 78 brands, John Jones concluded that single-source data are beginning to fulfill their promise now that more measurements are available.[11]

Tracking Print/Broadcast Ads   One of the more useful and adaptable forms of posttesting involves tracking the effects of the ad campaign by taking measurements at regular intervals. **Tracking studies** measure the effects of advertising on awareness, recall, interest, and attitudes toward the ad and/or brand as well as purchase intentions. (Ad tracking may be applied to both print and broadcast ads but is much more common with the latter.) Personal interviews, phone surveys, mall intercepts, and even mail surveys have been used. Sample sizes typically range from 250 to 500 cases per period (usually quarterly or semiannually). Tracking studies yield perhaps the most valuable information available to the marketing manager for assessing current programs and planning for the future. (See Exhibit 9-4.)

The major advantage of tracking studies is that they can be tailored to each specific campaign and/or situation. A standard set of questions can track effects of the campaign over time. The effects of various media can also be determined, although with much less effectiveness. Tracking studies have also been used to measure the differential impact of different budget sizes, the effects of flighting, brand or corporate image, and recall of specific copy points. Finally, when designed properly tracking studies offer a high degree of reliability and validity.[12]

Some of the problems of recall and recognition measures are inherent in tracking studies, since many other factors may affect both brand and advertising recall. Despite these limitations, however, tracking studies are a very effective way to assess the effects of advertising campaigns.

(L04) IMC Planning: Program for Measuring Effectiveness

In this section, we offer prescriptions for managers planning evaluative research. Some time ago, the largest U.S. ad agencies endorsed a set of principles aimed at improving the research used in preparing and testing ads.[13] (We include it here due to the U.S. connection of many Canadian agencies.) The principles, called **PACT (Positioning Advertising Copy Testing)**, define *copy testing* as research "which is undertaken when a decision is to be made about whether advertising should run in the marketplace. Whether this stage utilizes a single test or a combination of tests, its purpose is to aid in the judgment of specific advertising executions."[14] The nine principles of good copy testing are shown in Figure 9-13. Adherence may not make for perfect

1. Provide measurements that are relevant to the objectives of the advertising.
2. Require agreement about how the results will be used in advance of each specific test.
3. Provide multiple measures (single measures are not adequate to assess ad performance).
4. Be based on a model of human response to communications—the reception of a stimulus, the comprehension of the stimulus, and the response to the stimulus.
5. Allow for whether the advertising stimulus should be exposed more than once.
6. Require that the more finished a piece of copy is, the more soundly it can be evaluated and require, as a minimum, that alternative executions be tested in the same degree of finish.
7. Provide controls to avoid the biasing effects of the exposure context.
8. Take into account basic considerations of sample definition.
9. Demonstrate reliability and validity.

Figure   9-13

Positioning Advertising Copy Testing (PACT)

testing, but it goes a long way toward improving the state of the art and providing guidelines for effectiveness research.

CRITERIA FOR EFFECTIVE RESEARCH

When testing methods are compared to the criteria established by PACT, it is clear that the principles important to good copy testing can be accomplished readily. Principle 1 (providing measurements relative to the objectives sought) and principle 2 (determining *a priori* how the results will be used) are consistent with DAGMAR (i.e., Chapter 5) and are basic advertising management prescriptions along with principle 6 (providing equivalent test ads). Principles 3, 5, and 7 are largely in the control of the researcher. Principle 3 (providing multiple measurements) may require little more than budgeting to make sure more than one test is conducted. Likewise, principle 5 (exposing the test ad more than once) can be accomplished with a proper research design. It might seem that principle 7 (providing a nonbiasing exposure) would be easy to accomplish, however lab measures are artificial and vulnerable to testing effects while offering control while field measures are realistic with less control. Research should likely find a balance by using both types over time. Principle 8 (sample definition) requires sound research methodology; any test should use the target audience to assess an ad's effectiveness. If a study is properly designed, and by that we mean it addresses principles 1 through 8, it should be both reliable and valid. Principle 9 (concern for reliability and validity) includes two critical distinctions between good and bad research, however most of the measures discussed are lacking in at least one of these criteria.

Principle 4, which states the research should be guided by a model of human response to communications that encompasses reception, comprehension, and behavioural response, requires careful consideration because it is the principle least addressed by practising researchers. Even though response models (recall Chapter 4 and 5) have existed for many years, few if any common research methods attempt to integrate them into their methodologies. Models that do claim to measure such factors as attitude change or brand preference change are often fraught with problems that severely limit their reliability. An effective measure must include a relationship to the communications process.

GUIDELINES FOR EFFECTIVE TESTING

Good tests of advertising effectiveness must address the nine principles established by PACT. One of the easiest ways to accomplish this is by following the decision sequence model in formulating promotional plans.

- *Use a consumer response model.* Early in this text we reviewed hierarchy of effects models and cognitive response models, which provide an understanding of the effects of communications and lend themselves to achieving communications goals. We also presented Rossiter and Percy's model for stating communication objectives, which could also be a basis for measurement.

- *Establish communications objectives.* It is nearly impossible to show the direct impact of advertising on sales. The marketing objectives established for the promotional program are not good measures of communication effectiveness. On the other hand, attainment of communications objectives can be measured and leads to the accomplishment of marketing objectives.
- *Use both pretests and posttests.* From a cost standpoint—both actual cost outlays and opportunity costs—pretesting makes sense. It may mean the difference between success or failure of the campaign or the product. But it should work in conjunction with posttests, which avoid the limitations of pretests, use much larger samples, and take place in more natural settings. Posttesting may be required to determine the true effectiveness of the ad or campaign.
- *Use multiple measures.* Many attempts to measure the effectiveness of advertising focus on one major dependent variable—perhaps sales, recall, or recognition. As noted earlier in this chapter, advertising may have a variety of effects on the consumer, some of which can be measured through traditional methods, others that require updated thinking (recall the discussion on physiological responses). For a true assessment of advertising effectiveness, a number of measures may be required.
- *Understand and implement proper research.* It is critical to understand research methodology. What constitutes a good design? Is it valid and reliable? Does it measure what we need it to? There is no shortcut to this criterion, and there is no way to avoid it if you truly want to measure the effects of advertising.

A major study sponsored by the Advertising Research Foundation (ARF) addressed these issues, involving interviews with 12,000 to 15,000 people.[15] While we do not have the space to analyze this study here, note that the research was designed to evaluate measures of copy tests, compare copy testing procedures, and examine the PACT principles. Information on this study has been published in a number of academic and trade journals and by the ARF.

Learning Objectives Summary

 Identify the reasons for measuring promotional program effectiveness.

This chapter introduced issues and decisions concerning the measurement of advertising and promotion effectiveness. All marketing managers want to know how well their promotional programs are working. This information is critical for planning the next period, since program adjustments and/or maintenance are based on evaluation of current strategies.

While the need for understanding how programs are working appears critical, this chapter summarized the debate regarding whether measurement is in fact needed. We conclude that research measuring the effectiveness of advertising is important to the promotional program and should be an integral part of the planning process.

 Describe the measures used in assessing promotional program effectiveness.

We summarized many types of decisions for advertising research. Managers must consider what parts of the promotional message need to be tested. We identified both creative strategy and creative tactic decisions as being important for testing. We also suggested that most other IMC tools had a key message that required effectiveness testing and that these advertising research methods were applied accordingly. Moreover, research could occur prior to a campaign (i.e., pretesting) or after the campaign (i.e., posttesting), which represents another key decision.

Whether a lab or field test is required also should be determined. Lab tests offer greater control with the cost of a lack of realistic setting while features of field tests are reversed. While there are many choices for research, a comprehensive, yet expensive, evaluation program would test all message variables, before and after a campaign, with both lab and field methods.

 Evaluate alternative methods for measuring promotional program effectiveness.

The chapter described many research methods that cover the stages of developing a promotional program. Many of the tests originated with one firm and were later adapted by other firms. Many companies have developed their own testing systems in conjunction with their advertising or communication agency.

Concept tests, focus groups, and mall intercepts are used to test initial ideas for creative strategies and promotional messages. Comprehension and reaction tests along with consumer juries appeared useful to testing rough or preliminary examples of print ads and television storyboards.

Finished ads are also tested prior to launching the campaign. Investment in these tests reassures managers so that costly media buys can be avoided. We reviewed portfolio tests, readability tests, and dummy advertising vehicles for evaluating completed print ads. Finished broadcast ads can be examined with theatre tests, on-air tests, and physiological measures.

Evaluations after the ads have been launched, known as posttests, offer greater confirmation of the promotion effectiveness. Print ad posttests include inquiry tests, recognition tests, and recall tests. Broadcast posttests include day-after recall tests, comprehensive measures, test marketing, single-source tracking studies, and tracking studies. Single-source research data offer strong potential for improving the effectiveness of ad measures since commercial exposures and reactions may be correlated to actual purchase behaviours.

 Appraise the requirements of proper effectiveness research.

Finally, we reviewed the criteria (defined by PACT) for sound research and suggested ways to accomplish effective studies. It is important to recognize that different measures of effectiveness may lead to different results. Depending on the criteria used, one measure may show that an ad or promotion is effective while another states that it is not. This is why clearly defined objectives, evaluations occurring both before and after the campaigns are implemented, and the use of multiple measures are critical to determining the true effects of an IMC program.

Key Terms

Review key terms and definitions on Connect.

Review Questions

1. What are the reasons why a company should measure the effectiveness of their promotional programs?

2. Discuss the differences between pretesting and posttesting, and lab testing and field testing.

3. Why might a firm use theatre testing, on-air tests, and physiological measures to pretest its finished broadcast ads?

4. Why are the PACT criteria important for testing effectiveness?

Applied Questions

1. Imagine how a creative director who worked on an exciting, daring, and provocative ad campaign for months would react if the campaign were to be scrapped prior to launch after preliminary research indicated it did not resonate with audiences tested.

2. Select a popular ad campaign and explain whether it should have tested different creative strategy options or different creative tactics options.

3. Explain why you would or would not want to personally participate in each of the studies described.

4. For any of the print ads located in the previous chapters, design a testing approach based on the final section of this chapter.

GO ONLINE

For more information on the resources available from McGraw-Hill Ryerson, go to www.mcgrawhill.ca/he/solutions.

Media Planning and Budgeting for IMC

CHAPTER TEN

10

LEARNING OBJECTIVES

LO1 Illustrate how a media plan is developed.

LO2 Explain the process and identify the decisions for implementing media strategies.

LO3 Explain the process and identify the decisions for implementing media tactics.

LO4 Distinguish among the theoretical and managerial approaches for media budget setting.

LO5 Apply the methods for allocating the media budget to relevant IMC tools and market situations.

B!G Awards Find Big Advertising Spenders

Strategy's B!G Awards recognizes advertisers with budgets over $10 million that represent at least $1 million in revenue for the agency. The challenge recognizes work that addresses a communication opportunity with an innovative and creative approach and a mix of media and other elements of marketing communication to further show the interrelationship between creative and media. A recent year saw Sid Lee Architecture garner gold for its work with Red Bull Amsterdam, MacLaren McCann strike silver for its effort with MasterCard, and Cundari be bronzed with its BMW initiative.

Sid Lee's work with Red Bull demonstrated its movement into areas beyond expected agency services. Red Bull Amsterdam moved into a vacant heritage ship-building factory as the popular brand looked for an energizing design to foster employee creativity and also act as a functioning work space. Red Bull's interest in art and sports beyond its established place in the drink market is seen with music and dancing, and auto-racing downhill ice-cross provided the right kind of image for when outsiders visited for meetings. The result featured such things as sports-related design with interior skateboard ramps and ski cliffs that act as desks. In the end, the ultimate design overwhelmed management and employees with complete and total satisfaction.

MacLaren McCann found a way to deliver for Master-Card when the "priceless" brand looked to fill four intern positions requiring digital technology skills. Rather than take the tried route of a corporate recruitment page or on-campus postings and receive the standard applications, MasterCard tasked the agency to find a digital solution to finding digital specialists. Enter the "Social Interview," where applicants experienced a pre-screening process to find the best and brightest. Campus posters had QR codes and URLs to permit smartphone access to program information. A Facebook page instructed students to submit their résumé to LinkedIn with a link to their creative digital work and a Twitter feed notified the lucky recipients of a one-day workshop and an interview. Impressive results occurred with 532 social interviews, 400 percent growth in Facebook fans during four weeks, and half the Twitter conversations focused on the intern program. MasterCard hired a fifth intern due to the high-quality applicant pool, and the social interview is now part of worldwide recruitment.

After many years of sponsoring the Air Canada Maple Leaf Lounges, BMW desired a new approach to improve exposure levels as users of the high-end facility tended to not value the images and messages as in the past. The sporty car brand looked to Cundari for insight to find something that this target group would find interesting while waiting for their air travel. Cundari filled the lounge with stunning one-of-a-kind stylishly mounted and framed BMW photography. Appreciative viewers could bid on a piece knowing that the proceeds would go to the Air Canada Foundation, the charitable part of the airline. Signage, social media, and e-mails encouraged viewing and the agency subsequently expanded with strong consumer interest when it commissioned Canadian photographers to create more. These captivating pieces became the focal point of publicity in numerous publications while the agency completed a documentary about the art, subsequently posted on YouTube. The initiative raised $20,000, improved BMW's database, increased sales leads, and sold more cars.

Sources: Emily Jackson, "The B!G Awards," *Strategy,* August 29, 2012; Emily Jackson, "B!G Gold: Sid Lee Architecture Sets Up Shop for Red Bull Amsterdam," *Strategy,* August 2012; Emily Jackson, "B!G Silver: MacLaren McCann Finds a Social Intern for MasterCard," *Strategy,* August 29, 2012; Emily Jackson, "B!G Bronze: Cundari's BMW Art Auction Takes Flight," *Strategy,* August 29, 2012.

Questions:

1. Do you agree with the placing of the three winners?
2. How do these examples influence our thoughts about IMC?

As the opening vignette suggests, a marketer has many media opportunities available that require in-depth knowledge of all the alternatives. Media planners must now consider new options as well as recognize the changes that are occurring in traditional sources. Planning when, where, and how the message will be delivered is a complex and involved process resulting in a media plan. The purpose of the media plan is to identify and justify the decisions that will deliver the message to the target audience cost-efficiently and will communicate the product, brand, and/or service message effectively.

This chapter illustrates the media planning process, expresses the development of decisions for media strategy and tactics, and distinguishes approaches of setting and allocating an IMC budget. We include budget setting for IMC in this chapter because of the inherent trade-off between media decisions and financial resources. We do not exclusively discuss budget issues for other IMC tools for two reasons. First, the remaining IMC tools are often dependent on media expenditures. For example, advertisers use media to direct visitors to their websites or other digital media alternatives, and public relations campaigns use media to encourage visits to events or participate in brand activities. Second, the planning process for all marketing communication tools follows or is consistent with established planning processes of advertising. Thus, the budgeting concepts with reference to advertising described here are directly used for or transferred to other IMC tools.

(L01) Media Planning

In this section we provide an overview of media planning to highlight the context in which messages are delivered, describe the content of a media plan to understand how its content is consistent with other elements of IMC planning, and indicate the unique challenges with media planning not found in other areas of IMC planning.

OVERVIEW

Media planning is the series of decisions involved in delivering the promotional message to prospective purchasers and/or users of the product or brand. Media planning is a process whereby the decisions may be altered or abandoned as the plan develops. One primary decision is the type of media selected. Options include mass media such as television, newspapers, radio, and magazines, as well as out-of-the-home media such as outdoor advertising and transit advertising and Internet content publishers and social media (Figure 10-1). Each media has its own particular strengths and limitations that must be considered in light of the communication problem or opportunity with which the marketer is faced. This makes the media selection and all other media decisions very difficult. For example, the media planning process becomes even more complicated when the manager has to choose among alternatives within the same medium, like different television stations or shows and different magazine titles.

A number of decisions must be made throughout the media planning process. The promotional planning model in Chapter 1 identified decisions such as selecting target audiences, establishing objectives, and formulating strategies for attaining them. The development of the media plan and strategies follows a similar path, except that the focus is to determine the best way to deliver the message. Thus, the media plan is generally comprised of a short section containing **media objectives**, an explanation of the **media strategy** decisions, and fine-tuning details that are known as media execution or **media tactics**. The activities involved in developing the media plan and the purposes of each are presented in Figure 10-2. Although this simplified template shows a few media for illustrative purposes, the general process is similar for all media and IMC tools.

Media planning certainly occurs for advertising, but it is also necessary as part of the decision for other IMC tools as suggested above. Sales promotions often require media expenditure to communicate the offers available or for distribution. Public relations activities use media to communicate corporate activities with respect to sponsorship or community events. A

Figure 10-1 Canadian market data: Net advertising revenues

Media		2005	2006	2007	2008	2009	2010	2011	2012
Television	Total	3,014	3,241	3,299	3,393	3,104	3,391	3,552	3,467
	Conventional	2,226	2,335	2,326	2,345	2,084	2,262	2,302	2,189
	Specialty	769	882	948	1,027	1,001	1,113	1.233	1,263
	Infomercial	19	24	24	22	19	16	17	15
Daily Newspaper	Total	2,659	2,635	2,572	2,489	2,030	2,102	1,971	2,019
	National	610	605	590	571	406	736	709	804
	Local	1,174	1,163	1,135	1,099	974	631	709	719
	Classified	875	867	846	819	650	462	335	289
	Inserts						273	217	207
Community Newspaper	Total	1,016	1,094	1,154	1,211	1,186	1,143	1,167	1,266
	National						292	131	193
	Local						741	705	611
	Classified						110	113	103
	Inserts						219	360
Radio	Total	1,316	1,391	1,468	1,558	1,470	1,517	1,576	1,585
	National	323	352	379	408	376	409	442	454
	Local	993	1,039	1,089	1,149	1,094	1,108	1,134	1,131
Internet	Total	562	900	1,241	1,602	1,822	2,232	2,593	2,925
	Search	197	343	478	622	741	907	1,081	1,308
	Display	230	314	432	490	578	688	840	916
	Classifieds/Directories	124	223	305	460	467	587	576	584
	Email	11	20	17	18	13	11	13	12
	Video—	—	—	9	12	20	37	73	92
	Video Gaming—	—	—	—	—	3	2	10	13
Mobile		—	1	2	7	23	47	81	160
General Magazines		665	682	718	692	590	606	593	573
Out-of-Home		344	370	422	463	416	482	485	486
Total Reported		**9,579**	**10,314**	**10,876**	**11,415**	**10,641**	**11,520**	**12,017**	**12,481**
Catalogue/Direct Mail		1,532	1,608	1,595	1,542	1,207	1,313	1,243	1,257
Yellow Pages		1,068	1,058	1,033	1,000	815	844	791	811
Miscellaneous		480	493	519	500	426	438	428	414
Total Unreported		**3,080**	**3,159**	**3,147**	**3,042**	**2,511**	**2,595**	**2,462**	**2,482**
Total Advertising		**12,656**	**13,473**	**14,023**	**14,457**	**13,152**	**14,115**	**14,479**	**14,963**
Population (Millions)		32.2	32.6	32.9	33.3	33.7	34.1	34.9	35.1
Per Capita Total Advertising		393	414	426	434	389	413	415	426

Sources: Television: CRTC; Daily & Community Newspaper: Newspaper Canada; Radio: CRTC; Internet: IAB; General Magazine: Magazines Canada; Outdoor: Estimate of net revenue based on NMR; Direct Mail: Canada Post; Yellow Pages: Estimate based on last report by TeleDirect (1999); Miscellaneous: includes estimates for Trade & Other Print; Population: Statistics Canada Mid-Year Population by Year.

Source: Media Digest, Canadian Media Director's Council, 2012–2013, p. 8.

number of media are available for direct marketing, and many aspects of media planning are applicable. In general, the guiding principles for media strategy and media tactics are applicable for the use of media to implement other IMC activities beyond advertising.

Finally, media planning experiences the challenge of developing a plan with limited financial resources as plans have a prescribed budget that the media planner must respect. All decisions

Figure   10-2   Activities involved in developing the media plan

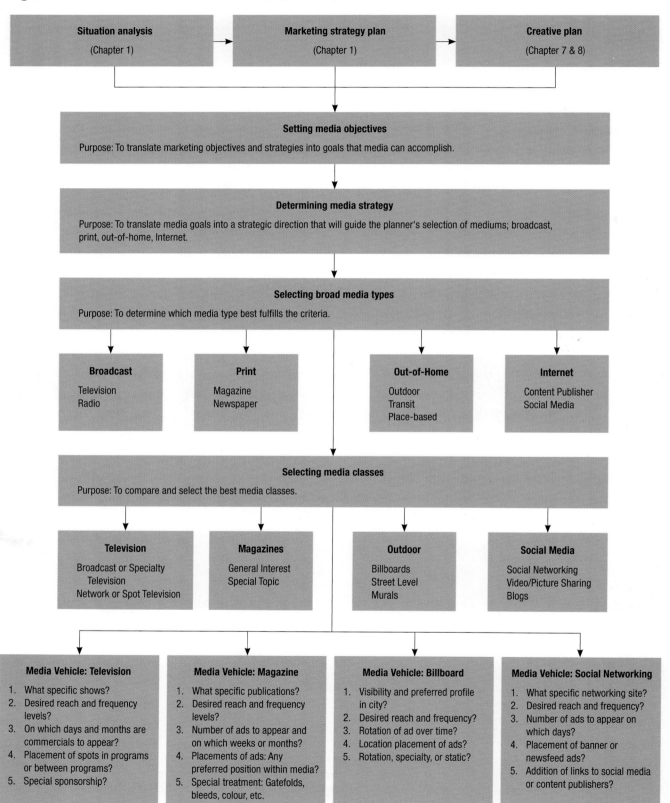

within media planning for advertising face trade-offs to maximize or optimize communication and behavioural objectives. When extended beyond advertising the promotional planner is faced with the task of allocating expenditures across all IMC tools to achieve broader target audience objectives. In fact, the pressure of marketing managers to spend wisely in the promotional domain is more critical with pressures holding the marketing task more financially accountable as firms now calculate their return on marketing investment (ROIM).[1]

MEDIA PLAN

The media plan documents the decisions for finding the best way to get the advertiser's message to the market. In a basic sense, the goal of the media plan is to find the combination of media that enables the marketer to communicate the message in the most effective manner to the largest number of the target audience at the lowest cost. In this section, we review the media plan content regarding media objectives, media strategy, and media tactics.

Media Objectives   Just as the situation analysis leads to establishment of marketing and communication objectives, it should also lead to specific media objectives. The media objectives are not ends in themselves. Rather, they are derived from and are designed to lead to the attainment of communication and behavioural objectives, and contribute to achieving marketing objectives. Media objectives are the goals for the media program and should be limited to those that can be accomplished through media strategies. We now present examples of media objectives that are derived from three communication and two behavioural objectives.

Category Need

- Select media to sufficiently demonstrate how the target audience requires the product category.
- Provide sufficient number of exposures to ensure 80 percent of target audience understands the need for the product category.

Brand Awareness

- Select media to provide coverage of 80 percent of the target audience over a six-month period.
- Provide sufficient number of exposures to ensure 60 percent target audience brand recognition.
- Concentrate advertising during the target audience's peak purchasing time.

Brand Attitude

- Select media to ensure that 40 percent of the target audience have favourable beliefs regarding the brand's benefits and have positive emotions associated with the brand.
- Schedule creative executions over six months to heighten emotions associated with the brand and minimize message fatigue.

Brand Trial

- Select media to allow immediate purchase of brand.
- Schedule sufficient number of opportunities for target audience brand engagement.

Brand Repeat Purchase

- Select media to remind target audience of brand purchase.
- Provide sufficient advertising throughout the year to minimize target audience switching.

The content and exact number of media objectives is at the promotional planner's discretion. These examples merely illustrate the degree to which the link between objectives is not an easy step. The media objectives give direction for the media strategy and tactics decisions. After implementation, marketers need to know whether or not they were successful. Measures of effectiveness must consider two factors: (1) How well did these strategies achieve the media objectives? (2) How well did this media plan contribute to attaining the overall marketing and communications objectives? If the strategies were successful, they should be used in future plans. If not, their flaws should be analyzed.

Media Strategy   As Figure 10-2 indicates, the primary media strategy decision concerns the use of media, moving from a broad perspective to a more specific one. The **medium** is the general category of available delivery systems, which includes broadcast media (like TV and radio), print media (like newspapers and magazines), out-of-home media (like transit, outdoor, place-based), and Internet media (like content publishers and social media). **Media type** refers to the individual media within a medium, so TV is a media type, as is radio, and the term is often shortened to "media." After or during this evaluation, the media planner will consider the relative strengths and limitations of broad **media class** options. IMC Perspective 10-1 shows how the advertising industry recognizes good media selection.

In making the media strategy decisions, a media planner will consider the strategic implications of three concepts. **Reach** is a measure of the number of different audience members exposed at least once to a media vehicle in a given period of time. **Coverage** refers to the potential audience that might receive the message through a vehicle. Coverage relates to potential audience; reach refers to the actual audience delivered. (The importance of this distinction will become clearer later in this chapter.) Finally, **frequency** refers to the number of times the receiver is exposed to the media vehicle in a specified period.

Media Tactics   After the general strategic direction of the media plan has been established, the media planner looks to more specific media decisions like the media vehicle. The **media vehicle** is the specific carrier within a media class. For example, *Maclean's* is a print vehicle; *Hockey Night in Canada* is a television vehicle. As described in later chapters, each vehicle has its own characteristics as well as its own relative strengths and limitations. Specific decisions must be made as to the value of each in delivering the message.

While making the media vehicle decision, the media planner evaluates the options carefully to maximize coverage, reach, and frequency, and to minimize costs. For example, according to Figure 10-2, once print has been established the media planner has to decide which specific magazine(s) to select. In addition, certain placement factors need to be carefully evaluated. The tactical decisions include relative cost estimates that may lead to refinements in the allocation of the media dollars. Finally, the complete plan is summarized in a blocking chart. The chart may indicate gaps in media coverage or another concern that would lead the media planner to perform additional evaluation prior to completing the media plan.

MEDIA PLANNING CHALLENGES

Since media planning is a series of decisions, a number of challenges contribute to the difficulty of establishing the plan and reduce its effectiveness. These problems include insufficient information, inconsistent terminologies, need for flexibility, role of media planner, and difficulty measuring effectiveness.

Insufficient Information   While a great deal of information exists about markets and the media, media planners often require more than is available. Some data are just not measured, either because they cannot be or because measuring them would be too expensive. The timing of measurements is also a problem; audience measures are taken only at specific times of the year. This information is then generalized to succeeding months, so future planning decisions must be made on past data that may not reflect current behaviours. Think about planning for TV advertising for the fall season. There are no data on the audiences of new shows, and audience information taken on existing programs may not indicate how these programs will do in the fall as most shows eventually lose their audience. The lack of information is even more of a problem for small advertisers, who may not be able to afford to purchase the information they require and rely on limited or out-of-date data.

IMC PERSPECTIVE 10-1

Excitement Reigns at Nissan

With the tagline "Innovation That Excites," Nissan Canada launched its new Altima and won Media Innovation of the Year from *Marketing Magazine*. A highlight featured a holographic video of the car projected onto water as part of Canada Day fireworks celebrations in Vancouver, Toronto, and Halifax. The car emerged from the water, accelerated with a growling engine, splashed water all around with its spinning wheels, and dove and reappeared from the water a few times before it eventually stopped front and centre with #2013 Nissan Altimas superimposed above the stylish vehicle, designed to compete against Toyota's Camry.

It was so impressive a feat that one judge commented, "I would have been talking about that thing forever." The campaign included print, digital, and social media to go along with this experiential open-air imagery, and won other awards: gold for Experiential/Special Events/Stunts, Car and Automotive Services, and silver for newspaper. With so much going for it no wonder another judge summarized the feelings of the panel this way: "This was the campaign that passed the all-important I-wish-I-had-done-that test."

The print execution proved innovative as well. Working with the *National Post,* Nissan used Layar technology that permitted readers to scan the photo with their phone and access additional content. According to the chief executive of OMD, Nissan's media agency, "Layar technology was not only part of the Nissan advertising, but it was also being introduced to consumers. It was completely new to Canadians, which added that extra degree of difficulty because was not only the launch of a technology, it also involved having to educate consumers about the technology before it would work."

Chosen from 20 other gold winners, it is clear that Nissan placed itself well above the competition that included a very strong roster of media innovation from the automotive industry. Ford won best video with its "Ford Focus Time Play." VW won gold for Out-of-Home for its "Beetle AR." Honda Dealers placed first in Ambient/Place–based for the "CR-V Conveyor Belt." Infiniti's JX hit gold in the Digital category. McDonald's hit a winner with its "Our Food, Your Questions" and was named Marketer of the Year.

And while Nissan gets the glory, they praised their agency suppliers, OMD and TBWA, and highlighted the significance of winning in a press release. "We are so honoured to have our innovative work recognized by one of the most prestigious and important media industry awards programs in Canada," said Judy Wheeler, Director of Marketing at Nissan Canada Inc. "There has never been a more exciting time at Nissan and we are thrilled to continue to share this excitement and connect with customers through ground-breaking, multi-platform marketing initiatives."

Source: Dave Brown, "Nissan and OMD Win Media Innovation of the Year Awards Best of Show," *Marketing Magazine,* November 16, 2012; Hollie Shaw, "Nissan Canada Wins Best in Show at Media Innovation Awards," *National Post,* November 14, 2012; http://nissannews.com/fr-CA/nissan/canada/releases/nissan-wins-five-marketing-media-innovation-awards.

Question

1. How could Nissan have leveraged the experiential component of the plan beyond obtaining press coverage?

Compared to media planners in the United States, Canadian media planners face additional pressures of insufficient information. The size of the American population permits extensive economies of scale, so it is not unexpected that larger U.S.-based media-buying organizations would have valuable resources. Combined with similar media consumption (e.g., popular television shows) between Americans and English-speaking Canadians, there is a movement to coordinate media purchasing across North America. The end result may be improved efficiency and effectiveness of the media purchase with the sharing of information.[2]

Inconsistent Terminologies   Problems arise because the cost bases used by different media often vary and the standards of measurement used to establish these costs are not always consistent. For example, print media may present cost-efficiency data in terms of the cost to reach a thousand people (cost per thousand, or CPM), while broadcast and outdoor media use the cost per ratings point (CPRP). Audience information that is used as a basis for these costs has also been collected by different methods. Finally, terms that actually mean something different (such as *reach* and *coverage*) may be used synonymously, adding to the confusion.

Need for Flexibility   Most media plans are written annually so that all participants are well informed and results can be measured against objectives. However, media planners juggle between requiring a document for action with the need for flexibility due to changes in the marketing environment. An opportunity to advertise within a new media vehicle might arise and the planner may shift its expenditure from one medium to another. A competitor may spend more money in certain media and the planner decides a change is required to defend against the threat. Preliminary decisions may not be feasibly implemented in terms of medium availability, thus requiring an adjustment. Poor audience size data in a media vehicle may necessitate a movement of money to another.

Role of Media Planners   Media planners often face a number of expectations from other organizational players. Procurement specialists often put extensive pressure on the media decisions in an effort to save money. Clients request media plans prior to contracting services. Decision makers of all the main IMC tools often look to media planners as the implementer instead of being a key decision-making participant. There also is never-ending debate as to whether media planning buying should be part of an advertising agency or an independent agency.[3]

Difficulty Measuring Effectiveness   Because of the potential inaccuracies of measuring the effectiveness of advertising and promotions, it is also difficult to determine the relative effectiveness of media or media vehicles. While progress has occurred across most media, the media planner must usually balance quantitative data with subjective judgments based on experience when comparing media alternatives. The next section explores how media strategies are developed and ways to increase their effectiveness.

 Media Strategy Decisions

Having determined what is to be accomplished, media planners consider how to achieve the media objectives. They develop and implement media strategies that consist of five main topics for decision: media mix, target audience coverage, geographic coverage, scheduling, and reach and frequency.

THE MEDIA MIX

A wide variety of media are available to advertisers. While it is possible that only one might be employed, it is much more likely that a number of alternatives will be used. The behavioural and communication objectives, the characteristics of the product or service, the size of the budget, the target audience, and individual preferences are primary factors that determine the combination of media used. While an evaluation of each media occurs within the perspective of the communication situation a media planner faces, each medium has certain degrees of use with Canadians, as shown in Figure 10-3.

The context in which the ad is placed may also affect viewers' perceptions, and the creative strategy may require certain media. Therefore, within the media mix a single media becomes the primary media where a majority of the budget is spent or the primary effects occur. Because TV provides both sight and sound, it may be more effective in generating emotions than other media. The campaign to attract tourists to Newfoundland and Labrador used TV extensively to convey the experience of actually being in the province while viewing the ad. According to the agency, "Most tourism advertising around the world is an inventory of products, whereas our deep feeling is that the advertising should express and evoke the feeling of the place."[4]

Time Spent Weekly per Capita Hours	Total Canada
Television	25
Radio	18
Internet	18
Newspaper	2

Source: BBM Analytics RTS Fall 2012; TV Basics 2012–2013, p 26.

Figure 10-3

Where is the time spent?
Adults 18+

Magazines may create different perceptions from newspapers, so we regularly see products in one form of print versus another.

It is possible to increase the success of a product significantly through a strong creative campaign. In some situations, the media strategy to be pursued may be the driving force behind the creative strategy, as the media and creative departments work closely together to achieve the greatest impact with the audience of the specific media. For example, in the case of the "Must drink more milk" campaign, six original ads ran on TV but eight cruder and cooler ads with animation ran on YouTube.[5]

As noted at the end of Chapter 5, media planners examine how each medium influences the stages of the consumer decision-making process. For the "All In" campaign for Adidas, the agency viewed its TV and cinema ads and its out-of-home (digital and high impact) as ways of "getting consumers off the couch." The YouTube video and Facebook executions brought all product information together and let consumers enjoy and participate with the "All In" experience. A strong retail presence of display material at Sport Chek and Foot Locker completed the "All In" message.[6]

By employing a media mix advertisers can add more versatility to their media strategies, since each medium contributes its own distinct advantages. By combining media, marketers can increase coverage, reach, and frequency levels while improving the likelihood of achieving overall communications and marketing goals. Chapters 11, 12, and 13 summarize the characteristics of each medium that make it better or worse for attaining specific communication objectives. We have organized these as media and media-usage characteristics.

Media Characteristics

- target audience selectivity
- target audience coverage
- geographic coverage
- scheduling flexibility
- reach
- frequency
- cost efficiency
- absolute cost for placement

Media-Usage Characteristics

- control for selective exposure
- attention
- creativity for cognitive responses
- creativity for emotional responses
- amount of processing time
- involvement
- clutter
- media image and production

Figure 10-4 provides a summary of the strengths and limitations of the media reviewed in the next three chapters. We continue with these characteristics for direct marketing and Internet marketing in their respective chapters. With so many competing variables, it becomes clear why media planners spend considerable efforts getting the media mix decision right. Finally, keep in mind that these are general characteristics that give guidance to the media mix decision. Citing these to make a media mix decision is not sufficient. Each strength and limitation needs to be related to the communication situation a specific brand faces and how the media characteristics will help the brand reach its relevant objectives.

TARGET AUDIENCE COVERAGE

The media planner determines which target audiences should receive the most media emphasis. Developing media strategies involves matching the most appropriate media to this audience by

Figure   10-4

Strengths and limitations of
media characteristics

	Strengths	Limitations
Television	Target audience coverage Geographic coverage Creativity for emotional responses Creativity for cognitive responses Reach Frequency Scheduling flexibility Cost efficiency Attention Media image	Selective exposure Target audience selectivity Absolute cost Amount of processing time Involvement Clutter Media image
Radio	Cost efficiency Absolute cost Target audience selectivity Geographic coverage Scheduling flexibility Creativity for cognitive responses Reach Frequency Media image	Amount of processing time Selective exposure Attention Clutter Creativity for emotional responses without visual Involvement Target audience coverage
Magazines	Target audience selectivity Geographic coverage Selective exposure Attention Involvement Amount of processing time Creativity for cognitive responses Creativity for emotional responses Media image	Target audience coverage Reach Frequency Scheduling flexibility Cost efficiency Absolute cost Clutter
Newspapers	Scheduling flexibility Reach Frequency Geographic coverage Cost efficiency Absolute cost Target audience coverage Media image Involvement Processing time Creativity for cognitive responses	Target audience selectivity Clutter Selective exposure Attention Creativity for emotional responses
Outdoor	Frequency Attention Geographic coverage Reach Cost efficiency Selective exposure Creativity for emotional responses Scheduling flexibility	Amount of processing time Media image Target audience selectivity Target audience coverage Absolute cost Clutter Involvement Creativity for cognitive responses
Transit	Geographic coverage Reach Frequency Amount of processing time Selective exposure Scheduling flexibility Cost efficiency Absolute cost	Target audience coverage Target audience selectivity Creativity for cognitive responses Creativity for emotional responses Involvement Media image Clutter Attention

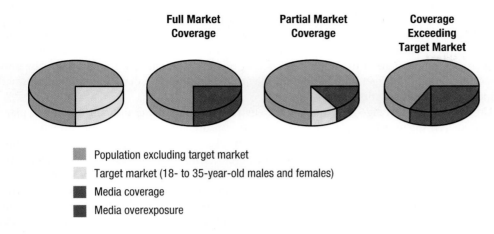

Full Market Coverage **Partial Market Coverage** **Coverage Exceeding Target Market**

Figure 10-5

Marketing coverage possibilities

Population excluding target market

Target market (18- to 35-year-old males and females)

Media coverage

Media overexposure

asking, "Through which media and media vehicles can I best get my message to prospective buyers?" The issue here is to get coverage of the audience, as shown in Figure 10-5. The optimal goal is full audience coverage, shown in the second pie chart. Business marketing organizations often get close to full audience coverage due to the small numbers of customers and potential customers. A B.C.-based firm, 4 Refuel, advertised in trade and industry association publications to attract new customers and obtained considerable leverage for its $100,000. A newsletter offered for publication in the magazines acted as additional publicity and garnered the equivalent of $500,000 in exposure.[7]

More realistically, conditions shown in the third and fourth charts are likely to occur in most marketing situations. In the third chart, the coverage of the media does not allow for coverage of the entire audience, leaving a portion without exposure to the message. In the fourth chart, the marketer is faced with a problem of overexposure (also called **waste coverage**), in which the media coverage exceeds the targeted audience. If media coverage reaches people who are not sought as buyers and are not potential users, then it is wasted. This term is used for coverage that reaches people who are not potential buyers and/or users. Consumers may not be part of the intended target audience but may still be considered as potential—for example, those who buy the product as a gift for someone else.

The goal of the media planner is to extend media coverage to as many members of the target audience as possible while minimizing the amount of waste coverage. The situation usually involves trade-offs. Sometimes one has to live with less coverage than desired; other times, the most effective media expose people not sought. In this instance, waste coverage is justified because the media employed are likely to be the most effective means of delivery available and the cost of the waste coverage is exceeded by the value gained from their use.

The target audience coverage decision relies on primary research and published (secondary) sources. This research can show the number of consumers for a particular product category across many demographic variables and their media consumption habits. We review audience information in Chapters 11, 12, and 13, as each medium has its own method.

When examining these data, media planners are often more concerned with the percentage figures and index numbers than with the raw numbers. This is largely due to the fact that the numbers provided may not be specific enough for their needs, or they question the numbers provided because of the methods by which they were collected. Another key reason is that index numbers and percentages provide a comparative view of the market.

Overall, the **index number** is considered a good indicator of the potential of the market. This number is derived from the formula

$$\text{Index} = \frac{\text{Percentage of users in a demographic segment}}{\text{Percentage of population in the same segment}} \times 100$$

An index number over 100 means use of the product is proportionately greater in that segment than in one that is average (100) or less than 100. Depending on their overall strategy, marketers may wish to use this information to determine which groups are now using the product and target them or to identify a group that is currently using the product less and attempt to develop that segment. While the index is helpful, it should not be used alone. Percentages and product usage figures are also needed to get an accurate picture of the market. Just because the index for a particular segment of the population is very high, that doesn't always mean it is the only attractive segment to target. The high index may be a result of a low denominator (a very small proportion of the population in this segment).

Understanding coverage in a multimedia environment is proving difficult for media planners. Research suggests that consumers frequently consume more than one medium at a time. It suggests that 50 percent use a laptop computer while watching television. Corresponding numbers for other devices include: mobile phone (40%), game console (25%), desktop computer (24%), and tablet (12%).[8] This is a significant trend since coverage historically implied a reasonably close association with exposure and processing of the advertising message. Clearly, the communication is limited even further if other media are competing for the people's attention. However, communication is intensified for an individual brand if viewers go to a social media site after a TV ad prompt, thereby affecting subsequent TV ads for other brands.

GEOGRAPHIC COVERAGE

The question of where to promote relates to geographic considerations. The question is, where will the ad dollars be more wisely spent? Should we allocate additional promotional monies to those markets where the brand is already the leader to maintain market share, or does more potential exist in those markets where the firm is not doing as well and there is more room to grow? Perhaps the best answer is that the firm should spend advertising and promotion dollars where they will be the most effective—that is, in those markets where they will achieve the desired objectives. Two useful calculations that marketers examine to make this decision are the Brand Development Index and the Category Development Index.

The **Brand Development Index (BDI)** helps marketers factor the rate of product usage by geographic area into the decision process.

$$\text{BDI} = \frac{\text{Percentage of brand to total Canadian sales in the market}}{\text{Percentage of total Canadian population in the market}} \times 100$$

The BDI compares the percentage of the brand's total sales in a given market area with the percentage of the total population in the market to determine the sales potential for that brand in that market area. An example of this calculation is shown in Figure 10-6. The higher the index number, the more market potential exists. In this case, the index number indicates this market has high potential for brand development.

The **Category Development Index (CDI)** is computed in the same manner as the BDI, except it uses information regarding the product category (as opposed to the brand) in the numerator:

$$\text{CDI} = \frac{\text{Percentage of product category total sales in market}}{\text{Percentage of total Canadian population in market}} \times 100$$

The CDI provides information on the potential for development of the total product category rather than specific brands. When this information is combined with the BDI, a much more insightful promotional strategy may be developed. One might first look at how well the product category does in a specific market area. In Alberta, for example, the category potential

Figure 10-6

Calculating BDI

$$\text{BDI} = \frac{\text{Percentage of total brand sales in Ontario}}{\text{Percentage of total Canadian population in Ontario}} \times 100$$

$$= \frac{50\%}{34\%} \times 100$$

$$= 147$$

$$CDI = \frac{\text{Percentage of product category sales in Alberta}}{\text{Percentage of total Canadian population in Alberta}} \times 100$$

$$= \frac{8\%}{11\%} \times 100$$

$$= 73$$

$$BDI = \frac{\text{Percentage of total brand sales in Alberta}}{\text{Percentage of total Canadian population in Alberta}} \times 100$$

$$= \frac{15\%}{11\%} \times 100$$

$$= 136$$

Figure 10-7

Using CDI and BDI to determine market potential

is low (see Figure 10-7). The marketer analyzes the BDI to find how the brand is doing relative to other brands in this area. This information can then be used in determining how well a particular product category and a particular brand are performing and figuring what media weight (or quantity of advertising) would be required to gain additional market share, as shown in Figure 10-8.

In addition to the BDI and CDI considerations, some geographic decisions are based on the availability of the product. For example, Primus launched the first national Web telephone service in North America using voice over Internet protocol (VOIP) technology. The Talk Broadband offering promises long-distance savings of 15 percent and attempts to pre-empt cable companies in the long-distance phone market and sway current telephone users. While national in scope for the long term, the radio, print, and transit ads are shown in Toronto, Montreal, Vancouver, Halifax, Calgary, Ottawa, and Edmonton, cities where the product is initially sold.[9]

SCHEDULING

Companies would like to keep their advertising in front of consumers at an appropriate level to maintain their behavioural and communications objectives and support to their brand positioning strategy. The primary objective of scheduling is to time promotional efforts to coincide with the highest potential buying times and other important brand-building opportunities. For some products these times are not easy to identify; for others they are very obvious. Three

Figure 10-8

Using BDI and CDI indexes

	High BDI	Low BDI
High CDI	High market share Good market potential	Low market share Good market potential
Low CDI	High market share Monitor for sales decline	Low market share Poor market potential

High BDI and high CDI	This market usually represents good sales potential for both the product category and the brand.
High BDI and low CDI	The category is not selling well, but the brand is; probably a good market to advertise in but should be monitored for declining sales.
Low BDI and high CDI	The product category shows high potential but the brand is not doing well; the reasons should be determined.
Low BDI and low CDI	Both the product category and the brand are doing poorly; not likely to be a good place for advertising.

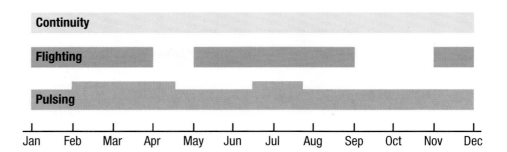

Figure   10-9

Three methods of promotional scheduling

scheduling methods available to the media planner—continuity, flighting, and pulsing—are shown in Figure 10-9.

Continuity refers to a continuous pattern of advertising, which may mean every day, every week, or every month. The key is that a regular (continuous) pattern is developed without gaps or nonadvertising periods. It is important to note that continuity is entirely predicated on the time period. For example, placing an ad in the newspaper every Monday for a whole year is continuous on a weekly basis, but not continuous on a daily basis. Such strategies might be used for advertising for food products, laundry detergents, or other products consumed on an ongoing basis without regard for seasonality.

A second method, flighting, employs a less regular schedule, with intermittent periods of advertising and nonadvertising. At some time periods there are heavier promotional expenditures, and at others there may be no advertising. Snow skis are advertised heavily between October and April; less in May, August, and September; and not at all in June and July. The weekly newspaper placement could be viewed as flighting on a daily basis since there is no advertising for the other days of the week.

Pulsing is actually a combination of the first two methods. In a pulsing strategy, continuity is maintained, but at certain times promotional efforts are stepped up. In the automobile industry, advertising continues throughout the year but may increase in April (tax refund time), September (when new models are brought out), and the end of the model year.

There are certain advantages and disadvantages to each scheduling method, as shown in Figure 10-10. One comprehensive study indicates that continuity is more effective than flighting. On the basis of the idea that it is important to get exposure to the message as close as possible to when the consumer is going to make the purchase, the study concludes that advertisers should continue weekly schedules as long as possible.[10] The key here may be the "as long as possible" qualification. Given a significant budget, continuity may be more of an option than it is for those with more limited budgets.

An interesting twist on scheduling occurs with Campbell's soup, where ads are run when the temperature drops below −5 degrees. A 10-second ad appearing on the Weather Network demonstrates the falling temperature of a thermometer turning into a Campbell's soup can. The voiceover concludes with, "When it's cold outside . . . warm up with Campbell's," while the visual shows a bowl of soup and the Campbell's slogan "M'm! M'm! Good!" The campaign also features a Web banner in ads in daily e-mails sent by the Weather Network and in newspaper ads adjacent to the weather information in some Toronto newspapers.[11]

As implied above, advertisers decide on the exact day, week, or months in which to advertise, so a good media plan provides extensive details on the exact timing of the placement. For example, a brand might want a magazine placement during spring months, TV placement could only occur on weekends, and a planner may decide to place banner ads only in the morning. Sport Chek decided to use TV during August to December to coincide with back-to-school, hockey, and holiday gift-giving, and used digital throughout the year.[12]

In a battle for market share in the $2 billion market for back-to-school supplies, Staples and Walmart raised the stakes with different approaches. Walmart jump-started the spending spree in July with cinema ads for laptop computers. Thinking that consumers required more time to consider their purchases for more expensive ticket items, the month-earlier beginning coincided with more targeting toward university and college students. The timing also fit with the idea of encouraging consumers to make fewer trips to stores, and of course to visit only one store, Walmart. Faced with the prospect of Walmart having the ability to advertise both school

Continuity	
Advantages	Serves as a constant reminder to the consumer
	Covers the entire buying cycle
	Allows for media priorities (quantity discounts, preferred locations, etc.)
Disadvantages	Higher costs
	Potential for overexposure
	Limited media allocation possible

Flighting	
Advantages	Cost efficiency of advertising only during purchase cycles
	May allow for inclusion of more than one medium or vehicle with limited budgets
Disadvantages	Weighting may offer more exposure and advantage over competitors
	Increased likelihood of wearout
	Lack of awareness, interest, retention of promotional message during nonscheduled times
	Vulnerability to competitive efforts during nonscheduled periods

Pulsing	
Advantages	All of the same as the previous two methods
Disadvantages	Not required for seasonal products (or other cyclical products)

Figure 10-10

Characteristics of scheduling methods

supplies and clothing, Staples responded with a joint effort with Old Navy, offering discounts at the clothing chain with purchases of its supplies. Staples also showed back-to-school ads on its Facebook page in July.[13]

Another scheduling decision involves the order in which each medium occurs when multiple media are in the plan. Which medium should occur first if TV, magazines, and outdoor are used in the campaign? Alternatively, should all media be placed simultaneously? Media placement constraints remove a planner's ability to completely control this decision, but nevertheless, the order is an important consideration. Procter & Gamble releases its ads digitally prior to TV with the aim of consumers forwarding them to others so that more people will attend to the messages when they see them on TV. For its Olympic messages, P&G found one-third of the online viewers shared the video link.[14]

REACH AND FREQUENCY

Advertisers usually must trade off reach and frequency because they face budget constraints when trying to attain objectives. They must decide whether to have the message be seen or heard by more people (reach) or by fewer people more often (frequency). This trade-off requires a complex investigation to answer these two questions for any media, and by extension, the whole media plan and the entire IMC plan.

How Much Reach Is Necessary? A universal communication objective is product and/or brand awareness. The more consumers are aware, the more they are likely to consider the brand throughout the decision-making process. Achieving awareness requires reach—that is, exposing the target audience to the message. New brands or products need a very high level of reach since the objective is to make all potential buyers aware. High reach is also desired at later purchase-decision stages since a promotional strategy might use a free sample. An objective of the marketer is to reach a larger number of people with the sample in an attempt to make them learn of the product, use it, and develop a favourable attitude toward it that may lead to an initial brand trial purchase.

Reach is the number of target audience individuals exposed at least once to a media vehicle in a specific time period. Media planners use weekly, monthly, or quarterly time periods that are known as *advertising cycles*. The reach number is usually expressed as a percentage provided the number of target audience individuals is clearly identified.

For example, the most watched TV show each week is about 3.4 million, according to Bureau of Broadcast Measurement (BBM), and the population of Canada is about 34 million according to Statistics Canada as reported in the Media Digest. Thus the reach of an ad placed on this show is approximately 10 percent for the advertising cycle of one week.

$$\text{Reach} = \frac{\text{Number of people watching TV ad}}{\text{Number of people in Canada}} = \frac{3.4 \text{ million}}{34 \text{ million}} = 10\%$$

Reach can be compiled over any time period (i.e., week, month, year), geographically (i.e., city, province), or any demographic (e.g., women 18–35). Reach can also be considered in terms of the stages of the buyer decision-making process and for any other media used for advertising or other IMC tools that have a media plan component. No matter what audience characteristics the media planner works with, the ratio remains as follows:

$$\text{Reach} = \frac{\text{Number of people in target audience exposed to the media vehicle}}{\text{Number of people in target audience}}$$

The concept of reach gets more complex and complicated going beyond the placement of one ad on one TV show. If one ad is placed on one TV show one time, the number of people exposed is the reach (Figure 10-11A). In order to achieve high levels of reach, brands often use multiple media (e.g., television, Internet). Alternatively, or in addition, brands use multiple media vehicles such as more than one TV station or TV show, or more than one magazine. Thus, it is possible for the target audience to be exposed to an ad more than once with multiple media and multiple media vehicles (Figure 10-11B).

The reach of the two shows, as depicted in Figure 10-11C, includes a number of people who were reached by both shows. This overlap is referred to as **duplicated reach**. If the ad is placed on two shows, the total number exposed once is **unduplicated reach** (Figure 10-11D). Both unduplicated and duplicated reach figures are important. Unduplicated reach indicates potential new exposures, while duplicated reach provides an estimate of frequency since some in the target audience saw the ad multiple times. Media plans should account for both unduplicated reach and duplicated reach, or acknowledge which is used, to provide a comprehensive reporting of the media buy.

Figure   10-11

Representation of reach and frequency

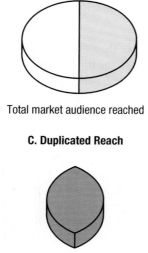

A. Reach of One TV Program

Total market audience reached

C. Duplicated Reach

Total market reached
with both shows

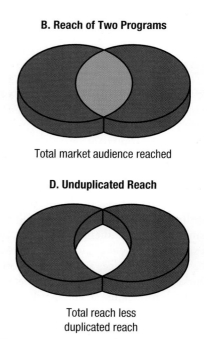

B. Reach of Two Programs

Total market audience reached

D. Unduplicated Reach

Total reach less
duplicated reach

The amount of reach can be estimated through the information contained in the target audience profile regarding customer group (i.e., loyal users or new category users) and other variables like demographics. Based on this information, media planners would know if the required reach is a niche market requiring a selective 10 percent or a broader audience of moving toward 50 percent, in whatever geographic or timing parameters are decided upon. While reach is an important decision, the duplicated reach resulting in a greater number of exposures for a portion of the target audience leads to the next question: What frequency of exposure is necessary for the ad to be seen and to have a communication effect?

What Frequency Level Is Needed?   With respect to media planning, *frequency* carries a particular meaning. Frequency is the average number of exposures a target audience individual receives from media vehicles in a specific time period. Frequency is dependent upon how much media target audience individuals consume. It can therefore range substantially, which raises the need to look at average frequency that is derived from a frequency distribution. Continuing with the TV example, ads placed once in each of the top ten shows in a given week would provide an average frequency of 1.36 (using BBM data from a randomly selected week).

$$\text{Frequency} = \frac{24 \text{ million exposures across 10 TV shows}}{17.6 \text{ million individuals exposed to ad}} = 1.36 \text{ exposures per person}$$

The 24 million exposures are calculated by adding the number of people who watched each show. However, some people watch two or more shows, resulting in fewer people actually exposed to the ad. Thus, the 17.6 million individuals exposed to the ad represent the total number of "unduplicated" viewers for all ten shows who potentially saw the 24 million exposures.

The 17.6 million is *estimated* by adding the unduplicated viewers for each of the ten shows. The most watched show was 3.216 million. To that number we add the unduplicated number of viewers for all the other nine shows. To calculate unduplicated numbers we adjust the actual ones downward by a percentage of possible repeat viewers.

The second most watched show reached 2.634 million, resulting in 2.384 million unduplicated viewers [i.e., $2.634 \times (34 - 3.216)/34$]. The percentage of people not watching the first show has an equal chance as those watching the second show. These calculations carry on for each subsequent show so that by the tenth show, the unduplicated audience is reduced; 1.946 million watching the tenth show but only .975 million new viewers. These calculations can be done for all media individually and combined across all media, but the general calculation remains as follows:

$$\text{Frequency} = \frac{\text{Total number of exposures}}{\text{Total number of unduplicated individuals exposed to media vehicle}}$$

The example with the BBM data is calculated with all viewers, but the data could be refined to a specific demographic and/or other variables used to profile the target audience. The general calculation remains the same, but the numbers will change correspondingly to observe the frequency of exposure for the target audience. Furthermore, actually calculating total exposures to estimate average frequency is generally done by computer software as the complexity intensifies exponentially with multiple media vehicles.

The above discussion suggests frequency is the number of times one is exposed to the media vehicle, not necessarily to the ad itself. While one study has estimated the actual audience for a commercial may be as much as 30 percent lower than that for the program, not all researchers agree.[15] Most advertisers do agree that a 1:1 exposure ratio does not exist. So while the ad may be placed in a certain vehicle, the fact that a consumer has been exposed to that vehicle does not ensure that it has been seen. As a result, the frequency level expressed in the media plan overstates the actual level of exposure to the ad. This overstatement has led some media buyers to refer to the reach of the media vehicle as "opportunities to see" an ad rather than actual exposure to it.

Having defined and illustrated the calculation of frequency, the question of how much frequency within an advertising cycle remains. Practitioners and researchers have investigated this question for decades, with one expert concluding that "Establishing frequency goals for an advertising campaign is a mix of art and science but with a definite bias toward art."[16] Figure 10-12 summarizes the effects that can be expected at different levels of exposure on the basis of research in this area. In addition to these results, research has shown that while the number of repetitions increases awareness rapidly, it has much less impact on attitudinal and behavioural responses.[17]

The idea of three exposures within an advertising cycle as being sufficient for communication effects to take hold implies that this average is the minimum; however, anyone in the target audience who receives only one or two exposures presumably would not be aware of the brand or understand its performance. Therefore, the average exposure level would have to be higher to ensure sufficient communication for all who were exposed to the message. Consider a media buy in which:

50 percent of audience is reached 1 time.
30 percent of audience is reached 5 times.
20 percent of audience is reached 10 times.

The average frequency is 4, which is slightly more than the number established as effective. Yet a full 50 percent of the audience receives only one exposure. Presumably a considerable portion of the money spent on advertising has been wasted because so many in the target audience were not exposed to the message.

Determining Effective Reach and Frequency   Since marketers have budget constraints, they must decide whether to increase reach at the expense of frequency or increase the frequency of exposure but to a smaller audience. A number of factors influence this decision. For example, a new product or brand introduction will attempt to maximize reach, particularly unduplicated reach, to create awareness in as many people as possible as quickly as possible. At the same time, for a high-involvement product or one whose benefits are not obvious, a certain level of frequency is needed to achieve effective reach.

Effective reach represents the percentage of a vehicle's audience reached at each effective frequency increment. This concept is based on the assumption that one exposure to an ad may not be enough to convey the desired message. As we saw earlier, no one knows the exact number of exposures necessary for an ad to make an impact, although advertisers have settled on three as the minimum. Effective reach (exposure) is shown in the shaded area in Figure 10-13 in the range of 3 to 10 exposures. Fewer than 3 exposures is considered insufficient reach, while more than 10 is considered overexposure and thus ineffective reach. This exposure level is no guarantee of effective communication; different messages may require more or fewer exposures. For example, Jack Myers, president of Myers Reports, argues that the three-exposure theory was valid in the 1970s when consumers were exposed to approximately 1,000 ads per day. Now that they are exposed to 3,000 to 5,000 per day, three exposures may not be enough. Adding in the fragmentation of television, the proliferation of magazines, and the advent of a variety of

Figure   10-12

The effects of frequency

1. One exposure of an ad to a target group within a purchase cycle has little or no effect.
2. Since one exposure is usually ineffective, the central goal of productive media planning should be to enhance frequency rather than reach.
3. The evidence suggests strongly that an exposure frequency of two within a purchase cycle is an effective level.
4. Beyond three exposures within a brand purchase cycle or over a period of four or even eight weeks, increasing frequency continues to build advertising effectiveness at a decreasing rate but with no evidence of decline.
5. Although there are general principles with respect to frequency of exposure and its relationship to advertising effectiveness, differential effects by brand are equally important.
6. Frequency response principles or generalizations do not vary by medium.
7. The data strongly suggest that wearout is not a function of too much frequency; it is more of a creative or copy problem.

Figure 10-13 Graph of effective reach

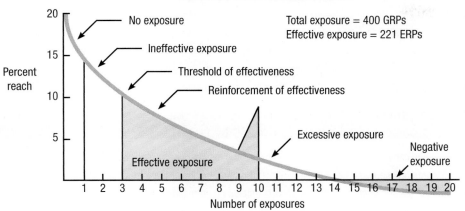

Total Exposure versus Effective Exposure of a Prime-Time Television Schedule

No exposure
Ineffective exposure
Threshold of effectiveness
Reinforcement of effectiveness
Effective exposure
Excessive exposure
Negative exposure

Total exposure = 400 GRPs
Effective exposure = 221 ERPs

GRPs = Gross rating points
ERPs = Effective rating points

Percent reach

Number of exposures

alternative media leads Myers to believe that 12 exposures may be the minimum level of frequency required. Also, Jim Surmanek, vice president of International Communications Group, contends that the complexity of the message, message length, and recency of exposure also impact this figure.[18]

Perhaps the best advice for determining optimal reach and frequency levels is offered by Ostrow, who recommends the following strategies:[19]

- Instead of using **average frequency**, the marketer should decide what minimum frequency goal is needed to reach the advertising objectives effectively and then maximize reach at that frequency level.
- To determine **minimum effective frequency**, one must consider marketing factors, message factors, and media factors. (See Figure 10-14.)

While the idea of minimum effective frequency has been used extensively in the advertising industry, there are some concerns with its use in more recent years.[20] In contrast, with the growth of more media outlets and enhanced syndicated data, minimum effective frequency within and across combinations of media provide opportunity for more efficient and effective use of media expenditures.[21]

Using Gross Ratings Points A summary indicator that combines the reach (duplicated) and the average frequency during an advertising cycle (e.g., one week, or 4 weeks) and is commonly used as a reference point is known as a **gross ratings point (GRP)**. The GRP can best be understood by an equation:

$$1 \text{ GRP} = \text{Reach of } 1\% \times \text{Frequency of } 1$$

Like both reach and frequency, GRP calculations are time dependent so that one can plan, calculate, or purchase a GRP on a weekly or monthly basis. We return to a TV placement example to see how this works. If one ad is placed on a top Canadian show with 10 percent reach, then the company has purchased 10 GRPs. If the show happens to be 60 minutes or 3 hours (e.g., a sports game), then the number of GRPs could grow to 20 or 30 if the ad is run two or three times, respectively. Of course, this assumes the audience size has remained the same throughout the show.

Extensive amounts of audience data exist, and combined with computer applications, the planning and scheduling of GRPs is a relatively routine practice. However, most media planners rely on their experience and judgment to complement the quantitative side. GRPs can be calculated for the total population aged 2+, adults 18+, adults 18–34, adults 18–49, or several other measured demographic groups.

Figure   10-14

Factors important in determining frequency levels

Marketing Factors

- *Brand history.* New brands generally require higher frequency levels.
- *Brand share.* The higher the brand share, the lower the frequency level required.
- *Brand loyalty.* The higher the loyalty, the lower the frequency level required.
- *Purchase cycles.* Shorter purchasing cycles require higher frequency levels to attain awareness.
- *Usage cycle.* Products consumed frequently usually require a higher level of frequency.
- *Share of voice.* Higher frequency levels are required with many competitors.
- *Target audience.* Target group's ability to learn and retain messages affects frequency.

Message or Creative Factors

- *Message complexity.* The simpler the message, the less frequency required.
- *Message uniqueness.* The more unique the message, the lower the frequency level required.
- *New versus continuing campaigns.* New campaigns require higher levels of frequency.
- *Image versus product sell.* Image ads require higher levels of frequency than product sell ads.
- *Message variation.* A single message requires less frequency; multiple messages require more.
- *Wearout.* Higher frequency may lead to wearout.
- *Advertising units.* Larger units of advertising require less frequency than smaller ones.

Media Factors

- *Clutter.* More frequency is needed to break through when a media has more advertising.
- *Editorial environment.* Less frequency is needed if the ad is consistent with the editorial environment.
- *Attentiveness.* Media vehicles with higher attention levels require less frequency.
- *Scheduling.* Continuous scheduling requires less frequency than does flighting or pulsing.
- *Number of media used.* The fewer media used, the lower the level of frequency required.
- *Repeat exposures.* Media that allow for more repeat exposures require less frequency.

Aggregating across multiple shows, media planners can calculate any number of GRPs to achieve their communication objectives. For example, 120 GRPs might be needed in a given week if the planner wants a reach of 30 percent and an average frequency of 4. In this example of 120 GRPs, a media planner would need to run ads on multiple shows and days to achieve these reach and frequency levels.

The purchase of 120 GRPs could mean 60 percent of the audience is exposed twice, or 20 percent of the audience is exposed six times, or 40 percent of the audience is exposed three times, and so on. Thus, for a fixed level of GRPs, there is an inverse relationship between reach and frequency. To know how many GRPs are necessary, the manager decides the minimum effective frequency and the amount of reach necessary based on the communication and media objectives established from the situation analysis, marketing strategy, and IMC strategy.

The chart in Figure 10-15 illustrates the trade-off between reach and frequency given a fixed number of GRPs. A purchase of 100 GRPs on one network yields a lower reach—just over 30 percent of the target audience, which translates into a frequency of about 3 ($100 = 33.3 \times 3$). The reach climbs to about 40 percent if two networks are used with a frequency of about 2.5 ($100 = 40 \times 2.5$). The reach then climbs to about 50 percent if three networks are used with a frequency of about 2 ($100 = 50 \times 2$). The increase in reach levels off as the incremental growth of adding more exposure does not affect very many new people in the target audience, and in fact the exposure growth begins to increase the amount of frequency as a greater number within the target audience see the ad more often. For example, at 600 GRPs the reach is 60 percent with a frequency of 10 ($600 = 60 \times 10$).

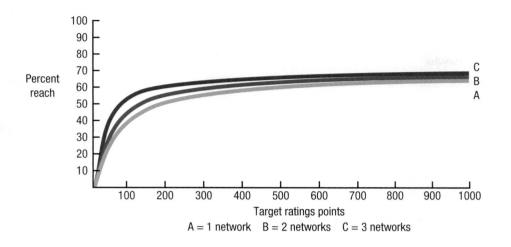

Figure 10-15

Estimates of reach for network GRPs

Media Tactics Decisions

Once the initial media strategy has been determined, the marketer addresses three media tactics decisions: media vehicle, relative cost estimates, and blocking chart.

MEDIA VEHICLE

Once the medium or media has been determined, the media planner must consider the most suitable media class and media vehicle. Certain media classes and media vehicles enhance the creativity of a message because they create a mood that carries over to the communication. The mood is much different on varying classes of TV channels such as sports, comedy, drama, or news. Also, think about the moods created by the following magazines: *NUVO, Golf Canada, Canadian Gardening,* and *Style at Home.* Each of these special-interest vehicles puts the reader in a particular mood. The promotion of clothing, golf equipment, gardening tools, and home products is enhanced by this mood. What different images might be created for a product advertised in the following media?

The National Post versus the *Toronto Star*
Hello! Canada versus *Tribute Magazine*
A highly rated prime-time TV show versus an old rerun

The message may require a specific media and a certain media vehicle to achieve its objectives. Likewise, certain media and vehicles have images that may carry over to the perceptions of messages placed within them. The explanation of these considerations is the **vehicle source effect**, which is defined as the differential impact that the advertising exposure will have on the same audience member if the exposure occurs in one medium versus another.[22] People perceive ads differently depending on their context.[23]

Sometimes advertisers find themselves objecting to the type of show or its content and decide not to advertise with a specific media vehicle. Microsoft initially planned to sponsor a special episode of *Family Guy* to promote Windows 7. The creators planned computer and Microsoft jokes; however, the "subversive and unique" humour regularly witnessed on the show proved too much for the executives (who, incidentally, watch the show themselves on a regular basis). In the end, Microsoft announced that the content "was not a fit with the Windows brand."[24]

An extension of this idea is the development of media engagement, where the media experiences of specific vehicles are identified along the global dimensions: inspiration, trustworthy, life enhancing, social involvement, and personal timeout. The purpose of this more detailed investigation of the media experience is to find a more specific link between the media vehicle and communication and behavioural effects.[25]

Related to the idea of directing messages to customers or non-customers, one author recommends finding a fit between the brand users and the media vehicle selected. Through the use of survey and syndicated data, the researcher concluded that demographic matching of target audience and media vehicle is less effective versus a similarity of brand and media vehicle users in terms of values. The author suggests that finding media vehicles that brand users are experiencing is possible for most major media.[26]

Once the media vehicle consideration is resolved, the media planner considers some other fine-tuning. The location within a particular medium (front page versus back page) and size of ad or length of commercial also merit examination. IMC Perspective 10-2 identifies award-winning marketing communication where both media strategy and key media tactics contributed significantly to the success.

RELATIVE COST ESTIMATES

The value of any strategy can be determined by how well it delivers the message effectively to the audience with the lowest cost and the least waste. The media planner strives for optimal delivery by balancing costs associated with each of the media strategy decisions. Media planning is inherently a series of trade-offs between reach and frequency or geographic coverage and scheduling, among others. As these trade-offs are investigated and finalized, the media planner estimates and compares costs. Advertising and promotional costs can be categorized in two ways, in terms of absolute cost and relative cost.

The **absolute cost** of the medium or vehicle is the actual total cost required to place the message. For example, a full-page four-colour ad in *Chatelaine* magazine costs about $42,000. **Relative cost** refers to the relationship between the price paid for advertising time or space and the size of the audience delivered. Relative costs are important because the manager must try to optimize audience delivery within budget constraints. Since a number of alternatives are available for delivering the message, the advertiser must evaluate the relative costs associated with these choices. For example, the media planner could compare the relative cost of reaching a member of the target audience in one magazine versus another. This decision can be influenced by the absolute cost of one magazine having a cheaper back page price versus another magazine. As the number of media alternatives rises, the number of comparisons grows considerably, potentially making this a tedious and difficult process. Media planners typically use two calculations, CPM and CPRP, to compare both media mix options or media vehicle options.

1. **Cost per thousand (CPM).** Magazines, and some other media, provide cost breakdowns on the basis of cost per thousand people reached. The formula for this computation is

$$\text{CPM} = \frac{\text{Cost of ad space (absolute cost)}}{\text{Circulation}} \times 1,000$$

Figure 10-16 provides an example of this computation for two vehicles in the same medium—*Canadian Living* and *Chatelaine*—and shows that *Canadian Living* is a more cost-efficient buy for a comparable full page ad. However, many might consider the difference not substantial enough to influence the decision on which vehicle to select.

Figure 10-16

Cost per thousand computations: *Canadian Living* versus *Chatelaine*

	Canadian Living	**Chatelaine**
Per-page cost	$50,360	$51,920
Circulation	556,859	552,647
Calculation of CPM	$\dfrac{\$50,360 \times 1,000}{556,859}$	$\dfrac{\$51,920 \times 1,000}{552,647}$
CPM	$90.44	$93.95

Advertising with Technology, Media, and Content

The AToMiC awards celebrate the achievements of combined efforts in advertising (A), technology (T), media creativity (M), and content (C). Media, digital, or creative agencies can enter their work for the competition presuming it is AToMiC—meaning the marketing communication is innovative by going against conventional thinking and uses elements in all four areas. A number of winners showed the talent found in Canada; here are a few snapshots showing key media tactical decisions in action.

With respect to when to execute messages, brands like Kraft Dinner, IKEA, and an ad agency itself all hit the mark with a perfect execution in the nick of time. Kraft Dinner, otherwise known as KD, counted down the hypothetical impending doom of the world (according to the Mayan calendar!) by inventing the "KD Pocalypse" where consumers discussed how KD would be their last meal. An out-of-home and social media campaign asked Canadians to tweet, "I want my last meal to be KD" with #KDpocalypse to receive a free sample. IKEA passed out branded packing boxes to apartment movers in Montreal on the July 1 weekend, an annual event as leases expire throughout the city. The message provided a key reminder of the household furniture and goods store as people likely perceived the need for new items after settling into their new digs. Finally, Taxi created a stunt where they put a car in a giant man-made pothole in Montreal and launched an app so drivers could identify potholes throughout the city. This celebrated their twentieth anniversary as an agency by highlighting their creativity and offering a public service as people found 7,000 needed repairs and the app communicated the information to the city.

When new car brands are launched, a difficult task is to get the brand into consumers' consideration set and prompt a visit to the dealership for a test drive or first-hand investigation of how it looks. Brands look to new ways, and these new ways need to be less expensive compared to alternative means. Audi set up slot-car racetrack in Toronto's financial district where 4,000 people took motorized

A4s for a spin on a mini-track resulting in 2,000 microsite visits and 118,000 YouTube channel views. VW let consumers use their smartphones and an augmented reality app to control an enhanced billboard and view the VW Beetle perform stunts. The event attracted 3 million website visits and 148 million online impressions.

Finally, brands look for specific media vehicles when implementing their plans, and Sony's Xperia Ion phone and P&G's Cheer detergent found a good fit with their executions. MTV.ca hosted four episodes of a Sony show that featured artists creating music with unusual items as instruments, all shot with the phone's HD video camera. A little over a half million viewers witnessed the performances and a total of 11 million media impressions ensued. A music video of the band Strange Talk included live links on colourful items (e.g., shirts, leggings); when clicked, users linked to the Cheer Facebook page to win the item, a free sample, and received the opportunity to read about the product. Cheer managers looked to young consumers, new users in this category, who wore colourful clothes since that fit with the key benefit claim of the brand. The "Dig It! Get It!" campaign lifted purchase intent by 7 percent and claimed 47,000 new Facebook fans.

Sources: Matthew Chung, "AToMiC Awards: Perfect Timing," *Strategy*, May 29, 2013; Matthew Chung, "AToMiC Awards: Car Brands Tune Up Test Drives," *Strategy*, May 29, 2013; Jennifer Horn, "AToMiC Awards: Brands Join the Band," *Strategy*, May 29, 2013.

Question:

1. Which of these media executions appears to be the most innovative?

Like magazines, newspapers now use the cost-per-thousand formula to determine relative costs. As shown in Figure 10-17, the *National Post* costs significantly less to advertise in than does *The Globe and Mail* based on a national advertiser spending $1 million annually.

Some media, such as Internet banner ads, quote their prices in terms of CPM. So if a banner ad placement has a CPM of $30, the media buyer would select the banner ad over these magazine and newspaper examples *if cost efficiency is deemed the only decision criterion.* However, virtually all media placement decisions involve multiple criteria beyond pure cost efficiency. In this case, the size of the ads is dramatically different as would be other factors.

2. **Cost per ratings point (CPRP).** The broadcast media provide a different comparative cost figure, referred to as cost per ratings point or *cost per point (CPP),* based on the following formula:

$$CPRP = \frac{\text{Cost of commercial time}}{\text{Program rating}}$$

An example of this calculation for a spot ad in a local TV market is shown in Figure 10-18. It indicates that Show A would be more cost-effective than Show B or Show C.

It is difficult to make comparisons across media. What is the broadcast equivalent of cost per thousand? In an attempt to standardize relative costing procedures, the broadcast and newspaper media have begun to provide costs per thousand, using the following formulas:

$$\text{Television: } \frac{\text{Cost of 1 unit of time} \times 1,000}{\text{Program rating}} \qquad \text{Newspapers: } \frac{\text{Cost of ad space} \times 1,000}{\text{Circulation}}$$

While the comparison of media on a cost-per-thousand basis is important, intermedia comparisons can be misleading. The ability of TV to provide both sight and sound, the longevity of magazines, and other characteristics of each medium make direct comparisons difficult. The media planner should use the cost-per-thousand numbers but must also consider the specific characteristics of each medium and each media vehicle in the decision.

The cost per thousand may overestimate or underestimate the actual cost efficiency. Consider a situation where some waste coverage is inevitable because the circulation exceeds the target audience. If the people reached by this message are not potential buyers of the product, then having to pay to reach them results in too low a cost per thousand, as shown in scenario A of

---

Figure   10-17

Comparative costs in newspaper advertising

	The Globe and Mail	National Post
Cost per page	$56,224	$34,490
Circulation	313,331	422,800
Calculation	$CPM = \dfrac{\text{Page cost} \times 1,000}{\text{Circulation}}$	
	$= \dfrac{\$56,224 \times 1,000}{313,331}$	$\dfrac{\$34,490 \times 1,000}{422,800}$
	= $179.44	$81.58

Figure   10-18

Comparison of cost per ratings point in a local TV market

	Show A	Show B	Show C
Cost per spot ad	$5,000	$10,000	$16,000
Rating	20	10	40
Calculation	$5,000/20	$10,000/10	$16,000/40
CPRP (CPP)	$250	$1,000	$400

Figure 10-19. We must use the potential reach to the target audience—the destination sought—rather than the overall circulation figure. A medium with a much higher cost per thousand may be a wiser buy if it is reaching more potential receivers. (Most media buyers rely on **target CPM (TCPM)**, which calculates CPMs based on the target audience, not the overall audience.)

CPM may also underestimate cost efficiency. Sellers of magazine advertising space have argued for years that because more than one person may read an issue, the actual reach is underestimated. They want to use the number of **readers per copy** as the true circulation. This would include a **pass-along rate**, estimating the number of people who read the magazine without buying it. Scenario B in Figure 10-19 shows how this underestimates cost efficiency. Consider a family in which a father, mother, and two teenagers read each issue of *Maclean's*. While the circulation figure includes only one magazine, in reality there are four potential exposures in this household, increasing the total reach.

While the number of readers per copy makes intuitive sense, it has the potential to be extremely inaccurate. The actual number of times the magazine changes hands is difficult to determine. While research is conducted, pass-along estimates are very subjective and using them to estimate reach is speculative. These figures are regularly provided by the media, but managers are selective about using them. At the same time the art of media buying enters, for many magazines' managers have a good idea how much greater the reach is than their circulation figures provided.

A majority of the cost data for media is found with Canadian Advertising Rates and Data (CARD). This subscription service offers extensive information regarding all media. For example, it identifies every media outlet and gives a description of its service and audience. The resource also provides the actual costs of many media for computing the media budget. Data regarding some media are not provided (e.g., TV), while some promotional media costs (e.g., coupon book) are included. Students can typically retrieve this information through the library's computer network or the monthly reports kept in the periodical section of their school's library. We will address specific media costs in each of the subsequent media chapters, but as the past

Scenario A: Overestimation of Efficiency

Target audience	18–49
Magazine circulation	400,000
Circulation to target audience	65% (260,000)
Cost per page	$15,600

$$\text{CPM} = \frac{\$15,600 \times 1,000}{400,000} = \$39$$

$$\text{CPM (actual target audience)} = \frac{\$15,600 \times 1,000}{260,000} = \$60$$

Scenario B: Underestimation of Efficiency

Target audience	All age groups, male and female
Magazine circulation	400,000
Cost per page	$15,600
Pass-along rate	3

$$\text{CPM (based on readers per copy)} = \frac{\text{Page cost} \times 1,000}{260,000 + 3(260,000)} = \frac{\$15,600 \times 1,000}{1,040,000}$$

$$= \$15.00$$

*Assuming pass-along was valid.

Figure 10-19

Cost per thousand estimates

several figures indicate, most media are purchased on a per unit basis; page for print, time for broadcast, and some, like Internet banner ads, on a CPM basis.

BLOCKING CHART

The media planning process typically concludes with a blocking chart. The **blocking chart** summarizes many of the media-strategy and media-tactics decisions made thus far, and includes extensive implementation details that guide the media buyers as they attempt to achieve their objectives. An example for Shreddies cereal is shown in Figure 10-20 for both the test market and the launch.

A blocking chart is typically formatted according to some type of calendar. While it is often done on a weekly basis, a firm with limited communications may organize it monthly. On the other hand, a firm with extensive communications may produce a blocking chart on a daily basis for all or critical parts of its annual media plan. For example, if a firm launches a new product, daily communications during the first few weeks can be critical and specific media exposure is planned in minute detail.

A synopsis of the media choice decisions with respect to television, print, and out-of-home media may also be contained in the blocking chart. In this age of IMC, the blocking chart can also contain elements of other communication tools such as marketing events, public relations, or direct-response tools. In all likelihood, the blocking chart will break these media choices down by different vehicles and different geographic markets.

Another key detail of the blocking chart is showing the relative weight of media expenditures. For example, it could illustrate the number of GRPs per week for each city. Related to this is a clear indication of the reach and frequency of each media decision.

Figure   10-20   The Shreddies blocking chart shows all media and IMC tools

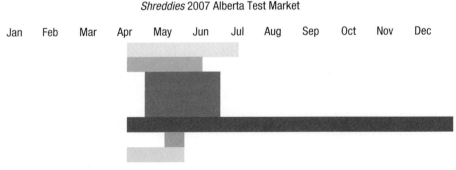

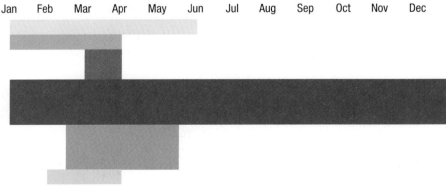

Because the blocking chart concludes the media planning process, the media expenditures have to be included either in summary form or accompanying the blocking chart. This information allows managers to assess the quality of the media plan and to determine whether any adjustments need to be made during the planning time frame.

While we have briefly highlighted the nature of a blocking chart, it may in fact be more than one chart. If a firm is using multiple media across many months and geographic markets, it may have one summary chart and other supporting charts that break the information down into more readable and action-oriented subsections. Remember that a blocking chart is also a communication tool that has to be organized and presented so that all participants are familiar with all decisions.

(L04) Budget Setting

This section begins with a brief overview of the budget setting process, provides insight into underlying theory with respect to budget setting, discusses how companies budget for promotional efforts, and demonstrates the inherent strengths and weaknesses associated with these theoretical and managerial approaches.

OVERVIEW

Establishing media and communication objectives is an important part of the media planning process; however, the degree to which these objectives can be attained is a function of the media budget or how much the firm wishes to invest in advertising. No organization has an unlimited budget, so objectives must be set with the budget in mind and the budget has to be realistic to achieve any media and communication objectives. We discus many budgeting methods even if they are not recommended. It is important to understand the methods since they are commonly employed by marketers, despite having disadvantages that limit their effectiveness. Tradition and top management's desire for control are probably the major reasons why certain managerial methods are so popular even though other methods offer stronger logic, but other issues are at play as well.

In a study of how managers make decisions regarding advertising and promotion budgeting decisions, researchers interviewed 21 managers in eight consumer-product firms and found that the budget-setting process is a perplexing issue and that institutional pressures led to a greater proportion of dollars being spent on sales promotions. The authors concluded that to successfully develop and implement the budget, managers must (1) employ a comprehensive strategy to guide the process, (2) develop a strategic planning framework that employs an integrated marketing communications philosophy, (3) build in contingency plans, (4) focus on long-term objectives, and (5) consistently evaluate the effectiveness of programs.[27]

Advertising agencies are involved in developing the messages for their clients, but curiously, they are not as involved with the managers of their client organizations when it comes to determining the budget.[28] The authors of this study identify factors inhibiting this opportunity: industry, organizational structure, politics, tradition, compensation system, trust, and length of relationship. They conclude that both agencies and clients could benefit with stronger partnerships on the budget amount. Clients would get a more complete recommendation from communication objectives to message and finally to media purchase while agencies would better understand the client's business and the pressures faced.

THEORETICAL APPROACHES IN BUDGET SETTING

Most of the approaches used to establish advertising budgets are based on marginal analysis or sales response models. These approaches are viewed as theoretical since academics have long debated the overall effects of advertising on sales, a topic that continually perplexes managers as well.

Marginal Analysis   Figure 10-21 graphically represents the concept of **marginal analysis**. As advertising/promotional expenditures increase, sales and gross margins also increase to a point, but then they level off. Profits are shown to be a result of the gross margin minus advertising expenditures. A marginal analysis theory suggests that a firm would continue to spend advertising/promotional dollars as long as the marginal revenues created by these expenditures exceeded the incremental advertising/promotional costs. As shown on the graph, the optimal expenditure level is the point where marginal costs equal the marginal revenues they generate (point A). If the sum of the advertising/promotional expenditures exceeded the revenues they generated, one would conclude the appropriations were too high and scale down the budget. If revenues were higher, a higher budget might be in order.

The logic of marginal analysis is weak due to two assumptions. The first is that sales are a direct result of advertising and promotional expenditures and this effect can be measured. In studies using sales as a direct measure, it has been almost impossible to establish the contribution of advertising and promotion.[29] Furthermore, it is generally believed that sales result from the successful attainment of behavioural and communication objectives relevant for target audience. The second is that advertising and promotion are solely responsible for sales. This assumption ignores the remaining elements of the marketing mix which do contribute to a company's success.

Sales Response Models   The sales curve in Figure 10-21 shows sales levelling off even though advertising and promotions efforts continue to increase. The relationship between advertising and sales has been the topic of much research and discussion designed to determine the shape of the response curve. Almost all advertisers subscribe to one of two models of the advertising/sales response function: the concave-downward response curve or the S-shaped response function.

According to the **concave-downward response curve** (Figure 10-22A), the effects of advertising expenditures on sales quickly begin to diminish. Researchers concluded that the effects of advertising budgets follow the microeconomic law of diminishing returns.[30] That is, as the amount of advertising increases, its incremental value decreases. The logic is that those with the greatest potential to buy will likely act on the first (or earliest) exposures, while those less likely to buy are not likely to change as a result of the advertising. For those who may be potential buyers, each additional ad will supply little or no new information that will affect their decision.

According to the **S-shaped response function** (Figure 10-22B), the effects of advertising expenditures on sales follow an S-shape. Initial outlays of the advertising budget have little impact (as indicated by the essentially flat sales curve in range A). After a certain budget level has been reached (the beginning of range B), advertising and promotional efforts begin to have an effect, as additional increments of expenditures result in increased sales. This incremental gain continues only to a point, however, because at the beginning of range C additional expenditures begin to return little or nothing in the way of sales. The logic is that advertising takes time before its effects (awareness, etc.) take hold.

Figure   10-21

Marginal analysis

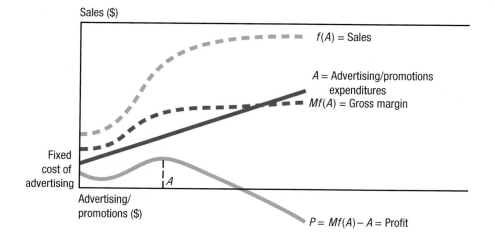

Figure 10-22 Advertising sales/response functions

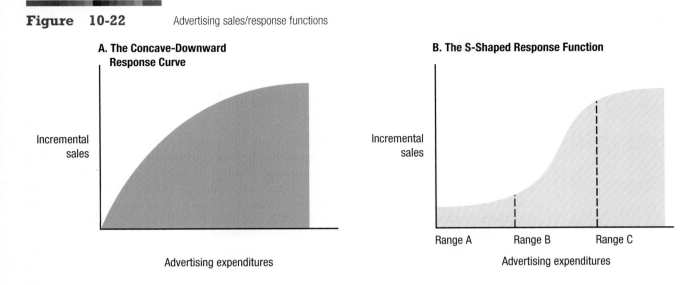

Even though marginal analysis and the sales response curves may not apply directly, they give managers insight into a theoretical basis of how the budgeting process should work. Empirical evidence indicates the models may have validity, however the advertising and sales effects may be reversed as we cannot be sure whether the results actually demonstrate the advertising/sales relationship or vice versa.

A weakness in attempting to use sales as a direct measure of response to advertising is the effect of situational factors as shown in Figure 10-23. For a product characterized by emotional buying motives, hidden product qualities, and/or a strong basis for differentiation, advertising

Figure 10-23 Factors influencing advertising budgets

Factor	Relationship of Advertising/Sales	Factor	Relationship of Advertising/Sales
Customer Factors		**Product Factors**	
Industrial products users	—	Basis for differentiation	+
Concentration of users	+	Hidden product qualities	+
Market Factors		Emotional buying motives	+
Stage of product life cycle		Durability	—
Introductory	+	Large dollar purchase	—
Growth	+	Purchase frequency	Curvilinear
Maturity	—	**Strategy Factors**	
Decline	—	Regional markets	—
Inelastic demand	+	Early stage of brand life cycle	+
Market share	—	High margins in channels	—
Competition		Long channels of distribution	+
Active	+	High prices	+
Concentrated	+	High quality	+
Pioneer in market	—	**Cost Factors**	
		High profit margins	+

Note: + relationship indicates a positive effect of advertising on sales; — relationship indicates little or no effect of advertising on sales.

would have a noticeable impact on sales. Products characterized as large-dollar purchases and those in the maturity or decline stages of the product would be less likely to benefit. These factors should be considered in the budget appropriation decision but should not be the sole determinants of where and when to increase or decrease expenditures.

MANAGERIAL APPROACHES IN BUDGET SETTING

This section reviews methods developed through practice and experience for setting budgets and the relative advantages and disadvantages of each. It is important to review many approaches since firms may employ more than one method and budgeting methods also vary according to the size and sophistication of the firm. One approach is **top-down budgeting** because an amount is established at an executive level and then the monies are passed down to the departments (as shown in Figure 10-24). Top-down methods include the affordable method, arbitrary allocation, percentage of sales, competitive parity, and return on investment (ROI). A flaw of these judgmental top-down methods is that it leads to predetermined budget appropriations not linked to the objectives and strategies designed to accomplish them. A more effective budgeting strategy would be to consider the firm's communication objectives and budget for the necessary promotional mix strategies to attain these goals. This is known as **bottom-up budgeting** and we review two approaches: the objective and task method and payout planning.

The Affordable Method   In the **affordable method**, the firm determines the amount to be spent in production and operations (and so on), and then allocates the remainder to advertising and promotion. The task to be performed by the advertising/promotions function is not considered, and the likelihood of under- or overspending is high, as no guidelines for measuring the effects of budgets are established. This approach is common among small firms where cash flow concerns are prominent. Unfortunately, it is also used in large firms, particularly those that are not marketing-driven and do not understand the role of advertising and promotion.

The logic for this approach stems from "We can't be hurt with this method" thinking. That is, if we know what we can afford and we do not exceed it, we will not get into financial problems. While this may be true in a strictly accounting sense, it does not reflect sound managerial decision making from a marketing perspective. Often this method does not allocate enough money to get the product off the ground and into the market. In terms of the S-shaped sales response

Figure   10-24

Top-down and bottom-up approaches to budget setting

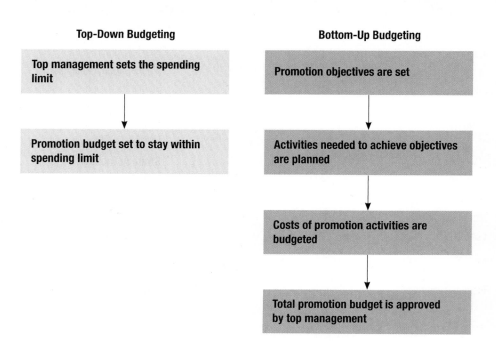

model, the firm is operating in range A. Or the firm may be spending more than necessary, operating in range C. When the market gets tough and sales and/or profits begin to fall, this method is likely to lead to budget cuts at a time when the budget should be increased.

Arbitrary Allocation   Perhaps an even weaker method than the affordable method for establishing a budget is **arbitrary allocation**, in which virtually no theoretical basis is considered and the budgetary amount is often set by fiat. That is, the budget is determined by management solely on the basis of what is felt to be necessary. The arbitrary allocation approach has no obvious advantages. No systematic thinking has occurred, no objectives have been budgeted for, and the concept and purpose of advertising and promotion have been largely ignored. Other than the fact that the manager believes some monies must be spent on advertising and promotion and then picks a number, there is no good explanation why this approach continues to be used. Yet budgets continue to be set this way, and our purpose in discussing this method is to point out only that it is used—not recommended.

Percentage of Sales   A commonly used method for budget setting is the **percentage-of-sales method**, in which the advertising and promotions budget is based on sales of the product. Management determines the amount by either (1) taking a percentage of the sales dollars or (2) assigning a fixed amount of the unit product cost to promotion and multiplying this amount by the number of units sold. These two methods are shown in Figure 10-25.

Proponents of the percentage-of-sales method cite a number of advantages. It is financially safe and keeps ad spending within reasonable limits, as it bases spending on the past year's sales or what the firm expects to sell in the upcoming year. Thus, there will be sufficient monies to cover this budget, with increases in sales leading to budget increases and sales decreases resulting in advertising decreases. The percentage-of-sales method is simple, straightforward, and easy to implement. Regardless of which basis—past or future sales—is employed, the calculations used to arrive at a budget are not difficult. Finally, this budgeting approach is generally stable. While the budget may vary with increases and decreases in sales, as long as these changes are not drastic the manager will have a reasonable idea of the parameters of the budget.

At the same time, the percentage-of-sales method has some serious disadvantages, including the basic premise on which the budget is established: sales. Letting the level of sales determine the amount of advertising and promotions dollars to be spent reverses the cause-and-effect relationship between advertising and sales. It treats advertising as an expense associated with making a sale rather than an investment.

Another problem with this approach was actually cited as an advantage earlier: stability. Proponents say that if all firms use a similar percentage that will bring stability to the marketplace. But what happens if someone varies from this standard percentage? The problem is that this method does not allow for changes in strategy either internally or from competitors. An

Method 1: Straight Percentage of Sales		
Year 1	Total dollar sales	$1,000,000
	Straight % of sales at 10%	$100,000
Year 2	Advertising budget	$100,000

Method 2: Percentage of Unit Cost		
Year 1	Cost per bottle to manufacturer	$4.00
	Unit cost allocated to advertising	$1.00
Year 2	Forecast sales, 100,000 units	
	Advertising budget (100,000 × $1)	$100,000

Figure 10-25

Alternative methods for computing percentage of sales

aggressive firm may wish to allocate more monies to the advertising and promotions budget, a strategy that is not possible with a percentage-of-sales method unless the manager is willing to deviate from industry standards.

The percentage-of-sales method of budgeting may result in severe misappropriation of funds. If advertising and promotion have a role to perform in marketing a product, then allocating more monies to advertising will, as shown in the S-shaped curve, generate incremental sales (to a point). If products with low sales have smaller promotion budgets, this will hinder sales progress. At the other extreme, very successful products may have excess budgets, some of which may be better appropriated elsewhere.

The percentage-of-sales method is also difficult to employ for new product introductions. If no sales histories are available, there is no basis for establishing the budget. Projections of future sales may be difficult, particularly if the product is highly innovative and/or has fluctuating sales patterns.

Finally, if the budget is contingent on sales, decreases in sales will lead to decreases in budgets when they most need to be increased. Continuing to cut the advertising and promotion budgets may just add impetus to the downward sales trend (Figure 10-26). Some argue that more successful companies allocate additional funds during hard times or downturns in the cycle of sales and are rewarded in future years.

A variation on the percentage-of-sales method uses a percentage of projected future sales as a base. This method also uses either a straight percentage of projected sales or a unit cost projection. One advantage of using future sales as a base is that the budget is not based on last year's sales. As the market changes, management must factor the effect of these changes on sales into next year's forecast rather than relying on past data. The resulting budget is more likely to reflect current conditions and be more appropriate. While this appears to be a remedy for some of the problems discussed here, the reality is that problems with forecasting, cyclical growth, and uncontrollable factors limit its effectiveness.

Competitive Parity   In many industries or product categories, we observe firms with similar advertising expenditures resulting from a competitive analysis. Competitors' advertising expenditures are available from market research firms, trade associations, advertising industry periodicals, and media tracking firms. This method is typically used in conjunction with other methods (e.g., percentage-of-sales).

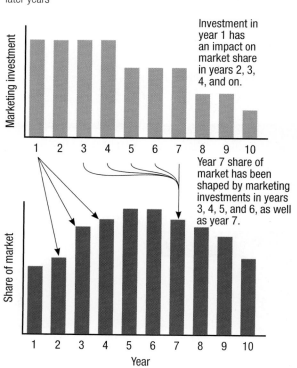

Figure   10-26

Investments pay off in later years

In the **competitive parity method**, managers establish budget amounts by matching the competition's percentage-of-sales expenditures, essentially taking advantage of the collective wisdom of the industry. It also takes the competition into consideration, which leads to stability in the marketplace by minimizing marketing expenditure battles. If companies know that competitors are unlikely to match their increases in promotional spending, they are less likely to take an aggressive posture to attempt to gain market share.

The competitive parity method has a number of disadvantages. First, it ignores the fact that advertising and promotions are designed to accomplish specific objectives by addressing certain problems and opportunities. Second, it assumes that because firms have similar expenditures, their programs will be equally effective. This assumption ignores the success of creative executions, media allocations, and/or promotion. Third, it ignores advantages of the firm itself—some companies simply make better products than others. A study by Yoo and Mandhachitara indicates that a competitive parity strategy must consider the fact that a competitor's advertising can actually benefit one's own firm, and that one competitor's gain is not always the other's loss. As shown in Figure 10-27 there are four different situations to determine how the competitive budgets may impact sales—only one of which involves the zero-sum scenario.[31]

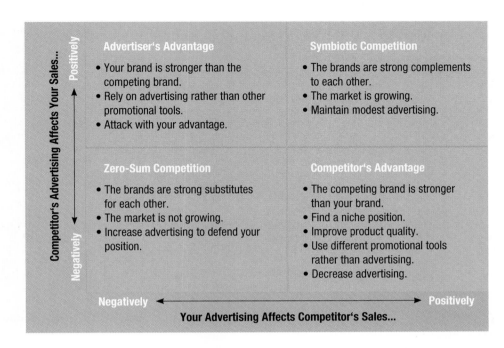

Figure 10-27

Competitors' advertising outlays do not always hurt

Fourth, there is no guarantee that competitors will continue to pursue their existing strategies. Since competitive parity figures are determined by examination of competitors' previous years' promotional expenditures, changes in market emphasis and/or spending may not be recognized until the competition has already established an advantage. Further, there is no guarantee that a competitor will not increase or decrease its own expenditures, regardless of what other companies do.

Return on Investment (ROI)   In the percentage-of-sales method, sales dictate the level of advertising appropriations. But advertising causes sales as seen in the marginal analysis and S-shaped curve approaches; incremental investments in advertising and promotions lead to increases in sales. The key word here is *investment*. In the **ROI budgeting method**, advertising and promotions are considered investments, like plant and equipment. Thus, the budgetary appropriation (investment) leads to certain returns. Like other aspects of the firm's efforts, advertising and promotion are expected to earn a certain return.

While the ROI method looks good on paper, the reality is that it is rarely possible to assess the returns provided by the promotional effort—at least as long as sales continue to be the basis for evaluation. Thus, while managers are certain to ask how much return they are getting for such expenditures, the question remains unanswered, and ROI remains a virtually unused method of budgeting.

Objective and Task Method   It is important that objective setting and budgeting go hand in hand rather than sequentially. It is difficult to establish a budget without specific objectives in mind, and setting objectives without regard to how much money is available makes no sense. The **objective and task method** of budget setting consists of three steps: (1) defining the communications objectives to be accomplished, (2) determining the specific strategies and tasks needed to attain them, and (3) estimating the costs associated with performance of these strategies and tasks. The total budget is based on the accumulation of these costs. As shown in Figure 10-28, this process involves several steps:

1. *Isolate objectives.* A company will have marketing and communication objectives to achieve. After the former are established, the firm determines the specific communications objectives needed to accomplish these goals. Communication objectives must be specific, attainable, and measurable, as well as time limited.
2. *Determine tasks required.* A number of elements are involved in the strategic plan designed to attain the objectives established. These tasks may include advertising in media, sales

Figure   10-28

The objective and task method

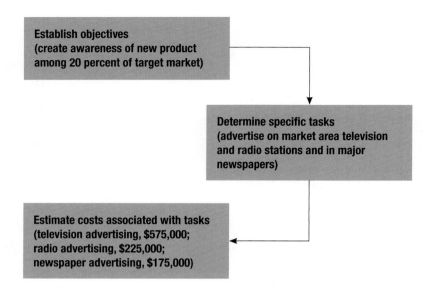

promotions, and/or other elements of the promotional mix, each with its own role to perform.

3. *Estimate required expenditures.* Buildup analysis requires determining the estimated costs associated with the tasks developed in the previous step. For example, it involves costs for developing awareness through advertising, trial through sampling, and so forth.

4. *Monitor.* As we saw in Chapter 9 on measuring effectiveness, there are ways to determine how well one is attaining established objectives. Performance should be monitored and evaluated in light of the budget appropriated.

5. *Reevaluate objectives.* Once specific objectives have been attained, monies may be better spent on new goals. Thus, if one has achieved the level of consumer awareness sought, the budget should be altered to stress a higher-order objective such as evaluation or trial.

The major advantage of the objective and task method is that the budget is driven by the objectives to be attained. The managers closest to the marketing effort will have specific strategies and input into the budget-setting process.

The major disadvantage of this method is the difficulty of determining which tasks will be required and the costs associated with each. For example, specifically what tasks are needed to attain awareness among 50 percent of the target audience? How much will it cost to perform these tasks? While these decisions are easier to determine for certain objectives—for example, estimating the costs of sampling required to stimulate trial in a defined market area—it is not always possible to know exactly what is required and/or how much it will cost to complete the job. This process is easier if there is past experience to use as a guide, with either the existing product or a similar one in the same product category. For this situation, payout planning is offered as an alternative bottom-up approach.

Payout Planning   The first months of a new product's introduction typically require heavier-than-normal advertising and promotion appropriations to stimulate higher levels of awareness and subsequent trial. After studying more than 40 years of Nielsen figures, James O. Peckham estimated that the average share of advertising to sales ratio necessary to launch a new product successfully is approximately 1.5:2.0.[32] This means that a new entry should be spending at approximately twice the desired market share, as shown in the two examples in Figure 10-29. For example, brand 101 gained a 12.6 percent market share by spending 34 percent of the total advertising dollars in this food product category.

To determine how much to spend, marketers often develop a **payout plan** that determines the investment value of the advertising and promotion appropriation. The basic idea is to project the revenues the product will generate, as well as the costs it will incur, over two to three years. Based on an expected rate of return, the payout plan will assist in determining how much advertising and promotions expenditure will be necessary when the return might be expected.

New Brands of Food Products

Brand	Average share of advertising	Attained share of sales	Ratio of share of advertising to share of sales
101	34%	12.6%	2.7
102	16	10.0	1.6
103	8	7.6	1.1
104	4	2.6	1.5
105	3	2.1	1.4

Figure 10-29

Share of advertising/sales relationship (two-year summary)

A three-year payout plan is shown in Figure 10-30. The product would lose money in year 1, almost break even in year 2, and finally begin to show substantial profits by the end of year 3.

The advertising and promotion figures are highest in year 1 and decline in years 2 and 3 reflecting additional outlays needed to make a rapid impact. For example, retailers expect immediate success otherwise they will move on to other products needing their limited shelf space. The budget also reflects the firm's guidelines for new product expenditures, since companies generally have set deadlines to establish profitability. Finally, building market share may be more difficult than maintaining it—thus the substantial dropoff in expenditures in later years. When used in conjunction with the objective and task method, payout planning provides a logical approach to budget setting.

(L05) IMC Planning: Budget Allocation

Once the overall budget has been determined, the next step is to allocate it. The allocation decision involves determining the relative expenditures across IMC tools and markets while accounting for market-share goals, client/agency policies, and organizational characteristics.

IMC TOOLS

The promotional budget is allocated to broadcast, print, and out-of-home media as suggested in the media plan, and among other IMC tools such as sales promotion, public relations, Internet, and direct marketing. As noted in Chapter 1, firms are increasingly evaluating and employing all IMC tools to achieve their communication and behavioural objectives. The degree to which a firm uses more tools to achieve its objectives influences the relative emphasis. Figure 10-31 summarizes examples of traditional media plans and others with evolving IMC tools.[33]

These examples are reflected in macro statistics cited earlier. As shown in Figure 10-1, total Canadian expenditures for media advertising, Internet, and catalogue/direct mail total $15 billion. Some of these IMC tools continue their strength over time. For example, television advertising consistently commands approximately one-quarter of all media expenditures at

	Year 1	Year 2	Year 3
Product sales	15.0	35.50	60.75
Profit contribution (@ $0.50/case)	7.5	17.75	30.38
Advertising/promotions	15.0	10.50	8.50
Profit (loss)	(7.5)	7.25	21.88
Cumulative profit (loss)	(7.5)	(0.25)	21.63

Figure 10-30

Example of three-year payout plan ($ millions)

Figure   10-31   Summary of examples of target and media choices

Brand	Target	Media
Newfoundland & Labrador Tourism $5 million	Sophisticated travelers 45+, 25-34 (no-nesting) Desiring intriguing experiences	TV (Specialty channels), Newspaper (display & insert) Cinema, In-flight video Online Rich Media (Weather Network/Fresh Air)
Nissan Sentra SE-R $1 million	Auto enthusiasts Men Desiring commuter transport	YouTube channel, YouTube take-over Pre-roll, Page domination (*Sympatico/Top Gear*) TV teaser ads
Knorr Sidekicks $4 million	Users of competing product Moms Desiring lower salt product	Pre-launch: Direct mail to current users Wave 1: TV, Magazine, Digital (banner), In-store Wave 2: Wave 1 plus Premium, Social Media

about $3.5 billion; however, the dispersion between conventional and specialty channels is closer. Radio continues with consistent year after year growth and a strong local presence while receiving $1.6 billion in advertising revenue.

Representing print media, daily newspapers, community newspapers, and consumer magazines constitute one-quarter of all media expenditures at almost $3.7 billion. Other estimated media that is mostly print, catalogue/direct mail, Yellow Pages, and miscellaneous represents $2.5 billion. In contrast, Internet grew from $562 million in 2005 to $3.1 billion in 2012, accounting for 21 percent of all media expenditures, and appears as a key part of most IMC plans.

In comparison, other promotional tools constitute extensive expenditures. Public relations activities like sponsorship approach $1 billion, while promotional products approximate $2 billion in Canada. And while an accurate accounting for all sales promotion expenditures is difficult to achieve, a conservative estimate of sales promotion expenditures at 2 percent of all Canadian retail sales culminates in a total of $7 billion.

As these macro statistics indicate, firms have a variety of tools and approaches for delivering messages to their target audiences, and careful consideration of the allocation across the tools each year is a central task for IMC planning. The budget allocation across media has been the focus of some research to find the right combination of media, and providing the optimal expenditure levels is a critical decision that has long-lasting communication and financial implications. A study of the SUV market found that the effects of the media mix for the Ford Explorer outperformed the effects of the media mix for the Jeep Grand Cherokee. The authors conclude that balance between image-oriented media versus more tactical media had stronger effects for this set of data.[34] Another study concludes that some media have longer carryover effects versus other media, which should also guide the media allocation decision for advertising.[35] The next research step is to assess the relative effects across different combinations of IMC tools.

MARKET SHARE GOALS

While the budget should be allocated according the specific promotional tools needed to accomplish the objectives, the size of the market affects the amount of money invested in promotion. In smaller markets, it is often easier and less expensive to reach the target audience and high expenditure in these markets will lead to wasted overage. In larger markets, the target audience may be more dispersed and thus more expensive to reach. Also, a marketing manager may allocate additional monies to markets that hold higher potential; just because a market does not have high sales does not mean it should be ignored. The key is potential, since a market with low sales and high growth potential may be a candidate for additional appropriations.

Two studies in the *Harvard Business Review* discussed advertising spending with the goal of maintaining and increasing market share.[36] John Jones compared the brand's share of market with its share of advertising voice (the total value of the main media exposure in the product category). Jones classified the brands as "profit taking brands, or underspenders" and "investment brands, those whose share of voice is clearly above their share of market." His study indicated that for those brands with small market shares, profit takers are in the minority; however, as the brands increase their market share, nearly three out of five have a proportionately smaller share of voice.

Jones noted three factors explained this change. First, new brands generally receive higher-than-average advertising support. Second, older, more mature brands are often "milked"—that is, when they reach the maturity stage, advertising support is reduced. Third, there's an advertising economy of scale whereby advertising works harder for well-established brands, so a lower expenditure is required. Jones concluded that for larger brands, it may be possible to reduce advertising expenditures and still maintain market share. Smaller brands, on the other hand, have to continue to maintain a large share of voice.

James Schroer addressed the advertising budget in a situation where the marketer wishes to increase market share. His analysis suggests that marketers should focus on markets where competition is weak and/or underspending instead of advertising nationally. Figure 10-32 shows Schroer's suggestions for spending priorities in different markets.

One factor influencing these suggestions is **economies of scale** in advertising. It is argued that larger advertisers can maintain advertising shares that are smaller than their market shares because they get better advertising rates, have declining average costs of production, and accrue the advantages of advertising several products jointly. In addition, they are likely to enjoy more favourable time and space positions, cooperation of intermediaries, and favourable publicity.

Some studies have presented evidence that firms and/or brands maintaining a large share of the market have an advantage over smaller competitors and thus can spend less money on advertising and realize a better return.[37] Reviewing the studies in support of this position and then conducting research over a variety of small-package products, Kent Lancaster found that this situation did not hold true and that in fact larger brand share products might actually be at a disadvantage.[38] His results indicated that leading brands spend an average of 2.5 percentage points more than their brand share on advertising. The results of this and other studies suggest there really are no economies of scale to be accrued from the size of the firm or the market share of the brand.[39]

ORGANIZATIONAL FACTORS

A review on how allocation decisions are made between advertising and sales promotion concluded that organizational factors play an important role.[40] The authors noted the following factors influence the decision: organizational structure, power and politics, use of expert opinions (e.g., consultants), preferences and experiences of the decision maker, approval and negotiation channels, and pressure on senior managers to arrive at the optimal budget.

One example of how these factors influence allocations relates to the level of interaction between marketing and other functional departments, such as accounting and operations. The authors note that the relative importance of advertising versus sales promotion might vary from department to department. Accountants, being dollars-and-cents minded, would argue for the sales impact of promotions, while operations would argue against sales promotions because

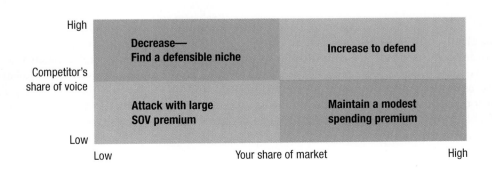

Figure 10-32

The share of voice (SOV) effect and ad spending: priorities in individual markets the sudden surges in demand that might result would throw off production schedules. The marketing department might be influenced by the thinking of either of these groups in making its decision.

The tendencies can also be seen with the agency that may discourage the allocation of monies to sales promotion, preferring to spend them on the advertising area. The agency may take the position that these monies are harder to track in terms of effectiveness and may be used improperly if not under its control. Furthermore, ad agencies are managed by officers who have ascended through the creative ranks and are inclined to emphasize the creative budget while others may have preferences for a specific medium. Finally, both the agency and the client may favour certain aspects of the promotional program, perhaps on the basis of past successes, that will substantially influence where dollars are spent.

Learning Objectives Summary

 Illustrate how a media plan is developed.

Media planning involves delivering the marketing communications message through different channels such as television, radio, print, and out-of-home, among others. Media planning is required for advertising to deliver the creative strategy but also for any other IMC tool. For example, a sales promotion offer might be communicated over the radio, a charity event that a brand sponsors could be found in a local city newspaper, or a transit ad possibly directs commuters to a firm's website.

A media plan is generally the end result of the media planning process, and it contains sections for objectives, strategy decisions, and tactical decisions. The media plan's objectives must be designed to support the overall marketing objectives and help achieve the behavioural and communications objectives determined for each target audience.

The basic task involved in the development of media strategy is to determine the best matching of media to the target audience, given the constraints of the budget. The media planner attempts to balance reach and frequency and to deliver the message to the intended audience with a minimum of waste coverage. Media strategy development has been called more of an art than a science, because while many quantitative data are available the planner also relies on creativity and non-quantifiable factors.

 Explain the process and identify the decisions for implementing media strategies.

This chapter discussed five media strategy decisions, including developing a proper media mix, determining target audience coverage, geographic coverage, scheduling, and balancing reach and frequency. A summary chart of strengths and limitations of media alternatives was provided. The list provides a starting point for planners who select the right combination of media based on the communication problem or opportunity.

 Explain the process and identify the decisions for implementing media tactics.

The chapter also looked at key tactical decisions that fine-tune the media strategy. The media vehicle plays a key part in the media plan as the media planner makes a careful match among the viewers, listeners, and readers of the media and the profile of the target audience. Relative cost estimates guide the media planner's final decisions for vehicle selection by finding the most cost-efficient placement. Fine-tuning scheduling details are finalized with the realization of a blocking chart that summarizes all media decisions and costs across relevant time periods and geographic locations.

Distinguish among the theoretical and managerial approaches for media budget setting.

This chapter summarized theoretical and managerial approaches for budget setting. Theoretical methods feature economic models (i.e., marginal analysis, sales response) that attempt to demonstrate the effects of advertising on sales, often without accounting for the effects of other marketing mix variables. Top-down managerial approaches include affordable, arbitrary allocation, percentage of sales, competitive parity, and return on investment. The methods are often viewed as lacking in any theoretical basis while ignoring the role of advertising and promotion in the marketing mix.

Bottom-up managerial approaches include the objective and task method and payout planning. In particular, the former connects the cost of advertising and promotion to the communication and behavioural objectives expected for the communication program as opposed to broader marketing objectives expected for the marketing program. While the objective and task method offers an improvement over the top-down approaches, firms continue to use a combination of approaches to make the budget decision.

 Apply the methods for allocating the media budget to relevant IMC tools and market situations.

Once the overall budget has been determined, it is allocated to the individual media for advertising and any other IMC tool requiring expenditures. Often times, the money for an individual tool will be allocated to certain markets depending on level of the brand's current market share. Sometimes markets are developed requiring a boost in expenditures, while other times markets are in a profit mode and less investment may be forthcoming. Some allocation decisions are affected by unique organizational or inter-organizational factors that may be tangential to the primary goals of achieving communication objectives.

Key Terms   ![McGraw Hill Education] **connect**

Review key terms and definitions on Connect.

Review Questions

1. Explain why media planning involves a trade-off between reach and frequency.

2. Describe what is meant by waste coverage. The decision must often be made between waste coverage and undercoverage. Give examples when the marketer might have to choose between the two, and when it may be acceptable to live with waste coverage.

3. What is meant by readers per copy? How is this different from CPM? Explain the advantages and disadvantages associated with the use of both.

4. Identify the information resources required to calculate the budget using the objective and task method.

5. What factors influence the budget allocation to different media or different IMC tools?

Applied Questions

1. One long-time advertising agency executive noted that buying planning is both an art and a science, with a leaning toward art. Explain what this means and provide examples.

2. Visit the websites for two magazines of the same genre and locate their media kit that tries to attract advertisers to their particular media vehicle. Investigate how each magazine tries to persuade advertisers and decide which magazine would be most suitable to advertise in.

3. Calculate the CPM for five or six different media vehicles that are interesting or topical.

4. Assume that a new entry-level car brand wants to achieve 30 percent awareness among graduated students aged 21 to 24. Calculate how much would have to be in the budget to achieve this objective.

5. For an up-and-coming brand of fashionable jeans, a re-branded local night club for dancing, and an established energy drink, identify the most appropriate media budget allocation (in percentages) to create awareness. Do the same for all three brands with respect to IMC tools.

GO ONLINE

For more information on the resources available from McGraw-Hill Ryerson, go to www.mcgrawhill.ca/he/solutions.

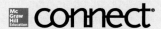

Broadcast Media

11

LEARNING OBJECTIVES

LO1 Describe different types of television advertising, specialty television advertising, alternative time periods and program format, and measurement of television audiences.

LO2 Summarize the strengths and limitations of television as an advertising medium.

LO3 Describe different types of radio advertising, alternative time periods and program format, and measurement of radio audiences.

LO4 Summarize the strengths and limitations of radio as an advertising medium.

LO5 Apply the media knowledge of TV and radio for strategic IMC decisions.

Sports Channels Battle It Out

The battle for sports TV viewers and radio listeners heated up in the past few years between TSN, owned by Bell, and Sportsnet, owned by Rogers, as both brands re-tooled their lineup for that all important stretch drive to increase their numbers. Both brands raised the bar by hiring high-profile names for on-air presentation and in the upper management suite. Rogers renamed its Fan-branded radio stations to Sportsnet Radio Fan in a couple of cities, while TSN also established its radio presence as each brand went toe-to-toe for new listeners. TSN beefed up its roster by signing UEFA, MLS, and Tour de France, while Sportsnet countered with tennis and extensive and customized regional programming.

Advertised as Canada's Sports Leader, TSN commanded top spot in viewership with its double the average-minute audience compared to Sportsnet. Further, TSN boasted 25 percent more subscribers and 20 percent more advertising revenue, fuelled by its successful presentation of the Grey Cup and the World Juniors, and reached new heights with its successful development of TSN2.

But new Sportsnet executives attempted to challenge for number one, with comments like "Can we be number one in the sports game? I don't know. But you don't want to do anything but set your sights on being number one, that's for sure." This is especially true after one TSN executive suggested that it could not possibly have any defections from its all-star roster to Sportsnet when it responded to the issue and claimed, "Not many people want to leave the Pittsburgh Penguins to go play for Nashville."

Sportsnet upped the ante with an overhaul of the brand and a new logo that drops the corporation identification of Rogers. After 13 years, only a quarter of English-speaking Canadians could accurately identify the previous logo of a stylized blue stick man with a red ball. Other aspects of the new brand included reconstruction of new sets for its main TV programs, expansion of new stations like Sportsnet World and Sportsnet One, and a more integrated approach to sell its media options to advertisers.

This step, for example, featured identification of Coors Light sponsorship across all of its media properties, TV, radio, magazine, website, and mobile. This exemplified the transition of Sportsnet moving from a purely TV offering or TV and digital offering to a branded media organization offering multiple exposure opportunities for advertisers to reach their target audiences through several channels as their media tastes evolve. This seems to be a key opportunity, as concluded by the head of media for Molson Coors Canada: "We all know that media consumption habits continue to expand. As such, we will continue to promote key brand programs across a wide spectrum of media channels and platforms."

With battle lines drawn and Sportsnet's revamped approach underway, TSN took notice and responded, "Sportsnet over its history has had a good offering, and the changes they are making over there I would presume are for improvement, as we try to do the same on our end. Any type of competition should breed that type of self-reflection towards improvement." And this looks like another battle round is shaping up to attract eyes and ears.

Source: Susan Krashinsky, "Rogers Bundles Up Its Sportsnet Ad Offering for Brewery," *The Globe and Mail*, February 14, 2012, p. B7; Chris Powell, "Dropping the Gloves," *Marketing Magazine*, February 28, 2011, pp. 10–12; Susan Krashinsky, "Sportsnet Unveils a Whole New Look," *The Globe and Mail*, September 29, 2011, p. B7; "In Quotes," *Marketing Magazine*, February 28, 2011, pp. 12, 15.

Questions:

1. Is Sportsnet more attractive for advertisers with its changes?

TV is in virtually every Canadian household and is a mainstay in most people's lives. The large number of television viewers are important to the TV networks and stations because they can sell time on these programs to marketers who want to reach that audience with their advertising messages. Moreover, the qualities that make TV a great medium for news and entertainment also encourage creative ads to influence current and potential customers. Radio is also an integral part of people's lives as it is a constant companion in their cars, at home, and even at work for information and entertainment. Radio listeners are an important audience for marketers just like TV viewers.

In this chapter, we describe the types of TV and radio media that advertisers may select within the media strategy, how advertisers buy TV and radio time, and how audiences are measured and evaluated for each medium. We summarize the specific strengths and limitations of each medium. Finally, we explain how advertisers use TV and radio as part of their advertising and media strategies. We follow this structure for TV and then radio.

(L01) Television

A number of options are available to advertisers that choose to use TV as part of their media mix. They can purchase ads on shows that are shown across a national or regional network, a local or spot announcement in a few cities, or sponsor an entire program. With the growth of new television services, advertisers decide the degree to which they want to advertise on specialty channels. They can purchase advertising in different time periods and in a variety of program formats that appeal to various types and sizes of audiences. We explore these three decisions in this section.

The purchase of TV advertising time is a highly specialized part of the advertising business, particularly for large companies spending huge sums of money. Large TV advertisers generally use agency media specialists or specialized media buying services to arrange the media schedule and purchase TV time. We conclude this section with a discussion on measuring TV audiences because it is a critical input for TV advertising decisions.

TYPES OF TELEVISION ADVERTISING

A basic decision for all advertisers is allocating their TV media budget to network, local, or spot announcements. Most national advertisers use network schedules to provide national coverage and supplement this with regional or local spot purchases to reach markets where additional coverage is desired. Periodically we see major advertisers do sponsorship advertising as well.

Network Advertising   A common way advertisers disseminate their messages is by purchasing airtime from a **television network**. A network assembles a series of affiliated local TV stations, or **affiliates**, to which it supplies programming and services. These affiliates, most of which are independently owned, contractually agree to pre-empt time during specified hours for programming provided by the networks and to carry the national advertising within the program. The networks share the advertising revenue they receive during these time periods with the affiliates. The affiliates are also free to sell commercial time in non-network periods and during station breaks in the pre-empted periods to both national and local advertisers. Figure 11-1 summarizes the Canadian and U.S. networks and independent stations, along with the amount of consumption for each. There are 138 conventional stations in Canada.[1]

Canada's television industry features six national networks. The Canadian Broadcasting Corporation (CBC) is a Crown corporation of the federal government of Canada and its network reaches virtually all English-language homes. Radio-Canada is the CBC cousin for the French-language network, reaching viewers in Quebec and other Canadian provinces and territories. The Canadian Television Network (CTV) and Global both operate as a national English-language service in most Canadian provinces. CITY is a semi-national network in most populated provinces of Canada. Finally, TVA, a private French-language network, broadcasts

Figure 11-1

Share of hours tuned by station group

Station Group	Fall			
	2009	**2010**	**2011**	***2012**
CBC O&O	4.7	4.9	4.5	3.2
CBC Affiliates	0.6	0.6	0.4	0.3
CBC TOTAL	**5.4**	**5.5**	**4.9**	**3.5**
City				2.7
CTV	10.9	11.2	10.7	11.0
Independent English	7.7	7.3	7.1	5.6
Global	6.6	6.5	6.5	7.3
Radio Canada O&O	3.7	3.8	3.7	4.2
Radio Canada Affiliates	0.1	0.1	0.1	0.1
RADIO CANADA TOTAL	**3.8**	**3.9**	**3.8**	**4.3**
TVA	8.0	7.6	7.4	7.3
Télé-Québec	0.6	0.5	0.6	0.6
Quatre Saisons	1.3	1.3	1.5	1.5
Total CDN Conventional	**44.3**	**43.8**	**42.5**	**43.8**
US: ABC Affiliates	1.5	1.3	1.2	1.4
NBC Affiliates	1.2	1.1	1.1	1.4
CBS Affiliates	2.0	2.1	1.9	2.2
FOX Affiliates	1.4	1.5	1.4	1.4
PBS	0.9	0.9	0.9	1.1
Independent/UPN/WB	1.5	1.4	1.4	1.5
Total U.S. Conventional	**8.5**	**8.3**	**7.9**	**9.0**
Cable/Prov.	0.3	0.3	0.3	0.3
International	0.6	0.5	0.4	0.4
VCR	3.8	3.3	3.3	—
PVR	3.1	3.4	4.6	—
DVD				2.0
Demand	0.5	0.6	0.6	0.7
CDN. Specialty/Pay	32.1	33.3	33.3	34.7
U.S. Specialty/Pay	5.6	5.0	5.2	6.3
Others	0.8	0.9	1.1	2.7
Total Hours (Millions)	**697.7**	**674.8**	**678.1**	**595.6**

Source: BBM Fall Surveys (Mon-Sun 6A-2A), Television Audience by Station Groups All Persons 2+ Canada *The methodology used to collect data changed significantly in Fall 2012 with the introduction of the Personal Diary. Prior years were based on set-top diary methodology. Due to these changes, it is not recommended that data from Fall 2012 be trended with past surveys. The hockey lockout also substantially impacted TV viewing in Fall 2012.

Source: TV Basics 2012–2013.

to most Quebec households and a significant number of French-speaking viewers throughout Canada. Many regional networks also dot the Canadian landscape: CBC, CTV, OMNI, Quatre Saisons, and Tele-Quebec.

The networks generally have affiliate stations throughout the country or region. As the list implies, some of the national networks operate regionally as well. When an advertiser purchases airtime from one of the national or regional networks, the commercial is transmitted through the affiliate station network. Network advertising truly represents a mass medium, since the

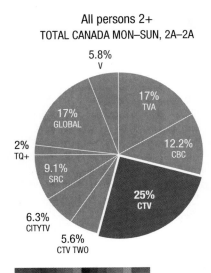

All persons 2+
TOTAL CANADA MON–SUN, 2A–2A

- 5.8% V
- 17% TVA
- 17% GLOBAL
- 2% TQ+
- 12.2% CBC
- 9.1% SRC
- 25% CTV
- 6.3% CITYTV
- 5.6% CTV TWO

Figure 11-2

National television audience share across available Canadian conventional channels

Source: Media Digest 2012–2013.

advertiser can broadcast its message simultaneously through many networks (Figure 11-2). Another advantage of this advertising is a simplified purchase process as the advertiser works with only one party or media representative to air a commercial.

The larger networks (e.g., CTV) offer the most popular programs and generally control prime-time programming. Advertisers interested in reaching larger audiences generally buy network time during the prime viewing hours of 8 p.m. and 11 p.m. Availability of time can be a problem as many advertisers turn to network advertising to reach mass markets. Traditionally, most prime-time commercial spots, particularly on the popular shows, are sold during the buying period in May/June/July that occurs before the TV season begins. Advertisers hoping to use prime-time network advertising must plan their media schedules and often purchase TV time as much as a year in advance. Demands from large clients who are heavy TV advertisers force the biggest agencies to participate in the upfront market. However, TV time is also purchased during the scatter market that runs through the TV season. Some key incentives for buying up front, such as cancellation options and lower prices, are available in the quarterly scatter market. Network TV can also be purchased on a regional basis, so an advertiser's message can be aired in certain sections of the country with one media purchase.

Spot Advertising Spot advertising refers to commercials shown on local TV stations, with time negotiated and purchased directly from the individual stations or their national station representatives. Station reps act as sales agents for a number of local stations in dealing with national advertisers.

Spot advertising offers the national advertiser flexibility in adjusting to local market conditions. The advertiser can concentrate commercials in areas where market potential is greatest or where additional support is needed. This appeals to advertisers with uneven distribution or limited advertising budgets, as well as those interested in test marketing or introducing a product in limited market areas. National advertisers sometimes use spot television advertising through local retailers or dealers as part of their cooperative advertising programs and to provide local dealer support. This attractive option is most prevalent in Canada, with about 60 percent of all TV ads.

Sponsorship Advertising Under a sponsorship arrangement, an advertiser assumes responsibility for the production and usually the content of the program and advertising that appears within it. In the early days of TV, most programs were produced and sponsored by corporations and were identified by their name. Today most shows are produced by either the networks or independent production companies that sell them to a network; however, sponsorship is a good option in some situations. However, the original approach to sponsorship returned with a new name, "branded entertainment," that is reminiscent of what occurred decades ago. President's Choice cooked up a reality show, *Recipes to Riches*, where contestants used the branded products to develop their own recipes. The show attracted over 600,000 viewers and reached the number one most watched video on FoodNetwork.ca. With company chairman Galen Weston as a judge, the show offered contestants an opportunity to demonstrate their culinary flair.[2]

This kind of arrangement is moving toward the Internet with Canada's media conglomerates. A high-profile example occurred with *Canada's Best Beauty Talent*, produced by Rogers Media in association with L'Oréal. The 12-part series showed beauty experts competing to see who is the most talented and appeared only on the Internet, much like watching original-content shows on YouTube. Although Internet represents only a very small percentage of people's average weekly viewing, advertisers like L'Oréal are very interested to see how many are watching and to what degree there is follow-up social media communication.[3]

A company might choose to sponsor a program for several reasons. Sponsorship allows the firm to capitalize on the prestige of a high-quality program, enhancing the image of the company and its products. Another reason is that the sponsor has control over the number, placement, and content of its commercials. Commercials can be of any length as long as the total amount of commercial time does not exceed network or station regulations. Advertisers introducing a new product line often sponsor a program and run commercials that are several minutes long to introduce and explain the product. For example, Becel sponsored (in part) the *2010 Academy Awards* on CTV and showed a mini-film (i.e., a two-minute commercial) that depicted the brand's support for the Heart & Stroke Foundation's campaign for women's heart health. While these factors make sponsorship attractive to some companies, the high costs of sole sponsorship limit this option to large firms.

SPECIALTY TELEVISION ADVERTISING

Canada has an extensive variety of specialty networks and digital specialty networks that advertisers run commercials on to reach specific target audiences. These specialty networks require either cable or satellite technology on the part of consumers to access this entertainment. We will briefly review these two technologies and then discuss the advertising on these specialty channels.

Cable and Satellite Technology A historic development in broadcast media has been the expansion of **cable television**. Cable, or CATV (community antenna television), which delivers TV signals through fibre or coaxial wire rather than the airways, was developed to provide reception to remote areas that could not receive broadcast signals. Canadians readily accepted cable in the 1970s since it was also the easiest (or only) method of receiving American channels. Today, cable penetration stands at about 67 percent, down from 76 percent in 1995.[4]

Direct broadcast satellite (DBS) services emerged in the 1990s. TV and radio programs are sent digitally from a satellite to homes equipped with a small dish. DBS companies marketed their service, superior picture quality, and greater channel choice as subscribers receive as many as 200 channels in crisp, digital video. The pendulum swung back the other way as cable operators offered digital cable that allows them to match the number of channels received on satellites. In addition, telecommunications firms (telco) offer other services and the term "television service provider" has emerged. Total satellite, digital cable, and telco penetration reached 83 percent in 2012.[5] Combined basic cable, digital cable, and satellite penetration in Canada stands at 94 percent.[6] Figure 11-3 summarizes how Canadians receive television service.

Subscribers pay a monthly fee and receive many channels, including the local Canadian and American network affiliates and independent stations, specialty networks, American

Figure 11-3   Connected TV in Canada

Year	Operating Systems	Cable Subs. (000)	Digital Cbl (000)	HDTV Subs (000)	DTH (000)	Telco (000)	Total TV Subs (000)
2012	2,172	8,212	6,234	2,461	2,879	737	11,858
2011	2,160	8,430	5,826	1,783	2,942	440	11,843
2010	2,145	8,465	5,359	1,291	2,884	358	11,743
2009	1,940	8,352	4,779		2,774	306	11,432
2008	1,941	8,316	3,783		2,647	201	11,191
2007	1,943	8,167	3,348		2,701	170	11,038
2005	2,097	7,984	2,784		2,597	105	10,686
2000^	2,001	8,285	500		1,167		9,452
1995^	1,915	8,102					*8,252

Source: Media Stats, ^Canadian Cable and Television Association, *BBM

*** All cable TV subscribers (including residential and commercial)

Source: TV Basics 2012–2013.

superstations, and local cable system channels. Operators offer programming that is not supported by commercial sponsorship and is available only to households willing to pay a fee beyond the monthly subscription charge (e.g., The Movie Channel). Program options available to viewers broaden advertisers' options by offering specialty channels, including all-news, pop music, country music, sports, weather, educational, and cultural channels as well as children's programming.

Another feature offered by these television service providers is time shifting, which allows viewers to watch network feeds from other time zones. If viewers in Toronto miss their favourite show at 8 p.m., for example, they can watch the Vancouver feed three hours later. The problem is that those viewers are also seeing ads intended for Vancouver residents. So, while a national company may run a price promotion intended only for Western Canada, someone in the East may see the ad while watching a time-shifted signal and become annoyed when the promotion doesn't seem to exist.

TV networks offer their shows online with commercials embedded within them much like regular television viewing. Television service providers also offer "on-demand" services where subscribers can access shows not seen during regularly scheduled times. The movement of watching "television" programming anytime, anywhere, with any device is expanding TV viewing opportunities and potentially opening up new avenues for advertising as consumers adapt to changing technology.[7]

Specialty Networks   The proliferation of channels has influenced the nature of television as an advertising medium. Expanded viewing options have led to considerable audience fragmentation. Much of the audience growth of specialty networks has come at the expense of national and regional networks. Specialty networks now have about 50 percent of the viewing audience (Figure 11-4). Many specialty networks have become very popular among consumers, leading advertisers to re-evaluate their media plans and the prices they are willing to pay for network and spot commercials on network affiliate stations. Advertising on specialty networks reached $1,263 million in 2012, more than double the amount for 2002. In comparison, television ad revenue from the 138 conventional channels increased only 11 percent from 2002 to 2012 and now sits at $2,189 million.[8]

This change in advertising revenue indicates that advertisers are using specialty networks to reach specific target audiences. Advertisers are also interested in specialty networks because of their low cost and flexibility. Advertising rates on specialty channels are much lower than those for the shows on the major networks. This makes TV a much more viable media option for smaller advertisers with limited budgets and those interested in presenting their commercials to a well-defined target audience. Also, specialty network advertisers generally do not have to make the large upfront commitments the networks require, which may be as much as a year in advance.

In addition to costing less, specialty networks give advertisers much greater flexibility in the type of commercials that can be used. While most network commercials are 30- or 15-second spots, commercials on specialty networks can be longer (e.g., **infomercials** ranging from 3 to 30 minutes in length). Direct-response advertisers often use these longer ads to describe their products or services and encourage consumers to call in their orders during the commercial. The use of infomercials by direct-response advertisers is discussed in Chapter 16. Finally, specialty network advertising can be purchased on a national or a regional basis. Many large marketers advertise on specialty networks to reach large numbers of viewers across the country with a single media buy. Regional advertising on specialty networks is available but limited.

While specialty networks have become increasingly popular among national, regional, and local advertisers, they still have limitations. One concern is that specialty networks are overshadowed by the major networks. The average person will watch more hours per week of a CBC or CTV affiliate than a single specialty network, although this is changing. Figure 11-5 tabulates how much individuals watch specialty TV in Canada. Across all age groups and both languages, Canadians watch between 11

Figure   11-4

Viewing habits of Canadians ages 2+ by station groups

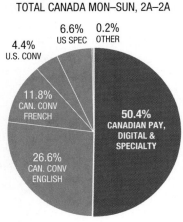

Share of Hours Tuned
TOTAL CANADA MON–SUN, 2A–2A

4.4% U.S. CONV
6.6% US SPEC
0.2% OTHER
11.8% CAN. CONV FRENCH
26.6% CAN. CONV ENGLISH
50.4% CANADIAN PAY, DIGITAL & SPECIALTY

Source: Media Digest 2012–2013.

Figure 11-5 Average weekly hours per viewer tuned and reach percentage of pay-TV and specialty services

	Total Canada									
	All 2+		Adults 18+		Women 18+		Teen 12–17		Children 2–11	
Stations	AvWk Hrs	AvWk Rch%	AvWk Hrs	AvWk Rch%	AvWk Hrs	AvWk Rch%	AvWk Hrs	AvWk Rch%	AvWk Hrs	AvWk Rch%
CDN SPEC/PAY ENG	11.1	81.6	11	82	10.8	81.4	11	78.4	12.1	80.3
CDN DIGITAL ENG	3.3	49.1	3.4	49.4	3.5	47.7	2.3	42	2.8	51.7

	Francophone Quebec									
	All 2+		Adults 18+		Women 18+		Teen 12–17		Children 2–11	
Stations	AvWk Hrs	AvWk Rch%	AvWk Hrs	AvWk Rch%	AvWk Hrs	AvWk Rch%	AvWk Hrs	AvWk Rch%	AvWk Hrs	AvWk Rch%
CDN SPEC/PAY FR	13.1	91.8	13.5	92.3	13	92.5	12.3	93.8	10.2	87
CDN DIGITAL FR	3.6	49.6	3.6	49.4	4	47.8	2.3	41.6	4.1	56.6

*Non-U.S., includes Digital stations

Source: Media Digest 2012–2013.

and 13 hours of TV per week on specialty, pay, or digital stations, reaching a substantial portion of the population.

Figure 11-6 shows a summary of the more highly viewed specialty channels. An equal number is not included as their reach falls below 1 percent of all Canadians. In contrast, the average viewer watches TSN an average of 4 hours per week and the station reaches just under 20 percent of Canadians (5.9/34 million) and is the most watched specialty channel. Although specialty networks' share of the TV viewing audience has increased significantly, the viewers are spread out among the large number of channels available. Collectively, the specialty channels contribute to greater audience fragmentation as the number of viewers who watch any one cable channel is generally quite low.

The emergence a few years ago of dozens of digital specialty channels raises the question as to how well they are performing in attracting audiences in sufficient numbers for advertisers to consider them as a viable television vehicle. While their share of 1 or 2 percent of the television market may be considered disappointing, another perspective suggests that a more realistic benchmark should be used. Since access to a specific digital specialty channel requires a subscription similar to that of magazines, a more important comparison is to look at the leaders for each medium. In fact, about three-quarters of the digital specialty channels have more than half a million subscribers, something only three subscription magazines can claim.

TIME PERIODS AND PROGRAMS

Another decision in buying TV time is selecting the right program and time period for the advertiser's commercial messages. The cost of TV advertising time varies depending on the particular program and the time of day, since audience size varies as a function of these two factors. As for the particular program, *Hockey Night in Canada* is a popular selection due the audience size and composition. For these reasons, Red Baron beer, produced by Brick Brewing Co., selected this program to launch its first-ever TV ad after extensive use of radio and out-of-home for many years.[9] IMC Perspective 11-1 describes network competition for TV shows.

Figure   11-6   Average hours watched per week for selected specialty channels

Specialty	Fall 2010			Fall 2011		
	Hours (000)	Reach (000)	Avg. Hrs	Hours (000)	Reach (000)	Avg. Hrs
ARTV (ARTV)	1,297	610	2.1	1,766	723	2.4
BBC Canada (BBCCA)	888	523	1.7	925	485	1.9
Business News Network (BNN)	1,859	479	3.9	1,714	453	3.8
Bravo! (BRAVO)	3,255	1,653	2.0	3,788	1,883	2.0
Canal D (CANALD)	2,042	1,024	2.0	2,120	1,034	2.0
Canal Vie (VIE)	2,945	1,235	2.4	2,524	1,151	2.2
CBC News Network (CBC NN)				7,392	2,489	3.0
Comedy Network, the (COMEDY)	2,662	1,786	1.5	2,678	1,814	1.5
Country Music Television (CMT)	3,274	1,904	1.7	2,903	1,713	1.7
CP24 (CP 24)	3,058	1,086	2.8	4,259	1,268	3.4
CTV NewsNet (CTVNCH)	3,625	1,493	2.4	3,366	1,329	2.5
Discovery Channel (DISCVY)	5,523	3,194	1.7	5,462	2,910	1.9
Family Channel, The (FAMILY)				9,782	2,808	3.5
Food Network Canada (FOOD)	4,352	2,126	2.0	4,835	2,273	2.1
Golf (GOLF)	1,484	461	3.2	1,857	567	3.3
HGTV Canada (HGTV)	5,794	2,734	2.1	5,751	2,654	2.2
Historia (HISTFR)	1,686	723	2.3	1,451	672	2.2
History Television (HISTTV)	6,775	3,118	2.2	7,406	3,425	2.2
MTV Canada (MTVCAN)	930	619	1.5	759	485	1.6
MuchMoreMusic (MMM)	1,068	674	1.6	961	596	1.6
MuchMusic (MMUSIC)	1,539	1,005	1.5	1,262	798	1.6
OLN: Outdoor Life Network (OLN)	2,298	1,142	2.0	2,113	1,290	1.6
RDI (RDI)	5,008	1,255	4.0	5,396	1,280	4.2
RDS—Le Reseau des Sports (RDS)	11,536	2,432	4.7	10,434	2,289	4.6
Rogers SportsNet (ROGRSP)	13,861	4,706	2.9	12,978	4,427	2.9
Score Television Network, the (SCORE)	1,431	734	2.0	1,541	706	2.2
Series+ (SERIES)	4,024	930	4.3	3,115	767	4.1
Showcase (SHWCSE)	4,210	1,966	2.1	3,992	1,912	2.1
Showcase Action (ACTION)	1,377	599	2.3	1,561	716	2.2
Showcase Diva (DIVA)	2,013	784	2.6	2,039	822	2.5
Space (SPACE)	3,734	1,359	2.7	3,067	1,151	2.7
Star TV (E)	1,040	827	1.3	794	606	1.3
Teletoon English (TOON E)	3,494	1,575	2.2	3,781	1,797	2.1
Teletoon French (TOON F)	1,477	617	2.4	1,690	727	2.3
Treehouse (TREE)	6,290	1,642	3.8	6,146	1,456	4.2
TSN (TSN)	20,193	5,456	3.7	23,455	5,857	4.0
TV5 (TV5)	1,882	605	3.1	1,954	628	3.1
TVTropolis (TV TROP)	2,299	1,639	1.4	2,420	1,457	1.7
Vision TV (VISION)	2,871	1,149	2.5	3,079	1,198	2.6
W Network (WNET+)	5,719	2,491	2.3	5,933	2,529	2.3
Weather Network, the (WEATHR)	3,026	1,922	1.6	2,603	2,529	1.6
YTV	7,583	2,833	2.7	6,255	2,618	2.4
Ztele	1,743	823	2.1	1,174	640	1.8

Source: TV Basics 2012–2013, pp. 42, 43.

IMC PERSPECTIVE 11-1

Top Show Competition

TV networks continuously try to outmanoeuvre one another to grow their audiences by getting the top shows and placing them on the right day and the right time. And these decisions are crucial, since in spring 2013 a top-ranked show like *The Big Bang Theory* attracted about 4 million English-speaking viewers, and *Voix La* attracted almost 3 million French-speaking viewers. Even anticipating what will be the next top show is a key factor in their success, as they identify shows that fit their media brand identity to sell advertisers on the merits of their network offering.

CTV has dominated the top spots for the past while, with hits like *The Big Bang Theory, The Mentalist, Grey's Anatomy, The Amazing Race, Two and a Half Men, Blue Bloods,* and *Survivor* all in the top ten during the spring of 2013. And, as occurred for most age demographics, CTV battled Global for the 18–34 age range. CTV nurtured a show like *The Big Bang Theory* and placed it right after the popular *Two and a Half Men,* where it found a strong audience and eventually became a lead show when prime time starts at 8 p.m. According to CTV's executives, "Our goal here is to win every timeslot." And they continued to do so by giving each evening an identity of certain types of programming, making periodic adjustments when a few shows did not work out.

CBC ran a higher concentration of American programming recently in comparison to what it has done historically, and in contrast to CTV sticking with mostly American programming, CBC moved back toward a stronger ratio of Canadian shows. With the success of *Dragons' Den, Battle of the Blades, Heartland,* and *The Rick Mercer Report,* the public broadcaster found the initiative to drop the popular *Jeopardy* and *Wheel of Fortune.* And despite increased pressure from the expansion of sports channels like TSN and Sportsnet, the CBC believed it could maintain a presence with sports programming as the content provider looked to spread its exposure and licensing across many media partners for increased audience reach since

it naturally competes with drama and comedy TV vehicles for advertising dollars. Furthermore, it still viewed itself as a leader for "nation-building" events like the Olympics, relevant regional or local content reflecting Canadian culture, and movements like "Live Right Now" that had a strong emphasis on health with sponsorship from the President's Choice brand across multiple media. And these plans appear to bear fruit, as advertising revenue gained reasonably over the past few years.

However, big networks compete against cable or specialty channel programming that may have no advertising or less advertising than the networks. Popular shows there feature fewer episodes and become more like event television with greater anticipation to see the shows. On commentator concluded, "The kind of buzz that comes with event television is very difficult for a CTV or a CBC or Global to match because the restrictions on over-the-air television mean you can't have shows that are as sexy, as compelling … that have foul language."

Source: David Brown, "Predictable Network Fare Pales in Comparison to Sexy Cable Programming," *Marketing Magazine,* March 14, 2011, pp. 22; Chris Powell, "It's Not What You Air, It's How You Air," *Marketing Magazine,* March 14, 2011, p. 20; Kristin Laird, "CTV," *Marketing Magazine,* March 14, p. 16; Kristin Laird, "Cool Under Fire," *Marketing Magazine,* February 28, 2011, p. 8; Alicia Andorich, "CBC/Radio-Canada," *Marketing Magazine,* November 14, 2011, p. 35; www.bbm.ca.

Question:

1. Explain why the selection of shows is so important to networks.

TV time periods are divided into **dayparts**, which are specific segments of a broadcast day. The time segments that make up the programming day vary from station to station. The various daypart segments attract different audiences in both size and nature, so advertising rates vary accordingly. Figure 11-7 shows how the viewership distribution varies across different dayparts. Prime time draws 38 percent of per capita television consumption. Since firms that advertise during prime time must pay premium rates, this daypart is dominated by the large national advertisers.

The various dayparts are important to advertisers since they attract different demographic groups. For example, daytime TV generally attracts women; early morning attracts women and

Figure   11-7   Percentage distribution of weekly per capita hours by daypart: total Canada

Audiences Dayparts	Ind. 2+ % T min	A18+ % T min	F18+ % T min	M18+ % T min	T12–17 % T min	C2–11 % T min
M–F 2a–4:30p	22.9	22.7	23.8	21.5	19.7	26.7
M–F 4:30p–7p	12.1	11.9	12.0	11.7	13.0	13.7
M–Su 7p–11p	38.0	38.1	38.1	38.5	40.2	33.7
M–Su 11p–2a	10.1	10.7	10.2	11.2	8.0	5.2
Sa 2a–7p	7.9	7.6	7.4	7.9	9.2	10.1
Su 2a–7p	9.0	8.8	8.5	9.1	9.9	10.6

Source: Media Digest 2012–2013, p. 19.

children. The late-fringe (late-night) daypart period has become popular among advertisers trying to reach young adults. Audience size and demographic composition also vary depending on the type of program.

MEASURING THE TELEVISION AUDIENCE

One of the most important considerations in TV advertising is the size and composition of the viewing audience. Audience measurement is critical to advertisers as well as to the networks and stations. Advertisers want to know the size and characteristics of the audience they are reaching when they purchase time on a particular program. And since the rates they pay are a function of audience size, advertisers want to be sure audience measurements are accurate. Audience size and composition are also important to the network or station, since they determine the amount it can charge for commercial time. Shows are cancelled once they fail to attract enough viewers to make their commercial time attractive to potential advertisers. In this section, we examine how audiences are measured and how advertisers use this information in planning their media schedules.

Audience Measurement   Television audiences are measured and communicated by the Bureau of Broadcast Measurement of Canada (BBM). BBM is a not-for-profit broadcast research company based on cooperation among the Canadian Association of Broadcasters, the Association of Canadian Advertisers, and Canadian advertising agencies. BBM Canada collects TV audience measurement data with two methods: portable people meter (PPM) for national and some local markets, and diary for remaining local markets. This current data collection arrangement has undergone tremendous change over the past few years.

Historically, BBM measured local market audiences with the diary method and Nielsen Media Research measured national audiences technologically. A meter attached to the household TV recorded when individuals watched. Over time, Nielsen expanded to a few local cities and BBM followed by introducing the same meter technology for national and some local markets. During this development, BBM introduced PPM technology to measure French-speaking audiences in Quebec. For a period of a few years, duplication of audience measurement in Canada existed between the two organizations until the current situation emerged.

Currently, BBM's portable people meter collects data nationally and in the four largest local markets: Montreal (French), Toronto-Hamilton, Calgary, and Vancouver-Victoria. People in the panel wear a device that automatically records a silent audio signal emitted from programming. In fact, the PPM is capable of receiving the signal from other media such as radio, cinema, or any medium that emits a sound. The device records information regarding station, program, and time. Each evening, the device is placed in a docket and the data are transferred to BBM.

The new method offers numerous measurement benefits over the previous technology; we highlight four major ones here:

- unobtrusive, as the person does not interact with the device while measurement occurs
- measures on an individual level instead of a household or television basis
- measures exposure to multiple media for each individual
- measures exposure of recorded programming from any technology (e.g., PVR)

Criticism of the PPM emerged as specialty channel executives believed the system worked best for measuring audience sizes for large networks. A decline in viewership for children, teens, and young adults appeared in the data, possibly due to the research method since the device needs to be continually worn and placed in the docket each night; two actions that some thought might not be happening consistently enough with younger members of the sampling panel. Part of the problem lies in the fact that it is chronically difficult to obtain data from young people, and now the pager does not look as "cool" as it used to when first established. A sleeker and wireless version is under development.[10] While the measurement technology may explain a portion of the audience decline, online viewing for music videos is hitting the specialty music channels, as shown in Figure 11-6 with a corresponding drop in ad revenue the past few years.[11]

BBM Canada also uses the diary research method for collecting television audience information in 40 local markets. A booklet for each television owned in the household is sent to a representative sample of households. BBM gathers viewership information from this sample and then projects this information to the total viewing area. The diary method works as follows. Each person aged two years or older records his or her viewing for one week in the booklet. The recordings are based on 15-minute increments from 6:00 a.m. until 2:00 a.m. Viewers write down station call letters, channel numbers, programs, and who is watching. The booklet also contains a number of basic demographic questions. As expected, the diary method is a substantially weaker measurement system than the original (and new) meter technology; however, the cost efficiencies and ease of use of the PPM will likely lead to expansion to local markets in future.

Figure 11-8 shows the amount of TV watched across different groups over the past 20 years. Despite the prevalence of the Internet during this time, TV viewing held its own. The introduction of the PPM with its enhanced accuracy shows that TV viewership remains strong in 2012.

To help its customers understand the data, BBM Canada provides an extensive array of products. Market reports are a summary of the audience sizes across all markets by time block, program listings, and time period. Their reach book summarizes the demographic information across each province, data area, and station. BBM Canada also offers guidelines on population estimates and booklets that assist its members in understanding the geographic boundaries studied and the research methodology. BBM Canada's television data book breaks down viewing habits across different markets with user-friendly graphs and charts. The EM Stats Card provides detailed information for each extended market in terms of cable, satellite, PVR, and VCR penetration in addition to other similar macro-level data. Finally, two different documents tabulate

Figure 11-8 Average weekly hours tuned per capita

Demographic	1995	2000	2005	2009	2010	2011	*2012
All Persons 2+	24:36	21:30	24:12	20:48	20:24	20:12	25:36
Adults 18+	26:06	23:15	26:15	22.42	22:18	22:06	27:00
Women 18+	28:24	25:28	28:54	25.06	24:24	23:48	28:24
Men 18+	23:48	20:56	23:36	20.18	20:12	20:24	25:30
Teens 12–17	18:55	14:04	13:42	11.24	10:54	10:12	19:00
Children 2–11	19:36	15:27	13:48	12.54	12:12	12:18	19:18

Source: BBM Fall Surveys—diary, *BBM PPM

Source: TV Basics 2012–2013.

the audiences for the different television shows. As a complement, BBM Canada also offers four different software packages that allow its members to analyze the data in a variety of ways.

Audience Measures   The data collected allow for the calculation of two critical audience measures, program rating and share of audience. A **program rating** is the percentage of people in a geographic area tuned in to a specific program during a specific time period. The program rating is calculated by dividing the number of people tuned to a particular show by the total number of people in the geographic area. A **ratings point** represents 1 percent of all the people in a particular area tuned to a specific television program. As suggested above, a program rating is calculated nationally and for each local market.

The program rating is the key number to the stations, since the amount of money they can charge for commercial time is based on it. Ratings points are very important to the networks as well as to individual stations. A 1 percent change in a program's ratings over the course of a viewing season can gain or lose substantial dollars in advertising revenue. Advertisers also follow ratings closely, since they are the key measure for audience size and commercial rates.

Another important audience measurement figure is the **share of audience**, which is the percentage of people using TV in a specified time period that are tuned to a specific program. Audience share is always higher than the program rating unless all people are watching television (in which case they would be equal). Share figures are important since they reveal how well a program does with the available viewing audience. For example, late at night the size of the viewing audience drops substantially, so the best way to assess the popularity of a late-night program is to examine the share of the available audience it attracts relative to competing programs. Again, share of audience is calculated nationally and for each local market.

Since the data are recorded on a minute-by-minute basis for the PPM and 15-minute increments for the diary method, the program ratings and share of audience can be examined over different time intervals. In fact, some believe that the ability of new technology to measure audiences with short time intervals on a minute basis will provide unexpected research results regarding TV viewing behaviour in the future.[12] Also, since the demographic and other consumer data are recorded, these measures can be investigated in great detail for many target audience profile variables. The sheer complexity and extensiveness of the data makes advanced software and analysis paramount.

Audience Measurement Reporting   The collected television data are analyzed with software applications from different suppliers. BBM Analytics is a subsidiary of BBM and offers numerous solutions for examining the program ratings and share of audience data extensively by time, and by different audience characteristics. While Nielsen no longer collects TV audience data in Canada, it remains a major player as a third-party processor with its sophisticated software. For example, it is capable of determining the audience size by person and by household with various distribution skews, many reach levels over time (i.e., daily, weekly, monthly), and other usage statistics in terms of amount of TV consumed. Numerous other third-party processors exist as it is a competitive market for turning data into valuable media planning information.

Media buying agencies and advertising agencies subscribe to these data and analytic services and use the information for developing media plans for their clients. Advertisers can access some of this aggregate information through the Television Bureau. The TVB is an industry association for television networks, television stations, and firms that sell television advertising time. It offers resources to those in the television industry to demonstrate the value and importance of television as a medium versus competing media (e.g., magazines). It publishes basic facts garnered from the aforementioned sources and conducts primary research through independent market research firms.

(L02) **Evaluation of Television**

Television is an ideal advertising medium because of its ability to combine visual images, sound, motion, and colour. It presents the advertiser with the opportunity to develop creative and imaginative appeals. However, TV does have certain characteristics that limit or even prevent its use by many advertisers.

STRENGTHS OF TELEVISION

TV has numerous strengths compared to other media, including creativity, target audience coverage, cost efficiency, attention, scheduling flexibility, geographic coverage, reach, frequency, and media image.

Creativity for Cognitive and Emotional Responses Perhaps the greatest advantage of TV is the opportunity it provides for presenting the advertising message. The interaction of sight, sound, and motion offers tremendous creative flexibility and makes possible dramatic, lifelike representations of products and services. TV commercials can be used to convey a mood or image for a brand as well as to develop emotional or entertaining appeals that help make a dull product appear interesting. The overall impact of TV's characteristics provides unlimited options for generating optimal cognitive and emotional responses to highly imaginative ads. For example the ads for Newfoundland and Labrador tourism showing fjords in Gros Morne National Park, the province's unique heritage architecture, and L'Anse aux Meadows national historical site all come alive with beautiful cinematography and the directional skills of Alar Kivilo.[13]

Television is an excellent medium for demonstrating a product. Print ads are effective for showing a product such as a high-definition television and communicating information regarding its features. However, a TV commercial like the acclaimed "Power Unleashed" spot for the Hitachi UltraVision plasma set shown in Exhibit 11-1 is very effective in portraying its rich colour, vivid detail, and lifelike picture.

Target Audience Coverage Television advertising makes it possible to ensure that advertisers achieve audience coverage. Nearly everyone, regardless of age, sex, income, or educational level, watches at least some TV. The average Canadian watches TV 28 hours per week, thereby consuming this medium more than any other. In fact, for all age groups TV is consumed considerably more than Internet media, including among young adults (see Figure 11-9). And, interestingly, the 18–24 age group per capita TV consumption increased by 20 to 25 percent for the most recent five years compared to the previous five years, with no change in all other demographic groups.[14] Most people watch on a regular basis: 99 percent of all Canadian households own a TV, 94 percent subscribe to a TV service, and 74 percent have more than one TV. Marketers selling products and services that appeal to broad target audiences find that TV lets them cover mass markets or large groups of target consumers.

Cost Efficiency Compared to many other media, the cost to reach individuals by television is reasonably affordable. For example, one of the most expensive placements is an ad shown during the Super Bowl costing $130,000, yet with a viewership of 6.5 million the average

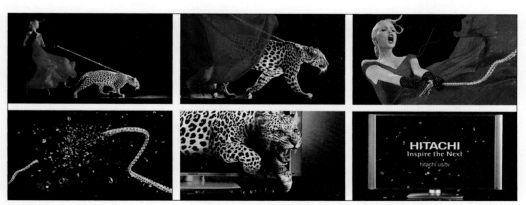

Exhibit 11-1 A television ad is an effective way to communicate the picture quality of this Hitachi plasma TV.

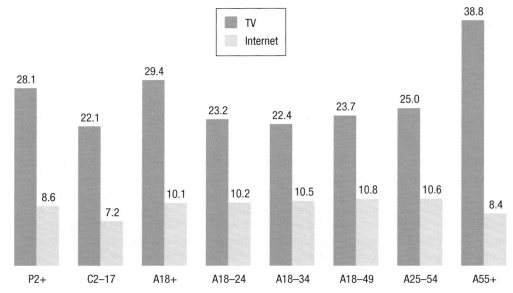

Figure   11-9

Weekly per capita hours
of TV and Internet media
consumption

Source: Media Digest 2012–2013, p. 26.

cost per thousand (CPM) is about $20, which is on par with basic banner ad rates.[15] Because of its ability to reach large audiences in a cost-efficient manner, TV is a popular medium among companies selling mass-consumption products. Companies with widespread distribution and availability of their products and services use TV to reach the mass market and deliver their advertising messages at a very low cost per thousand. Television has become indispensable to large consumer packaged-goods companies, car makers, and major retailers. In fact, Hyundai Auto Canada produced its own ad for the Canadian Super Bowl broadcast after a previous poor response from showing the American ad on Canadian TV.[16]

Attention   Television is basically intrusive in that commercials impose themselves on viewers as they watch their favourite programs. Unless we make a special effort to avoid commercials, most of us are exposed to thousands of them each year. This seemingly continuous exposure implies that viewers devote some attention (i.e., selective attention) to many advertising messages. As discussed in Chapter 4, the low-involvement nature of consumer learning and response processes may mean TV ads have an effect on consumers simply through heavy repetition and exposure to catchy slogans and jingles. Research suggests that consumers watching their favourite programs pay greater attention to the program and subsequently to the embedded television commercial.[17]

Scheduling Flexibility   Television has often been criticized for being a nonselective medium, since it is difficult to reach a precisely defined target audience through the use of TV advertising. But some selectivity is possible due to variations in the composition of audiences as a result of broadcast time and program content. For example, Saturday morning TV caters to children; Saturday and Sunday afternoon programs are geared to the sports-oriented male; and weekday daytime shows appeal heavily to homemakers. With the growth of specialty channels, advertisers refine their coverage further by appealing to groups with specific interests such as sports, news, history, the arts, or music.

Geographic Coverage   Advertisers can also adjust their media strategies to take advantage of different geographic markets through spot ads in specific market areas. Ads can be scheduled to run repeatedly in more favourable markets. Alternatively, advertisers can obtain national coverage or regional coverage depending upon their marketing objectives.

Reach   Television viewing is a closely monitored activity such that the size of the audience for a television program is known fairly quickly. Placement of TV ads on certain combinations of shows allows an advertiser to reach as many in its target audience as it feels necessary. As

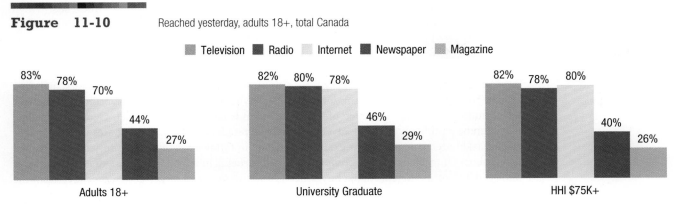

Figure 11-10 Reached yesterday, adults 18+, total Canada

Source: TV Basics 2012–2013.

Figure 11-10 shows, TV reaches about 80 percent of Canadians on a daily basis and virtually everyone on a weekly basis with 97 percent reach.[18] Availability of airtime and amount of budget are the main constraints on allowing an advertiser to reach as large an audience as possible.

Frequency Scheduling television permits frequency in concentrated blocks throughout a program, evening, week, month, or season. Heightened frequency may be necessary for a new product launch or an effort to obtain switching, while lower levels of frequency may be feasible for advertisers desiring more continuous exposure.

Media Image Given the prominence television has with its mass-market characteristic, TV advertising often carries a high degree of acceptability. Television is usually viewed favourably due to the higher costs of placement and production, which demonstrates a level of acceptance or establishment for those who advertise with this medium. Figure 11-11 summarizes BBM data reported by TV Basics. The evolution of advertisers putting their ads on video hosting sites is a testament for media image. A 60-second ad for the redesigned Subaru Forester featured a collection of sumo wresters washing their filthy vehicle. With Forester virtually in every second of the ad, the message "Japanese SUVs just got a little sexier" is humorously communicated with the imagery of the wrestlers engaged in a variety of manoeuvres. So humorous, in fact, that it racked up 700,000 online views that helped spur a 5 percent increase in the Japanese SUV market.[19]

LIMITATIONS OF TELEVISION

Although television is unsurpassed from a creative perspective, the medium has several limitations that preclude its use by many advertisers. These problems include absolute cost, target audience selectivity, processing time, clutter, selective exposure, involvement, and media image.

Absolute Cost Despite the efficiency of TV in reaching large audiences, it is an expensive medium in which to advertise. The high cost of TV stems not only from the expense of buying airtime but also from the costs of producing a quality commercial. More advertisers are using

	TV	Radio	Internet	Newspaper
Authoritative	40%	7%	10%	22%
Influential	59%	5%	15%	11%
Effective	56%	5%	18%	12%
Persuasive	58%	5%	11%	12%

Source: TV Basics 2012–2013.

Figure 11-11

Major media comparisons of attitudes, adults 18+, total Canada

media-driven creative strategies that require production of a variety of commercials, which drive up their costs. Even local ads can be expensive to produce and often are not of high quality. The high costs of producing and airing commercials often price small and medium-sized advertisers out of the market.

Target Audience Selectivity   Selectivity is available in television through scheduling by day, time, or type of program, but advertisers who are seeking a very specific, often small, target audience find the coverage of TV often extends beyond their market. Geographic selectivity can be a problem for local advertisers such as retailers, since a station bases its rates on the total market area it reaches. For example, stations in Ottawa reach viewers in western Quebec and eastern Ontario. The small company whose market is limited to the immediate Ottawa area may find TV an inefficient media buy, since the stations cover a larger geographic area than the merchant's trade area.

Selectivity is possible within a network's portfolio as Corus Television reaches women with three channels. W Network offers a wide variety of entertainment for women of all ages. Cosmopolitan TV "promises fun, flirty and irreverent entertainment" for women aged 18–34. W Movies is expected to reach women aged 25–54. The flanking strategy of having two niche channels to support the mainstream one is consistent with media vehicle options found with magazines. For example, Transcontinental has *Elle Canada* for women in their 20s, *Canadian Living* and *Homemakers* for women in their 30s and 40s, and *More* and *Good Times* for women older than 40.

Processing Time   TV commercials usually last only 30 or 15 seconds and leave nothing tangible for the viewer to examine or consider. Commercials have become shorter as the demand for a limited amount of broadcast time has intensified and advertisers try to get more impressions from their media budgets. Commercials lasting 15 seconds have grown from 13 percent in 1995 to 30 percent in 2012, while 30-second commercials moved from 76 percent to 52 percent as shown in Figure 11-12.

Rising media costs are a factor in the decline in commercial length. A 15-second spot typically sells for about two-thirds the price of a 30-second spot. Since these advertisers believe shorter commercials can deliver a message just as effectively as longer spots, the use of 15-second commercials allows advertisers to run additional spots to reinforce the message through greater frequency, reach a larger audience, or advertise in more purchase cycles.

Clutter   The problems of short messages are compounded by the fact that the advertiser's message is only one of many spots and other nonprogramming material seen during a commercial break, so it may have trouble being noticed. One of advertisers' greatest concerns with TV advertising is the potential decline in effectiveness because of such *clutter*.

Imagine counting the number of commercials, promotions for the news or upcoming programs, or public service announcements that appear during a station break and the concern for clutter becomes obvious. With all of these messages competing for target audiences' attention, it is easy to understand why the viewer comes away confused or even annoyed and unable to remember or properly identify the product or service advertised.

One cause of clutter is the use of shorter commercials and **split-30s**, 30-second spots in which the advertiser promotes two different products with separate messages. The Canadian

Figure   11-12

Canadian commercial lengths

	5 seconds	10 seconds	15 seconds	30 seconds	60 seconds	120 seconds	other
2012	0.4%	2.7%	29.8%	51.7%	4.5%	5.6%	5.2%
2005	0.2%	1.3%	26.8%	61.8%	5.6%	2.7%	4.2%
2000	0.5%	2.1%	22.5%	59.9%	8.8%	2.7%	6.2%
1995			13.4%	76.2%	6.7%		3.7%

Source: TV Basics 2012–2013, p. 19.

Radio-television and Telecommunications Commission (CRTC), which regulates television, permits 12 minutes of commercials per hour for specialty channels and unlimited number of minutes for conventional channels. However, when simulcast Canadian commercials are run, there may be extra time since U.S. TV stations often show more commercial minutes. To fill this time, Canadian stations run ads for other shows, public service announcements, or news/entertainment vignettes. Thus, Canadian viewers sometimes experience a different kind of clutter than their American counterparts.

Selective Exposure   When advertisers buy time on a TV program, they are not purchasing guaranteed exposure but rather the opportunity to communicate a message to large numbers of consumers. There is evidence that the size of the viewing audience shrinks during a commercial break for a variety of reasons and viewers also have selective exposure to television ads resulting from zapping and zipping.

Zapping refers to changing channels to avoid commercials. An observational study found as much as a third of program audiences may be lost to electronic zapping when commercials appear.[20] Zapping occurs because commercials are viewed as unbelievable, a poor use of time, and annoying—and TV ads suffer from greater ad avoidance than other media like radio, magazines, and newspapers.[21] Research shows that young adults zap more than older adults, and men are more likely to zap than are women.[22]

A study on zapping behaviour found that people stop viewing TV during a commercial break because they have a reason to stop watching television altogether or they want to find out what is being shown on other channels. The number of people zapping in and out during breaks was not caused by the type of products being advertised or by specific characteristics of the commercials.[23] Research has also shown that zappers recalled fewer of the brands advertised than non-zappers and that most of the brands that were recalled by zappers were placed near the end of the commercial break, which is when viewers would be likely to return to a program.[24] Figure 11-13 shows the incidence of zapping by Canadians.

A challenge facing television networks and advertisers is how to discourage viewers from zapping. The networks use certain tactics like previews to hold viewers' attention. Some programs start with action sequences before the opening credits and commercials. Some advertisers believe that producing different executions of a campaign theme is one way to maintain viewers' attention. Others think the ultimate way to zap-proof commercials is to produce creative advertising messages that will attract and hold viewers' attention.

Zipping occurs when customers fast-forward through commercials as they play back a previously recorded program. PVR technology entered Canada in 2001, about five years after the launch of the TiVo and Relay brands in the United States. By 2012, household penetration reached 39 percent in Canada and 44 percent in the U.S.[25] A study by Forrester Research in the United States suggests that users watch 60 percent of their viewing from recorded programming and skip about 90 percent of the ads. However, another study released by *Mediaweek* found

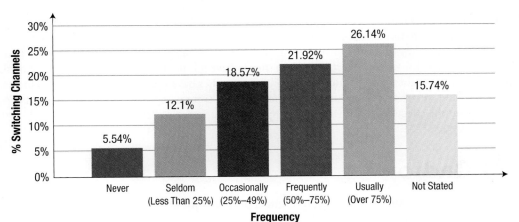

Figure   11-13

Frequency of Canadians switching channels

Source: PMB 2012 Fall Media and Product Study.

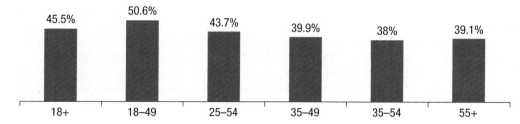

Figure   11-14

Percentage of Canadians who
view ads while using a PVR

Source: TV Basics 2012–2013.

that most consumers could recognize the brands advertised as they zipped through the commercials.[26] A Bureau of Broadcast Measurement of Canada study finds that the vast majority
of Canadians using PVR are aware of the brands advertised when zipping past commercials
and that half stop zipping and view the ads because the brand was of interest to them or they
found the ad entertaining.[27] Figure 11-14 shows the distribution of those who watch the ads
with a definite skew to those in the 18–24 age range. Finally, the study indicates that only one
hour out of 25 hours watched (i.e., 4%) is from a PVR. In conclusion, one author suggests that
the data showing how and when viewers avoid commercials will provide valued information to
make advertising more relevant and efficient.[28] IMC Perspective 11-2 summarizes some current
information on the future of TV due to technological changes.

Involvement   The cumulative effect of the varied television characteristics generally implies
that it is a low-involvement medium. While its invasiveness can expose the message to us readily
and perhaps hold our attention with significant creative strategies and tactics, the relatively
short processing time and clutter make for less effective media for an advertiser to significantly
persuade a target audience. While this assertion of television appears historically accurate, some
alternative ideas are emerging. For example, some shows attract a devout cohort of viewers that
are so engaged or connected with the program their attention to advertising is heightened.[29]

Linking ads with the program content also tries to alleviate this concern. For the Friday
night movies on W, Dare Simple Pleasures cookies brand received multiple 5-second billboards,
30-second ads, and 10-second closed-captioning spots from Corus. The station also developed
ads for the movies and used a similar "reinvention and transformation" theme consistent with
Dare's message. The ads use an image of the cookie along with images from the movie and start
with the following copy:

> This is a Simple Pleasures cookie—it has no cholesterol. That's good for your heart. What else is
> good for your heart? Finding true love, like in *Sense and Sensibility*. What else is sensible? Simple
> Pleasures cookies and Gwyneth Paltrow, who plays a first-class flight attendant. First Class has
> lots of leg room and Sandra Bullock has great legs in *Miss Congeniality*. How'd they get so strong?
> Calcium, like in Simple Pleasures cookies.[30]

Media Image   To many critics of advertising, TV commercials personify everything that is
wrong with the industry. Critics often single out TV commercials because of their pervasiveness
and the intrusive nature of the medium. Consumers are seen as defenceless against the barrage
of TV ads, since they cannot control the transmission of the message and what appears on their
screens. Viewers dislike TV advertising when they believe it is offensive, uninformative, or shown
too frequently, or when they do not like its content.[31] Studies have shown that of the various forms
of advertising, distrust is generally the highest for TV commercials.[32] Also, concern has been
raised about the effects of TV advertising on specific groups, such as children or the elderly.[33]

 **Radio**

In contrast to television, radio has evolved into a primarily local advertising medium characterized by highly specialized programming appealing to very narrow segments of the population.

TV Viewing Trends

What is to become of TV viewing? One idea is that it is in fact not dying, but thriving for several reasons. One, people's desire to watch TV shows online actually means that current TV shows are very good. Two, people have no awareness of TV shows until they are on TV first. Three, people are watching TV content on other platforms, which is fine for the content producers but not so fine for the future of TV service providers. Four, nothing replaces the experience of watching live sports on a big screen except actually being there. Five, it appears unlikely that the next generation of consumers will forgo buying a big-screen TV after leaving a family home that has one. Finally, online content is not even in the same league as first-run TV content.

Furthermore, original TV content is continually uploaded and viewed illegally by millions. However, one enterprising firm, Vancouver-based BroadbandTV, sends its search algorithms to find the clips and package advertising around them, thereby giving revenue to the original creators and not penalizing the original poster through prosecution. For example, one of its customers is the NBA, whose millions of fans upload mashups of the best dunks. With this situation, there is a new TV content package that now has advertising sponsoring just like the model used in so many other traditional media. BroadbandTV expanded the concept to original online content and to video games and currently works with Electronic Arts to package advertising online.

From the actions of TV networks, it appears they do not envision the end of TV as we know it now that all major networks are entrenched in the market and owned by major telecommunications firms. Their annual visits to Los Angeles continue with increased intensity as they bid for shows that will attract advertisers. Some TV executives estimate that Canadian networks will try to outbid one another for the top shows as the funnel of good-quality production continues across all the major American producers. Growth in programming expenditures grew substantially in the past eight years despite the recession.

Continuing with the idea of the strength of TV is research indicating that 95 percent of all programs are watched live or within 24 hours of broadcast on a TV, computer, smartphone, or tablet. So technology has given consumers more flexibility, but they are still watching TV content even if the device is not a TV! Research finds that 2 percent and 4 percent of French- and English-speaking Canadians watch TV only online, respectively; one-third of English-speaking Canadians watch TV online; and PVR playback occurs on the same day 46 percent of the time and within three days 82 percent of the time.

And while it seems that some people want to watch TV without commercials, evidence suggests maybe viewers do not mind them and that TV will survive despite some online brands' predictions or wishes that it might not. Witness the anticipation for watching new ads during big TV events, the interest in watching shows that show commercials as the content, the YouTube viewing of TV commercials, and the way people share TV ads with one another via e-mail or social media!

Source: John Doyle, "Watch How You Want: TV Is Still the Future," *The Globe and Mail,* May 21, 2012, p. R3; Chris Daniels, "BroadbandTV," *Marketing Magazine,* November 14, 2011, p. 31; Jamie Sturgeon, "Building Outside the Box," *National Post,* May 14, 2011, p. FP1; Doug Picklyk, "Who's Watching TV?" *Marketing Magazine,* March 12, 2012, p. 66; John Doyle, "In Praise of Commercials, Sort Of," *The Globe and Mail,* July 25, 2012, p. R3.

Question:

1. How is viewing a TV show on TV the same as or different from viewing it online at the broadcaster's website?

The pervasiveness of this medium continues as radio advertising revenue grew from $1.391 billion in 2006 to $1.585 billion in 2012.[34] In this section, we show how buying radio time is mostly similar to that of television. We also review radio's strengths for advertisers to communicate messages to their current and potential customers and summarize the inherent limitations that affect its role in the advertiser's media strategy.

TYPES OF RADIO ADVERTISING

The purchase of radio time is similar to that of television; advertisers can make either network or spot buys. Since these options were reviewed in the section on buying TV time, we discuss them here only briefly.

Network Radio   Advertising time on radio can be purchased on a network basis. This is a relatively new option for advertisers, who can now run ads on the CHUM radio network, the Team Sports Radio Network, and a few others. Using networks minimizes the amount of negotiation and administrative work needed to get national or regional coverage, and the costs are lower than those for individual stations. However, the number of affiliated stations on the network roster and the types of audiences they reach may vary, so the use of network radio reduces advertisers' flexibility in selecting stations. National advertising revenue topped $454 million in 2012.[35] Syndicated radio operators offer an alternative for radio advertising as they offer packages for advertising across their whole network.

Spot Radio   National advertisers can also use spot radio to purchase airtime on individual stations in various markets. The purchase of spot radio provides greater flexibility in selecting markets, individual stations, and airtime and adjusting the message for local market conditions. Local advertising revenue reached $1.131 billion in 2012.[36] By far the heaviest users of radio are local advertisers; the majority of radio advertising time is purchased from individual stations by local companies. Auto dealers, retailers, restaurants, and financial institutions are among the heaviest users of local radio advertising.

Station Formats   Canada has 1,208 over-the-air radio stations with 904 in English, 266 in French, and 38 in other languages. According to the CRTC, there are 143 commercial AM stations and 543 commercial FM stations.[37] Both network and spot advertising is offered across all these format options. Figure 11-15 shows that FM listening is substantially stronger than AM listening. Satellite radio, offered by SiriusXM, is a subscription service for consumers and this lone competitor offers advertising opportunities on a limited basis.

TIME CLASSIFICATIONS

As with television, the broadcast day for radio is divided into various time periods or dayparts, as shown in Figure 11-16. The size of the radio listening audience varies widely across the dayparts, and advertising rates follow accordingly. The largest radio audiences (and thus the highest rates) occur during the early morning and late afternoon drive times. Radio rates also vary according to the number of spots or type of audience plan purchased, the supply and demand of time available in the local market, and the ratings of the individual station. Rate information is available directly from the stations and is summarized in Canadian Advertising Rates and Data (CARD). Some stations issue grid rate cards. However, many stations do not adhere strictly to rate cards. Their rates are negotiable and depend on factors such as availability, time period, and number of spots purchased. The majority of radio ads are 30 seconds in length; however, stations will book 60-second spots and the majority do not book 15-second spots.

Figure   11-15

Weekly reach and share hours by station format and demographics

Canada	Reach			Share		
	All (%)	AM (%)	FM (%)	AM (%)	FM (%)	Misc (%)
12+	89	28	79	19	78	3
Women 18+	91	26	81	19	79	2
Men 18+	90	32	79	20	77	4
Teens 12–17	78	10	75	5	92	3

Source: BBM Fall 2011, National, AQH Audience, p. 31.

Time Block		Women 18+	Men 18+	Teens
Breakfast	M-F 6-10a	48	49	3
Mid-day	M-F 10a-4p	50	49	1
Drive	M-F 4-7p	46	49	4
Evening	M-F 7p-12a	44	49	7

Source: BBM Fall 2011, National, AQH Audience, p. 31.

Figure 11-16

Audience composition by daypart (%)

MEASURING THE RADIO AUDIENCE

As noted earlier, BBM Canada also provides information on radio listenership using the PPM and a diary method similar to television. Surveys are done twice per year in over 130 radio markets. BBM Canada publishes many reports associated with these surveys. Market reports summarize each radio station's audience by occupation, language, and other important characteristics. Other similar reports with greater aggregation across regions are also published. As for television, BBM Canada provides its members with many supporting documents to understand how to use radio as a communication tool. It also offers many software applications so that advertisers can purchase radio media effectively and efficiently. The three basic elements in the BBM Canada reports are:

- Person estimates—the estimated number of people listening.
- Rating—the percentage of listeners in the survey area population.
- Share—the percentage of the total estimated listening audience.

These three estimates are further defined by using quarter-hour and cume figures. The **average quarter-hour (AQH) figure** expresses the average number of people estimated to have listened to a station for a minimum of five minutes during any quarter-hour in a time period. This figure helps to determine the audience and cost of a spot schedule within a particular time period. Figure 11-17 is a summary of such data by daypart and three demographics.

Cume stands for cumulative audience, the estimated total number of different people who listened to a station for at least five minutes in a quarter-hour period within a reported daypart. Cume estimates the reach potential of a radio station.

The **average quarter-hour rating (AQH RTG)** expresses the estimated number of listeners as a percentage of the survey area population. The **average quarter-hour share (AQH SHR)** is the percentage of the total listening audience tuned to each station. It shows the share of listeners each station captures out of the total listening audience in the survey area.

Audience research data on radio are often limited, particularly compared with TV, magazines, or newspapers. The BBM audience research measurement mostly focuses on demographics and a handful of lifestyle factors. Most users of radio are local companies that cannot support research on radio listenership in their markets. Thus, media planners do not have as much audience information available to guide them in their purchase of radio time as they do with other media. Figure 11-18 shows an example of breaking down the audience share of listening by location.

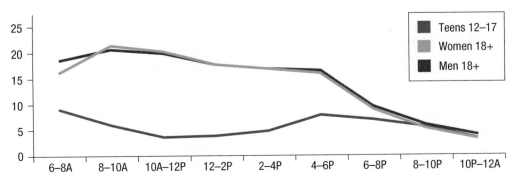

Source: BBM Fall 2011, National, AQH Audience, p. 32.

Figure 11-17

Average quarter-hour ratings by daypart

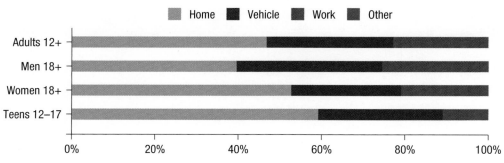

Figure   11-18

Percentage of listening by location and demographic

Source: BBM Fall 2011, National, AQH Audience, p. 33.

L04 Evaluation of Radio

Radio is an important advertising medium because of its ability to inform consumers of factual information and influences with rational appeals that often help facilitate their shopping needs. Consumers feel radio keeps them connected; locally with important information, socially with radio personalities, musically with ideas for music not considered, and conveniently with no online search hassles.[38] However, radio does have certain characteristics that limit or even prevent its use by advertisers.

STRENGTHS OF RADIO

Radio has many strengths compared to other media, including cost efficiency and absolute cost, reach and frequency, target audience selectivity, geographic coverage, scheduling flexibility, creativity for cognitive responses, and image.

Cost Efficiency and Absolute Cost   One of the main strengths of radio as an advertising medium is its low cost. Radio commercials are very inexpensive to produce. They require only a script of the commercial to be read by the radio announcer or a copy of a prerecorded message that can be broadcast by the station. The cost for radio time is also low. The low relative costs of radio make it one of the most efficient of all advertising media, and the low absolute cost means the budget needed for an effective radio campaign is often lower than that for other media. Figure 11-19 highlights the value of radio compared to other major media. It shows that the amount of money spent on radio compared to the amount of time people consume the media is disproportionate.

Reach and Frequency   The low cost of radio means advertisers can build more reach and frequency into their media schedule within a certain budget. They can use different stations to broaden the reach of their messages and multiple spots to ensure adequate frequency. Radio commercials can be produced more quickly than TV spots, and the companies can afford to run them more often. Many national advertisers also recognize the cost efficiency of radio and use it as part of their media strategy. Figures 11-20 and 11-21 indicate the degree of reach.

Target Audience Selectivity   Another major advantage of radio is the high degree of audience selectivity available through the various program formats and geographic coverage of the numerous stations. Radio lets companies focus their advertising on specialized audiences such as certain demographic and lifestyle groups. Most areas have radio stations with formats such as adult contemporary, easy listening, classical music, country, news/talk shows, jazz, and all news, to name a few. BBM tracks radio listeners across 20 different radio formats. Elusive consumers like teenagers, students, and working adults can be reached more easily through radio than most other media. Furthermore, light television viewers spend considerably more time with radio than with TV and are generally an upscale market in terms of income and education level. Light readers of magazines and newspapers also spend more time listening to radio.

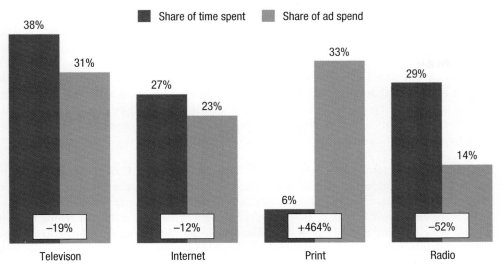

Source: Canadian Association of Broadcasters Radio Ahead Study (http://radioahead.ca/), p. 51.

Figure 11-19

Value of radio compared to other major media

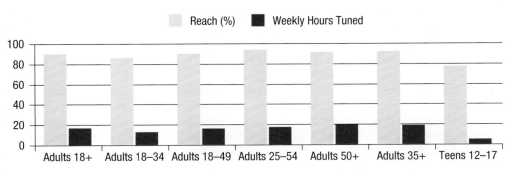

Source: BBM Survey 2011, National, p. 32.

Figure 11-20

Percentage weekly reach and hours tuned by major demographic

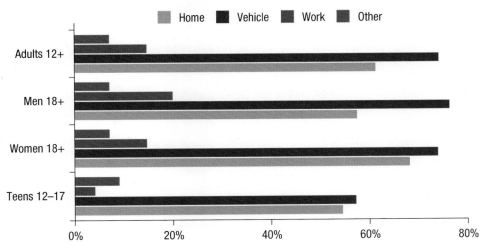

Source: BBM Fall 2011, p. 33.

Figure 11-21

Percentage weekly reach by major demographic, by location

Geographic Coverage   Radio is essentially a local medium. In this respect, since all listeners can tune in, it offers excellent coverage within its geographic scope. Radio stations become an integral part of many communities, and the deejays and program hosts may become popular figures. Advertisers often use radio stations and personalities to enhance their involvement with a local market and to gain influence with local retailers. Radio also works very effectively in conjunction with place-based/point-of-purchase promotions. Retailers often use on-site radio broadcasts combined with special sales or promotions to attract consumers to their stores and get them to make a purchase. Live radio broadcasts are also used in conjunction with event marketing.

Scheduling Flexibility   Radio is probably the most flexible of all the advertising media because it has a very short closing period, which means advertisers can change their message almost up to the time it goes on the air. Radio commercials can usually be produced and scheduled on very short notice. Radio advertisers can easily adjust their messages to local market conditions and marketing situations.

Creativity for Cognitive Responses   The verbal nature of radio ads makes them ideal for long copy to select target audiences who may appreciate greater detailed information for some products. Alternatively, radio ads can also provide more concise brand information in a timely manner. Moreover, both of these factors are highly relevant for those listening in their car, which is a significant percentage of radio listenership. In either case, the informative nature of radio advertising makes it an opportunistic medium to connect with a target audience on a more rational level.

Lay's potato chips used a radio call-in show as the style for its national ad campaign to take advantage of this strength. Farmer Joe Oulton, the same person featured in three TV spots, received calls from people asking for directions. Instead of actually helping them, Joe directed the questioner to the local farm where Lay's grew its potatoes. The 20 ads featured local scenarios—like a lost Calgarian on the Edmonton Trail—to add a bit of folksy humour to the message of authentic home-grown potatoes in every bite.[39]

Media Image   Radio advertising in general has a good media image. Consumers rely on radio for news, weather, and traffic information, not to mention the obvious program content. Thus, radio is well appreciated and this spills over to the ads, as 77 percent of Canadians feel that radio advertising is acceptable. Figure 11-22 demonstrates positive aspects of radio media. Additional data from this research indicate strong connection to the radio station and its shows and personalities via social media.

Figure   11-22

Reasons why consumers like radio

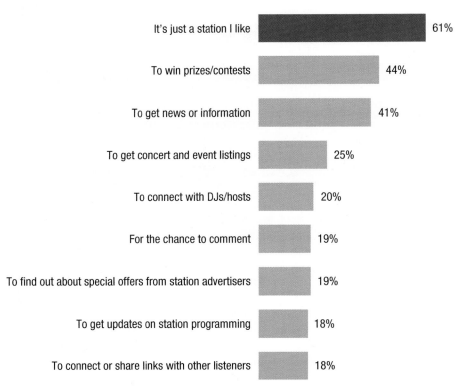

It's just a station I like	61%
To win prizes/contests	44%
To get news or information	41%
To get concert and event listings	25%
To connect with DJs/hosts	20%
For the chance to comment	19%
To find out about special offers from station advertisers	19%
To get updates on station programming	18%
To connect or share links with other listeners	18%

Source: Vision Critical.

LIMITATIONS OF RADIO

Several factors limit the effectiveness of radio as an advertising medium, among them creativity for emotional responses, amount of processing time, target audience coverage, listener attention, selective exposure, clutter, and involvement. The media planner must consider them in determining the role the medium will play in the advertising program.

Creativity for Emotional Responses   A major drawback of radio as an advertising medium is the absence of a visual image. The radio advertiser cannot show the product, demonstrate it, or use any type of visual appeal or information. While the creative options of radio are limited, many advertisers take advantage of the absence of a visual element to let consumers create their own picture of what is happening in a radio message. Some ads encourage listeners to use their imagination when processing a commercial message.

Radio may also reinforce television messages through a technique called **image transfer**, where the images of a TV commercial are implanted into a radio spot.[40] First the marketer establishes the video image of a TV commercial. Then it uses a similar, or even the same, audio portion (spoken words and/or jingle) as the basis for the radio counterpart. The idea is that when consumers hear the radio message, they will make the connection to the TV commercial, reinforcing its video images. Image transfer offers advertisers a way to make radio and TV ads work together. This promotional piece put out by the Radio Advertising Bureau in the United States shows how the image transfer process works (Exhibit 11-2).

James Ready Beer successfully transferred its creative concept from outdoor to radio. Long known for its inexpensive price, "Help Us Keep This Beer a Buck," the brewery used only half a billboard, saying that it was saving money so the price of the beer would stay reasonable. The ad invited consumers through other media channels to create the rest of the ad, which culminated in over 100 unique "co-op" messages. For radio, the concept emerged as "Share Our Radio Space," where fans could complete the ending of the radio spots. The ads could be anything from marriage proposals to band gigs, or whatever an individual wanted to market.[41]

Amount of Processing Time   A radio commercial is, like a TV ad, a short-lived and fleeting message that is externally paced and does not allow the receiver to control the rate at which it is processed.

Target Audience Coverage   Another problem with radio is the high level of audience fragmentation due to the large number of stations. The percentage of the market tuned to any particular station is usually very small. The top-rated radio station in many major metropolitan areas with a number of AM and FM stations may attract less than 10 percent of the total listening audience. Advertisers that want a broad reach in their radio advertising media schedule have to buy time on a number of stations to cover even a local market. With recent media mergers in Canada, syndicated radio stations now provide advertisers with greater coverage, thus minimizing this limitation to a lesser degree.

Listener Attention   Another problem that plagues radio is that it is difficult to retain listener attention to commercials. Radio programming, particularly music, is often the background to some other activity and may not receive the listener's full attention. Thus they may miss all or some of the commercials. This is slightly less of a concern because radio is with consumers throughout the day while doing many activities (Figure 11-23). Advertisers use creativity in radio ads to minimize the effects listener attention. For example, Boston Pizza used radio in Quebec for a 13-week campaign to promote its "Mangiare, Mangiare" theme for special meals at $9.95. A popular star, Marc Hervieux, sings opera in Italian for a while until he humorously ends the solo due to his lack of rhyming skills. The 10-second spot's use of Italian intended to break through the clutter and remind consumers that Boston Pizza offered authentic Italian food.[42]

Exhibit 11-2   The Radio Advertising Bureau promotes the concept of imagery transfer.

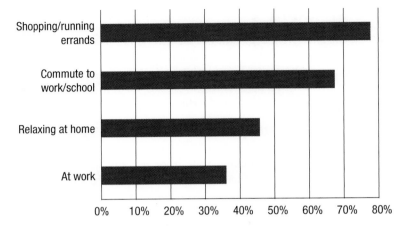

Figure   11-23

Activities while listening to radio—18+, some/most of the time

Source: Radio Marketing Bureau, Foundation Research Study 2009.

Selective Exposure   One environment where radio has a more captive audience is in cars. But getting listeners to expose themselves to commercials can still be difficult. Most people preprogram their car radio and change stations during commercial breaks. A study by Avery Abernethy found large differences between exposure to radio programs versus advertising for listeners in cars. They were exposed to only half of the advertising broadcast and changed stations frequently to avoid commercials.[43] While radio, like television, does suffer from a degree of selective exposure, research suggests ad avoidance is about 30 percent for radio and 40 percent for television.[44] Figure 11-24 shows that radio's limitation in this regard is less than some other media as well.

Clutter   Clutter is just as much a problem with radio as with other advertising media. Radio stations can play as many minutes of advertising as they like. Most radio stations carry an average of nearly 10 minutes of commercials every hour. During the popular morning and evening rush hours, the amount of commercial time may exceed 12 minutes. Advertisers must create commercials that break through the clutter or use heavy repetition to make sure their messages reach consumers.

Involvement   Similar to television, radio is generally considered a low-involvement medium since it is faced with the same characteristics of short processing time and clutter. In fact, it may be seen as being less involving because it has the additional limitation of no visual.

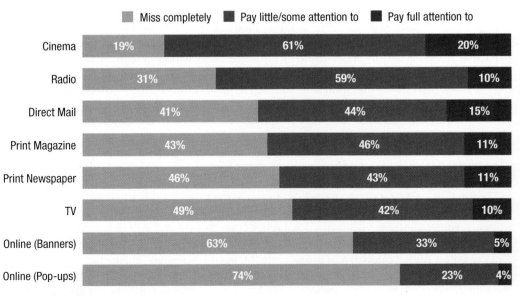

Figure   11-24

Percentage of ads missed or avoided completely

Source: Canadian National Omnibus, Vision Critical.

LO5 IMC Planning: Strategic Use of Broadcast Media

We continue with our IMC planning sections by relating the use of TV and radio with respect to achieving communication and behavioural objectives in general and in terms of the different stages of the consumer decision-making process for the target audience. This builds on our discussions in earlier chapters and highlights the importance of planning creative and media together.

TELEVISION

The creative opportunities and many types of television allow it to play a variety of roles in the decision-making process for the target audience. We link the different types of ads with communication objectives and decision-making processes because the integration of television with other media or tools is predicated upon which types of TV ads will be run. For example, the suggestion to combine TV with Internet advertising, an event sponsorship, or perhaps out-of-home media is contingent on how the two media are planned to influence the target audience. As promotional planners decide upon TV as part of their IMC plan, it is critical to consider its communication objectives in relation to the objectives the other tools will contribute.

Promotional managers can plan for ads to influence their target audience at the pre-purchase and need recognition stages. These kinds of ads could focus on one key benefit or consumption experience, and identify the brand sufficiently to contribute to awareness. For example, some car ads fit this role quite nicely, like the commercials positioning the Toyota Corolla as a reliable vehicle. The plan included other media to encourage further progress through the decision-making process. In this case, the Corolla utilized newspaper advertising for additional explanation and support of the reliability (e.g., information search), and transit station posters as a reminder for a test drive (e.g., purchase decision). For Corolla, the media selection, including television, planned a particular role for each selection to encourage all aspects of the decision-making process, each with particular attitudinal communication objectives.

Alternatively, marketers could provide a television message with information to influence their target audience while evaluating alternative brands. WestJet ads communicated the enhanced service level compared to its previous discount offering to encourage Air Canada consumers to switch; this message would be critical at the alternative evaluation stage. The many executions showed the variety of customer experiences enhanced by the commitment level of the staff to serve its customers in an exemplary manner.

Finally, planners often schedule ads that have more immediate purchase intention or purchase facilitation objectives for the target to take action. An additional type of car ad communicates a promotional event or encourages a dealer visit for a test drive. Virtually all car brands resort to TV ads like this, yet the intensity of the "call to action" and the frequency varies considerably. When these ads are run, car brands typically are not running other types of TV ads but might have instructions to consult the newspaper for additional information. Another example from the social marketing realm is the United Way of Toronto's TV ads that showed a "helping hand" in two different scenarios with a verbal message requesting donations and the Internet address shown visually.

RADIO

While all media are inherently in competition for advertising revenue spent by media planners, radio finds itself with a very significant niche of flexibility that allows it to be in the plans for national brands like Bell and for local advertisers like the pizzeria just around the corner. Moreover, the characteristics of the medium allow planners to integrate radio with virtually any other media or IMC tool.

Whether we are considering a national advertiser like Bell or a local business, oftentimes the purchase decision stage is the one where maximum influence occurs. For example, many radio messages have a time frame for encouraging purchase through participation with a price promotion. Retailers use radio extensively for various sales, for instance. Alternatively, other radio messages might remind the target audience of entertainment and leisure activities occurring in the city or province within a time frame requiring more immediate action. In these situations, the key communication objectives attained are brand purchase intention or brand purchase facilitation. As we can see from these points, the scheduling flexibility of radio permits attainment of particular communication objectives or messaging consumers exactly when they are planning to make a purchase decision.

The lower costs associated with radio can contribute to building brand equity or an identifiable positioning through the affordability of repetition. A recent example of this is the prevalent use of radio by Sleep Country Canada, with owner Christine McGee as the spokesperson. The radio ads give the central positioning as a leading mattress retailer much added frequency beyond its television commercials, thus indicating a natural way to build brands by integrating a consistent message across two broadcast media (see Figure 11-25 and Figure 11-26).

Radio's flexibility and cost implications allow it to support other IMC tools. It can suggest that the target audience visit a brand's Internet site or look for a direct mail piece sent to their home—again, both are action-oriented with a time frame—or with some kind of intention on the part of the receiver of the message. One study found a high percentage of listeners check the Internet, perform a search, type in a Web address, or visit the radio station's website after hearing about something on the radio.[45]

As noted above with price promotions, many other sales promotions can be communicated through radio, particularly those affiliated with sponsorships. Radio can be a key integrating medium to generate awareness of the other IMC tools for further communication in the target audience's decision making.

Figure   11-25   Radio's influence on Internet, adults 18+

Agree/Strongly Agree to Statement	Adults 18+	Working adults	Adults w/kids	A18–34	A25–54	HHI $100K+
I check the Internet after hearing about something on radio	41%	42%	47%	46%	44%	43%
Radio ads prompted search the Internet	45%	45%	54%	45%	48%	50%
I have typed website address in my browser just after heard on radio	35%	35%	43%	35%	38%	35%

Source: Radio Marketing Bureau, Foundation Research Study 2009.

Figure   11-26

Local radio stations online

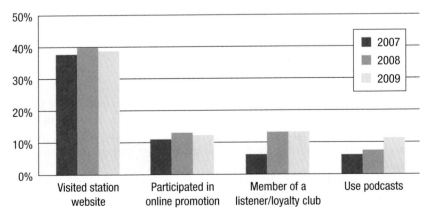

Source: Radio Marketing Bureau, Foundation Research Study 2009.

Learning Objectives Summary

 Describe different types of television advertising, specialty television advertising, alternative time periods and program format, and measurement of television audiences.

Television advertising is time dependent rather than space-oriented like print advertising. Advertisers select the time, day, week, and month in which they want their ads to be seen. Television is a system of affiliated stations belonging to a network, as well as individual stations, which broadcast programs and commercial messages. Advertising can be done on national or regional network programs or purchased in spots from local stations. The growth of specialized stations in recent years offers advertisers niche audiences and stronger selectivity than in the past.

Information regarding the size and composition of national and local TV audiences is provided by BBM Canada. The amount of money a network or station can charge for commercial time on its programs is based on its audience measurement figures. This information is also important to media planners, as it is used to determine the combination of shows needed to attain specific levels of reach and frequency with the advertiser's target audience.

 Summarize the strengths and limitations of television as an advertising medium.

Television is a pervasive medium in most consumers' daily lives and offers advertisers the opportunity to reach vast audiences with very frequent messages. Over the past 60 years, national advertisers, and many local ones, employed TV as their leading medium. No other medium offers its creative capabilities; the combination of sight, sound, and movement give the advertiser a vast number of options for presenting a commercial message. As a primary medium for these advertisers, the creative opportunities of television contribute to the brand's awareness and help in establishing or maintaining a brand's position. Television also offers advertisers mass coverage at a low relative cost. Variations in programming and audience composition are helping TV offer scheduling opportunities and some audience selectivity to advertisers.

While television is often viewed as the ultimate advertising medium, it has several limitations, including the high absolute cost of producing and airing commercials, low target audience selectivity, short processing time, extensive clutter, high selective exposure, and distrustful image. Despite these concerns, consumers generally appreciate brands more if they are advertised on television because the expenditure signals a stronger and more reputable brand.

 Describe different types of radio advertising, alternative time periods and program format, and measurement of radio audiences.

As with TV, the rate structure for radio advertising time varies with the size of the audience delivered. It differs from television in that purchases are not tied to individual shows or programs. Instead, packages are offered over a period of days, weeks, or months. The primary source of listener information is BBM. The new PPM technology for television works with radio as well, although the diary method remains for smaller radio markets.

 Summarize the strengths and limitations of radio as an advertising medium.

The role of radio as an entertainment and advertising medium has evolved into a primarily local one that offers highly specialized programming appealing to narrow segments of the market. Radio offers strengths in terms of cost efficiency and absolute cost, reach and frequency, target audience selectivity, geographic coverage, scheduling flexibility, creativity for cognitive responses, and media image. The major drawback of radio is its weak creativity owing to the absence of a visual image. The short and fleeting nature of the radio commercial, the highly fragmented nature of the radio audience, low involvement, and clutter are also problems.

LO5   **Apply the media knowledge of TV and radio for strategic IMC decisions.**

TV and radio still command almost $5 billion in advertising revenue and remain very good media for achieving broad reach and frequency objectives to achieve or maintain brand awareness and establish or reinforce existing brand image perceptions. No doubt these media feel pressure from Internet media and the use of personal devices to listen to music; however, creative advertising in these media with the right connections to digital brand exposure makes them a strong part of major brands' advertising.

Key Terms

Review key terms and definitions on Connect.

Review Questions

1. Television is described as a mass medium that offers little selectivity to advertisers. Do you agree with this statement? What are the ways selectivity can be achieved through TV advertising?

2. Discuss the strengths of television as an advertising medium and the importance of these factors to major national advertisers and to smaller local companies.

3. Discuss the methods used to measure radio audiences. Do you think the measurement methods used for each are producing reliable and valid estimates of the viewing audiences?

4. What are the strengths and limitations of advertising on radio? What types of advertisers are most likely to use radio?

5. How can TV best be used to work with social media?

Applied Questions

1. Watch a show on TV and make notes on what ads are shown. Find the equivalent show on the network's website and make notes on what ads are shown. What similarities and differences do you notice?

2. Watch TV or listen to the radio and make note of whether the ads direct the receiver to any aspect of digital media (e.g., a social network).

3. Listen to the radio and make notes on what ads are aired. What similarities and differences do you notice in comparison to TV advertising?

4. Listen to a radio station and pay attention to the ads to assess whether any use the idea of image transfer.

5. How can radio best be used to work with social media?

GO ONLINE

For more information on the resources available from McGraw-Hill Ryerson,
go to www.mcgrawhill.ca/he/solutions.

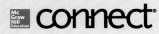

Print Media

12

LEARNING OBJECTIVES

LO1 Identify the different types of magazines available for advertising, how circulation and readership levels are determined, how audience size and its characteristics are measured, and the factors that influence advertising rates.

LO2 Evaluate the strengths and limitations of magazines as an advertising medium.

LO3 Identify the types of newspapers offered for advertising, how circulation and readership levels are determined, how audience size and its characteristics are measured, and how advertising rates are determined.

LO4 Evaluate the strengths and limitations of newspapers as an advertising medium.

LO5 Apply the media knowledge of magazines and newspapers for strategic IMC decisions.

A Tale of Two Media Giants

Two giants in Canada, Torstar and Vice Media, continue to change the media landscape here and abroad. Torstar got its start with the establishment of the *Toronto Star* newspaper 120 years ago, while Vice Media began from humble beginnings with a single magazine 30 years ago in Montreal and is now a global youth media company. Each innovated with media properties available for advertisers to reach their audiences and further blurred the lines between media and other players in the marketing communication world.

One of Torstar's main divisions is the Star Media group, comprising the *Toronto Star, Metro* newspapers in numerous cities, *The Grid* magazine, *Sing Tao,* a Chinese-language newspaper, and Star Content Studios. Another big division is Metroland, with many community newspapers, magazines, and specializations in printing, delivery, digital flyers and promotional transmissions, and the execution of consumer shows. Torstar Digital is an online presence in various types of services. Finally, Harlequin publishes many genres of publications directed to women. With digital a forefront point across most of these divisions, the ability of Torstar to offer advertisers options for ad placement and ad integration across vehicles is substantial.

Perhaps the most interesting development from an advertising perspective is Star Content Studios. Its primary mandate is to construct customized content for all media—print, online, online video, and social media—with the intention to make an attractive environment for advertisers. This customized content is tailored to ensure the topic is relevant and fitting to be associated with an accompanying ad placement. Often the content would look like the content of the host media. For example, in a newspaper this customized content would look like a news story, with similar printing and typeface. In Torstar's case, the head of the unit maintains that a clear divide between this custom content and journalism will be respected.

Vice Media's story started in 1994 with a newsprint magazine, *Voice of Montreal,* reflecting Montreal's underground culture; it changed its name to *Vice* two years later, and linked with *Shift* magazine and started Viceland.com in 1999. Since then it has diverged many ways: a record label to promote unsigned musicians, pubs for them to play in, travel DVDs aligned with MTV, a communications agency to connect advertisers to youth markets, film production within the magazine unit, launch of online television channel VBS.TV, an Internet site for new bands and music, and finally a partnership with WPP. The latter move gave the international mega-agency the opportunity to further develop its content capabilities.

While all of this appears new and different, the essence of the original magazine holds true—Vice Media is a content producer with many capabilities so that it can get placed in many different digital avenues as the digital world expands by building many new channels to reach youth. According to the original owners, it is not tied down to old media models on how things should work: they just make content and make sure it gets to the right audience they are creating.

Questions:

1. Why are these print media firms diverging into other types of media?

Thousands of magazines are published in Canada and throughout the world. They appeal to nearly every consumer interest and lifestyle, as well as to thousands of businesses and occupations. The magazine industry has prospered by becoming a highly specialized medium that reaches specific target audiences. Newspapers are a primary advertising medium in terms of both ad revenue and number of advertisers. Newspapers are particularly important as a local advertising medium for retail businesses and are often used by large national advertisers.

The role of print media differs from that of broadcast media because detailed information can be presented that readers may process at their own pace. Print media are not intrusive like radio and TV, and generally require effort on the part of the reader for the advertising message to have an impact. For this reason, magazines and newspapers are often referred to as *high-involvement media*.[1] This chapter focuses on these two forms of print media as it identifies important information to assist in determining when and how to use magazines and newspapers in the media plan and examines their unique strengths and limitations.

🔘 Magazines

Magazines serve the educational, informational, and entertainment needs of a wide range of readers and are a specialized advertising medium. While certain magazines are general mass-appeal publications, most are targeted to a very specific audience. There is a magazine designed to appeal to nearly every type of consumer in terms of demographics, lifestyle, activities, interests, or fascination. Magazines are targeted toward specific industries and professions as well. Magazine advertising reached $573 million in 2012, down from a peak of $718 million in 2007. Average issue circulation climbed from 63 million to 69 million during the 2004 to 2011 time period. In this section, we review different types of magazines, circulation and readership information, audience measurement, and magazine advertising rates to understand how to plan for magazine advertising placement.

CLASSIFICATIONS OF MAGAZINES

To gain perspective on the types of magazines available and the advertisers that use them, consider the way magazines are generally classified. Canadian Advertising Rates and Data (CARD), the primary reference source on periodicals for media planners, divides magazines into four broad categories based on the audience to which they are directed: consumer, ethnic, farm, and business publications. Each category is then further classified according to the magazine's editorial content and audience appeal. We also examine the opportunity of foreign publications.

Consumer Magazines   Consumer magazines are bought by the general public for information and/or entertainment. CARD divides over 800 domestic consumer magazines into 48 classifications, among them general interest, women's, city/regional, entertainment, and sports, as seen in Figure 12-1. Figure 12-2 shows that the majority of all magazines have circulations below 50,000 and only 27 publications (3 percent) have circulations above 500,000. Figures 12-3 and 12-4 show the top Canadian magazines in terms of circulation for both official languages. Magazines can also be classified by frequency—weekly, monthly, and bimonthly are the most common—and by distribution—subscription, store distribution, or controlled (free).

Consumer magazines are best suited to marketers interested in reaching general consumers of products and services as well as to companies trying to reach a specific target audience. For example, the ad in Exhibit 12-1 could be found in general magazines to encourage people to consider Australia as a destination early in their vacation plans, while the TaylorMade ad in Exhibit 12-2 might fit better in a specialty golf magazine. Figure 12-5 shows the most prevalent advertising product categories.

Rank	Editorial Category	2011 Circulation (000's)		
		Total	English	French
1	General Interest	8,537	7,658	879
2	Homes/Gardening	7,063	5,789	1,277
3	Women's	6,165	4,720	1,445
4	City & Regional	5,723	5,015	708
5	Entertainment	5,047	4,651	396
6	Food and Beverage	3,840	2,461	1,379
7	Travel	3,076	1,606	1,470
8	Sports/Recreation	2,998	1,194	1,804
9	Senior/Mature Market	2,951	2,551	400
10	Lifestyle	2,786	2,570	216

Source: CARD, Magazines Canada.

Figure 12-1

Top editorial circulation

Circulation Size	# of Titles	% of Total Titles	Group Circulation	% of Total Circulation
1 million+	6	0.7	7,847,297	11.3
500,000 to 999,999	21	2.4	12,505,193	18.0
250,000 to 499,999	28	3.2	8,977,224	13.0
100,000 to 249,999	125	14.3	18,278,639	26.4
50,000 to 99,999	148	16.9	10,300,147	14.9
20,000 to 49,999	287	32.7	8,728,198	12.6
1 to 19,999	262	29.9	2,683,333	3.9

Source: Titles Reporting Circulation in CARD, 2011.

Figure 12-2

Circulation distribution

Publication	Magazine Class	Circulation (000's)	Readership (PMB 2012 All 12+ 000's)
CAA Magazine	General Interest	1,568	2,293
Westworld	General Interest	1,299	1,489
What's Cooking	Food & Beverage	1,171	3,332
Reader's Digest	General Interest	707	5,340
Cineplex Magazine	Entertainment	700	2,468
Chatelaine	Women's	547	3,280
Canadian Living	Women's	512	3,892
Teen Tribute	Youth	501	594
Tribute	Entertainment	500	1,864
Food & Drink	Food & Beverage	499	2,269
Canadian Health & Lifestyle	Health & Fitness	398	1,937
Movie Entertainment	Entertainment	389	1,500
Maclean's	News	354	2,426

Source: Media Digest 2012–2013, pp. 70–71

Figure 12-3

Top English-language magazines by circulation and readership

Figure 12-4

Top French-language magazines by circulation and readership

Publication	Magazine Class	Circulation (000's)	Readership (PMB 2008 All 12+ 000's)
Châtelaine	Women's	183	994
Coup de Pouce	Women's	218	1,105
Le Magazine Cineplex	Entertainment	198	326
Primeurs	TV & Radio	349	300
Qu'est-ce qui mijote	Food & Beverage	515	1,234
Selection du Reader's Digest	General Interest	201	84,664
Touring (French & English)	General Interest	790	1,092

Source: Media Digest 2012–2013, p. 72.

While large national advertisers tend to dominate consumer magazine advertising in terms of expenditures, consumer magazines are also important to smaller companies selling products that appeal to specialized markets. Special-interest magazines assemble consumers with similar lifestyles or interests and offer marketers an efficient way to reach these people with little wasted coverage or circulation. For example, a manufacturer of ski equipment such as Nordica, Rossignol, or Salomon might find *Ski Canada* magazine the best vehicle for advertising to serious skiers. Not only are these specialty magazines of value to firms interested in reaching a specific market segment, but their editorial content often creates a very favourable advertising environment for relevant products and services.

The growth of free, customized magazines from retailers with controlled distribution is an emerging trend. Foremost are *Food & Drink* and *Chill* distributed in the liquor and beer stores in Ontario. HBC's *Belle* targets upscale females ages 35 to 55 with household income greater than $100,000—representing HBC's best customers. Past purchasing behaviour through credit cards and rewards cards identified this attractive segment as being interested in fashion, beauty, and home décor. *Belle* offers editorial content to fit the target's lifestyle while showing selective products and brands. Harry Rosen's *Harry* magazine is distributed to the chain's top 100,000 customers and has a newsstand presence of about 10,000. It features 50 pages of paid advertising from selective advertisers like Mercedes, Lexus, Armani, and Hugo Boss (Exhibit 12-3)

Exhibit 12-1 Tourism Australia's ad appeals well in general consumer magazines.

Exhibit 12-2 TaylorMade ads appeal well in specialty golf magazines.

Advertiser Category	2011 Rank*	
	English	French
Toiletries & Toilet Goods	1	1
Retail Stores	2	3
Food & Food Products	3	2
Business & Consumer Services	4	5
Drugs & Remedies	5	4
Apparel, Footwear, & Accessories	6	6
Travel, Hotels, & Resorts	7	8
Automotive	8	9
Entertainment & Amusement	9	20
Household Equipment & Supplies	10	11

*Advertising dollars

Source: LNA 2011.

Figure   12-5

The most prevalent advertising product categories

Ethnic Publications   CARD currently lists 136 magazines directed to persons with many backgrounds based on ethnicity. The majority of these are written in English (75), French (24), and Arabic (23), with many other languages (Chinese, German, Greek, Korean, Polish, Punjabi, Romanian, Russian, Spanish, Urdu) in the four to seven range. Some of these publications have low circulation figures or do not have an authenticated circulation. Thus, the cost of advertising in these publications is currently very low.

Farm Publications   The third major CARD category consists of all the magazines directed to farmers and their families. About 98 publications are tailored to nearly every possible type of farming or agricultural interest (e.g., *Ontario Milk Producer, Ontario Produce Farmer*). A number of farm publications are directed at farmers in specific provinces or regions, such as *Alberta Beef*. Farm publications are not classified with business publications because historically farms were not perceived as businesses.

Business Publications   Business publications are those magazines or trade journals published for specific businesses, industries, or occupations. CARD lists over 700 business magazines and trade journals, and breaks them into 80 categories. The major categories include:

- Magazines directed at specific professional groups, such as *Canadian Lawyer* for lawyers and *Canadian Architect* for architects.
- Industrial magazines directed at businesspeople in manufacturing and production industries—for example, *Process Equipment and Control News* and *Heavy Construction*.
- Trade magazines targeted to wholesalers, dealers, distributors, and retailers, among them *Canadian Grocer*.
- General business magazines aimed at executives in all areas of business, such as *Canadian Business*.

The numerous business publications reach specific types of professional people with particular interests and

Exhibit 12-3   Retailer Harry Rosen's store magazine.

Exhibit 12-4   Lenovo increases awareness in the business market.

give them important information relevant to their industry, occupation, and/or careers. Business publications are important to advertisers because they provide an efficient way of reaching the specific types of individuals who constitute their target market. Much marketing occurs at the trade and business-to-business level, where one company sells its products or services directly to another. The Lenovo ad could be found in a business publication to increase brand awareness for those who need a laptop for work (Exhibit 12-4).

FOREIGN PUBLICATIONS

Canadian magazines face competition from foreign publications, particularly American consumer magazines that account for about 90 percent of newsstand sales for foreign publications. These U.S. print vehicles are another means for Canadian advertisers to reach Canadian consumers. Current legislation allows for foreign publications to accept up to 18 percent of their advertising space from Canadian advertisers for magazines sold in Canada. In addition, foreign publications can accept greater amounts of advertising if the majority of editorial content is Canadian.[2]

Figure 12-6 shows circulation for the top five U.S. publications; the opportunity for Canadian advertisers is to a degree limited in comparison to circulation figures for Canadian titles shown in Figures 12-3 and 12-4. As Figure 12-7 shows, the spillover of American magazines has declined substantially over the past decade; the growth of Canadian magazine pages has risen sharply during the same time period, as shown in Figure 12-8. Research done by the Canadian Magazine Publishers indicates that Canadians prefer domestic magazines but have difficulty identifying them in the face of foreign competition. An extensive communications campaign over the past decade to brand Canadian magazines appears to have contributed to a steady increase in the number of pages and Canadian titles.[3]

MAGAZINE CIRCULATION AND READERSHIP

Two of the most important considerations in deciding whether to use a magazine in the advertising media plan are the size and characteristics of the audience it reaches. Media buyers evaluate

Figure   12-6

U.S. magazines with a circulation of 100,000+ in Canada

Magazine Name	Total Paid CDN Circ.
National Geographic	343,707
Cosmopolitan	274,190
People	150,531
O, The Oprah Magazine	141,920
Women's World	129,100
Prevention	116,847
Men's Health	116,081
First	115,558
Women's Health	110,146
In Touch Weekly	105,146
Sports Illustrated	99,172

Source: ABC; Media Digest 2012–2013, p. 73

Year	Total Spill Circ (000's)	Index	Avg. Circ/Title	Index
1983	10,705	100	26,303	100
1989	9,969	93	21,031	80
1998	9,155	86	16,203	62
2000	8,518	80	15,716	60
2002	8,160	76	15,396	59
2004	7,899	74	14,055	53
2006	7,666	72	13,664	52
2008	7,322	68	13,435	51
2010	6,349	59	14,235	54
2011	6,201	58	14,799	56

Source: ABC.

Figure 12-7

U.S. spill trends

magazines on the basis of their ability to deliver the advertiser's message to as many people as possible in the target audience. To do this, they must consider the circulation of the publication as well as its total readership, and match these figures against the audience they are attempting to reach.

Circulation   Circulation figures represent the number of individuals who receive a publication through either subscription or store purchase, or through controlled distribution (free). Given that circulation figures are the basis for a magazine's advertising rates and one of the primary considerations in selecting a publication for placement, the credibility of circulation figures is important. Most major publications are audited by the Alliance for Audited Media (AAM), a North America–wide organization founded in 1914, and is sponsored by advertisers, agencies, and publishers. AAM collects and evaluates information regarding the subscriptions and sales of magazines and newspapers to verify their circulation figures. Only publications with 70 percent or more paid circulation (which means the purchaser paid at least half the magazine's established base price) are eligible for verification audits. Certain business publications are audited by the Business Publications Audit (BPA) of Circulation. Many of these are published on a **controlled-circulation basis**, meaning copies are sent (usually free) to individuals who the publisher believes can influence the company's purchases.

AAM provides media planners with reliable figures regarding the size and distribution of a magazine's circulation, which helps them evaluate its worth as a media vehicle. The AAM statement also provides detailed circulation information that gives a media planner an indication of the quality of the target audience. For example, it shows how the subscription was sold, the

Year	Canada		US	
	# Titles	Index	# Titles	Index
1997	818	100	7,712	100
1999	908	111	9,311	121
2001	961	117	6,336	82
2003	1,032	126	6,234	81
2005	1,160	142	6,325	82
2007	1,244	152	6,809	88
2009	1,276	156	7,110	92
2011	1,286	157	7,179	93

Source: Magazines Canada; US Spill into Canada.

Figure 12-8

Canada continues to outpace the U.S. in magazine titles growth

percentage of circulation sold at less than full value, the percentage of circulation sold with an incentive, and the percentage of subscriptions given away. Many advertisers believe that subscribers who pay for a magazine are more likely to read it than are those who get it at a discount or for free. Media buyers are generally skeptical about publications whose circulation figures are not audited and will not advertise in unaudited publications. Circulation data, along with the auditing source, are available from CARD or from the publication itself.

Readership   Advertisers are often interested in the number of people a publication reaches as a result of secondary, or pass-along, readership. **Pass-along readership** can occur when the primary subscriber or purchaser gives a magazine to another person or when the publication is read in doctors' waiting rooms or beauty salons, on airplanes, and so forth.

Advertisers generally attach greater value to the primary in-home reader than the pass-along reader or out-of-home reader, as the former generally spends more time with the publication, picks it up more often, and receives greater satisfaction from it. Thus, this reader is more likely to be attentive and responsive to ads. However, the value of pass-along readers should not be discounted. They can greatly expand a magazine's readership.

The **total audience**, or **readership**, of a magazine is calculated by multiplying the readers per copy (the total number of primary and pass-along readers) by the circulation of an average issue. For example, *Flare* has a circulation of 160,000 and 11 readers per copy for a total audience of 1.5 million. However, rate structures are generally based on the more verifiable primary circulation figures, and many media planners devalue pass-along readers by as much as 50 percent. Total readership estimates are reported by the Print Measurement Bureau (PMB), to which we now turn our attention.

MAGAZINE AUDIENCE MEASUREMENT—PMB

The Print Measurement Bureau (PMB) is a non-profit Canadian industry association of nearly 500 members drawn from advertisers, print magazine publishers, and advertising agencies. Its primary mandate is to collect readership information for print magazines, which allows all three constituents to make more effective advertising decisions. Its foremost research is known simply as the **PMB study**.

The first national PMB study was conducted in 1973 and originally concerned print magazines only. It has grown since then and is now Canada's primary syndicated source for print and non-print media exposure, as well as responses to survey questions. The current study has resulted in a two-year database of 30,000 respondents, over 2,500 products, and over 3,500 brands.

The research method is an in-home interview conducted throughout the year. Respondents are screened by asking whether they have read any of the listed publications within the past 12 months; they are subsequently qualified if they have read the publications recently enough, depending upon the frequency of publication (e.g., weekly, monthly). A number of reading-related questions are asked, including frequency of reading, number of reading occasions, time spent reading, source of copy, where read, and interest.

Respondents are then asked many demographic, lifestyle, media consumption, product usage, retail shopping, and psychographic questions. The demographic questions are quite exhaustive and total over 20 in number. The lifestyle questions include life events, leisure activities, education, sporting activities, and attendance of sporting events. Media consumption questions are very extensive and include TV viewing, radio listening, community and daily newspaper reading, transit usage, distance travelled, shopping mall trips, and Yellow Pages usage. Product usage data are recorded for 17 broad product categories (e.g., personal care, groceries, financial, business, and so on). Questions pertaining to shopping at approximately 30 different retail environments are also asked. And finally, many questions are asked to determine psychographic clusters for nine broad product categories and one general societal category.

The data available for analysis represent a virtual gold mine of information for media planners. They can relate many of the variables together to accurately reach a specific target audience in terms of their behaviour (i.e., the primary target variable), demographics, lifestyle, and psychographics. The database works with specialized software to allow media planners to make their effective decisions efficiently.

One final useful feature of the PMB study is "return to sample." Individual firms can confidentially re-contact respondents to ask them proprietary questions with respect to specific brand attitudes, purchase intentions, or purchase influences. An advertiser would then have the broad data tied in with specific measures of its own brand.

MAGAZINE ADVERTISING RATES

Magazine rates are primarily a function of circulation; the greater the circulation, the higher the cost of the ad. Ads in controlled circulation magazines (i.e., free) are generally cheaper than ads in paid circulation magazines. Advertising space is generally sold on the basis of space units, such as full-page, half-page, quarter-page, or double-page spread (two facing pages); a greater cost is incurred for ads requiring more space.

Rates for magazine ad space can also vary according to the number of times an ad runs and the amount of money spent during a specific period. The more often an advertiser contracts to run an ad, the lower the space charges. Volume discounts are based on the total space purchased within a contract year, measured in dollars or number of insertions. The following table from CARD shows the cost per ad (4 colour) per month by size and the number of insertions (i.e., ti) for *Ski Canada Magazine,* which publishes four issues per year.

	1 ti	2 ti	3 ti	4 ti
Full page	$4,990	$4,745	$4,242	$3,990
2/3 p.	$4,142	$3,935	$3,520	$3,106
1/2 p.	$3,393	$3,224	$2,884	$2,545
1/3 p.	$2,246	$2,133	$1,909	$1,684
1/6 p.	$1,098	$1,043	$933	$823
1/12 p.	$749	$711	$636	$561

Other variables that increase the cost of an ad include the colours used, its position in the publication, the particular editions (geographic, demographic) chosen, any special mechanical or production requirements, and the number and frequency of insertions. *Ski Canada Magazine* charges an additional 15 percent, 10 percent, and 25 percent for ad placement on front inside cover, back inside cover, and back cover, respectively.

Ads can be produced or run using black and white, black and white plus one colour, or four colours. The more colour used in the ad, the greater the expense because of the increased printing costs. Colour ads are so prominent in magazines that many do not even quote a non-colour cost in their CARD listing. Recall and action taken are stronger with colour ads vs. non-colour ads.[4] Larger ads produce stronger recall and action taken. For example, a full page ad can have 20 percent stronger communication effects.[5] Ads placed inside the front cover, inside the back cover, and outside the back cover yield 15 percent, 10 percent, and 20 percent stronger recall than a regularly placed ad.[6]

Finally, the CARD listing for *Ski Canada Magazine* shows an audited circulation of about 27,000, broken down as individual subscription 10,000, sponsored placement for in-room reading at hotels and ski resorts 9,000, sponsored individually addressed delivery to ski associations and ski travel companies 6,000, and sponsored distribution to ski retailers 2,000. The CPM is about $185 for a one-page ad (i.e., $4,990/27), but the CPM per reader is much lower with the placement in public locations. At three readers per copy, the CPM approaches $60 (i.e., $185/3).

(L02) **Evaluation of Magazines**

Magazines have a number of strengths and limitations in comparison to other media. We review each of these according to the criteria of Chapter 10. Astute readers will acknowledge that each evaluation represents a generalization across all classifications of magazines. As such, exceptional anomalies maybe found thereby rendering debate upon the assessment.

STRENGTHS OF MAGAZINES

Magazines have a number of characteristics that make them attractive for advertisers. Strengths of magazines include their target audience selectivity, geographic coverage, creativity, reader involvement and amount of processing time, media image, and selective exposure and attention.

Target Audience Selectivity   One of the main advantages of using magazines is their selectivity, or ability to reach a specific target audience. Magazines are the most selective of all media except direct communication where the receiver's identity is known (e.g., addressed direct mail). Most magazines are published for readers with very specific reading requirements. The magazines reach all types of consumers and businesses and allow advertisers to target their advertising to groups that are consistent with their segmentation strategies along the lines of demographics, socio-economics, and lifestyle (e.g., activities and interests). For example, *PhotoLife* is targeted toward camera buffs, *Exclaim!* reaches those with an avid interest in music, and *What!* claims to be "the voice and choice of Canadian youth."

One Canadian success story is the lifestyle magazine *Nuvo*, a refined publication (non-paid circulation) catering to the very affluent who appreciate a refined lifestyle of luxury. It claims to be Canada's premier lifestyle magazine with an audited circulation hitting 45,000.[7] Another successful interest magazine is *Hello!*, which features photos of and articles about celebrities. The uniquely Canadian edition found a niche where its focus on celebrities did not follow old ways of telling the stories but found a distinctive voice. It faced the challenge of advertisers reluctant to run ads in consecutive weeks due to their familiarity with buying monthly magazine ad placements.[8] Homeowners interested in decoration and renovation ideas can select *Canadian House and Home,* with an audited circulation of 246,000 (160,000 subscribers, 86,000 single-copy sales). This is one of Canada's largest special-interest magazines with a paid circulation. Its readership of 2.4 million implies 10 readers per copy resulting in a CPM per reader just under $9, a good balance of selectivity and cost efficiency for advertisers of household decor.[9]

In addition to providing selectivity based on interests, magazines can provide advertisers with high demographic selectivity. *Demographic selectivity,* or the ability to reach specific demographic groups, is available in two ways. First, most magazines are, as a result of editorial content, aimed at fairly well-defined demographic segments. *Canadian Living* and *Chatelaine* (Exhibit 12-5) are read predominantly by women; *The Hockey News* is read mostly by men. Older consumers can be reached through publications like *FiftyPlus.*

Selectivity can be applied effectively by tailoring the message by language since Canada naturally has magazines written in both English and French. In fact, the latter has seen tremendous change with the relaunching of several titles prompting significant readership and ad revenue growth.[10] International ad campaigns like Heineken's are translated for use in French publications (Exhibit 12-6).

Two technological developments allow advertisers to deliver personalized messages to tightly targeted audiences: selective binding and ink-jet imaging. **Selective binding** is a computerized production process that allows the creation of hundreds of copies of a magazine in one continuous sequence. Selective binding enables magazines to target and address specific groups within a magazine's circulation base. They can then send different editorial or advertising messages to groups of subscribers within the same issue of a publication. **Ink-jet imaging** reproduces a message by projecting ink onto paper rather than using mechanical plates. This process makes it possible to personalize an advertising message. These innovations permit advertisers to target their messages more finely and let magazines compete more effectively with direct mail and other direct-marketing vehicles.

Exhibit 12-5 *Chatelaine* allows for demographic selectivity.

Exhibit 12-6 Translated versions of Heineken's international campaign appeared in Canadian and worldwide publications.

Geographic Coverage One way to achieve specific geographic coverage is to use a vehicle that is targeted toward a particular area like city magazines. *Toronto Life, Vancouver Magazine,* and *Montréal Scope,* to name a few, provide residents of these areas with articles concerning lifestyle, events, and the like in these cities and their surrounding metropolitan areas (Exhibit 12-7). Toronto enjoyed an expansion of titles much like what occurred 30 years ago due to an energized street scene, new inexpensive publishing technology, and post-recession optimism.[11]

Another way to achieve selective geographic coverage in magazines is through purchasing ad space in specific geographic editions of national or regional magazines. A number of publications (e.g., *Maclean's, Chatelaine*) divide their circulation into groupings based on regions or major metropolitan areas and offer advertisers the option of concentrating their ads in these editions.

CARD lists the consumer magazines offering geographic editions. Regional advertisers can purchase space in editions that reach only areas where they have distribution, yet still enjoy the prestige of advertising in a major national magazine. National advertisers can use the geographic editions to focus their advertising on areas with the greatest potential or those needing more promotional support. They can also use regional editions to test-market products or alternative promotional campaigns in regions of the country.

Ads in regional editions can also list the names of retailers or distributors, thus encouraging greater local support from the trade. The trend toward regional marketing is increasing the importance of having regional media available to marketers. The availability of regional and demographic editions can also reduce the cost per thousand for reaching desired audiences.

Creativity for Cognitive and Emotional Responses A valued attribute of magazine advertising is the reproduction quality of the ads. Magazines are generally printed

Exhibit 12-7   City magazines such as *Toronto Life* offer advertisers high geographic selectivity.

Toronto Life, August 2010. Printed with permission.

on high-quality paper stock and use printing processes that provide excellent reproduction in black and white or colour. Since magazines are a visual medium where illustrations are often a dominant part of an ad, this is a very important property. Figure 12-9 presents evidence of the importance of quality and creativity. The reproduction quality of most magazines is far superior to that offered by the other major print medium of newspapers, particularly when colour is needed. The use of colour has become a virtual necessity in most product categories. The creative HTC ad in Exhibit 12-8 encourages both types of responses with its interesting people photos.

In addition to their excellent reproduction capabilities, magazines also offer advertisers options in terms of the type, size, and placement of the advertising material. Good magazines offer (often at extra charge) a variety of special opportunities to enhance the creative appeal of the ad such as gatefolds, bleed pages, inserts, and creative space buys.

Gatefolds enable an advertiser to make a striking presentation by using a third page that folds out and gives the ad an extra-large spread. Gatefolds are often found at the inside cover of large consumer magazines, or on inside pages. Advertisers use gatefolds to make a very strong impression, especially on special occasions such as the introduction of a new product or brand. For example, automobile advertisers often use gatefolds to introduce new versions of their cars each model year. **Bleed pages** are those where the advertisement extends all the way to the end of the page, with no margin of white space around the ad. Bleeds give the ad an impression of being larger and make a more dramatic impact.

Inserts are used in magazines designed for promotion such as recipe booklets, coupons, and even product samples. Cosmetics companies use scented inserts to introduce new fragrances,

Figure   12-9   Effects of ad quality

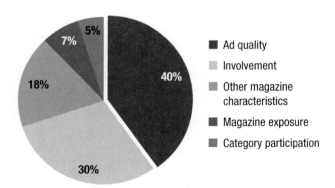

Ad recall that can be explained

- Ad quality — 40%
- Involvement — 30%
- Other magazine characteristics — 18%
- Magazine exposure — 7%
- Category participation — 5%

Source: Identifying Key Metrics for Magazine Planning, Ware (Meredith Corp.), Baron (DRAFTFCB) & Edge (Knowledge Networks), worldwide Readership Research Symposium (Prague). Base: 27% of ad recall that could be explained. September 2011

Source: Magazines Canada Fact Book 2012, p. 70.

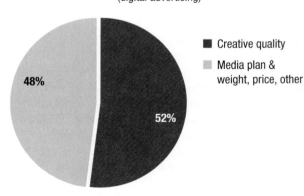

Influence on shifts in brand sales
(digital advertising)

- Creative quality — 52%
- Media plan & weight, price, other — 48%

Source: comScore ARS Global Validation Summary. Numbers represent the percent variance in sales shifts explained by the corresponding factors. Creative quality is based on the ARS Consumer Choice Score/ A lift in the score is highly correlated with brand sales results. October 2010

and others use them to promote products for which scent is important (e.g., deodorants, laundry detergents). Exhibit 12-9 shows an example of a creative insert. Cost-effective technologies enhance the reading of advertising messages through options like anaglyphic images (three-dimensional materials that are viewed with coloured glasses); lenticular (colour) images printed on finely corrugated plastic that seem to move when tilted; and pressure- or heat-sensitive inks that change colour on contact. **Creative space buys** allow advertisers to purchase space units in certain combinations to increase the impact of their media budget. IMC Perspective 12-1 describes new creative approaches for magazines.

Exhibit 12-8 This HTC ad evokes all sorts of responses.

Reader Involvement and Amount of Processing Time A distinctive strength offered by magazines is that they are generally read over several days. TV and radio are characterized by fleeting messages that have a very short life span. Readers devote about 40 minutes to reading a magazine with a high degree of interest.[12] Figure 12-10 highlights the valuable effects of the longer processing time. Magazines are retained in the home longer than any other media and are referred to on several occasions; nearly 73 percent of consumers retain magazines for future reference.[13] One benefit of the longer life of magazines is that reading occurs at a less hurried pace and there is opportunity to examine ads in considerable detail. This means ads can use longer and more detailed copy, which can be very important for complex products or services. The permanence of magazines also means readers can be exposed to ads on multiple occasions and can pass magazines along to other readers.

Media Image Another positive feature of magazine advertising is the prestige the product or service may gain from advertising in publications with a favourable image. Companies whose products rely heavily on perceived quality, reputation, and/or image often buy space in prestigious publications with high-quality editorial content whose consumers have a high level of interest in the advertising pages. For example, *Flare* covers young women's fashions in a very favourable environment, and a clothing manufacturer may advertise its products in these magazines to enhance the prestige of its lines. *Canadian Geographic* provides an impressive editorial environment that includes high-quality photography. The magazine's upscale readers are likely to have a favourable image of the publication that may transfer to the products advertised on its pages. Media planners rely on their experiences to assess a magazine's prestige and reader opinion surveys in order to select the best magazine title. Data in Figure 12-11 indicate how much consumers enjoy advertising in magazines.

Exhibit 12-9 The show *Supernatural* used a creative insert for promotion.

Selective Exposure and Attention With the exception of newspapers, consumers are more

IMC PERSPECTIVE 12-1

Magazines Get Creative and Digital

While magazine advertising revenue stabilized at the $600 million level over the past few years, Print Measurement Bureau research shows that readership interest and the number of readers per copy remains positively strong despite numerous media alternatives for consumers. Publishers look to innovate to make these personal media all the more worthwhile for advertisers—and, indeed, these customers are in the same position as their media counterparts, since both are trying to acquire and retain business to remain profitable. So it is not too surprising to see that they work together to ensure joint success along the lines of websites, social media, and databases.

At TC Media the publisher often acts as a full service provider by developing advertising programs that include social media, creative, research, contests, and video. A related initiative of this is its Media Lab, where a dedicated magazine team works with clients to build customized marketing communication packages to achieve their communication objectives. For example, TC Media put together a comprehensive package for the Export Development Corporation of Canada, a federal government agency assisting companies with international trade, to reach executives in Quebec. The package included magazine placements, website communication, and mobile apps to inform potential exports with valuable information that all produced excellent exposure numbers.

Fashion magazine helped with the launch of the new Calvin Klein fragrance Beauty by offering a contest via its magazine's website. *Fashion* invited its Twitter and Facebook followers to submit a photo that represented beauty and to explain what beauty meant to them. The communication involved 5,300 readers who commented on the photos and who subsequently received a sample. *Canadian Living* worked with P&G to identify possible leads from the former's reader panel for an Herbal Essences promotion. Participants provided online feedback in social media that proved to be useful content for future testimonial advertising.

Loulou customized its magazine with different versions for Centre a la Mode customers who fit into three groups based on their shopping behaviour derived from their database: impulsive, thoughtful, and habitual. Eight unique pages of clothing matched the three profiles so that consumers could visit the location with just the right shopping plans. Databases played an important role for Curel in working with *Reader's Digest* and *Selection* magazines, which wrote editorials about dry skin and sent e-mail using addresses from their subscription lists to those who had indicated having skin concerns. Combined with e-mails from an Environics list, the communication achieved 190,000 unique visits. *Canadian Family* used its database to recruit readers for an event for both the magazine and for Mattel and its line of Barbie products. It reached its limit of 400 in just two days and unfortunately turned away many.

The end result is that magazines no longer see themselves simply as publishers of magazines. "I now consider myself not a publisher, I consider myself a media brand manager," commented one TC Media executive. However, one critic ventured that as magazines carried on acting as advertising agencies, the development of producing quality content and building an audience for advertisers could suffer. But despite this, magazines with digital presence reported stronger overall readership as duplication levels across the website or app versus the printed version appeared minimal. Magazines that have made this transition successfully include *Toronto Life, Fresh Juice, The Walrus, Alberta Venture,* and *The Hockey News.* Finally, with all this direct connection between publishers and consumers, one wonders if an idea from the United States might take hold in Canada, with publishers guaranteeing sales levels to the advertisers in exchange for their business.

Source: Alica Androich, "Canada's Magazines Aren't Doomed," *Marketing Magazine,* May 16, 2011, pp. 26–29, 31–32; Jeff Hayward, "Gloss Leaders," *Marketing Magazine,* June 4, 2012, pp. 30–36; Jeromy Lloyd, "Printing Promises," *Marketing Magazine,* August 29, 2011, pp. 16–17.

Question:

1. How is the experience of reading a print magazine similar to or different from a digital version of the same title?

	Editorial Article	Advertisement
Noting score	54%	54%
Read any of content	50%	45%
Read most of content	33%	25%
Information Gathering:		
Used for ideas	18%	—
Gathered more info after seeing article/ad	13%	18%
Visited brand website	11%	16%
Cut it out	7%	7%
Impact Actions:		
Discussed/referred it to someone	19%	—
Passed to someone	13%	—
Have a more favourable opinion of product	—	19%
Recommended the product	—	14%
Consideration & Purchase:		
Considering purchase	12%	22%
Purchased	4%	9%
Net action score	66%	63%

Source: Magazines Canada Fact Book 2012, p. 64.

Figure 12-10

Behavioural effects of high involvement processing of magazines

Figure 12-11   Magazines offer a good media image for advertisers

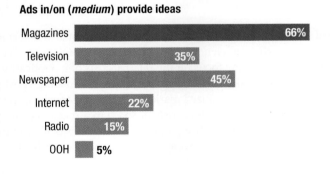

Ads in/on (*medium*) provide ideas

Magazines	66%
Television	35%
Newspaper	45%
Internet	22%
Radio	15%
OOH	5%

Ads in/on (*medium*) contain important details

Magazines	57%
Television	34%
Newspaper	39%
Internet	21%
Radio	14%
OOH	2%

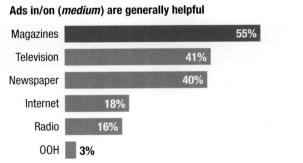

Ads in/on (*medium*) are generally helpful

Magazines	55%
Television	41%
Newspaper	40%
Internet	18%
Radio	16%
OOH	3%

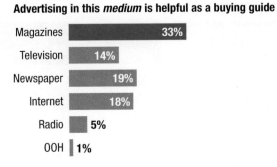

Advertising in this *medium* is helpful as a buying guide

Magazines	33%
Television	14%
Newspaper	19%
Internet	18%
Radio	5%
OOH	1%

Source: Magazines Canada Fact Book 2012, p. 55.

receptive to advertising in magazines than in any other medium. Magazines are generally purchased because the information they contain interests the reader, and ads provide additional information that may be of value in making a purchase decision. Magazines, such as bridal or fashion publications, are purchased as much for their advertising as for their editorial content.

In addition to their relevance, magazine ads are likely to be received favourably by consumers because, unlike broadcast ads, they are nonintrusive and can easily be ignored. The majority of magazine readers welcome ads; only a small percentage have negative attitudes toward magazine advertising. Consumers generally enjoy magazines over other media along many measures such as advertising receptivity, inspirational, trustworthy, life-enhancing, social interaction, and personal timeout. Furthermore, readers believe advertising contributes to the enjoyment of reading a magazine more strongly than other media and they have stronger attitudes to magazine ads versus ads in other media.[14] Figure 12-12 shows that magazines hold readers' attention better than other media as fewer people gravitate to other media for simultaneous consumption.

Advertisers take advantage of this strength with clever creative tactics. For example, Audi and *Maclean's* teamed up to put an ad on the magazine cover that looked entirely normal except for a discreetly placed "open here" message. Readers lifted a small flap to reveal the car ad—which proclaimed the AQ was foxy compared to a generic "boxy" competitor.[15] *Vice* magazine managed to put a BMW ad on its cover that could be seen only in the dark. The publisher distributed copies to nightclubs, where the ad would become visible.[16]

LIMITATIONS OF MAGAZINES

Although the strengths offered by magazines are considerable, they have certain drawbacks too. These include the costs of advertising, their limited reach and frequency, the long lead time required in placing an ad, weak target audience coverage, and the problem of clutter.

Absolute Cost and Cost Efficiency   The cost of advertising in magazines varies according to size of audience reached and selectivity. Advertising in large mass-circulation magazines like *Maclean's* can be very expensive. For example, a full-page, four-colour ad in *Maclean's* national edition (circulation 362,000) had a cost of $37,000. Popular positions such as the back cover cost even more.

Magazines must be considered not only from an absolute cost perspective but also in terms of relative costs. Most magazines emphasize their efficiency in reaching specific target audiences at a low cost per thousand. Media planners generally focus on the relative costs of a publication in reaching their target audience. However, they may recommend a magazine with a high cost per thousand because of its ability to reach a small, specialized market segment. Of course, advertisers with limited budgets will be interested in the absolute costs of space in a magazine and the costs of producing quality ads for these publications. Strong brands like BMW are often in publications where the absolute cost is not a substantial deterrent for ad placement (Exhibit 12-10).

Figure   12-12

Incidence of simultaneous media consumption

	Read Magazines	Watch Tv	Listen To Radio	Read Newspapers	Go Online	Total*
Read Magazines	—	21%	13%	—	11%	45%
Read Newspapers	—	25%	14%	—	11%	50%
Listen to Radio	10%	11%	—	13%	21%	55%
Watch TV	11%	—	6%	12%	33%	62%
Go Online	10%	44%	24%	13%	—	91%

*Totals calculated to provide an indication of multiple media use volume

Source: Magazines Canada Fact Book 2012, p. 53.

Reach and Frequency Magazines are generally not as effective as other media in offering reach and frequency. While adults in Canada read one or more consumer magazines each month, the percentage of adults reading any individual publication tends to be much smaller. As Figure 12-2 showed, the circulation of 80 percent of all titles is below 50,000. An ad in a magazine with this circulation reaches less than half a percent of all households.

Advertisers seeking broad reach must make media buys in a number of magazines, resulting in greater costs with multiple transactions. For a broad reach strategy, magazines are used in conjunction with other media. Since most magazines are monthly or at best weekly publications, the opportunity for building frequency through the use of the same publication is limited. Using multiple ads in the same issue of a publication is an inefficient way to build frequency, although a product category like fashion finds success with this approach as volume discounts are offered.

Despite these concerns from an individual titles view, total magazine reach is as impressive as any other media. About 9 out of 10 Canadians (aged 12–17, 18–24, 25–34) read magazines within the most recent three months, and readership averages about 80 percent. Six out of 10 Canadians (aged 12 to 64) read a magazine within the past week.[17]

Scheduling Flexibility Another drawback of magazines is the long lead time needed to place an ad, thus reducing scheduling flexibility. Most major publications have a 30- to 90-day lead time, which means space must be purchased and the ad must be prepared well in advance of the actual publication date. No changes in the art or copy of the ad can be made after the closing date. This long lead time means magazine ads cannot be as timely as other media, such as radio or newspapers, in responding to current events or changing market conditions.

Target Audience Coverage The flipside of the strength of target audience selectivity is the limitation of magazines in providing extensive target audience coverage. Even though a magazine may draw an audience with a particular interest, for example, hockey with *The Hockey News,* the number of people reading the publication versus the number of people who actually play hockey is substantially disproportionate. The ability to achieve coverage with young adults 18–24 is limited as purchase and subscription levels are quite low; however, one study finds that young adults are vastly more receptive to reading print versions of magazines versus digital versions and prefer ads in magazines over digital ads.[18] And one expert sees great opportunity for continued development for magazines—and subsequently advertisers—with the growth of tablets, as long as the content resonates with the young audience.[19]

Clutter Advertising clutter is not a serious issue for print media as data show strong communication effects even with a competitor's ad in the same issue.[20] Consumers are more receptive and tolerant of print advertising and control their exposure to a magazine ad simply by turning the page; however, the many pages of ads in a magazine raises an issue of concern when planning print ad placement. And this issue is a paradox for magazines since successful titles attract more advertising pages potentially leading to greater clutter. Magazine publishers control clutter by maintaining a reasonable balance of editorial pages to advertising. Advertisers control the clutter with the use of strong visual images, catchy headlines, or other creative techniques to gain a reader's attention. In fact, new creative executions in magazines over many issues minimize ad wear-out, another factor contributing to issues of clutter.[21]

Advertisers create their own custom magazines to sidestep advertising clutter as well as to have control over editorial content. Fashion retailer Holt Renfrew custom-published its own shopping magazine, *Holt's,* to reach a sophisticated clientele who shop all around the world.

Exhibit 12-10 Brands like BMW can afford the high absolute cost of ad placement in upscale magazines.

Exhibit 12-11 *Rouge* is a custom magazine published by Procter & Gamble.

This contributed to Holt Renfrew's established connections with the high-profile publication *Lucky,* where the fashion retailer consistently linked its brand with the world-renowned fashion and beauty brands through product placement and cooperative media opportunities. In the future, Holt Renfrew looks to establish more permanent advertising placements in Canada's newest fashion magazines—*Loulou, Fashion Shops,* and *Shopping: Clin d'oeil*—and achieve an optimal balance between custom-published and regular magazines.[22] Procter & Gamble's *Rouge* is a custom publication targeted to consumers who are active in buying personal enhancement or beauty products (Exhibit 12-11). The brand leader established the publication in Canada four years prior to its American launch.

 # Newspapers

Newspapers are another form of print media and are one of the largest of all advertising media in terms of total dollar volume. In 2012 $2 billion was spent on daily newspaper advertising, or about 13 percent of the total advertising expenditures in Canada. Community newspapers hit $1.2 billion or 8 percent, and online newspaper notched in at almost $.3 billion but this amount is counted as Internet advertising revenue. The total of $3.5 billion rivaled TV's $3.5 billion. Newspapers are an especially important advertising medium to local advertisers, particularly retailers, and are also valuable to national advertisers. In this section we review different types of newspapers, the types of advertising newspapers offer, audience circulation and readership, audience measurement, and finally newspaper advertising rates.

TYPES OF NEWSPAPERS

The traditional role of newspapers has been to deliver prompt news information and features that appeal to readers as shown in Figure 12-13. In short, they provide detailed coverage of news, events, and issues concerning the local area as well as business, sports, and other relevant information and entertainment. The vast majority of newspapers are daily publications serving a local community. However, weekly, national, and special-audience newspapers have special characteristics that can be valuable to advertisers.

Daily Newspapers   Daily newspapers, which are published each weekday, are found in cities and larger towns across the country. Some areas have more than one daily paper and are known as competitive markets, while the vast majority of smaller Canadian cities and towns have one publication. Daily newspapers are read by 46 percent of adults each weekday and nearly 73 percent each week. In 2011, there were 121 daily newspapers in Canada; of these, 108

Figure   12-13

Secondary topics, read after news

Men 18+		Women 18+	
Sports	56%	Arts/Entertainment	52%
Business/Finance	43%	Health	48%
Editorial/Opinion	36%	Food	46%
Health	27%	Fashion/Lifestyle	40%
Arts/Entertainment	26%	Editorial/Opinion	39%
Source: 2012 NADbank.			

were English-language papers and 13 were French-language papers, with a total circulation of 5.8 million. The newspaper formats included 67 broadsheet style and 54 tabloid style. Most daily newspapers charge a price (or subscription fee); however, free dailies emerged on the market a decade ago and now represent substantial circulation and advertising revenue. There are 18 free daily newspapers in 11 markets under the *Metro* or *24 Hours* banner.[23]

Community Newspapers   Most community newspapers publish weekly and originate in small towns where the volume of news and advertising cannot support a daily newspaper. Canada had 1,100 community newspapers in 2011 with a total circulation of 15 million. Community newspapers also dot the suburbs of many larger Canadian cities. These papers focus primarily on news, sports, and events relevant to the local area and usually ignore content covered by the city-based daily newspaper. Community newspapers appeal primarily to local advertisers because of their geographic focus and lower absolute cost. Most national advertisers avoid community newspapers because of their duplicate circulation with daily papers in the large metropolitan areas.

National Newspapers   Newspapers in Canada with national circulation include the *National Post* and *The Globe and Mail*. Both are daily publications and have editorial content with a national appeal. The *National Post* has a weekday circulation of about 142,000 and a Saturday circulation of almost 132,000, and *The Globe and Mail* has a weekday circulation of about 355,000 and a Saturday circulation of approximately 293,000.[24] National newspapers appeal primarily to large national advertisers and to regional advertisers that use specific geographic editions of these publications.

Internet Newspapers   Major Canadian daily newspapers, the two national newspapers, and community newspapers offer an Internet version of their publications. Regular newspapers charge for subscription or individual papers at newsstands and rely on advertising revenue to support the distribution of editorial content. Internet versions are similar in this respect; the publishing firms have experimented with different combinations of fees and banner ads. CanWest allowed newspaper subscribers free access to the complete digital version of the newspaper. Online readership has grown from 10 percent in 2001 to almost 20 percent, but it is substantially lower than the 80 percent for the original version. Consumers are currently in the process of evolving their newspaper consumption habits, as shown in Figures 12-14 to 12-17. Newspapers are packaging online and print ads for advertisers, and larger media companies are adding TV ads to the overall sale. However one industry executive suggested, "We need to think more about selling our audiences, because that is something that is sincere and heartfelt and resonates with advertisers."[25]

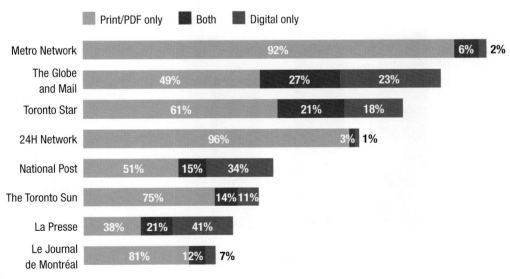

Figure 12-14

Readership by channel varies by newspaper

Source: 2012 NADbank Study.

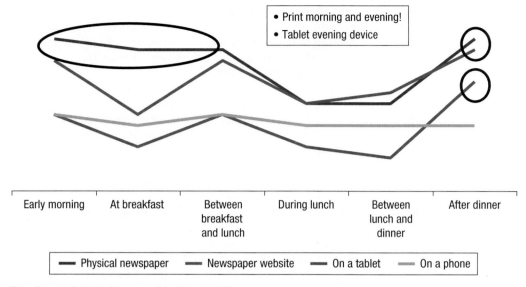

Figure   12-15

Newspaper access by time of day

Source: Newspapers Canada 24-7 Study.

Totum Research; Canadians 18+, any weekday, December 2011

Special-Audience Newspapers   A variety of papers offer specialized editorial content and are published for particular groups, including labour unions, professional organizations, industries, and hobbyists. Many people working in advertising and marketing read *Marketing Magazine*. Specialized newspapers are also published in areas with large foreign-language-speaking ethnic groups, among them Chinese. Newspapers targeted at various religious and educational groups compose another large class of special-interest papers. A trend has been the establishment of local business newspapers.

Newspaper Supplements   Although not a category of newspapers per se, papers include magazine-type supplements. For example, *The Globe and Mail* publishes a glossy *Report On Business* magazine at the end of each month. Newspapers are also in the game of custom publishing magazine supplements for advertisers. This is a relatively new field for this media as titles look to replace lost advertising revenue with classified ads shifting to digital vehicles. In contrast, as noted in the magazine section, this kind of activity occurred with great frequency in that media,

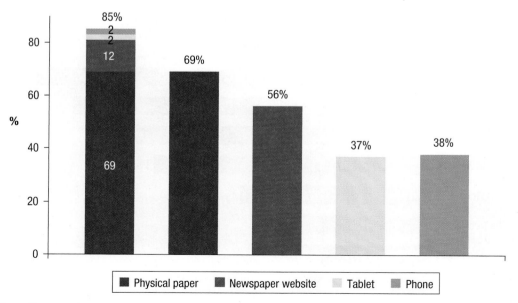

Figure   12-16

Weekly reach by type of access

Source: Newspapers Canada 24-7 Study.

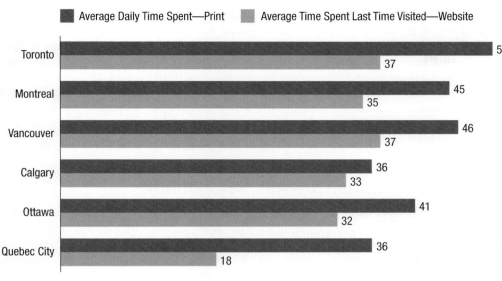

■ Average Daily Time Spent—Print   ■ Average Time Spent Last Time Visited—Website

Figure   12-17

Time spent reading, weekday and weekend, in minutes

Source: 2012 NADbank.

but newspapers struggle with the balance of journalistic integrity with the need to please advertisers. One example is the twice-yearly publication Sunnybrook put together by *The Globe and Mail*. This publication provides extensive information regarding all of the hospital's activities and is a key tool for generating donations as it is sent to 50,000 *G&M* subscribers and 30,000 donors.[26]

TYPES OF NEWSPAPER ADVERTISING

The ads appearing in newspapers can also be divided into different categories. The major types of newspaper advertising are display and classified. Other special types of ads and preprinted inserts also appear in newspapers.

Display Advertising   Display advertising is found throughout the newspaper and generally uses illustrations, headlines, white space, and other visual devices in addition to the copy text. The two types of display advertising in newspapers are local and national (general).

Local advertising refers to ads placed by local organizations, businesses, and individuals who want to communicate with consumers in the market area served by the newspaper. Supermarkets and department stores are among the leading local display advertisers, along with numerous other retailers and service operations such as banks and travel agents.

National or general advertising refers to newspaper display advertising done by marketers of branded products or services that are sold on a national or regional level. These ads are designed to create and maintain demand and to complement the efforts of local retailers that stock and promote the advertiser's products. Major retail chains, automakers, and airlines are heavy users of newspaper advertising.

Classified Advertising   Classified advertising provides newspapers with revenue; however, online classifieds have eaten into this market considerably. These ads are arranged under subheads according to the product, service, or offering being advertised. While most classified ads are just text set in small type, newspapers also accept classified display advertising. These ads are run in the classified section of the paper but use illustrations, larger type sizes, white space, borders, and even colour to stand out.

Special Ads   Special advertisements in newspapers include a variety of government and financial reports and notices and public notices of changes in business and personal relationships. Other types of advertising in newspapers include political or special-interest ads promoting a particular candidate, issue, or cause.

Inserts Preprinted inserts do not appear in the paper itself; they are printed by the advertiser and sent to the newspaper to be inserted before delivery. Many retailers use inserts such as circulars, catalogues, or brochures in specific circulation zones to reach shoppers in their particular trade areas. Car companies often include poster-like inserts that people may choose to keep. A trend is for inserts to become more creative. Belairdirect insurance used inserts that looked like file folders similar to what consumers would use while researching this purchase. For the holiday season a Molson insert looked like a beer fridge; upon opening, consumers could see cases on flaps that could be opened that had promotional information underneath, like PIN codes for an online contest to win a beer fridge or links to Facebook fan pages.[27]

NEWSPAPER CIRCULATION AND READERSHIP

The media planner must understand the size and reading usage characteristics of the audience reached by a newspaper when considering its value in the media plan. Like any other media, advertisers are concerned with the size of the audience reached through a particular vehicle. Thus, the circulation, or number of readers, is an important statistic evaluated. And while the size is important, advertisers are also interested in the amount of reading occurring and similar usage statistics prior to making their decision regarding newspapers.

Circulation The basic source of information concerning the audience size of newspapers comes from circulation figures available through CARD, discussed earlier in this chapter. The Alliance for Audited Media (AAM) verifies circulation figures for many newspapers, as illustrated in the magazine media section. Advertisers using a number of papers in their media plan generally find CARD to be the most convenient source. The Canadian Community Newspapers Association (CCNA) verifies the circulation if an advertiser decides to use this vehicle.

The CCNA is a network of regional newspaper associations and membership of an individual community newspaper in a regional association includes membership in the national association. CCNA currently represents about 750 of the 1,100 community newspapers with a total first-edition circulation of more than 14 million copies per week. The CCNA gives an individual community newspaper a national voice in working with the public, business, and government, and its mission is to ensure a strong community newspaper industry. For advertisers, the CCNA plays a strong role in coordinating the placement of ads throughout the network. Its services include a "one-order, one-bill" system, ROP ads and pre-printed inserts, digital transmission of ads, Geographic Information System (GIS), and national or regional classified advertising. CCNA claims that community newspapers offer key benefits: precise coverage of specific markets with no wasted circulation, strong household penetration, state-of-the-art newspaper reproduction, and audited circulation figures.

Newspaper circulation figures are generally broken down into three categories: the city zone, the retail trading zone, and all other areas. The **city zone** is a market area composed of the city where the paper is published and contiguous areas similar in character to the city. The **retail trading zone** is the market outside the city zone whose residents regularly trade with merchants within the city zone. The "all other" category covers all circulation not included in the city or retail trade zone.

Sometimes circulation figures are provided only for the primary market, which is the city and retail trade zones combined, and the "all other" area. Both local and national advertisers consider the circulation patterns across the various categories in evaluating and selecting newspapers.

Readership Circulation figures provide the media planner with the basic data for assessing the value of newspapers and their ability to cover market areas. However, the media planner also wants to match the characteristics of a newspaper's readers with those of the advertiser's target audience. Data on newspaper audience size and characteristics are available from NADbank. Figures 12-18 to 12-21 give an overview of the Canadian newspaper reader.

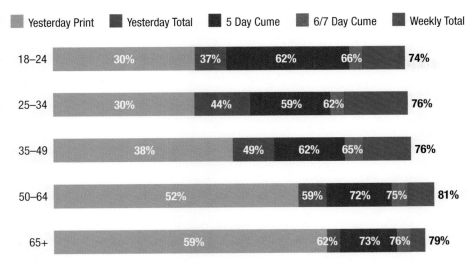

Figure 12-18

Daily newspaper readership by age, all markets, adults 18+

Legend: Yesterday Print · Yesterday Total · 5 Day Cume · 6/7 Day Cume · Weekly Total

18–24	30%	37%	62%	66%	74%
25–34	30%	44%	59%	62%	76%
35–49	38%	49%	62%	65%	76%
50–64	52%	59%	72%	75%	81%
65+	59%	62%	73%	76%	79%

Source: 2012 NADbank Study.

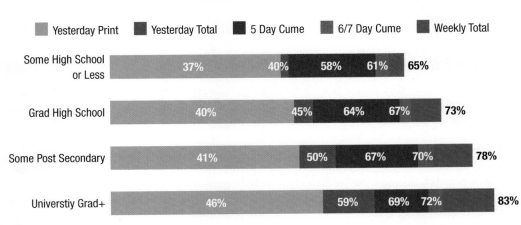

Figure 12-19

Daily newspaper readership by education, all markets, adults 18+

Legend: Yesterday Print · Yesterday Total · 5 Day Cume · 6/7 Day Cume · Weekly Total

Some High School or Less	37%	40%	58%	61%	65%
Grad High School	40%	45%	64%	67%	73%
Some Post Secondary	41%	50%	67%	70%	78%
Universtiy Grad+	46%	59%	69%	72%	83%

Source: 2012 NADbank Study.

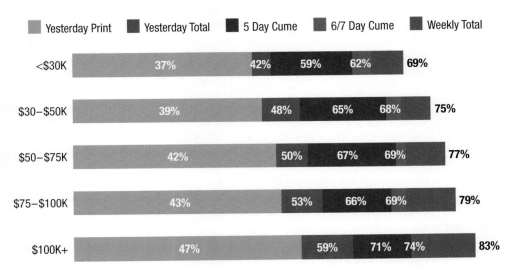

Figure 12-20

Daily newspaper readership by income, all markets, adults 18+

Legend: Yesterday Print · Yesterday Total · 5 Day Cume · 6/7 Day Cume · Weekly Total

<$30K	37%	42%	59%	62%	69%
$30–$50K	39%	48%	65%	68%	75%
$50–$75K	42%	50%	67%	69%	77%
$75–$100K	43%	53%	66%	69%	79%
$100K+	47%	59%	71%	74%	83%

Source: 2012 NADbank Study.

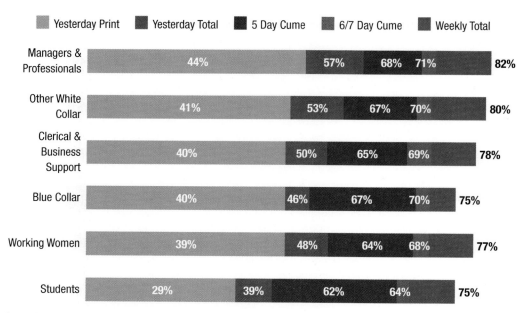

Figure   12-21

Daily newspaper readership
by occupation, all markets,
adults 18+

Source: 2012 NADbank Study.

DAILY NEWSPAPER AUDIENCE MEASUREMENT

For newspapers, we summarize two important organizations that are involved with audience measurement: NADbank and ComBase. The former concerns itself with city newspapers, while the latter's focus is community newspapers.

NADbank   Newspaper Audience Databank Inc. (NADbank) is an organization comprising newspaper, advertising agency, and advertiser members. Its primary mandate is to publish audience research information for Canadian daily newspapers. The purpose of this research is to provide its members with valid readership information to facilitate the buying and selling of newspaper advertising space.

NADbank uses a phone interview of respondents that takes approximately 15 minutes. The interview asks questions pertaining to readership of local and non-local newspapers, time spent reading, frequency of reading, method of receipt of newspapers into the home or outside the home, readership of TV magazine publications, radio listening, TV viewing and magazine readership, Internet readership of online newspapers, demographics, and media reliance. Product usage data are collected by a self-completion questionnaire that is sent to respondents after the telephone interview. These questions focus on 29 product categories and 20 retail shopping categories.

The study is conducted in 53 Canadian urban markets covering 83 Canadian paid daily newspapers. Twenty-two markets annually are measured for both the readership and product data, while 31 markets are measured for readership data every three years. The measurement period for NADbank comprises two waves. The Winter/Spring wave covers the period from January to June. The Fall wave measures the period from September to December.

The readership study indicated that adults read the newspaper an average of 48 minutes per weekday and an average of 88 minutes on the weekend. The reach of newspapers is quite pervasive even though there are many media choices and reading is more time-consuming and involving than other media. For example, 46 percent of adults 18 and older across all markets read a newspaper yesterday, 44 percent read a newspaper last weekend, and 7 percent have read a newspaper in the past week.[28]

As we have seen in the audience measurement for other media, the NADbank data are available to use with specialized software from two authorized suppliers (IMS and Harris/Telmar). It provides consultation services to assist its members who use the information. Proprietary questions may also be added to the survey if an advertiser or marketer wants to link brand-specific data with the media and product usage data.

ComBase ComBase administers the audience measurement for CCNA. ComBase is also the name of the study. ComBase is an organization with a composition and mandate similar to that of NADbank. The independent board features newspapers, advertisers, and advertising agencies. Its mandate is to publish audience research information of the community newspapers throughout Canada to allow them to sell their advertising space more effectively. The most current study occurred in 2009.

The "Recent Reading" methodology used by ComBase is as thorough as the NADbank and PMB studies. In fact, an independent organization, the Canadian Advertising Research Foundation (CARF), appraised and endorsed the methodology. Of note, the survey determines all the publications read with an intensive investigation over a three-month time period. The survey also features excellent sample sizes and response rates and conducts the survey appropriately over time to ensure authenticity.

ComBase conducts 10-minute telephone interviews in English with adults selected at random. The interviewer asks questions pertaining to readership of community newspapers, local and non-resident; readership of daily newspapers, including nationals; readership of other print press including shoppers, agricultural press, and alternative publications; number of papers read; frequency of reading; newspaper preferred if more than one is read; rating of newspapers read; radio listening and TV viewing; and demographic information about the respondent and household.

Results of the data can be compiled along a number of dimensions: Census Metropolitan Area (CMA) with population of 100,000 or more in an urbanized core; Census Agglomeration (CA) with population of 10,000 or more in an urbanized core; suburbs; newspaper distribution areas; Census Subdivisions (CSD) like towns and villages; economic regions with areas of common economic interests as defined by Statistics Canada; and provinces. Data can be accessed and used with existing media software, similar to the situation with NADbank. The following results demonstrate the significance of community newspapers: 74 percent read a community newspaper (weekend or weekday), one-third read only a community newspaper, and the average reading time is about 40 minutes.[29]

NEWSPAPER ADVERTISING RATES

Advertisers are faced with a number of options and pricing structures when purchasing newspaper space. The cost of advertising space depends on the circulation, and whether the circulation is controlled (free) or paid. It also depends on factors such as premium charges for colour in a special section, as well as discounts available. National rates can be about 15 percent higher than local rates, to account for agency commission. Figures 12-22 and 12-23 provide a summary of newspaper advertising rates.

Newspaper space is sold by the **agate line** and **column width**. A line (or agate line) is a unit measuring one column wide and 1/14-inch deep. One problem with this unit is that newspapers

Figure 12-22   Daily newspaper circulation and cost by region

	Atlantic	Quebec	Ontario	Prairies	BC & Yukon	Total
Number of Markets	13	6	34	14	21	88
Number of Dailies	14	13	45	21	25	121
Circulation	341,229	1,259,549	2,530,336	945,049	708,401	5,784,204
Full Page BW ($)	62,303	114,377	436,099	151,357	99,699	1,024,625
Full Page Colour ($)	73,049	142,447	507,355	184,673	117,101	

Source: CARDonline May 2012, Media Digest 2012–2013, p. 55.

Figure   12-23   Daily newspaper circulation and cost by population groups

	1MM+	500M– 1MM	100M– 500M	50M– 100M	Under 50M	Total
Number of Markets	6	3	25	23	31	88
Number of Dailies	30	6	31	23	31	121
Circulation	3,928,084	513,944	897,813	270,333	174,030	5,784,204
Full Page BW ($)	460,579	60,366	192,661	76,723	73,506	863,835
Full Page Colour ($)	540,794	83,861	222,468	90,260	87,242	1,024,625

Source: CARDonline May 2012, Media Digest 2012–2013, p. 55.

use columns of varying width, from 6 columns per page to 10 columns per page, which affects the size, shape, and costs of an ad. (Note that these columns are not the actual columns viewed while reading the newspaper.) This results in a complicated production and buying process for national advertisers that purchase space in a number of newspapers.

Advertisers need to know the number of lines and number of columns on a newspaper page in order to calculate the cost of an ad. For example, the following calculation is for the weekday cost of a full-page ad in the national edition of the *National Post*. The paper has 301 lines and 10 columns per page, and the open cost per line is $17.69.

$$10 \text{ columns} \times 301 \text{ lines} \times \$17.69/\text{line per column} = \$53,247$$

This calculation could be done differently with the same result when the entire length of the paper is known (301 lines/14 agate lines per column inch).

$$10 \text{ columns} \times 21.5 \text{ inches} \times 14 \text{ agate lines per column inch} \times \$17.69 = \$52,247$$

This principle can be used to calculate the cost of ads of various sizes. For example, for an ad that is 5 columns wide and 6 inches deep, the calculation would then be the following:

$$5 \text{ columns} \times 6 \text{ inches} \times 14 \text{ agate lines per column inch} \times \$17.69 \text{ per column inch} = \$7,430$$

Newspaper rates for local advertisers continue to be based on the column inch, which is 1 inch deep by 1 column wide. Advertising rates for local advertisers are quoted per column inch, and media planners calculate total space costs by multiplying the ad's number of column inches by the cost per inch.

Most newspapers have an **open-rate structure**, which means discounts are available. These discounts are generally based on frequency or bulk purchases of space and depend on the number of column inches purchased in a year. The above calculations used the most expensive cost based on a one-time ad. The maximum discount puts the cost per line at $11.82, about one-third less expensive. A full-page ad would drop from $53,247 to $35,578, a savings of $17,669.

Newspaper space rates also vary with an advertiser's special requests, such as preferred position or colour. The basic rates quoted by a newspaper are **run of paper (ROP)**, which means the paper can place the ad on any page or in any position it desires. While most newspapers try to place an ad in a requested position, the advertiser can ensure a specific section and/or position on a page by paying a higher **preferred position rate**. Colour advertising is also available in many newspapers on an ROP basis or through preprinted inserts or supplements.

Advertising rates have come under fire from media buyers with an equally contentious response from the media vendors. Historically, media buyers paid what newspapers set as their price without much criticism. However, newspaper rates have been questioned from larger advertising agencies and media buying organizations that have emerged with amalgamations in the industry. While media buyers usually investigate and evaluate the audience size and price for television advertising rates, this behaviour was not generally expected with newspapers. In particular, the *National Post* and *The Globe and Mail* reacted strongly to those buyers who have put increased pressure on lower rates as they represent very large advertisers who purchase millions of agate lines per year. To contribute to the discussion, *The Globe and Mail* worked with an independent data analysis firm that tracked the sales impact of newspaper ad placement.[30]

 Evaluation of Newspapers

Newspapers have a number of strengths and limitations in comparison to other media. We review each of these according to the criteria of Chapter 10. Newspapers present unique opportunities for ad placement that varies its strengths and limitations, as does the use of national, city, or community publications. Despite this the generalizations are reasonably consistent no matter the situation.

STRENGTHS OF NEWSPAPERS

Newspapers have a number of characteristics that make them popular among both local and national advertisers. These include their reach and frequency, scheduling flexibility, geographic coverage, reader involvement and amount of processing time, media image, creativity for cognitive responses, absolute cost and cost efficiency, and target audience coverage.

Reach and Frequency   One of the primary strengths of newspapers is the high degree of market coverage they offer an advertiser. In most areas, 40 to 50 percent of households read a daily newspaper each day, and the reach figure hits the higher end among households with higher incomes and education levels. Most areas are served by one or two daily newspapers.

The extensive penetration of newspapers makes them a truly mass medium and provides advertisers with an excellent opportunity for reaching all segments of the population. Also, since many newspapers are published and read daily, the advertiser can build a high level of frequency into the media schedule. Figure 12-24 shows reach information for print and print/website options.

Scheduling Flexibility   Another strength of newspapers is the flexibility they offer advertisers in terms of requirements for producing and running the ads. Newspaper ads can be written, laid out, and prepared in a matter of hours. For most dailies, the closing time by which the ad must be received is usually only 48 hours before publication (although closing dates for supplements and for special ads, such as those using colour, are longer). The short production time and closing dates make newspapers very suitable for responding to current events or presenting timely information to consumers.

Geographic Coverage   Newspapers generally offer advertisers targeted geographic or territorial coverage. Advertisers can vary their coverage by choosing a paper—or combination of papers—that reaches the areas with the greatest sales potential. National advertisers take

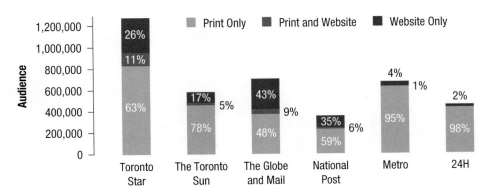

Figure   12-24

Total reach including online readership, 18+

Source: 2012 NADbank Study.

advantage of the geographic coverage of newspapers to concentrate their advertising in specific areas they can't reach with other media or to take advantage of strong sales potential in a particular area. For example, more expensive automobile manufacturers advertise in Toronto newspapers that reach the greater Toronto area and beyond with their wide distribution.

A number of companies use newspapers in their regional marketing strategies. Newspaper advertising lets them feature products on a market-by-market basis, respond and adapt campaigns to local market conditions, and tie in to more retailer promotions, fostering more support from the trade.

Local advertisers like retailers are interested in geographic coverage within a specific market or trade area. Their media goal is to concentrate their advertising in the areas where most of their customers are. Many newspapers now offer advertisers geographic areas or zones for this purpose. Figure 12-25 shows readership in Canada's large geographic markets.

Reader Involvement and Amount of Processing Time   Another important feature of newspapers is consumers' level of acceptance and involvement with papers and the ads they contain. The typical newspaper reader spends considerable time each day reading. Most consumers rely heavily on newspapers not only for news, information, and entertainment but also for assistance with consumption decisions.

Many consumers actually purchase a newspaper *because* of the advertising it contains. Consumers use retail ads to determine product prices and availability and to see who is having a sale. One aspect of newspapers that is helpful to advertisers is readers' knowledge about particular sections of the paper. Most of us know that ads for automotive products and sporting goods are generally found in the sports section, while ads for financial services are found in the business section. The weekly food section in many newspapers is popular for recipe and menu ideas as well as for the grocery store ads and coupons offered by many stores and companies.

Media Image   The value of newspaper advertising as a source of information has been shown in several studies. One study found that consumers look forward to ads in newspapers more than in other media. In another study, 80 percent of consumers said newspaper ads were most helpful to them in doing their weekly shopping. Newspaper advertising has also been rated the most believable form of advertising in numerous studies. IMC Perspective 12-2 reflects on the positive changes of newspaper advertising.

Creativity for Cognitive Responses   Newspapers offer the opportunity for extremely long copy, perhaps a thousand words extolling the attributes and benefits of a product. The option of considerable explanation of a product could be quite important for marketers looking to persuade consumers who are at the information search stage of the decision-making process. Furthermore, newspapers offer numerous creative options as ads can be run in different sizes, shapes, and formats to persuade the reader. Magazine innovations described earlier are adapted to newspapers as well. *Metro* agreed to print all 540,000 copies of an entire edition on

Figure   12-25

Yesterday readership 18+ in 1MM+ markets

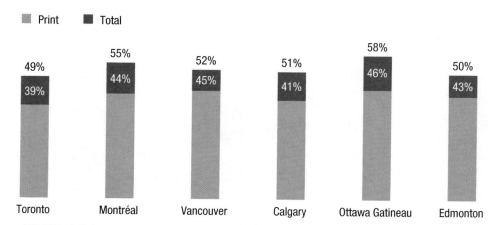

Source: 2012 NADbank Study.

IMC PERSPECTIVE 12-2

Newspaper Innovations

Popular opinion suggests that newspapers are on their deathbed and no longer represent a viable advertising medium; however, nothing could be further from the truth. Most Canadian newspapers remain quite strong as readers continue to seek out information, which keeps readership levels steady. Further, readers seek content from a credible and trusted source like a newspaper in the face of less credible sources found on the Internet. Newspapers have found a growing niche in readers getting news through different digital avenues, which raises a significant concern about having to charge for "free" online service. However, some inventive techniques for both content and advertising may hold off the pay-for-service model for a while.

Many newspapers raced to develop apps so readers could consume their media on new reading and mobile devices. This growth of digital media permitted accurate tracking of reader consumption. As expected, reading via mobile devices peaks during commute times and shifts to desktop access during the day, thereby giving newspapers the opportunity to adjust content and give advertisers direction for targeting.

Another innovation without widespread dissemination is reader participation through opening a file on the publication's Internet site and adding to the story, raising the possibility of a new and unique advertising approach. Furthermore, social media is now an important source for reporters to be on the scene for changes in stories, thereby giving content a new meaning of importance as readers are letting publishers know what stories are relevant; this approach should permit stronger reader interest in the long run. Continuing with this idea is that publishers are trying to stay more connected with the community to ensure local stories are covered more thoroughly.

Another aspect is the development of customized content on a topic for which the publisher knows it will be able to attract stronger advertising interest and revenues. Innovation with news content production and the selling of advertising occurs with newspaper reporters now doing video news and continually updating their stories, and account reps selling paper and digital space for ads. Digital technology permits sourcing of content from all over the world, which allows cultural targeting for advertising as publishers compile the more customized news in a format that works for both readers and advertisers.

Torstar offered its subscription list and put Internet ads on its publication with group-buying promoters, so that when a customer responded to the offer the publisher would receive a commission from the promoter while the business would avoid the advertising fee. New features for presenting ads emerged in a presumably more enjoyable format, like the ones where the ad expands outward so that consumers can see and experience the message. Another approach put together different kinds of front pages that are in fact ads on the actual newspaper, known as "front page wraps," to obtain reader attention. Some are concerned that this detracts from the delivery of the news product, but others are finding success. Other inventions—like "belly bands," which are advertising strips surrounding the paper like a belt, and "French doors," which are section wraps split down the middle—are making headway as well.

Source: Susan Krashinsky, "Paying for the News: Media Companies Push Online Readers to Open Their Wallets," *The Globe and Mail,* December 28, 2011, p. B1; Susan Krashinsky and Simon Houpt, "The Battle for the Digital Newsstand," *The Globe and Mail,* February 26, 2011, p. B6; Susan Krashinsky, "Papers Step Up in Battle for Eyeballs," *The Globe and Mail,* April 28, 2011; Matt Semansky, "Paper Tigers," *Marketing Magazine,* January 24, 2011, pp. 15–16, 18, 20, 22.

Question:

1. Why are newspapers a stronger or weaker alternative as an advertising medium compared to online blogs?

---

special green paper for Dove's Cool Moisture product line. The special media buy included a front-page ad, a double-page spread inside, and a product sample attached to the front.[31]

Absolute Cost and Cost Efficiency Newspapers assist small companies through free copywriting and art services. Small advertisers without an agency or advertising department often rely on the newspaper to help them write and produce their ads. Production costs of ads are reasonable since many are comprised of simple copy with a standard image or photo-stock visual. The creative flexibility of newspapers in terms of size and format of the ad makes it difficult to exactly conclude the cost implications of this medium. Small and local businesses can run a small ad with a reasonable CPM (cost per thousand) compared to magazines.

Target Audience Coverage   Coverage of a specific target audience is argued to be a limitation for the newspaper in comparison to its print cousin, the magazine. However, placement of ads in certain newspaper sections that recur every day (e.g., sports, business, entertainment) or once a week (e.g., food, cars, finance) can be advantageous for marketers. Figure 12-26 shows some content readership levels.

LIMITATIONS OF NEWSPAPERS

While newspapers have many strengths, like all media they also have limitations that media planners must consider. The limitations of newspapers include their creativity for emotional responses, selective exposure and attention, target audience selectivity, and clutter.

Creativity for Emotional Responses   A significant limitation of newspapers for advertising is their poor reproduction quality. The coarse paper stock used for newspapers and the absence of extensive colour limits the quality of most newspaper ads. Newspapers have improved their reproduction quality, and colour reproduction has become more available. Also, advertisers desiring high-quality colour in newspaper ads can turn to such alternatives as free-standing inserts or supplements. However, these are more costly and may not be desirable to many advertisers. As a general rule, if the visual appearance of the product is important, the advertiser will not rely on newspaper ads. Ads for food products and fashions generally use magazines to capitalize on their superior reproduction quality and colour.

Selective Exposure and Attention   Unlike magazines, which may be retained around the house for several weeks, a daily newspaper is generally kept less than a day. So an ad is unlikely to have any impact beyond the day of publication, and repeat exposure is very unlikely.

Figure   12-26

Content readership, all markets

Source: 2012 NADbank Study.

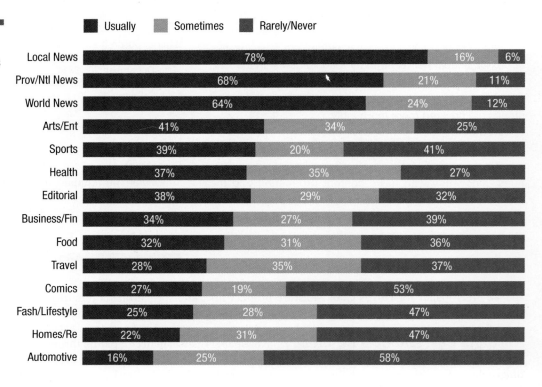

Compounding this problem are the short amount of time many consumers spend with the newspaper and the possibility they may not even open certain sections of the paper. Media planners can offset these problems somewhat by using high frequency in the newspaper schedule and advertising in a section where consumers who are in the market for a particular product or service are likely to look.

Target Audience Selectivity While newspapers can offer advertisers geographic selectivity, they are not selective in terms of demographics or lifestyle characteristics. Most newspapers reach broad and very diverse groups of consumers, which makes it difficult for marketers to focus on narrowly defined market segments. For example, manufacturers of fishing rods and reels will find newspapers very inefficient because of the wasted circulation that results from reaching all the newspaper readers who don't fish. Thus, they are more likely to use special-interest magazines. Any newspaper ads for their products will be done through cooperative plans whereby retailers share the costs or spread them over a number of sporting goods featured in the ad.

Clutter Newspapers, like most other advertising media, suffer from clutter. Because a substantial amount of the average daily newspaper in Canada is devoted to advertising, the advertiser's message must compete with numerous other ads for consumers' attention and interest. Moreover, the creative options in newspapers are limited by the fact that most ads are black and white. Thus, it can be difficult for a newspaper advertiser to break through the clutter without using costly measures such as large space buys or colour. Advertisers use creative techniques like island ads—ads surrounded by editorial material. Island ads are found in the middle of the stock market quotes on the financial pages of many newspapers.

LO5 IMC Planning: Strategic Use of Print Media

In the previous chapter, we ended with a discussion of the use of broadcast media to achieve strategic IMC objectives. In this IMC planning section, we investigate the use of magazines and newspapers to achieve communication and behavioural objectives at different stages of the target audience's decision-making process.

MAGAZINES

The selectivity and creativity options for magazines allow promotional planners a multitude of opportunities for establishing and maintaining very unique brand positions across all potential target audiences. For example, if research indicates a high proportion of non-users in certain lifestyle publications, the promotional planner can develop print ads with extensive copy to build category need as well as sufficient brand coverage for awareness while communicating the most appropriate brand benefit message for persuasion. Alternatively, research in other publications might indicate strong brand development and a high degree of current customers, thus allowing the promotional planner the opportunity to use messages that maintain the strong brand equity. This might suggest a more emotional message with enticing visuals for low-involvement processing.

While the decision to offer more customized messages to each audience is met with a certain amount of risk, it is mitigated by the consistency in the creative theme and creative tactics such as the design elements (e.g., layout). This possible scenario for promotional planners suggests that ads directed toward non-users could be developed to influence the pre-purchase and need recognition stages, whereas the ads for the customer could attempt to influence the purchase decision stage, as the brand would be encouraging a repeat purchase objective.

Extending this argument geographically is another strategic opportunity for promotional planners. For example, if the brand has a low brand development index in one part of the country, more persuasive switching messages directed to consumers at the purchase decision stage might be considered through regional or city editions. Alternatively, other regional editions could be examined if the brand has a high brand development index and the promotional planner concentrates on brand maintenance messages that focus, for example, on post-purchase satisfaction.

As the use of these key strengths of magazines implies, promotional planners can use magazines to attain virtually any of the communication objectives with any type of target audience and create the unique brand positions desired. Magazines are also strong for attaining purchase intention objectives and shopping objectives; ads generate action or planned action in 50 to 60 percent of respondents.[32] Magazine ads are useful for prompting Internet searches and website visits, with 26 to 36 percent of respondents reporting such behaviour.[33] Granted, certain costs are associated with this strategic use of magazines; the promotional planner can schedule the placements over time so as not to break the budget.

These strengths of magazines allow print to work with other media and IMC tools. Visuals can be the same as those from TV commercials to enhance message frequency. Headlines could be consistently used across out-of-home media and print ads. Sales promotions can be added to the message, like coupons or Internet site links to register for samples. Brand-building charity sponsorship or events can be communicated if they especially resonate with the readership audience. In short, magazines offer a degree of potential integration in the IMC plan.

NEWSPAPERS

The strategic use of newspapers is similar to radio in that national and local advertisers design messages with related objectives. National advertisers employ newspapers for brand-building messages they wish to disseminate across the country or in select regions. These ads take a few general forms. One kind of ad builds awareness and benefit beliefs at the pre-purchase and need recognition stages due to the broad reach of newspapers. With the majority of Canadian households reading newspapers on a regular basis, brands naturally reach their target audience and those who may not be in the market for such products. Other types of ads contribute at the information search stage for the target audience. The involved nature of the messages that can be creatively communicated in a more rational manner to fit the editorial context permits promotional planners to persuade their audience via high-involvement, informational brand attitude. One limitation with the opportunity is that the number of consumers actually in the market at this stage is fewer, thus making the purchase less cost-efficient. Finally, national advertisers utilize newspapers for executing information regarding sales promotions. For example, automobile manufacturers and large retailers are the largest advertisers who communicate their price and other promotions in newspapers to influence consumers at the purchase decision stage.

As noted in the cost implications discussion, newspapers offer local advertisers and small businesses (e.g., retailers, services) a tremendous opportunity for reaching an entire city for a reasonable cost. These advertisers can design ads to meet any communication objectives. A perusal of the local newspaper will identify ads that are clearly trying to build awareness and communicate certain brand benefits. However, the daily/weekly time frame of newspapers reveals that many ads have stronger purchase intention objectives.

Like magazines, newspapers offer good potential for integrating with other media and IMC tools. Oftentimes, television and radio commercials suggest that consumers "see newspaper for details." In this case, the initial ads are influencing the target audience at the need recognition stage and the newspaper is influencing the information search stage. Many public relations activities like sponsorship of charity events in the local community are conveyed in newspapers since they act as a planning resource for things to do in one's city.

Learning Objectives Summary

 Identify the different types of magazines available for advertising, how circulation and readership levels are determined, how audience size and its characteristics are measured, and the factors that influence advertising rates.

Magazines are a very selective medium and are valuable for reaching specific types of customers and market segments. The four broad categories of magazines are consumer, ethnic, farm, and business publications. Each of these categories can be further classified according to the publication's editorial content and audience appeal. Readership is verified with an audit function so advertisers are confident that the number claimed by the individual titles is accurate. Extensive information about magazine readers is available to those who subscribe to the PMB data. The PMB is one of the most sophisticated and extensive readership studies in the world.

Advertising space rates in magazines vary according to a number of factors, among them the size of the ad, position in the publication, particular editions purchased, use of colour, and number and frequency of insertions. Rates for magazines are compared on the basis of cost per thousand, although other factors such as the editorial content of the publication and its ability to reach specific target audiences must also be considered.

 Evaluate the strengths and limitations of magazines as an advertising medium.

The strengths of magazines include their target audience selectivity, geographic coverage, creativity, reader involvement and amount of processing time, media image, and selective exposure and attention levels. Limitations of magazines include their high cost, limited reach and frequency, long lead time, weak target audience coverage, and the advertising clutter in most publications.

 Identify the types of newspapers offered for advertising, how circulation and readership levels are determined, how audience size and its characteristics are measured, and how advertising rates are determined.

A variety of newspapers are available for advertisers, including, daily, community, national, Internet, and special audience. Newspapers offer great flexibility regarding the type of ad including display, classified, and inserts. Extensive research is conducted to ensure that the number of readers is accurate. Additional research of newspaper readers provides a detailed profile of their characteristics.

Newspaper ads are sold as a full page or any partial page the advertiser desires. The line and column characteristics of newspapers allow nearly unlimited sizes, although most ads follow conventional sizes of half-page, quarter-page, and so on, with smaller advertisers selecting smaller spaces. Advertising rates are determined by the size of the ad and the circulation.

 Evaluate the strengths and limitations of newspapers as an advertising medium.

Newspapers are a very important medium to local advertisers, especially retailers. Newspapers are a broad-based medium and reach a large percentage of households in a particular area. Newspapers' other advantages include scheduling flexibility, geographic coverage, reader involvement and amount of processing time, media image, creativity for cognitive responses, and absolute cost and cost efficiency. Drawbacks of newspapers include their creativity for emotional responses, selective exposure and attention, target audience selectivity, and clutter. The use of special inserts and supplements allows advertisers to overcome these limitations to a degree. However, newspapers face increasing competition from Internet media as the World Wide Web continues to grow as an information resource for consumers.

Apply the media knowledge of magazines and newspapers for strategic IMC decisions.

Print media are important for IMC plans as their potential for long-form copy, lengthy reading, and selectivity for magazines and coverage for newspapers makes expenditures worthwhile for certain product categories or for when consumers are in the information or purchase decision stage. Given their importance for providing information, print media are readily linked with other media as ads may suggest connection to digital media or follow-up on messages found in broadcast or out-of-home media that have broader coverage.

Key Terms

Review key terms and definitions on Connect.

Review Questions

1. Discuss how circulation figures and readership composition are used in evaluating magazines as part of a media plan and setting advertising rates.

2. Discuss the strengths and limitations of magazines for advertising. How do magazines differ from television and radio as advertising media?

3. Discuss how circulation figures and readership composition are used in evaluating newspapers as part of a media plan and setting advertising rates.

4. Discuss the strengths and limitations of newspapers for advertising. How might the decision to use newspapers in a media plan differ for national versus local advertisers?

5. How do magazines and newspapers help achieve brand behavioural and communication effects?

Applied Questions

1. Explain why advertisers of products such as cosmetics or women's clothing would choose to advertise in magazines such as *Flare, Elle Canada,* or *Chatelaine.*

2. Select an enjoyable print ad from a magazine and apply the earlier text material. Identify the target audience, behavioural objectives, communication objectives, brand positioning strategy, and creative strategy and tactics decisions, and associate these points with the key strengths of magazines as an advertising medium.

3. Explain why advertisers of products such as smartphones or men's clothing would choose to advertise in newspapers such as *The Globe and Mail, Vancouver Sun,* or *Metro.*

4. What differences might one conclude exist between national newspapers and community newspapers regarding the strengths and limitations of newspapers?

5. Identify how newspapers and magazines can be used for each stage of the decision-making process for automobile purchases.

GO ONLINE

For more information on the resources available from McGraw-Hill Ryerson,
go to www.mcgrawhill.ca/he/solutions.

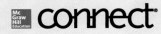

Out-of-Home and Support Media

13

LEARNING OBJECTIVES

LO1 Identify the options within out-of-home media for developing an IMC program and for audience measurement, and their strengths and limitations.

LO2 Apply the concepts of out-of-home media to promotional products and product placement to construct support programs within an IMC plan.

LO3 Show how out-of-home and support media are important elements of IMC planning.

Outdoor Adventures with Nivea and Others

What do Nivea skin care, Dempster's bagels, Axe shampoo, MAAX bathroom fixtures, and Xbox Kinect all have in common? Each found a unique way to present the brand in public places to deliver a unique experience to consumers. Moving beyond ads, sales promotions, and even digital communication, brands see the need to allow consumers to participate in a demonstration of product usage to fully enjoy what it has to offer. With agencies like Launch specializing in developing and executing these kinds of programs, it appears consumers have exciting brand experiences to look forward to.

Nivea opened up a temporary pop-up shop in Toronto called Nivea Haus that included interactive skin tests, personalized skin care suggestions, photo shoots, product shots, and Your Shape: Fitness Evolved, an Xbox Kinect game. Ads, public relations, a microsite, samples, and a contest all supported the experiential effort designed to communicate how one's skin is an important part of one's physical and emotional well-being. News media invited to a preview provided extensive coverage resulting in 20 million impressions, and 20,000 consumers visited Nivea Haus.

Dempster's reconfigured a previously used shipping container into a giant toaster with inflatable half bagels situated on the top as they toasted 6,000 real bagels and handed them out to consumers in Toronto's Dundas Square. According to one manager of Steel Space, the container provider, the events associated with the containers help foster strong goodwill of the brand to consumers and provide an enjoyable way to consume the sample rather than at home or actually getting but forgetting to use a sample.

Axe's "Hair Action" campaign featured a Virtual Hair Play Van where men received the touch of a woman as she attended to his hair, all in a virtual simulation of course. The van visited numerous locations including campuses and events such as the Warped Tour and Montreal Jazz Festival. Photos of the experience gave the participants the opportunity to upload pictures to their Facebook account where friends could "like" it and give the guy a chance to win a $10,000 prize.

Steel Space also created a showroom for MAAX, a bathroom fixtures manufacturer based in Montreal, with five functional bathtubs in an open-air display shown at 175 events for retailers, wholesalers, and distributors in Canada and the United States. According to a manager at MAAX, "It was all about living the experience and enjoying the experience. People have actually gotten into the bathtubs in the hotter states, but it is more about really showing people what the system does, the quiet pump, the whirlpool." Experience translated into stronger product inquiries and sales where the showroom visited.

Xbox set up a massive Kinect Hubs adjacent to the Eaton Centre malls in Toronto and Montreal where gamers played with the console via infrared technology. Full station subway ads and videos of participants uploaded to Facebook proved successful. Created by Mosaic Experiential Marketing, the effort gave consumers a true feel for the new way to play. "Kinect was one of those products that until you got in front of it and played a game, you would have no idea how great it is," commented one of Mosaic's managers.

As shown in these examples, experiential promotional activities are the result of working with specialized agencies with significant expertise in this field. Some of Launch's other work includes the rejuvenation of the Pepsi Taste Challenge and a huge event for Carlsberg beer during the World Cup.

Sources: Hollie Shaw, "Mobile Showroom; Street Marketing Key to Steel Space's Containers," *National Post,* February 17, 2012, p. FP14; Theras Wood, "See Me, Touch Me, Feel Me," *Strategy,* June 3, 2011, p. 34; Chris Powell, "Experiential Marketing Firm Launch Names New CEO," *Marketing Magazine,* February 21, 2013; www.launchthis.com.

Question:

1. Why are advertisers turning toward experiential messages?

Every time we step out of the house, we encounter media directing an advertising message to us. Often we see ads while travelling. Many places we go to for leisure have advertising. **Out-of-home media** is quite pervasive as it delivers advertising messages that we experience while moving throughout our town or city while accomplishing our day-to-day activities. Some are new to the marketplace, and others have been around a while. In this chapter, we review three broad categories of out-of-home media: outdoor, transit, and place-based (see Figure 13-1) that generated $486 million in advertising revenue in 2012. The term out-of-home media is adopted because it encompasses media that are located in public spaces.

We also encounter messages from **support media**. These media are used to reach those in the target audience that primary media may not, or to reinforce the message contained in primary media. We conclude this chapter by summarizing two types: promotional products and product placement. The term "promotional media" might be more appropriate; however, the notion of support media has existed for a while and remains relatively accurate. Its function as a public dissemination of a brand's messages is similar to out-of-home media, allowing this chapter to have a consistent theme. Finally, for each out-of-home and support medium, we offer a summary of strengths and limitations; these are generalizations, however, and advertisers can certainly find exceptions as these media continue to flourish and innovate.

(LO1) Outdoor Media

Outdoor media are pervasive, and it appears that we are surrounded. However, the amount spent on this medium is a portion of the $486 million spent on out-of-home media. In contrast, advertising on the Internet is about four times larger than out-of-home. Despite this paradox of both large and small scale, the growth of outdoor media options and its contribution to sales may be a key factor in its continued interest to advertisers. For example, a study showed that outdoor advertising can have a significant effect on sales, particularly when combined with a promotion.[1] We now describe outdoor media options available, the audience measurement, and their strengths and limitations as an advertising medium.

OUTDOOR MEDIA OPTIONS

A variety of outdoor media options are available, as shown in Figure 13-1. **Posters** describe the typical billboard, which can be horizontal (e.g., 3m by 6m) or vertical (e.g., 4m by 5m). These displays are front lit for visibility at night and are located in areas with high vehicle traffic (see Exhibit 13-1). They may be purchased on an individual basis or for a certain level of GRPs in cities such as Toronto or in smaller markets such as Timmins, Ontario. As the name implies, **backlit posters** are posters of generally the same size that have a light behind them so that they

Figure 13-1

Out-of-home media

Outdoor	Transit	Place-Based
Horizontal/vertical poster	Interior horiz./vert. poster	Bar, restaurant, hotel
Backlit poster	Exterior bus poster	Mall, cinema
Superboard, spectacular	Super-bus, bus mural	Airport poster/video display
Video/electronic display	Station video display	Arena, stadium
Street level/transit shelter poster	Station poster	Golf, ski, fitness centre
Wall banner, mural	Station domination	Office building
Mobile signage	Taxi	University, college
Aerial, bench, receptacle, parking lot, bike rack	In-flight video/magazine	Washroom, elevator

Exhibit 13-1 Example of a poster ad.

Exhibit 13-2 Example of a backlit poster.

are more clearly illuminated (see Exhibit 13-2). These units are located at major intersections or high-traffic-volume areas in or near major cities in Canada.

Creativity is possible with billboards. The Quebec Federation of Milk Producers comforted Quebecers with cheery messages that changed weekly and reminded consumers to drink milk. Montreal and Quebec businesses could win visits featuring heartwarming messages along with milk and cookies to keep them happy and chase away the winter blues. Additional comforting messages occurred in the subway system.[2]

Larger billboards, known as **bulletins**, **superboards**, or **spectaculars**, are larger displays (two to three times larger) that have a variety of sizes depending upon the media company (see Exhibit 13-3). These displays are sold on a per location basis due to their size and the low number of options available in major Canadian markets. Trivisions and permanents are two specialized forms of bulletins. The former are horizontal or vertical posters with rotating blades that allow three different ads to be shown. The latter features unique sizes and formats and are erected in specific locations permanently.

Research on billboards is lacking in comparison to other media, but one study on why billboards are used found that managers rated visibility and media efficiency as more influential than local presence and tangible results (e.g., sales). The most critical factors for billboard success included name identification, location, readability, and clarity. A secondary set of factors suggested IMC and visuals, while the third group indicated creative and information. This implies that allowing the target audience to clearly read the brand identification at the right place is paramount over the most creative or informative ad.[3]

Smaller backlit displays, known as **street-level posters** and measuring about 2m by 1m, are available across the country and are also posted in transit shelters. Industry people also refer to this as "street furniture"; a couple of examples are shown in Exhibits 13-4 and 13-5. A study conducted in Europe makes a number of conclusions regarding their usefulness:[4]

- Clear branding and inclusion of new-product information enhances product recognition.
- Large amounts of text and pictures of people delay product recognition.
- Lengthy, large headlines, information cues, and humour delay brand recognition.
- Short headlines, longer body text, and a product shot enhance the creative appeal.
- Specifying a brand name in the headline or providing price information reduces appeal.

Exhibit 13-3 Example of a superboard.

Exhibit 13-4   Example of a transit shelter poster.

Exhibit 13-5   Example of a street poster.

A number of innovative outdoor tools have emerged in Canada, with firms setting up large video-display units that have full animation and colour. For example, Dundas Square, near the Eaton Centre in downtown Toronto, features a 12-metre-wide by 9-metre-high full-colour video screen in addition to eight display faces and Canada's largest neon sign, at 18 metres in diameter. With its high-profile location, Dundas Square is ideal for brands looking to extend their reach. For example, a billboard for Cadbury's Creme Egg relied on precipitation to completely reveal a gooey adventure for all to see in person or online. A pendulum-like device with a giant egg at one end and a box that collected snow and rain at the other eventually tilted so that the egg made contact with a fan. The ensuing contact broke the egg and released the faux cream filling upon the billboard.[5]

Electronic message signs offer short ads (e.g., 10 seconds) on a 2- or 3-minute rotation. As expected, both of these displays are located in high-traffic locations in a few large urban markets, with various sizes and packages available depending on the media firm. The growth of outdoor video displays is such that the firms offer network services, thereby reaching many viewers across the country. Murals and wall banners are sold in a few major markets in Canada (e.g., Toronto, Vancouver) with varying sizes (Exhibit 13-6).

The Media Merchants of Vancouver projected video images onto building walls in Montreal, Toronto, Calgary, and Vancouver using a hand-held projector with ads for a Burger King promotion connected to the movie *Transformers: Revenge of the Fallen*. Operators handed out coupons and carried the speakers in backpacks. The technology allowed advertising at night in places where outdoor ads do not exist and vehicle ads cannot reach.[6]

A number of firms offer **mobile signage** by placing displays on trucks or vehicles. These are sold by the number of vehicles and the number of months. And mobile messages with advertising-wrapped cars are driving into Canada, after growing substantially in the United States in the past decade. CityFlitz offers a fleet of 35 Minis with a cost of $4,500 per month for the advertiser. With a claimed exposure of at least 50,000 people, the CPM clicks in at a mere $3, far cheaper than static billboards located in the same place for one month. In addition, the cars are WiFi equipped, offering additional opportunity for inventive marketers. The logistics of driving are covered by members who join the company and rent the car for only $1 per day.[7] Finally, we find outdoor media in unusual outdoor locations. Signage is placed on benches, parking lots, bicycle racks, garbage receptacles, and in the air through aerial advertising on airplanes or hot-air balloons. It seems that no matter where we turn outside, there will be a form of advertising message directed toward us.

Exhibit 13-6   Murals are part of the outdoor landscape.

IMC TECHNOLOGY PERSPECTIVE **13-1**

www.isignmedia.com

Out-of-Home Technological Creativity

Application of digital technology for out-of-home media reached new heights with movement on three significant fronts. Digital signage is a small portion of the facings in Canada, but media companies are moving toward greater penetration. Secondly, Bluetooth technology used with billboard ads that directed messages to passersby's phones emerged a few years ago; however, it felt like spam to some recipients and this technology is not applied to retail situations. Finally, considerable adaptations of Bluetooth and other technology to various types of displays permit enhanced communication.

Industry specialists estimate about 9,000 digital advertising faces in Canada, about 5 percent of the overall total. Pattison, one of the leaders with 10,000 advertising faces (digital and non-digital), is the largest digital firm with its acquisitions and new placements. Other firms like Astral and Lamar Outdoor are converting their static outdoor ads to digital, which means the media landscape will certainly grow beyond the 5 percent level in the coming years. A similar trend is occurring with Newad, which is converting to digital for many of its place-based ads in restaurants, bars, and fitness centres. A key advantage of digital is the ability to instantly change the message and lower production costs since a physical change is no longer necessary.

Mac's and Couche-Tard introduced a network of mobile antennae from iSign Media Corporation in their 1,500 convenience stores to push advertising messages to those within 100 metres who had a phone with Bluetooth technology. Consumers received a "tile" pop-up on their phone screen and would authorize receiving the message, giving permission if any information were to be tracked and recorded. Generally the message would contain a promotional offer to ensure the acceptance. The technology allowed the stores to feature specific products and allowed consumers a more useful exposure beyond flyers and radio ads.

New technology inserted into vending machines surprised those walking by when it asked for a smile and returned an ice-cream. This clever execution won a Gold Lion at Cannes and showed the future of technological advertising. A similar vending machine presentation was accompanied with a large LCD touch screen that showed video, flash graphics, and responded to hand motions, all while distributing phone wallpapers and ring tones to those who passed by.

As can be seen in these examples, out-of-home advertising will feature facial recognition, touch screens, gesture, control, augmented reality, and interactive projections to entice consumers to witness advertisers' embellished messages. Royal Bank tested a Microsoft Surface tabletop that allows consumers to explore products and services at the touch of their fingers. Telus implemented large, gesture-controlled storefront screens to explore its new product lineup that featured its most current icon, a dolphin. Maxwell House presented images of a cup of coffee on public walls and asked consumers to vote online whether the cup was half full or half empty as they offered uplifting messages on Twitter. The Bay "employed" virtual salesperson Anna, who greeted those who entered La Boutique; Anna happened to be a computer-generated image who spoke when motion-sensor technology picked up the presence of a consumer. Anna could also interact with customers about products that consumers evaluated.

Source: Chris Powell, "Out-of-Home Run," *Marketing Magazine,* April 24, 2011, p. 11; Jonathan Paul, "The Future Starts Now," *Strategy,* June 3, 2011, p. 21; Susan Krashinsky, "Ads That Reach Out to the Passing Pedestrians," *The Globe and Mail,* February 28, 2012, p. B3; Hollie Shaw, "The Reality of Virtual Sales," *National Post,* March 2, 2012, p. FP6.

Question:

1. Which of these ideas appears to be the most creative use of new technology?

Historically, advertisers considered outdoor advertising as a support medium to broadcast or print. However, current usage indicates outdoor ads can be used successfully as a primary medium, as shown by Clover Leaf's strategic emphasis. Hoping to expand the overall tuna category to both men and women with its flavoured varieties (e.g., sun-dried tomato and basil), the only nationally distributed tuna producer showed interesting and innovative ways of thinking about tuna (e.g., salad or wraps) with its more exotic taste sensations. Outdoor (e.g., posters, transit shelters, street columns) became the focal point to communicate the images and messages that easily transferred to other out-of-home media (e.g., in-store, health club posters) and sales promotions (e.g., coupons, samples).[8] Technology Perspective 13-1 identifies examples where out-of-home ads use technology very creatively.

Figure 13-2

Share of COMB-approved
outdoor advertising faces
in Canada

	2008	2009	2010	2011	2012
CBS Outdoor	37.6%	37.4%	36.8%	37.1%	36.4%
Pattison Outdoor	41.9%	42.3%	43.6%	42.4%	43.1%
Astral Out-of-Home	15.8%	15.5%	16.9%	17.7%	17.9%
All Others	4.7%	4.8%	2.7%	2.8%	2.6%

Source: COMB Data Reports 2008–2012.

Total No. of Outdoor Panels—All formats

The major outdoor operators are shown in Figure 13-2. These companies can present examples of past outdoor campaigns producing awareness and other communication effects. The examples can be for a product category or for individual campaigns. The operators can also provide maps to illustrate the locations and other relevant data (e.g., demographics). The aforementioned outdoor options are typically purchased for four weeks and provide anywhere from 25 GRPs to 150 GRPs per day, depending upon the number of displays or showings chosen within a local market. Recall from Chapter 10 that one GRP represents one percent of the market exposed to the ad once. Thus, buying 50 GRPs possibly implies that the marketer reaches 50 percent of the market once per day. The costs for placing outdoor advertising are not readily available with CARD any longer; however, the locations and other basic data are still offered.

AUDIENCE MEASUREMENT

COMB   Audience measurement is done by the Canadian Out-of-Home Measurement Bureau (COMB); an independent organization comprising members from advertisers, advertising agencies, and media firms. Founded in 1965, its members provide guidance, funding and oversight of the measurement process. COMB maintains a national database of all products for outdoor and place-based media firms in order to compile the audience measurement data. COMB publishes circulation and market data for approximately 80,000 out-of-home facings in about 280 markets.

COMB's methodology to determine advertising exposure (impressions) of out-of-home media is comprehensive with its unbiased, accurate and independently collected quantitative data; however the methodologies for outdoor and place-based are customized to a degree to account for the unique travel patterns of each media type. Important characteristics of the research are the visibility criteria which identify the number of people that have a reliable opportunity to see the message within a standardized distance for each advertising format, the use of sound statistical procedures, the inclusion of market-specific data, and reliable data collection procedures.

For the outdoor research, COMB begins with data from municipalities for road planning purposes, which is then assessed on how it can be used for measuring the regular traffic flow. This data is adjusted for the visibility criteria, the average number of people in the vehicle, and the number of hours an ad is illuminated. This is augmented with pedestrian data that also meets the visibility criteria in order to calculate the average daily circulation per face. As might be expected, all of this data is examined with advanced mapping technologies to visually see the volume of people potentially exposed to an advertising message.

These circulations are applied to each poster along a certain part of the road called a link. The numbers are adjusted to account for time-of-day variations throughout the week to arrive at an adjusted circulation. An important refinement of the data is the use of GPS technology that tracks traffic moving into a Census Metropolitan Area (CMA) in Canada's five larger cities which accounts for commuters who are exposed to advertising messages.

From this data, COMB calculates the number of people (5+) who have a reasonable opportunity to see an ad and estimates reach and frequency levels with sophisticated mathematical models. Advertisers confidently purchase the advertising space knowing that rigorous standards and exceptional research methodology provide accurate exposure levels. To facilitate their planning, COMB offers two planning software tools. The COMB Data Report is a comprehensive system for identifying all of the 80,000 facings with a number of reporting options. The COMBNavigator® allows planners to select media vehicles to attain reach and frequency levels for various target audience profiles.

OMAC The Out-of-Home Marketing Association of Canada (OMAC), formed in 2005, is a membership among five founding media companies—Astral Media Outdoor, Newad, Pattison Outdoor, CBS Outdoor, and Zoom Media—and four others that have joined—Lamar Transit, Metromedia Plus, OBN, and Titan 360. OMAC's mission is to develop the market for this medium, implement new industry initiatives, establish guidelines, and act on behalf of the industry on any issues. Like other organizations that represent a particular medium, OMAC commissions research to demonstrate its effectiveness that acts as key information for decision makers.

OMAC undertook two "Day in the Life" (DIL) studies. The first, DIL I, investigated time spent inside/outside home, out-of-home exposure, commuting habits, and related shopping behaviour. Based on telephone interviews with 2,500 Canadians age 12+ in major markets, the study found that the average person spends 55 percent of the day (while awake) out of the home and one-third in the home. On a typical weekday, urban Canadians spend as much time exposed to out-of-home media (3.8 hours) as to television and the Internet (Figure 13-3). The typical urban Canadian drives nearly 130 kilometres a week, with commuting to and from work accounting for half this distance and taking 65 minutes. Many urban workers (73 percent) use a vehicle to get to work, with the incidence of travelling by vehicle increasing significantly among suburbanites.

Figure 13-4 shows when people do their shopping: more than 50 percent shop on their way to work or home. From a measurement standpoint, advertisers can be confident that out-of-home media reach a substantial portion of the population while they are planning to or actually shopping. In fact, 87 percent either shop closer to work, closer to home, or somewhere equally

	Average Time Exposed per Day (Hours)		
	Week Day	**Saturday**	**Sunday**
Out-of-Home Stimulus	3.8	4.7	4.7
Radio	2.2	1.3	1.1
Internet	3.6	2.6	2.4
Newspapers	0.5	0.6	0.4
Magazines	0.4	0.3	0.2
Television	3.8	3.1	3.1

Source: Out-of-Home Marketing Association of Canada (OMAC).

Figure 13-3

Time exposed to various media

Figure 13-4

Time of day when workers shop

Source: Out-of-Home Marketing Association of Canada (OMAC).

close to both places. Out-of-home advertising also wields considerable influence on purchase decisions. The study found that in the past three months, 30 percent of people visited a specific website after seeing it promoted on out-of-home advertising; 25 percent learned about a store/product/sale that motivated them to visit a specific store; and 17 percent were prompted to purchase or seek information about a new product.

The second Day in the Life study, DIL II, investigated the relevance and impact of out-of-home media versus other media. Figure 13-5 suggests that consumers do not believe there is too much out-of-home advertising compared to other media.[9]

Another source of measurement is innovative technology that tracks a driver's eye movement to assess which ads are actually seen while driving. Taking into account the size of the ad and the distance from the road, this new method is well established in the United Kingdom and is demonstrating more accurate numbers and some believe it has led to a growth of advertising revenue that now stands at 8 percent.[10] Member companies of OMAC (Pattison, Astral, CBS) commissioned the Outdoor Advertising Consumer Exposure Study (OACES) to investigate the usefulness of this research for Canada. The study used 27 randomly selected drivers and passengers from Ottawa and Montreal, who were asked to drive a predetermined route that passed by a variety of outdoor advertising products and consisted of a variety of different driving conditions. The route was driven at different times of day, respondents' eye movements were tracked using a headband eye camera, and the entire visual interaction was also video recorded. An outdoor ad was considered "seen" if a driver or passenger fixated on it for at least 200 milliseconds. The study found that 55 percent of the ads selected for analysis were seen by the 27 drivers and passengers tested. Passengers, unsurprisingly, were more likely to see them (73 percent, versus 52 percent of drivers who saw them). Those people who looked at advertising looked at an ad an average of 2.04 times on a single drive-by. Out-of-home ads with three rotating faces were looked at more often, 2.46 times, compared with 1.9 times for a standard poster. In total, 535 outdoor exposures were eye-tracked during the study. Neither drivers nor passengers knew the study was related to advertising, with most of them thinking it was something to do with the transport ministry.[11]

STRENGTHS OF OUTDOOR MEDIA

Reach   With proper placement, a broad base of exposure is possible in a given market, with both day and night presence. A 100 GRP showing (the percentage of duplicated audience exposed to an outdoor poster daily) could yield exposure to an equivalent of 100 percent of the marketplace daily! This level of coverage is likely to yield high levels of reach. Behavioural responses toward outdoor media are considerable, with extensive reach possibilities as documented in Figure 13-6.

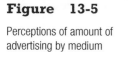

Figure   13-5

Perceptions of amount of advertising by medium

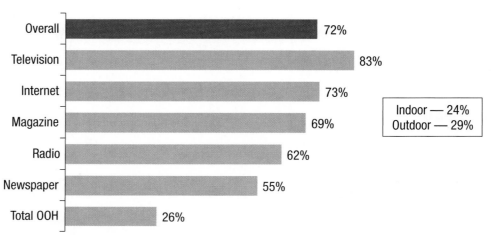

Source: Out-of-Home Marketing Association of Canada (OMAC).

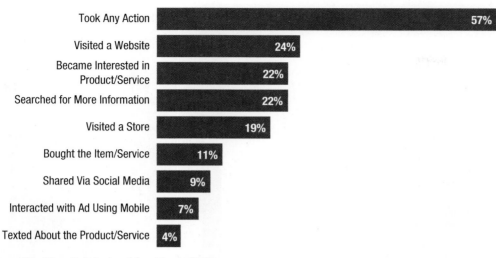

Source: Out-of-Home Marketing Association of Canada (OMAC).

Figure   13-6

Behavioural responses to outdoor ads in past six months

Frequency   Because purchase cycles for outdoor media are typically for 4-week periods, consumers are usually exposed a number of times, resulting in high levels of frequency. The importance of frequency is substantiated with the results of a study shown in Figure 13-7.

Geographic Coverage   Outdoor media can be placed along highways, near stores, or on mobile billboards, almost anywhere that the law permits. Local, regional, or even national markets may be covered.

Creativity for Emotional Responses   As shown in Exhibits 13-1 and 13-2, outdoor ads can be very creative. Large print, colours, and other elements attract attention and tend to generate short emotional responses that connect the target audience to the brand. Presumably

Figure   13-7   Out-of-home ads support other media when part of the budget

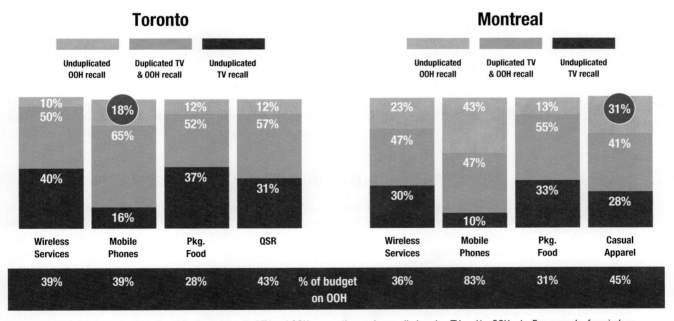

The bar chart shows the unduplicated and duplicated recall of TV and OOH among those who recalled seeing TV and/or OOH ads. For example, for wireless in Toronto: 10% recalled OOH only, 50% recalled both OOH and TV, and 40% recalled TV only.

Source: Out-of-Home Marketing Association of Canada (OMAC).

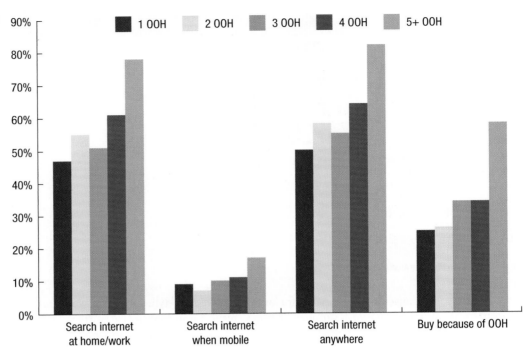

Figure   13-8

Behavioural effects of out-of-home advertising

Source: Out-of-Home Marketing Association of Canada (OMAC).

this emotional involvement contributes to the strong brand building leading to strong follow-up behaviour for continued shopping due to out-of-home media as shown in Figure 13-8.

Cost Efficiency   Outdoor ads usually have a very competitive CPM when compared to other media. The average CPM of outdoor ads is less than that of radio, TV, magazines, and newspapers.

Scheduling Flexibility   Modern technologies have reduced production times for outdoor advertising to allow for rapid turnaround time. Placement can be done on a monthly basis assuming availability exists.

Selective Exposure   On the one hand, outdoor ads are difficult for consumers to avoid since they are so pervasive. Moreover, a consumer has little control like television or radio to change the channel or station. On the other hand, consumers can deliberately ignore outdoor ads; however, the high profile of the ads makes this a difficult task at times.

Attention   The sheer size, strategic placement, and the creative elements of colour make outdoor advertising an attractive medium to draw the attention of the target audience.

LIMITATIONS OF OUTDOOR MEDIA

Target Audience Coverage   With the broad base reach of outdoor advertising, it is difficult to ensure that the specific target audience coverage is sufficient. While it is possible to reach an audience with select location placement, in many cases the purchase of outdoor ads results in a high degree of waste coverage. It is not likely that everyone driving past a billboard is part of the target audience.

Amount of Processing Time   Because of the speed with which most people pass by outdoor ads, exposure time is short, so messages are limited to a few words and/or an illustration. Despite this concern, there appears to be sufficient amount of processing that encourages consumers to text a response (Figure 13-9).

Invitation to Special Event — 18–34: 36%, 35+: 26%
A Promotional Offer — 18–34: 38%, 35+: 28%
Contest — 18–34: 31%, 35+: 26%

18–34
35+

Figure   13-9

Likelihood* of texting in response to digital OOH advertising by age

*Very/Somewhat likely

Source: Out-of-Home Marketing Association of Canada (OMAC).

Creativity for Cognitive Responses   Lengthy appeals are not physically possible in many instances, and if they were, they have less likelihood of complete comprehension. Thus, it is expected that outdoor ads suffer from their inability to fully persuade consumers with an involved message.

Absolute Cost   A basic level of 25 GRPs per day over four weeks in ten—or even three—major cities can be quite prohibitive for many advertisers. For smaller businesses, selecting a few strategic locations in a local market could overcome this limitation.

Media Image   Outdoor advertising has suffered image problems and disregard among consumers. This may be in part due to fatigue of the high frequency of exposures that may lead to wearout—people are likely to get tired of seeing the same ad every day.

Target Audience Selectivity   Reaching a specific target audience is challenging due to the broad exposure of outdoor media in general. However, strategic use can overcome this limitation, for example by using reminder ads for a type of product near the retail outlets.

Clutter   By its very nature, outdoor ads have competing messages. At any streetscape or location where outdoor ads are featured, it is very likely that other messages will be also vying for consumer attention, as seen in Exhibit 13-7.

Low Involvement   The overall effect of the short repeated message is that outdoor ads tend to be considered a low-involvement media.

Transit Media

Another form of out-of-home advertising is transit advertising. While similar to outdoor in the sense that it uses posters, digital, and video messages, transit is targeted at the millions of people who are exposed to commercial transportation facilities, including buses, subways, light-rail trains, and airplanes. Transit revenue is a noticeable but small portion of overall transit revenue. For example, the Toronto Transit Commission reported $19 million advertising revenue and but well over $900 million in fares annually. It looked to increase its advertising

Exhibit 13-7   Competing messages present a challenge with outdoor media.

revenue to $27 million/year for 12 years in a deal with Pattison.[12] We now describe transit media options available, and their strengths and limitations as an advertising medium.

TRANSIT MEDIA OPTIONS

Common transit ads viewed are **interior transit cards** placed above the seating. Ads are positioned in backlit units above windows and along both sides of the bus, streetcar, subway, or light-rail transit cars (see Exhibit 13-8). **Interior door cards** are available in major markets where there is subway-like transit. These cards are placed on both sides of the doors and are about 50 percent larger than the aforementioned cards. **Exterior posters** may appear on the sides, backs, and/or roofs of buses, taxis, trains, and subway and street cars (see Exhibit 13-9). Various sizes are available depending on the media company and the transit vehicles; however, the two most common are "seventies" (.5 m × 1.8 m) and "king" (.75 m × 3.5 m) that are seen on buses and so on. The former gets its name from the length actually sold with a width of 70 inches.

Transit offers creative opportunities with innovative thinking. For example, a rejuvenated campaign for the Caramilk "Secret" featured 50 interactive audioboards in the Toronto subway system among other media like TV, print, and online. A series of interpretive reveals of the secret kept the mystery and discovery experience exciting for consumers. Cadbury promoted consumption with a Chocolate Couture Fashion Show where fashion designers and chocolate artists teamed up to create an outfit made of chocolate.[13]

Station posters are of varying sizes and forms that attempt to attract the attention of those waiting for a subway-like ride. The most common size is 1 m by 2 m. As Exhibit 13-10 shows, station posters can be very attractive to gain attention. Similar-sized posters are found at bus or streetcar **transit shelters** and often provide the advertiser with expanded coverage where other outdoor boards may be restricted. Many of these are sold by outdoor media companies as they are identical to street-level posters, but others are listed in transit. Larger station posters are available as well; Metromedia offers super vertical subway posters and platform posters, for example.

Innovations in transit media include the super-bus, where an advertiser "owns" the bus and places a vinyl ad on its entire surface. This is often done for a longer-term contract of a half- or full year because of the application on the bus (see Exhibit 13-11). On a less grand scale in a few select markets, smaller bus murals can be applied to the side or tail for a shorter period of time. Similar wraps are also possible for subway cars. The Toronto and Montreal subway systems have featured station domination, where a single advertiser can be the sole sponsor of all points of communication within that station. This could include wrapping a number of different parts of the infrastructure and erecting sizable murals and posters. **Subway online** is located in the 10

Exhibit 13-8   Example of interior transit ad.

Exhibit 13-9   Example of exterior transit ad.

Exhibit 13-10 Station posters can be used to attract attention.

busiest subway stations in Toronto. It features digital news centres with video capabilities that deliver news, sports, and weather highlights with 20-second ads. Video applications are coming to taxis where screens show 15-minute video clips, of which five minutes are advertising. Play Taxi installed screens in 4,000 vehicles by 2012 and major advertisers looked to use the interactive features creatively by offering ads consumers wanted to see, games, and promotions.[14]

The Toronto group of Venture Communications turned the stairway of Toronto's Union Station from street level to track level with a virtual trek down a ski hill with wall-to-wall images of the Alberta Rockies. "We felt our ski messaging would have a large impact on the quarter-million commuters who frequent the station on a daily basis," commented a director of Travel Alberta. Other media complemented the initial eye-opener and included store kiosks, direct mail, and a website (skicanadianrockies.com) where visitors could experience video clips of the hills and plan a vacation.[15]

Transit media are sold in select markets on a four-week basis with a certain desired level of GRPs. The range of GRPs is quite varied, going from a low of 5 GRPs to a high of 100 GRPs. Other purchases of transit media are based on the number of showings. For example, if an operator has the rights to 400 buses or subway cars, then an advertiser could typically buy displays in varying numbers (i.e., 25 percent, 50 percent, 75 percent, 100 percent) over a four-week time period. Unlike outdoor advertising, there is no industry association to document circulation or authenticate reach and frequency levels despite their use in pricing of the media purchase. However, information is gained from the research conducted by BBM so that rough estimates of exposure are possible. OMAC's DIL research also touches on transit to a degree, as shown in Figure 13-10 where most people find transit advertising acceptable.

Transit media viewed while travelling *between* cities and towns presents similar transit and terminal (i.e., airport, train, bus) options. Free magazines are published by travel operators (see Exhibit 13-12) and in-flight videos are common on longer flights. For example, Air Canada sells different packages depending on the type of show (e.g., news, movie) and these commercial messages can last up to three minutes. In-flight radio is a pleasant way to pass the time while flying, and offers another opportunity for advertisers to deliver an audio message beyond standard radio. Ads can be placed on collateral material such as boarding passes, ticket jackets, and meal trays. The design

Exhibit 13-11 Example of a bus wrap.

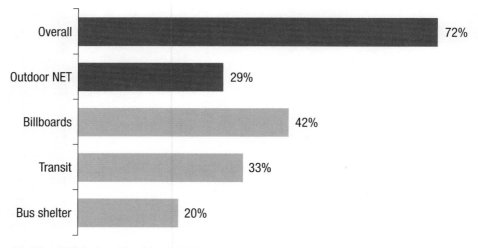

Figure 13-10

Perceived amount of advertising by outdoor medium

Source: Out-of-Home Marketing Association of Canada (OMAC).

of these media is important as both Air Canada and WestJet put considerable effort into their in-flight magazines to reflect their positioning. Air Canada looks more a like a sophisticated life-style magazine with luxurious full-page ads, fitting with its international and business clientele, while WestJet offers a more utilitarian offering with functional travel tips.[16]

STRENGTHS OF TRANSIT MEDIA

Amount of Processing Time Long length of exposure to an ad is a major strength of indoor forms. The audience is essentially a captive one, with nowhere else to go and nothing much to do. As a result, riders are likely to read the ads—more than once.

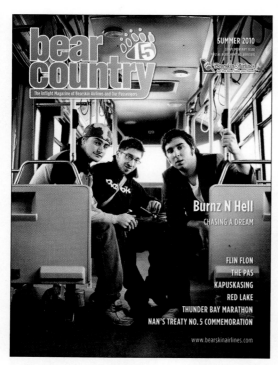

Exhibit 13-12 In-flight magazines are available on most carriers.

Reach Transit advertising benefits from the absolute number of people exposed. Millions of people ride mass transit every week, providing a substantial number of potential viewers that can be reached.

Frequency Because our daily routines are standard, those who ride buses, subways, and the like are exposed to the ads repeatedly. If one rode the same subway to work and back every day, in one month one would have the opportunity to see the ad 20 to 40 times. The locations of station and shelter signs also afford high frequency of exposure.

Geographic Coverage For local advertisers in particular, transit advertising provides an opportunity to reach a very select segment of the population. A purchase of a location in a certain neighbourhood will lead to exposure to people of specific ethnic backgrounds, demographic characteristics, and so on.

Absolute Cost and Cost Efficiency Transit advertising tends to be one of the least expensive media in terms of both absolute and relative costs. An ad on the side of a bus can be purchased for a very reasonable CPM.

Selective Exposure Similar to outdoor advertising, transit ads are quite pervasive for those using the service and consumers have little control over the use of the media.

Scheduling Flexibility   The capacity available for transit ads makes it fairly good for placement. Ads can be produced quickly and inserted internally or externally.

LIMITATIONS OF TRANSIT MEDIA

Media Image   To many advertisers, transit advertising does not carry the image they would like to represent for their products or services. Thus, advertisers may think having their name on the side of a bus or in a bus does not reflect well on the firm.

Target Audience Selectivity   While a strength of transit advertising is the ability to provide exposure to a large number of people, this audience may have certain lifestyles and/or behavioural characteristics that are not true of the target audience as a whole. For example, in rural or suburban areas mass transit is limited or nonexistent, so the medium is not very effective for reaching these people.

Target Audience Coverage   While geographic selectivity may be an advantage, not everyone who rides a transportation vehicle or is exposed to transit advertising is a potential customer. For products that do not have specific geographic segments, this form of advertising incurs a good deal of waste coverage. Another problem is that the same bus may not run the same route every day. To save wear and tear on the vehicles, transit companies alternate city routes (with much stop and go) with longer suburban routes. Thus, a bus may go downtown one day and reach the desired target group but spend the next day in the suburbs, where there may be little market potential.

Creativity for Emotional and Cognitive Responses   It may be very difficult to place colourful and attractive ads on cards, thus limiting their emotional content. And while much copy can be provided on inside cards, the short copy on the outside of a bus provides less rational persuasion.

Clutter   Inside ads suffer from clutter of competing ads and outside ads feel the pressure of other street-level ads. Furthermore, the environment is cluttered in another sense as sitting or standing on a crowded subway may not be conducive to reading advertising, let alone experiencing the mood the advertiser would like to create.

Attention   The smaller size and location of interior transit ads make it difficult to use the creative elements to attract attention. The movement of transit vehicles makes it difficult to perceive the message.

Involvement   Like outdoor advertising, with shorter copy and seemingly fleeting messages of short copy, transit ads are generally considered to be low-involvement media.

Place-Based Media

The variety of out-of-home media continues to increase, and the idea of bringing an advertising medium to consumers wherever they may be underlies the strategy behind place-based media. In this section we summarize a few of the more prevalent options that include both print and video messages and highlight their strengths and limitations.

PLACE-BASED MEDIA OPTIONS

As Figure 13-1 indicated at the start of this chapter, there are a number of locations in which advertising messages reach consumers. Many of these options occur where consumers enjoy leisure or recreational activities, while others are where consumers work or study. Figure 13-11 shows that Canadians are aware of many forms of place-based advertising. Many of these media occur indoors, which is a term that is also used. The three main media companies offering place-based media are Zoom Media, Newad, and Pattision.

In all of these locations there are poster or print messages, and in many there are video or digital applications. There is also growth in these locations that allows consumers to interact with their hand-held mobile device. Given the interaction with websites and text messages after viewing ads (Figure 13-12 and Figure 13-13), it appears this "on-the-spot" follow-up to messages will be a new evolution in advertising and consumer response behaviour.

An original example of place-based media is the mall poster. It is often backlit, like the transit shelter or transit-station poster, and is located throughout a shopping mall. The key feature of the mall poster is that it is in the shopping environment and therefore one step closer

Figure 13-11

Awareness of place-based media

	Total %	18–34 %	35+ %
Shopping Malls	48	58	45
Outdoor	47	53	45
Airport	28	30	27
Public Transit	25	36	21
Restaurants	25	36	20
Medical Waiting Rooms	21	23	20
Bars/Nightclubs	18	28	14
Office Elevators	12	16	10
Health/Fitness Clubs	9	17	6

Source: Out-of-Home Marketing Association of Canada (OMAC).

Figure 13-12

Percentage visiting a website within past three months after seeing indoor/outdoor ad

	DITL 1	DITL 2
Toronto	29.5	36.9
Montreal	27.8	37.7
Vancouver	27.6	38.3
Females	29.5	38.5
Males	29.0	35.7

Source: Out-of-Home Marketing Association of Canada (OMAC).

Figure 13-13

Percentage sending a text message within past three months after seeing indoor/outdoor ad

	DITL 1	DITL 2
Toronto	4.8	4.7
Montreal	3.2	6.0
Vancouver	3.2	6.9
Females	2.7	4.3
Males	4.4	6.5

Source: Out-of-Home Marketing Association of Canada (OMAC).

to the actual purchase. These posters are sold in most markets across the country similarly to outdoor posters with individual spot buys and varying levels of GRPs. Firms also sell various sizes of mall posters for branding or interaction purposes. Advertisers use these posters for interaction purposes by including QR codes so consumers can use their smartphone and receive additional information (Exhibit 13-13). Video or digital displays are growing in retail locations as well.

An example of video messages occurring out-of-home at a specific location is cinema or movie theatre ads. Today, it is estimated that about $25 million to $30 million in advertising is spent in theatres on commercials, slides, posters, and sales promotions, with about $15 million of that for the commercials. Since the commercials last 60 to 90 seconds, advertisers have a unique opportunity to communicate for a longer period of time than with a typical TV ad. In fact, 95 percent of the theatre ads are also shown on television, albeit in a shortened format. Cinema ads lead other public video media as it now reports audience measurement information. One study estimated that total recall (aided plus unaided) reached 74 percent compared to 37 percent for radio and 32 percent for television.[17]

Research on consumer attitudes toward cinema ads in general found a number of sources of negativity in terms of restriction (e.g., less communication, captive, delayed gratification, minimizing escapism) and equity (unfair, time-waster, payment); however, many people enjoy the experience of specific ads (entertaining, liking the ad, involved, ad congruent with movie) as long as it is not shown too many times. It appears this, like other media, has a tension of both positive and negative reactions.[18]

Despite this mixed view, advertisers sometimes develop ads specifically for cinemas; Toyota took advantage of that idea with a scene set in a car at a drive-in movie theatre. The movie showed a montage of Toyota vehicles over the past 20 years to reinforce the message that 80 percent of all Toyotas sold in the past 20 years are still on the road. A creative director for the agency commented, "Toyota likes cinema. We get good recall results from it. Those ads create good drama for the brand."[19]

Airport terminals are another place where extensive signage occurs; an airport is very similar to a mall, with shopping concourses and restaurant areas. Displays are available ranging from smaller backlit posters in the terminal to superboards near the terminal and other types of displays depending upon the media company and terminal (Exhibit 13-14). An exploratory study of airport terminal advertising reports the following conclusions.[20] One, ads are more likely to be processed when in the main concourse or near retail outlets. Two, the situational variable of the person's activity influences their degree of processing. Three, repetition of a simple message is necessary, but with less frequency. Four, elements of the ad influence recall and recognition differently, thus necessitating decisions on design and communication objective. Five, frequent flyers' responses are strong up to a point then taper off after receiving a repetitious message.

Lexus innovated with a touch screen attached to the window of its new luxury crossover vehicle. The screen allowed consumers to interact with the vehicle's advanced features. A high-contrast rear-projection film adhesive located inside allowed the touch screen to be seen from the outside. Lexus

Exhibit 13-13 Backlit poster ads encourage further digital communication.

ignore or interact?

Exhibit 13-14 While picking up luggage, airport travellers viewed an ad encouraging them to consider certain services.

Exhibit 13-15   Ads in unusual locations provide a unique vehicle for advertising.

used the message "Reinventing the vehicle that invented it all" and placed the RX in Toronto's major airport for 13 weeks to obtain 64,000 interactions and 1.3 million envious glances.[21]

Like malls, a number of place-based media are outdoor media brought into a particular environment. Backlit posters, superboards, electronic message signs, and video displays are used in many locations for leisure such as movie theatres, hotels, restaurants and bars, sports stadiums or arenas, athletic venues such as golf, ski, or fitness centres, or wherever a sufficient number of people congregate. Advertisers extend these media to locations where consumers cannot avoid receiving the message (Exhibit 13-15). The OMAC DIL research estimates that the average Canadian spends 1.3 and 2.2 hours per weekday and weekend day on leisure, respectively. For example, 55 percent visited a restaurant or bar four times per month for an average of two hours, and 24 percent visited a health club eight times per month for an average of 1.4 hours. Advertising in office buildings or convention centres or similar venues also reaches those who are at work, where a considerable amount of time is spent. The method of selling the time or space is similar to that described above.

Continuing this idea of bringing a message to a target audience based on where they are illustrates two emerging place-based media outlets. Firms attempt to reach younger consumers on the campuses of many universities and colleges with various sizes of indoor posters that are standard and non-standard. Research confirms the average student's experience as each campus visit averages five hours—plenty of exposure time for messages in various university/college buildings. Furthermore, with closed-circuit television, firms attempt to reach travellers in hotels, or patients in medical waiting rooms. And to reach virtually anyone and everyone, it is possible to place print and video ads inside elevators or washrooms, and print ads on floors or escalator handrails. Despite the prevalence of all these place-based media, Canadians do not believe it is too much (Figure 13-14).

Creativity with place-based media is possible. The Vancouver team of the Taxi agency created a pint-sized outdoor campaign that fit its client, West Valley Market. The local independent store wanted to distance itself from the ads for big-box stores, so the miniature campaign proved to be a perfect contrast. About 500 small pots planted with vegetables found their way to doorsteps and public places for consumers to take and had the message "A small taste of the farm—West Valley Market."[22] The Vancouver team of the Rethink agency demonstrated Parissa Wax Strips on the beach with help from a man with a hairy back. The brand name—groomed using wax

Figure   13-14

Perceived amount of advertising by indoor medium: percentage having "too much" advertising

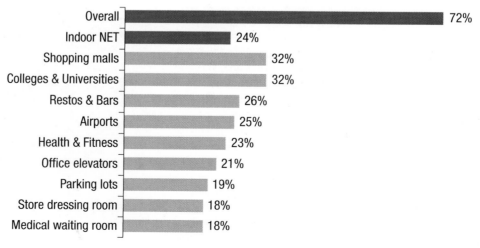

Source: Out-of-Home Marketing Association of Canada (OMAC).

into the man's hair—attracted the attention of sunbathers, who clearly perceived the need for the product! Rethink estimated the resulting publicity garnered $250,000 in exposure. Rethink also promoted a personal trainer's services by having a person ride a stationary bike beside morning commuters with the message "Escape your boring gym."[23]

STRENGTHS OF PLACE-BASED MEDIA

Target Audience Selectivity   The main purpose of place-based media is to reach a specific target audience or to reach the target audience while closer to the purchase decision in terms of time and space. For example, ads in fitness clubs could contain messages for athletic gear, mall posters could have ads for food outlets that are located in the mall food court, and movies could attract a certain crowd who fit with particular brands more than others.

Absolute Cost and Cost Efficiency   The absolute cost and CPM are generally reasonable compared to other media options.

Creativity for Cognitive and Emotional Responses   Because the target and place are intertwined, the message may generate more in-depth cognitive responses or stronger emotional responses. For example, creative lifestyle messages can be prominent in poster ads located in clubs or bars. Large-scale spectaculars have been used to create fantastic visual effects to generate positive feelings. The special mood created in the movie theatre compared to at-home consumption makes the experience richer, and advertisers use theatre ads as an emotional spike that can transfer to the product more readily, especially if the theatre is located next to a mall or store where the product may be sold.

Control for Selective Exposure   Since many of these media options have captive or nearly captive audiences, the opportunity for consumers to avoid the ads or direct their attention elsewhere is minimal compared to other media. For example, once sitting in a movie theatre, it is very difficult for the average person to not watch the ad.

Attention and Involvement   With the above strengths of many place-based media options, the collective conclusion suggests that the target audience may be more involved with the advertising message than similar media in different contexts. The growth of video and digital messages in many locations offers greater opportunity to gain attention, and with a degree of target audience selectivity the creative can be customized with appropriate headlines for print messages.

LIMITATIONS OF PLACE-BASED MEDIA

Media Image   Often, place-based media are exposed to consumers when they do not expect a selling message to occur, which may cause displeasure. Consumers appear to be generally accustomed to ads in malls since they are so similar to the store signage. Cinema ads, in contrast, experienced negative reaction when first introduced.[24] However, we find mixed research results; one study reports a high percentage of viewers claim to not mind this form of advertising.[25] Other research suggests a negative image remains concerning how the ad infringes upon patrons' time prior to the movie, removes control for avoidance, delays movie enjoyment, minimizes the escapism feeling of being in the theatre, makes too much money for the theatre, steals personal time, and represents an unwarranted cost.[26] We have provided additional details for cinema ads as research exists compared to other media and to suggest that certain points may be relevant for other place-based media.

Clutter   The clutter that consumers feel while watching television may be similar as the video displays generally play a block of commercials, although this can be lessened in options like cinema ads where one or two video ads could play. Similarly, locations have multiple posters of varying sizes, thus giving a similar clutter experience as reading the newspaper or magazine.

Reach and Frequency Place-based media plays more of a supporting role to other media since it is very difficult to ensure high levels of either reach or frequency. Exceptions can be considered, but in general media planners will look for other media to maximize these two factors.

Target Audience and Geographic Coverage The logistical availability of these types of media makes full target audience coverage difficult or quite challenging to implement, or nearly impossible to get complete geographic coverage.

Amount of Processing Time For the most part, place-based media suffer from very short messages to target audiences that are more likely preoccupied with other tasks. Evidence of strong recall suggests that the processing may be stronger for more creative executions, where additional processing occurs.

Scheduling Flexibility While not a complete or comprehensive limitation, the logistics of changing place-based media, which is done on a monthly basis, put certain restrictions on an advertiser for scheduling a timely message. Placement for cinema ads generally requires eight weeks, and category exclusivity in certain distribution outlets further limits the availability and scheduling ease with this media option.

LO2 Promotional Products

The Promotional Products Association International (PPAI), a trade association, defines **promotional products marketing** as "the advertising or promotional medium or method that uses promotional products, such as ad specialties, premiums, business gifts, awards, prizes, or commemoratives." Promotional product marketing is a name for what used to be called specialty advertising. Specialty advertising has now been provided with a new definition:

> A medium of advertising, sales promotion, and motivational communication employing imprinted, useful, or decorative products called advertising specialties, a subset of promotional products. Unlike premiums, with which they are sometimes confused (called advertising specialties), these articles are always distributed free—recipients don't have to earn the specialty by making a purchase or contribution.[27]

Specialty advertising is often considered both an advertising and a sales promotion medium. In our discussion, we treat it as an advertising medium in the IMC program, as it often communicates or represents the brand and its positioning. For example, IKEA offered a gift bag at an event that fit perfectly with the brand: USB key, Jansjo lamp, ice cube tray, Kort design cards, and a sewing kit, all useful household items that communicate the style and functionality IKEA is known for.[28]

The promotional product industry in Canada is substantial; the Canadian trade association is known as the Promotional Product Professionals of Canada (PPPC) (see www.promocan.com). One of its main tasks is to compile research information for its members, which we highlight briefly. Distributor revenue topped $3.9 billion in 2008, up from $1.2 billion in 1998 (Figure 13-15). The 2008 figure is two times greater than all Internet advertising in 2008. Figure 13-16 shows the percentage of sales by product category. Wearables/apparel accounted for the bulk at 30 percent, while the next highest, writing instruments, clipped in at 9 percent. Figure 13-17 shows the percentage of sales by program type. Business gifts, brand awareness, public relations, and trade shows account for nearly half of all revenue.[29]

Thanks to the Internet, it is now logistically easier to distribute the products than in the past. Clothing is the largest product category, its growth stemmed from a steady change toward more casual dressing at work and from many name brands such as Nike getting into the market. Other big

Figure 13-15

Promotional products revenue

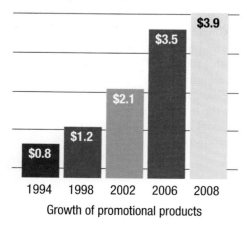

Growth of promotional products

Source: Promotional Product Professionals of Canada.

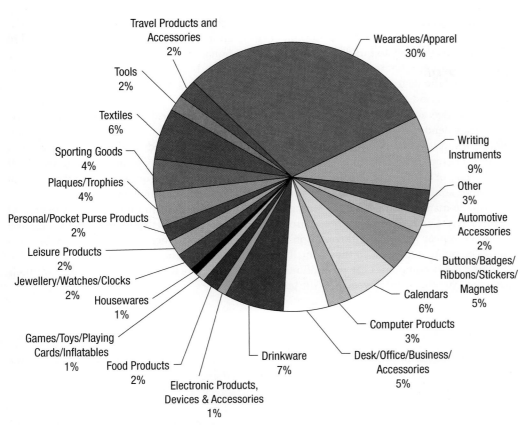

Source: Promotional Product Professionals of Canada.

Figure 13-16

Distribution product category breakdown

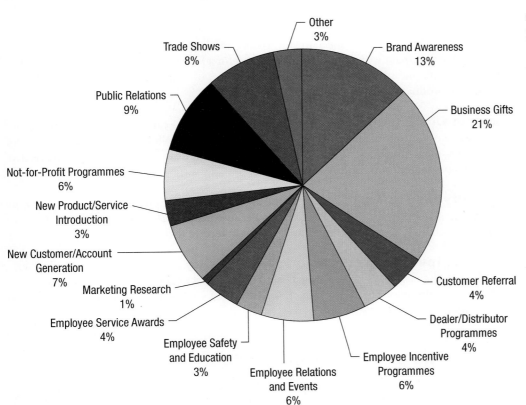

Source: Promotional Product Professionals of Canada.

Figure 13-17

Distributor sales by program type

brands like Apple make their product lines available, thus spurring on the overall demand for promotional products. Promotional product organizations have become more sophisticated in their selling as they try to build a brand with promotional planners. For example, both parties carefully consider whether the promotional product needs to be directly tied to the type of product, and the degree to which the promotional product needs to last a long time or for a shorter time period.[30]

As suggested above, thousands of advertising specialty items exist—pens, mugs, glassware, key rings, calendars, T-shirts, and USB flash drives. Unconventional specialties such as plant holders, wall plaques, and gloves with the advertiser's name printed on them are also used to promote a company or its product. Specialty items are used for many promotional purposes. It can generate or improve awareness when introducing new products or reinforcing the name of an existing company or products. The variety of promotional products makes it a virtual certainty that a manager will be able to strengthen attitudes with an item that represents the brand appropriately. Oftentimes promotional products are used to thank customers for patronage and encourage repeat purchasing. Promotional products support other IMC tools like sales promotion or public relations, so they contribute substantially to the overall promotional mix. In summary, many companies use promotional products as a way to fully communicate with their customers, suppliers, employees, and the general public.

STRENGTHS OF PROMOTIONAL PRODUCTS

Target Audience Selectivity and Coverage   Because specialty advertising items are generally distributed directly to target customers, the medium offers a high degree of selectivity. The communication is distributed to the desired recipient, reducing waste coverage.

Creativity for Cognitive Responses   As the variety of specialty items in Figure 13-14 demonstrates, this medium offers a high degree of flexibility. A message as simple as a logo or as long as is necessary can be distributed through a number of means. Both small and large companies can employ this medium, limited only by their own creativity.

Frequency   Most forms of specialty advertising are designed for retention. Key chains, calendars, and pens remain with the potential customer for a long time, providing repeat exposures to the advertising message at no additional cost. One set of statistics suggests 50 percent of all promotional products are kept for a year or longer.

Absolute Cost and Cost Efficiency   Specialty items can be expensive (e.g., leather goods), but most are affordable to almost any size organization. While they are costly on a CPM basis when compared with media, the high number of repeat exposures drives down the relative cost per exposure of this advertising medium.

Creativity for Emotional Responses   Promotional products are perhaps the only medium that generates goodwill in the receiver. Because people like to receive gifts and many of the products are functional, consumers are grateful to receive them.

Attention, Involvement, Amount of Processing Time   These would all be considered strengths of promotional products assuming the recipient appreciates the actual item, whether it is clothing or an office product. Certainly the selection of the item in question will heavily influence consumer reaction.

LIMITATIONS OF PROMOTIONAL PRODUCTS

Media Image   While most forms of specialty advertising are received as friendly reminders of the store or company name, the firm must be careful choosing the specialty item. The company image may be cheapened by a chintzy or poorly designed advertising form.

Clutter With so many organizations using this advertising medium, the marketplace may become saturated. While one can always use another pen the value to the receiver declines if replacement is too easy, and the likelihood that one will retain the item or even notice the message is reduced. The more unusual the specialty, the more value it is likely to have to the receiver.

Scheduling Flexibility The lead time required to put together a promotional products message can be longer than that for most other media due to supply and printing requirements.

Reach An advertiser hoping to expand the market through wider reach would likely find promotional products a weaker choice. As a support media, it thrives on assisting existing media that have reach as their strength.

Geographic Coverage While promotional products can be distributed essentially anywhere, the cost implications would severely curtail this as a feasible feature for most advertisers.

Selective Exposure Recipients of promotional products are in complete control as to whether they choose to display or show the item. It is entirely possible that a tremendous investment could receive very minimal exposure to the intended target audience.

PROMOTIONAL PRODUCTS RESEARCH

Owing to the nature of the industry, specialty advertising has no established ongoing audience measurement system. Research conducted to determine the impact of this medium is archived with PPAI (www.ppai.org) and shows the pronounced communication effect of promotional products when combined with media. The results of one experiment shown in Figure 13-18 illustrate the stronger impressions that occur when a promotional product is combined with TV and print ads for a local pizzeria. Another survey of more than 550 business travellers at a U.S. airport found that 71 percent had received a promotional product within the past 12 months; 34 percent actually had the item with them at the time of the survey; and 76 percent recalled the brand name. A field experiment at a trade show indicated that visits to a firm's booth increased significantly when a modest promotional product (i.e., magnet) and a promise to receive a more valuable item (i.e., T-shirt) were mailed to registrants prior to the show compared with a simple invitation. Finally, research shows that recipients have strong brand recall and keep and use the promotional product for up to two years. Most recipients were current customers or received the item as they were in the process of becoming a customer.[31]

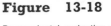

Figure 13-18

Respondents' evaluation of a brand or product

Product Placement

Product placement occurs when a brand name, logo, the actual product or an ad for it is part of a movie, TV show, or video game. Like specialty advertising, product placement is sometimes considered a promotion rather than an advertising form. This distinction is not a critical one, and we have decided to treat product placement as a form of advertising. We review a few key product placement decisions and their corresponding strengths and limitations.

PRODUCT PLACEMENT OVERVIEW

The global market for product placement reached $7.4 billion for 2011 with eight countries accounting for close to

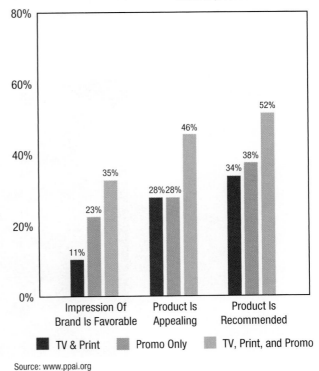

Source: www.ppai.org

$4.25 billion	United States
$ .50 billion	Brazil, Mexico
$ .10 billion	Australia, Japan, France, UK, Italy

Source: http://www.pqmedia.com/about-press-201212.html.

Figure   13-19

Expenditures on product
placement worldwide

$6 billion (Figure 13-19). TV and movies represented 90 percent of the amount spent as estimated by PQMedia.[32] The media tracking firm calculated the total based on actual financial transactions and excluded non-paid placements for in-kind exposure. The high-level deal-making environment of this decision makes it difficult to develop accurate reporting; however, developments have improved the situation.[33]

Much of the logic behind product placement is that since the placement is embedded in the script or program setting it cannot be avoided, thereby increasing exposure. Given the lack of intrusiveness of the placement, consumers may not have the same negative reactions to it as they may to a commercial. Assuming a marketer selected the right movie or TV vehicle, product placement contributes to higher awareness by its sheer volume of exposure (see Exhibit 13-16). Product placement appears promising, but its greatest strength may lie in maintaining existing loyalty of current customers who see the product they favour actually consumed by a character in a situation they can relate to. Research into product placement finds that it contributes to brand attitude and awareness and that consumers do not mind the prevalence of product placement.[34]

Product placement on Canadian television is not of the same magnitude as in the United States. One executive noted, "If you're a U.S. network getting a $200,000 fee for placement, that kind of money is worth the trouble. But as a Canadian broadcaster charging one-tenth of that, $20,000 just isn't worth it." Despite this concern the product placement has grown in Canada. CBC integrated brands into a number of shows such as *Being Erica, Little Mosque on the Prairie,* and *Heartland.* However, producers of one hit show find the product placement proposals far too blatant and uninspired and avoid the concept altogether. Although open to the idea, a commercial-like premise of the placement cannot be a natural fit with the characters. Another concern is the time delay where the show's production may not coincide with the advertising schedule and message evolution. Some are also concerned with the ability to accurately measure the effects in comparison to established procedures in advertising.[35]

Interestingly, products are placed in shows as part of the story and character without fees from the brand. Don Draper, a character in the hit show *Mad Men,* regularly drinks Canadian Club whisky. When the vintage bottle looked fatigued after a few seasons, the distiller Beam Inc. gladly provided an update—the first time any contact between the show and the company occurred.[36] So, technically, if there is no fee involved it is not product placement and more akin to publicity via a non-news medium.

Exhibit 13-16   Audi's
Spyder was a hit in
Ironman 2.

PRODUCT PLACEMENT DECISIONS

A summary of product placement research identifies seven execution decisions that influence processing and communication and behavioural effects.[37] A primary issue to decide concerns the source as represented by the type of movie or TV show. Much like there are media vehicle source effects upon the receiver's mood, the right entertainment selected creates a positive mood effect for the brand. Many TV programs feature product placement as data indicate that it occurs every three minutes, with storied shows having the fewest and game shows and news shows having the most.[38]

Secondly, the placement can be an actual product filmed, or digitally embedded afterward or added via overlay for live sports. Growth of this has occurred in sports broadcasts, however league organizers are not adopting the concept as quickly as suppliers had hoped.[39] These virtual products are added to the background or foreground of a scene. But transition shots—usually outdoor city images—provide a blank canvas on which to plaster ads. Virtual ads can be cheaper than standard product placement at $10,000 an episode; a 30-second spot on the same broadcast is $36,000.[40]

TV ads are most frequently 30 seconds, and other media have corresponding processing times. Thus, the amount of time the product is featured and how many different vehicles a marketer wants to be exposed in represent a third decision. While a marketer and its agent obviously try to negotiate the most favourable situation on these issues, they are also dependent upon the director's final artistic decision. TV show exposure averaged about five seconds with many of the incidents as simple "plugs" where the brand is mentioned.[41]

Much like advertising messages, the fourth decision is that the message can be visual or verbal or a combination of both, and a dual approach is generally hypothesized to improve effects. For example, the creative use of the product profoundly impacts the experience ranging from a central role in the scene to a mere showing of the product to having a central character use or talk about the product. Most ads are visual or verbal, with a dual approach rarely occurring.[42] Related to this is priming the product placement message via advertising or media publicity, or not priming the existence of the product placement ahead of time. This fifth decision regarding priming could be visual, verbal, or both.

A sixth decision is the amount and type of brand information presented. Generally, product placements are more concerned with brand exposure as the opportunity to say in-depth meaningful information is limited to the plot, scene, and character development. However, related to the fourth decision, the nature of the presentation can provide transformational experiences beyond information.

Finally, the brand personality and its positioning must "fit" with the characters, story, editorial content, and media vehicles. Much like message and source congruence found with other messages, product placements much make sense to the receiver; otherwise, the placement faces rejection like any other promotional message.

As a support medium, product placement needs to work with other marketing communication tools to achieve its maximum contribution. One expert suggests that product placement cannot possibly work on its own, and that it needs to be linked with all other aspects of the marketing communication plan. Furthermore, the communication effect can take time, much like other IMC tools, so brand managers need to be patient before seeing their investments pay off.[43] IMC Perspective 13-1 explores product placement trends in Canada.

Innovation in product placement occurred on a few fronts, but they are all a partial return to historical activities. Advertisers insert ads for brands that naturally fit in a storyline. For example, if the story has a restaurant scene, then an ad for a restaurant could play immediately thereafter. One network that tested the idea found improved measures of overall effectiveness and brand resonance.[44] Additionally, content sponsorship occurs when an advertiser sponsors a specific program and receives product placement, brand integration into the story, and other promotional considerations in return. In reality this is somewhat of a return to the early days of television, when shows were sponsored by advertisers. Another approach is the use of "advertainment," which is the creation of video and/or music content by an advertiser in an attempt to entertain viewers while advertising their products. All of these innovations are sometimes

IMC PERSPECTIVE 13-1

Which Way to Place a Product?

BARBIE and KEN are registered trademarks of Mattel, Inc. and these trademarks and images are being used with permission.

TV got its start with complete sponsorship of shows from consumer products, where the pauses between live scenes spliced in their messages. Nowadays, the placement ranges from obvious promotional messages in TV, movies, and talk shows to much more subtle visuals as the product is seen and noticed but becomes part of the natural storyline, to situations where the sponsorship is hardly noticed. And this placement gravitated beyond established entertainment locations to new and unexpected places and formats.

The pinnacle of product placement occurs with substantial brand recall, where viewers can recite the brand they saw in a movie or TV show the next day when questioned in follow-up research. For example, double the norm recalled a red Ferrari racing in lower Manhattan in an episode of *Castle*. Perhaps readers can recall what brand of beer James Bond drank while in recluse during *Skyfall*? While these recent overt displays are consistent with historical exposures, marketers are looking at more subtle approaches that revert to the original sponsorship idea. For example, Coke released three short films on the Internet featuring a rapper, snowboarders, and skateboarders with an ending that identified Burn.com, a Coke-owned beverage. Denny's restaurants distributed short clips of comedian Dave Koechner chatting with entertainment guests at the diner, much like people do when eating there. Called "Always Open," the mini show will feature actors with a project they want promoted, so in the end it will be a promotion within a promotion.

This notion of the brand as the star within a show is more blurring of content and advertising. For example, MTV's live hosts played the Apples to Apples board game while on-air. In a significant move, Mattel reunited Ken and Barbie after their 40-year-plus relationship ended in 2004 in a series of media activities that spanned Twitter, Facebook, *eTalk Canada*, out-of-home and print ads, a six-page fashion spread in *Elle*, and a contest that allowed fashion designers to create outfits for the couple with full-scale versions modelled by want-to-be Ken and Barbie.

Following up on the clothing idea, research finds that when people select avatars for simulation games they often select clothing they wear or aspire to wear—giving an unusual opportunity for clothing companies to place an identity that people can virtually purchase with points, and purchase for real as they buy virtual currency to adjust their swag. Xbox Live users have made 290 million customization adjustments to their avatars! Clothing brands adapted uses by users for their avatar grew awareness by 44 percent, and purchase intent by 31 percent. With such success it is no wonder Billabong updates the virtual lineup as often as its in-store selection!

Avatar clothing is but one of many options for in-game placements. Embedding brands within big-name games produced by Electronic Arts (EA) is one avenue that used to be quite expensive with a long lead time. However, programming changes make this cheaper and easier with gaming networks. In-game product placement hit $1 billion in 2010 in North America, up from $115 million in just five years. With 172 million consoles worldwide and about 5 million in Canada, the reach and frequency potential is strong. Dynamic in-game placement is a new and popular option, with Gatorade obtaining a 24 percent increase in sales with one usage and the Canadian Armed Forces finding a 200 percent increase in military career interest.

Sources: Kristin Laird, "Money for Nothing," *Marketing Magazine*, September 12, 2011, p. 11; Peter Nowak and Jeromy Lloyd, "Press Start," *Marketing Magazine*, January 24, 2011, pp. 24, 26, 28, 31–32; Simon Houpt, "And Now a Word from Our Sponsor," *The Globe and Mail*, May 7, 2011, p. R1; Theras Wood, "Brands' New Star Roles, *Strategy*, June 3, 2011.

Question

1. In what way is product placement effective?

referred to as "branded entertainment," signalling a blurring of the promotional message and the original creative content. In this respect, these promotional activities circumvent advertising laws as the distinction between the advertising message and the editorial content is strictly adhered to for TV shows and TV commercials, and print ads in magazines and newspapers.

STRENGTHS OF PRODUCT PLACEMENT

Reach   A large number of people see movies each year. The average film is estimated to have a life span of 3½ years, and most of these moviegoers are very attentive audience members. When this is combined with home rentals, movies on demand, specialty movie channels, and finally network viewing, the potential exposure for a product placed in a movie is enormous. A similar logic holds true for TV shows that are available with similar distribution intensities.

Frequency   Depending on how the product is used in the movie or program, there may be ample opportunity for repeated exposures due to those who like to watch a program or movie more than once.

Creativity for Emotional Responses   We previously discussed the advantage of source identification that occurs with a creative message. When consumers see their favourite movie star wearing Oakley sunglasses, drinking Gatorade, or driving a Mercedes, this association may lead to a favourable product image. Most of those involved in product placement believe that association with the proper source is critical for success.

Cost Efficiency   While the cost of placing a product may range from free samples to a million dollars, the CPM can be very low because of the high volume of exposures it generates.

Geographic Coverage   The potential for geographic coverage is substantial as a top movie or television show could have national or international coverage. We emphasize the importance of this qualifying aspect, as entertainment viewers can be fickle.

Selective Exposure   It is very difficult for a theatre audience member to physically avoid the product placement through zipping or zapping! Similarly, it is unlikely to expect many viewers at home to skip a product placement while enjoying the drama, action, or comedy of a movie or program.

Clutter   With category exclusivity rights within a vehicle and the fact that any show or movie has only a few product placements, the potential for clutter is very low. However, the plot, scenes, and dialogue act as a form of clutter that can be overcome with creative use of product placement.

Involvement   A product placement done properly has direct relevance for the character or situation and is almost a transformational experience for the audience member who is paying full attention to the entertainment.

LIMITATIONS OF PRODUCT PLACEMENT

Absolute Cost   While the CPM may be very low for product placement in movies, the absolute cost of placing the product may be very high, pricing advertisers out of the market.

Amount of Processing Time and Attention   Product placement in a movie or TV show has an attitudinal impact due to the vehicle source effect; there is no guarantee viewers will notice the product. Product placements range in whether they are conspicuous or not. When the product is not featured prominently or lasts for only a few seconds, the advertiser runs the risk of not being seen.

Creativity for Cognitive Responses   The appeal that can be made in this media form is limited. There is no potential for discussing product benefits or providing detailed information. Rather, appeals are limited to source association, use, and enjoyment. The endorsement of the product is indirect, and the flexibility for product demonstration is subject to its use in the film.

Scheduling Flexibility   In many movies, the advertiser has no say over when and how often the product will be shown. Fabergé developed an entire Christmas campaign around its Brut cologne and its movie placement, only to find the movie was delayed until February.

Media Image   Many TV viewers and moviegoers are incensed at the idea of placing ads in programs or movies. These viewers want to maintain the barrier between program content and commercials. If the placement is too intrusive, they may develop negative attitudes toward the brand.

Target Audience Selectivity   By its very nature of being cast in a movie, the potential for exposure beyond a brand's target audience is enormous. Although a certain amount of selectivity is viable through the type of movie or show, there is likely considerable wasted coverage.

Target Audience Coverage   Movie attendance is historically strong; however, in many cases it will be difficult to reach a substantial portion of one's audience with a single movie. Similarly, even a hit television show may reach only a portion of a brand's target audience.

AUDIENCE MEASUREMENT FOR PRODUCT PLACEMENT

Research studies and companies attempting to monitor and measure the impact of product placement have not resulted in an accepted industry standard like TV; however, companies offer service in this area. Nielsen Media Research, the TV ratings company in the United States, currently tracks product placement on network television. Nielsen-IAG Research maintains a panel where 5,000 daily viewers take an online quiz about the previous night's prime-time programs, the commercials, and product placements therein. The information is used to determine which ads work best; what shows, spots, and placements are being remembered; and viewers' attitudes toward the same. An advertising agency and product placement valuation company, Deutsch and iTVX, combined their efforts to measure effects. Their method values the quality of each hundredth of a second of a placement, and then translates them into a product placement/commercial cost ratio and compares it to the value of a commercial. Two studies have demonstrated the potential effectiveness of product placement. One showed that prominently displayed placements led to strong recall.[45] Another study indicated that viewers are accepting of promotional products and in general evaluate them positively, though certain products (alcohol, guns, cigarettes) are perceived as less acceptable.[46] As measurement systems develop, planners can rely on this preliminary information and may still make decisions based on their own creative insights (see Exhibit 13-17) or rely on the attractiveness and credibility of the source.

(L03) IMC Planning: Strategic Use of Out-of-Home and Support Media

Previously, the strategic use of out-of-home and support media might have been considered an oxymoron, as both types appeared in promotional planners' budgets after money had been allocated to other more "valuable" media. An IMC perspective toward media selection provides a new look at how these types of opportunities can achieve communication and behavioural objectives, primarily at the pre-purchase and purchase decision stages.

OUT-OF-HOME MEDIA

For the most part, outdoor, transit, and place-based media tend to have two primary objectives. The first is awareness, as these media share common strengths of cost efficiency with extensive reach and frequency levels in the geographic areas in which the media are located or placed. The ability to use clever images and headlines or very short-copy messages permits these messages to have emotional relevance to help ensure brand recognition or recall. Moreover, these two design elements can be consistent with creative messages from other media to ensure additional message frequency with the intention to build awareness more strongly.

Exhibit 13-17   Ads often appear in the strangest places.

In general, these media are limited in their ability to build category need or influence brand attitudes beyond maintaining the current attitude of the target audience. Many brands will use these media as an inexpensive, yet cost-effective way of communicating simple brand preference messages directed toward current customers or messages to reinforce the general market position of the brand to all potential consumers. Given the limited nature of these media to influence attitudes extensively with short messages, they typically are good for building communication effects at the pre- and post-purchase stages.

Most place-based media typically offer the opportunity for promotional planners to achieve a second objective: brand purchase intention. Since the messages for place-based media are context-dependent in terms of location or time, they can provide the right situational motive to spur on a store visit or more immediate sale. Particular place-based media, like movie theatres, are vehicles for additional exposure of the more traditional broadcast and print media ads and thus permit strong brand positioning strategy opportunities. As noted in the chapter, movie theatres can show longer and more specialized ads that brands may be reluctant to show in a broadcast environment.

Given the broad reach and public nature of these media, oftentimes they are more general and have a less clear behavioural objective. However, given that many messages are reinforcing existing attitudes, it appears a substantial number of these ads attempt to influence repeat purchasing. Application of out-of-home messages including connections to mobile hand-held devices suggests greater opportunity for brand switching for trial purchases.

From an integration perspective, out-of-home or transit media provide additional frequency of a creative message that has been placed in broadcast or print media. Typically, we do not see advertisers using these media for executing sales promotions except in poster locations. This medium is also used for public relations activities, and we infrequently observe any connection to direct marketing or Internet applications.

SUPPORT MEDIA

The size and growth of support media such as promotional products and product placement is almost hidden given the degree to which it fits into our everyday life or our normal TV, movie, and video game consumption habits. In this regard, they are similar to out-of-home media that are a part of our everyday experiences. However, for these two support media, the exposure is both more widespread and more narrow. Promotional products are more widespread as we are selectively observing them virtually everywhere depending on the product. Given that a high percentage is wearable, we witness brand names on shirts, hats, and so on almost constantly. Product placement is clearly narrower, as it is limited within the time frame and scope of the vehicle it is delivered in. These characteristics suggest that both are excellent for building awareness, much like out-of-home media, and could be especially useful for all stages of the target audience's decision-making process.

Promotional products and product placement offer brand-building capabilities much like specialized place-based media such as movie theatres. The vehicle in which the brand is associated provides an additional source effect that puts significant context around the brand experience. For example, observing a particular brand in a movie approximates an endorsement from both the character and the actor. This is consistent with viewing a television commercial with the same actor, but even more so as the emotion and involvement with the movie compounds the positive effect. Given this more profound viewing experience, it is no wonder advertisers are willing to pay substantial parts of their budget to have the brand featured in a few seconds of a popular movie.

The independence of these kinds of media suggests more limited opportunity for integration, but opportunities are pursued. Public relations activities are often used to connect the brand and its product placement in a movie or television show. For example, for blockbuster placements, like showing a new car model in a movie, news media will report the appearance in both traditional versions and on the Internet. News media have reported upon the placement of brands in video games. Naturally, the Internet offers a wide variety of information content, and a brand can highlight its placement on its own site.

Learning Objectives Summary

 Identify the options within out-of-home media for developing an IMC program and for audience measurement, and their strengths and limitations.

This chapter introduced three types of out-of-home media available to marketers: outdoor, transit, and place-based. Within each, there are numerous options for promotional planners to use to achieve their objectives. Many provide the opportunity to creatively express the brand message in a very appropriate location depending on where people live, work, or play.

Outdoor advertising audience measurement is very strong in Canada. The industry association COMB has established a strong research methodology for ensuring accurate estimates of exposure levels. This research has expanded to place-based media such as those found in restaurants and hotels as well as health and fitness outlets. Documentation for transit audiences is less thorough, although a degree of assessment is possible.

Collectively, the three outdoor media offer consistent strengths. For the most part, the public nature of these media leads to high numbers of people reached, which in turn suggests relatively positive cost efficiency allowing advertisers to extend their frequency levels. Secondly, each medium allows for creativity for either emotional or cognitive responses. In addition, many of the media discussed here have effectively demonstrated their power to obtain positive communication and business effects. Perhaps the major weakness is the lack of audience measurement and verification for transit and place-based media in comparison to out-of-home; however, the developments in the latter offer potential development in the former ones in the future.

 Apply the concepts of out-of-home media to promotional products and product placement to construct support programs within an IMC plan.

Support media include promotional products and product placement. Each of these media are public displays of brand messages that are more fitting with the unique situation in which it is delivered. Research of audience size for the support media of promotional products and product placement is mixed. Clearly, product placements in movies and TV shows rely on movie ticket sales (and later video purchase and rentals) and audience size estimates for television viewing. Similarly, marketers know the number of promotional product items given out since they pay the bill, and could estimate pass-along rates and readership rates much like is done in magazines. But in both cases, estimates of exposure level and subsequent achievement of objectives is incomplete or mixed.

 Show how out-of-home and support media are important elements of IMC planning.

In many instances, IMC planners require broad exposure levels for the brand name and basic positioning message to be reinforced for many consumers. Out-of-home and support media are very good at achieving these tasks, and with the development of digital communication, these media are contenders for initiating consumer contact for product information or participation with various kinds of brand experiences or sales promotions. As such, their potential for moving into the realm as a primary media continually improves over time.

Key Terms

Review key terms and definitions on Connect.

Review Questions

1. Explain how out-of-home ads can be creative and foster emotional responses. Why would brands use outdoor ads for this purpose?

2. What are promotional products? List the advantages and disadvantages of this medium. Provide examples where the use of this medium would be appropriate.

3. How do out-of-home media and support media help achieve awareness objectives?

Applied Questions

1. While travelling through a town or city, look for the most unusual place-based ad and decide whether it represents effective advertising.

2. The James Bond movie *Skyfall* had many product placement deals. Watch the movie and try to figure out which brands used this strategy; then do an Internet search to find the real answers.

3. Explain how out-of-home and support media might be used as part of an IMC program. Take any three of the media discussed in the chapter and explain how they might be used in an IMC program for automobiles, cellular telephones, and Internet services.

GO ONLINE

For more information on the resources available from McGraw-Hill Ryerson,
go to www.mcgrawhill.ca/he/solutions.

Sales Promotion

14

LEARNING OBJECTIVES

LO1 Explain the role of sales promotion in a company's integrated marketing communications program and examine why it is increasingly important.

LO2 Identify the objectives, strategy, and tactical components of a sales promotion plan.

LO3 Describe consumer sales promotion strategy options and evaluate the factors to consider in using them.

LO4 Describe trade sales promotion strategy options and evaluate the factors to consider in using them.

LO5 Apply key IMC issues related to sales promotion decisions.

Consumer Contests Go Digital

Consumers love contests, and it seems advertisers love them too, as we see interesting examples where consumer participation is quite exemplary compared to something simple like filling out an entry form online, in a retail store, or at an event. From retro Cougar boots, to Nivea skincare products, to Magnum ice cream, it seems contests work well in different product categories.

Decades ago, Cougar achieved success with its popular tan-coloured pillow boots that featured a red felt lining and inner tongue and were worn by fashionably trendy young women. After the company floundered for a period and then resurrected in the 1990s, the new brother-owners looked back to their history and saw the success their father and uncle had with the iconic pillow boot during the 1970s and 1980s. "In 1981, that boot made us the biggest manufacturer of footwear in Canada," commented one of the two brothers. Working with an online fashion site that had many Facebook and Twitter followers, Cougar conceived a contest to attract young women who had no awareness of the brand. Entrants suggested what they would do to win a limited-edition pair of boots, with the possibility that the online fashion site would show up at their door and record them doing what they claimed they would do! Hundreds of entrants resulted in many video uploads, with each winning video receiving at least 30,000 views. The $100,000 campaign cost resulted in higher sales for Cougar, increased website traffic due to stronger search results, and greater retailer purchases.

Nivea coordinated a contest with its pop-up store (see Chapter 13) and other promotional tools to celebrate its 100th anniversary. "We know from our proprietary research that our consumer is totally interested in educating themselves about skincare," commented one executive. As such, after a visit to the pop-up store and a skincare consultation, consumers received a branded bag containing a their after-effects photo, samples, and coupons, and offered a chance to win a $10,000 "body and soul regimen for two" featuring the services of a beauty and well-being expert, a Nivea skincare expert, a massage therapist, a fashion stylist, a personal trainer, a chef, and a nutritionist. One-hundred gift sets rounded out the prize list. Other promotion of the contest included direct mail, national magazines ads in both languages, and a microsite.

Magnum ice cream searched for an heir to the fictitious Baron Leopold Ferdinand von Magnum upon his death and looked to its customers, who uploaded video explaining why they deserved the nobility title while eating the ice cream. Picking up on research findings, Magnum realized that its consumers saw the brand as manifesting the life of a rich and famous VIP. The winning video claimed a $250,000 prize that included $100,000 in cash and vacation stops in Europe and New York each worth $50,000. Promotion for the contest included international ads that reflected the image of the brand bestowing regal status upon its consumers. Media partnerships with CTV and TVA where *eTalk* and *Gala Arts* hosts featured the search on their shows, newspaper ads, and out-of-home transit stops that looked like throne rooms rounded out the exposure levels. Ivanka Trump, an heiress in her own way, assisted with a media blitz launch in Toronto and with the judging to reduce the 400 entries to final list of 10 from which consumers voted for the winner, who was featured on Erica Ehm's Yummy-Mummy blog.

Source: Melinda Mattos, "Nivea Pops Up for 100th Anniversary," *Strategy*, May 1, 2011, pp. 10; Jonathan Paul, "Magnum Seeks an Heir to the Empire," *Strategy*, May 1, 2011, p. 12; Denise Deveau, "Video Contest Kicks Retro Up a Notch, *National Post*, January 16, 2012, p. FP1; http://www.yummy mummyclub.ca/blogs/erica-ehm-exposed/inspired-by-the-magnum-heir.

Questions:

1. Why are consumers motivated to participate in contests like these?

Advertising alone may not be enough to convince consumers to switch brands, try a new product category, or return to the same brand purchased previously. Companies also use sales promotion methods targeted at both consumers and the wholesalers and retailers that distribute their products to stimulate demand. Most IMC programs include consumer and trade promotions that are coordinated with advertising, direct marketing, and publicity/public relations campaigns as well as salesforce efforts.

This chapter focuses on the role of sales promotion in a firm's IMC program. We explain how marketers use both consumer and trade promotions to influence the purchase behaviour of consumers and wholesalers and retailers, respectively. We identify the objectives of sales promotion programs and describe the types of sales promotion tools that can be used at both the consumer and trade level. We also consider how sales promotion can be integrated with other elements of the promotional mix, and look at problems that can arise when marketers become overly dependent on consumer and trade promotions.

(L01) Sales Promotion Planning

Of all the IMC tools available to a promotional planner, sales promotion potentially allows brands to achieve multiple objectives or provides the opportunity to enhance an IMC plan due to the nature of its characteristics and the many types that are available. We review these two topics in this section and highlight the reasons why sales promotion has grown so tremendously, thus indicating the relative strengths of sales promotion.

CHARACTERISTICS OF SALES PROMOTION

Sales promotion has been defined as "a direct inducement that offers an extra value or incentive for the product to the salesforce, distributors, or the ultimate consumer with the primary objective of creating an immediate sale."[1] This definition indicates two distinguishing features of sales promotion.

First, sales promotion involves an inducement that provides an *extra incentive* to buy. This incentive is usually the key element in a promotional program: it may be purely financial (i.e., coupon, price reduction, refund or rebate), emotionally based (i.e., opportunity to enter a contest or sweepstakes, gift or premium), value-oriented (e.g., extra amount of product, sample a free product), or experiential (i.e., attend a marketing event). The financial incentive can be seen as extrinsic while the intrinsic non-financial incentives are hedonic in nature, demonstrating entertainment, personal exploration, and value expression.[2] Furthermore, sales promotions also reinforce consumers' feelings about themselves as finding deals is seen as an achievement and a personal reward for being a good shopper, thereby increasing the frequency of purchases.[3]

A second point is that sales promotion is essentially an *acceleration tool,* designed to speed up the buying process of consumers and maximize sales volume.[4] By providing an extra incentive, sales promotion techniques can motivate consumers to purchase a larger quantity of a brand or shorten the purchase cycle of consumers by encouraging them to take more immediate action. Companies also use limited-time offers such as price-off deals or a coupon with an expiration date to accelerate the purchase process.[5] Sales promotion attempts to maximize sales volume by motivating customers who have not responded to advertising. The ideal sales promotion program generates sales that would not be achieved by other means. However, sales promotion offers may end up being used by current users of a brand rather than attracting new users.

TYPES OF SALES PROMOTION

Sales promotion activities can be *targeted to different audiences* in the marketing channel. As shown in Figure 14-1, sales promotion can be directed to consumers and trade members. Activities involved in **consumer sales promotion** include sampling, couponing, premiums, contests and sweepstakes, refunds and rebates, bonus packs, price-offs, programs, and event

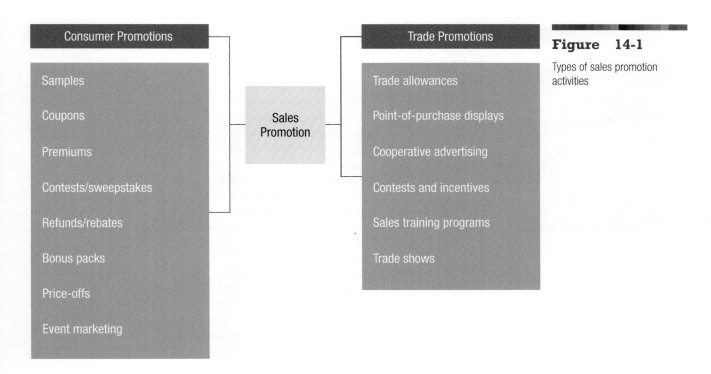

marketing. These promotions are directed at consumers, the end purchasers of goods and services, and are designed to induce them to purchase the marketer's brand. Consumer promotions are also used by retailers to encourage consumers to shop in their particular stores. Sales promotion can also be directed to intermediaries like wholesalers, distributors, and retailers, known as trade members. **Trade sales promotion** includes dealer contests and incentives, trade allowances, point-of-purchase displays, sales training programs, trade shows, cooperative advertising, and other programs designed to motivate organizations in the distribution channel to carry and merchandise a product.

Marketing programs usually include both trade and consumer promotions, since motivating both groups maximizes effectiveness. Programs designed to persuade the trade to stock, merchandise, and promote a manufacturer's products are part of a **promotional push strategy**. The goal of this strategy is to push the product through the channels of distribution with promotional activities. A push strategy tries to convince resellers they can make a profit on a manufacturer's product and to encourage them to order the merchandise and communicate and promote the brand to their customers. Company sales representatives call on resellers to explain the product, discuss the firm's plans for building demand among ultimate consumers, and describe and offer the trade promotion programs. The company may use **trade advertising**, generally publications that serve the particular industry, to generate reseller interest.

Companies also employ a **promotional pull strategy**, spending money on sales promotion efforts directed to the ultimate consumer with the goal of creating demand among consumers. Effort directed toward the end-user encourages the reseller to stock and promote the product. Thus, stimulating demand at the end-user level pulls the product through the channels of distribution.

Whether to emphasize a push or a pull strategy depends on a number of factors, including the company's relations with the trade, its promotional budget, and demand for the firm's products. Companies that have favourable channel relationships may prefer to use a push strategy and work closely with channel members. A firm with a limited promotional budget may not have the funds for sales promotion that a pull strategy requires and may find it more cost-effective to build distribution and demand by working closely with resellers. When the demand outlook for a product is favourable because it has unique benefits, is superior to competing brands, or is very popular among consumers, a pull strategy may be appropriate. Companies often use a combination of push and pull strategies, with the emphasis changing as the product moves through its life cycle.

Exhibit 14-1   Aspen Marketing Services touts its IMC capabilities.

GROWTH OF SALES PROMOTION

Sales promotion has been part of marketing for years; however, its role and importance in an IMC program has evolved. Historically, advertising received the major budget allocation for most consumer-products companies' plans. In the 1980s and 1990s, the proportion of the marketing budget allocated to sales promotion rose sharply, mostly due to increased trade promotion but also due to more attractive and creative consumer promotions. Many factors have led to the shift in marketing dollars to sales promotion. Among them are the strategic importance, reaching a specific target audience, promotional sensitivity, declining brand loyalty, brand proliferation, short-term focus, accountability, power of retailers, and competition.

Strategic Importance   In the past, sales promotion specialists participated in planning after key strategic branding decisions were made to develop a promotional program that could create a short-term increase in sales. However, companies now include promotional specialists as part of their strategic brand-building team, and promotional agencies offer integrated marketing services and expertise to enhance brand equity (see Exhibit 14-1). Critics contend that if the trend toward spending more on sales promotion at the expense of media advertising continues, brands may lose the equity that advertising helped create. However, not all sales promotion activities detract from the value of a brand, as the next example illustrates.

With the mystique of the Stanley Cup, the NHL, and CBC's *Hockey Night in Canada,* corporate partners Pepsi, Lay's, and Gatorade invited fans to submit a video or photo showing their ritual for watching NHL playoff hockey and what the Cup means to them (Exhibit 14-2). The winner of the inaugural promotion received a $25,000 grand prize package comprising a hockey shrine built in their home designed by *Hockey Night in Canada,* a Samsung HDTV home theatre system, *HNIC* leather chairs and memorabilia, an Xbox 360 game system, and a supply of Pepsi, Lay's, and Gatorade products. This ultimate playoff party was captured for broadcast during a playoff game on *HNIC,* punctuated by six-time Stanley Cup champion Mark Messier delivering the Holy Grail itself as the guest of honour. The campaign was supported by *HNIC* broadcasts, a dedicated website, retail point-of-purchase creative, and special-edition Pepsi, Lay's, and Gatorade packaging. The public viewed the three finalists online a total of 40,000 times and voted for the ultimate winner, which was announced during game 2 of the Stanley Cup final featuring the Anaheim Ducks and Ottawa Senators. During the promotion, the website attracted more than 100,000 visitors, 70 percent of them unique, and produced more than 700,000 page views.[6]

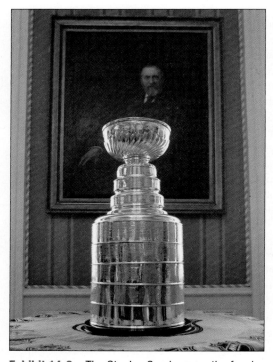

Exhibit 14-2   The Stanley Cup became the focal point of the promotion.

Reaching a Specific Target Audience   Marketing efforts focus on specific market segments, and firms use sales promotions to reach geographic, demographic, psychographic, and ethnic audiences. Sales promotion programs can also be targeted to specific user-status groups such as customers or non-customers, as well as non-category users or light versus heavy users. Sales promotion tools have become one of the primary vehicles for geographic-based programs tied into local flavour, themes, or events.

Promotional Sensitivity   Marketers are making greater use of sales promotion in their marketing programs because consumers respond favourably to the incentives it provides. Since the incentive can be financial, emotionally based, value-oriented, or experiential, it seems likely that consumers for most goods and services typically look for a little extra, which is consistent with economic theory.

Declining Brand Loyalty Consumers are always willing to buy their preferred brand at full price without any type of promotional offer. However, consumers can also be loyal coupon users and/or are conditioned to look for deals when they shop. They may switch back and forth among a set of brands they view as essentially equal. These brands are all perceived as being satisfactory and interchangeable, and favourable brand switchers (discussed in Chapter 3) purchase whatever brand is promoted.

Brand Proliferation Mature product categories are often saturated with new brands that may lack significant advantages that can be communicated in an advertising campaign. Thus, companies depend on sales promotion to encourage consumers and trade members to try or adopt these brands. Marketers also rely on sales promotion tools to achieve consumer trial of their brand's extensions (Exhibit 14-3). Marketers face competitive pressure to obtain shelf space for new products in stores as retailers favour new brands with strong sales promotion support.

Exhibit 14-3 A premium offer is used to provide extra incentive to purchase Kellogg's Corn Flakes.

Short-Term Focus Marketing plans and reward systems are geared to short-term performance measures of quarterly and yearly market share and sales volume. Critics believe the packaged-goods brand management system has contributed to marketers' increased dependence on sales promotion at the expense of brand building activities. Marketing or brand managers use promotions to help them move products into the retailers' stores at the request of the salespeople, who also face short-term quotas or goals.[7] Managers view consumer and trade promotions as the most dependable way to generate short-term sales, particularly when they are price-related.

Accountability Senior management puts pressure on marketing or brand managers and the sales force to produce an acceptable return on investment of marketing expenditures. In companies struggling to meet their sales and financial goals, top management is demanding measurable, accountable ways to relate promotional expenditures to sales and profitability. Managers held accountable to produce results often use price discounts or coupons, since they produce a quick and easily measured jump in sales as compared to advertising, which takes longer to show impact and the effects are more difficult to measure.

Power of Retailers Marketers also feel pressure from the trade as retailers demand sales performance from their brands. Real-time data available from computerized checkout scanners makes it possible for retailers to monitor promotions and track the results they generate on a daily basis. With optical checkout scanners and sophisticated in-store computer systems retailers estimate how quickly products turn over, which sales promotions are working, and which products make money. Retailers use this information to analyze sales of manufacturers' products and then demand discounts and other promotional support from manufacturers of lagging brands. Companies that fail to comply with retailers' demands for more trade support may have their shelf space reduced or even their product dropped.

Competition Manufacturers rely on trade and consumer promotions to gain or maintain competitive advantage. Exciting, breakthrough creative ideas are difficult to achieve on a regular basis, so there can be an overreliance on sales promotion. Companies tailor their trade promotions to key retail accounts and develop strategic alliances with retailers that include both trade and consumer promotional programs to achieve differentiation. A major development is **account-specific marketing**, whereby a manufacturer collaborates with an individual retailer to create a customized promotion that accomplishes mutual objectives. For example, when Unilever launched its new Sunsilk hairspray line the company developed 14 different

Exhibit 14-4   Sunsilk developed an account-specific promotion for Walmart.

account-specific promotions to get retailers to stock and promote the brand. For Shoppers Drug Mart, they published 600,000 copies of a mini-magazine called *Hairapy* that was made available in the store and sent out with *Glow,* the retailer's in-house magazine. For Walmart, Sunsilk "Hairapy guys" appeared in stores; this was supported by cinema ads designed to drive traffic to the retailer[8] (see Exhibit 14-4).

(L02) Sales Promotion Plan

In this section, we examine the various parts of a sales promotion plan. First, we consider objectives marketers have for sales promotion programs. Next, we illustrate why the sales promotion decisions are strategic options. Finally, we discuss the key tactics that are critical for all sales promotions. We focus on the consumer market to illustrate these ideas. Application to the trade market is readily done once the concept is understood.

OBJECTIVES OF CONSUMER SALES PROMOTION

As with any promotional mix element, marketers plan consumer promotions by conducting a situation analysis and determining sales promotion's specific role in the IMC program. They must decide what the promotion is designed to accomplish and to whom it should be targeted. Setting clearly defined objectives and measurable goals for their sales promotion programs is consistent with the planning process explained in previous chapters. While the goal is to induce brand purchase, the marketer may have different objectives for new versus established brands or new versus current customers. We use the ideas developed in Chapter 5 to highlight how sales promotions can help achieve behavioural and communication objectives. In particular, the latter considers the long-term cumulative effect on the brand's image and position.

Trial Purchase   One of the most important uses of sales promotion techniques is to encourage consumers to try a new product or service. While thousands of new products are introduced to the market every year, many fail within the first year due to a lack of the promotional support needed to encourage initial brand trial by enough consumers. Often, new brands are merely new versions of an existing product without unique benefits, so advertising alone cannot induce trial. Sales promotion tools have become an important part of new brand introduction strategies; the level of initial trial can be increased through techniques such as sampling, couponing, and refund offers.

A trial purchase objective is also relevant for an established brand that uses a sales promotion to attract nonusers of the product category. Attracting nonusers of the product category can be very difficult, as consumers may not see a need for the product. Sales promotions can appeal to nonusers by providing them with an extra incentive to try the product, but a more common strategy for increasing sales of an established brand is to attract consumers who use a competing brand. This can be done by giving them an incentive to switch, such as a sample, coupon, premium offer, bonus pack, or price deal.

Repeat Purchase   The success of a new brand depends not only on getting initial trial but also on inducing a reasonable percentage of people who try the brand to repurchase it and establish ongoing purchase patterns. Promotional incentives such as coupons or refund offers are often included with a sample to encourage repeat purchase after trial. For example, when Peek Freans introduced its Lifestyle Selections brand of cookie, it distributed free samples along with a 50-cent coupon and a contest offer with the winner receiving a trip to Las Vegas. The samples allowed consumers to try the new cookie, while the coupon provided an incentive to purchase it.

A company can use sales promotion techniques in several ways to retain its current customer base through continued repeat purchases. One way is to load them with the product, taking them out of the market for a certain time. Special price promotions, coupons, or bonus packs can encourage consumers to stock up on the brand. This not only keeps them using the company's brand but also reduces the likelihood they will switch brands in response to a competitor's promotion.

Increasing Consumption Many marketing managers are responsible for established brands competing in mature markets, against established competitors, where consumer purchase patterns are often well set. Awareness of an established brand is generally high as a result of cumulative advertising effects, and many consumers have probably tried the brand. These factors can create a challenging situation for the brand manager. Sales promotion can generate new interest in an established brand to help increase sales or defend market share against competitors.

Marketers attempt to increase sales for an established brand in several ways, and sales promotion can play an important role in each. One way to increase product consumption is by identifying new uses for the brand. Sales promotion tools like recipe books or calendars that show ways of using the product often can accomplish this. One of the best examples of a brand that has found new uses is Arm & Hammer baking soda. Exhibit 14-5 shows a clever freestanding insert (FSI) coupon that promotes the brand's new fridge–freezer pack, which absorbs more odours in refrigerators and freezers.

Build Brand Equity A final objective for consumer promotions is to enhance or support the brand's IMC effort. Although maintaining or building brand equity and image has traditionally been viewed as being accomplished by media advertising, it has also become an important objective for sales promotions. Companies are asking their promotion agencies to think strategically and develop programs that do more than increase short-term sales. They want promotions that require consumer involvement with their brands. Sales promotion techniques such as contests or sweepstakes and premium offers are often used to draw attention to an ad, increase involvement with the message and product/service, and help build relationships with consumers.

Exhibit 14-5 Arm & Hammer used this FSI to promote a specific use for the product.

CONSUMER SALES PROMOTION STRATEGY DECISIONS

Strategic decisions for sales promotions fall into three broad categories: sales promotion strategy options, application across product lines, and application across geographic markets.

Sales Promotion Strategy Options Our view of sales promotions is that the options identified in Figure 14-1 are important strategic choices for a marketer. Essentially, the key strategic decision for a marketer concerns the most appropriate sales promotion option that will best achieve the behavioural objective for the target audience. Two characteristics of sales promotions help guide the strategic direction of the sales promotion plan: the degree to which the sales promotion is "franchise building," and whether the incentive of the sales promotion is immediate or delayed.

Franchise-Building Characteristic Sales promotion activities that communicate distinctive brand attributes and contribute to the development and reinforcement of brand identity are **consumer franchise-building (CFB) promotions**.[9] Consumer sales promotion efforts cannot make consumers loyal to a brand that is of little value or does not provide them with a specific benefit. But they can make consumers aware of a brand and, by communicating its specific features and benefits, contribute to the development of a favourable brand attitude. Consumer franchise-building promotions are designed to build long-term brand preference and help the company achieve the ultimate goal of full-price purchases that do not depend on a promotional offer. Specialists in the promotional area stress the need for marketers to use sales promotion tools to build a franchise and create long-term continuity in their promotional programs. Well-planned CFB activities can convert consumers to loyal customers.

For years, franchise or image building was viewed as the exclusive realm of advertising, and sales promotion was used only to generate short-term sales increases. But now marketers are recognizing the image-building potential of sales promotion and realizing its CFB value. The Peek Freans contest mentioned above contributed to building the brand as it reinforced the image of the cookie as being better for the consumer (e.g., healthier). Since the cookie was good, the winner had to go to "Sin City in order to be bad."

Nonfranchise-Building Characteristic   **Nonfranchise-building (non-FB) promotions** are designed to accelerate the purchase decision process and generate an immediate increase in sales. These activities do not communicate information about a brand's unique features or the benefits of using it, so they do not contribute to the building of brand equity and image. Price-off deals, bonus packs, and rebates or refunds are examples of non-FB sales promotion techniques. Short-term non-FB promotions have their place in a firm's promotional mix, particularly when competitive developments call for them since they can switch customers from other brands. But their limitations must be recognized when a long-term marketing strategy for a brand is developed.

Trade promotions are mostly viewed as being nonfranchise-building. First, promotional discounts and allowances given to the trade are passed on to consumers intermittently. Second, trade promotions that are forwarded through the channels reach consumers in the form of lower prices or special deals and lead them to buy on the basis of price rather than brand benefits. Like consumer sales promotions, a franchise-building characteristic can be built into the trade promotion program with activities that do not have a price focus.

Incentive Characteristic   Sales promotions provide consumers with an extra incentive or reward to influence their behaviour, such as purchasing a brand. For certain sales promotion tools the incentive that the consumer receives is immediate, while for others the reward is delayed and not realized immediately. Using their situation analysis, marketers decide the relative balance between immediate or delayed incentives. The decision is based on the target audience(s) and the intended behavioural objective(s). The chart in Figure 14-2 outlines which sales promotion tools can be used to accomplish behavioural objectives and identifies whether the extra incentive or reward is immediate or delayed.[10] Some of the sales promotion techniques are listed more than once because they can be used to accomplish more than one objective with both immediate and delayed incentives, and with trial and repeat purchase behaviour.

Figure   14-2   Consumer sales promotion tools for various objectives

Communication and Behavioural Objectives

Consumer Reward Incentive	Trial purchase	Repeat purchase/ customer loading	Support IMC program/ build brand equity
Immediate	• Sampling • Instant coupons • In-store coupons • In-store rebates	• Price-off deals • Bonus packs • In- and on-package free premiums	• Events • In- and on-package free premiums
Delayed	• Media- and mail-delivered coupons • Mail-in refunds and rebates • Free mail-in premiums • Scanner- and Internet-delivered coupons	• In- and on-package coupons • Mail-in refunds and rebates • Loyalty programs	• Self-liquidating premiums • Free mail-in premiums • Contests and sweepstakes

One explanation for how sales promotion incentives work lies in the theory of **operant conditioning**. Individuals act on an aspect of the environment that reinforces behaviour. In a promotion context, if a consumer buys a product with a sales promotion and experiences a positive outcome, the likelihood that the consumer will use this product again increases. If the outcome is not favourable, the likelihood of buying the product again decreases. Two aspects of reinforcement relevant to sales promotion strategies are schedules of reinforcement and shaping.

Different **schedules of reinforcement** result in varying patterns of learning and behaviour. Learning occurs most rapidly under a *continuous reinforcement schedule,* in which every response is rewarded—but the behaviour is likely to cease when the reinforcement stops. This implies promotional offers like earning points in an online branded game should carry on indefinitely so that customers would not switch. Learning occurs more slowly but lasts longer when a *partial or intermittent reinforcement schedule* is used and only some of the individual's responses are rewarded. This implies that an IMC program should have a sales promotion with partial reinforcement schedule. The firm does not want to offer the incentive every time (continuous reinforcement), because consumers might become dependent on it and stop buying the brand when the incentive is withdrawn. A study that examined the effect of reinforcement on bus ridership found that discount coupons given as rewards for riding the bus were as effective when given on a partial schedule as when given on a continuous schedule.[11] The cost of giving the discount coupons under the partial schedule, however, was considerably less.

Reinforcement schedules can also be used to influence consumer behaviour through a process known as **shaping**, the reinforcement of successive acts that lead to a desired behaviour pattern or response.[12] In a promotional context, shaping procedures are used as part of the introductory program for new products. Figure 14-3 provides an example of how samples and discount coupons can be used to introduce a new product and take a consumer from trial to repeat purchase. Marketers must be careful in their use of shaping procedures: if they drop the incentives too soon the consumer may not establish the desired behaviour, but if they overuse them the consumer's purchase may become contingent on the incentive rather than the product or service.

Application across Product Lines   Another part of the strategic sales promotion decision is the degree to which each sales promotion tool is applied to the range of sizes, varieties, models, or products. Overall, there are three important product decisions for sales promotions. The first concerns whether the sales promotion should be run on the entire line or on individual items. If the latter option is selected (i.e., selective application), the second decision concerns which specific items. The marketer could run a promotion on either the more or less popular items. Similarly, the marketer could focus on higher or lower price points. Sometimes, a sales promotion is offered on a unique product format or size instead of the regular product. For example, Kellogg's bundled three brands of cereal with plastic in one sales promotion in which each size was not the standard size typically distributed. Thus, the third strategic issue concerns whether the sales promotion is run on the "regular" stock or another special version.

Application across Geographic Markets
Sales promotions can be run nationally or in select markets. Local or regional market conditions, with respect to consumer demand and competitive intensity, tend to dictate the degree of tailoring sales promotions for each geographic market. Intuitively, it appears that marketers would be faced with situations where offering unique sales promotions for each geographic market would achieve optimal communication and

Figure 14-3

Applications of shaping procedures for sales promotion

Behaviour Change	Type of Sales Promotion
Induce product trial	Free samples distributed; large discount coupon
Induce purchase with little financial obligation	Discount coupon prompts purchase with little cost; coupon good for small discount on next purchase enclosed
Induce purchase with moderate financial obligation	Small discount coupon prompts purchase with moderate cost
Induce purchase with full financial obligation	Purchase occurs without coupon assistance

behavioural effects; however, there are three factors that marketers need to consider. First, a regional focus requires additional managerial commitment in planning and implementation. Second, achieving objectives more specifically may result in greater expense, thus necessitating a cost–benefit analysis. Finally, national accounts may not be too receptive, with different types of sales promotions in one province versus another.

CONSUMER SALES PROMOTION TACTICS DECISIONS

A coupon can be received with a value anywhere from 50¢ to $2.00 for many consumer products, early in the year or later in the year, often or not so often, or from any number of outlets (e.g., direct mail, magazine). As this implies, for each sales promotion option the marketer faces a number of key tactical decisions: value of the incentive, timing, and distribution. We briefly describe each of these in order to put together a comprehensive sales promotion plan.

Value of Incentive   Whether the marketer is offering a price discount or a consumer franchise-building sales promotion such as a premium, eventually the marketer has to decide the value of the sales promotion. For example, should the coupon be the equivalent of a 10- or a 20-percent discount? This decision is contingent upon the threshold at which consumers will respond to a sales promotion and the number of potential consumer responses; each will contribute to the total cost of the sales promotion. Similarly, if a beer company is offering a premium, a strategic decision has to be made as to the relative value of the premium: for example, a T-shirt worth $10 to $15 or perhaps a "cozy" worth a couple of dollars.

A non-economic interpretation of value is also possible. Hostess Frito-Lay has used in-pack collectibles (e.g., stickers) of well-known entertainment or pop-culture icons (e.g., *The Simpsons, Star Wars*) that attract young, impulse-purchase consumers. The focus of these sales promotions transfers well to point-of-sale displays to attract consumers' attention and to meet retailers' need for innovative merchandising to move product off the shelves. For example, Hostess Frito-Lay has used Marvel comic-book characters on packaging and convenience-store point-of-sale displays, and offered limited-edition comic books as part of a trivia challenge in association with Teletoon.[13]

Timing   The time element of the sales promotion is important in a few directions that are mutually dependent. A marketer has to decide during which months, weeks, or days the sales promotion will be offered. Seasonal or some other consumption pattern discovered through market research or the situation analysis may guide this choice. Secondly, sales promotions can be offered for one day, one week, a few weeks, or even a few months. Target audience and behavioural objectives typically guide this duration decision. Finally, the frequency of the sales promotion is a final timing consideration. If coupons have been decided, the marketer needs to decide whether one will be offered every six months or perhaps two every six months.

Distribution   For most sales promotions, there is a logistical consideration as to how the promotion will get to the consumer or how the consumer will get to the sales promotion. There are many choices for sales promotions, such as coupons (e.g., direct mail, in-ad), while for others, such as premiums, the choices may be limited. We discuss the distribution options for each sales promotion in the next section, where we describe each sales promotion and its strengths and limitations. Technology Perspective 14-1 identifies new ways to distribute discounts digitally.

(L03) Consumer Sales Promotion Strategy Options

A number of consumer sales promotions that managers may select from to develop a strategic sales promotion plan were identified in Figure 14-1. Each of these options can assist the promotional planner in achieving the objectives just discussed. We now review each of these options by describing their characteristics, distribution methods, and strengths and limitations.

Let's Make a Deal

The desire by many to get online deals, better known as price discounts, prompted operators to set up group buying services whereby reduced prices for retail stores and other locations are accepted if sufficient pre-purchases are made online. The concept requires a considerable number of "subscribers" so that operators have sufficient buyers to match the amount of business desired by the sellers—that is, companies using price discounts to attract new customers. At the forefront of this trend is Groupon, which spends a substantial amount of money to attract its subscribers. In its growth phase Groupon was on pace to spend $700 million, about the same amount sought from an IPO, before moving on to a phase of encouraging current subscribers to participate in the promotional purchasing more frequently or reacquiring lost subscribers.

Similar competitors popped up, and as the concept caught on interesting deals appeared that prompted many to wonder whether the idea was a new type of Ponzi scheme. The Butchers, a store in Toronto, offered $175 of organic meat for $55, selling 11,500 coupons culminating in $632,500 in sales and attaining a loss leader price discount—something done by retailers for decades—with a digital distribution twist. According to the owner, just about every customer who arrives with the discounted coupon purchases other products, putting him ahead in the end. Furthermore, he has everyone's email address and could conceivably offer the same deal directly down the road.

With the notoriety, consumers questioned whether the supply chain could handle the increased demand, others wondered if the meat qualified as organic, and more worried that the owner might close shop and take off with the cash. The answers cleared the hurdle positively for all three questions. However, the increased demand caused considerable service-level concerns with so many new customers arriving and making it difficult for regular long-term customers to enjoy their shopping.

Other means of offering deals are in the works as well with the development of Facebook Deals. Users who check in with their location on their status can retrieve a special deal from a nearby retailer, which they show on their touchscreen phone to instantly get the price discount. The approach is a good deal for retailers as they do not pay a fee to the operators like Groupon; however, they are required to pay for the ad announcing the sales promotion on Facebook. And while this sounds pretty good, the privacy of the transaction is questionable since the purchase is presented on the user's Facebook news feed, thus turning basic personal content into an ad.

Finally Swiss Chalet found an innovative way to bypass fees to operators like Groupon and Facebook altogether by inventing the Rotisserie Channel on Rogers, where viewers could watch chicken roasting 24 hours a day, 7 days a week, for 3 months. Of course the channel offered promotional codes, redeemed for deals at the restaurant's Internet site and Facebook page. Chicken orders rose 30 percent and 13,000 coupons were downloaded in the first week; the number of Facebook fans grew 12,000 from a base of 70,000 in a month; Rogers claimed one million households watched the channel for an average of eight minutes; and the media placement won a Cannes Silver Lion!

Sources: Alistair Barr, "Groupon Targets Zero Spending on New Users," *National Post,* January 16, 2012, p. FP1; Katie Bailey, "Swiss Chalet Roasts with Rogers," *Strategy,* May 1, 2011, p. 9; Simon Houpt, "There Could Be a Deal Right Where You Are Standing," *The Globe and Mail,* February 19, 2011, p. B9; Tim Kiladze, "Ninety-Nine Bucks for $400 Worth of Organic Meat. Seriously?" *The Globe and Mail,* April 16, 2011, p. M1; Jeromy Lloyd, "BBDO and Proximity Win Silver and Bronze in Media Lions," *Marketing Magazine,* June 21, 2011.

Question:

1. What is the appeal for consumers to receive discounts like this versus finding a coupon or receiving the discount in-store while shopping?

SAMPLING

Sampling involves a variety of procedures whereby consumers are given an amount of a product for no charge to induce trial. Sampling is generally considered the most effective way to generate trial, although it is also the most expensive. Sampling is often used to introduce a new product or brand to the market and can be used for established product; however, it may not induce satisfied users of a competing brand to switch and may simply reward the firm's current customers who would buy the product anyway.

Sampling can have strong consumer franchise–building strength if supported within the IMC program. McDonald's initiated its free coffee offer with extensive advertising: TV, billboard, and out-of-home spectaculars. The ads conveyed that it was a premium roast coffee made with 100 percent Arabica beans, hand-picked and fire-roasted for a full-bodied flavour—a clear reason to enjoy the sample even more and increase the likelihood of actual purchase with a change in consumer attitude.[14]

Packaged goods (e.g., food, health care) producers are heavy users of sampling since their products meet the three criteria for an effective sampling program:

- The products are of relatively low unit value, so samples do not cost too much.
- The products are divisible, which means they can be broken into small sample sizes that are adequate for demonstrating the brand's features and benefits to the user.
- The purchase cycle is relatively short, so the consumer will consider an immediate purchase or will not forget about the brand before the next purchase occasion.

One of the cleverest samples that seems to satisfy these criteria occurred within four subway ads in Toronto. Commuters plugged their headphones into an audio jack to hear book excerpts, much like sampling music online or in a store. The recording ended with "HarperCollins: We tell the world's greatest stories."[15]

Strengths of Sampling   Samples are an excellent way to induce a prospective buyer to try a product or service. A major study conducted by the Promotion Marketing Association in 2002 found that the vast majority of consumers receiving a sample either use it right away or save it to use later.[16] Sampling generates much higher trial rates than advertising or other sales promotion techniques.

Getting people to try a product leads to a second benefit of sampling: consumers experience the brand directly, gaining a greater appreciation for its benefits. This can be particularly important when a product's features and benefits are difficult to describe through advertising. Food, beverage, and cosmetic products have subtle features that are most appreciated when experienced directly. Nearly 70 percent of the respondents in the PMA survey indicated that they have purchased a product they did not normally use after trying a free sample. The study also found that samples are even more likely to lead to purchase when they are accompanied with a coupon.

Limitations of Sampling   While samples are an effective way to induce trial, the brand must have some unique or superior benefits for a sampling program to be worthwhile. Otherwise, the sampled consumers revert back to other brands and do not become repeat purchasers. The costs of a sampling program can be recovered only if the program gets a number of consumers to become regular users of the brand at full retail price.

Another possible limitation to sampling is that the benefits are difficult to gauge immediately, and the learning period required to appreciate the brand may require supplying the consumer with larger amounts of the brand than are affordable. An example would be an expensive skin cream that is promoted as preventing or reducing wrinkles but has to be used for an extended period before any effects are seen.

Sampling Methods   One decision the promotional manager must make is how to distribute the sample. The sampling method chosen is important not only in terms of costs but also because it influences the type of consumer who receives the sample. The best sampling method gets the product to the best prospects for trial and subsequent repurchase. Promotional planners are not limited to one method. In fact, **multiple methods** for sample requests and delivery can occur. We now review the distribution options available.

Door-to-door sampling, in which the product is delivered directly to the prospect's residence, is used when it is important to control where the sample is delivered. This distribution method is very expensive because of labour costs, but it can be cost-effective if the marketer has information that helps define the target audience and/or if the prospects are located in a well-defined geographic area.

Sampling through media, in which goods are delivered through print media as they are delivered to residences. Newspapers use bags with advertising on the outside and the sample is tucked inside with the reading material, or an extension is put on the bag allowing greater visibility of the promotional offer. Magazines have similar capabilities but for smaller products. Companies use Internet media for consumers to sample their products. Software, information, or entertainment products can be easily delivered electronically in the digital age. Samples that are physical goods can be delivered to consumers, who can easily make a request using the Internet.

Sampling through the mail is common for small, lightweight, nonperishable products. This gives the marketer control over where and when the product will be distributed and can target the sample to specific market areas. Marketers use information from geodemographic target marketing programs to better direct their sample mailings. Sampling requests obtained from various sources (e.g., phone, Internet, mail) are usually mailed to consumers. The main drawbacks to mail sampling are postal restrictions and costs.

In-store sampling occurs when the marketer hires temporary demonstrators who set up a table or booth, prepare small samples of the product, and pass them out to shoppers. This approach can be very effective for food products, since consumers get to taste the item and the demonstrator can give them more information about the product while it is being sampled. Demonstrators may offer a financial incentive for the sampled item to encourage immediate trial purchase. This sampling method can be very effective with direct product experience but it requires greater investment, extensive planning, and retailer cooperation.

On-package sampling, where a sample of a product is attached to another item (see Exhibit 14-6) can be very cost-effective, particularly for multiproduct firms that attach a sample of a new product to an existing brand's package. A drawback is that since the sample is distributed only to consumers who purchase the item to which it is attached, the sample will not reach nonusers of the carrier brand. Marketers can expand this sampling method by attaching the sample to multiple carrier brands and including samples with products not made by their company.

Event sampling occurs at venues such as concerts, sporting events, and cultural festivals and the brand's event marketing activities. Marketers use sampling programs that are part of integrated marketing programs that feature events, media tie-ins, and other activities that provide consumers with a total sense of a brand rather than just a few tastes of a food or beverage or a trial size of a packaged-goods product.

Location sampling allows companies to use specialized sample distribution services that help the company identify consumers who are nonusers of a product or users of a competing brand and develop appropriate procedures for distributing a sample to them. For example, university and college students receive sample packs at the beginning of the semester that contain trial sizes of such products as mouthwash, toothpaste, headache remedies, and deodorant.

COUPONS

The oldest, most widely used, and most effective sales promotion is the coupon. These characteristics are a function of options with its tactical considerations: the variability in discount offered (e.g., $.50, $1.00), time flexibility in terms of offer and expiration (e.g., limited, unlimited), and how it is distributed (e.g., media, direct, package, retailer), allowing it to fit in many of the cells of Figure 14-2. Research indicates that the average Canadian household receives about 200 coupons per year and uses about eight coupons, a 4 percent redemption rate.[17]

Exhibit 14-6 Armor All uses on-package samples for related products.

Currently, extensive research on coupons in Canada is not available; however, we present a couple of items from the United States in Figure 14-4. The average U.S. household received considerably more coupons—as many as 10 times more—yet the redemption is only about one percent. The face value and length of time data in Figure 14-4 are reasonably consistent with historical Canadian data. Consumer use of "extreme couponing" demonstrated on TV shows is not possible in Canada due to retailers' acceptance of only one coupon per purchase and their reluctance to offer "double-up" options with redemptions; however, some consumers have found great savings with effort to locate coupons and plan their shopping accordingly.[18]

Strengths of Coupons   Coupons have a number of strengths that make them popular sales promotion tools for both new and established products. First, coupons make it possible to offer a price reduction only to those consumers who are price-sensitive. Such consumers generally purchase because of coupons, while those who are not as concerned about price buy the brand at full value. Coupons also make it possible to reduce the retail price of a product without relying on retailers for cooperation, which can often be a problem. Coupons are generally regarded as second only to sampling as a promotional technique for generating trial. Since a coupon lowers the price of a product, it reduces the consumer's perceived risk associated with trial of a new brand. Coupons can encourage repurchase after initial trial. New products might include a coupon inside the package to encourage repeat purchase. Coupons can also be useful promotional devices for established products. They can encourage nonusers to try a brand, encourage repeat purchase among current users, and get users to try a new, improved version of a brand. Coupons may also help coax users of a product to trade up to more expensive brands.

Limitations of Coupons   There are a number of problems with coupons. First, there is potential that coupons will not achieve their intended objective. Coupons intended to attract new users to an established brand can be and are redeemed by consumers who already use the brand. Rather than attracting new users, coupons can end up reducing the company's profit margins among consumers who would probably purchase the product anyway. Due to the incentive, conditions, and expiry date, coupons remain less effective than sampling for inducing initial product trial in a short period.

Second, it can be difficult to estimate how many consumers will use a coupon and when. Response to a coupon is rarely immediate; it typically takes anywhere from two to six months to redeem one. A study of coupon redemption patterns found that coupons are redeemed just before the expiration date rather than in the period following the initial coupon drop.[19] Marketers are attempting to expedite redemption by shortening the time period before expiration. The uncertainty in knowing the redemption rate and timing makes for more difficult financial planning for coupons.

A third problem with coupons involves low redemption rates and high costs. Couponing program expenses include the face value of the coupon redeemed plus costs for production, distribution, and handling of the coupons. Figure 14-5 shows the calculations used to determine the costs of a couponing program using an FSI (freestanding insert) in the newspaper and a

Figure 14-4		**2011**
U.S. coupon facts	Value distributed	470 billion
	Quantity distributed	305 billion
	Quantity redeemed	3.5 billion
	Average face value coupons *distributed*	$1.54
	Average face value coupons *redeemed*	$1.32
	Average valid period	70 days
	Consumer savings	$3.7 billion

Source: NCH 2010 Coupon Facts Report.

Cost per Coupon Redeemed: An Illustration	
1. Distribution cost 5,000,000 circulation × $15/M	$75,000
2. Redemptions at 2%	100,000
3. Redemption cost 100,000 redemptions × $1.00 face value	$100,000
4. Retailer handling cost and processor fees 100,000 redemptions × $0.10	$10,000
5. Total program cost (Items 1 + 3 + 4)	$185,000
6. Cost per coupon redeemed Cost divided by redemption	$1.85
7. Actual product sold on redemption (misredemption estimated at 10%) 100,000 × 90%	90,000
8. Cost per product moved (Program cost divided by amount of product sold)	$2.06

Figure 14-5

Calculating couponing costs

coupon with an average face value of one dollar. The marketer should track costs closely to ensure the promotion is economically feasible.

Research on coupon face value indicates that testing for the most appropriate level is important for determining the most efficient (i.e., cost per coupon redeemed) coupon program. Since a coupon program combines redemption, printing, distribution, and handling costs, the face value and corresponding redemption rate can influence the overall efficiency of the program. The research tested a number of direct mail and FSI offers from firms selling major grocery brands with different face values and consistent communication elements across all offers. The results indicate that moving from $.50 to $1.00 off nearly doubles the redemption rate (e.g., 2 percent to 4 percent), while moving from $1.00 to $1.50 off improves the redemption rate at a slower rate (e.g., 4 percent to 5 percent). Overall, this curvilinear relationship between face value and redemption rate made the $1.00 offer 20 percent and 12 percent more cost-efficient versus the $.50 and $1.50 offers, respectively. Conclusions from the research suggest the choice of face value should not make the program go over budget, the face value and redemption rate connection will vary by brand, lower face values may not be the most cost-efficient program, higher face values are good for brand trial, and lower face values are good for brand retrial.[20]

A final problem with coupon promotions is misredemption, or the cashing of a coupon without purchase of the brand. Coupon misredemption or fraud occurs in a number of ways, including:

- Redemption of coupons by consumers for a product or size not specified on the coupon.
- Redemption of coupons by salesclerks in exchange for cash.
- Gathering and redeeming coupons by store managers/owners without actually selling the product.
- Printing of counterfeit coupons that are redeemed by unethical merchants.

Coupon Distribution   Coupons can be disseminated to consumers in a number of ways, including newspaper freestanding inserts, direct mail, newspapers (either in individual ads or as a group of coupons in a cooperative format), magazines, packages, and the Internet. Figure 14-6 summarizes the U.S. coupon redemption rates for each media type.

Freestanding inserts (FSIs) are distributed through newspapers and are used for a number of reasons, including their high-quality four-colour graphics, competitive distribution costs, national same-day circulation, market selectivity, and the category exclusivity given by the FSI company. Because of their consumer popularity and predictable distribution, coupons distributed in FSIs are also a strong selling point with the retail trade. On the other hand, FSIs suffer from a low redemption rate and their widespread distribution may lead to a clutter problem.

Figure 14-6

U.S. coupon redemption rates, 2011

Freestanding Insert	0.9%
Newspaper	0.5%
Magazine	1.3%
Direct Mail	3.1%
Regular In-Pack	4.0%
Regular On-Pack	6.3%
In-Pack Cross-Ruff	3.4%
On-Pack Cross-Ruff	4.1%
Instant On-Pack	21.0%
Instant On-Pack Cross-Ruff	8.4%
On-Shelf Distributed	10.0%
Handout Electronically Dispensed	8.3%
All Other Handouts In-Store	2.3%
All Other Handouts Away from Store	2.3%
Internet	17.4%

Source: NCH 2010 Coupon Facts Report.

Direct mail coupons are sent by local retailers or through co-op mailings where a packet of coupons for different products is sent to a household. Direct mail couponing has several advantages. First, the mailing can be sent to a broad audience or targeted to specific geographic or demographic segments. Second, firms that mail their own coupons through addressed mail can be quite selective about recipients. Third, direct-mail coupons can also be combined with a sample, greatly enhancing communication and behavioural effects. Finally, the above strengths generally give this method a redemption rate higher than FSI. The major disadvantage of direct-mail coupon delivery is the expense relative to other distribution methods. The cost per thousand for distributing coupons through co-op mailings ranges from $10 to $15, and more targeted promotions can cost $20 to $25 or even more. Also, the higher redemption rate of mail-delivered coupons may result from the fact that recipients are already users of the brand who take advantage of the coupons sent directly to them.

The use of *newspapers* and *magazines* as couponing vehicles offers a print media alternative. The advantages of newspapers as a couponing vehicle include market selectivity, shorter lead times with timing to the day, cooperative advertising opportunities that can lead to cost efficiencies, and promotional tie-ins with retailers. Other advantages of newspaper-delivered coupons are the broad exposure and consumer receptivity. Consumers actively search the newspaper for coupons, especially on "food day" (when grocery stores advertise their specials). This enhances the likelihood of the consumer at least noticing the coupon. Distribution of coupons through magazines can take advantage of the selectivity of the publication to reach specific target audiences, along with enhanced production capabilities and extended copy life in the home. One feature of these print options is that the distribution cost is not a factor if the advertiser was planning to run a print ad in the first place.

Placing coupons either *inside* or on the *outside of the package* has virtually no distribution costs and a much higher redemption rate than other couponing methods. An in/on pack coupon that is redeemable for the next purchase of the same brand is known as a **bounce-back coupon**. Bounce-back coupons are often used with product samples to encourage the consumer to purchase the product after sampling. They may be included in or on the package during the early phases of a brand's life cycle to encourage repeat purchase, or they may be a defensive manoeuvre for a mature brand that is facing competitive pressure and wants to retain its current users. The main limitation of bounce-back coupons is that they go only to purchasers of the brand and thus do not attract nonusers. A bounce-back coupon placed on the package for a Kellogg's cereal bar is shown in Exhibit 14-7.

Another type of in/on pack coupon is the **cross-ruff coupon**, which is redeemable on the purchase of a different product, usually one made by the same company but occasionally through a tie-in with another manufacturer. Cross-ruff coupons can be effective in encouraging consumers to try other products or brands. Yet another type of package coupon is the **instant coupon**, which is attached to the outside of the package so that the consumer can rip it off and redeem it immediately at the time of purchase. They can be selectively placed in terms of promotion timing and market region.

In-store coupons are distributed to consumers while shopping via tear-off pads, handouts, on-shelf dispensers, and electronic dispensers. These in-store coupons can reach consumers when they are ready to make a purchase, increase brand awareness on the shelf, generate impulse buying, encourage product trial, and provide category exclusivity.

Coupon distribution also occurs *online*. Couponclick.ca distributes coupons that can be instantly downloaded and printed. Each voucher contains a code tracked to the individual consumer for measurement effectiveness and security purposes. Two websites, Coupons.com and Save.ca, allow consumers to print or receive coupons in the mail, respectively. The famous blue Valpak, distributed to households through the mail system, is now available online

Exhibit 14-7   Kellogg Company uses an on-package coupon to encourage repurchase.

(Exhibit 14-8). Online coupon distribution got off to a slow start relative to other aspects of marketing, but growth finally arrived as the number grew from 1.6 million in December 2007 to 2.6 million in 2009 according to comScore.[21]

Another step in the digitization of coupons is the capability of using them with *mobile* devices. The process begins with a website (Sample saint.com) to transmit the offer to an Internet-enabled phone. Upon purchase, a cashier scans the bar code on the phone's screen, thereby redeeming the coupon and deleting it from the phone. Another application allows manual entry of the coupon code; however, retailers find the process cumbersome as mistakes get made, and costly as the process requires more time leading to higher labour costs. So there is hope to implement online coupons with a streamlined process. A significant advantage of digital distribution is a higher redemption rate (mid-teens), since consumers are seeking out a desired brand rather than sorting through newspaper inserts.[22]

PREMIUMS

Premiums are a sales promotion device used by marketers. A **premium** is an offer for an item of merchandise or service either free or at a low price that is an extra incentive for purchasers. Marketers are eliminating toys and gimmicks in favour of value-added premiums that reflect the quality of the product and are consistent with its image and positioning in the market.

Strengths of Premiums Premiums are usually small gifts or merchandise included in a product package or sent to consumers who mail in a request along with a proof of purchase. In/on-package free premiums include toys, balls, trading cards, or other items included in cereal packages, as well as samples of one product included with another. Thus, package-carried premiums provide an extra incentive to buy the product as a key distinguishing feature. McDonald's is a leader in the restaurant market for giving free premiums with its Happy Meal for children (Exhibit 14-9). As this example shows, premiums build or reinforce a brand image and work with co-branding. Premiums also have high impulse value that can lead to frequent purchases. Research concluded that premium usage is a function of deal-proneness, compulsive buying tendency, and variety-seeking tendency.[23]

A fourth benefit of premiums is their ability to work with rest of the IMC program effectively to build the brand image. For example, Labatt had a winner with the Labatt Blue NHL Crazy Coldie Program during the Stanley Cup playoffs. Each case of Double Blue (i.e., 12 Blue and 12 Blue Light) had a "coldie" (i.e., holder to keep beer cold) in the shape of the jersey of one of the 30 teams. While the in-pack premium is relatively inexpensive, it resonated with the 19–34 male market that pushed sales to a 300-percent market share growth during the promotional program. Success can be partly attributed to the promotion's ads, where three humorous spots showed consumers trying to wear the "coldie jersey" despite its obvious small size, and a host of other promotional support activities such as a contest and special events.[24]

Finally, premiums can also encourage trade support and gain in-store displays for the brand and the premium offer. General Mills Canada was at it again

Exhibit 14-8 Valpak's coupons are now available online.

Exhibit 14-9 McDonald's Happy Meal uses toys to help attract children.

with a successful premium during the Christmas season. Customers received a beanbag version of the Pillsbury Doughboy for $2.99 with the purchase of two refrigerated-dough products. This marked the first time the brand icon had ever been directly merchandised! Pillsbury had the perfect opportunity because the Doughboy is the second-most recognized icon in North America, after Coca-Cola's Polar Bears. Even more impressive was the retailer participation and consumer acceptance. All retailers in Canada ran with the deal, and more than 200,000 Doughboys found a new home. And just to make sure that consumers liked the idea even more, the Doughboy came in three models: one holding a candy cane, another, a stocking, and the third, gifts.[25]

Limitations of Premiums   There are limitations associated with the use of premiums. First, there is the cost factor, which results from the premium itself as well as from extra packaging that may be needed. Finding desirable premiums at reasonable costs can be difficult, particularly for adult markets, and using a poor premium that costs less may do more harm than good. A solution to this is to offer self-liquidating premiums requiring the consumer to pay a portion or all of the cost of the premium (as described above). The marketer usually purchases items used as self-liquidating premiums in large quantities and offers them to consumers at lower-than-retail prices. The goal is not to make a profit on the premium item but rather just to cover costs and offer a value to the consumer. A second limitation is that offers usually require the consumer to send in more than one proof of purchase to receive the premium. This requires effort from the consumer and money for the mailing and does not offer an immediate reinforcement or reward. A third limitation is that the marketer faces the risk of poor acceptance and is left with a supply of items with brand identification (e.g., logo) that makes them hard to dispose of. Thus, it is important to test consumers' reaction to a premium incentive and determine whether they perceive the offer as valuable. Another option is to use premiums with no brand identification, but that detracts from their consumer franchise-building value.

CONTESTS AND SWEEPSTAKES

Contests and sweepstakes are an increasingly popular consumer sales promotion since they seem to have an appeal and glamour that other promotions like coupons lack. A contest is a promotion where consumers compete for prizes or money on the basis of skills or ability. The company determines winners by judging the entries or ascertaining which entry comes closest to predetermined criteria. Contests usually provide a purchase incentive by requiring a proof of purchase or an entry form that is available from a dealer or advertisement. Some contests require consumers to read an ad or package or visit a store display to gather information. Marketers must be careful not to make their contests too difficult to enter, as doing so might discourage participation among key prospects in the target audience.

A sweepstakes is a promotion where winners are determined purely by chance; it cannot require a proof of purchase as a condition for entry. Entrants need only submit their names for the prize drawing. While there is often an official entry form, handwritten entries must also be permitted. One form of sweepstakes is a game, which also has a chance element or odds of winning. Scratch-off cards with instant winners are a popular promotional tool. Some games occur over a longer period and require more involvement by consumers. Promotions where consumers must collect game pieces are popular among retailers and fast-food chains as a way to build store traffic and repeat purchases. For example, McDonald's has used promotions based on the game Monopoly several times.

Because they are easier to enter, sweepstakes attract more entries than do contests. They are also easier and less expensive to administer, since every entry does not have to be checked or judged. Choosing the winning entry in a sweepstakes requires only the random selection of a winner from the pool of entries or generation of a number to match those held by sweepstakes entrants. Experts note that the costs of mounting a sweepstakes are also very predictable. Companies can buy insurance to indemnify them and protect against the expense of awarding a big prize. In general, sweepstakes present marketers with a fixed cost, which is a major advantage when budgeting for a promotion. Exhibit 14-10 shows an ad for a sweepstakes where the prize and brand are closely aligned to build brand equity, another key feature of these promotions.

Strengths of Contests and Sweepstakes A study suggests that sales can be enhanced by trial and repeat purchases through a sweepstakes advertised via in-store ad-pads. A 12-week experiment of 20 mass-merchandiser outlets—10 test and 10 control stores—revealed that a major household product increased its sales by 70 percent in the test stores during the four-week test period compared to the previous four-week period that featured no advertising or promotion. Furthermore, during the posttest four-week period that had no ad-pad, sales hit a 30 percent increase.[26] Clearly, non-customers either recalled the sales promotion and ad message, or new or existing customers returned for a repeat purchase. In either case, the improved communication and behavioural effects of the promotion make it useful for both manufacturers and retailers.

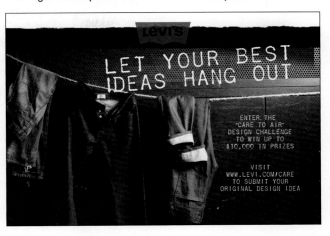

Exhibit 14-10 Advertisements are often used to deliver messages about promotions such as a sweepstakes.

Contests and sweepstakes can involve consumers with a brand by making the promotion product relevant or by connecting the prizes to the lifestyle, needs, or interests of the target audience. Part of Honda's marketing communication for its compact car is the Civic Nation, an approach to building strong feeling through driving the vehicle and a way for individual consumers to customize their experience with a mass-marketed product. The "United We Drive" theme took a new direction with a contest where musical souls could create an "Anthem for a Nation" using samples of music from hip-hop artist Saukrates. Multimedia directed those interested to a website (civicnation.ca) where they developed a 30-second electronica, hip-hop, or electropop track. After voting, the winning selections played as the intro for a radio show. The second and third phases of the campaign culminated in a full Civic Nation anthem.[27]

The Canadian division of LG conceived the inaugural LG "Life's Good" Film Festival, where aspiring filmmakers from all over the world could submit a high-definition film up to five minutes in length that expressed an uplifting message consistent with the brand's slogan. LG partnered with Google, YouTube, and Film.com and a dedicated website (LGfilmfest.com) to announce the contest and allow viewership. Categories included animation, sports, narrative, and fashion and music, with three category winners receiving $10,000 and a fourth overall winner receiving $100,000.[28]

Limitations of Contests and Sweepstakes Sweepstakes and/or contest promotions rarely contribute to consumer franchise building for a product or service and may even detract from it. The sweepstakes or contest often becomes the dominant focus rather than the brand, and little is accomplished other than giving away substantial amounts of money and/or prizes. Promotional experts question the effectiveness of contests and sweepstakes. The following example raises this question, although executives accepted the results.

Using Facebook, Absolut invited Vancouver's artists, writers, visual artists, musicians, curators, filmmakers, and gallery owners to create artwork, series, or educational programs that reflected the brand's values of "engaging," "visionary," "bold," and "perfection." The best effort received an award of $120,000. The popular vodka maker obtained only 30 entries, with about half worthy of serious evaluation. Given the historical close connection of Absolut and artists the low number appears startling, yet executives were satisfied because the task demanded excellence in order to find a long-lasting artistic partner to portray the brand. In fact, for complete success the artistic work had to demonstrate a partnership with the brand and its values.[29]

Numerous legal considerations affect the design and administration of contests and sweepstakes.[30] But companies must still be careful in designing a contest or sweepstakes and awarding prizes. Most firms use consultants that specialize in the design and administration of contests

Exhibit 14-11   Pennzoil uses a refund offer that is tied to a future purchase.

and sweepstakes to avoid any legal problems, but they may still run into problems with promotions.

A final problem with contests and sweepstakes is participation by professionals or hobbyists who submit entries but have no intention of purchasing the product or service. Because it is illegal to require a purchase as a qualification for a sweepstakes entry, people can enter as many times as they wish. Professional players sometimes enter one sweepstakes several times, depending on the nature of the prizes and the number of entries the promotion attracts. There are even newsletters that inform them of all the contests and sweepstakes being held, the entry dates, estimated probabilities of winning, how to enter, and solutions to any puzzles or other information that might be needed. The presence of these professional entrants not only defeats the purpose of the promotion but also may discourage entries from consumers who think their chances of winning are limited.

REFUNDS AND REBATES

Refunds (also known as rebates) are offers by the manufacturer to return a portion of the product purchase price, usually after the consumer supplies proof of purchase. Consumers are generally very responsive to rebate offers, particularly as the size of the savings increases. Rebates are used by makers of all types of products, ranging from packaged goods to major appliances, cars, and computer software (Exhibit 14-11).

Packaged-goods marketers often use refund offers to induce trial of a new product or encourage users of another brand to switch. Consumers may perceive the savings offered through a cash refund as an immediate value that lowers the cost of the item, even though those savings are realized only if the consumer redeems the refund or rebate offer. Redemption rates for refund offers typically range from 1 to 3 percent for print and point-of-purchase offers and 5 percent for in/on-package offers.

Refund offers can also encourage repeat purchase since they require consumers to send in multiple proofs of purchase. The size of the refund offer may even increase as the number of purchases gets larger. Packaged-goods companies are switching away from cash refund offers to coupons or cash/coupon combinations. Using coupons in the refund offer enhances the likelihood of repeat purchase of the brand.

Strengths and Limitations of Refunds and Rebates   Rebates can help create new users and encourage brand switching or repeat purchase behaviour, or they can be a way to offer a temporary price reduction. The rebate may be perceived as an immediate savings even though consumers do not follow through on the offer. This perception can influence purchase even if the consumer fails to realize the savings, so the marketer can reduce price for much less than if it used a direct price-off deal.

Limitations are associated with refunds and rebates; not all consumers are motivated by a refund offer because of the delay and the effort required to obtain the savings (e.g., completing forms and mailing receipts). A study of consumer perceptions found a negative relationship between the use of rebates and the perceived difficulties associated with the redemption process.[31] The study also found that consumers perceive manufacturers as offering rebates to sell products that are not faring well. Nonusers of rebates were particularly likely to perceive the redemption process as too complicated and to suspect manufacturers' motives. This implies that companies using rebates must simplify the redemption process and use other promotional elements such as advertising to retain consumer confidence in the brand.

When small refunds are being offered, marketers may find other promotional incentives such as coupons or bonus packs more effective. They must be careful not to overuse rebate offers and confuse consumers about the real price and value of a product or service. Also, consumers can become dependent on rebates and delay their purchases, or purchase only brands for which a rebate is available.

BONUS PACKS

Bonus packs offer the consumer an extra amount of a product at the regular price by providing larger containers or extra units (Exhibit 14-12). Bonus packs result in a lower cost per unit for the consumer and provide extra value as well as more product for the money. There are several advantages to bonus pack promotions. First, they give marketers a direct way to provide extra value without having to get involved with complicated coupons or refund offers. The additional value of a bonus pack is generally obvious to the consumer and can have a strong impact on the purchase decision at the time of purchase.

Bonus packs can also be an effective defensive manoeuvre against a competitor's promotion or introduction of a new brand. By loading current users with large amounts of its product, a marketer can often remove these consumers from the market and make them less susceptible to a competitor's promotional efforts. Bonus packs may result in larger purchase orders and favourable display space in the store if relationships with retailers are good. They do, however, usually require additional shelf space without providing any extra profit margins for the retailer, so the marketer can encounter problems with bonus packs if trade relationships are not good. Another problem is that bonus packs may appeal primarily to current users who probably would have purchased the brand anyway, or to promotion-sensitive consumers who may not become loyal to the brand.

Exhibit 14-12 Bonus packs provide more value for consumers.

PRICE-OFF DEALS

Another consumer sales promotion tool is the direct **price-off deal**, which reduces the price of the brand. Price-off reductions are typically offered right on the package through specially marked price packs, as shown in Exhibit 14-13. Typically, price-offs range from 10 to 25 percent off the regular price, with the reduction coming out of the manufacturer's profit margin, not the retailer's. Keeping the retailer's margin during a price-off promotion maintains its support and cooperation.

Marketers use price-off promotions for several reasons. First, since price-offs are controlled by the manufacturer, it can make sure the promotional discount reaches the consumer rather than being kept by the trade. Like bonus packs, price-off deals usually present a readily apparent value to shoppers, especially when they have a reference price point for the brand and thus recognize the value of the discount.[32] So price-offs can be a strong influence at the point of purchase when price comparisons are being made. Price-off promotions can also encourage consumers to purchase larger quantities, preempting competitors' promotions and leading to greater trade support.

Price-off promotions may not be favourably received by retailers, since they can create pricing and inventory problems. Most retailers will not accept packages with a specific price shown, so the familiar X amount off the regular price must be used. Also, like bonus packs, price-off deals appeal primarily to regular users instead of attracting nonusers. Finally, the federal government has regulations regarding the conditions that price-off labels must meet and the frequency and timing of their use.

Services also offer discounts, as seen with the Milestones "Wednesday Date Night" promotion. Each Wednesday the casual dining chain offered patrons dinner for two for $50 when ordering off a special menu. Radio communicated the promotion and the dating theme prevailed in the execution. Management saw the promotion as a way of distinguishing the brand from competitors like The Keg and Moxies.[33]

Electronic products are often discounted, and one market where fierce discounting has occurred is e-books. The whole book market is in a degree of turmoil, with two formats—print and electronic versions—and royalty arrangements based on the initial print form, thus influencing the cost structure. Consequently, publishers discounted e-books to $10 when selling hardcover equivalents for $30.[34] Vehicles are often discounted via money reduced from the manufacturer or from the dealer, and the delivery method is a straight discount or special finance rates. These discounts can be regularly scheduled or used to clear inventory as model year changes occur.

Exhibit 14-13 Examples of price-off packages.

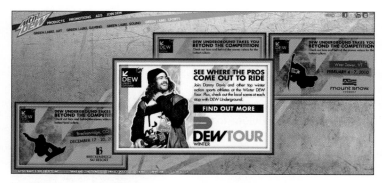

Exhibit 14-14 Pepsi established the AST Dew Tour.

The Honda Civic, Canada's number one car sold for more than ten years in a row, faced significant challenges from the aggressive marketing efforts of numerous brands that coveted the title. In response, Honda immediately increased its advertising and provided a low-interest financing option to retain its market share.[35]

EVENT MARKETING

It is important to make a distinction between *event marketing* and *event sponsorships,* as the two terms are often used interchangeably yet refer to different activities. **Event marketing** is a type of promotion where a company or brand is linked to an event or where a themed activity is developed for the purpose of creating experiences for consumers and promoting a product or service. Pepsi associated its Mountain Dew brand with various action sports (Exhibit 14-14), while an energy drink company established Red Bull Crashed Ice, where the finals are televised. Event marketing allows marketers to develop integrated marketing programs including promotional tools that create experiences for consumers in an effort to associate their brands with certain lifestyles and activities. Marketers use events to distribute samples as well as information about their products and services, or to let consumers actually experience the product. IMC Perspective 14-1 describes the thrilling Red Bull event that one must see live. Exhibit 14-15 shows competitors celebrating at the finish line of the team race at the Red Bull Crashed Ice event held in Saint Paul, Minnesota.

An **event sponsorship** is an integrated marketing communications activity where a company develops actual sponsorship relations with a particular event (e.g., concert, art exhibition, cultural activity, social change, sports) and provides financial support in return for the right to display a brand name, logo, or advertising message and be identified as a supporter of the event. Part of the confusion between these two promotions arises from the fact that event marketing often takes place as part of a company's event sponsorship. We describe examples of the former concept here and address the latter in the next chapter as it relates more closely to public relations activities.

Perrier fans who signed up online (Societeperrier.ca) received a special PIN code that allowed them to attend "soirees" at upscale nightclubs. These exclusive parties occurred in branded VIP areas and offered a free Perrier cocktail, a taxi voucher, and complimentary Perrier all evening.

Exhibit 14-15 Adam Skube, Ghyslain Hotte, and Daniel Guolla of Team Ottawa celebrate their second place finish at a Red Bull Crashed Ice event.

IMC PERSPECTIVE 14-1

Crash This Marketing Event

Red Bull Crashed Ice (RBCI) is an event established by the sports energy drink marketer 12 years ago that features a new sport, downhill ice-cross, which combines downhill skiing, hockey, and boarder-cross. Today, a series of events in North America and Europe culminates with the world champion crowned at the final competition in Quebec City each year to the delight of 100,000 spectators, Canadian TV viewers, and a worldwide audience via live streaming. Due to its popularity in Canada, an additional competition occurred in Niagara Falls for 2012–2013 and the city immediately began requesting a repeat performance after an overwhelming success.

Competitors decked out with full hockey gear race in groups of four to the bottom of the track, with the top two moving on to the next round. The final race determines the winner after a series of elimination rounds. In the past few years, a points system based on the performance across all five competitions within the year determined the annual champion with the final race in Quebec deciding the winner. World rankings are computed based on an athlete's most recent eight races. A new twist to the competition in 2012–2013 featured two three-man teams competing head-to-head, thereby putting six racers on the track at once.

In each city where the competition occurs, Red Bull builds a track covered with ice in the city streets at a cost of a couple million dollars and about a month to construct. Starting near the Chateau Frontenac, the Quebec track winds its way down the hill toward the St. Lawrence River through the Historic District of Old Quebec, a UNESCO World Heritage Site. Designers of the track challenge the competitors with steep drops, tight curves, various bumps and ledges, uphill climbs, and a 360-degree corkscrew.

The reconfigured Quebec track reached almost 600 metres with a 60-metre vertical drop as racers attained speeds up to 50 km/hour. Some twists and stretches are mere metres away from buildings that have stood in the fortified city for 400 years. With cheering spectators along the walls of the track drinking Red Bull and big-screen viewing available, the electric atmosphere is a true party for all who attend. Red Bull attracts considerable media coverage in the cities leading up to the competition, and in the cities where qualifier races occur. For the Canadian events, preliminary races occurred in a dozen cities with spectators turning out to watch novice racers try out for glory in Niagara Falls and Quebec City.

RBCI is one of many events the brand created beyond advertising that "Red Bull Gives You Wings." With worldwide distribution, the energy drink creates or sponsors events in other sports, games, and music to promote the brand. So it is not too surprising to find RBCI primarily featured in the land of snow and ice where hockey rules. And while many nations are represented, Canadians are found in the final rounds and near the top of the world rankings. Brothers Kyle and Scott Croxall are ranked one and two, and nine Canadians are ranked in the top 32 and are considered to be on the RBCI tour at end of the 2012–2013 season.

Sources: http://www.newswire.ca/en/story/1024845/ice-cross-downhill-charges-into-canada-with-two-races-in-the-true-north; http://www.newswire.ca/en/story/1130527/switzerland-s-derek-wedge-takes-ice-cross-downhill-win-in-quebec-city-in-season-finale; http://www.newswire.ca/en/story/1066133/ice-cross-downhill-crashes-into-niagara-falls-for-a-thrilling-2013-season-opener; http://www.redbull.com.

Question:

1. How does Red Bull Crashed Ice help build the brand?

Each club displayed bar mats, coasters, stirsticks, candles, and tent cards describing the three cocktails. Brand reps gave out business cards to invite registrations, and other communication occurred with wild postings via e-mail, Facebook, and Twitter.[36]

A Montreal agency, Sid Lee, developed the first global campaign for Adidas Originals products, a line-up that celebrates the authentic fashion of the three stripes. The theme "Celebrate Originality" expressed the wide-ranging cultural presence of the brand and youth culture. A house party with international stars and regular young people played a key part as clips played on Canadian music stations. For example, a three-minute segment appeared on *Much on*

Demand, a two-minute ad sponsored the show, and VJs wearing Adidas clothing announced a contest for gear to allow winners to host their own house party.[37]

Fido sponsored a series of underground artsy events/parties called Fido Sessions that centred on art, culture, design, and fashion in areas where young, hip people live, work, and play. The location and the events remained a mystery until two giant dolls eventually joined after eight days of getting closer together. The four-storey, white, featureless dolls had no identity except for a text shortcode where people could learn about the events. A team of people dressed as mini dolls deployed the message as well through wild postings, chalk art, night projections, tree hangers, and flying cloud logos. The lack of branding fit with the underground nature of the events—although participants could order drinks with Fido phones.[38]

(L04) Trade Sales Promotion

Trade sales promotions that managers may select from to develop a strategic sales promotion plan were identified in Figure 14-1. Each of these options can assist the promotional planner in achieving the objectives with resellers. The objectives are similar to those of consumer sales promotions since the promotion acts as a behavioural incentive. We now review objectives and strategic options for trade sales promotions.

OBJECTIVES OF TRADE SALES PROMOTION

Like consumer promotions, sales promotion programs targeted to the trade should be based on well-defined objectives and measurable goals and a consideration of what the marketer wants to accomplish. Typical objectives for promotions targeted to marketing intermediaries such as wholesalers and retailers include obtaining distribution for new products, maintaining trade support for established brands, building retail inventories, and encouraging retailers to display established brands.

Obtain Distribution for New Products   Trade promotions are often used to encourage retailers to give shelf space to new products. Essentially, this translates into a trial purchase objective like we saw with consumer promotions. Manufacturers recognize that only a limited amount of shelf space is available in supermarkets, drugstores, and other major retail outlets. Thus, they provide retailers with financial incentives to stock new products. While trade discounts or other special price deals are used to encourage retailers and wholesalers to stock a new brand, marketers may use other types of promotions to get them to push the brand. Merchandising allowances can get retailers to display a new product in high-traffic areas of stores, while incentive programs or contests can encourage wholesale or retail store personnel to push a new brand.

Maintain Trade Support for Established Brands   Trade promotions are often designed to maintain distribution and trade support for established brands. Clearly, this objective is akin to a repeat purchase objective that we saw with consumer sales promotion. Brands that are in the mature phase of their product life cycle are vulnerable to losing wholesale and/or retail distribution, particularly if they are not differentiated or face competition from new products. Trade deals induce wholesalers and retailers to continue to carry weaker products because the discounts increase their profit margins. Brands with a smaller market share often rely heavily on trade promotions, since they lack the funds required to differentiate themselves from competitors through media advertising. Even if a brand has a strong market position, trade promotions may be used as part of an overall marketing strategy.

Build Retail Inventories   Manufacturers often use trade promotions to build the inventory levels of retailers or other channel members, another form of repeat purchasing. There are several reasons why manufacturers want to load retailers with their products. First, wholesalers and retailers are more likely to push a product when they have high inventory levels rather than storing it in their warehouses or back rooms. Building channel members' inventories also ensures they will not run out of stock and thus miss sales opportunities.

Manufacturers of seasonal products offer large promotional discounts so that retailers will stock up on their products before the peak selling season begins. This enables the manufacturer to smooth out seasonal fluctuations in its production schedule and pass on the inventory carrying costs to retailers or wholesalers. When retailers stock up on a product before the peak selling season, they often run special promotions and offer discounts to consumers to reduce excess inventories.

Encourage Retailers to Display Established Brands   Another objective of trade-oriented promotions is to encourage retailers to display and promote an established brand. This could be analogous to increased consumption as seen with consumer sales promotion objectives, since the retailer demonstrates increased commitment. Marketers recognize that purchase decisions are frequently made in the store and promotional displays are an excellent way of generating sales. An important goal is to obtain retail store displays of a product away from its regular shelf location. A typical supermarket has approximately 50 display areas at the ends of aisles, near checkout counters, and elsewhere. Marketers want to have their products displayed in these areas to increase the probability shoppers will come into contact with them. Even a single display can increase a brand's sales significantly during a promotion. Manufacturers often use multifaceted promotional programs to encourage retailers to promote their products at the retail level. For example, a manufacturer will combine its advertising and consumer sales promotions and offer them at the same time as the trade promotion.

TRADE SALES PROMOTION STRATEGY OPTIONS

Manufacturers use a variety of trade promotion tools as inducements for wholesalers and retailers. Next we examine the most often used types of trade promotions and factors marketers must consider in using them. These promotions include trade allowances, point-of-purchase displays, cooperative advertising, contests and incentives, events, sales training programs, and trade shows.

Trade Allowances   Probably the most common trade promotion is some form of **trade allowance**, a discount or deal offered to retailers or wholesalers to encourage them to promote, display, or stock the manufacturer's products. Types of allowances offered to retailers include buying allowances, promotional or display allowances, and slotting allowances.

Buying Allowances   A buying allowance is a deal or discount offered to resellers in the form of a price reduction on merchandise ordered during a fixed period. These discounts are often in the form of an **off-invoice allowance**, which means a certain per-case amount or percentage is deducted from the invoice. A buying allowance can also take the form of *free goods*; the reseller gets extra cases with the purchase of specific amounts (for example, 1 free case with every 10 cases purchased).

Promotional (Display) Allowances   Manufacturers often give retailers allowances or discounts for performing certain promotional or merchandising activities in support of their brands. These merchandising allowances can be given for providing special displays away from the product's regular shelf position, running in-store promotional programs, or including the product in an ad. The manufacturer generally has guidelines or a contract specifying the activity to be performed to qualify for the promotional allowance. The allowance is usually a fixed amount per case or a percentage deduction from the list price for merchandise ordered during the promotional period.

Slotting Allowances   Retailers often demand a special allowance for agreeing to accept a new product. *Slotting allowances,* also called *stocking allowances, introductory allowances,* or *street money,* are fees retailers charge for providing a slot or position to accommodate the new product. Slotting fees range from a few hundred dollars per store to $50,000 or more for an entire retail chain. Manufacturers that want to get their products on the shelves nationally can face substantial slotting fees. Retailers charge slotting fees because of their power and the limited availability of shelf space in supermarkets relative to the large numbers of products introduced each year. Large manufacturers with popular brands are less likely to pay slotting fees than smaller companies that lack leverage in negotiating with retailers.

A study examined the views of manufacturers, wholesalers, and grocery retailers regarding the use of slotting fees. Their findings suggest that slotting fees shift the risk of new product introductions from retailers to manufacturers and help apportion the supply and demand of new products. They also found that slotting fees lead to higher retail prices, are applied in a discriminatory fashion, and place small marketers at a disadvantage.[39]

Strengths of Trade Allowances   Buying allowances are used for several reasons. They are easy to implement and are well accepted, and sometimes expected, by the trade. They are also an effective way to encourage resellers to buy the manufacturer's product, since they will want to take advantage of the discounts being offered during the allowance period. Manufacturers offer trade discounts expecting wholesalers and retailers to pass the price reduction through to consumers, resulting in greater purchases.

Promotional allowances provide brands that sell in retail stores the opportunity to have specialized displays to feature their product. Promotional allowances also permit a brand to obtain a favourable end-of aisle location or another prominent place where high traffic occurs, thus ensuring greater exposure. Brands would like to reproduce the imagery from their commercials or any other advertising vehicle where brand recognition at the point of sale is required. Extensive and elaborate displays would also reinforce the positioning strategy of the brand and contribute to its overall brand development. Thus, retailers prefer to merchandise a brand that has a consistent and well thought out strategy so that they will not be stuck with inventory unsold due to a lack of in-store communication.

Limitations of Trade Allowances   Marketers give retailers these trade allowances so that the savings will be passed through to consumers in the form of lower prices, but companies claim that only one-third of trade promotion discounts actually reach consumers because one-third is lost in inefficiencies and another one-third is pocketed by the trade. Moreover, marketers believe that the trade is taking advantage of their promotional deals and misusing promotional funds.

For example, retailers and wholesalers do **forward buying**, where they stock up on a product at the lower deal or off-invoice price and resell it to consumers after the marketer's promotional period ends. Another common practice is **diverting**, where a retailer or wholesaler takes advantage of the promotional deal and then sells the product purchased at the low price to a store outside its area or to an intermediary that resells it to other stores.

In addition to not passing discounts on to consumers, forward buying and diverting create other problems for manufacturers. They lead to huge swings in demand that cause production scheduling problems and leave manufacturers and retailers always building toward or drawing down from a promotional surge. Marketers also worry that the system leads to frequent price specials, so consumers learn to make purchases on the basis of what's on sale rather than developing any loyalty to their brands.

Point-of-Purchase Displays   Point-of-purchase (POP) displays are an important promotional tool because they can help advertisers obtain more effective in-store merchandising of products. In one sense, a display acts as a "medium" since it is an important method of transmitting an advertising-like message when consumers are making a purchase decision. We put medium in quotes because often displays do not appear to be typical media; in fact, however, a display shares similar characteristics with place-based media (discussed in Chapter 13). A display is also viewed as a sales promotion since the messages include a sales promotion and most require the participation of retailers that necessitates a payment that is often recorded as a trade promotion expense in the budget.

Figure 14-7 identifies different types of point-of-purchase displays. Exhibit 14-16 shows an award-winning POP display created by E-B Display Co. to promote the SeaKlear family of

On-premise sign	Pre-assembled display	Display card	TV display
Window display	Display shipper	Shelf sign	LED board
Modular display rack	Wall display	Stand-up rack	End-of-aisle display

Figure 14-7

Types of point-of-purchase displays

pool and spa treatments. The display holds 16 different pool and spa products and the unique octagonal shape allows for 360 degrees of display availability in a relatively small footprint. The display also has large graphic areas to educate consumers regarding specific uses and applications and help them make their purchase decisions.

The Point of Purchase Advertising Institute (POPAI) is an organization serving marketers and retailers worldwide with research information and examples of successful display innovations. Its main study classifies purchases into four groups, as shown in Figure 14-8, with the following breakdown: specifically planned 24 percent, generally planned 15 percent, substitutes (i.e., brand switch) 6 percent, and unplanned 55 percent. The top two reasons provided by respondents on why an unplanned purchase occurred were that they remembered they needed or wanted an item once in the store, and that they took advantage of a sale.[40] These results suggest the importance of displays as they prompt existing beliefs through recognition at the point of purchase.

Strengths of Point-of Purchase Displays   It is easy to see why advertisers use point-of-purchase displays extensively. The main purpose is to reach the target audience while they are making the brand choice, so naturally a message or promotion attempting to influence a decider appears imperative. Indeed, key or deterministic benefits can be communicated just prior to purchase as these benefits may become salient only during the final choice decision. Innovations in point-of-purchase options—such as video screens at cash registers—attempt to bring the emotion of television commercials to the store environment so that consumers feel the same way just prior to purchasing the product. Since consumers are in the process of shopping, point-of-sale media have a tremendous opportunity for attracting the attention of the target audience. In general, consumers are seeking additional information or sensory experience as they consider the product selection. Coverage objectives also can be achieved by distributing point-of-purchase displays across the country through retail chains. For example, a brand could have displays in virtually all grocery stores at the same time with placement agreed among personnel at a few head offices. A key strength of point-of-sale display is that it is communicating to virtually all people who are considering purchasing in a particular category except those going direct through the Internet or catalogues. It may be difficult to suggest

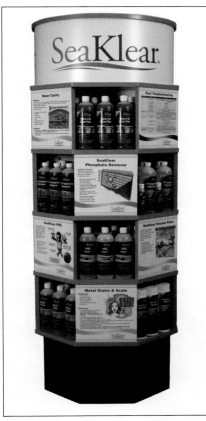

Exhibit 14-16   This award-winning point-of-purchase display plays an important role in the merchandising of SeaKlear pool and spa treatments.

Specifically Planned	Purchases the shopper specifically identified by name in a pre-shopping interview and bought.
Generally Planned	Purchases that were referred to generically in a pre-shopping interview and bought on impulse.
Substitutes	Purchases that were specifically identified by name in a pre-shopping interview, but actual purchase reflected a substitute of brand or product.
Unplanned	Purchases that were not mentioned in the pre-shopping interview and bought on impulse.

Source: http://www.popai.com/engage/docs/Media-Topline-Final.pdf. Used by permission of POPAI.

Figure 14-8

Classification of purchases for POPAI research

that point-of-purchase displays are universally involving. However, it appears reasonable to suggest that if the target audience has not avoided a certain part of the store and also paid attention to a display, then the potential is strong that the relevant messages will resonate such that a sufficient amount of consideration will be given. And finally, the absolute cost and CPM are generally reasonable compared to other media options.

Limitations of Point-of Purchase Displays   Despite these strengths, point-of-purchase displays have limitations. One source of discontent for a consumer is that the shopping experience may be hindered by numerous promotional messages. Consumers have complete control over where they want to look in a store, how much time they prefer to stay in one area, and whether they want to look at any form of in-store communication. If an advertiser desires to be there, so does the competition. The clutter consumers feel while watching television or reading a magazine may be felt in the purchase environment. Processing of point-of-sale media requires a consumer's presence in the retail environment. So, except for circumstances where a consumer is entering an establishment repeatedly, the likelihood of an advertiser achieving sufficient frequency through this medium is quite limited. Finally, a marketer is reliant on the retailer, who may not install or set up the display correctly and also requires payment.

Cooperative Advertising

Cooperative Advertising   A trade promotion that has consumer effects like point-of-purchase display is **cooperative advertising**, where the cost of advertising is shared by more than one party. There are three types of cooperative advertising. Although the latter two are not exactly trade promotion, they involve the trade at times and are consistent with cooperative advertising.

The most common form of cooperative advertising is **vertical cooperative advertising**, in which a manufacturer pays for a portion of the advertising a retailer runs to promote the manufacturer's product and its availability in the retailer's place of business. Manufacturers generally share the cost of advertising run by the retailer on a percentage basis (usually 50/50) up to a certain limit.

The amount of cooperative advertising the manufacturer pays for is usually based on a percentage of dollar purchases. If a retailer purchases $100,000 of product from a manufacturer, it may receive 3 percent, or $3,000, in cooperative advertising money. Large retail chains often combine their co-op budgets across all of their stores, which gives them a larger sum to work with and more media options.

Cooperative advertising can take on several forms. Retailers may advertise a manufacturer's product in, say, a newspaper ad or a flyer insert featuring a number of different products, and the individual manufacturers reimburse the retailer for their portion of the ad. Or the ad may be prepared by the manufacturer and placed in the local media by the retailer. Research supports the value of retail ads like these as advertised products are purchased in greater numbers and dollar amounts.[41] Exhibit 14-17 shows a cooperative ad format that retailers can use by simply inserting their store name and location.

Horizontal cooperative advertising is advertising sponsored in common by a group of retailers or other organizations providing products or services to the market. For example, automobile dealers who are located near one another often allocate some of their ad budgets to a cooperative advertising fund. **Ingredient-sponsored cooperative advertising** is supported by raw materials manufacturers; its objective is to help establish end products that include the company's materials and/or ingredients. Perhaps the best-known, and most successful, example of this type of

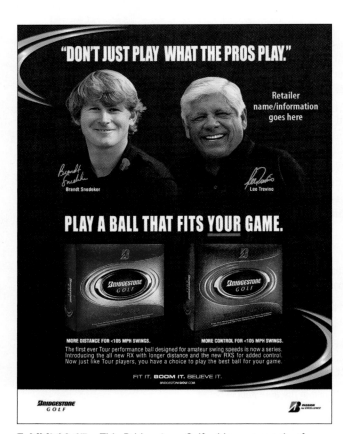

Exhibit 14-17   This Bridgestone Golf ad is an example of vertical cooperative advertising.

cooperative advertising is the "Intel Inside" program, sponsored by Intel Corporation (Exhibit 14-18).

Contests and Incentives   Manufacturers may develop contests or special incentive programs to stimulate greater selling effort and support from reseller management or sales personnel. Contests or incentive programs can be directed toward managers who work for a wholesaler or distributor as well as toward store or department managers at the retail level. Manufacturers often sponsor contests for resellers and use prizes such as trips or valuable merchandise as rewards for meeting sales quotas or other goals.

Contests or special incentives are often targeted at the sales personnel of the wholesalers, distributors/dealers, or retailers. These salespeople are an important link in the distribution chain because they are likely to be very familiar with the market, more frequently in touch with the customer (whether it be another reseller or the ultimate consumer), and more numerous than the manufacturer's own sales organization. Manufacturers devise incentives or contests for these sales personnel. These programs may involve cash payments made directly to the retailer's or wholesaler's sales staff to encourage them to promote and sell a manufacturer's product. These payments are known as **push money** (pm) or *spiffs*. For example, an appliance manufacturer may pay a $25 spiff to retail sales personnel for selling a certain model or size. In sales contests, salespeople can win trips or valuable merchandise for meeting certain goals established by the manufacturer. As shown in Figure 14-9, these incentives may be tied to product sales, new account placements, or merchandising efforts.

While contests and incentive programs can generate reseller support, they can also be a source of conflict between retail sales personnel and management. Retailers want to maintain control over the selling activities of their sales staff. They don't want their salespeople devoting an undue amount of effort to trying to win a contest or receive incentives offered by the manufacturer or becoming too aggressive in pushing products that serve their own interests instead of the product or model that is best for the customer.

Sales Training Programs   Products sold at the retail level may require knowledgeable salespeople who provide consumers with information about the features and benefits of various brands and models (e.g., cosmetics, appliances, computers). Manufacturers provide

Exhibit 14-18   The "Intel Inside" cooperative advertising program has been extremely successful.

- **Product or Program Sales**
  Awards are tied to the selling of a product, for example:
      Selling a specified number of cases
      Selling a specified number of units
      Selling a specified number of promotional programs

- **New Account Placements**
  Awards are tied to:
      The number of new accounts opened
      The number of new accounts ordering a minimum number of cases or units
      Promotional programs placed in new accounts

- **Merchandising Efforts**
  Awards are tied to:
  Establishing promotional programs (such as theme programs)
  Placing display racks, counter displays, and the like

Figure   14-9

Three forms of promotion targeted to reseller salespeople

assistance to retail salespeople through training sessions so that retail personnel can increase their knowledge of a product line and understand how to sell the manufacturer's product. A manufacturer's sales force also provides sales training assistance to retail employees. The reps provide ongoing sales training as they come into contact with retail sales staff on a regular basis and can update them on changes in the product line. Sales reps often provide resellers with sales manuals, product brochures, reference manuals, videos, and product-use demonstrations. These selling aids are also presented to customers.

Trade Shows   A forum where manufacturers display their products to current as well as prospective consumers and resellers is a trade show. According to the Trade Show Bureau, nearly 100 million people attend the 5,000 trade shows each year in the United States and Canada, and the number of exhibiting companies exceeds 1.3 million. Trade shows are a major opportunity to display one's product lines and interact with customers. They are often attended by important management personnel from large retail chains as well as by distributors and other reseller representatives.

A number of promotional functions can be performed at trade shows, including demonstrating products, identifying new prospects, gathering customer and competitive information, and even writing orders for a product. Trade shows are particularly valuable for introducing new products, because resellers are often looking for new merchandise to stock. Shows can also be a source of valuable leads to follow up on through sales calls or direct marketing. The social aspect of trade shows is also important. Companies use them to entertain key customers and to develop and maintain relationships with the trade. An academic study demonstrated that trade shows generate product awareness and interest and can have a measurable economic return.[42]

(L05) IMC Planning: Strategic Use of Sales Promotion

Rather than separate activities competing for a firm's promotional budget, advertising and sales promotion should be viewed as complementary tools. When properly planned and executed to work together, advertising and sales promotion can have a more complete and persuasive communication effect that is much greater than that of either promotional mix element alone. Proper coordination of advertising and sales promotion is essential for the firm to take advantage of the opportunities offered by each tool and get the most out of its promotional budget. Successful integration of advertising and sales promotion requires decisions concerning not only the allocation of the budget to each area but also the coordination of the ad and sales promotion themes, the timing of the promotional activities, the brand equity implications of sales promotion, and the measuring of sales promotion effectiveness.

BUDGET ALLOCATION

It is difficult to say just what percentage of a firm's overall promotional budget should be allocated to advertising versus consumer and trade promotions. The allocation will likely vary according to a brand's stage in the product life cycle as there are different promotional objectives. In the introductory stage, a large amount of the budget may be allocated to sales promotion techniques such as sampling and couponing to induce trial. In the growth stage, however, promotional dollars may be used primarily for advertising to stress brand differences and keep the brand name in consumers' minds.

When a brand moves to the maturity stage, advertising is primarily a reminder to keep consumers aware of the brand. Consumer sales promotions such as coupons, price-offs, premiums, and bonus packs may be needed periodically to maintain consumer loyalty, attract new users, and protect against competition. Trade promotions are needed to maintain shelf space and accommodate retailers' demands for better margins as well as encourage them to promote the brand. When a brand enters the decline stage of the product life cycle, most of the promotional support will probably be removed and expenditures on sales promotion are unlikely.

Some brands never move on to the decline stage as their equity remains for decades or even longer. In this situation, promotional managers examine the competitive dynamics of new entrants or old foes who may attempt to steal share, and plan accordingly with appropriate allocations based on the objectives determined to ward off the threat. Alternatively, long-standing brands remain so as they periodically encourage new cohorts of consumers to try the brand with the right balance of advertising and sales promotion initially, and then retain them with an alternative ratio as these consumers remain loyal to the newfound brand.

CREATIVE THEMES

To integrate the advertising and sales promotion programs successfully, the theme of consumer promotions should be tied in with the advertising and positioning theme wherever possible. Sales promotion tools should attempt to communicate a brand's unique attributes or benefits and to reinforce the sales message or campaign theme. In this way, the sales promotion effort contributes to the consumer franchise-building effort for the brand.

At the same time, media advertising and other IMC tools should be used to draw attention to a sales promotion program such as a contest, sweepstakes, or event or to a special promotion offer such as a price reduction or rebate program. An excellent example of this is the award-winning "Win 500 Flights" sweepstakes that was developed by MasterCard and its promotional agency, Armstrong Partnership. The sweepstakes was developed under the umbrella of MasterCard's "Priceless" campaign theme and thus was designed to deliver on the brand promise that MasterCard understands what matters most to consumers—in this case travelling for any reason at all. The primary objective of the integrated marketing campaign was to drive MasterCard use during the key summer travel season. Consumers using their MasterCard from July 1 to August 31 were automatically entered in the sweepstakes for a chance to win 500 airline tickets to anywhere and that could be shared with family and friends. Media advertising, including television, print, out-of-home, and online banner ads, was used to promote the sweepstakes, along with an extensive public relations campaign. Exhibit 14-19 shows one of the print ads used to promote the "Win 500 Flights" sweepstakes.

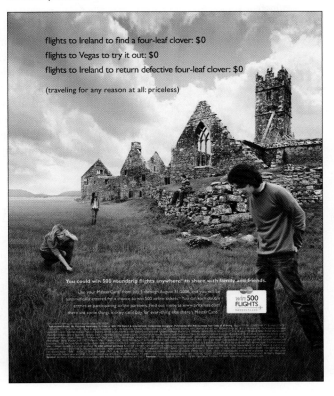

Exhibit 14-19 MasterCard used media advertising to promote its sweepstakes.

MEDIA SUPPORT

Media support for a sales promotion program should be coordinated with the media program for the ad campaign since it is used to deliver sales promotion materials (e.g., coupon, contest entry form, premium offer). It is also needed to inform consumers of a promotional offer as well as to create awareness and favourable attitudes toward the brand. By using advertising in conjunction with a sales promotion program, marketers can make consumers aware of the brand and its benefits and increase their responsiveness to the promotion. Consumers are more likely to redeem a coupon or respond to a price-off deal for a brand they are familiar with than one they know nothing about.

Using a promotion without prior or concurrent advertising can limit its effectiveness and risk damaging the brand's image. If consumers perceive the brand as being promotion dependent

Exhibit 14-20   Dove Men+Care coordinated advertising, sales promotion, and other IMC tools for its launch.

or of lesser quality, they are not likely to develop favourable attitudes and long-term loyalty. Conversely, the effectiveness of an ad can be enhanced by a sales promotion as well for a reciprocal effect. Dove's Men+Care launch relied on multiple IMC tools requiring coordination for success (Exhibit 14-20).

To coordinate their advertising and sales promotion programs more effectively, companies are getting their sales promotion agencies more involved in the advertising and promotional planning process. Rather than hiring agencies to develop individual, nonfranchise-building types of promotions with short-term goals and tactics, firms are having their sales promotion and advertising agencies work together to develop integrated promotional strategies and programs. Figure 14-10 shows how the role of sales promotion agencies is changing.

BRAND EQUITY

The increasing use of sales promotion in marketing programs is a fundamental change in strategic decisions about how companies market their products and services. These concerns lead to a conclusion that sales promotion can be overused by too much frequency, too valuable an economic offering, or offering too many promotions. A brand that is constantly promoted may lose perceived value. Consumers often end up purchasing a brand because it is on sale, they get a premium, or they have a coupon, rather than basing their decision on a favourable attitude they have developed. When the extra promotional incentive is not available, they switch to another brand.

One study examined whether price promotions affect pretrial evaluations of a brand.[43] The study found that offering a price promotion is more likely to lower a brand's evaluation when the brand has not been promoted previously compared to when it has been frequently promoted; that price promotions are used as a source of information about a brand to a greater extent when the evaluator is not an expert but does have product or industry knowledge; and that promotions are more likely to result in negative evaluations when they are uncommon in the industry. The findings suggest that marketers must be careful in the use of price promotions as they may inhibit trial of a brand in certain situations.

Marketers must consider both the short-term impact of a promotion and its long-term effect on the brand. The ease with which competitors can develop a retaliatory promotion and the

Figure   14-10

The shifting role of the promotion agency

Traditional	New and Improved
1. Primarily used to develop short-term tactics or concepts.	1. Used to develop long- and short-term promotional strategies as well as tactics.
2. Hired/compensated on a project-by-project basis.	2. Contracted on annual retainer, following formal agency reviews.
3. Many promotion agencies used a mix—each one hired for best task and/or specialty.	3. One or two exclusive promotion agencies for each division or brand group.
4. One or two contact people from agency.	4. Full team or core group on the account.
5. Promotion agency never equal to ad agency—doesn't work up front in annual planning process.	5. Promotion agency works on equal basis with ad agency—sits at planning table up front.
6. Not directly accountable for results.	6. Very much accountable—goes through a rigorous evaluation process.

Our Firm

All Other Firms	Cut back promotions	Maintain promotions
Cut back promotions	Higher profits for all	Market share goes to our firm
Maintain promotions	Market share goes to all other firms	Market share stays constant; profits stay low

Figure 14-11

Competitive dynamic of sales promotion

likelihood of their doing so should also be considered, as shown in Figure 14-11. Marketers must be careful not to damage the brand franchise with sales promotions or to get the firm involved in a promotional war that erodes the brand's profit margins and threatens its long-term existence. Marketers are often tempted to resort to sales promotions to deal with declining sales and other problems when they should examine such other aspects of the marketing program as channel relations, price, packaging, product quality, or advertising.

MEASURING SALES PROMOTION EFFECTIVENESS

Elizabeth Gardener and Minakshi Trivedi offer a communications framework to allow managers to evaluate sales promotion strategies over a given set of specific criteria. Borrowing from advertising applications, and using four communications goals—attention, comprehension (understanding), persuasion, and purchase—the researchers show the impact of four promotional tools and everyday low pricing (EDLP) on each goal (Figure 14-12).[44]

The implication of this study is that sales promotions can be evaluated with a framework similar to the one we summarized in Chapter 5. Much of the advertising research methods and measures discussed in Chapter 9 can be used in the context of sales promotions. For example, pre- or post-surveys can be used to assess brand awareness or brand attitude (i.e., attribute or benefit beliefs) associated with the sales promotion. Furthermore, assessment of attention, cognitive, and emotional responses of the promotional offer can also be measured with the appropriate method. From a behavioural standpoint, measurement of switching and loyalty is assessed with scanner data. Other aspects of behaviour can be measured by counting the number of inquiries, coupon redemptions, and contest entries.

Figure 14-12   Conceptual framework analysis

		Communication Factors		
		Attention/ Impression	Communication/ Understanding	Persuasion	Purchase
Sales Promotions	FSI coupons	✓✓	✓✓✓	✓✓	✓✓
	On-shelf coupons	✓✓✓	✓✓✓	✓✓✓	✓✓✓
	On-pack promotions	✓	✓	✓✓	✓
	Bonus packs	✓✓✓	✓✓	✓✓	✓✓
	EDLP	✓	✓✓	✓✓	✓

Promotional tendency to fulfill factor: ✓✓✓ = Strong; ✓✓ = Moderate; ✓ = Weak

Learning Objectives Summary

 Explain the role of sales promotion in a company's integrated marketing communications program and examine why it is increasingly important.

Sales promotion is an incentive and an acceleration tool that is offered as value to any person or organization within the overall marketing system, such as consumers and any trade members like wholesalers and retailers. Marketers have been allocating more of their promotional dollars to sales promotion to influence purchasing behaviour. Reasons for this shift include the strategic importance of sales promotions, reaching a specific target audience, promotional sensitivity, declining brand loyalty, brand proliferation, short-term focus of managers and accountability of promotional managers, and power of retailers and the competition.

 Identify the objectives, strategy, and tactical components of a sales promotion plan.

The objectives of sales promotion are often stated in terms of brand behaviour such as trial, re-trial, and repeat purchases, or product category trial or re-trial. Sales promotions can be characterized as either franchise building or nonfranchise building. The former contribute to the long-term development and reinforcement of brand identity and image; the latter are designed to accelerate the purchase process and generate immediate increases in sales. Sales promotion can also be looked at in terms of their incentive characteristic that can be immediate or delayed. Tactical considerations for sales promotion include the amount of the incentive, the timing of the promotion in terms of schedule and duration, and the distribution of the sales promotion.

 Describe consumer sales promotion strategy options and evaluate the factors to consider in using them.

A number of consumer sales promotion techniques were examined, including sampling, couponing, premiums, contests and sweepstakes, refunds and rebates, bonus packs, price-off deals, and event marketing. The characteristics of these promotional tools were discussed, along with their strengths and limitations. Promotional planners can select any combination of these tools for their IMC plans to achieve trial and repeat purchasing objectives and execute them with appropriate tactics to reinforce brand communication effects. The selection of the right combination reinforces the direction of the plan to influence both customers and non-customers.

 Describe trade sales promotion strategy options and evaluate the factors to consider in using them.

We also identified trade promotions including trade allowances, point-of-purchase displays, cooperative advertising, contests and incentives, sales training programs, and trade shows. These have different terminology and are similar to consumer sales promotion, but are intended for resellers who are in a similar buying process with more business-like objectives instead of personal objectives. Strategic and tactical decisions for each sales promotion are as critical here as they are with consumer promotions.

 Apply key IMC issues related to sales promotion decisions.

Advertising and sales promotion should be viewed as complementary tools. When planned and executed properly, advertising and sales promotion can produce a synergistic effect that is greater than the response generated from either promotional mix element alone. To accomplish this, marketers must coordinate budgets, advertising and promotional themes, media scheduling and timing, and target audiences. Extensive sales promotion can result in diminished brand equity when marketers become too dependent on the use of sales promotion techniques and sacrifice long-term brand position and image for short-term sales increases. Many industries experience situations where competitors use promotions extensively and it becomes difficult for any single firm to cut back on promotion without risking a loss in sales. Overuse of sales promotion tools can lower profit margins and threaten the image and even the viability of a brand.

Key Terms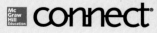

Review key terms and definitions on Connect.

Review Questions

1. What are the differences between consumer and trade sales promotion? Discuss the role of each in a marketer's IMC program.

2. Discuss how sales promotion can be used as an acceleration tool to speed up the sales process and maximize sales volume.

3. Post-secondary educational institutions do not usually use sales promotions. Consider which ones could be used and identify the target audience in which they could be effective.

4. Explain how trade promotions are similar and dissimilar to consumer trade promotions.

5. Explain why it is important for sales promotion to contribute to brand equity. In what circumstances will brand equity enhancement not be a priority?

Applied Questions

1. Explain how the consumer sales promotions identified in Figure 14-1 can be executed with Internet media.

2. What are the differences between consumer franchise-building and nonfranchise-building promotions? Find an example of a promotional offer you believe contributes to the equity of a brand and explain why.

3. Phone service providers do not offer premiums all that often. Identify good ones for different brands.

4. Consider all the trade sales promotions that a major brand like Tassimo would use and explain how they would be effective or ineffective for increasing sales of the machine and the coffee discs.

5. Why does the Red Bull Crashed Ice event not use the imagery from the advertising with the slogan "Red Bull Gives You Wings"?

GO ONLINE

For more information on the resources available from McGraw-Hill Ryerson, go to www.mcgrawhill.ca/he/solutions.

Public Relations

15

LEARNING OBJECTIVES

LO1 Recognize the role of public relations in the promotional mix.

LO2 Explain how to compile a public relations plan.

LO3 Examine how public relations is generated through media publicity and argue the strengths and limitations of media publicity.

LO4 Illustrate how public relations is managed through corporate advertising.

LO5 Apply the ideas of public relations within the development of an IMC plan.

Award-Winning Socially Responsible Marketing

The vast majority of Canadians believe it is important for companies to implement programs that improve society, social causes, or the environment, so it seems natural to see *Strategy* recognize corporate social responsibility efforts in various categories.

Bell pledged $50 million in support of mental health and initiated the "Let's Talk" idea to communicate the importance of mental health. Bell invited Canadians to talk about mental health by talking or texting to loved ones, with $0.05 going to the cause for every form of communication. In 2011, Bell customers sent 66 million messages and raised $3.3 million. In 2012, Bell customers included tweets, sending 78 million messages and raising $3.9 million. And in 2013 the initiative included Facebook shares, for a total of 96 million messages and $4.8 million. Over five years, Bell pledged a total of $50 million.

Widespread support for the cause included TV, radio, before and after print ads, in-store, billboard, out-of-home digital, digital at the Bell Centre, rink boards, banner ads, Internet site (letstalk.bell.ca), and public relations via *Hockey Night in Canada,* CTV's *eTalk,* and *Canada AM.* Messages featured Clara Hughes as a spokesperson for 2012, who has publicly communicated her personal story on this matter. One judge commended Bell, saying that "Targeting mental health for cause-related efforts was an exceedingly brave choice for Bell. Taking the risk of tackling an issue which could be view as controversial, Bell was able to assist those who may have otherwise hesitated to open up in the past."

"Extraordinary, Authentic Nourishment for All" is Campbell Canada's contribution to CSR with an emphasis since 2004 to alleviate hunger, prepare better meals, and eat nutritious food. Food Bank Canada and Campbell's worked together for over a decade and each year the company donated one million pounds of food and agreed to provide additional funds, supplies, and personnel support in the coming years.

A new ambitious task is Campbell's product Nourish, a complete meal in an easy-open can requiring no heating or water for preparation that is suitable for food banks and disaster relief situations. The product features a protein-rich grain developed by federal government scientists and is the result of committed Campbell's employees who desired the company do more for hunger. Campbell's with its partners, donated 100,000 cans initially and sought public support for increased levels. Campbell's placed ads in multiple media and used public relations to encourage Canadians to participate in the cause by sharing on Facebook, tweeting on Twitter, or watching the "Story of Nourish" on YouTube, with each step leading to a donation of one can of Nourish. After five weeks, the campaign achieved a total of 85,000 additional cans donated. Campbell's placed additional funds into the food system with each can sold to consumers, who were also encouraged to buy and donate to food banks.

Other companies recognized by *Strategy* included Shoppers Drug Mart for its commitment to women's health; Cadbury for its effort to provide bicycles to people in less developed countries who face transportation problems for everyday living—for example children cycling instead of walking too far to attend school; and Stanfield's underwear for its support of testicular cancer.

Sources: Emily Wexler, "Bell Tackles Tough Topic," *Strategy,* May 1, 2011, p. 31; Carey Toane, "For the Creative," *Strategy,* June 3, 2011, p. 24; Emily Wexler, "Stanfield's Battles Cancer in Its Underwear," *Strategy,* May 1, 2011, p. 30; Emily Wexler, "Cadbury Cycles Change," *Strategy,* May 1, 2011, p. 28; Melinda Mattos, "Bringing CSR into Focus," *Strategy,* May 1, 2011, p. 20; www.letstalk.bell.

Question:

1. What is the key redeeming characteristic of each of these award winners?

Public relations, publicity, and corporate advertising all have promotional program elements that may be of great benefit to marketers. They are integral parts of the overall promotional effort that must be managed and coordinated with the other elements of the promotional mix. However, these three tools do not always have the specific objectives of product and service promotion, and often involve other methods of reaching their target audiences. Typically, these activities are designed more to change attitudes toward an organization or issue than to promote specific products or affect behaviours directly. Aspects of these tools assist the marketing of products periodically for firms with a new view of the role of these tools. This chapter explores the domain of public relations, its related topic of publicity generated by news media, corporate advertising, the strengths and limitations of each, and the process by which they are planned and implemented.

L01 Public Relations

What is public relations? How does it differ from other elements of marketing communication discussed thus far? Perhaps a good starting point is to define what the term *public relations* has traditionally meant, to introduce its new role, and to compare it to publicity.

TRADITIONAL VIEW OF PR

Public relations is the management function that evaluates public attitudes, identifies the policies and procedures of an organization with the public interest, and executes a program of action and communication to earn public understanding and acceptance.[1] In this definition, public relations requires a series of stages: the determination and evaluation of public attitudes, the identification of policies and procedures of an organization with a public interest, and the development and execution of a communications program designed to bring about public understanding and acceptance. An effective public relations program continues over months or even years as it builds public trust between citizens and the organization.

This definition reveals that public relations involves much more than activities designed to sell a product or service. The PR program may involve promotional program elements previously discussed but use them in a different way. For example, a press release may announce a new product launch or an organizational change, a special event may be organized to create goodwill in the community, and advertising may be used to state the firm's position on an issue. In addition, the *management* aspect means that public relations is not limited to business management but extends to other types of organizations, including government and nonprofit institutions.

NEW ROLE OF PR

An increasing number of marketing-oriented companies have established new responsibilities for public relations. PR takes on a broader (and more marketing-oriented) perspective, designed to promote the organization as well as its products and/or services. For example, McDonald's looked to continue its efforts at eroding Tim Hortons' hold on the coffee market by sponsoring minor hockey, a long-time sponsorship activity of the leading coffee retailer in the quick service market.[2]

The way companies and organizations use public relations might best be viewed as a continuum. On one end of the continuum is the use of PR from a traditional perspective. In this perspective public relations is viewed as a nonmarketing function whose primary responsibility is to maintain mutually beneficial relationships between the organization and its publics. In this case, customers or potential customers are only part of numerous publics—employees, investors, neighbours, special-interest groups, and so on. Marketing and public relations are separate departments; if external agencies are being used, they are separate agencies.

Exhibit 15-1 The Grey Cup stage offered a venue for public relations activities.

At the other end of the continuum, public relations is considered primarily a marketing communications function. All noncustomer relationships are perceived as necessary only in a marketing context.[3] In these organizations, public relations reports to marketing. Thus, the PR function is moving more and more toward a "new role," which is much closer to a marketing function than a traditional one. The new role of public relations envisions both strong marketing and strong PR departments. Rather than each department operating independently, the two work closely together, blending their talents to provide the best overall image of the firm and its product or service offerings. Big events like the Grey Cup allow brands to present their public image (Exhibit 15-1).

Writing in *Advertising Age,* William N. Curry notes that organizations must use caution in establishing this relationship because PR and marketing are not the same thing, and when one becomes dominant, the balance required to operate at maximum efficiency is lost.[4] He says losing sight of the objectives and functions of public relations in an attempt to achieve marketing goals may be detrimental in the long run. Others take an even stronger view that if public relations and marketing distinctions continue to blur, the independence of the PR function will be lost and it will become much less effective.[5] In fact, as noted by Cutlip, Center, and Broom, marketing and public relations are complementary functions, "with each making unique but complementary contributions to building and maintaining the many relationships essential for organizational survival and growth. To ignore one is to risk failure in the other."[6] This position is consistent with our perception that public relations is an important part of the IMC process, contributing in its own way but also in a way consistent with marketing goals.

PUBLICITY

Publicity refers to the generation of news about a person, product, service, or organization that appears in broadcast or print media, and now on the Internet. It often appears that publicity and public relations occur at the same time or in close proximity. For example, Maple Leaf Foods faced the absolute worst experience in its long history when consumers perished or became severely ill from eating its contaminated meat products. In response, CEO Michael McCain took a strong leadership role in reassuring Canadians. In doing so, Maple Leaf Foods used extensive public relations activities at varying stages of the identification and solution of the problem to address the situation such that consumers were exposed to both publicity (i.e., information coming from the media) and public relations (i.e., information coming from Maple Leaf

Exhibit 15-2 Maple Leaf Foods responds to a crisis.

Foods itself). Mr. McCain met with journalists on a regular basis at press conferences and acted as the main spokesperson in corporate advertising messages that communicated the actions the company had undertaken to prevent further problems. Maple Leaf's television messages reached Canadians and became a key part of the Maple Leaf Foods channel on YouTube (see Exhibit 15-2).

In other instances, it seems that publicity is the end result or effect of the public relations effort. Because marketers like to have as much control as possible over the time and place where information is released, they often provide the news media with pre-packaged material. One way to do this is with a **video news release (VNR)**, a publicity piece produced by publicists so that stations can air it as a news story. Print media publications also receive material from brands with the intention of getting an editorial story written. A branded flower company, FLO, successfully used this idea by having gardening stories written in women's magazines that prominently featured the brand name and its imagery. The campaign included out-of-home, print, and radio media along with vibrant point-of-sale display carts, banners, and labels. Additional support occurred with signature information on delivery trucks along with the website address (flocanada.ca). By all accounts, the plan firmly planted FLO as a quality brand in the undifferentiated flower market.

Given the above scenarios, there are at least three complications for understanding public relations and publicity. First is the fact that publicity typically lasts for a short period of time. The communication effect of an article in the newspaper about a new product may last for a few weeks. Alternatively, public relations is a concerted program, with several exposures extending over a period of time that have a lasting communication effect. A second complication is that public relations is designed to provide positive information about a firm and is usually controlled by the firm or its agent. Publicity, on the other hand, is not always positive and is not always under the control of, or paid for by, the organization. One factor that distinguishes publicity from the other IMC program elements is its sheer power as a form of communication, which gives rise to the final complication. The more powerful incidents of publicity are unplanned by the corporation, and the focus is on the successful and unsuccessful reactions of the organization to positive or negative events. IMC Perspective 15-1 identifies the publicity a brand received resulting from a previous decision.

Public Relations Plan

Public relations is an ongoing process requiring formalized policies and procedures for dealing with problems and opportunities. A public relations plan is required, as in the case for an advertising plan or a sales promotion plan. Moreover, the public relations plan needs to be integrated into the overall marketing communications program. A public relations plan can be structured like the other IMC tools we have discussed thus far. It starts with a situation analysis and includes decisions with respect to target audiences, behavioural objectives, communication objectives, strategy, and tactics. Once the plan is written, marketers should ask themselves the questions in Figure 15-1 to determine whether their public relations plan is complete. Given the broad nature of public relations, there are options for each part of the plan that we now discuss.

SITUATION ANALYSIS

Elements of the situation analysis from the marketing plan or IMC plan are reviewed. An additional key piece of information is a current assessment of people's attitudes toward the firm, its product or service, or specific issues beyond those directed at a product or service. Why are

IMC PERSPECTIVE 15-1

A PR Battle

The neverending volley between public relations and publicity is often seen in controversial issues among multiple stakeholders, especially if the motives of each party diverge. An incident between the National Hockey League (NHL) and one of its sponsors, Air Canada, took an interesting turn of events following a hit by Zdeno Chara of the Boston Bruins on Max Pacioretty of the Montreal Canadiens during a Habs home game in which the local hero received a concussion and left the game.

As directed by Air Canada's CEO, Calvin Rovinescu, the company subsequently wrote a letter to NHL Commissioner Gary Bettman, addressed from the airline's Director of Marketing and Communications Denis Vandal. The letter voiced their concern over the on-ice hit and others that occurred throughout the league, and expressed how the company experienced difficulty justifying its NHL sponsorship with the league's apparent disregard for player safety. The letter closed with the following: "Unless the NHL takes immediate action with serious suspensions to the players in question to curtail these life-threatening injuries, Air Canada will withdraw its sponsorship of hockey." The league responded by telling Air Canada to stop meddling in internal affairs and to withdraw its sponsorship if it desired. After this, Air Canada declined to wade into the matter since it believed the original communication would remain private and not leaked to the media.

Given this situation, a number of stakeholders commented on the matter in the media thus generating even more publicity. One brand consulting expert suggested, "If you're going to start a debate, you have to be ready to join the debate." Other NHL sponsors like Labatt and Visa declined to comment on the issue, and Pepsi stated it had no plans to change any sponsorship of the NHL or the players' association. Molson, which replaced Labatt as the league's beer sponsor shortly after the incident, offered that it was "firmly on the side of hockey." Another sponsor, a coffee retailer that features Sidney Crosby in its ads, stated, "Tim Hortons encourages the NHL, the teams and general managers and the NHL Players' Association to continue to work towards addressing concerns with head injuries."

Interestingly, Bell—an NHL sponsor and partial owner of the Montreal hockey club—provided a balanced point of view: "Bell is fully behind the Canadiens' plan to engage all NHL owners and the league in addressing safety concerns as quickly as possible. Bell agrees that player safety is paramount, and we are confident in the NHL's willingness and ability to effectively manage the issue." Another major sponsor also made its perspective known: "Scotiabank will continue to work with the NHL, and the NHLPA to educate future generations of hockey players on respect, safety and team work, and we do this through skills clinics at a minor level. Our approach is to be very active in the educational area on concussion and drive moral passion on the issue."

Marketing experts concluded that Air Canada's point would be well taken by the general public since the airline echoed the sentiment of many Canadians; however, some expressed concern about an idle threat of sponsorship removal that could be potentially damaging in the long run. With the NHL locking out its players a year later for about four months, it remains uncertain as to who lost in terms of long-run credibility.

Sources: Jeromy Lloyd, "Hurts So Good," *Marketing Magazine,* June 13, 2011, pp. 20–22, 24, 26–29; Simon Houpt, Brent Jang, and Susan Krashinsky, "On Hockey Violence, Air Canada Jabs, Then Ducks," *The Globe and Mail,* March 11, p. B1; David Brown, "Don't Stop, Air Canada," *Marketing Magazine,* March 28, 2011, p. 9.

Question

1. What is your assessment of how each party handled the situation?

firms so concerned with the public's attitudes? One reason is that these attitudes may affect sales of the firm's products. Second, no one wants to be perceived as a bad citizen. Corporations exist in communities where their employees work and live. Negative attitudes carry over to employee morale and may result in a less-than-optimal working environment internally and in the community.

Figure 15-1

Ten questions for evaluating public relations plans

1. Does the plan reflect a thorough understanding of the company's business situation?
2. Has the PR program made good use of research and background sources?
3. Does the plan include full analysis of recent editorial coverage?
4. Do the PR people fully understand the product's strengths and weaknesses?
5. Does the PR program describe several cogent, relevant conclusions from the research?
6. Are the program objectives specific and measurable?
7. Does the program clearly describe what the PR activity will be and how it will benefit the company?
8. Does the program describe how its results will be measured?
9. Do the research, objectives, activities, and evaluations tie together?
10. Has the PR department communicated with marketing throughout the development of the program?

Due to their concerns about public perceptions, privately held corporations, publicly held companies, utilities, and the media survey public attitudes for a few reasons. One, initial public attitudes become the starting point in the development of programs designed to maintain favourable positions or change unfavourable ones. Two, these initial attitudes might signal a significant potential problem, which allows the firm to handle it proactively. Three, it will be much easier for the PR team to gain the support it needs to address this problem. Finally, optimal communication can occur if the firm understands a problem completely.

DETERMINE RELEVANT TARGET AUDIENCES

The target audiences for public relations efforts vary, and as we saw earlier each will have unique behavioural and communication objectives. These audiences may be internal or external to the firm. **Internal audiences** are connected to the organization and include the employees of the firm, shareholders and investors, members of the local community, suppliers, and current customers. **External audiences** are those people who are not closely connected with the organization (e.g., the public at large). It may be necessary to communicate with both groups on an ongoing basis for a variety of reasons and it is likely that those who are not in the target audience will in fact receive the message, like we observe with product advertising.

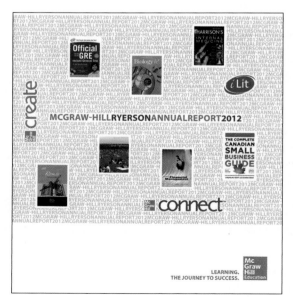

Exhibit 15-3   Annual reports serve a variety of purposes.

Employees of the Firm   Maintaining morale and showcasing the results of employees' efforts are often prime objectives of the public relations program. Organizational newsletters, notices on intranet resources, mail/e-mail, and annual reports are methods used to communicate with these groups. Personal methods of communicating may be as formal as an established grievance committee or as informal as an office party. Other social events such as corporate sports teams, picnics, or cause-related or community activities are also used to create goodwill.

Shareholders and Investors   An annual report like the one in Exhibit 15-3 provides shareholders and investors with financial information regarding the firm. While this is one purpose, annual reports are also a communications channel for informing this audience about why the firm is or is not doing well, future plans, and other information that goes beyond numbers.

For example, McDonald's has successfully used annual reports to fend off potential PR problems. One year the report described McDonald's recycling efforts to alleviate consumers' concerns about waste; another report included a 12-page spread on food and nutrition. Other companies use similar strategies, employing shareholders' meetings, video presentations, and other forms of direct mail. Companies have used these approaches to generate additional investments, to bring more of their shares "back home" (i.e., become more locally controlled and managed), and to produce funding to solve specific problems, as well as to promote goodwill.

Community Members   People who live and work in the community where a firm is located or doing business are often the target of public relations efforts. Such efforts may involve ads informing the community of activities that the organization is engaged in—for example, reducing air pollution, or cleaning up water supplies. Demonstrating to people that the organization is a good citizen with their welfare in mind may also be a reason for communicating to these groups. Exhibit 15-4 features an ad to draw community members' attention to AMEX's concern for society.

Suppliers and Customers   An organization wishes to maintain *goodwill* with its suppliers as well as its consuming public. If consumers think a company is not socially conscious, they may take their loyalties elsewhere. Suppliers may be inclined to do the same. Indirect indications of the success of PR efforts may include more customer loyalty, less antagonism, or greater cooperation between the firm and its suppliers or consumers. Historically, most people viewed public relations as a communications strategy to maintain customers.

The Media   Perhaps one of the most critical external publics is the media, which determine what is read in a newspaper or seen on TV, and how this news will be presented. Because of the media's power, they should be informed of the firm's actions. Companies issue press releases and communicate through conferences, interviews, and special events. The media are generally receptive to such information so long as it is handled professionally; reporters are always interested in good stories.

Exhibit 15-4   AMEX demonstrates concern for the public.

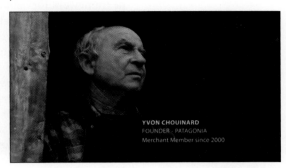

Educators   A number of organizations provide educators with information regarding their activities. The Canadian Marketing Association and the Promotional Products Association of Canada, among others, keep educators informed in an attempt to generate goodwill as well as exposure for their causes. These groups and major corporations provide information regarding innovations, state-of-the-art research, and other items of interest.

Civic and Business Organizations   Local nonprofit civic organizations also serve as gatekeepers of information. Companies' financial contributions to these groups, speeches at organization functions, and sponsorships are all designed to create goodwill. Corporate executives' service on the boards of nonprofit organizations also generates positive public relations.

Governments   Public relations often attempts to influence government bodies directly at both local and national levels. Successful lobbying may mean immediate success for a product, while regulations detrimental to the firm may cost it millions.

Financial Groups   In addition to current shareholders, potential shareholders and investors may be relevant target markets. Financial advisers, lending institutions, and others must be kept abreast of new developments as well as financial information, since they offer the potential for new sources of funding. Press releases and corporate reports play an important role in providing information to these publics.

BEHAVIOURAL OBJECTIVES

The framework for behavioural objectives discussed in Chapter 5 is readily applicable for public relations. Recall that behavioural objectives are trial purchase, repeat purchase, shopping, or consumption. No matter what target audiences are selected in the prior step, an astute marketer will know that it is important to understand the type of behaviour desired as a result of the communication. The idea of a "purchase" seems incongruous for certain public relations situations, so the marketer may have to view this as the target audience "buying into the idea" or another specific behaviour in order to carefully define the objectives. The RBC Blue Water Project encourages considerable involvement of citizens to actively improve Canada's water supply, such as drinking less bottled water and volunteering with watershed cleanups. The initiative includes social media where citizens discuss water issues and raise awareness.[7]

COMMUNICATION OBJECTIVES

The communication objectives of Chapter 5 can similarly be used for public relations. Communication objectives include category need, brand awareness, brand attitude, and purchase intention. Each of these can be the focus of the public relations plan, although slight modifications are needed. For example, the "brand" may in fact be the corporation itself or a new product that is talked about in a press release. In addition, the notion of a "category" has to be adjusted. Some target audiences want to be affiliated with "good corporate citizens" that are responsible to the community, the environment, or another issue. Often, the "category" will be related to the particular topic or the public relations message content.

Awareness is critical for a brand and is important for the organization. Organizations support social causes because the exposure of their name will enhance the general public's recall and recognition at a later point in time. For example, Cisco created a social networking site (onemillionactsofgreen.com) focused on environmental sustainability (Exhibit 15-5). The site fit the technology company's global "Human Network" campaign and allowed Canadians to post their "green" ideas such as riding a bike to work. Cisco partnered with the CBC for outreach to encourage participation by having the program featured on *Hockey Night in Canada* and *The Hour*. Extensive direct communication occurred with online video, newsletters, and e-mail. Organizations jumped onboard by encouraging employee involvement. At the time of the award, the site had hit 1.3 million acts from 33,000 registered users, with 186,000 unique visitors having spent an average of 17 minutes on the site. Positive publicity through numerous articles in media and comedians spoofing the initiative proved such remarkable acceptance that this Canadian idea went global.[8]

We started off by highlighting the importance of existing attitudes of the target audiences. Clearly, then, the public relations plan should have a specific section that outlines the attitude change or modification desired. It should also illustrate the key motives addressed and what attributes or benefits of the firm or product the message should focus on. Automobile firms are good examples of where positive publicity via news media is desired and encouraged. New product launches include media releases and feature interviews for articles appearing in the car section, a weekly feature in national and most large daily newspapers. Further positive press occurs with trade shows that occur in major cities, which typically get coverage resulting in framing initial consumer attitudes about a vehicle model.[9]

Exhibit 15-5   Cisco's distinctive corporate imagery is the face of many of its public relations activities.

STRATEGY

The strategy decisions for public relations are twofold, as we saw with advertising: message and media. The primary message decisions concern the degree to which the message will have a marketing or corporation focus, and the creative associated with the message. We will briefly describe issues related to this decision in this section. Like advertising, there are a number of options to disseminate the message—news media, advertising media, and events. We will discuss these in more detail in the next major section.

Message Content Thomas L. Harris has referred to public relations activities designed to support marketing objectives as **marketing public relations (MPR)** functions.[10] Marketing objectives that may be aided by public relations activities include raising awareness, informing and educating, gaining understanding, building trust, giving consumers a reason to buy, and generating consumer acceptance. These points are consistent with the behavioural and communications objective of our framework. Marketing public relations can be used effectively in the following ways:

- Building marketplace excitement before media advertising breaks
- Creating news about a new advertising or promotional campaign
- Introducing a product with little or no advertising
- Influencing the influentials—that is, providing information to opinion leaders
- Defending products at risk with a message of reassurance
- Constructively promoting a product

IKEA Canada's innovative activities successfully increase media exposure and exemplify marketing public relations. In fact, a key source of zany ideas originated from its consumer surveys—shopping at IKEA was seen as a bit stressful for couples so it hosted relationship seminars on Valentine's Day. IKEA's Relax event noted the fact that Canadians found relaxing to be more naughty than sex. This prompted IKEA to issue instructions for making a restful home along with an "IKEA Adrenaline Index" on the website featuring humorous questions to assess people's stress levels. Store openings and catalogue launches both receive ambitious events to ensure the media cover the story. IKEA sees the value of these activities and invests heavily, with a 50 percent budget increase and each event receiving a $500,000 allotment.[11]

The historical role of public relations is one of communicating a favourable image of the corporation as a whole. The domain of this image, or reputation management, concerns every facet of how the organization interacts with its social, economic, political, and charitable constituents, in addition to the general public locally, nationally, and internationally.

During GM's difficulties during the recession, the U.S. division moved toward the "Rebirth of the American Car" message in its ads to restore its corporate reputation, but the Canadian version of the ad made no reference to the bankruptcy and did not have American imagery (i.e., the U.S. flag). Instead, a message of reinvention that highlighted the strong brands and models emphasized a more positive and future-oriented direction. According to the advertising director for GM Canada, "The early feedback on the campaign is extremely positive. We are thinking it is coming across in the right tone and manner—acknowledging the situation we are in and moving forward in a positive direction."[12]

Given the two broad directions of the actual message, marketing versus corporate, an organization has to decide the relative degree of the message's impact over the course of a year or even longer, as public relations tends to have a lasting communication effect. Too much of a focus in either direction and the organization loses the opportunity to communicate fully.

Message Creativity We will discuss the tools for public relations shortly; however, in deciding what message to communicate, the marketer is faced with the decision as to whether the creative strategy of advertising or other IMC tools should be adopted for public relations. On the one hand, there is the argument that all communications should have a common look and feel to them. To counter this, one could argue that unique target audiences with a specific message should have an appropriate associated creative.

Honda developed the "Blue Skies for Our Children" theme and directed messaging to children with TV, print, online banner, POS ads, elevator wraps, and digital brochures as part of an Earth Day launch of Honda's long-standing commitment to the environment. Its website (hondabluesky.ca) contained three sections, Yesterday, Today, and Tomorrow, with the latter

Exhibit 15-6   Toyota's managing director Stephen Beatty addressed a recall issue in media outlets.

showing interviews of children to symbolically show what Honda plans to do beyond its current Insight vehicle.[13]

Message Delivery   In the course of defining public relations and publicity, and explaining the content of a public relations plan, we have generally described two mechanisms for the delivery of the message. News media outlets are available and the media have the choice of publishing or not publishing the materials that organizations submit for their consideration. Alternatively, organizations can turn to other options where they control the dissemination of the message through different types of corporate advertising opportunities in which the organization is responsible for the costs, much like regular product advertising we have covered thus far.

During Toyota's major recall a few years ago, the U.S. division halted sales of the affected models and its advertising response to the negative publicity focused on its reputation for quality. The managing director for Toyota Canada released a four-minute online video that clarified the situation in Canada. Since the problem of the gas pedal sticking affected only one Canadian model, the extensiveness of the problem was not as severe. However, Toyota Canada did offer a "voluntary safety improvement campaign," where it replaced the parts on models recalled only in the United States even though the parts on the Canadian versions were manufactured with different materials and would not cause problems. Toyota Canada executives also appeared on television news shows. Extensive communication occurred on the company's website, and Toyota directly contacted all owners to explain the solution and how it planned to resolve the problem (Exhibit 15-6).[14]

TACTICS

The choice of news media or corporate advertising dictates the types of tactics employed. When using news media, a marketer would need to know how to make a media presentation, whom to contact, how to issue a press release, and what to know about each medium addressed, including TV, radio, newspapers, magazines, and direct-response advertising. In addition, decisions have to be made regarding alternative media such as news conferences, seminars, events, and personal letters, along with insights on how to deal with government and other legislative bodies. Because this information is too extensive to include as a single chapter in this text, we suggest students peruse additional resources for further insight. For corporate advertising, numerous considerations have been addressed in the advertising message chapters (Chapters 7 and 8) and the media chapters (Chapters 10 to 13).

PUBLIC RELATIONS EFFECTIVENESS

As with the other promotional program elements, it is important to evaluate the effectiveness of the public relations efforts. In addition to determining the contribution of this program element to attaining communications objectives, the evaluation tells management how to assess what has been achieved through public relations activities, measure public relations achievements quantitatively, and judge the quality of public relations achievements and activities.

In measuring the effectiveness of PR, one author suggests three approaches: media content analysis that systematically and objectively identifies the messages appearing in the media and analyzes the content to determine trends and perceptions relevant to the product or brand, survey research that quantitatively assesses consumers' attitudes toward the product or brand, and marketing mix modelling that draws data from multiple sources and integrates them to provide insight into the process.[15] Figure 15-2 summarizes a number of exposure measures

A system for measuring the effectiveness of the public relations program has been developed by Lotus HAL. The criteria used in the evaluation process follow:

- Total number of impressions over time
- Total number of impressions on the target audience
- Total number of impressions on specific target audiences
- Percentage of positive articles over time
- Percentage of negative articles over time
- Ratio of positive to negative articles
- Percentage of positive/negative articles by subject
- Percentage of positive/negative articles by publication or reporter
- Percentage of positive/negative articles by target audience

Figure 15-2

Criteria for measuring the effectiveness of PR

that may be used to assess the effects of PR programs through news media that are consistent with the first step.

Others suggest comprehensive approaches like we have seen with advertising. Walter Lindenmann says three levels of measures are involved: (1) the basic, which measures the actual PR activities undertaken; (2) the intermediate, which measures audience reception and understanding of the message; and (3) the advanced, which measures the perceptual and behavioural changes that result.[16] As a reminder, this approach is entirely consistent with the exposure, processing, and communications effects model described in Chapter 4.

Media Publicity

In this section, we discuss how organizations can achieve public relations communication objectives through publicity generated through the media. We refer to this as *media publicity*; that is, publicity that the firm attempts to control by influencing the media to report an organization's story to the public. In this section we review different ways to reach the media and consider the strengths and limitations of this option. When considering the significance of this assessment, keep in mind that consumers receive the message through all the media discussed thus far, so the effects can be varied.

MEDIA OPTIONS

A number of media options are available for communicating with target audiences, including press releases, press conferences, exclusives, interviews, and community involvement.

Press Releases   One of the most important publics is the press. To be used by the press, information must be factual, true, and of interest to the medium as well as to its audience. The source of the **press release** can do certain things to improve the likelihood that the "news" will be disseminated, such as ensuring that it reaches the right target audience, making it interesting, and making it easy to pass along.

The information in a press release won't be used unless it is of interest to the users of the medium it is sent to. For example, financial institutions may issue press releases to business trade media and to the editor of the business section of a general-interest newspaper. Information on the release of a new rock album is of more interest to radio disc jockeys than to TV newscasters; sports news also has its interested audiences.

Press Conferences   We are all familiar with **press conferences** held by political figures. While used less often by organizations and corporations, this form of delivery can be very effective as scenes of corporate spokespeople will be viewed on television. The topic must be of major interest to a specific group before it is likely to gain coverage. Companies often call press conferences when they have significant news to announce, such as the introduction of a new product or advertising campaign. On a local level, community events, local developments, and the like may receive coverage. Sports teams use this tool to attract fan attention and interest when a new star is signed. The development of technology has allowed the delivery of press conferences to occur remotely where reporters receive the presentation and participate in the follow-up question and answer session.

Exclusives   Although most public relations efforts seek a variety of channels for distribution, an alternative strategy is to offer one particular medium exclusive rights to the story if that medium reaches a substantial number of people in the target audience. Offering an **exclusive** may enhance the likelihood of acceptance, and sometimes the media actually use these exclusives to promote themselves.

Interviews   Interviews occur on a variety of news or information shows. Usually, someone will raise specific questions and a spokesperson provided by the firm will answer them. Oftentimes, the president or owner will give interviews when there is important news about the firm.

Community Involvement   Corporations enhance their public images through involvement in the local community that often is covered by the media. This involvement may take many forms, including membership in local organizations and contributions to or participation in community events. For example, Rogers employees work throughout neighbourhoods on Halloween night to promote community safety. It also includes organizations participating in emergencies.

Exhibit 15-7   Edward Jones promotes its J.D. Power Award.

STRENGTHS OF MEDIA PUBLICITY

Credibility   Public relations communication through media publicity is not perceived in the same light as advertising. Consumers understand that most advertising is directly paid for by the sponsoring organization. Obviously exceptions occur, such as public service announcements heard on the radio, for example. The fact that the media are not being compensated for providing the information may lead receivers to consider the news more truthful and credible. For example, an article in newspapers or magazines discussing the virtues of ibuprofen may be perceived as much more credible than an ad for a particular brand of ibuprofen. And while firms present the media with news releases or press kits and incur a cost, consumers generally perceive the media source to be reasonably trustworthy with its reporting expertise.

Endorsement   Information from media publicity may be perceived as an endorsement by the media vehicle in which it appeared. Automotive awards presented in magazines such as *Motor Trend* carry clout with potential car buyers, and car companies often advertise their achievements. A number of auto manufacturers advertised their high customer satisfaction ratings reported by J. D. Power & Associates, an independent research firm specializing in satisfaction research. Exhibit 15-7 shows that it extends to other industries. Taken together, the credibility and endorsement effects constitute a significantly positive media image.

Cost In both absolute and relative terms, the cost of media publicity is very low, especially when the possible effects are considered. While a firm can employ public relations agencies and spend millions of dollars, for smaller companies this form of communication may be the most affordable alternative available. Public relations programs require little more than the time and expenses associated with putting the program together and getting it distributed, yet they still accomplish their objectives.

Avoidance of Clutter Because they are typically perceived as news items, media publicity messages are not subject to the clutter of ads. A story regarding a new product introduction or breakthrough is treated as a news item and is likely to receive attention.

Reach Specific Audiences Because certain products appeal only to small market segments, it is not feasible to implement advertising and/ or promotions to reach them. If the firm does not have the financial capabilities for promotional expenditures, the best way to communicate to these groups is through media publicity.

Image Building Effective public relations helps to develop a positive image for the organization. The examples discussed thus far have indicated strong image-building capabilities with proactive public relations. News about a product may in itself serve as the subject of an ad. Exhibit 15-8 demonstrates how General Mills used favourable publicity from a variety of sources to promote the importance of whole grains in a healthy diet and promote the use of whole grains in its cereal.

Frequency Potential Still another reason for publicity's power is the frequency of exposure it generates. For example, a successful public relations activity could generate exposure in multiple media (i.e., broadcast, print, Internet).

Exhibit 15-8 General Mills capitalizes on positive publicity.

LIMITATIONS OF MEDIA PUBLICITY

Weaker Brand or Corporate Identification Effect Perhaps the major disadvantage of media publicity is the potential for not completing the communications process. While these messages can break through the clutter of commercials, the receiver may not make the connection to the source. A firm's PR efforts are rarely associated with their sponsors in the public mind.

Inconsistent Message Media publicity may also misfire through mismanagement and a lack of coordination with the marketing department. When marketing and PR departments operate independently, there is a danger of inconsistent communications or redundancies in efforts.

Timing Timing of media publicity is not always completely under the control of the marketer. Unless the press thinks the information has very high news value, the timing of the press release is entirely up to the media—if it gets released at all. Thus, the information may be released earlier than desired or too late to make an impact.

Accuracy The information contained in a press release can get lost in translation—that is, it is not always reported the way the provider wishes it to be. As a result, inaccurate information, omissions, or other errors may result.

(LO4) Corporate Advertising

For purposes of this text we use the term **corporate advertising** for marketing communication implemented for the direct benefit of the corporation rather than its products or services. This method of delivery is selected over media publicity since the firm exerts complete control over the communication process rather than relying on the media acceptance for publicity to occur. Marketers seek attainment of corporate advertising's objectives by implementing image advertising, cause-related advertising, and sponsorship. The latter two have moved to the product level in communications strategy so the distinction has blurred. We cover these three topics in this section, but first we look at the purpose of corporate advertising, namely the management of corporate reputation.

CORPORATE REPUTATION

Earlier in this text we suggested that the communications framework described for advertising can be applied to other communication tools, and previously in this chapter we highlighted that it can be used for public relations tools. This thought is echoed with a summary of the planning process used by executives of a leading public relations firm, FleishmanHillard Canada, in its efforts to assist clients with reputation management[17]:

- Gain a detailed, forward-looking understanding of corporate business objectives, competitive positioning, and the desired corporate reputation or corporate brand. This is best accomplished through interviews with senior corporate and business unit executives.
- Define the key audience, and derive audience-specific behavioural and attitudinal objectives and audience-specific corporate positioning attributes.
- Assess current perceptions of the company held by each key stakeholder group or audience on each of the key reputational attributes.
- Implement reputation-management programs throughout the corporation.
- Establish an ongoing plan to measure and monitor corporate reputation, and use reputation measurement to refine communications programs.

We highlight the issue of corporate reputation, a term that is used in public relations to convey the idea of corporate image, since a key outcome of corporate advertising is to influence overall perceptions of the organization. Clearly, the notion of corporate reputation is attitudinal, thus indicating that the general framework suggested in this text can be applied to all IMC tools. Furthermore, all methods described in Chapter 9 (e.g., focus groups, interviews, surveys) are readily applied for measuring corporate advertising effectiveness. News organizations publish polls that ask Canadians their opinion about corporations. Figure 15-3 summarizes the findings from the 2012 corporate reputation survey by *Marketing Magazine*/Leger, where 1,500 respondents rated the quality of products offered by the companies.[18]

Heinz appeared at the top of the list in 2011 in its first year of being included in the survey, knocking Google off its perch as number one. Heinz prides itself on its ketchup and baby food, naturally, as well as its other quality products. Strong efforts for the United Way and organizations devoted to health and nutrition keep Heinz at the forefront as a reputable corporation in the eyes of Canadians. Tim Hortons clinched a top spot once again; executives for Canada's famous coffee retailer believe organizational commitment of $10 million to the Tim Hortons Children's Foundation during 2011, along with $3.6 million to charities, hospitals, and communities from sales of its "Smile Cookies," makes the iconic company a strong performer.[19]

Other entities beyond big brands look to develop their reputation. For example, cities often are looking to promote themselves in a positive light for reasons related to tourism, business investment, and overall citizen goodwill. Vancouver and Calgary sought to enhance their reputations with both domestic and international audiences. Tourism Vancouver needed a quick response to the post-hockey-playoff difficulties and worked with the theme of "This Is Our Vancouver," undertaking extensive activity in social media. "Calgary: Be Part of the Energy" tried to develop an image and build people's interest in moving to the city for employment as labour demand continued to mount.[20]

2012 Rank	Company	Score	% Good Opinion	% Bad Opinion	2011 Rank
1	Heinz	84.6	87.6	3.0	—
2	Google	84.5	88.1	3.6	1
3	Kellogg	82.6	87.2	4.6	3
4	Sony	79.0	84.5	5.5	2
5	Kraft	78.5	85.8	7.3	7
6	Tim Hortons	77.7	86.8	9.1	6
7	Campbell	77.6	83.9	6.3	—
8	Canadian Tire	76.2	86.4	10.2	5
9	Subway	75.5	82.5	7.0	10
10	Staples	75.3	81.6	6.3	4

Source: *Marketing Magazine*, May 10, 2012.

Available online at http://www.marketingmag.ca/news/marketer-news/best-brand-reputations-2012-52296

Figure 15-3

The top 10 companies in the 2012 *Marketing Magazine/* Leger Corporate Reputation Survey

IMAGE ADVERTISING

One form of corporate advertising is devoted to promoting the organization's overall image. **Image advertising** may accomplish a number of objectives, including creating goodwill both internally and externally, creating a position for the company, specifying a firm's perspective on an issue, and generating resources, both human and financial.

Positioning   Firms, like products, need to establish a position in the marketplace, and corporate image advertising activities are one way to accomplish this objective. A well-positioned product is much more likely to achieve success than is one with a vague or no image. The same holds true of the firm. Companies with strong positive corporate images have an advantage over competitors that may be enhanced when they promote any aspect of their organization or products. As shown in Exhibit 15-9, ads are often designed to create an image of the firm in the public mind. The exhibit shows how Dow is attempting to create an image of itself as an innovator and leader in putting healthy food on the world's table. The ad is designed to demonstrate Dow's concern for science and humanity.

Television Sponsorship   A firm often runs corporate image advertising on TV programs or specials. By associating itself with high-quality or educational programming, the firm hopes for a carryover effect that benefits its own image. IBM acted as the sponsor (i.e., sole advertiser) for a number of newscasts on CBC and Canwest that addressed seven major themes, such as "The Smart City" and "Building Sustainable Value." As part of IBM's "Smarter Planet" brand positioning, the effort encouraged the media partners to investigate the themes within their existing news programs. For instance, the CBC investigated the topics on *The Nature of Things* and *Mansbridge One on One,* while Canwest linked in its *Global News* and *Financial Post* properties.[21]

Recruitment   The promotional piece presented in Exhibit 15-10 is a good example of corporate image advertising designed to attract new employees. The employment section of major metropolitan

Exhibit 15-9   Dow uses image advertising.

Exhibit 15-10 Corporate image advertising designed to attract employees.

Exhibit 15-11 Citizens protest the development of wind turbines citing numerous concerns.

newspapers (*National Post, The Globe and Mail*) is an excellent place to see this form of corporate image advertising at work. Notice the ads in these papers and consider the images the firms are presenting. This form of communication has taken on new meaning with online recruitment ads and with business networking sites (e.g., LinkedIn).

Financial Support   Corporate advertising is also designed to generate investments in the corporation. By creating a more favourable image, the firm makes itself attractive to potential share purchasers and investors. More investments mean more working capital, more monies for research and development, and so on. In this instance, corporate image advertising is almost attempting to make a sale; the product is the firm.

Advocacy   Firms often take positions on certain social, business, or environmental issues that influence their image and the public's perception. Such **advocacy advertising** is concerned with propagating ideas and elucidating controversial social issues of public importance in a manner that supports the interests of the sponsor.

While still portraying an image for the company or organization, advocacy advertising does so indirectly, by adopting a position on a particular issue rather than promoting the organization itself. The ads may be sponsored by a firm or by a trade association and are designed to tell readers how the firm operates or management's position on a particular issue. The reason for the advertising can be due to the firm's negative publicity or the firm's inability to place an important message through public relations channels, or because the firm just wants to get certain ideas accepted or have society understand its concerns. Renewable energy producers like Samsung devote a considerable portion of their website communicating the environmental advantages of wind turbines to fulfill future energy needs. The rationale is to build an understanding of the potential benefits and to likely thwart the efforts of protestors who have health, safety, and economic criticisms (Exhibit 15-11).[22]

CAUSE-RELATED ADVERTISING

An increasingly popular method of image building is **cause-related marketing**, in which companies link with charities or nonprofit organizations as contributing sponsors. The company benefits from favourable publicity, while the charity receives much-needed funds. Companies also take the opportunity to advertise their involvement (Exhibit 15-12). Spending on cause-related marketing has increased considerably in the past decade. Proponents of cause marketing say that association with a cause may differentiate one brand or store from another, increase consumer acceptance of price increases, generate favourable publicity, and even win over skeptical officials who may have an impact on the company.[23]

Cause marketing relationships historically took a variety of forms; making outright donations to a nonprofit cause, having companies volunteer for the cause, donating materials or supplies, or running public service announcements. However, like most marketing communication activities, brands look for unique opportunities to facilitate the communication process effectively and efficiently with innovations such as a total commitment with complete IMC exposure, fundraising, and inventing causes to fit their brand.

As part of its marketing communication, Becel has supported the Heart & Stroke Foundation for decades with a variety of activities. Exhibit 15-13 shows cyclists participating in Becel's Heart & Stroke Ride for Heart. It took a huge step in a new direction when it became the founding sponsor for the Foundation's Heart Truth campaign designed to inform the public that heart disease is the leading cause of death among women. The key message focused on how supporters could help save the life of a woman they loved (e.g., mother, sister, friend). Extensive TV ads and sponsorship of women's shows heightened awareness during February's Heart Month. Print and PR communicated the Foundation's Red Dress Fashion Show featuring Canadian celebrities and benefit concerts. All communication drove women to the website (loveyourheart.ca) for resources and media content. After three months, awareness of heart disease increased from 13 percent to 23 percent, and Becel's sales grew by 9 percent.

Becel also sponsored a two-minute film entitled *The Heart* that premiered during the Academy Awards. The message of the film took a new direction by artistically encouraging women to think of themselves and their heart health. A montage of images of a woman's life as she cared for her family ensued as heartfelt music kept pace. Pre-broadcast publicity occurred with *eTalk Daily* host Tanya Kim and stories placed in print and broadcast media. Post-broadcast messaging with *eTalk* continued along with placement of the film in Cineplex movie theatres and online placements on YouTube, VideoEgg, CTV pre-roll, and Facebook. Becel filmed a separate execution for Quebec that aired during the French-language Cinematic awards show *Les Jutra*.[24]

These next two activities show examples where a brand creatively fundraises for a nonprofit organization and receives a marketing communication benefit in return. Virgin Mobile's Re*Generation program raised money for clothing for at-risk and homeless youth and donated the money to nonprofit organizations like the Broadway Youth Resource Centre in Vancouver. One

Exhibit 15-12 Whirlpool supports the effort for affordable housing.

Exhibit 15-13 Becel supports the Heart & Stroke Foundation with sponsorship events.

Exhibit 15-14 Indigo's support of reading fits the image of the brand perfectly.

fundraising activity saw Lady Gaga perform at a Toronto nightclub, while another featured contributions for every Samsung Re*Generation phone sold.[25] And Food Banks Canada received a total of $2.5 million from Kraft over the past few years in a matching donations program. Kraft extended the idea with a recipe program that included a partnership with American Greetings. For every recipe e-card forwarded to a friend Kraft donated $2, up to a maximum of $50,000.[26]

Companies also become involved in causes that reinforce their brand or corporate mandate by establishing a worthy cause themselves rather than working with an existing organization as described above. For example, Indigo established the Love of Reading Foundation and donated $7.5 million to 70 schools in support of library renovations and book purchases (Exhibit 15-14). It teamed up with a publisher of children's books, where a portion of sales contributed to the fund. A 60-second public service announcement and other media advertised the initiative, which also helped the publisher expand its franchise to a new merchandising product line based on a book character.[27] An international chocolate brand established the Cadbury's Cocoa Partnership, a 10-year, $80 million program to help cocoa farmers in developing countries where its beans are purchased. The Canadian division launched a Bicycle Factory program to send 5,000 bicycles to Ghana, allowing the recipients to travel. Cadbury featured a host of advertising and promotional activities designed to get Canadian consumers involved. For example, a website allowed consumers to enter the code on its package to "buy" one part for a bike. Each bike requires 100 parts, so after 500,000 chocolate bars the collaboration achieved its mandate.[28]

At the same time, not all cause marketing is a guarantee of success. Cause marketing requires more than just associating with a social issue, and it takes time and effort. Companies can get into trouble by misleading consumers about their relationships. It is also possible to waste money by hooking up with a cause that offers little connection or relation to their brand. Firms need to avoid picking the wrong cause, and finding that their customers and potential customers either have little interest in or don't like the cause. Finally, the results of cause-marketing efforts can be hard to quantify.

SPONSORSHIP

Corporate sponsorship of different events plays a major role in the public relations plans of organizations. While companies sponsor specific events with primarily traditional public relations objectives in mind, a separate and more marketing-oriented use of sponsorships is also on the increase; event sponsorship occurs for product-level brands compared to corporate brands. In either case, the decisions involved are comparable—we turn to these in this section, beginning with a brief overview.

Overview   Activities where a fee is paid in exchange for marketing communication benefits for an organization are known as **event sponsorship**. An organization agrees to sponsor an event since it provides exposure to a selective audience, and potentially a larger audience with television coverage or photos or video posted on the Internet. A further benefit includes the ability to have the organization associated with the event, thus providing additional development of the corporate or product brand.

A survey of managers found that sponsorship contributes to brand differentiation and financial success provided that advertising and sales promotion supported the initiative.[29] Furthermore, academic research conducted in lab experiments suggest that sponsorship

	1998	2002	2006	2009	2012
Sports	$4.56	$6.43	$8.94	$11.28	$13.01
Entertainment	0.68	0.87	1.38	1.64	$1.93
Festivals, fairs, events	0.61	0.83	0.61	0.76	$0.83
Causes	0.54	0.83	1.30	1.51	$1.70
Arts	0.41	0.61	0.74	0.82	$0.89
Associations/membership organizations			0.40	0.50	$0.55
Total	$6.80	$9.57	$13.371	$16.51	$18.91

Source: Adapted from *Promo*, June 1, 2002; *Promo Xtra*, January 24, 2007; *Promo*, January 28, 2010, Sponsorship.com 2012.

Figure   15-4

Annual sponsorship spending in North America by property ($ billions)

contributes to brand recall and stronger brand attitudes, and initial field research supports this conclusion as well.[30] However, factors like too many sponsors, controversial co-sponsors, a poor product association with the event, and weak initial brand attitude can all contribute to less desirable outcomes regarding brand attitude among others.[31]

Sponsorship can take on a variety of forms, as shown in Figure 15-4. Sports sponsorship leads the way every year and Molson's deal with the NHL confirms the importance of hockey for selling beer. The seven-year deal worth $375 million breaks out as $100 million for the rights, $100 for guaranteed advertising buys, $100 million for events and special promotions, and $75 million for unreported marketing activities.[32] In response to the growth of sponsorship, industry members established the Sponsorship Marketing Council of Canada to demonstrate sponsorship as a valuable communication tool by establishing practices and measurement tools to validate the investment.[33] Other activities include establishing an awards program recognizing the best sponsorship in four categories: arts and entertainment, sports, causes, and special interest.

One award-winning sponsorship campaign was Kraft Hockeyville, which won gold in the sports category, gold for continued success, and Best of Show for 2009 (following up its 2007 Best of Show recognition) at the Sponsorship Marketing Awards. The program launched in 2006 as a grassroots competition to find the place where hockey lives in Canada, bringing together Kraft Canada, the CBC, the NHL, and the NHL Players' Association. To enter, people submitted a 500-word essay plus photos to support their community. Kraft Hockeyville 2009 attracted 7,183 entries and 481 community profiles. The final ballot beat all previous records, with 9.3 million votes cast. As title sponsor, Kraft attempted to increase brand loyalty, showcase community responsibility, and create retail excitement to drive sales. A number of key metrics support achievement. Consumers completely accepted the retail-level initiatives; consumption grew by 4.4 percent for 2009. Each year, Kraft Hockeyville became the number one CBC show website. PR coverage attained 330 million media impressions—close to triple the previous record (Exhibit 15-15).[34]

A high-profile Canadian festival where international stars make an appearance is the Toronto Film Festival, which has celebrated its 34th anniversary. Like other star-studded affairs, a pre-eminent occasion is the walk down the red carpet taken by the noted celebrities—the perfect location for sponsorship. And so thought the executives at Holt Renfrew; the upscale retailer had its logo imprinted at close intervals along the path toward the gala

Exhibit 15-15   Kraft Hockeyville celebrates with the NHL.

Exhibit 15-16   Holt Renfrew sponsors the Toronto International Film Festival.

theatre entrance (Exhibit 15-16). Holt Renfrew began its sponsorship of the red carpet in 2004, and its executives appear pleased with the relationship: "In many red carpet pictures you can see the Holt Renfrew logo," and "It's a nice fit, the worlds of fashion and film coming together." The fashion leader spends its marketing dollars on traditional and digital media, catalogues, fashion shows, glitzy parties, and eye-catching store windows, yet the film sponsorship has represented only one percent of its marketing budget and produces the strongest impact.[35]

As expected, a number of decisions are associated with event sponsorship, including the types of sponsorship, target audience fit, target audience exposure, and brand positioning. We explore these important sponsorship decisions in the context of sports sponsorship for illustrative purposes because it represents the dominant expenditure—more than $13 billion in North America in 2012. Each idea can be readily adapted to other domains, for example entertainment or arts festivals. Sports sponsorship can be successful with clear objectives, a good positioning strategy, adequate budget, the appropriate sporting vehicle, and key tactical implementation; characteristics we have seen in other types of promotional plans.[36] IMC Perspective 15-2 describes a few sporting sponsorships.

Types of Sponsorship   Sport sponsorship involves endorsement deals or sponsoring a team, league, event, athlete, or organization, along with stadium naming or broadcast rights. The goal is to associate a brand with its target audience's entertainment consumption or lifestyle, thus enriching the overall brand experience. One thought on the topic suggested three levels of sponsorship.[37] *Proprietary* has little or no external sanctioning or partnerships; Nike's Run TO featured a running event throughout the entire city of Toronto (Exhibit 15-17). *Affiliated advertising* utilizes the assets of a sponsorship or association. For example, the Esso Legends of Hockey brings together the Hockey Hall of Fame, NHL, NHL Players' Association, and NHL Alumni. *Programming* lives within a larger event or sponsorship, for example Powerade's "Thirst for Soccer" that visits youth soccer tournaments across Canada.

Working with an athletic sponsorship is similar to sponsorship with a team, but with a few unique issues. Foremost is ensuring a fit between the athlete and the company or brand. Exposure arrangements regarding an athlete's identity (i.e., name, image, and likeness), amount and type of service, and corporate logo placement need to be established. Rounding out the arrangement is the strategic communication use of an athlete in advertising, public relations, or sales promotion and conditions for the sponsor to protect its investment (e.g., an ethics clause).[38]

Brand Positioning   Companies are attracted to event sponsorships because effective IMC programs can be built around them and promotional tie-ins can be made to local, regional, national, and even international markets. Companies are finding event sponsorships an excellent platform from which to build equity and gain affinity with target audiences as well as a good public relations tool for the corporation in general.

While the overall market position of the brand may be well established throughout

Exhibit 15-17   Participants in the Nike Run TO event.

Sponsorships Everywhere

Sponsorship deals exist internationally with the Olympics, nationally with the NHL, and locally with companies supporting local communities with ways to associate their brand. And this is supported with recent statistics. The sponsorship industry in Canada is worth about $1.6 billion. Furthermore, companies spend considerably more of their budget, moving up from 15 percent to 30 percent over the past few years. The average amount spent on the largest sponsorship is $1.25 million. Many companies do not use an agency, but this has changed moving from 25 percent to almost 40 percent corresponding to the growth in expenditures. Festivals, fairs, and annual events comprised 25 percent, with 19 percent for sports.

On the international stage, Canadians witnessed sponsorship activity with the 2010 Winter Olympic Games. After losing the sponsorship bid to Hudson's Bay to supply clothing, Lululemon looked to capitalize in its own way with a line of clothing that celebrated a "Cool sporting event that takes place in British Columbia between 2009 and 2011." Although Lululemon did not technically break the law, the Vancouver Olympic Committee scolded the company, saying it expected better sportsmanship. Scotiabank similarly wanted to associate itself with the nation with its "Show Your Colours" campaign that invited Canadians to share photos and stories to demonstrate their pride. These kinds of battles are also seen with the NHL, for example when Molson Coors Canada swept the beer sponsorship rights from its main competitor right when Labatt was negotiating an extension with the NHL. One commentator suggested that the value of NHL sponsorship had changed dramatically, becoming a much more valuable property, and that Labatt misread the situation.

Other companies prefer a smaller stage but see great value in sponsorship. Kraft's Hockeyville promotion allowed communities to compete to be named the country's best hockey town, with the winner announced on *Hockey Night in Canada* after online fan voting. Leading up to this, Kraft narrowed down the towns and cities to a final list. The winner received $100,000 in rink upgrades, and the four runners-up received $25,000 each. The promotion continued yearly with sales up noticeably during the eight-week campaign. Several brand measures were strong, like "Kraft has great community spirit," and Kraft "actively cares and supports my community." These results are what Kraft

looked for when the promotion began, as its research indicated that most Canadians' lives revolved around the local community centre with a rink for hockey, figure skating, public skating, ringette, and sledge hockey—the assistance to improve the facilities appeared a natural fit for the company that makes family products.

Picking up on the success of this community sponsorship, BMO turned to a similar idea with its support for soccer. The participation level for soccer is 33 percent, double the rate of hockey. Over a period of four months, after being named the team of the week 15 teams would compete for votes to win the prize of $125,000 for field improvements and an opportunity to see a professional soccer game in Toronto or Vancouver. This promotion supported BMO's sponsorship of professional soccer and its naming rights of Toronto's BMO field. BMO's VP of sponsorship commented, "We really started to look at the growth of soccer in this country, and the linkages between the Canadians who are playing soccer and our BMO customer base, and recognizing that soccer certainly touches a lot of our customers, just like it touches a lot of Canadians." Overall, BMO spent 20 percent of its corporate marketing on soccer activities, with 40 percent directed toward sponsorship.

Sources: Alicia Androich, "Ring Around the Poser," *Marketing Magazine,* July 9, 2012, pp. 16–17; Chris Daniels, "Want to Be Part of Something Bigger," *Marketing Magazine,* August 21, 2012; Chris Powell, "Molson Roughs Up Labatt for the Good Ol' Hockey Game," *Marketing Magazine,* March 28, 2011, pp. 10–11; Simon Houpt, "BMO Finds Fertile Sponsorship Ground on the Soccer Pitch," *The Globe and Mail,* March 31, 2011; Simon Houpt, "When Sponsorship Becomes the Whole Point," *The Globe and Mail,* May 7, 2011.

Question:

1. Do each of these sponsorship strategies fit the brand?

Exhibit 15-18 A competitor on the half-pipe at the Telus Festival.

the marketing plan, sport sponsorship permits a brand positioning strategy to a unique and well-defined target audience toward which the brand has specific communication and behavioural objectives. For example, a sports sponsorship could enable a brand to establish awareness and new brand associations as it reaches new customers to develop trial purchases.

However, brands should be prepared to spend accordingly to achieve their objectives, as the initial sponsorship investment requires additional advertising or sales promotion expenditures. As the foundation is critical, brands should ensure that the rights and benefits of the sports sponsorship allow the brand to achieve its objectives and positioning. For example, sponsorship in hockey can have limits without the clearance from its stakeholders (e.g., NHL, NHL Players' Association, and Hockey Canada). Finally, picking the right sponsorship that has the right profile at the right time and a partner that is receptive to making the deal work is paramount for successful implementation.

Target Audience Fit   Most companies focus their marketing efforts on specific market segments and are always looking for ways to reach these target audiences. Marketers are finding that event sponsorships are very effective ways to reach specific target audiences based on geographic, demographic, psychographic, and ethnic characteristics. For example, golf tournaments are a popular event for sponsorship by marketers of luxury automobiles and other upscale products and services. The golf audience is affluent and highly educated, and marketers believe that golfers care passionately about the game, leading them to form emotional attachments to brands they associate with the sport. Alternatively, brands will look to similar venues to reach a consistent target audience that fits. For example, BMO Financial supports Figure Skating Canada, Equestrian at Spruce Meadows in Calgary, and the Canadian Opera Company.[39] The Telus World Ski and Snowboard Festival allows the national telecommunications firm to reach its youth market with its sponsorship investment (Exhibit 15-18).[40]

Target Audience Exposure   Marketers are attracted to event sponsorship because it gets their company and/or product names in front of consumers. By choosing the right events for sponsorship, companies can get visibility among their target audience. Clearly this appears to be a key reason why Molson spent its money sponsoring the NHL as it anticipates that hockey viewers are also beer drinkers. Curiously, sponsorship deals raise interesting questions as to the target audience exposure of a sponsorship messages as shown in Exhibit 15-19. While exposure is no doubt important, the degree to which the sponsorship is noticed is concern for managers since most events offer varying exposure levels for different amounts of dollars invested. Thus, the risk of potential clutter due to the prominence of a major sponsor can inhibit the exposure of secondary sponsors.

Exhibit 15-19   Zurich Insurance saw a connection between its target audience and viewers of beach volleyball.

Brand Activities   Most sponsored properties include guidelines on what level of marketing the brand's support permits in terms of the number and size of signs, for example. Sponsored

Exhibit 15-20 Crankworx draws sponsors for its bike events.

properties allow extensive brand activation to occur, while others place significant limitations on the type of brand activities permitted during the exposure. For example, Levi Strauss & Co. was a secondary sponsor of Crankworx (Exhibit 15-20), a mountain bike festival in Whistler, B.C. To gather momentum, Levi's staged mock photo shoots where staff acted as "model scouts" and approached festival attendees in the brand's 17–24 target to pose for mock ads. The posters were put up on-site, and event attendees were encouraged to vote for their favourite "model" via text messages or ballots (two winners later appeared in a real Levi's ad published in *Exclaim!* magazine). Levi's did the same thing at a Virgin Festival in Toronto with a "Best Impressions" competition. Music festival goers voted for their favourite Levi's "model," and the winner appeared in the November issue of *Exclaim!* In contrast, events like the Calgary Stampede and the Rogers Cup tennis tournament place companies in strict sponsorship categories based on their investment level and take steps to ensure that each sponsor receives a level of exposure consistent with their investment. For example, sampling is closely controlled because this method often attracts greater attention.[41]

Measuring Sponsorship Effectiveness As we have seen with other communication tools, sponsorship planning follows a general framework of performing a situation analysis with relevant consumer and competitive research, establishing objectives (i.e., marketing, communication, behavioural), developing strategy and tactics, and outlining the criteria and measures of effectiveness to assess whether objectives have been met. A major issue that faces the event sponsorship industry is incomplete research. As marketers become interested in targeted audiences, they will want more evidence that event sponsorship is effective and a good return on their investment.

Despite this concern, the growth in sponsorship investments has led to a corresponding emergence of measuring the effectiveness of sponsorships. Essentially, measures of sponsorship effectiveness can be categorized as exposure-based methods or tracking measures[42]:

- *Exposure methods.* Exposure methods can be classified as those that monitor the quantity and nature of the media coverage obtained for the sponsored event and those that estimate direct and indirect audiences. These measures have been commonly employed by corporations, but heavily criticized by scholars. Pham argues that media coverage is not the objective of sponsorships and should not be considered a measure of effectiveness. He argues that the measures provide no indication of perceptions, attitude change, or behavioural change and should therefore not be considered as measures of effectiveness.[43]
- *Tracking measures.* These measures are designed to evaluate the awareness, familiarity, and preferences engendered by sponsorship based on surveys. A number of empirical studies

have measured recall of sponsors' ads, awareness of and attitudes toward the sponsors and its products, and image effect including brand and corporate images. Moreover, the tracking measures could be done for current customers, potential customers, and the general public before, during, and after the event to get a complete picture of the sponsorship.[44]

While each of these measures has its advantages and disadvantages, we suggest using several in assessing the impact of sponsorships. In fact, the selection of appropriate measures is so critical that they may have to be customized for each sponsorship activity.[45] One innovative and comprehensive measurement system is SponsorScope, developed by Fusion Alliance Marketing, a division of Cossette Communication Group. Their tool examines items like the media used, media and sponsor visibility, and usage of sales promotion tools, along with items like the number of event sponsors, the event's reputation, category exclusivity, leveraging potential for employees, and the event's communication plan.[46]

Finally, at the conclusion of investigating numerous studies of the persuasion effects of sponsorship, the researcher makes a number of managerial prescriptions based on the findings. Sponsorship content should be visible. An organizer should clearly thank the sponsor at the event; this can be implemented in the media as well. Planners should avoid multiple-sponsor events. The sponsorship should offer true value to the audience, who should perceive it as being distinct from brand advertising.[47]

(L05) IMC Planning: Strategic Use of PR

As discussed in this chapter, public relations activities often communicate infrequently to a broader population and attempt to persuade the target audience on more global or abstract attributes of the company and its brand. With this in mind, public relations generally does not influence the decision-making process because the activities are not sequenced to match the purchase and consumption behaviour of consumers, as they are in advertising or sales promotion. For that matter, it is unlikely that a single public relations activity would coincide exactly with decision making for any other stakeholder that might be a target audience for the organization.

For example, CIBC is the title sponsor for Run for the Cure, an annual event to raise funds for the Canadian Breast Cancer Foundation (Exhibit 15-21). The late-September event features considerable lead-up media exposure funded by CIBC and other sponsors; however, this timing does not necessarily fit for all customers and non-customers of CIBC since financial products and services are purchased year-round. Presumably, CIBC expects this sponsorship activity to have a broad, long-term benefit associated with the corporate brand that consumers and all other internal and external stakeholders would retain during the year and until the event returns.

Advertising and PR often reinforce one another. The launch of a new advertising campaign is helped with additional exposure through news media in the form of announcements in the newspaper, clips shown on television, or information and complete ads posted on the Internet. Sometimes, brands take advantage of favourable publicity and make note of this in their advertising or make it a central theme in a particular message. Alternatively, if the corporation involved itself with sponsorship of arts, a cause, or sports,

Exhibit 15-21   CIBC's Run for the Cure draws enthusiastic supporters.

the advertising can make reference of this for regular brand messages beyond advertising messages dedicated to communicating information about the sponsorship. For these reasons, it is no wonder we have seen extensive proliferation of public relations expenditures.

PR and sales promotion often work hand-in-hand, and Tabi International provides a good example of this. Each season Tabi, like most fashion retailers or clothes designers, provides press releases to fashion, lifestyle, and marketing/business media with the intention of obtaining exposure through news articles in magazines, newspapers, or the Internet. To spark the presentation, the upscale retailer established the Tabi Face of 40+ contest as the central theme to launch its autumn fashions. The contest encouraged women over 40 to enter and be selected to model in a photo shoot published in the 40th anniversary edition of *Homemakers* magazine, along with *Canadian Living* magazine.[48]

Internet sites for corporations are a primary vehicle for communicating basic facts, especially the corporation's social and community interests, and for disseminating common public relations tools. For example, firms regularly put copies of their press releases on their sites and also include video clips of corporate activities like speeches or annual shareholder meetings. The ability of virtually anyone to obtain basic company information through the Internet makes it a desirable tool for firms to project their best image with timely content to ensure strong reputation management. However, the darker side of the Internet appears in the form of unwarranted negative publicity for brands. Even the average person may try to sabotage organizations that have appropriate corporate missions, sell legitimate products, and follow the laws of the land.

Learning Objectives Summary

 Recognize the role of public relations in the promotional mix.

This chapter examined the role of public relations. Public relations is typically accomplished through publicity generated through news media and corporate advertising. We noted that these areas are all significant to the marketing communication effort and are usually considered differently from the other promotional elements. The reasons for this special treatment stem from the facts that (1) they are typically not designed to promote a specific product or service, and (2) in many instances it is harder for the consumer to make the connection between the communication and its intent.

PR is often a separate department operating independently of marketing; in others, it is considered a support system. Many large firms have an external public relations agency, just as they have an outside ad agency. Thus, public relations is useful with its traditional responsibilities; however, increasingly more marketing-oriented firms use this tool at the brand or product level for enhanced communication efforts.

 Explain how to compile a public relations plan.

Like all aspects of IMC, a public relations plan begins with a situation analysis, in particular an evaluation of public attitudes to the firm through a survey methodology in order to gauge an accurate reading. Influencing the right audience is another critical element as the organization must decide to communicate with groups such as employees, investors, community, suppliers, customers, media, educators, and any other relevant societal stakeholder. Objectives need to be set, consistent with the behaviour and communication ideas suggested earlier in this book.

An appeal of sorts is also established for public relations much like we saw in advertising examples; a clear message with a focus that often has creative elements. The delivery of the message can occur through established media channels discussed already, and through the media to generate publicity. Finally, tactical considerations and effective measures need to be established for full implementation.

Examine how public relations is generated through media publicity and argue the strengths and limitations of media publicity.

News about a person, product, service, or organization that appears in broadcast or print media or on the Internet is known as publicity. It can occur through a story a journalist decides to write. In this case, publicity can be positive or negative and the firm is in more of a reactionary mode; preparedness for this scenario is certainly possible and recommended. Alternatively, a firm can seek media coverage for important news by communicating with the media through tools with the planned intention of receiving positive stories. Firms use press releases, press conferences, exclusives, interviews, and community involvement, and may use other creative means to persuade journalists to cover them.

Messages about a company that consumers receive through the media have strengths, including credibility, endorsement, low cost, less clutter, ability to reach specific audiences, image building, and frequency potential. Limitations include whether the brand is actually stronger, and a lack of control leading to an inconsistent message, poor timing, and possible inaccuracy.

 Illustrate how public relations is managed through corporate advertising.

Corporate advertising involves the reputation management of the firm through advertising and promotional activities designed to put the firm in the most favourable public position. Corporate advertising is a general term to cover all marketing communication that usually includes image advertising, cause-related advertising, and sponsorship. Corporate advertising can be controversial because sometimes the source of the message is top management, who may have their own intentions and motivations. This element of communication definitely has its place in the promotional mix but should follow the planning suggestions outlined in this chapter in order to be effective.

 Apply the ideas of public relations within the development of an IMC plan.

Public relations is an integral part of an IMC program as PR potentially reaches so many different constituents in the general public and those immediately connected to the organization. Furthermore, public relations both supports and can lead other IMC tools like advertising, sales promotion, and digital communication. As such, the execution of public relations should be carefully planned with objectives, strategies, and tactics much like any other aspect of marketing communication.

Key Terms   McGraw Hill Education **connect**

Review key terms and definitions on Connect.

Review Questions

1. Identify the key differences between public relations and media publicity. In what ways are the two interdependent?

2. Describe the reasons why firms use public relations in an IMC program. Provide an example of an appropriate use of public relations in this mix.

3. Many companies are now trying to generate as much free publicity as they can. Cite examples, and discuss the advantages and disadvantages associated with this strategy.

4. Companies are now taking the position that their charitable contributions should lead to something in return—for example, sales or increased visibility. Discuss the pros and cons of this position.

5. Explain how public relations activities and media publicity can be executed with Internet media.

Applied Questions

1. Some marketers and PR people believe public relations should replace advertising as the primary tool for introducing new products. Explain why this would or would not be a good plan.

2. Who are the target audiences for Bell's work described in the opening vignette?

3. How do music artists take advantage of media publicity? Which strengths do they predominantly use? How do they minimize the limitations of media publicity?

4. Identify the sponsors of different concerts or entertainment activities you have attended and make a conclusion as to why this type of sponsorship may be successful.

5. Explain why a company like RBC would use the tools described in the chapter, including media publicity, corporate image advertising, cause-related advertising, and sponsorship.

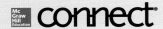

Direct Marketing

16

LEARNING OBJECTIVES

LO1 Define direct marketing and summarize the importance of a database for making marketing communication decisions.

LO2 Express the decisions of a direct-marketing plan.

LO3 Describe the content of a loyalty program.

LO4 Evaluate the strengths and limitations of direct marketing.

LO5 Apply the ideas of direct marketing within the development of an IMC plan.

Direct Marketing with Loyalty Programs

Loyalty programs are all around us, it seems, and the data prove this belief. Virtually all Canadians are enrolled in a loyalty program; each of us is a member of about six programs, on average, that can be mentioned top-of-mind such as Air Miles, Aeroplan, or Scene. About 50 percent of consumers modify when and where they shop, and about 40 percent modify the brands purchased to maximize loyalty benefits. Sixty percent of consumers claim continued transactions with brands they participate in. Moreover, 50 percent focus on collecting with one program to maximize points.

Attitudes are just as strong. Most consumers feel that loyalty programs are worth participating in (70 percent) and form a part of their relationship with a company (50 percent). Furthermore, about a third of all consumers value the programs that offer special services. Finally, 30 percent would switch their current credit card if not for the loyalty program. These behavioural and attitudinal responses are stronger for higher-income households and lower for lower-income households, indicating a very strong correlation.

While the success of loyalty programs appears strong, marketers are faced with the continued issue of whether the program merely rewards behaviour that would have occurred anyway since consumers generally sign up for programs with brands that they are already emotionally attached to and have a purchase history with. Research suggests that hard benefits of financial rewards in terms of discounts, cash, or merchandise are critical; softer rewards with respect to privilege, access, and information are very important for fostering strong loyalty over time. Furthermore, consumers become attached to brands with loyalty programs for regular purchases and are more likely to use the brand once again for infrequent larger purchases.

The experience of being in a loyalty program is also a strong consideration as consumers value seeing the rewards accumulating over time. Furthermore, the experience of "cashing in" for a big-ticket item is seen as an important consumption event that helps strengthen the relationship with the brand. In fact, one-quarter of all Canadians "splurge" with their rewards claim. And this loyalty is seen in the 40 percent of major loyalty program members who have stayed with a program for over 10 years, especially since many "save up" for big-ticket items. Continued communication, usually via direct mail and e-mail, is also valued by consumers. So, if even if the rewards are great, the softer relationship side is important as well.

Loyalty programs are at varying levels of sophistication, so a number of prescriptions have emerged to guide successful implementation. A primary one concerns customer information within the database to allow behavioural (level, amount purchased) and attitudinal (brand associations and feeling) segmentation. Second, customized and personalized communication is critical as a one-size-fits-all approach is not viable even though companies pursue it. Third, marketers should consider moving beyond direct mail and e-mail for communication within the loyalty program and augment with social media to forge a stronger relationship with consumers who have connected with the brand (e.g., Facebook fan pages). Finally, greater smartphone penetration allows loyalty programs to adjust their offerings or communicate ways to earn rewards more immediately through the use of location-based apps.

Sources: Maritz Loyalty Report 2011; Maritz Loyalty Report 2012; "Crunch," *Marketing Magazine*, March 28, 2011, p. 46; Alicia Androich, "Secrets of Canada's Top Loyalty Programs," *Marketing Magazine*, March 28, 2011, pp. 23–24.

Question:

1. Why are loyalty programs different across different product categories or goods versus services?

In this chapter, we discuss direct marketing and its role as a communications tool. Direct marketing includes programs that use direct-response media such as direct mail, catalogues, telephones, TV infomercials, and newer methods of digital communication. In essence, it uses the media we have discussed thus far and others, but with a more immediate behavioural objective in addition to communication objectives. We begin with an overview of direct marketing and the use of databases, a critical implementation resource. We then identify key decisions for direct-marketing programs, the use of direct-response media, and loyalty programs. The chapter concludes with a summary of the strengths and limitations of this marketing tool and an IMC application.

(L01) Direct Marketing

While companies rely primarily on the other promotional mix elements to move their products and services through intermediaries, an increasing number are going directly to the consumer. These companies believe that the traditional promotional mix tools, such as advertising and sales promotion, are effective in creating brand image, conveying information, and/or creating awareness. However, going direct with these same tools can generate an immediate behavioural response that makes direct marketing a valuable tool in the integrated communications program. For this section we briefly define the purpose of direct marketing and illustrate the importance of databases for implementation.

DEFINING DIRECT MARKETING

As noted in Chapter 1, **direct marketing** is the interactive use of advertising media to stimulate an (immediate) behaviour modification in such a way that this behaviour can be tracked, recorded, analyzed, and stored on a database for future retrieval and use.[1] Direct marketing involves marketing research, segmentation, strategic and tactical decisions, and evaluation as shown in our planning model in Chapter 1. For the execution, direct marketing uses a set of **direct-response media**, including direct mail, telephone, interactive TV, print, the Internet, mobile devices, and other media to reach both customers and prospective customers. Exhibit 16-1 shows how advertising encourages direct communication and purchasing via the Internet.

The use of direct-response media differs depending on whether the identity of an individual within the target audience is known. For example, direct mail can be addressed, where the person's name and address is on the communication sent to the home (or business) location. In contrast, unaddressed mail reaches homes and is delivered in bulk to selective geographic areas, or the use of another segmentation variable, decided by the promotional planner. In either case, an important element of direct marketing and the selection of the most appropriate direct-response media is the development and use of a database. We briefly examine the content and use of a database for the purpose of marketing communication as it has implications for all direct-response media described in this chapter and for Internet media discussed in the next chapter.

Bose® SoundDock® Portable digital music system

Compare it to any other sound system
for the iPod. Portable or not.

1-XXX-XXX-XXXX, ext. xxxxx | Bose.com/SoundDock   **BOSE**
Better sound through research.

Exhibit 16-1   Bose uses multiple methods to promote its products.

DEVELOPING A DATABASE

As we have discussed throughout this text, market segmentation and targeting are critical components of any promotional program. Direct-marketing programs employ these principles even more than others, since the success of a direct-marketing program is in large part tied to the ability to reach a very specific target audience. To segment and target their audiences, direct marketers use a **database**, a listing of customers and/or potential customers. This database is a tool for **database marketing**—the use of specific information about individual customers and/or prospects to implement more effective and efficient marketing communication. In this section we look at using database information, the sources of database information, and how to determine the effectiveness of the database.

Using Database Information   Figure 16-1 demonstrates how database marketing works. The creation and development of the database is the first and obviously a necessary step for this program. The database contains names, addresses, and postal codes; more sophisticated databases include information on demographics and psychographics, purchase transactions and payments, personal facts, neighbourhood data, and even credit histories (see Figure 16-2). With the development of electronic communication, databases may also contain e-mail addresses and consumers' social media identification. Canada's privacy legislation places limitations on what marketers can do with information stored in their databases. We refer you to www.privcom.gc.ca for a complete guide.

The database permits extensive and advanced statistical analysis to identify specific audiences for which a customized and/or personalized message or promotional offer can be delivered through a direct-response medium. For example, Knorr entered the frozen food category and delivered direct-mail pieces, also containing a coupon, to households according to demographic and purchase behaviour potential along 10 different characteristics. Those most likely to respond included past Knorr consumers of other product categories who were interested in the frozen food category and who had sufficient disposable income to afford a premium product. The various combinations of the 10 characteristics provided opportunities to reach different target audiences ranging from very low to extremely high levels of audience attractiveness. The results indicated a 10 percent response rate, substantially higher than the projected 3 percent. One of the more attractive target audiences attained a response rate of 50 percent.

As this Knorr example illustrates, certain consumers are more likely to be potential purchasers than others. By analyzing the characteristics of the database, a marketer like Knorr can target potential audiences that have a stronger likelihood of responding to the offer (e.g., use coupon, trial purchase) and the database serves as the foundation to profile the target audience and achieve a trial purchase objective.[2] Finally, this example shows how brands

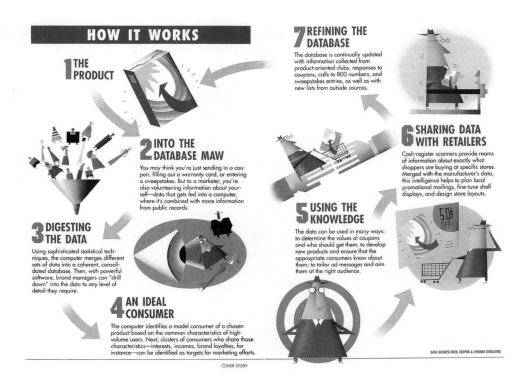

Figure   16-1

How database marketing works

Figure 16-2

Contents for a comprehensive database

Consumer Database	Business-to-Business Database
Name	Name of company, Name and title of contact
Address/postal code	Address/postal code
Telephone number	Telephone number
E-mail, social media coordinates	E-mail, social media coordinates
Age	Credit history
Gender	Industrial classification
Marital status	Size of business
Family	Revenues
Education	Number of employees
Income	Time in business
Occupation	Source of order/inquiry or referral
Transaction history	Purchase history
Promotion history	Promotion history
Inquiry history	Inquiry history
Unique identifier	Unique identifier

cross-sell by offering new products or related products to customers who have bought in another product category.

Similarly, direct marketing also helps achieve repeat purchasing objectives. Once an initial purchase occurs, the customer's name and other information may be entered into the database. These people are proven users who offer high potential for repurchase. Magazines, for example, routinely send out renewal letters and/or call subscribers before the expiration date. Companies like lawn care services and car dealers build a base of customers and contact them when they are "due" to repurchase. These activities are examples where the timing of repeat purchasing are important, as identified in Chapter 5. Costco mails promotions to members regularly to encourage return visits (Exhibit 16-2), which likely improves the frequency objective identified in Chapter 5.

Another aspect of repeat purchasing occurs through customer relationship management (CRM), where marketers develop and maintain a significant amount of information about their clients. The aim is to establish and maintain a relationship with customers through personalized communication and customized product/service offerings. CRM relies on software technology and an extensive database specifically designed to implement the management of customer relationships. For example, Exhibit 16-3 shows brands that have a loyalty program, a key part of CRM since it provides an incentive for repeat purchase.

Timely communication and appropriate promotional offers that fit with the customer's past purchase behaviour are the hallmark of CRM, of which a database and direct-response media are imperative. The Canadian division for American Express promotes the credit card to its

Exhibit 16-2 Costco mails promotional offers to its members.

members as a tool for enhanced service with its "Front of the Line" program. It expanded the offering with faster security clearance and taxi service in a sponsorship arrangement with the Toronto Airport. As part of the package, AMEX sponsored free Wi-Fi and entertainment to all waiting passengers.[3]

Despite this promise, research suggests that up to two-thirds of all organizations did not experience the full benefit of CRM initiatives. Collectively, they spent about $220 billion from 2000 to 2005 and achieved a return of only $50 billion in the intervening years to date. Criticism focused on the fact that even though companies bought leading-edge call centres, databases, software, hardware, and Internet sites, they did not appropriately adjust how they operated or trained personnel to build these relationships. The researchers suggested that business moved too quickly to expand the program rather than exerting patience and learning with a smaller base of customers prior to full implementation.[4]

Numerous companies have established comprehensive databases on existing and potential customers both in North America and internationally. Database marketing has become so ubiquitous that people are concerned about invasion of privacy. Direct marketers are concerned as well. The Canadian Marketing Association (CMA) and the Canadian Advertising Foundation (CAF) have asked members to adhere to ethical rules of conduct in their marketing efforts. They point out that if the industry does not police itself, the government will do it.

Exhibit 16-3 The databases for these brands help facilitate CRM.

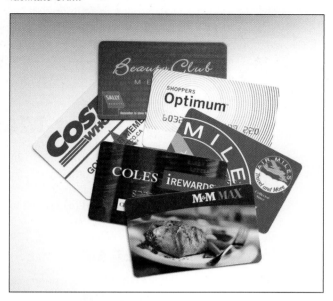

Sources of Database Information

There are numerous sources of information for direct-marketing databases:

- *Statistics Canada.* Census data provide information on almost every household in Canada. Data include household size, demographics, income, and other information.
- *Canada Post.* Postal codes provide information on both household and business locations.
- *List services.* Many providers of lists are available. The accuracy and timeliness of the lists vary.
- *Info Canada.* Provincial business directory provides information regarding business lists. Direct Mail List Rates and Data contains thousands of list selections, published by province.
- *Marketing research houses.* Large research houses conduct annual studies of customers who buy at home via mail or telephone. They compile information on total orders placed, types of products purchased, demographics, and purchase satisfaction, among others.
- *Loyalty programs.* Continuity programs designed to enhance loyalty are a new source of consumers with precise purchase patterns.
- *Others.* The Canadian Marketing Association, Dunn and Bradstreet, Fortune 500, *The Book of Lists,* and other published periodicals of this nature all contain listed information that can be used for these purposes.

Consumer-goods manufacturers, banks, credit bureaus, retailers, charitable organizations, and other business operations also sell lists and other selected information. Companies can build their own databases through completed warranty cards, surveys, and so on.

Determining the Effectiveness of the Database

While companies maintain a database, many do not use them effectively. Collecting names and information is not enough; the list must be kept current, purged of old and/or inactive customers, and updated frequently. The more information about customers that can be contained in the database, the more effective it will be. An **RFM scoring method** is often used for this purpose. RFM stands for the recency, frequency, and monetary transactions between the company and the customer. More specifically, data need to be entered each time there is a transaction so that the company can track how recently purchases have been made, how often they are made, and what amounts of money are being spent. In addition, tracking which products and/or services are used increases the ability for databases to conduct the activities previously mentioned in this section. By analyzing the database on a regular basis, the company or organization can identify trends and buying patterns that will help it establish a better relationship with its customers by more effectively meeting their needs.

(L02) Direct-Marketing Plan

To successfully implement direct-marketing programs, companies must make a number of decisions. As in other marketing programs, they must determine (1) whom to target by using a database; (2) what the program's objectives will be; (3) what direct-response media strategy will be employed; and (4) how to measure direct-marketing effectiveness.

TARGET AUDIENCES FOR DIRECT MARKETING

As the database description suggested, direct marketing is especially useful to target current customers. Well-managed firms have extensive records of their customers in terms of their purchases and other relevant characteristics, allowing for much more meaningful communication as it can be personalized and customized. Alternatively, the database section identified other sources to compile a database of non-customers. Businesses are often expanding geographically or along another dimension (e.g., demographic, socio-economic) where an accurate database and direct marketing could generate trial among prospects. As the earlier Knorr example showed, other segmentation variables are used to accurately profile the target audience for the marketing communication.

Targeting with direct marketing to other known individuals is a key strength of this IMC tool. The agency Target Marketing and Communications won Best in Show honours and Direct Mail Gold with its execution for its client the Canadian Sea Turtle Network (CSTN) at the ICE Awards. The agency arranged to have an issue of *National Geographic* dedicated to CSTN's efforts to save the leatherback turtles, which included a handwritten note from the executive director of the CSTN and was wrapped in an actual fish net. The recipients, journalists, and bloggers with environmental and conservation background, who had the most potential to be key influencers, had to physically cut the net to read the magazine and card. Commenting on the creative, Target's president said, "We wanted to differentiate it from everything else that landed in their 'in' tray. It's differentiated in every way, not only their shape, size and weight, but they actually have to free the magazine, which is relevant with what CSTN is working to do."[5]

Thus far we have discussed direct marketing and the use of databases with the idea that the identity of the receiver is known. While this is true, direct marketing is also used with broader media (i.e., television) and with media that allow for delivery without identity (i.e., unaddressed direct mail). In these situations, databases are (or should be) used to identify the most relevant profile variables to ensure the highest response rate possible. A planner can use census data and postal codes to select attractive regions within a vicinity for unaddressed direct mail. For example, Nubody's Fitness targeted its unaddressed monthly mail drop of 190,000 pieces with key demographic variables, leading to stronger retail visits and phone enquiries.[6] In rare situations, an addressed direct mail piece is sent to "resident" since the company's database indicates the household is not a customer. For example, Rogers mails promotional pieces such as the one in Exhibit 16-4 to exact addresses where its database indicates no current customer.

A third idea for targeting occurs through profiling current customers and using the information to select prospective customers from an alternative database. Working with Canada Post, the Canadian Cancer Society followed this approach with an experiment. They identified four different groups: (1) profiled postal code and receive mail, (2) profiled postal code and receive no mail, (3) non-profiled postal code and receive mail, and (4) non-profiled postal code and receive no mail. The results found a 13.5 percent higher response rate for profiled segments, with net revenue being 19.2 percent higher.[7]

DIRECT-MARKETING OBJECTIVES

The direct marketer seeks an immediate behavioural response. As such, the behavioural objectives identified in Chapter 5 become much more salient in direct marketing. Direct marketers can attempt to achieve brand trial, re-trial, switching, or category trial objectives. A databases of consumers' past purchase history information helps identify those who have not previously purchased the brand. For databases containing current customer purchase history, the direct marketer can attempt to influence the rate, amount, or timing of purchases. Oftentimes, direct marketing attempts to bring consumers along in their decision-making process. Thus, purchase-related behaviour can be an objective through retail visits that manifest in ways such as test driving cars or trying on shoes and clothes, requests for service such as obtaining free estimates, or experiencing other marketing communication. Repeat consumption is also an objective with current customers. For example, financial-service firms can use direct marketing to encourage additional visits by customers for yearly financial planning advice. Exhibit 16-5 shows an ad for a car inviting customers to take a test drive at an exclusive club.

A behavioural response is not the only objective for direct marketing. All communication objectives and how the message and offers influence attitudes is still very relevant for direct marketing. As we noted in Chapter 5, brand objectives (i.e., awareness, attitude) are considerations for all pieces of marketing communication. In fact, direct marketers are very innovative, with clever creative approaches to attract attention and encourage processing the message so that a communication effect occurs even if the receiver declines the call to action. A typical objective of perhaps a 2 to 3 percent response rate suggests that communication objectives are as valuable here as in other marketing communication tools, since more than 90 percent are viewing the direct marketing in the same light.

DIRECT-RESPONSE MEDIA

Direct-response media include media like direct mail, catalogue, broadcast, and telemarketing. To help achieve the previously identified objectives, these media generally follow a couple of approaches. In the **one-step approach**, the medium is used directly to obtain an order. For example, TV commercials for products such as workout equipment urge viewers to phone a toll-free number to place an order immediately. The **two-step approach** involves the use of more than one medium. The first effort is designed to screen, or qualify, potential buyers. The second effort generates the response. For example, business marketing companies use telemarketing to screen on the basis of interest, then follow up to interested parties with more information designed to achieve an order or use personal selling to close the sale.

Direct Mail Direct mail is a significant medium; combined with catalogue distribution, advertising revenue hit $1.25 billion in 2012, down from a peak of $1.6 billion in 2006 and 2007. This amount is equivalent to the amount spent on radio, and the combined amount spent on specialty television or Internet search advertising, or local radio. The material shown in

Exhibit 16-4   Rogers uses direct mail to entice switching.

Exhibit 16-5   Acura invites new customers to take a test drive.

Exhibit 16-6   Maserati used direct mail to introduce its new automobiles.

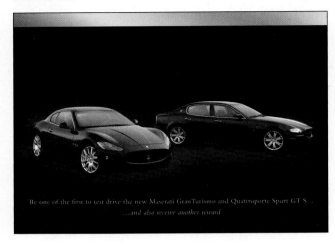

Be one of the first to test drive the new Maserati GranTurismo and Quattroporte Sport GT S...
...and also receive another reward

Exhibit 16-6 is just one piece that was sent by Maserati to market its new Gran Turismo and Quattroporte Sport GT S automobiles, which indicates that high-end brands see considerable value in this direct-response medium.

Canada Post has a strong interest in developing the market for direct mail and provides extensive research and service to facilitate this goal, especially for small businesses concerned with reaching their customers and prospects with a low-cost option. Canada Post research statistics show that 66 percent of Canadians read addressed direct mail right away when it arrives. Another 27 percent of Canadians keep it to review later at a time more convenient to them. Attitudinally, 72 percent of Canadians look forward to seeing what is in their mailbox, and 63 percent claim receiving mail is a real pleasure. Consumers are quite favourable to reading mail if they are a customer of the sender, it is a promotional offer, or they have seen previous ads. Currently, Canadians prefer mail over e-mail from businesses marketing their products by a four to one ratio.[8]

Creativity is possible with direct mail as Grey Advertising won a Gold Lion at the 2010 Cannes Awards with its innovative execution for its client, GGRP, a premier sound design house located in Vancouver. GGRP needed a message to rejuvenate its image for creativity in sound to existing and new North American clients who truly appreciated the audio art the company could produce. The idea picked up on the love audiophiles have for vinyl, an expressive medium for sound that has resurged in popularity. The direct-mail piece featured a cardboard record player that also acted as the envelope along with a vinyl 45. Users spun the record with a pencil and the cardboard naturally amplified the vibrations going through the needle. A response rate of almost 100 percent resulted, as all recipients either talked about it or wanted more copies. It also became an Internet hit, with hundreds of blog reports, extensive YouTube hits on the video showing how to set up the record player, and 70,000 hits to the GGRP website.[9]

Direct mail works well as the first step in the two-step approach for message delivery. Tourism Yukon's direct-mail initiative obtained a 20 percent response rate for website visits versus 5 percent for its online ads presenting the same message. Bear Mountain Resort delivered brochures to two selective markets that encouraged online registration to view their new condominiums and garnered a 37 percent response versus a 14 percent response for past newspaper ads.[10]

Keys to the success of direct mail are the **mailing list**, comprising the database from which names are generated, and the ability to segment markets on the basis of geography, demographics, and lifestyles. Lists have become more current and selective, thereby eliminating waste coverage and increasing effectiveness. The importance of the list itself has led to a standalone business as companies profit from selling the names of purchasers of their products and/or services to list firms. Canadian mailing lists sorted by association or type of vocation are available, and Canadian companies such as www.interactdirect.com, based in London, Ontario, are becoming more common.

Catalogues   Certain companies rely solely on catalogue sales. For example, Yves Rocher is a firm that markets botanical beauty care products for women. It expanded into Canada with its small catalogues and sells directly to consumers. Lee Valley Tools of Ottawa began as a mail-order catalogue company years ago, but has branched out to retail stores across the country and online sales. Exhibit 16-7 is an example of a catalogue where the brand eventually moved to physical retail locations.

Exhibit 16-7   RoadRunner offers both catalogue and in-store sales.

Companies also use catalogues in conjunction with their more traditional sales and promotional strategies. For example, companies such as Canadian Tire and Sears sell directly through catalogues but also use them to inform consumers of product offerings available in the stores. Canadian Tire revamped its catalogue and presented it online with a much different look than its Internet site. Entitled "The Canadian Way," the virtual presentation featured four sections—living, fixing, playing, and driving—with customized options. Executives saw it directed toward families with young children with its colour photos and demonstration-like presentation.[11]

IKEA prints 6 million catalogues per year; its executives view the catalogue as the company's "main marketing tool" since it naturally encourages consumers to visit a retail outlet or the Internet site. But, more importantly, the catalogue is a strong brand-building tool to demonstrate how IKEA's products can improve the homes of millions of consumers. IKEA also developed a mobile app to allow consumers to interact with the catalogue by looking behind closed doors or altering decorative items.[12]

E-Mail   Direct mail on the Internet is essentially an electronic version of regular mail. Like regular mail, it is highly targeted, relies heavily on lists, and attempts to reach consumers with specific needs through targeted messages. Consumers can opt to have specific types of e-mail sent to them and other types not sent. Consumers also receive unwanted e-mails, referred to as spam. However, legitimate and enlightened marketers accept the practice of permission-based marketing as described above. Figure 16-3 summarizes the different types of advertising and promotion messages that Canadian consumers are most interested in receiving via e-mail.

Consumers also subscribe to publications and receive them via e-mail. A detailed and sophisticated database is developed from consumers agreeing to opt in since they provide segmentation-like information. Two successful sites (thrilllist.com, urbandaddy.com) send out publications to men that are consistent with the regular content not sent digitally. Each publication has a growing e-mail list and sends customized content that is quite distinct from one another with unique positioning approaches.[13]

Research investigated two of the behavioural responses to receiving e-mail: visiting the brand's website, and forwarding the e-mail to a friend. In a study for cosmetic and body care products sold in retail stores, more useful permission-based e-mail messages yielded fewer website visits, presumably because the information satisfied consumer requirements. However, more useful, more interesting, and more frequent e-mail messages resulted in more store visits, presumably to examine or buy the product. Consumers perceived useful e-mails as offering sales promotion information, or information about new products.[14]

Another study found pass-along rates for different types of e-mail: humour (88 percent), news (56 percent), health care and health information (32 percent), finance (24 percent), and sports (24 percent). Overall, 89 percent of the U.S. sample shared content with others via e-mail, with 63 percent sharing content at least once a week, and a whopping 75 percent forwarding content to as many as six others. However, 75 percent contend branded content makes no impact on whether they forward a message. Heather Clark, associate director of creative strategy at Henderson Bas in Toronto, who has worked on campaigns for ING Direct and Levi's, cautions there is potential for dismal failure as the chance of a commercial message being passed along using e-mail is extremely low. Apart from humour, one tactic that will help is incentives, such as

	2004	2010
Entertainment	48%	40%
E-Commerce/Retail	30%	28%
Travel	26%	28%
Health/Fitness	29%	27%
News/Information	36%	27%
Finance/Banking	20%	27%

Source: Ipsos-Reid, 2004 E-mail Marketing Study, 2010 Inter@ctiv Reid Report

Figure   16-3

Registering to receive e-mail/ types of sites registered

an extra entry in a sweepstakes contest. A third factor is recognizing the consumer is in charge with an optional "send to a friend" feature and a chance for recipients to personalize the message before they forward it.[15]

In another sample of 1,259 forwarded e-mails from 34 participants, a study found extraordinary dispersion in the number forwarded during the one-month time frame. One person forwarded 177 messages and two others forwarded more than 100, while three people sent one each. Overall, participants forwarded about 40 percent of the e-mails received, which ranged from 0 percent to 100 percent. The implication of finding a "lead sender" for an e-mail forwarding campaign appears critical for success, much like a lead user in a diffusion of innovation. Additional qualitative research in the study finds that participants experienced substantial positive and negative emotional responses when receiving forwarded e-mail.[16]

It is important to note that the pass-along of e-mail is an outcome and not a strategy.[17] It is a manifestation of the cognitive and emotional responses of the receiver to the message. The similarity to a TV ad would be to recall the ad and tell someone about it, or to call out to a family member ("Hey Dad, come check out this ad on TV"). Secondly, e-mail can experience extensive pass-along yet have minimal benefit for the brand since it entails a single exposure of a brand message for many of the receivers, who simply delete it after viewing.[18]

Broadcast Media   Two broadcast media are available to direct marketers: television and radio. While radio was used quite extensively in the 1950s, its use and effectiveness have dwindled substantially. Thus, the majority of direct-marketing broadcast advertising now occurs on TV. Direct-response TV encompasses direct-response TV spots, infomercials, and home shopping shows (teleshopping).

TV Spots   Referred to in the direct-marketing industry as *short-term programs,* these spots include direct-response commercials for products such as health and beauty, fitness, and household goods. In **direct-response advertising**, the product or service is offered and a sales response is solicited through either the one- or two-step approach. Toll-free phone numbers are included so that the receiver can immediately call to order and companies run direct-response television commercials to encourage website visits.

Infomercials   An **infomercial** is a long commercial that ranges from 3 to 60 minutes. Infomercials are usually produced by the advertisers and are designed to be viewed as regular TV shows. Relatively speaking, infomercials in Canada are less significant in terms of expenditures, with only $15 million in revenue for 2012, a decline of $7 million since peaking in 2006 and 2007.[19] The video capabilities of the Internet may diminish this further in future. Despite this, infomercials are popular with small firms and have been adopted by both mainstream marketers and niche marketers like Bentley (Exhibit 16-8). One study compared the communication effects of a one-minute ad, 15-minute infomercial, 30-minute infomercial, and direct experience (i.e., interacting with the product). The authors concluded that infomercials provided results more closely related to direct experience than a one-minute ad, presumably because both messages allow for extensive cognitive and emotional process during a longer duration.[20]

Thane Direct, with world headquarters located in Toronto, operates in over a dozen countries and controls 250,000 half-hour time slots and 500,000 short-time-frame slots globally, demonstrating strong commitment to direct TV ads and infomercials. Specific targeting at a low cost is possible with more TV options via specialty channels. And despite Internet growth where consumers are actively searching, advertising responses when consumers are passively watching TV is still a fruitful channel according to Thane's CEO: "The message has to be clear, concise, it has to solve a real problem which the consumer is experiencing.

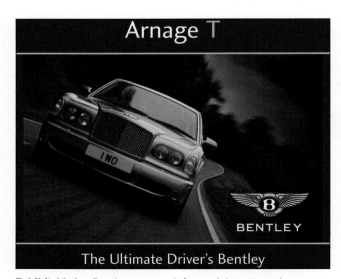

Exhibit 16-8   Bentley uses an infomercial to attract buyers.

It has to provide the consumer with instant gratification, be a good price point, provide value, and be demonstrable."[21]

Home Shopping   The Shopping Channel (TSC) is Canada's broadcast retailer available on all delivery formats (cable, satellite) across the country. It claims a reach of 6.5 million households, viewership of 1.5 million Canadians each week, and a 70:30 female–male ratio. TSC recruits its audience like other channels, via direct mail and e-mail, broadcast ads, print ads, paid Internet search, and social media. The lines of communication get blurred a little as TSC is available in catalogue form and on the Internet.[22]

Telemarketing   Communication resulting in sales via the telephone is known as **telemarketing**. There are two types of telemarketing. *Outbound telemarketing* refers to calls made by a company or its sponsor to a potential buyer or client, soliciting the sale of products, services, donations, votes, or any other "value" issue. *Inbound telemarketing* occurs when a company has advertised its toll-free number or its website address, for example asking the customer to call the number, visit the store, or log on to the website. Both for-profit and charitable organizations have employed this medium effectively in one- and two-step approaches.

Problems associated with telemarketing include its potential for fraud and deception and its potential for annoyance. However, data on call centres in Canada show that most call centres are well managed. The majority communicate clearly if the interaction is recorded, follow the laws governing telemarketing, and work with their employees to ensure appropriate interactions.[23] Those in the telemarketing and telemedia industry have responded to public criticisms. As more large companies use telemedia, its tarnished image will likely brighten up.

DIRECT-MARKETING EFFECTIVENESS

For direct-marketing programs that do not have an objective of generating an immediate behavioural response, traditional measures of advertising effectiveness can be applied. In those situations requiring a direct response, measuring the effectiveness should include specific behavioural measures in addition to the communication measures. Using the cost per order (CPO), advertisers can evaluate the relative effectiveness of an ad in only a few minutes based on the number of calls generated. By running the same ad on different stations, a direct marketer can determine the relative effectiveness of the medium itself. For example, if the advertiser targets a $5 return per order and a broadcast commercial (production and print) costs $2,500, the ad is considered effective if it generates 500 orders. Similar measures have been developed for print and direct mail ads.

 LOYALTY PROGRAMS

One significant direct-marketing program is a *loyalty program*. Loyalty programs are common in many product categories, particularly travel and hospitality, as well as retailers. Virtually every airline, car rental company, and hotel chain features a loyalty program. They are also used by a variety of retailers, including grocery stores, department stores, home centres, and bookstores. A number of other names are used, such as *rewards program, frequency program,* and *continuity program*; however, a literature review concludes that the term loyalty program is the most useful.[24]

Marketers view these programs as a way of encouraging consumers to use their products or services on a continual basis and as a way of developing strong customer loyalty. Companies realize the importance of customer retention and understand that the key to retaining and growing market share is building relationships with loyal customers. Loyalty programs provide marketers with the opportunity to develop databases containing valuable information on their customers that can be used to better understand their needs, interests, and characteristics as well as to identify and track a company's most valuable customers. One study of a convenience store loyalty program found that the program increased the dollar amount of goods purchased by light and

Exhibit 16-9   The WD-40 FanClub is a popular customer loyalty program.

medium volume purchasers. Heavy volume consumers did not alter their purchase patterns.[25]

These databases can also be used to target specific programs and offers to customers to increase the amount they purchase and/or to build stronger relationships with them. Careful management of databases is necessary to identify and track valuable customers and their purchase history and to make strategic use of targeted loyalty rewards. For example, the WD-40 FanClub is a loyalty program for the brand that provides members with product information, usage tips, newsletters, game downloads, and other benefits (Exhibit 16-9).

As the above example suggests, loyalty programs have significant characteristics that distinguish them from sales promotions. Furthermore, brands often compete on loyalty program characteristics since they could be a significant factor in consumer decision making. Figure 16-4 shows five characteristics of loyalty programs based on a substantial review of the topic.[26]

It is suggested that loyalty programs influence consumers in three ways. The *points-pressure mechanism* occurs when consumers earn points and then realize they are close to achieving a reward level and make additional purchases to achieve it. The *rewarded-behaviour mechanism* occurs after reward redemption as this process contributes to positive attitudinal and behavioural responses. The *personalized marketing mechanism* occurs with the use of the database marketing activities. The design of the loyalty programs affects each of these mechanisms. Design includes the structure in terms of the time frame and whether the reward is based on frequency or tiered customer groups. Another characteristic is whether the program is a single brand or partnerships. A third design consideration is whether the rewards are monetary vs. non-monetary, or brand vs. non–brand related. Finally, the reward could be immediate or delayed.[27]

The popular Air Miles loyalty program offers an example of these design decisions. Air Miles is a partnership approach where shoppers collect points while buying goods and services at retail locations or online, among others like using a credit card. Air Miles offers tiered customer groups with its gold level for those who collect a certain number of points from a minimum number of brands. Air Miles originally offered non-monetary rewards when consumers redeemed points for goods and services, including air travel. For many items, it would require a time delay to collect points and redeem them. Air Miles currently offers consumers the option of using points collected as cash when making purchases at a point of sale. While a minimal delay is incurred, it is substantially less so since the minimum $10 purchase can be made with 95 points, a level someone could accumulate in a month.[28]

Air Miles also retains the characteristics of a loyalty program. It is a major strategic initiative for its participating brands. For example, Shell Canada offers Air Miles and regularly promotes additional offers to encourage repeat visits. Shell recently sent a direct-mail piece that contained a card designed to be kept in one's wallet to receive a bonus when buying Shell gas. Air Miles

Figure   16-4

Characteristics of loyalty programs

Characteristic	Customer Effect
Strategic with goals	Maintains strong brand attitude
	Encourages purchase frequency, purchase amount, purchasing timing
Structured	Customer formally enrolls as a member
Long-term	Customer participates continually over time
Rewarding	Purchases recognized via goods/services, preferential treatment, or financial gain
Ongoing	Receives regular communication and offers

Source: Tammo Bijmolt, Matilda Dorotic, and Peter Verhoef, "Loyalty Programs: Generalizations on Their Adoption, Effectiveness and Design," *Foundations and Trends in Marketing, 5*(4), 2010, pp. 197–258.

is clearly structured as members enroll, receive a card, and track points totals on their online account. The accumulation of points takes time, and monetary and non-monetary rewards are a strong incentive. Consumers regularly receive direct mail and e-mail notifications of offers to accumulate additional points.

Retailers use points systems in Canada with brand names like Hudson's Bay Rewards and PC Points, while others are attempting to innovate. The Gap tested a new loyalty program in Vancouver with the idea of launching it globally if successful. Called Sprize, it allows consumers to buy an item at full price and receive an automatic credit on future purchases if the item goes on sale within 45 days. Communication of the program used the theme "Shopping turned on its head." Stores literally turned signage upside down, and radio also supported the announcement.[29]

Other retailers that began or augmented their loyalty programs include Sobeys and Canadian Tire. Club Sobeys passed the one-million-member mark in the first six weeks of its points program, which allows redemption for in-store savings, food rewards, and Aeroplan miles. Canadian Tire "money" is obtained by consumers for cash purchases that can be used for future purchases—about $100 million is distributed annually (Exhibit 16-10). Speculation abounds that the program may be discontinued; however, the chain offered a $1 coin instead of its normal paper currency for a two-day December promotion to invigorate the offer and drive traffic for holiday purchases.[30] Canadian Tire tested a new loyalty program similar to others where consumers collect points to be redeemed for merchandise with a tie-in to a credit card for enhanced collection and the option to donate points to a worthy cause.[31] IMC Perspective 16-1 highlights the characteristics of other popular loyalty programs in Canada.

Exhibit 16-10 Canadian Tire money represents an iconic loyalty incentive.

Communication with existing members and providing promotional offers is a value-enhancing approach to foster greater use of the loyalty program and greater purchases. Shoppers Drug Mart continues to use e-mail, and lately personalizes the e-mail message even more—with considerable success, as these types of messages enjoyed an opening rate 10 percent higher than non-personalized messages and stronger purchase levels.[32]

While loyalty programs worked with direct mail and e-mail to administer and communicate with members, more are moving toward social media, mobile, and Internet site interactions to permit timely or customized offers.[33] Much of the improvements are designed to provide an experience that is similar to buying and consuming the brand. For example, members of the Jack Astor's loyalty program can design a unique identity on Facebook and receive SMS messages and promotions.[34]

Industry experts consider the possibility that these channels might permit brands to bring their loyalty programs "in-house," away from plans like Air Miles or Aeroplan, while others envision much more personalized and customized offerings, or perhaps profile sites where consumers share their profile to select brands rather than signing up for multiple loyalty cards.[35] In turn, Air Miles is testing an enhancement of its offerings through a mobile app allowing members to visit a participating retailer's site and promotional incentives with more frequent visits. Shoppers Drug Mart instituted a game to create a friendly online experience associated with the program.[36]

🗨 Evaluation of Direct Marketing

We presented strengths and limitations of direct marketing thus far, but summarize these factors in a concluding section as we have done in previous chapters. Given that direct marketing employs different media, each with its own characteristics, these conclusions are generalizations in which variation can be expected.

IMC PERSPECTIVE 16-1

Popular Loyalty Programs Innovate

With consumers participating in so many loyalty programs, questions arise about which characteristics work for each program. Scene, the joint Scotiabank and Cineplex effort, is popular with moviegoers. Best Buy's Reward Zone is useful for those buying electronics and other related items. My Starbucks Rewards provides coffee lovers with even more opportunities to enjoy the brand. And Aeroplan, one of the original loyalty programs in Canada, continues to innovate with its extensive offerings.

The Scene card allows 3.3 million members to collect reward points by attending movies, using products associated with Scotiabank (e.g., a Scene debit or credit card), buying goods at the concession stand, and ordering tickets in certain ways (e.g., online). Consumers also receive discounts and special promotion offers and contests, and can spend their rewards on free tickets or on restaurants, music, or magazines. The Scene loyalty program was augmented to result in more points if members formed online groups and attended movies together. It also offered a mobile app and SMS alerts for keeping in touch and offering improved services. Many of the improvements to the program are the result of the annual survey Scene does with its members.

Best Buy's Reward Zone offers monetary reward certificates for qualifying purchases that work out to approximately a one percent rebate. To enhance the program, Best Buy used e-mail where consumers could participate in a contest when they followed a link. Click-through rates hit about 20 percent as Best Buy customized the message for different demographics. Improvements to the program included gifts like show tickets, free movie rentals, and private shopping events for program members only.

My Starbucks Rewards gives "stars" to customers with their purchases and offers food and drink products along three collection levels. At the Welcome level consumers get a drink for their birthday; at the Green level consumers can get a free refill with five stars; and at the Gold level consumers receive free food or drink once they hit 30 stars within

a year and obtain status with a gold card. Many tweeted a positive response to the gold card as recognition for their high volume of purchases. A new smartphone app allows consumers to track their stars in a fun way consistent with the brand image. Members can interact with one another for ideas on improving the Starbucks experience.

Aeroplan arrived on the scene in 1984 as an Air Canada promotion for business travellers, and after 20 years it became its own entity. With its 4.5 million members, it is one of the biggest and most established programs—branching out from earning and spending points on travel to a whole host of sponsoring organizations in which members can collect and redeem rewards. However, for the most part, it still retains its travel orientation, and this brand position is one that its current managers continue to support. Considerable communication and promotion occurred over the past few years with sponsorship of the Juno Awards and the Art Gallery of Ontario, and promotional activities with key media partners like *The Walrus*. It also allows members to pool rewards into designated accounts for worthy causes and international activities like Veterinarians Without Borders, and offered chartered airline flights for members to head south during spring break. All told, Aeroplan gives out about two million rewards per year, with 65 percent for travel.

Sources: Alicia Androich, "The Loyalty Treatment," *Marketing Magazine,* December 3, 2012, pp. 33–39; Melinda Mattos, "Aeroplan's Passion Play," *Strategy,* May 1, 2011 p. 15; Alicia Androich, "Scene, Gamifies, Gets Mobile to Keep Movie Buffs Loyal," *Marketing Magazine,* December 22, 2011.

Questions:

1. What are the similarities and differences among these loyalty programs?
2. Could any of them be adapted given what occurs with the others?

STRENGTHS OF DIRECT MARKETING

Target Audience Selectivity   Marketers can purchase lists of recent product purchasers (e.g., car buyers), and these lists may allow segmentation on the basis of geographic area, occupation, demographics, and job title. Combining this information with the geocoding capabilities of PRIZM C2 (discussed in Chapter 3), marketers can develop effective segmentation strategies.

Target Audience Coverage   Direct marketing lets the advertiser reach a high percentage of the selective target audience and reduces or eliminates waste coverage. Since the database allows precise target audience profiles, the direct-response medium selected can achieve a strong level of hits. For example, while not everyone drives on highways where there are billboards or pays attention to TV commercials, virtually everyone receives mail. A good list allows for minimal waste, as only those consumers with the highest potential are targeted. For example, a political candidate can direct a message at a very select group of people (those living in a certain postal code, or members of McGill University Alumni, or the Royal Vancouver Yacht Club, say); in the same vein, a music club can target recent purchasers of MP3 players, or a medical software supplier can target all cardiac surgeons in a medical association directory.

Frequency   Depending on the medium used, it may be possible to build frequency levels. The program vehicles used for direct-response TV advertising are usually the most inexpensive available, so the marketer can afford to purchase repeat times. Frequency may not be so easily accomplished through the mail, since consumers may be annoyed to receive the same mail repeatedly.

Creativity for Cognitive and Emotional Responses   Direct marketing can take on a variety of creative forms. For example, the Discovery Network sent 17-inch TV sets to media buyers through the mail. The only message accompanying the TV sets was one on the cord that said "Plug me in" and another on a videotape that read "Play me." Upon doing so, the recipient was greeted with a 7-minute promotional video. Direct-mail pieces also allow for detailed copy that provides a great deal of information. The targeted mailing of CDs or DVDs containing product information has increased dramatically, as companies have found this a very effective way to provide potential buyers with product information.

Scheduling Flexibility   While some media require long-range planning and have long closing dates, direct-response advertising can be much more timely. Direct mail, for example, can be put together very quickly and distributed to the target population. TV programs typically used for direct-response advertising are older, less sought programs that are likely to appear on the station's list of available spots. Another common strategy is to purchase available time at the last possible moment to get the best price.

Personalization   No other advertising medium can personalize the message as well as direct media. Parents with children at different age levels can be approached, with their child's name included in the appeal. Car owners are mailed letters congratulating them on their new purchase and offering accessories. Computer purchasers are sent software solicitations. Graduating college and university students receive very personalized information that recognizes their specific needs and offers solutions (such as credit cards). With the ability of direct marketing to personalize and customize its messages through a relevant direct-response medium, we suggest that a considerable amount is fairly strong for attention and involvement of the message.

Costs   While the CPM for direct mail may be very high on an absolute and a relative basis, its ability to specifically target the audience and eliminate waste coverage reduces the actual CPM. The ads used on TV are often among the lowest-priced available, and a video can be delivered for less than $1 (including postage). A second factor contributing to the cost-effectiveness of direct-response advertising is the cost per customer purchasing. Because of the low cost of media, each sale generated is very inexpensive.

LIMITATIONS OF DIRECT MARKETING

Media Image   Generally, people believe unsolicited mail promotes undesired products, and others dislike being solicited. Likewise, direct-response ads on TV are often low-budget ads for lower-priced products, which contributes to the image that something less than the best products are marketed in this way. Some of this image is being overcome by the home shopping channels, which promote very expensive products. Telemarketing is found to be irritating to consumers, as is spam e-mail.

Target Audience Coverage   One of the advantages cited for direct mail was targeting potential customers specifically. But the effectiveness of these methods depends on the accuracy of the lists used. People move, change occupations, and so on, and if the lists are not kept current, selectivity will decrease. Computerization has greatly improved the currency of lists and reduced the incidence of bad names; however, the ability to generate lists is becoming a problem.

Control for Selective Exposure   While target audience selectivity attempts to address this factor, consumers exert tremendous control with respect to direct marketing. It is easy to simply toss a direct-mail piece in one's paper recycling bin. As seen in the discussion for television, consumers can readily zip or zap a direct message, and consumers usually have to actively seek and select an infomercial.

Reach   The selectivity of direct marketing and the cost associated with it suggest that achieving high levels of reach are neither feasible nor even a realistic characteristic of the purpose of this marketing approach.

L05 IMC Planning: Strategic Use of Direct Marketing

Direct marketing is now an important component in the integrated marketing programs of organizations. In some cases it is used as a tool for an immediate response and in other cases it plays a key role in building the brand by moving through the target audience's decision-making process. In addition, direct-marketing activities support and are supported by other elements of the promotional mix.

DECISION-MAKING PROCESS

As described in this chapter, direct-marketing tools are typically employed to persuade immediate consumer action. At this point, it is critical that the promotional manager plan for a specific action in order to select the most appropriate direct-response media. In Chapter 5 we reviewed different types of behavioural objectives for promotional communication, which we will use to develop IMC planning prescriptions. Trial and repeat purchasing objectives suggest that much of direct marketing involves influence at the purchase decision stage.

Trial objectives require a broader-based direct-response medium, much like what is seen in advertising media decisions. Typically, wide-ranging direct-mail pieces targeted by census track and income dispersions allow firms to reach as many potential consumers as possible. In this situation, the database used relies on more public sources, and a manager may use unaddressed drop-offs. Alternatively, for more targeted messages, brands may rely upon the list services and provide addressed mailings. Alternatively, with a database of existing customers, cross-selling of other products is now a trial purchase for the promotional planner's brand in a new product category. This trial purchase may be relatively new and be viewed as a purchase within the product category, thus requiring a direct-response medium providing considerable information.

We mentioned that existing customer databases are used for repeat purchases. Repeat purchasing objectives involve the timing, amount, and rate of consumer purchases. These different options suggest other criteria for evaluating the different direct-media options. For example, repeat purchasing objectives for specific timing might suggest telemarketing if the managers have current databases and permission to call upon its current customers. A favourite direct-response medium is bill inserts delivered monthly to enhance frequency and thus improve the amount and rate of purchase. Thus, the opportunity of promotional planners to match the specific objectives with the right direct-response medium requires full consideration.

Purchase-related behaviour objectives frequently involve influencing consumers at earlier stages in their decision making. For example, direct-mail pieces may be delivered to encourage need recognition and prompt the target audience to make a sales inquiry at the retail location or over the telephone, or to visit the Internet site for further understanding of the brand during the information search stage. Alternatively, telephone calls can be made to follow up after the sales inquiry to ensure that the brand is seriously considered at the alternative evaluation stage.

DIRECT MARKETING AND IMC TOOLS

Obviously, direct marketing is in itself a form of advertising. Whether through mail, print, or TV, the direct-response offer is an ad. It usually contains a contact number, a form that requests mailing information, or a link to an Internet site. Sometimes the ad supports the direct-selling effort. Direct-response ads or infomercials are also referred to in retail outlet displays.

Public relations activities often employ direct-response techniques. Private companies may use telemarketing activities to solicit funds for charities or co-sponsor charities that use these and other direct-response techniques to solicit funds. Likewise, corporations and/or organizations engaging in public relations activities may include contact numbers or Internet addresses in their ads or promotional materials.

Telemarketing and direct selling are two methods of personal selling. Non-profit organizations such as charities often use telemarketing to solicit funds. For-profit companies are also using telemarketing with much greater frequency to screen and qualify prospects (which reduces selling costs) and to generate leads. Direct-mail pieces are often used to invite prospective customers to visit auto showrooms to test-drive new cars; the salesperson then assumes responsibility for the selling effort.

Direct mail is often used to notify consumers of sales promotions like sales events or contests. Ski shops regularly mail announcements of special end-of-season sales. Whistler Ski Resort and Intrawest constantly mail out promotions to their customer database announcing promotional and seasonal vacation packages, room rates, and lift ticket specials. Consumer packaged-goods firm Garnier used both addressed (5 percent redemption) and unaddressed mail (1.5 percent redemption) with extensive profiling to deliver a sample and coupon offer for its Long and Strong brand.[37] Hudson's Bay, Sears, and other retail outlets call their existing customers to notify them of special sales promotions. In turn, the sales promotion event may support the direct-marketing effort since databases are often built from the names and addresses acquired from a promotion, permitting other direct-marketing follow-up.

Learning Objectives Summary

 Define direct marketing and summarize the importance of a database for making marketing communication decisions.

This chapter introduced the field of direct marketing, which involves a variety of methods and media that seek to obtain a more immediate behavioural response from the target audience. The success of a direct-marketing program is predicated on a database. The database contains extensive information for each customer or prospect in terms of demographic variables. More thorough databases will have additional variables on purchase history, socio-economic characteristics, media exposure, and any other relevant segmentation variable the marketer believes necessary. The intrusive nature of the direct marketing and the use of databases make marketers hesitant to use direct-marketing tools. However, self-policing of the industry and involvement by large, sophisticated companies have led to significant improvements, allowing direct marketing to continue growing.

Express the decisions of a direct-marketing plan.

Direct marketing involves careful target audience profiling through the use of the database. Direct marketers can target lapsed customers in an attempt to generate re-trial. Alternatively, they can target current customers and try to encourage repeat purchasing of the brand, but with additional products (i.e., cross-selling). Databases garnered from other means can be compiled to develop stronger trial among non-category users or non-brand users. Thus, a critical part of the direct-marketing plan is profiling the target audience and selecting the corresponding objective, since this guides the promotional offer and the selection of the most appropriate direct-response media.

Direct marketing is executed with a variety of direct-response media including direct mail, catalogues, broadcast, telemarketing, and new digital applications. We summarized the former ones in this chapter and examine the latter in the next chapter. These media are used in a specific manner to encourage consumers to take action in terms of a purchase or getting involved with another medium or another IMC tool such as sales promotion.

 Describe the content of a loyalty program.

An important part of a direct-marketing plan is a loyalty program designed to maintain continued repeat purchasing from consumers who enroll and become members. Most of these consumers are behaviourally and attitudinally loyal; however, others join to collect points to earn rewards and might readily switch to an alternative provider if they did not have so much invested in the program. Despite this limitation, consumers are quite satisfied with these programs and Canada has one of the highest participation rates in the world.

 Evaluate the strengths and limitations of direct marketing.

Advantages of direct marketing include target audience selectivity, target audience coverage, frequency, creativity for cognitive and emotional responses, scheduling flexibility, personalization leading to stronger attention and involvement, and costs. At the same time, a number of disadvantages are associated with the use of direct marketing including media image, target audience coverage, control for selective exposure, and reach.

 Apply the ideas of direct marketing within the development of an IMC plan.

Direct marketing is one activity in marketing where activities are clearly demarcated with respect to targeting potential customers with a message to ensure a trial purchase or targeting existing customers to continue purchasing. The source of sending the message and offer is from a database of leads or current customers, so the most appropriate approach is possible unlike other forms of marketing communication. Direct marketing acts as the delivery mechanism for other IMC tools like sales promotion. As seen in some of the loyalty programs, promotional offers to members can enhance their experience. Similarly, public relations activities can be tied with direct marketing for stronger communication effect or cost efficiencies.

Key Terms

Review key terms and definitions on Connect.

Review Questions

1. Explain how companies use database marketing. How is the information derived from the database used to target audiences?

2. What is the difference between the one- and two-step approaches to direct marketing? Give examples of companies that pursue both methods.

3. Why are loyalty programs considered to be a direct-marketing program rather than a sales promotion?

4. One of the disadvantages associated with direct-marketing media is the high cost per exposure. Some marketers feel that this cost is not really as much of a disadvantage as is claimed. Argue for or against this position.

5. How does direct marketing influence each stage of the consumer decision-making process as it works with other IMC tools?

Applied Questions

1. Construct a list of variables that a fashion brand might desire in its database to market to students in college or university.

2. Collect any direct mail delivered to your household and evaluate whether it is effective.

3. Read up online about an interesting loyalty program and apply Figure 16-4 to identify the characteristics and give an assessment of the program's value.

4. How might a smartphone service improve its marketing communication with the use of direct marketing?

5. Provide examples for both consumer goods and services of how companies might use direct marketing as part of an IMC program.

GO ONLINE

For more information on the resources available from McGraw-Hill Ryerson, go to www.mcgrawhill.ca/he/solutions.

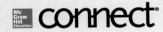

Norco John Henry Bikes

1,629 likes · 12 talking about this · 147 were here

✓ Liked   Message   ⚙

🏷 Bike Shop
📍 100–400 Brooksbank Ave., North Vancouver, Brit...
📞 (604) 986-5534
🕐 Today 10:00 am – 7:00 pm

About - Suggest a Change

Photos

The Seat Post Newsletter:
Sign up to recieve your
regular Live to ride
inspiration. Simply drop us
your name and email
below.

Sign up here

Events

Videos

Internet Media

CHAPTER SEVENTEEN

17

LEARNING OBJECTIVES

LO1 Describe the general characteristics of Internet users and explain website communication.

LO2 Identify the advertising formats of Internet media.

LO3 Illustrate how to use social media in an IMC plan.

LO4 Define measures of Internet media effectiveness.

LO5 Evaluate the strengths and limitations of Internet media.

LO6 Apply the ideas of Internet media within the development of an IMC program.

"Live to Ride" with John Henry Bikes

Burgeoning Internet media use has produced fantastic examples of effective marketing communication for small and large brands across all aspects: ads, banner ads, video, social networking, and blogging. Great stories here show that the creativity and the message connected to the brand is still crucial, with new ways for brands to communicate with their current and potential customers.

John Henry Bikes in Vancouver eventually turned to social media despite initial skepticism about using Facebook. The wheel got rolling when Twitter provided great success; this social media avenue gave an authentic voice to the brand's "live to ride" motto. When the shop sent technicians to Uganda to repair bicycles, its message on Twitter really resonated with clientele, who retweeted it endlessly. In contrast, messages about new products are now placed on radio after they returned virtual silence on Twitter. In the end, the bike shop became a fan of Facebook too as both social media vehicles helped in communicating the shop's events, biking excursions, and adventure camps. Interestingly, the social side of cycling is well communicated with social media!

Internet media advertising is so pervasive that specialized recognition now happens in the form of Webby Awards. Nominee Liberté Blueberry Greek Yogurt used a tablet-based mobile ad, located on the lower part of the page, where users played a game trying to put the blueberries on the banner ad back in the container by tipping and turning the device. The average game lasted 46 seconds. Locating the ad at the bottom of the page reinforced the attribute of the berries at the bottom of the container and reinforced the brand's natural positioning. Over on an automotive shopping website, nominee BMW created the world's longest banner ad—which expanded when touched by the cursor to reveal a witty story that "people could not put down" as the average time spent with the ad reached three minutes!

Martell Home Builders, a small and enterprising construction startup in Moncton, stumbled upon using YouTube with a video clip of industry tradespeople endorsing the owner to potential customers. With quick distribution of the video link within the real estate industry, Pierre Martell was in business. Subsequent videos describe the customized house building process so well that the owner can now close a sale in two hours, down from eight hours, because the video answers so many preliminary questions.

Finally, Kraft Dinner has continued its fascinating attachment with Canadians on Facebook. Since the product's name south of the border is Kraft Macaroni and Cheese, KD (as it is known here) retains its unique identity with home-grown advertising featuring the famous "Gotta Be KD" slogan, invented by a consumer more than 10 years ago during the brand's cross-country promotional tour. Playing on the sense of ownership Canadians feel with KD, the Facebook page presented challenges for its fans—including photo bombing with KD, making a KD .gif, putting captions on photos of KD, and "Make It Epic" recipe battles. TV ads with humorous battle scenes between two roommates drove traffic to Facebook. The campaign pumped up the fan roster from 120,000 to 270,000, an especially impressive result considering the challenges did not reward winners with prizes like most contests. Instead, winners received social media glory as KD victors!

Sources: Susan Krashinsky, "The Wild, Wacky, Weird World of Webby Advertising," *The Globe and Mail*, April 2, 2012, B7; Hollie Shaw, "Catering to the Kraft Dinner Cult," *National Post*, March 23, 2012, p. FP12; Ivor Tossell and John Lorinc, "Social Media Superstars," *The Globe and Mail*, April 25, 2012, p. 11.

Question:

1. Do social networking sites work better for attracting new customers or communicating with current customers?

The chapter opener illustrates a brand that effectively uses Internet media in its marketing communication program by viewing the Internet as a medium to reach a target audience. In this chapter we discuss Internet media from a communication perspective. First we describe general characteristics of Internet media users and explain website communication. Next, we identify the advertising formats of Internet media that promotional planners place in virtually any location within Internet media. We then illustrate how social media can be planned within an IMC program, as an approach for directly communicating with audiences, as a media vehicle for ad placement, and as a means for consumers to see and contribute user-generated content from customers and non-customers. To conclude, we define the options for measuring Internet media communication effectiveness, evaluate its key strengths and limitations, and apply the use of Internet media within an IMC program.

(L01) Internet Communication

The **Internet** and the **World Wide Web (WWW)** allow for marketers and consumers to conduct transactions for goods and services; however, our focus is to consider these digital tools as media for communication and facilitation of the promotional program. In the academic literature, there are many digital marketing domains investigated beyond advertising.[1] Our particular interest is Internet advertising research that examines the effectiveness of Internet media advertising, interactivity, how advertising works, attitude to Internet media ads (including websites), and finally comparisons to other media.[2] As this suggests, the Internet connects consumers— both current customers and potential customers—and marketers seeking or greeting both types of consumers through advertising and other tools. In this section, we describe Canadian Internet media users and explain the primary purpose of website marketing communication.

INTERNET USERS

Approximately 86 and 80 percent of all Canadians accessed Internet media at any location or home, respectively, in 2011. Mobile access to Internet media continued to grow and reached 37 percent (Figure 17-1). Access varies by age, with near universal access (95 percent) for those under 55 while those older than 55 hit 68 percent. Mobile showed similar access

Figure   17-1

Household Internet access

Source: The Ipsos Canadian Inter@ctive Reid Report, 2011, Issue 3. Base: National Sample of Canadian Adults (n = 1000). Copyright © 2012 Ipsos Reid Corporation.

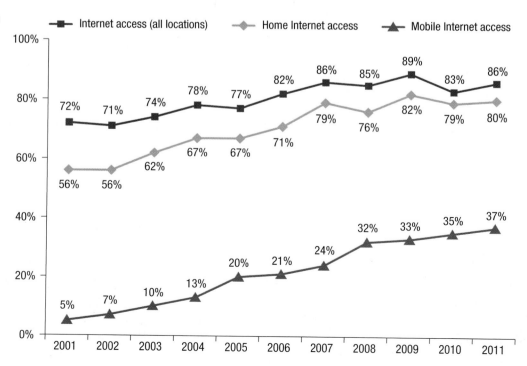

differences; under 55 at 47 percent and over 55 at 16 percent.[3] Clearly, these numbers confirm one's belief in the penetration of Internet use for Canadians.

Figure 17-2 illustrates that Internet media reaches 77 percent of Canadians on a weekly basis, substantially lower than broadcast media, on par with newspapers, and considerably higher than magazines. However, the growth is noticeable, moving from half the population to three-quarters over the past decade. And as the corresponding diagram illustrates, the amount of time more than doubled, with Canadians using Internet media for over 12 hours per week, not counting access via mobile devices. Figure 17-3 shows other data with slightly lower usage per week, but these data suggest that differences among key segmentation variables are minimal as Internet media is a mainstream media much like all others.

Figure 17-4 summarizes the types of usage during the past month uncovered by Media Technology Monitor. Clearly, the extensive activities Canadians experience on the Internet allow advertisers opportunities to reach specific customer groups, lifestyles, or virtually any marketing segmentation variable. In fact, some opportunities may be *very* good—the Internet appears to have spurred greater consumption of news when adding up the total exposure from traditional and digital media.[4] Further to this is the development of user-generated content such as product reviews, forum or journal posts, blogs, websites, wikis, audio files, video files, podcasts—all contribute to an enormous amount of word-of-mouth communication. One study documented how certain

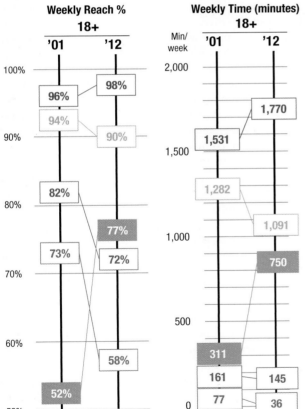

Figure 17-2 Internet exposure vs. other media

The Internet medium reaches 77% of adults 18+ in Canada weekly and has been the only medium to have registered any significant growth over the last decade. Adults spend 750 minutes with the Internet medium weekly (pc) and this does not include time accessing the Internet via smart phones and tablets. PHD estimates an additional 190 minutes per week is spent by accessing the Internet via these mobile devices. Again, the internet medium's growth rate has been significant (+141%) since 2001.

Source: Used with permission from PHD Network.

Figure 17-3 Time spent on Internet media by segmentation variables

Location	Global (Hours)	Canada (Hours)
Male	10.1	10.2
Female	9.5	9.7
Age <35	10.4	11.2
Age 35–49	9.6	9.9
Age 50+	8.8	8.6
Low HH Income	9.1	10.4
Medium HH Income	9.8	9.3
High HH Income	10.4	10.3
Married	9.3	9.3
Other	10.2	10.4
Low Education	9.4	9.9
Medium Education	9.9	9.8
High Education	10.0	10.4
TOTAL	**9.8%**	**9.9%**

Source: Global @dvisor, Social Media Survey, January 2012

Source: http://www.magazinescanada.ca/uploads/File/AdServices/FactBooks/2012/DigitalFactbook2012_EN.pdf

Figure 17-4

Internet use (%) by age groups and Internet activity (fall 2012, Canadians 18+)

	18 years +	18–34 years	35–49 years	50–64 years	65 years +
Use Internet	87	98	95	85	60
Use social networking site	59	84	67	46	22
Watch Internet video	71	92	80	62	35
Watch Internet TV	37	58	41	26	12
Stream radio	20	25	24	16	8
Stream YouTube audio	46	77	52	28	11
Listen to podcast	13	18	15	11	4

Source: Statscan, "Canadian Internet Use Survey," CANSIM 358-0153.

types of psychographic groups relied on these different Internet media sources of information when making purchase decisions.[5] With variations within Internet media, we can conclude that its viewers and readers use it like a specialized medium with limited mass communication effects similar to TV—even though virtually anyone can see anything at any time on the World Wide Web!

WEBSITE COMMUNICATION

We investigate website communication since the purpose of digital marketing communication tools is to direct users to a website and a website is where considerable Internet media persuasion occurs. One role of a **website** is to act as the place where information is made available to Internet users. To attract visitors to the site—and to have them return—requires a combination of creativity, updated information, and the use of other media to direct consumers. An additional role of a website is much more creative, with technological advances allowing fancier graphics, audio, and animation. With this new role, brands create unique messages and digital experiences unlike any consumers had previously experienced in any other advertising media. A third role of a website is to facilitate communication and interaction among consumers as witnessed by capability of two-way communication features. From a purely communication standpoint, websites typically achieve four broad communication objectives: develop awareness, disseminate information, build a brand image, and facilitate interaction.

These latter three are attitudinal in nature and are consistent with earlier chapters.

Develop Awareness   Communicating on a website can be useful in enhancing or creating awareness of an organization as well as its specific product and service offerings. Websites for well-established products offer additional interactive exposure of the brand in terms of its key messages and typical signature (e.g., logo, slogan, colours). Exhibit 17-1 shows how Red Bull creates a fun experience for consumers to enjoy the brand and keep awareness strong. For small companies with limited budgets, a website is an opportunity to create awareness well beyond what might be achieved through other media. Internet media may not be the optimal medium for awareness in these situations due to its limited reach without other communication to direct consumers to the website; however, these consumers are often in the information search stage of their decision making and are very good prospects for ensuring they do not forget about the brand when making a final decision or for when they want to buy on their next purchase occasion.

Exhibit 17-1   Red Bull offers a number of reasons to visit its website.

Disseminate Information A primary website objective is to provide in-depth information about a company's products and services. In most markets, a website is a necessity since buyers expect that a company will have a site providing them with detailed information about its offerings and where to buy, as shown in Exhibit 17-2. This is true for both consumer goods and services and business-to-business goods and services. In fact, three-quarters of all Canadians "window shop" or browse for information on goods or services in general, and similar numbers arise for things like medical and travel information and banking online. In the public sector, all levels of government use Internet media to provide citizens with a wide range of information on services and policies; two-thirds of all Canadians visit a government website each year.[6]

Build a Brand Image Websites are often designed to reflect the image a company wants to portray. Interestingly, one difficulty marketers have experienced is that of creating a brand image on the Internet. While companies have been successful, others have not fared as well and realize that branding and image-creating strategies must be specifically adapted to the medium. Websites also provide a transformational experience, with video, animation, and social media–like tools to make the brand experience truly unique and interactive beyond what consumers experience with other media.

For example, Internet sites for beer are excellent examples of image building. Molson Dry maintained its lively reputation with "party bottles," where a message appeared on the label when cold, a feature of thermal ink technology, and kept it up even stronger with augmented reality at its website (MolsonDry.com). After downloading an application, users could hold a "party bottle" up to their webcam and view three different live animated messages that appeared to spring forth from the bottle. Users recorded their "party bottle" antics and uploaded them to be used later in banner ads that directed new users to the site (see Exhibit 17-3).[7]

A study by the marketing research firm Millward Brown published in the *Journal of Advertising Research* concludes that Internet media is capable of building a brand like other established advertising media, although certain caveats seen elsewhere remain. For example, ensuring that the right message is communicated within the appropriate media vehicle is critical, a key conclusion that we have seen with more established media.[8] Since then, it is clear that Internet sites are a critical component of any brand's ability to project its image to customers, non-customers, and any other stakeholders. A few great Canadian examples include MAC Cosmetics, BlackBerry, Lululemon, Canada Goose, NRML, and Harry Rosen—check them out!

Facilitate Interaction Companies set up websites to interact with an audience on a regular basis, and may use a membership component to obtain personal information with permission and communicate afterward (e.g., e-mail). For example, Procter & Gamble established a website (www.vocalpoint.com) where moms share information (Exhibit 17-4). Vocalpoint's mission is to help companies develop products and services that moms care about and want to talk about. The site offers moms access to information, products, and samples as well as the ability to influence products and programs to help shape marketing programs. The Vocalpoint moms share their opinions and feedback and "spread the word" if they think the idea or product is worth talking about. Membership in the community and

Exhibit 17-2 OluKai's website is designed to provide easy access to information.

Exhibit 17-3 Molson uses the Internet to build its brands.

Exhibit 17-4 Vocalpoint is a website where mothers exchange ideas about goods and services.

the sharing of opinions is voluntary. Vocalpoint moms are asked occasionally to participate in research and are compensated like participants in any other paid consumer research program.[9] From another perspective, Nissan established its own game on a website (nissangooddecision.com) that provided an interactive feature to help consumers in their search for a new car.[10]

Interaction also occurs during the execution of sales promotions. To earn an entry into a contest for Coors Light Maxim Golf, contestants created a profile at the website (CoorsLight.ca) and uploaded photographs, videos, and text to make their case as to why they should be selected. This "Become Part of the Legend" contest encouraged the use of other social media tools in order to win an opportunity to play golf in British Columbia with the assistance of a female caddie. The overall campaign included increased social media, with Facebook links, a comments section, and video banner ads. A total of 73,000 fan votes determined the winner after looking at almost 4,000 entries; both numbers doubled over the previous year's "Help Wanted" contest.[11]

WEBSITE STRATEGY

Making a site work and having one work successfully are not the same thing; whether a site is effective is determined by what management hopes to achieve through the site. As already noted, some sites are offered for informational purposes only, while others approach the market with more transformational purposes as they become a valuable resource for important life experiences. And firms use more than one site to achieve their objectives. Wind Mobile used two websites when it entered the Canadian market. It had a branded site (windmobile.ca) and a website (wirelesssoapbox.com) that continued the dialogue with consumers after a series of ads that illustrated the state of Canada's wireless industry and demonstrated the need for increased choice for consumers.[12]

The Dove beauty bar (Exhibit 17-5) has a website that is an example of a newer trend, with multiple capabilities and an extensive array of text, video, graphics, and photos. Its main menu offers six selections: Products, Connections, Expertise, Features, Offers, and Campaign for Real Beauty. The website helps develop a long-term relationship with women and girls, contributes to the brand image for Dove, and supports sales. Its Products section is a clear approach for providing basic factual information for each type of product (e.g., bar/body wash). The Connections section allows for interaction with blogs and discussion forums along with writing from Dove personnel. Expertise is offered in its own menu item so that consumers can be more knowledgeable about self-care and the products. The Features menu provides video and interactive experiences for different ages. As the title implies, the Offers section highlights the latest promotions. And, finally, the overall theme of Dove's marketing, Campaign for Real Beauty, has its own section where consumers can learn about the esteem fund. Furthermore, this menu item offers information for specific individuals (e.g., girls, mothers, educators). Surrounding the content displayed for each menu item are "banner ad–like" boxes for multiple products. As this state-of-the-art example from Dove demonstrates, a website can be an effective marketing tool to achieve

Exhibit 17-5 A beauty bar like Dove uses many transformational features on its website.

any or all communication objectives, and in fact achieve different types of behavioural objectives (identified in Chapter 5) for multiple audiences at varying stages of the decision-making process (identified in Chapter 3). Other brands with interesting approaches for website communication include everycup.ca, fora.mtv.ca, and havanacultura.com.

A consumer interacting with a website raises the question as to what is meant by interactivity. **Interactivity** is the extent to which an actor involved in a communication episode perceives the communication to be reciprocal, responsive, speedy, and characterized by the use of nonverbal information.[13]

Applying this idea, a website demonstrates reciprocity when it offers multiple opportunities for the consumer to act upon, such as links, buttons, or connections to other utilities like social media. It also shows responsiveness if every action produces a relevant and appropriate outcome. Extensive use of pictures, sounds, and animation implies nonverbal information. Finally, quick response suggests the website is strong on the speedy characteristic. Notably absent from this definition is the notion of control, since it is a media usage characteristic of both interactive media and non-interactive media as described in Chapter 10. Empirical findings supported this definition of interactivity, which was also found to be a strong predictor of attitude to the website and media involvement.[14] Furthermore, preliminary research indicates that more interactive websites generate deeper information processing and message believability, leading to stronger attitudes to the brand and website.[15]

This attitudinal communication effect is another source of findings where researchers investigate what design factors lead to a consumer's positive attitude to the website.[16] Additionally, research investigates the impact of attitude to the website to brand attitude or company attitude.[17] This effect has been investigated for both high/low involvement and informational/transformational brand attitudes, previously discussed in Chapter 8.[18]

Research also looks at the attitudinal effects on purchase intentions.[19] Figure 17-5 summarizes these ideas, which are similar to the models described in Chapter 4. Several of the advertising principles established in other media are being investigated with Internet media, and it remains to be seen whether it will be completely similar or with variation. In the end, however, the notion of Internet advertising is now common terminology. Finally, consumers develop an affinity for or are very loyal to their favourite Internet sites for their information or entertainment needs. More loyal users tend to spend more time at these sites and have much more positive attitudes toward the site's relevance, content, and features. This is consistent with other media, where people have their favourite TV show or radio station.

To illustrate these ideas we turn to the microsite for Bull's-Eye barbecue sauce. Its creative video clips end with a merit theme as the viewer obtains a "badge of brotherhood," and its tips for grilling celebrate the barbecuing experience for men aged 25–45 who are very protective of the tools of their trade—in this case, cooking meat in the great outdoors of one's patio. Guys sent videos of their bolder endeavours to a social media site, where they could enter for chances in a contest for a trip to Las Vegas.[20] Presumably, the key design elements of the microsite lead to these consumers having a stronger attitude to both Bull's-Eye and the site, leading to increased intentions and actual trial.

But how do consumers get to the new microsite in the first place? In this case, the plan included radio and print that directed potential viewers. Alternatively, brands can use online

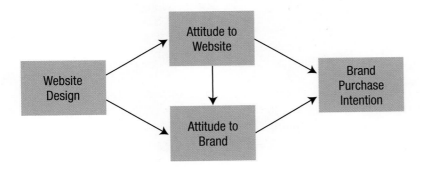

Figure   17-5

Model of website advertising effects

advertising or rely on social media, two topics we also examine in this chapter. Practitioners refer to each of these IMC tools as "owned" media (e.g., website), "paid" media (e.g., banner ad), and "earned" media (e.g., user-generated content). While this handy vocabulary works well to a degree, it does limit the innovativeness and creativity of a plan as we shall see.

(L02) Advertising

The Interactive Advertising Bureau (IAB) of Canada estimated that online advertising revenue reached $3 billion in 2012 (Figure 17-6). This is lower than the $3.5 billion spent on television and substantially lower than total broadcast of $5 billion and total print of $4 billion. Internet advertising revenue accounted for 21 percent of the total advertising revenue and 25 percent of the total reported advertising revenue in Canada. In comparison, this figure reached 36 percent for the United Kingdom.[21] By comparison, Internet advertising in the United States reached $31.7 billion for 2011 and $36.6 billion for 2012.[22]

The types of products advertised on the Internet in 2011 are shown in Figure 17-7. The top four online advertisers in Canada for 2012 were Netflix, Microsoft, Procter & Gamble, and

Figure 17–6   Canadian online advertising revenue ($ millions), excluding mobile

	2005	2006	2007	2008	2009	2010	2011	2012
Total Canada	562	900	1,241	1,602	1,822	2,232	2,593	2,925
% growth/yr	54	60	38	29	14	23	16	13
French Canada	124	189	260	317	352	428	490	559
% growth/yr	89	52	38	22	11	22	14	14

Source: © IAB Canada.

Figure 17-7

Distribution of online revenue by major product category, 2011

Source: © IAB Canada.

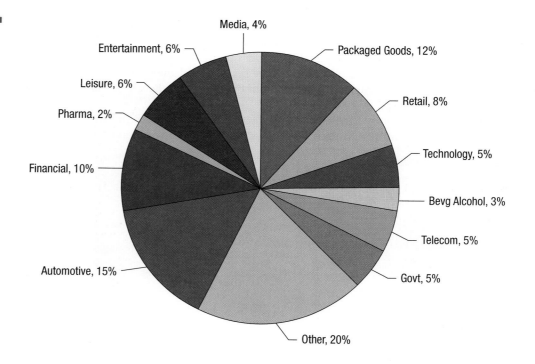

General Motors. Coastal Contacts, located in Vancouver, was fifth and is one of the world's largest online retailers of prescription eyewear.[23] Wind Mobile spent 30 percent of its $30 million to $40 million first-year budget on online advertising when it launched in Canada.[24] Expenditures of online advertising formats are shown in Figure 17-8 and are described in this section using the formats as headings to organize the topic for presentation purposes.

DISPLAY ADS

Display advertising revenue hit $916 million in 2012, up from $216 million in 2006, and clearly rivals magazines at $573 million. The original use of display ads occurred in print media and so it is not too surprising that Internet media ads look like the ads found in those media as well. Display ads are placed on virtually any Internet site, including social media Internet sites and within e-mail messages. Figure 17-9 shows where advertisers place display ads across different types of Internet media. As expected, advertisers are keenly interested in placing display ads on social media sites and these account for a substantial portion. Canada's top advertisers like Capital One and the federal government put half of their display ad expenditures in social media.[25]

Figure   17-8   Canadian online advertising revenue ($ million), by advertising vehicle, five-year trend

	2005	2006	2007	2008	2009	2010	2011	2012
Search	197	343	478	622	741	907	1,081	1,308
Display	230	314	432	490	578	688	840	916
Classifieds/ Directories	124	223	305	460	467	587	576	584
Video	—	—	9	12	20	37	73	92
E-mail	11	20	17	18	13	11	13	12
Video Gaming	—	—	—	—	3	2	10	12
Mobile	—	1	2	7	23	47	81	160
Total	551	881	1,243	1,609	1,845	2,279	2,674	3,085

Source: © IAB Canada.

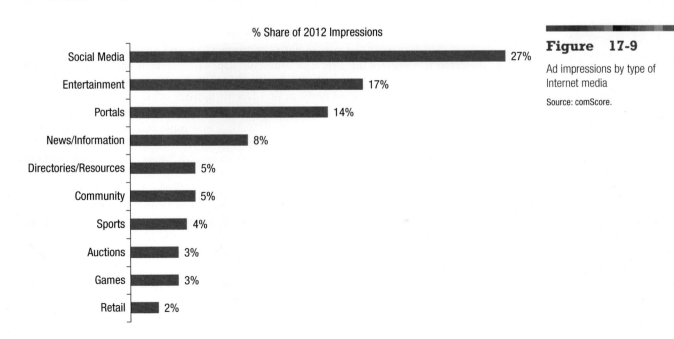

% Share of 2012 Impressions

Social Media	27%
Entertainment	17%
Portals	14%
News/Information	8%
Directories/Resources	5%
Community	5%
Sports	4%
Auctions	3%
Games	3%
Retail	2%

Figure   17-9

Ad impressions by type of Internet media

Source: comScore.

Exhibit 17-6
A leaderboard banner ad.

Display ad formats follow industry standardization; extensive demonstrations of these formats and their technical requirements are available (see iab.net and iabcanada.com). A major adjustment to the standardized formats occurred in 2012 with the deletion of old formats and the addition of new ones to take advantage of technological innovations. We now review the different ad formats that advertisers place in Internet media vehicles.

Banner Ad   A common advertising format is a **banner ad**. Banner ads take their name and format from ads found in newspapers. A banner ad is now referred to as Universal Ad Package (UAP; CAUP in Canada), with four formats: rectangle, medium rectangle, skyscraper, and leaderboard. Other ad units are available, like super leaderboard, half page, button 2, and micro-bar. Exhibit 17-6 shows a leaderboard banner ad that is a horizontal rectangle across the top of an Internet page. Various page locations are available for these ad units, with limitations due to industry standardization.

Banner ads are found in all sorts of vehicles on the Internet, and this revenue total includes ads also found in social media outlets like Facebook. Naturally, banner ads have a link embedded allowing users to move to another digital location, usually a brand or company website or a branded page on a social network, and developments allow for different interactive features. Click rates in Canada vary; however, all are very low, ranging from 0.04 percent to 0.10 percent. More innovative banner ads using Flash technology produce higher rates, but also have substantial processing times as automatic, 15-second ads are fully played half the time.[26]

Since banner ads are the original marketing communication found in Internet media and account for extensive advertising revenue, it is not surprising to see a number of academics investigating their usefulness. Much of this research builds on existing studies done for other media with an interest in predicting awareness (i.e., recall and recognition), attitude to the brand, attitude to the ad, attitude to the advertising format, purchase intention, and click-through rates—all communication and behavioural effects discussed earlier. A number of familiar topics have been investigated. One study looked at the effects of forced exposure; that is, whether the user had control to avoid the ad.[27] Other research has shown the importance of congruence between the website (i.e., media vehicle) or the search engine keywords imputed and the brand advertised.[28] Another inquiry looked at whether the audience was familiar or unfamiliar with the advertised brand, a key factor in advertising planning that has been covered extensively in this book.[29] Other research has begun to investigate the effects of message content design elements and format of the ads on both communication and behavioural effects.[30] For example, research investigates the effects of different shapes like vertical banner ads (Exhibit 17-7) much like what is done in print media. Furthermore, media scheduling and duration of exposure of the banner ads replicate findings of advertising from other media. For example, longer exposure and repetition are generally important in achieving desired effects.[31] And, while existing research begins to uncover how banner ads work, a new innovation comes along where banner ads will instantly turn into an interactive microsite without redirection that allows the downloading of promotional items (e.g., a coupon). Subsequently, these new ads will include provisions for feedback (e.g., sign-up) and transactions.[32]

Rich Media   Rich media ads are display ads that use newer computer software technology and permit user interaction such as expansion of the ad, additional product description, or movement that appears video-like. Approximately half of all display ads are rich media, offering greater creativity options.[33] Ads that occur within a video player are measured as digital video ads, not rich media.[34]

A major addition to the roster of ad formats is collectively referred to by IAB as Rising Stars Display Ad Units and includes six different presentations: billboard, filmstrip, portrait,

Exhibit 17-7
A vertical banner ad.

pushdown, sidekick, and slider. Research found that consumers were two and a half more times likely to interact with these ads and spent twice as much time interacting with the ads than standard banner ads. Consumers found the ads more enjoyable and claimed stronger website impressions for those using the new format.[35] Exhibit 17-8 shows a filmstrip ad unit where the sequence of the ad is user-controlled by moving the cursor over each part.

Advertisements that appear on the screen with a message are known as **pop-ups**. Pop-ups are usually larger than banner ads but smaller than a full screen. **Pop-unders** are ads that appear underneath the Internet page and become visible only when the user leaves the site. These ads have been delisted by IAB, but some websites do not adhere to IAB standards. **Floating** ads move along in front of the website's page. Research suggests people find pop-up ads annoying or very annoying.[36] In contrast, one academic study concludes that these ads may be welcomed when users are in an entertainment-minded mood, the ads are relevant, or the ads provide value.[37] The frequency and effectiveness of these ads have been greatly reduced given the opportunity for Internet users to use an application that blocks the ads before they appear on the screen.

Interstitials are ads that emerge on the screen while a site's content downloads. Although advertisers believe that interstitials are irritating and more of a nuisance than a benefit, one study found that only 15 percent of those surveyed felt that the ads were irritating (versus 9 percent for banner ads) and that 47 percent liked the ads (versus 38 percent for banners). Perhaps more importantly, while recall of banner ads was approximately 51 percent, recall of interstitials was much higher, at 76 percent. A new form of interstitial is in-person ads, where a person begins speaking to the user, so the effect is similar to experiencing a presentation from a salesperson.

A preliminary page that precedes the homepage of an Internet site is known as a **splash page**. Ads in this format typically disappear after a few seconds and permit the viewer to skip it. One clever splash page shows a hand with a scalpel that cuts the page open to reveal the homepage and a display ad requesting donations for Sunnybrook Hospital in Toronto. As this example shows, captivating creative executions are possible with short messages to enhance further exposure and processing. All of these display ads are bought and sold with a system undergoing change, as shown in Technology Perspective 17-1.

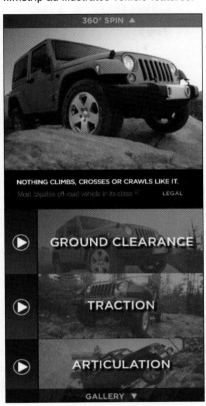

Exhibit 17-8 This IAB Rising Stars filmstrip ad illustrates vehicle features.

PAID SEARCH ADS

A substantial form of advertising on the Internet is **paid search**, or search engine advertising in which advertisers pay only when a consumer clicks on their ad or link from a search engine page (Exhibit 17-9). Other payment methods are also available depending on the search engine and other factors. Paid search ads in a link format are essentially primitive display ads received by the searcher who at that point in time has a particular target audience characteristic. Visually, link ads are text-only ads and are the most basic form of display ad, containing no visual and no or minimal copy. Search advertising revenue reached $1,308 million in Canada for 2012, accounting for almost half of all Internet advertising.

Google is the dominant provider, accounting for two out of every three searches. Google's application of AdSense and AdWords is an example of this form of

Exhibit 17-9 Results of a Google search for flowers.

IMC TECHNOLOGY PERSPECTIVE 17-1

Exchanges for Display Ads

Ad display networks offer a reasonably efficient and effective model to place display ads for advertising clients across millions of potential Internet sites that publish content. Literally hundreds of ad display networks operate around the world, with big names like Google commanding significant market share. The ad network's service is performed over four steps. First, the ad network provider obtains ad placement inventory from multiple Internet sites that publish content. As part of this step, it forecasts the inventory for the coming time frame (e.g., month) and organizes the inventory across multiple segmentation variables adhering to advertiser requirements. Second, the network negotiates and sells the ad placements to advertising clients. And finally, the network facilitates delivery of the ads from the advertiser to the publisher. The general idea of this process is reasonably consistent with the placement of ads in media existing prior to the Internet; however, the development of ad networks changed the game considerably.

An ad exchange, much like a stock exchange with a centralized computer, occurs directly between the publisher and the advertiser over a number of steps. The publisher provides information and requests an ad from the exchange. The exchange submits the request to advertisers. An advertiser then bids on the ad impression against other advertisers. The ad exchange selects the best bid and sends the ad to the publisher. The publisher completes the process, submitting the ad. The entire process is completed one ad at a time yet takes milliseconds! And it links the two systems, networks and exchanges, since the former will buy ad inventory from the latter.

A number of benefits are associated with ad exchange networks. Fewer parties involved results in less overall commission and greater dollars invested in advertising. Logistically, the whole process is simpler for all parties. The pricing mechanisms offer less risk to the publisher receiving minimal amounts of money for its space. Research suggests publishers stand to make more money. Advertisers know exactly where their ad will appear thus avoiding any negative media vehicle source effects. This takes care of the problem of ads for wholesome brands with respectable images appearing in unsavoury Internet locations. Finally, the instantaneous bidding permits dynamic allocations of the advertising budget.

In the United States ad exchanges account for about half of all display advertising, but the method is just getting started in Canada. Numerous companies organized themselves to begin selling with expectations that about a quarter of display ads would be bought this way by the end of 2013. One explanation for the domestic lag is a lack of quality advertisers, but big-name brands in Canada moved toward greater online presence providing a more encouraging environment of increased need for ad exchanges. Another contributing factor included the reluctance of publishers to release advertising space to the exchange. Together, we have the classic chicken or egg conundrum! A situation complicating the system is the fact that a few advertisers have represented three-quarters of the buying.

Canadian executives working with ad networks offered a number of trends based on their early exposure. Most agreed that expanding their database and using the behavioural data of where users visited would assist in the selection and placement of ads. Furthermore, they recognized the inherent trade-off of all media: high volume of consumers exposed to the message who are not in the market versus lower volume of consumers exposed to the message who are actively searching to buy. Many agreed that the exchange trading could move to other aspects of online sales in particular with the coming explosion of video ads.

Sources: Chris Powell, "It's About Real Time," *Marketing Magazine,* August 13, 2012, pp. 36–41; David Brown, "Exchange Is Good," *Marketing Magazine,* November 14, 2011; "The Round Table," *Marketing Magazine,* August 13, 2012, pp. 44-50; "Ad Networks vs. Ad Exchanges: How They Stack Up," *OpenX White-paper,* July 2010.

Question:

1. What are the essential differences between an ad display network and an ad exchange for buying and selling display ads?

advertising (Exhibit 17-10). Link ads with AdSense on an Internet site provide additional information and/or related materials at another site, much like the original link in the paid search. Almost all the company's revenue comes from selling advertisements associated with search keywords. A keyword-targeted advertising program called AdWords uses short text-only ads to maintain an uncluttered page design and to maximize page loading speed. These text ads are identified as "sponsored links" that appear at the top or far right side of the search results page and are separated for clear user distinction. Online advertisers compete for the privilege of having their ads displayed with the results of a particular keyword search in a higher position than their competitors' ads. Advertisers pay only when an ad is clicked (called cost-per-click, or CPC), which in turn takes the Web surfer to the advertiser's website. AdWords runs a specialized auction to decide which ads to show on the basis of (1) each advertiser's CPC bid and (2) the advertiser's *quality score,* which is a measure of the *relevance* of how well an ad matches a user's search query. The AdWords pricing system is designed to reward more relevant ads and keywords by showing them higher in the search results. Google does this by decreasing the amount that relevant ads must bid per click to beat their competition. This means that Google can display the advertisements that are the most targeted and relevant to a Google user's *search query,* which draws more users and click-throughs and thus generates more revenue for Google.[38] Paid search ads are considered very effective; one example by Yahoo finds a 60 percent higher click-through rate beyond display ads arising from a search versus display ads placed without connection to past search engine use.[39]

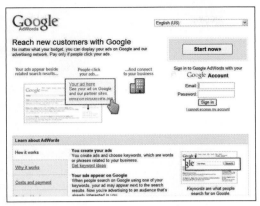

Exhibit 17-10   Google's AdWords provides links for advertisers to do search engine advertising.

In an effort to more specifically target customers who may be interested in their offerings, advertisers employ search engine optimization (SEO). SEO is the process of improving the volume of traffic driven to one's site by a search engine through unpaid results as opposed to paid inclusions. The belief is that the higher a site appears on the search results list, the more visitors it will receive. SEO considers how search engines work and edits its HTML and coding to increase its relevance to keywords and to remove barriers to the indexing activities of search engines. SEO is an integral part of an Internet marketing strategy of companies and organizations of all sizes.

Jeff Quipp, CEO of Toronto-based Search Engine People, makes the following recommendations for search success. One, the titles for the pages should be labelled and unique, and the text should not be embedded in visuals. Two, content should be unique and valuable so that designers of other sites will see value and include a link on their site. Three, to increase a ranking on search, pay the extra money for the search terms and do what is necessary in messaging to ensure strong click-through rates. Four, optimize customization through past search history.[40]

CLASSIFIED AND DIRECTORY ADS

Classified and directory ads are found on Internet sites where consumers search for information when comparison shopping or where consumers are planning a purchase and looking to complete a transaction. One noteworthy example of this is Kijiji; while the average Canadian can post an ad for free to sell used items, Kijiji offers display ad options and paid search capabilities for advertisers such as dealerships to sell new and used vehicles. For the most part, Kijiji sells its ad space on a CPM basis, ranging from $2 to $18. Similarly, Similarly, Auto Trader lets private sellers post ads for free and generates revenue from auto dealers who try to attract those who are searching for a new car in the free postings. And employment directories like Workopolis charge a set fee for a job posting ad with varying levels of service and exposure.

Each of the targeting options described above are possible with these online directories, giving this opportunity for advertising extensive sophistication over traditional newspaper advertising. In fact, a direct substitution effect from newspaper to online has occurred, stealing a significant portion of revenue from the former. Classified and directory advertising hit $584 million in 2012, up from $124 million in 2005, the first year in which the IAB tracked this

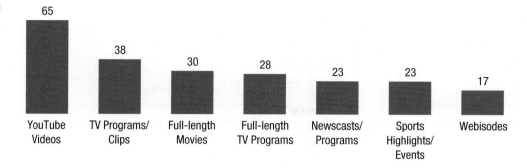

Figure   17-10

Types of video viewed online (spring 2013, anglophones 18+)

Source: CBC/Radio-Canada's Media Technology Monitor (MTM).

form of advertising separately. Classified ad revenue for newspapers peaked at $875 million in 2005 and declined to $289 million in 2012.

Classified and directory ads in newspapers and online are mostly local, as witnessed by the city designations in Kijiji and others, so it is not surprising to observe that local newspaper ads declined by $455 million during this same time period as well. While online gain of about $450 million is not quite in line with the newspaper's total loss of $1 billion ($585 million + $455 million), presumably the remaining half billion moved to other online avenues and has been erased as ordinary citizens now have a free option for personal selling of their goods.

VIDEO AND AUDIO ADS

Video on Internet media made great strides as it hit $92 million in advertising revenue for 2012—five times the level spent on TV infomericals! There are two perspectives for video: ones that appear on video hosting sites like YouTube, for which there is no placement fee, and placement of ads prior to seeing a content video that could be on a video hosting site or any content publisher of video material. Figure 17-10 identifies the type of online video viewing where a portion of video ads are placed, while Figure 17-11 shows that 85 percent is consumed by one-third of the viewers among anglophones.

Online Video Ads   The increased penetration of broadband into households has increased the use of streaming video advertising messages. The equivalent of traditional television commercials, online commercials are appearing on Internet media vehicles. Some companies create new video messages for the Internet, while others run the same spots they show on TV. Companies have also been successful in blending the two media, showing the commercial on TV and then directing interested viewers to their Internet site if they wish to see it again or to view longer versions. These viewings on a company's Internet site are usually hosted on YouTube or an equivalent video hosting service.

Figure   17-11

Share of total hours of video viewed online (spring 2013, anglophones 18+)

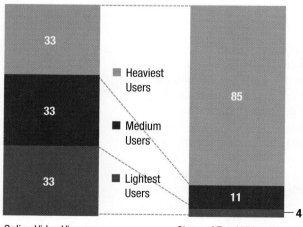

Online Video Viewers

Share of Total Video Hours Viewed Online

Source: CBC/Radio-Canada's Media Technology Monitor (MTM).

Alternatively, brands develop their own video ads or messages and host them on a devoted Internet site. For example, Dove's interactive romantic comedy—located at its own website (wakinguphannah.ca) to promote its new GoFresh product line of soap, shampoo, lotion, deodorant, and body mist targeted to women in their twenties—featured a storyline where users decided the ending by clicking different videos at the completion of each scene. With 19 clips and 7 possible endings, women experienced the highs and lows of Hannah's day (e.g., blind date, boss, etc.) while witnessing her e-mails, voicemails, text messages, and photos. A total of 270,000 visits occurred during the first six months, with an average length of over three minutes, to help Dove exceed its sales target by 48 percent.[41]

Digital Video Ads   Online video versions of entertainment activities or shows (which include ads or are sponsored) are also available through the Internet. CTV's Broadband Network ushered in a new route for advertisers to reach their audiences via Internet media. Viewers watch free shows along with embedded commercials, similar to the existing television model. Initial programming had five or six minutes of commercials per 22-minute show, running before, after, and during the show. As an alternative, CHUM offered its shows on specific Internet sites for each program, such as MuchMusic, rather than a central "network" location.[42]

The future of advertising through streamed television shows is a new and promising opportunity for promotional planners, even though the innovation is in the early stages of development for the sender and the receiver. All major TV broadcasters offer varying options for ad placement for the majority of their shows. Much of the targeting potential and fit of audience of a show is now possible via online video. The growth of consumers watching TV shows online has led to additional advertising revenue that is currently accounted for within the TV figures.[43]

Looking for even more revenue, YouTube offers the availability to see ads before viewing the intended video. Some have the option for viewers to skip the ad, while others are controlled so the viewer must watch the ad, much like the experience with television. Other media vehicles like news sites offer video ads prior to seeing the intended news video clip. These options are priced using CPM methods to account for instances when viewers do not watch the complete message. Future Internet media ad placement may move toward pricing and planning with GRPs like other media as advertisers look toward intermedia comparisons.[44]

Podcasting Podcasting is a medium that uses Internet media to distribute video and audio files for downloading to handheld devices for learning or entertainment purposes. The enhanced control of this medium allows users to time-shift and place-shift their media consumption (Exhibit 17-11). Like other media alternatives, advertising opportunities are present. For example, Volvo sponsored a podcast for $60,000 that was downloaded 150,000 times, while other initial sponsorships garnered $25 per thousand. In addition, metrics for understanding the audience size emerged similar to other media (e.g., podtrac.com). After this initial development, a study investigated how podcasting worked. The findings indicate an average of 2.4 ads per podcast with an average length of 16 seconds, consistent with a length seen on television and ads shown prior to video clips on news or portal sites. The majority of the ads (i.e., 75 percent) preceded or ended the podcast with a sponsorship message, much like the early days of television in the 1950s. In most cases, the content provider acknowledged sponsorship with familiar phrases like, "brought to you by" (19 percent), "support" (18 percent), "break" (16 percent), "sponsors" (13 percent), and "thanks" (6 percent). The specificity of the podcast content allowed for very targeted ads (60 percent), such as automobile brands sponsoring a car-care podcast; thus, we see a very strong media vehicle source effect much like magazines.[45] It appears a familiar advertising model with a sponsorship approach will continue to grow; however, the content of a podcast is also a message with possible commercial intent. For example, in order to increase demand for fine wine consumption, a podcast describing the nuances of grapes, vintages, tasting, and so on could act as a means of switching consumers who currently purchase less premium brands.

MOBILE ADS

Smartphone penetration reached 62 percent of the total mobile phone market in 2012, and 37 percent watched a "TV" program or video.[46] What Canadians look at with their devices is summarized in Figure 17-12. Advertising revenue for mobile totalled almost $160 million in 2012, as summarized in Figure 17-13 and Figure 17-14. Canadian data lags behind American, where mobile advertising revenue attained $3.4 billion in 2012.[47] Canadian revenue is about $5 per capita whereas the

Exhibit 17-11 Audiences for podcasts represent a new advertising opportunity.

Figure 17-12

Internet media vehicles accessed

Source: comScore.

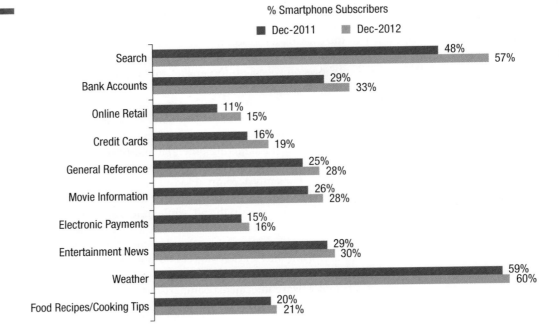

American per capita revenue is about $11, indicating weaker development of mobile advertising in Canada.

Three main mobile advertising formats are short message service (SMS), display/sponsorship, and mobile search. As Figure 17-13 indicates, IAB distinguished between ad placement revenue and ad production revenue for a period of time. However, production of mobile applications are no longer viewed as advertising revenue. We now briefly describe these three options and mobile apps due to their popularity and consumer appeal.

Short Message Service Canadian cellphone carriers agreed to connect their networks so that text messages could be sent to any cellphone handset regardless of the carrier used. For example, Telus customers could send a message to a friend who used Rogers, rather than only to another Telus user.[48] This technological evolution paved the way for marketers

Figure 17-13   Advertising revenue ($ millions) by mobile advertising vehicle

	2006	2007	2008	2009	2010
Ad Placement Revenue					
Mobile Messaging (SMS)	0.8	2.1	3.2	10.7	12.5
Mobile Display/Sponsorship	0.1	0.1	3.3	5.1	15.6
Mobile Search	0	0	0	6.7	17.1
Subtotal	1	2.3	6.5	22.8	46.6
Ad Production Revenue					
Mobile Content	0.1	0.2	5.1	0.6	0.3
Mobile Applications	0	0.1	0.2	3.5	5.2
Subtotal	0.1	0.3	5.4	4.2	5.5
Total	**1.1**	**2.7**	**11.9**	**26.9**	**52.1**

Source: © IAB Canada.

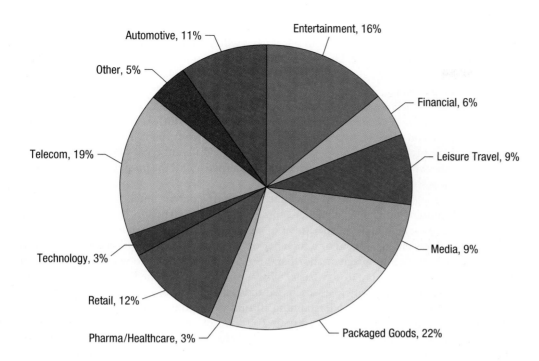

Figure 17-14

Product categories communicated in mobile advertising

Source: © IAB Canada.

to develop two-way communication. Rather than sending text messages one way, like e-mail, marketers conceived the idea of creating short codes as part of a short message service (SMS) so that consumers could immediately respond to relevant ads using their cellphone. For example, if "24BLUE" is seen on a billboard, the consumer could type this in and receive whatever promotional offer or information Labatt wanted to send as part of its overall promotional program. Overall, the SMS becomes a permission-based pull communication as only those interested in the promotional messages respond accordingly. Moreover, the marketer can reach any cellphone user with the technology standardization.[49]

Figure 17-15 shows that sending a text message is the most prevalent activity when using a phone, offering a number of opportunities for new communication and promotional offers. Coca-Cola put forth a promotion with under-the-cap PIN numbers and SMS codes that offered discounts for cellphone bills. In hindsight, the incentive did not completely fit the teen target audience, who usually did not pay for their bill; however, the new approach gave the soft drink brand strong results for future implementation that included iTunes downloads and a contest to win concert tickets. Air Miles sends permission-based text alerts customized by transaction activity to encourage shopping at affiliated sponsors; response rates of up to 8 percent have

Sent text message	65%	Search	21%
Took photos	49%	Captured video	20%
Used applications	41%	Listened to music	19%
News and information	35%	Maps	18%
Used web browser	33%	Sports information	13%
E-mail (work or personal)	30%	Entertainment news	13%
Played games	27%	Movie information	12%
Social networking site or blog	25%	Banking	11%
Weather	23%	Restaurant information	10%
Major instant messaging service	21%	Financial news or stock quotes	10%

Source: comScore.

Figure 17-15

Mobile behaviours in Canada (percentage of mobile subscribers)

occurred. Opt-in geolocation SMS provides offers to consumers who have not previously visited a store.[50] Consumers can send messages to select what will be viewed in digital display networks in malls and transit stations, or on large screens in public locations.[51] Additionally, mobile users can now collect reward points via their device with innovative approaches for those interested in continued brand patronage.[52]

One limitation of SMS codes is the time delay of four to six weeks for registration with the Canadian Wireless Telecommunications Association (CWTA), which is responsible for ensuring that legitimate codes are launched to protect consumers from spam. Another limitation is that carriers are not fully consistent in working with all the different types of codes, as Telus no longer accepts one type. Finally, marketers are still concerned about the proper metrics by which to measure success.[53]

As the above suggests, these promotional messages have content much like other forms of marketing communication with a particular source and message structure. A study investigated the effects of these variables in an experiment of short messages sent to gamers during a LAN party. The source was either a brand or a member of the party, while the message structure was either normal advertising language or shorthand text language, similar to what is sent in short text messages by users on a day-to-day basis.[54] Thus, while this new "medium" is an alternative for sending the message, the principles discussed thus far in terms of positioning and advertising messages remain relevant for understanding attitudinal responses and purchase intentions.

SMS codes eventually may be replaced with 2-D (two-dimensional) barcodes, also known as QR (quick response). Consumers snap a picture of the code—from an out-of-home ad, for example—and their browser locates the programmed destination (e.g., brand's website, promotion offer, social media). Labatt tested the idea with a tie-in to film festivals and received about 1,000 interested users for its Stella Artois beer. With consumers opting in at 20 percent, the software is picking up detailed exposure information on number of scans, who is scanning, and where.[55] However, data suggest that consumers are not positive on the use of QR codes, with minimal usage levels reported in market studies. Even though the idea of making static out-of-home ads becomes more exciting with handheld interactive features, one critique finds the idea unpalatable; the images are unattractive, distract from the main ad message, and there is no motivating reason to scan the code.[56] No wonder consumers are reluctant to get more involved.

Display   Mobile devices are used to connect to the Internet, so display ads are placed within the mobile versions of Internet pages. Most of the points raised earlier are entirely relevant in this wireless environment. Whether banner ads will be effective remains to be seen. When consumers access Internet media with their mobile device they are using a much smaller screen, and people often use their smartphone while walking around. How could a student possibly pay attention to an ad while passing people, dodging cars and skateboarders, and avoiding absent-minded professors? Nevertheless, IAB has established standard ad units for regular and high-resolution mobile advertising, which should spur greater use as ad placement will be easier logistically. Brands are beginning to offer rewards and discounts so that users will view mobile ads at the conclusion of a call. Click-through rates hit 20 percent.[57] However, research suggests that consumers are not receptive to receiving ads directly to their phone. Questions as to respondent interest in an incentive to receive a coupon or free app generate only 10 percent positive reception.[58]

Mobile Search   While searching with the mobile device occurs as in other computer environments, the GPS feature on new phones gives retailers and event marketers a greater opportunity to persuade consumers. The coordinates signalled from the device are tracked, allowing brand information to be placed higher in the search. This local search approach can be a better investment for smaller brands, such as single-shop retail outlets.[59]

Mobile Applications   Known as "apps" for short, these small programs can be downloaded to a smartphone for many purposes. They act as ads since they generally carry brand identification and a brand experience. An entertainment app like Carling's Fill & Drink lets a user pretend to be drinking a beer as the glass slowly empties after the phone is tipped—in a way, the experience is like watching a mini commercial. Apps allow consumers to keep up to date with a brand, such as one by Chanel that lets consumers know when fashion shows or other

Going Mobile

Advertising on mobile devices is a hot trend, with marketers experimenting with new ways of advertising and communicating with consumers. With 26 million mobile phone subscribers and about 60 percent having a smartphone, the opportunity for marketing communication via SMS, display ads, search, and apps appears unlimited. A signal that this may be even bigger news is that Proctor & Gamble signed on with a mobile agency of record to expand its presence in the burgeoning medium. And Cannes added a Mobile Lion to its prize list in 2012, with the Hospital for Sick Children's app announced as the winner.

While Canadian marketers lag behind American marketers, many are looking to establish news ways of interacting—especially since statistics show how much young consumers use their phones for almost everything these days. Usage is particularly strong with sports fans, who use social media to comment on a game they are watching live or at home. Snapping and posting a photo of a friend wearing an NHL sweater at the game creates additional digital brand exposure beyond those who witness it at the arena, showing another way in which user-generated content in social media contributes to brand development.

Of course one of the hottest trends in mobile is apps, where it seems like there is an app for everything a consumer could want. Poynt is a popular Canadian app that allows users to find restaurants, movies, people, and businesses based on their location. The app allows consumers to book an appointment or reservation, save it in the calendar, and access all the contact information without even exiting the app. The next step appears to be features that will deliver promotional offers to users based on their location and user profile. Working with data suppliers and other third-party developers, the app is a handy tool for consumers shopping virtually anywhere.

Despite the euphoria, experts caution that apps should have a useful function since consumers generally will not be motivated to download an app just to "interact with a brand" as if the brand were some kind of game. At least on one occasion, such an experiment received a rude response. Ford tested an app with Cineplex where consumers could vote on the next phase of an ad shown on the screen—after, of course, downloading the app. However, the audience in one Toronto theatre had no one participate and the crowd booed, exactly what occurred when cinema ads first played 30 years ago.

So it appears consumer adoption of new marketing ideas may take a while. But fundamentally, the use of a mobile phone to participate in marketing communication is not a regular activity for most consumers. Advertising and most promotional tools are passive exposures that interrupt people's lives and are for the most part tolerated. However, apps and increasingly interactive digital communication are wonderful from the marketer's point of view since consumers will spend more time processing brand information. However, consumers generally do not share the same perspective, at least not for every brand at all times.

Sources: Hollie Shaw, "Mobile Shoppers Are Moving Ad Targets, *National Post,* May 6, 2011, p. FP12; Susan Krashinsky, "These Ads Aim for Fingertips, Not Eyeballs," *The Globe and Mail,* June 22, 2012, p. B6; Jameson Berkow, "No Magic Formula," *National Post,* January 17, 2011; Susan Krashinsky, "Interactive Advertising? There's a Mobile App for That," *The Globe and Mail,* January 6, 2012, p. B14; Marina Strauss and Omar El Akkad, "A Handheld Way Retailers Are Fighting Online Store Wars," *The Globe and Mail,* December 20, 2011.

Question:

1. How are apps an effective method for marketing communication?

events occur. This kind of app seems to work like a mini website ad. Other apps have ads embedded in them and the ads appear like other media, supporting content.[60] IMC Perspective 17-1 highlights interesting uses of apps.

App penetration reached 70 percent (Figure 17-16), and hit 84 percent for weather information, 79 percent for social networking, 73 percent for travel, public transit, and maps, 64 percent for YouTube, and 61 percent for gaming. Age variation exists in the rates for types of apps as well,

Figure 17-16   App usage among smartphone users

	Smartphone '12	14–17	18–24	25–34	35–44	45–54	55+
Have downloaded apps	70%	72%	79%	79%	72%	59%	55%
# of apps downloaded	12	10	10	13	12	12	11
# of apps purchased	2	2	2	3	3	3	3

Source: Canadian Wireless Telecommunications Association.

with apps for social networks at virtually 100 percent for those aged 14 to 24. Indeed, penetration for all types of apps is higher for this group compared to all other groups. Interestingly, the number of apps varies considerably less across all age groups.[61] Exhibit 17-12 shows an innovative use of mobile technology where payment of transit services can be done with a swipe of a smartphone.

Mobile location apps (e.g., Foursquare) are increasingly being used by marketers and consumers alike. Brands like HarperCollins, Molson, the NHL, Metro News, and the Toronto International Film Festival have all used these kinds of apps for advertising and sales promotion purposes to achieve attitudinal and trial objectives. And the apps themselves offer rewards points for continued use of the app![62] Companies take advantage of the apps section on Facebook and mobile platforms by offering games with point or badge systems to encourage continued patronage to the site.[63] Mobile apps are also a driving force behind the successful implementation of group buying or group discount activities in social media vehicles as well, which suggests that handheld devices will be a main marketing communication tool if consumers desire to interact with brands in this manner.[64] TV broadcasters are developing apps for a second-screen experience for viewers while watching TV shows. Their rationale is to foster enhanced viewer participation of the show's content by commenting on it via social media or enrolling in promotions, and to develop new advertising revenue sources.[65]

As Figure 17-13 indicates, accounting for advertising revenue for mobile has undergone a change. Initially, mobile content took the form of multimedia messaging services (MMS). For example, CHUM offered snippets of its show *Fashion Television* but added additional clips for cellphone users, which had greater potential for e-mailing to friends. Also, P&G sponsored a MuchMusic VJ search video containing the advertiser's brand that was sent to cellphones.[66] However, it appears future data will no longer have mobile content; apps will rule and smartphones will be an important part of our lives. Furthermore, direct streaming of audio and video (Figure 17-17) offer similar advertising opportunities currently found via computer-based devices as the penetration levels continue upward (Figure 17-18).

INTERNET MEDIA VEHICLES

The advertising formats can be placed on virtually any Internet site to target a brand's audience. Promotional planners need guidance on how to structure this decision even though targeting on Internet media shares similarity with targeting in other media. Figure 17-19 applies the media terminology of Chapter 10 and compares broadcast and Internet media definitions. The Internet is a medium much like broadcast (i.e., TV and radio) is a medium. Since there are two types of broadcast it is plausible to group Internet media along the same lines. Pre-existing Internet sites that consisted of content publishers and entertainment venues (i.e., early non–social media that continues to exist)

Exhibit 17-12   Cellphone users in Asia have used their devices for payments much sooner than those in North America.

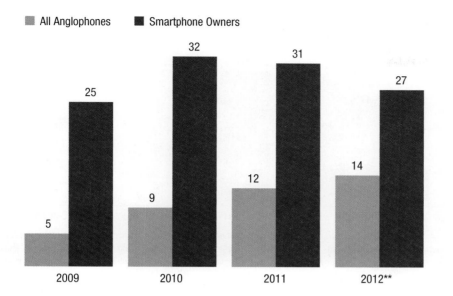

Figure 17-17

Video streaming on
smartphones, fall 2012

Source: CBC/Radio-Canada's Media
Technology Monitor (MTM).

	18 years +	18–34 years	35–49 years	50–64 years	65 years +
Smartphone ownership	51	75	62	39	14
Stream video	13	28	14	4	1
Stream audio	14	30	14	5	1

Source: CBC/Radio-Canada's Media Technology Monitor (MTM).

Figure 17-18

Smartphone adoption (%) and
use (%) by age, fall 2012,
Canadians 18+

Figure 17-19   Comparison of media

Medium	Internet media	Internet media	Broadcast media	Broadcast media
Media Type	Social media	Content publisher	Television	Radio
Media Class	Social networking	News and information	Sports	Modern rock
Media Vehicle	Facebook	Yahoo	TSN (World Jr. Hockey)	Live 88.5 (Ottawa)

provide opportunity for the placement of ads. We also have social media that accepts ads as well; however, the membership characteristics, ability for interaction, and facility for contributing user-generated content provides a new way of planning brand messaging.

This implies that ads can be placed in a specific media class within social media and a specific media class within content publishers. For example, a social networking Internet site would be a media class within social media. Carrying on, Facebook, Google+, and LinkedIn would be avenues for placing an ad and would be the equivalent of a media vehicle much like an ad placed on TSN's broadcast of the World Jr. Hockey tournament or placing an ad on a particular kind and name of radio station. For Internet content publishers, we see Yahoo as a media vehicle within the media class of news and information.

However, the targeting capabilities are much different even though the idea of a media vehicle is similar. An advertiser can be very precise on a number of segmentation variables to direct an ad in these social media environments for a particular time frame. In contrast, the TV advertiser

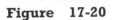

Figure   17-20

Display ads connected and within social media

Source: comScore.

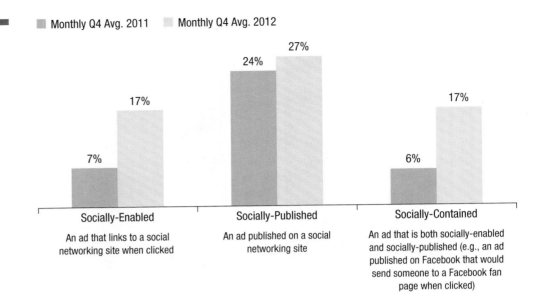

reaches an expected group of hockey fans during the game, with certain characteristics based on historical audience profile data. The importance of media vehicles within social media is conveyed with the data in Figure 17-20, which distinguish three different ways one could be advertising with social media.

We present this perspective to convey the importance and pervasiveness of social media and to understand that the avenues for placing a message via a display ad or within the social media itself offer many vehicles to select from. This is much like what occurs in other aspects of Internet media, like established content publishers such as Yahoo and content publishers from existing print media like *Maclean's* or *The National Post,* and content streamers like CTV. Furthermore, it is an extension of the idea of media vehicles in existing broadcast and print media.

As such, the notion of a media vehicle is critical for targeting in any medium and this is true for any aspect of Internet media since media vehicles assist promotional planners in directing their message to their target audience. Many applications for directing display ads through an ad network or ad exchange to any other Internet site or through a social networking site like Facebook rely completely on targeting, and this would necessitate understanding how media vehicle options are classified. Advertising on a particular Internet site based on its content is known as **contextual targeting**, and this concept is essentially an extension of the concept of a media vehicle. For example, an advertiser places an airline ad on a travel site, or a golf club ad on a golf site, or even in or near a story about golf on another site. This is much like putting an ad for tools on HGTV during a Mike Holmes renovation show. The RBC ads in Exhibit 17-13 illustrate ads for unique audiences that would be placed at the most appropriate Internet sites.

All segmentation variables identified in Chapter 3 can be applied for targeting with Internet media. The Advertising Research Foundation suggests behaviour, geography, and time of day as additional critical variables given the technical capabilities of Internet media.[67] **Behavioural targeting** lets advertisers target consumers according to their Internet viewing. By compiling

Exhibit 17-13 RBC targets different audiences in unique Internet media vehicles.

clickstream data and Internet protocol (IP) information, segments of potential buyers can be identified and ads directed specifically to them. For example, by tracking an individual's visits to a number of automobile websites, an ad for cars or a dealership could be served to that individual.

Geographic targeting lets advertisers adjust their brand messages depending upon where the user is located. This information can be determined technologically and with the user's voluntary declaration of residence (e.g., country, city, etc.). For example, different versions of travel websites (e.g., Travel Alberta) can emerge depending upon where the information seeker is living. Local display ads are presented even if the viewer is on a website without a local connection.

Time of day targeting lets advertisers direct a message to consumers when they are consuming certain Internet media vehicles. This consumer variation in media usage is akin to what occurs in television and radio media consumption. Television viewership composition and frequency vary across the day (e.g., early morning, daytime, prime-time). Similarly, radio's audience size and composition varies considerably, especially during driving to and from work. Internet media are following a similar pattern, with groups of working people accessing Internet media during the day for business purposes, primarily in the morning. It declines during the afternoon and dinner time and then peaks once again during the evening for leisure purposes.

(L03) Social Media

Without question, the most significant media trend is the consumer adoption of social media. Approximately half of all Canadians use social media regularly—media that did not even exist less than a decade ago. Moreover, they are using social media with multiple hardware avenues like TVs, personal computers, smartphones, game consoles, and tablets, and whatever future technology that may be available. In this section we review different classes of social media. While it is impossible to address all, we provide guidance on the major ones that may generalize to others for marketing communication purposes.

SOCIAL MEDIA CLASSIFICATION

Social media is an Internet-based application that allows the creation and exchange of user-generated content resulting in six social media classes: collaborative projects (e.g., wiki, social bookmarking), blogs, content communities (e.g., YouTube), social networking sites (e.g., Facebook), virtual game worlds, and virtual social worlds.[68] For our purposes in this chapter we investigate the first four of these six social media classes in this section. Virtual game world advertising is more closely aligned with product placement (see Chapter 13), and advertising implications of virtual social worlds remain open for further development.

The user-generated content is the key distinguishing feature, and further research expanded this idea and defined consumers' online brand-related activities (COBRAs) as being consuming, contributing, and creating. *Consuming* includes viewing a brand video, listening to brand audio, watching brand pictures, following brand threads in a forum, reading brand social network pages, reading product reviews, playing branded games, and downloading branded material (e.g., widgets). *Contributing* involves rating products, joining a brand social network page, participating in brand conversations in a forum, and commenting in brand blogs. *Creating* moves further by publishing a brand blog, uploading brand video, audio, or picture, writing brand articles, and writing product reviews.[69]

Figure 17-21 identifies numerous social media brands spanning different domains, illustrating the pervasiveness of this media and where all aspects of COBRAs occur. Another perspective suggests that there are 25 social media classes, as indicated in Figure 17-22. Although one might question such a broad view and some classes have stronger social dynamic characteristics than others, the point remains that social media is a significant media type with multiple classes and multiple vehicles within each class. As both the Internet and social media mature over the next 10 years, the significance of this will be more valuable as targeting precision strengthens.

Figure   17-21

Major social media vehicles

Source: Gary Hayes and Laurel
Papworth, 2008.

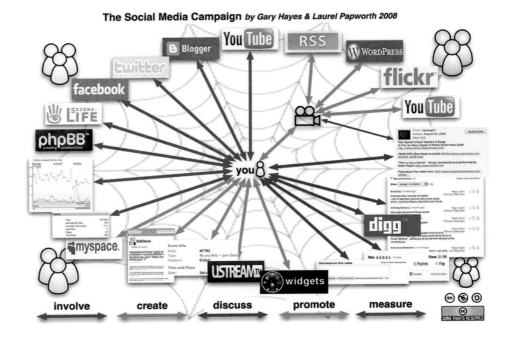

Figure   17-22

Main social media classes

Source: © ethority GmbH & Co. KG
2012. All Rights Reserved.

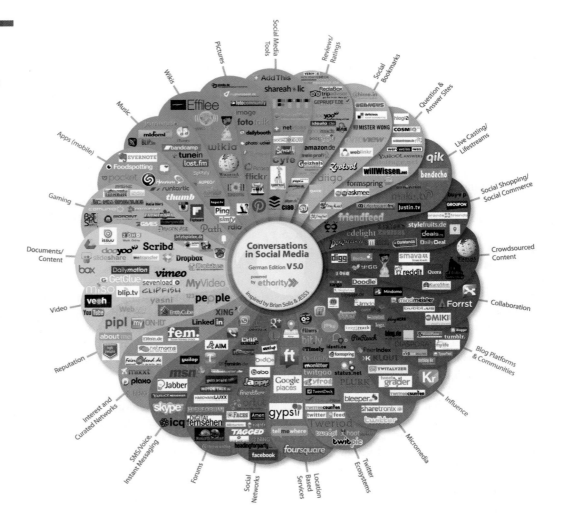

Marketing communication of brands occurs within the social media itself. For example, branded Facebook pages are unique extensions of the brand image promoted and undoubtedly resemble "owned" media—much like the brand's website, and other "owned" media that has existed for decades before the Internet. As we know, ads are displayed in social media like Facebook, which means "paid media" occurs here. And finally, consumers visit a branded page within Facebook, "like" it, and communicate positive and negative consumption experiences in a variety of ways. These activities are COBRAs and indicate user-generated content, a unique feature of social media leading to the designation of "earned" media. Thus, when we say we are going to use social media in an IMC plan, the promotional planner needs to carefully consider whether the plan is addressing one, two, or all three of these aspects. Clearly all are connected to a degree, but promotional planners want to influence optimally to achieve objectives and should consider how it will work prior to investing time and money.

The triple role of social media occurs with all other major players. Followers subscribe to a Twitter feed of their favourite brand, are exposed to paid messages, and converse with people whom they do not even know. Consumers witness a brand's video on YouTube, see ads for the brand on other videos, and forward links to others, comment on videos, or produce a response video. Consumers keep in touch with brands on blogs, see ads alongside the blog, and correspond seemingly as with a beloved friend as they respond to postings. Consumers use a wiki, a social bookmarking page, to creatively express their relationship to a brand, see paid ads, and understand something of a brand from the basic information provided. As all these behaviours imply, consumers digitally involve themselves in several ways with a brand; this section explores how communication occurs within social media among users, the placement of display ads within social media, and how brands convey the message they control.

The significance of social media and the resulting consumer participation can be seen with Mars Canada's campaign with its famous M&Ms candy treat that won a Cannes award. Using Google Street View, Foursquare, Twitter, and Facebook, the brand sent people on a scavenger hunt to locate three oversized red M&M candies hidden in Toronto and captured by Google's cameras. Winners drove away with a red Smart Car. While the uniqueness of the adventure is appealing, managers wondered what the significance of looking for the candy meant in terms of brand communication effects.[70] And here is the rub: with technology at our fingertips—for both planner and consumer alike—which direction should a brand go with social media and how can it marry the three approaches successfully?

SOCIAL NETWORKING

Social media exploded in popularity, with social networking sites as a prominent destination that appears to be levelling off (Figure 17-23) although many are very frequent users (Figure 17-24). Figure 17-25 summarizes what activities social networking users do when signed in. In fact, social networking users tend to watch more online video and listen to more online audio. Twitter and LinkedIn users consume 50 percent more Internet media than non–social media users.[71] Figure 17-26 shows data indicating the number of visits to specific social networking vehicles. Although critics might not agree that all are pure social networking sites, this ranking and others measure the visits and sees sufficient similarity to group them together.

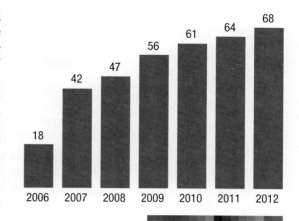

Figure 17-23

Social networking usage during the past month (fall 2012, anglophones 18+)

Source: CBC/Radio-Canada's Media Technology Monitor (MTM).

Figure 17-24 Frequency of social networking usage (fall 2012, anglophones 18+)

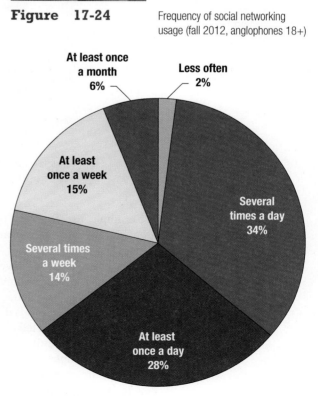

Source: CBC/Radio-Canada's Media Technology Monitor (MTM).

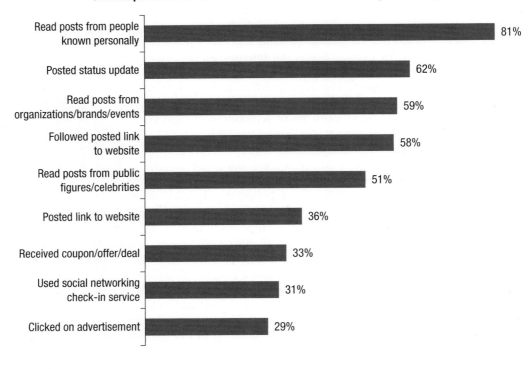

Figure   17-25

Usage of social networking sites

Source: comScore.

% Smartphone Subscribers Who Accessed Social Networking Site or Blog

- Read posts from people known personally — 81%
- Posted status update — 62%
- Read posts from organizations/brands/events — 59%
- Followed posted link to website — 58%
- Read posts from public figures/celebrities — 51%
- Posted link to website — 36%
- Received coupon/offer/deal — 33%
- Used social networking check-in service — 31%
- Clicked on advertisement — 29%

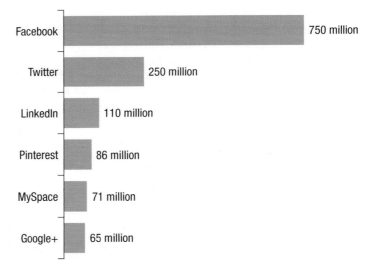

Figure   17-26

Estimated monthly visits to top social networking sites

Sources: www.ebizmba.com; www.quantcast.com; www.compete.com; www.alexa.com.

- Facebook — 750 million
- Twitter — 250 million
- LinkedIn — 110 million
- Pinterest — 86 million
- MySpace — 71 million
- Google+ — 65 million

For example, users create a personal profile and connect with others to digitally share content for all of these media.[72] We now take a look at couple of popular ones.

Facebook   From an advertising standpoint, Facebook and other social media offer themselves as media vehicles much like a specific magazine or television show might. There is placement of a print or video message within a content environment (or via a link). These messages are similar to the ads described above, such as a banner ad with a link to a brand's website or video messages created by the brand.

The targeting abilities of these tools make them a very attractive opportunity for advertisers, allowing for complete choice and substantial precision among all the methods described earlier. Facebook, for example, provides guidelines on how the targeting and costing operates in this new media environment, and for the most part the steps are similar to what we have seen for other media but with simpler, "point and click" options as opposed to other more involved logistical arrangements. Furthermore, the ability to target exceedingly precisely on key variables places a premium on the service, provided people pay attention to the ads.

In another sense these media are completely unique, with the development of "brand pages" that allow an instant connection to exciting brand content, making the whole page a commercial experience in which the user may not even perceive (or may not be concerned about) the advertising due to their pervasive brand loyalty. This idea of content on a branded Facebook page is not the same as content found in broadcast or print media where the content is a TV program, a radio show, a newspaper article on a topic like youth unemployment, or a magazine piece on how university and college students can live away from home economically. Much of the content presented by a brand on a Facebook brand page is a form of advertising or another kind of marketing communication messages.

Fan pages offer virtually any marketing communication tool depending on the brand's objective. For example, during the summer of 2010 the Molson Canadian Facebook page featured about 430,000 fans who could watch 6 Molson videos and 32 videos posted by fans or other consumers. Similarly, Molson posted 6 photo albums, while fans posted about 1,300 photos. Concert information and links to buy tickets for the Molson Canadian Amphitheatre could be found, as well as locations of bars to attend. True fans could read about and participate in the "Seize the Summer" promotion by earning badges for their summer experiences, much like a child's summer camp experience, that could be recorded on a personal page. This final step required the permission of the user, who had to agree to let Molson do the following four activities: "(1) access my basic information (i.e., name, profile picture, gender, networks, user ID, list of friends, and any other information I've shared with everyone); (2) send me an e-mail (i.e., Molson Canadian Seize the Summer may e-mail me directly at. . .); (3) post to my wall (i.e., Molson Canadian Seize the Summer may post status messages, notes, photos, and videos to my wall); (4) access my data any time (i.e., Molson Canadian Seize the Summer may access my data when I'm not using the application)".

The implications of giving this kind of access to a company are interesting. The data could, over time, be compiled into a database and act as a resource for other marketing activities. For example, for a product like a beer brand a sophisticated marketer might want to figure out when a group of friends are planning to go to a particular bar, and then send out a promotional team to the same bar. Additional direct digital marketing activities may be developed such that a group of friends could be invited to an event.

Facebook encourages extensive brand promotion in its literature designed to educate businesspeople that is quite consistent with advertising elsewhere.[73] The page has a cover photo, a visually attractive brand presentation much like a print ad in a magazine. The profile picture gives a prime location for brands to present their logo or any other identifying image, once again adapting a long-established advertising principle found in other media. The filmstrip-like row of activities that includes apps provides additional promotional experiences. For example, game developer EA recently purchased an interactive games company to pursue the path of playing games within a social networking site.[74] The ability to include brand information or photos in the pinned posts offers extended reading or viewing, and the experience is akin to reading feature magazine articles about a brand. But the distinction about content made earlier suggests that these posts are more like copy found in catalogues or other collateral material. Communications regarding sales promotions like contests or discounts are certainly familiar as they occur in all other types of media as well.

However, other aspects of the page where fellow Facebookers describe their buying and consumption experiences as a message to consumers is another important attribute that is distinctive for this social media. While these messages are not controlled by the advertiser like the initial photos and messages are, their content can be influenced by the brand since they can be reactions to what the brand initially posted. Nevertheless, clearly a degree of brand influence occurs from the social dynamic of people conversing—the extent, however, is open for investigation.

Twitter Twitter self-identifies as a "real-time information network" on its Internet site.[75] This contributes to difficulty in exactly classifying it, since "networking" implies it is similar to entities like Facebook, however "real-time information" implies a blog or micro-blog. However, the messages distributed are much like the newsfeed feature on Facebook, and the functions summarized in Figure 17-25 are relevant for Twitter, so it remains in the social networking domain. Twitter established an office in Canada and expanded services previously available only in the United States. Its managing director moved over from TV and sees Twitter as marrying with TV rather than in competition.[76]

To some degree, Twitter is entirely free—any brand or person (e.g., performing artist, athlete) can set up an account and send messages to followers, who will ultimately be influenced by such communication. The messages can be simple phrases and if desired include links to whatever digital content the author would like to associate, including video. In this manner, brands can distribute a controlled message to anyone who is following or motivated to seek out the messages, much like other Internet media that is owned. With so many users and so many messages there is considerable clutter, which led to Twitter offering advertising options for fees, otherwise moving into a world of paid media.

Twitter's ad products for marketing communication include promoted accounts, promoted tweets, and promoted trends.[77] Promoted accounts are identified by the brand name, like Cirque du Soleil, and are featured in the "Who to follow" account recommendation search engine. Cirque du Soleil wanted to announce tour dates and new shows to potential customers who can find this branded account among others. So this works much like a short link ad from a search engine to encourage repeat exposures to brand messages.

Promoted tweets are brand messages much like specific advertising messages found in other online media where consumers willingly seek brand information (i.e., Internet sites). It is also similar to brand messages placed in non-digital media like magazines. For one promoted tweet, Cirque requested followers to communicate their experience while seeing a show. In this respect, the social media message from a customer (i.e., source of the message) acts as a testimonial so that potential customers vicariously experience the spectacle. In this respect, the customer testimonial is the unique contribution of social media; this personal content acts as a brand message yet shares similar qualities since there is an identifiable source characteristic regarding similarity (see Chapter 7).

The message often has a link to the Internet site or any other type of digital communication the brand planned. Cirque made use of promoted tweets that include sales promotions for discounted tickets that linked to its Facebook page. Naturally, the links could go to a brand's Internet site, which Gongshow Gear successfully employed, or to a YouTube video for continued brand exposure, like Porsche did for its launch of the 911 model.

Promoted trends are listed in a designated trends section on Twitter, which acts as an automated search designed to encourage continued exposure to other messages. Again, this operates much like a link ad from a search engine. For example, Porsche initially established its hashtag in a promoted tweet and then listed the same hashtag in the promoted trends.

Twitter operates like any other media, offering an opportunity of brand exposure for fees. As of early 2013, a promoted trend cost $200,000 per day. Advertisers pay when people follow a promoted account, or when people retweet, reply, favourite, or click on a brand's promoted tweet. Cost for these two ad products is based on a bidding system and ranges from $0.50 to $2.50 per follower for the former and $0.50 to $1.50 per action for the latter.[78] The minimum price works out to a CPM of $500, a very expensive proposition compared to other media. Other agencies figured out a way to make money from Twitter by using it as a medium for celebrity endorsements. Brands pay the celebrity (with a cut to the agency) to talk about a product and the digital response is substantial with links to Internet sites.[79]

From a social marketing standpoint, brands encourage lots of interaction with fun activities like Twestivals, which raise funds for a worthy cause the brand sponsors; TweetUps, where people who follow a brand can meet up and socialize face-to-face; and Twitter parties, where consumers continually talk about a brand with multiple comments.[80] These and any other follow-up messages from consumers are the height of social media, with user-generated content (e.g., earned media). While these can have positive impact, there is tremendous risk for negative communication as the company loses control, something most brands historically do not desire. McDonald's experience with Twitter backfired as the campaign prompted consumers to write about their bad experiences; all this possibly was a factor in the YouTube marketing effort described in Chapter 1.

However the implementation side of Twitter remains a concern for brands. Organizations are grappling with this social media much like they did with others when they first arrived.[81] This opens the door to questions we ask for all media, and now for Twitter. What message should be sent via Twitter? Who in the organization should be sending the message? When should the messages be sent? How frequently should the messages be sent? Where should the brand digitally direct the user via its links? Why is someone motivated to receive our brand's Twitter feed?

Ford Canada claimed Twitter success with anecdotal stories of consumers reporting they purchased a Ford after seeing the company's Twitter presence or responses. Furthermore, the brand uses Twitter as a listening post to act upon negative experiences with a direct call once contact information is ascertained. A whole team constantly monitors the account, providing responses 24/7.[82] Ford Canada has a respectable number of followers at 23,000 and Ford Motor Company has 295,000—however, a brand like BlackBerry has 3.3 million followers!

PR executives feel strongly that Twitter responses and all social media communication are in their domain, since these professionals are trained and experienced with continual messaging with the press and the public as issues and topics emerge over time. On the other side, digital agencies believe they should be in charge since they have the technical skills and are stronger resources during our technological era.[83]

CONTENT COMMUNITIES

Content communities exist for users to share video, photo images, and audio media. For our purposes, we concentrate the first two for this section; there is no documented revenue stream for audio advertising revenue, and video advertising revenue hit $2.3 billion in the United States for 2012 (Canadian data were unavailable at publication time).

Video   Figure 17-27 identifies the top video sites; not unexpectedly, YouTube retains a considerable lead over the remaining contenders. For this reason, we concentrate on YouTube since it is the most dominant in its domain and the clear industry leader in new advertising practices. Like any other Internet site, YouTube generates revenue by selling display ads such as standard banner ads (including masthead ads with options) and rich media ads, and also offers in-video overlay display ads and specialized options for homepage ads. These types of ads are available for mobile delivery as well, demonstrating that YouTube is a paid media Internet media option.

YouTube offers the opportunity for channels—designated repositories of whatever videos a brand may want to post for viewers, from ads appearing on TV, another Internet location, or specifically customized. User channels are cost-free with the same functionality as for any other

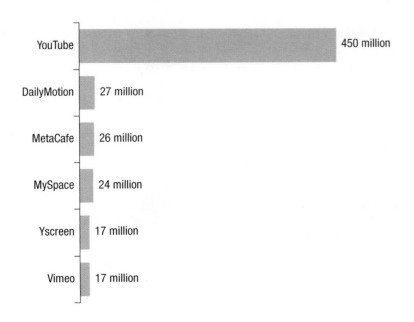

Figure   17-27

Estimated monthly visits to top video sites

Sources: www.ebizmba.com; www.quantcast.com; www.compete.com; www.alexa.com.

user. Thus, a YouTube channel retains the idea of owned media for brands desiring to host video messages. Brand channels are cost-free and offer additional avenues for brand identification and enhanced viewer experience. Custom brand channels offer interactive applications, user-generated submission, live streaming, and client services for fees. Channels can be used very creatively; for example, Koodo used a series of videos on its YouTube channel where consumers could chase a life-size gingerbread man through the streets—clearly from the imaginations of marketers![84]

In some respects the use of channels on YouTube is a wonderful opportunity for advertisers to initiate further social media communication among its viewers (e.g., owned media). Viewers might want to comment on Koodo and its advertising after experiencing the game. Similarly, the Skittles use of YouTube described in Chapter 8 presents ample opportunity for consumers to respond to the brand, much like the sensation with Old Spice a few years ago. And for some unknown reason consumers may decide to create tribute ads for brands they love. One enterprising former student created his own "BlackBerry There Then There Now—Z10 Commercial" on YouTube and picked up more than 35,000 views.

Curiously, major Canadian brand channels for vehicle brands have low subscription rates and low viewership, as shown in Figure 17-28. However, brands can see razor sharp returns—like Dollar Shave Club, with over 10 million views! And it seems that the old adage—familiar from media before Internet video—is that creativity, no matter where it is located or viewed, gets notoriety. A brand's video message in social media is passed along if it is original and creative, much like we see in all facets of advertising.[85]

As an alternative to YouTube, brands can move to less known video hosting vehicles beyond the most dominant player. For Canadian's "The Code" campaign, Molson put together an online video launch to reflect the unwritten rules of "guy social conduct" for targeted beer drinkers aged 19–24. The videos filmed at sporting and music events with comedienne Nicole Arbour interviewed audience members with questions like, "What do you do if you spill someone's beer?" or "Do you have a six-pack or a mega-keg?" Viewers streamed the nine videos on Heavy.com a total of seven million times and could really identify with what their peers were saying and instantly made a link to the brand.[86]

In commenting on the success of brand messages on video hosting sites, experts suggest that a positive ROI is achieved if a clip achieves the one million mark.[87] For example, a video costing $50,000 to produce results in a CPM of $50. This is a different cost comparison based on production since there is no media cost, for now. Canadian advertisers are taking creative risks by placing ads on these sites that they might not normally do with TV. For example, Lululemon posted a video mocking its very own customers in a humorous version of "stuff yogis say" as a take-off on other pop-culture examples.[88] Of course, the one million mark only happens if the video link ricochets throughout social media, another example of how the same ad units discussed in the previous section work in social media as well.[89] And the media cost for distribution is free, since ordinary consumers are doing the work that brands would normally pay media companies to do.

Streaming ads operate much like TV, showing a message while viewing a content video, with options. True View ads permit viewers to skip the ad after five seconds, and YouTube offers four versions: in-stream ads, in-slate ads, display, and search. Standard in-stream ads occur before, during, or after a video and do not have the skip feature. First Watch plays a brand's ad first no matter what video the viewer watches.

YouTube original channels offer similar media vehicles much like TV. There are a host of genres of shows in terms of sports, comedy, lifestyle, and others. Ads can be selectively placed on

Figure 17-28

YouTube subscriber and viewing statistics

	Ford	Chevrolet	Chrysler	Honda	Toyota	Nissan
Subscribers	1,239	2,413	54	920	751	1,311
Video Views	3,948,185	2,356,462	3,316	459,171	2,179,504	1,454,630

Source: Compiled by observation on June 4, 2013.

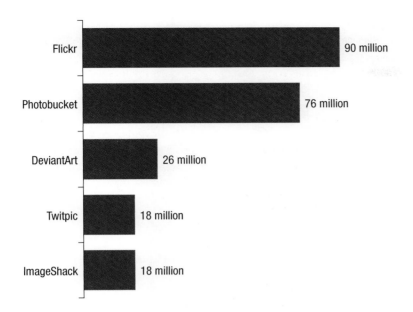

Figure 17-29

Estimated monthly visits to top image hosting sites

Sources: www.ebizmba.com; www.quantcast.com; www.compete.com; www.alexa.com.

any of these channels. Alternatively, advertisers can select placement on regular videos based on profiling characteristics seen in previous media placement.

Photo Images   Figure 17-29 identifies the top image hosting sites. The leader, Flickr, does not dominate this media market as YouTube does with video, yet the combined delivery of the top three easily distances them from the rest of the pack. All three of these organizations, and others, accept advertising placements. Yahoo owns Flickr and so placement in this media vehicle yields numerous options as it is part of the broad advertising tools available across all digital media. In contrast, Photobucket provides very basic information on its Internet site for advertising placement, with a request to call or e-mail them. These two ends of the spectrum show the variance in placing ads as Internet media remains fragmented.

The brand development in these forms of social media appears enormous for different types of advertisers. For example, for anything experiential, like travel, entertainment, and so on—essentially, any product category that has a transformational motive—the images or videos contribute to existing positive attitudes or begin to build new ones for non-users. If Canada wanted to foster more travel, what better way than to sprinkle videos and photos among the vehicles that people from other countries would eventually find when another social media to direct them. Or, to take advantage of the user-generated concept of social media, the travel organizations can merely seek out the video and photo postings of ordinary citizens and create a means for consumers to find them, like a social bookmarking site.

BLOGS

A **blog** (or weblog) is a publication consisting primarily of periodic articles, normally presented in reverse chronological order. Blogs reflect the writings of an individual, a community, a political organization, or a corporation. A blog set up for brand presentation is akin to a website in that it is owned media. Blogs also present the opportunity for ad placement (e.g., paid media). And the ability of consumers to participate with responses and by adding user-generated content permits both positive and negative brand communication. Thus, this social media vehicle is a multifaceted brand communication tool, like other social media. Figure 17-30 identifies the most-visited blogs. Blog sites where writers can set up their own blogs with varying levels of visitors include WordPress and Blogger.

Companies have experimented with corporate or brand blogs to put forth a friendly public relations face to the general public and allow some interactions. These can be within the corporate website or as a standalone. The imagery and tone of blogs provide a less formal

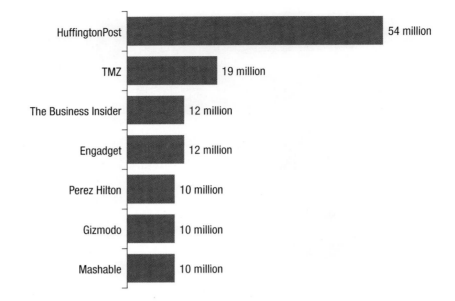

Figure   17-30

Estimated monthly visits to top
blog sites

Sources: www.ebizmba.com;
www.quantcast.com;
www.compete.com; www.alexa.com.

approach for communication, so companies look to blogs as a way of putting forth a friendlier face with an open dialogue. Brands can also look to blogs to address issues or ideas related to consumers who are more committed to the brand by virtue of their participation in viewing and interacting with the blog.

Blogs offer advertisers a potential way to reach their target audience at a small cost since they are specialized vehicles for placing display and video ads as described in the previous section. WordPress does not facilitate the placement of ads; however, Blogger, owned by Google, is associated with its system of ad placements. Individual blogs offer their own media kit for ad prices that are consistent with previous descriptions. For example, BlogTO, a blog about Toronto, offers different banner ad options with a CPM of $10 to $20, along with other customized options.[90] A Vancouver-based blog entitled Scout sells ads to small local businesses on a per placement basis in its "Locals We Recommend" section.[91] Extreme fragmentation occurs, with literally millions of blog media vehicles available in which an advertiser might place its ad. This problem supports the need for digital ad placement firms.

Personal bloggers often find themselves as key influencers for consumers while describing their product experiences. For certain consumers, a blogger has a strong source credibility effect. In this respect, bloggers are acting similarly to journalists who feature product stories in newspapers or magazines. Marketers are also starting to recognize that mothers who blog are particularly successful in this role, as mothers seem to trust other mothers considerably. For example, McDonald's recruited five mothers for behind-the-scenes tours. As they wrote about their experiences, the testimonials resonated like the most perfect commercial: "McDonald's hamburgers are made from 100% Canadian beef. No fillers, no additives. No preservatives. Beef. That's it. I promise. And I can make this promise to you because I was there to see it."[92]

Advertisers also sponsor personal blogs, or an individual blog that is part of a collection of blogs such as the yummymummyclub.ca. Erica Ehm, a famous media host, documented a trip to Alberta on her blog, which included photos taken with a Sony camera. One page of the blog ended with the brand prominently displayed with a sponsorship notice that provided full disclosure of the relationship between the blogger and the brand. Some are critical of this process and suggest that it circumvents the "idea" of a blog, while others are concerned that bloggers do not communicate the advertiser's exact financial contribution. In defence, bloggers cite industries (e.g., fashion, travel) where free goods are routinely passed along for endorsement. Currently, Advertising Standards Canada, the self-regulatory body for marketers, has no plans for potential disguised advertising techniques in blogs.[93] One Canadian lawyer suggests that Canadian bloggers should consider guidelines put forth by the FTC in the United States, where bloggers should clearly disclose the cash or in-kind benefits received from a brand and communicate the nature of the corporate relationship.[94]

Authentic blogs that are personal expressions exist with interested followers. For example, Justyna Baraniecki's fashion blog (Chameleonic) shows photographs of herself modelling the clothing of brands she enjoys wearing for her own personal style. Readers vote their "likes" or appreciate how she puts her collection together through comments. Justyna says, "Everyone has their own way of speaking through their clothes," and suggests fashion blogs are good for young girls learning their style rather than reading celebrity magazines.[95]

COLLABORATIVE PROJECTS

This type of social media includes wikis and social bookmarking Internet sites. Both of these share a common characteristic of having extensive user-generated content. Wikis permit users to add, remove, or change text-based content, and social bookmarking sites allow users to collect links to Internet sites and rate their quality. Figure 17-31 identifies the top reference sites, which include Wikipedia. Other sites do not completely reflect wikis, but their format resembles the idea of a collaborative project for the most part since users respond and converse on a multitude of topics.

Wikipedia does not accept advertising and encourages an active debate on its merits.[96] Many of the other top sites in Figure 17-31 do accept advertising. For example, Answers.com offers extensive placement options and provides a thorough media kit describing the standard and custom formats; this is similar to other social media and Internet sites that are not social media, as discussed in the advertising section.[97] These kinds of collaborative question and answer sites appear conducive for both positive and negative brand communication effects as consumers are in a role of communicating a testimonial by contributing their consumption experiences that may or may not resonate with readers.

Top social bookmarking sites are listed in Figure 17-32. This list demonstrates difficulty with exact classification given the overlapping features, as we see Twitter listed here as well. The drop-off in visitors relative to the other social media lists implies that this avenue for placing ads is less useful for promotional planners beyond a few vehicles. Reddit provides instructions for

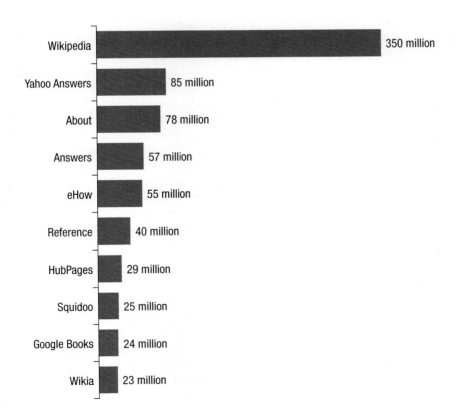

Figure 17-31

Estimated monthly visits to top reference sites

Sources: www.ebizmba.com; www.quantcast.com; www.compete.com; www.alexa.com.

Wikipedia — 350 million
Yahoo Answers — 85 million
About — 78 million
Answers — 57 million
eHow — 55 million
Reference — 40 million
HubPages — 29 million
Squidoo — 25 million
Google Books — 24 million
Wikia — 23 million

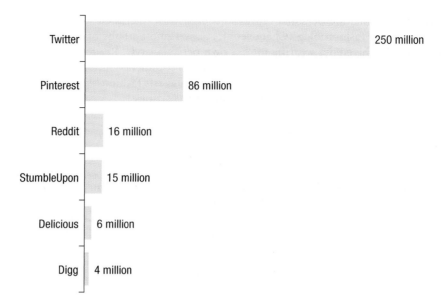

Figure   17-32

Estimated monthly visits to top social bookmarking sites

Sources: www.ebizmba.com; www.quantcast.com; www.compete.com; www.alexa.com.

how would-be advertisers can place ads alongside the content, while others appear to not offer advertising at all.

The user-generated content is quite fascinating from a marketing communication standpoint. For example, extensive lists of bookmarks of Internet sites on a site like Delicious appear very similar to a list of links from a search engine. Additionally, one might construe it as a list of link ads such that the whole site is merely a collection of ads. Alternatively, one could even view it along the same lines as a directory. In either of these cases, the user-generated content appears as if it were advertising of sorts, placed by the advertisers. However, since this "content" was placed by regular people known as "users," this would constitute non-advertising. Of course, all of this gets terribly complicated if the regular person is in fact paid by the advertiser, or its agent, to make the posting.

A site like Pinterest permits all kinds of repurposing of Internet content by users through a simple process of "pinning" images that retain the original link. The site has attracted a high proportion of women, with users spending an average of 16 minutes on the site—versus 3 and 12 minutes for Twitter and Facebook, respectively—and experts see it as a useful social media for expressive and transformational brands.[98] What more could a brand ask than for its customers to select photos from the Internet and comment to show others how great the product is? For example, in its literature to explain how businesses can use this social media, Pinterest cites the example of Sephora, where the retailer noticed that consumers selected pictures from its company Internet site and "pinned" them—which, of course, encouraged others to visit its site.[99] This is another example where "advertising material" became "social media content" as users moved it from one digital location to another. Sephora took advantage of this by adjusting its site with "Pin It" buttons to foster further postings in the social media and sent e-mails to encourage registered customers do more pinning. As this suggests, certain aspects of brand messages in social media occur because of consumer initiative, while others are responses to concerted marketing communication efforts by the brand.

SOCIAL MEDIA INCENTIVES

Promotional planners offer incentives (e.g., sales promotions) to consumers via Internet media. Most of the sales promotions are identical to the ones described in Chapter 14; as discussed in that chapter, Internet media is the delivery or execution mechanism instead of a store or delivery to the home. As mentioned, a coupon can be printed or digitally saved, or clipped from a newspaper flyer. Incentives are also used in Internet media to encourage continued media consumption, and this especially occurs in social media. Because of the interactive nature of social media, promotional planners continue to explore ways to ensure that users will try certain aspects of social media, and importantly continue using social media.

In social media environments, members often receive digital treats. Loyal customers are rewarded with related electronic items provided to them—such as ringtones, wallpapers, emoticons, skins, winks, and pictures for instant message services. In this sense, these services have become digital "gifts" or "premiums," as described in Chapter 14 on sales promotion. Although the non-virtual world usually considered tangible goods to be the premium, the digital age has spawned the concept of intangible gifts that become highly valued.

Another example occurs where various types of points systems allow repeat customers to generate even further rewards—a virtual continuity program for avid Internet media users who are brand loyal. Also, brands offer advergames, skill-challenging endeavours that keep customers amused while offering brand messages during play. Like other aspects of Internet media, games are associated with mobile apps and brands like Foursquare offer status badges for continued use of their service.[100] Molson established the "Seize the Summer" app with Foursquare where users collected badges for activities accomplished to share on Facebook, which translated to a 20 percent growth in fans. The NHL connected with Foursquare to get fans interested in the game with prizes to be won after collecting badges and greater use of the hockey's social media.[101] Thus, Internet media allow previously intangible sales promotions to create value through intangible benefits for continued usage.

Finally, one of the most significant rewards for loyal customers has been the delivery of enhanced content in terms of information or entertainment. Loyal customers are rewarded with exclusive video for their participation. To give thanks, advertisers provide enhanced levels of information where this is deemed valuable. In this sense, the content is not the product witnessed as it is perceived as a bonus—something fitting the original definition of a sales promotion.

 Measuring Internet Effectiveness

Measuring the effectiveness of Internet media is accomplished by a variety of methods, most of which can be done electronically. Audience information (demographics, psychographics, and so on) and exposure were the initial measures of effectiveness; however, fully measuring communication effects occurs.

AUDIENCE MEASURES

When Internet media first developed its own audience size measures, concerns with the research methods led to a slower adoption rate by traditional media buyers. In an attempt to respond to criticism of the audience metrics used, as well as to standardize the measures used to gauge effectiveness, the Interactive Advertising Bureau (IAB)—the largest and most influential trade group—formed a task force consisting of global corporations involved in advertising and research. The final reports of the task force are available from iab.net and contain both American and international guidelines (see also iabcanada.com).

The basic problem facing Internet media concerns a standardized method for determining the size of the audience. The report identified the technical procedures for accurately reporting whether an ad impression has occurred. This answers the fundamental expectation of advertisers as to whether the receiver of the message actually experienced an opportunity to see the ad (i.e., degree of exposure to the message). Another aspect concerns the accepted procedures for auditing the data, much like we see in traditional print media. Another key part of the report included guidelines for presenting data in terms of time of day, week, and month, much like we see in broadcast media. Finally, industry representatives agreed upon substantial guidelines for disclosure of research methodology, again consistent with all major media described in previous chapters. In future, advertisers can look forward to more authentic data to assess the viability of committing increased resources for Internet communication. Firms now use methods similar to those found in other media (i.e., PMB study) to measure demographics, psychographics, location and method of Internet access, media usage, and buying habits.

EXPOSURE AND PROCESSING MEASURES

The electronic recording of Internet user behaviour allows advertisers to investigate a multitude of ways of understanding what has been looked at on a website and for how long, along with user characteristics.[102] Figure 17-33 summarizes measures to track whether pages are actually loaded and therefore have an opportunity to be seen; this would be equivalent to the data recorded by the portable people meter that tracks exposure to TV and other signals. Figure 17-34 shows other measures that can be used as a proxy for the degree of processing since they show how long the browser is loaded.

COMMUNICATION EFFECTS MEASURES

The movement for comprehensive communication effects measurement reveals that the Internet has its own set of criteria for measuring effectiveness and is also borrowing from traditional measures. Companies that provide research information in traditional media now extend their reach to Internet media. Academics publish articles related to measuring communication effectiveness with Internet media, such as consumers' attitudes toward a site or consumers' attitudes to an ad (e.g., banner ads).[103]

A number of companies use traditional measures of recall and retention to test their Internet ads. The same measures have been used to pretest online commercials as well. Survey research, conducted both online and through traditional methods, is employed to determine everything from site usage to attitudes toward a site. Companies now provide information on specific communication measures like brand awareness, message association, brand attitude, and purchase intention.

One of the more extensive attempts to measure the effectiveness of integrating interactive and traditional media is through IAB's cross-media optimization studies (CMOST). These studies are designed to determine the optimal mix of online and offline advertising media vehicles, in terms of frequency, reach, and budget allocation for a given campaign to achieve its marketing goals.[104] What makes these studies important is that they provide insight into (1) the relative contributions of each medium in the mix, (2) the combined contribution of multiple media, (3) optimal media budget allocations, and (4) actionable media mix strategies.

Figure 17-33

Measures of exposure

Type of Measure	What Is Measured
Page impression	Number of users exposed to a Web page
Visits	Number of user sessions
Unique visitors	Number of unique users
Ad impression	Number of users exposed to an ad
Clicks	Number of user interactions with an ad
Click-through rate	Percentage of ads exposed that users click

Figure 17-34

Measures of processing

Type of Measure	What Is Measured
Average time per visit	Number of users exposed to a Web page
Average time per visitor	Number of user sessions

Type of Measure	What Is Measured
Repeat visitor percentage	Number of repeat visitors as a percentage of total visitors
Frequency	Number of visits by unique visitors
Recency	Average interval between user visits

Figure 17-35

Measures of behaviour

MEASURES OF BEHAVIOUR

Finally, Internet data are very adept at measuring the browsing behaviour of users through a variety of means, as shown in Figure 17-35.

Evaluation of Internet Media

As we have done for other media thus far in the text, we summarize the strengths and limitations of Internet media for delivering a message.

STRENGTHS OF INTERNET MEDIA

Target Audience Selectivity   A major strength of Internet media is the ability to target very specific groups of individuals with a minimum of waste coverage. Internet sites are tailored to meet consumers' needs and wants through personalization and other targeting techniques. As a result of precise targeting, messages can be designed to appeal to the specific needs and wants of the target audience. The interactive capabilities of Internet media make it possible to carry on one-to-one marketing with increased success. Social media vehicles are available for any taste in any of life's domains, permitting brands to set up a presence, put up display ads, or encourage or receive any type of COBRAs.

Involvement and Processing Time   Because Internet media is interactive, it provides strong potential for increasing customer involvement and almost immediate feedback for buyers and sellers. A main objective of most websites is to provide significant brand information or rich transformational experiences. By its very definition, the user-generated content requires extensive involvement and processing as do even the most basic levels identified with the COBRAs.

Control for Selective Exposure   Perhaps the greatest strength of Internet media is its availability as an information source. Internet users can find a plethora of information about almost any topic of their choosing merely by conducting a search using one of the search engines. Once they have visited a particular site, users can garner a wealth of information regarding product specifications, costs, purchase information, and so on. Links will direct them to even more information if it is desired. Moreover, this control is very quick compared to all other media.

Creativity   Creatively designed sites can enhance a company's image, lead to repeat visits, and positively position the company. Technological advances have made Internet media as enjoyable to use as broadcast and print media for both cognitive and emotional responses. Social media and interesting ways for consumers to involve themselves with a brand open the door for unlimited creative potential.

Costs   Internet media enables smaller companies with limited budgets to gain exposure to potential customers. For a fraction of the investment that would be required using traditional media, companies can gain national and even international exposure in a timely manner. A creative approach in social media can generate considerable consumer response, providing a significant return on investment for both small and large organizations.

LIMITATIONS OF INTERNET MEDIA

Target Audience Coverage   In the past, one of the greatest limitations of Internet media was the lack of reliability of the research numbers generated. A quick review of forecasts, audience profiles, and other statistics offered by research providers will demonstrate a great deal of variance—leading to a concern of validity and reliability. The actions by IAB to standardize metrics will help reduce these concerns. Tremendous improvement has occurred in the nearly 20 years since the first banner ad was placed online.

Clutter   As the number of ads proliferates, the likelihood of one ad being noticed drops accordingly. The result is that ads may not get noticed, and consumers may become irritated by the clutter. Studies already show that banner ads may be losing effectiveness for this very reason, while others show consistently declining click-through rates. Kantar Media reports an average of two display ads per page on Canadian Internet sites.[105] Certain social media vehicles contain vast amounts of information or video or pictures, leading to a great difficulty of consumers noticing ads competing for viewer attention. Moreover, the blurring between advertising messages and actual content limits consumers' perception and may heighten clutter.

Reach   While Internet media numbers are growing, the ability to reach vast numbers with a placement of a few ad messages or the ability to attract large numbers to a brand's website places strong concern regarding its ability to generate significant reach levels compared to TV. As a result, Internet media works well with traditional media to achieve reach and awareness goals.

Media Image   A poor media image is due to annoying characteristics, deception, and privacy concerns. Numerous studies have reported on the irritating aspects of Internet tactics—like spam, pop-ups, and pop-unders—that deter visitors from repeat visits. Attempts by advertisers to target children with subtle advertising messages have proven to be a significant concern. In addition, data collection without consumers' knowledge and permission, hacking, and credit card theft are problems confronting the Internet. Like direct marketing, Internet marketers must be careful to respect users' privacy. Again, IAB has issued guidelines to improve this concern. In contrast to these early Internet media issues, many consumers enjoy the abundance of social media experiences and find shopping with Internet media very useful for planning all sorts of purchases. In this respect, Internet media is looked upon more favourably, and we might say that this now leans toward being a paradox, both a strength and a limitation.

LO6 IMC Planning: Strategic Use of Internet Media

The text, video, and audio characteristics of Internet media, along with various types of applications (e.g., websites, banner ads, streaming video, sponsorship, promotions, social networks, etc.), positions it as being capable of communicating with customers and non-customers to achieve all communication and behavioural objectives, and to influence consumers at every stage of their decision-making process. The challenge for promotional planners is to select the correct application that fits the target audience and allows for the achievement of the most relevant objective along with the most appropriate message that supports the brand-positioning strategy. This is not an easy task, as there are multiple combinations of digital media opportunities for consideration. It makes their integration an interesting aspect of marketing communication, as seen in the following examples:

- Ben & Jerry's used e-mail, Facebook, Twitter, and finally a specialized website to run a contest for consumers to name a new flavour of ice cream.[106]
- Banff Lake Louise Tourism regularly used videos, blogs, Facebook, and Twitter, and quickly took them all to a new level when a squirrel from a photo taken at the lake began to appear in hundreds of other Internet photos. The "crasher" squirrel's popularity exploded so much, it was featured on billboards and other media.[107]
- Silk Canada created a microsite (sipsavoursmile.ca) to communicate the improved flavour of its soy beverages and allowed consumers to participate in a contest by uploading photos. Other activities included social networking, banner ads, in-store point-of-purchase, and mass media.[108]
- Pepsi sponsored an Internet radio station that broadcast live from a music event hosted by the Podcast Playground, ran a Twitter feed, and sent employees to post content on Twitter, YouTube, and a blog. The company also first communicated the new Pepsi online.[109]

One Canadian Google manager suggested that marketers will need to think about planning issues similar to those found in other media, like how to break through the clutter and how to deliver messages digitally across a wide spectrum of vehicles. At the same time, marketers would have to figure out a way to tap into the resources of the many online connections consumers have through their friends on social networking applications.[110] While this appears to be a solid recommendation, some brands seem to use every conceivable option for Internet media communication.

A second planning issue concerns how Internet media may or may not be better than other media for advertising purposes. Early research investigated whether Internet or TV produced better results and found that the former appeared stronger for high-involvement purchases only.[111] Other research compared the same ad delivered via print media to Internet media and found similar communication effects; however, ads with promotional messages (i.e., discounts) delivered better in print.[112]

A third planning issue pertains to how Internet media are integrated with other media for advertising purposes. One early study concluded that offline advertising increased awareness and subsequent website visits while online ads contributed to website visits. Neither affected the brand equity, as the actual visit to the website played more strongly in that regard.[113] Another study found that a combined TV–Internet message performed better in terms of processing and stronger communication effects versus two TV messages or two Internet messages.[114] The conclusions of a print and Internet study recommended that print ads convey clear reasons to motivate readers to visit the website versus merely placing the website address in the ad.[115]

A fourth planning issue is how Internet media are increasingly part of a complete IMC program. For example, *Gillette Drafted: The Search for Canada's Next Sportscaster* hooked up in a promotional tie-in with *The Score* and used virtually all IMC tools including its own website (Drafted.ca), product placements with contestants on the sports show *The Score*'s website, and mass media.[116] Other research uncovered the significant communication effect of direct-response media through mobile devices after viewers received advertising or promotional TV messages that prompted continued interaction.[117]

Internet media often work with other IMC tools. Promotional planners using print, broadcast, or out-of-home media would need to investigate the degree to which the advertising campaign in these media would be directly transferred to Internet advertising. This is commonly done and there are many examples. Alternatively, Internet advertising could take a substantially different direction—some microsites, for example, have allowed brands to take a more experiential or informational track and have a substantially different role and message compared to what is more publicly available. Finally, Internet media is consumed with other media, notably TV (Figure 17-36), and the communication effects of simultaneous brand exposure via a brand's TV ad and its Facebook page are promising avenues for future development especially for heavy multitasking users who tend to be younger (Figure 17-37).

Internet advertising supports sales promotion activities designed to encourage trial and repeat purchases with banner ads or sponsored search links that direct consumers to contests or price promotional offers. Internet advertising is used successfully for public relations activities as links to corporate websites are found on relevant Internet sites (e.g., financial information

Figure   17-36

Activities performed while watching TV (fall 2012, anglophones 18+)

Source: CBC/Radio-Canada's Media Technology Monitor (MTM).

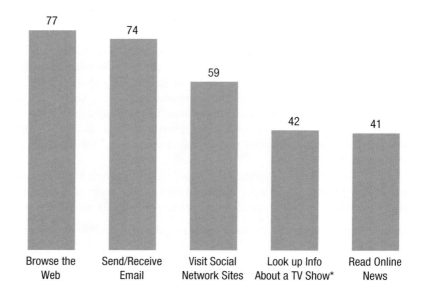

Figure   17-37

Frequency of Internet access and while watching TV (fall 2012, anglophones 18+)

Source: CBC/Radio-Canada's Media Technology Monitor (MTM).

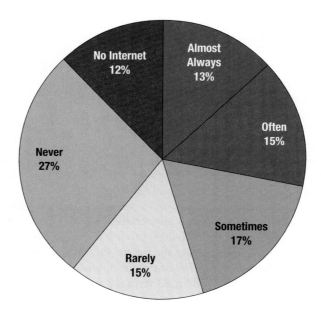

sites) and other mechanisms are available to direct consumers to corporate information to influence appropriate stakeholders. Finally, Internet advertising assists in direct-response marketing as it facilitates communication to the websites for conducting transactions.

Internet media as sales promotion is a new opportunity for marketers, with brands having success. This can work very well with media advertising and sales promotions, as seen in the decorative options delivered to computer users. These fun activities are consistent with both the brand image and consumer experience, with sales promotions offering additional exposure and increasing meaningful brand experiences.

Internet media as public relations supports considerable advertising for consumer packaged goods and food products. Broadcast and print ads for such products create images and persuade consumers with an appropriate brand-positioning strategy. However, consumers may desire more information on usage, or would like to know the exact ingredients in more detail. The Internet site for Becel margarine offers a wonderful array of information for consumers desiring a more involved message about the brand and acts as a tremendous public relations resource by presenting a comprehensive and honest assessment of the brand.

Internet media for direct-response advertising works very well for Belairdirect. The insurance company's print and radio ads suggest that consumers visit its Internet site to compare quotes from Belairdirect and up to five competitors. In this sense, Internet media function beyond mere communication like a regular informational website, especially considering that for a few years the focus of all the ads has been to encourage a direct response via the Internet.

In short, Internet media is capable of communicating all facets of the IMC program, and all aspects of Internet media can work with any other existing advertising media to achieve a brand's objectives. Careful planning is required like any other promotional decision, but the potential for positive results is limitless.

Learning Objectives Summary

 Describe the general characteristics of Internet users and explain website communication.

Internet communication is relatively common for a vast majority of the population. While older segments of the population rely on these media less than younger groups do, the fact that the average hourly per capita consumption reached significant levels suggests that Internet communication will be the significant media of the future. This appears especially true as consumers perform shopping activities online on company websites.

Website communication is used for any and all communication objectives described in this book. They contribute to building brand awareness, disseminating information, building a brand image, and fostering interaction between consumers and the company. The unlimited creativity we have witnessed with websites is remarkable, and something that many might not have dreamed possible two decades ago. This creativity has given rise to consumers, practitioners, and academics referring to it as website advertising or Internet advertising. They apply existing models to understand how attitudes to the website and brand attitude are influenced by strategic and tactical design elements, much like what occurs with print and broadcast media.

 Identify the advertising formats of Internet media.

Advertising formats of Internet media include display ads that involve various types of "banner" ads and rich media ads, link ads, paid search ads, and video ads including online commercials, video-on-demand, and podcasts. Internet media permits targeting of these ad formats across all segmentation variables described in Chapter 3 and in particular in terms of behaviour, geography, and time of day. Targeting occurs through the appropriate selection of the right Internet media vehicle. Whether that may be a news or entertainment portal, established media published from print or broadcast, new forms of publications found on the Internet, or many social media such as social networking, social bookmarking, blogging, etc., successful placement of ads in any of these media vehicles requires an understanding of the receivers or participants. Virtually all of these opportunities can express their audience or provide guidance in directing messages to the most appropriate target audience characteristics.

 Illustrate how to use social media in an IMC plan.

Social media includes collaborative projects, blogs, content communities, social networking sites, virtual game worlds, and virtual social worlds; this chapter investigated the first four. Social media provides three ways of garnering positive brand communication. It demonstrated that there is opportunity for bands to present their image with a degree of control much like their websites. For example, a Facebook page for a brand contains numerous pieces of brand information, photos, and videos.

The chapter concluded that each is a media vehicle for placing any type of ad unit. Most of the specific titles give detailed information on their audience and explain how to place an ad in their media, much like other media have done for decades. Social networking sites with vast amounts of individual information allow specific targeting much like direct marketing. In this respect, social media are very closely aligned with how advertising operates historically.

More significantly, social media gives its participants the opportunity to publish user-generated content in any of the four venues described. In some instances this is true user-generated content where people make videos or post their photos or write their thoughts. In other instances, the user-generated content is repurposed and is in fact someone else's content. Examples of user-generated content are content from a brand, otherwise known as advertising. The end result is that planning brand communication in social media is a delicate situation as brands encourage positive reactions and interactions with current and potential customers.

 Define measures of Internet media effectiveness.

Like other media we concentrated on different measures of effectiveness for each stage of the communication process. Measures are obtained for exposure, processing, and communication effects and behavioural responses. The majority of these are tracked digitally; however, communication effects require direct measurement or a proxy.

 Evaluate the strengths and limitations of Internet media.

We viewed the Internet as a means for communication to reach audiences much like other media, as a way to deliver a message and interact with current and potential customers. With this in mind, Internet media currently offers numerous strengths. Advertisers can direct tailored messages to very selective target audiences. And with technological advances, the creative messages can be richly experienced both cognitively and emotionally for considerable amounts of time as the users themselves decide what they would like to receive and not receive. Finally, this incredible messaging ability is possible at a reasonably low absolute and relative cost.

There are limitations, however. It is unclear to marketers the degree to which the target audience can be covered and reached. Internet media can be viewed as tremendous clutter as users move among websites and social media worlds. And, finally, severe problems regarding advertising delivery, illegal activities, and privacy concerns remain significant drawbacks.

 Apply the ideas of Internet media within the development of an IMC program.

Internet media has been the most rapidly adopted medium of our time. It holds great potential for communicating with all groups of consumers, and customers and non-customers alike. Moreover, it is useful for implementing all aspects of the IMC program including sales promotion, public relations, and direct marketing. Other stakeholders are potential audiences as well, making Internet media unlimited in its ability to persuade. However, contrary to popular belief, the Internet is not a standalone medium. Its role in an integrated marketing communications program strengthens the overall program as well as the effectiveness of Internet media itself.

Key Terms

Review key terms and definitions on Connect.

Review Questions

1. How has Internet media threatened other media? How has Internet media assisted other media?

2. Explain the different advertising formats that advertisers use with Internet media. Discuss the advantages and disadvantages associated with each.

3. Explain the three ways in which a promotional planner can achieve positive marketing communication effects in social media.

4. Describe the ways that marketers measure the effectiveness of their use of Internet media. How do these measures relate to more traditional measures?

5. Review the limitations of Internet media and assess whether these are as weak as the limitations of other media.

6. Discuss the advantages of Internet media. For which types of advertisers is Internet media best suited? Why?

Applied Questions

1. Select a favourite Internet site for a brand and investigate how it achieves the objectives outlined in this chapter.

2. Visit a number of Internet media vehicles and evaluate the effectiveness of the display ads in terms of creativity, message, and ability to reach the intended target audience.

3. Investigate the social media use, in as many vehicles as possible, of a favourite brand, and assess which social media appears most effective for that brand.

4. What measures of marketing communication effectiveness are relevant for each of the four types of social media investigated in this chapter?

5. Given the strengths and limitations of Internet media, how would a promotional planner use all the Internet media options to optimize a digital media plan?

6. Select a product of interest and explain how each of the four types of social media described in this chapter can be integrated effectively with other broadcast, print, and out-of-home media.

Regulatory, Ethical, Social, and Economic Issues for IMC

18

LEARNING OBJECTIVES

LO1 Describe the advertising regulation system in Canada.

LO2 Evaluate the ethical perspectives of advertising.

LO3 Explain the social effects of advertising.

LO4 Examine the economic role of advertising and its effects on consumer choice, competition, and product costs and prices.

Accuracy in Advertising

The 2012 annual report for Advertising Standards Canada upheld a total of 95 complaints violating code standards for message and price information accuracy and clarity. By comparison, the second highest number of complaints upheld reached a total of 16 for violating code standards for gender portrayal. Clearly, Canadians appeared very concerned about receiving the right messages for goods and services, and this issue spilled over in many directions for marketers to consider as they construct their advertising plans.

Product ingredients are a concern for many people, especially food products since these affect our bodies so significantly. With many words and phrases used to convey authentic quality, the term "natural" appeared important for brands to use—and the practice underwent criticism. Processed meats like deli meats, bacon, and hot dogs emerged as one particular target since many brands claimed to be using all-natural ingredients to distance themselves from the unhealthy image these foods have typically received. And, in particular, Schneiders Country Naturals took heat from critics when it claimed that its processed meats are "made with natural ingredients and no artificial additives or preservatives." Debate ensued when critics pointed out that one of the natural ingredients acted like a preservative that had unhealthy consequences. Schneiders disputed the claim; nevertheless, the issue of what exactly "natural" means remained with consumers.

Similarly, automobile consumers were perplexed when a Chrysler 300 ad claimed "Imported from Detroit" while the Detroit-born music star Eminem toured the city in one of the vehicles. Critics countered that the automobile, assembled in Brampton, could not possibly live up to that claim. However, Chrysler responded that, "Imported from Detroit is sort of a fanciful reference; it was never intended as a literal reference." They added that the notion of any car being from any one location appeared remote in the global car industry, where American states manufacture many Toyota brands and Ford cars are manufactured in Mexico and Europe.

With the growth of natural cosmetics (there's that word again!), consumers are concerned that they have not been given the whole truth regarding ingredients in the lipstick, mascara, and other products designed for beauty enhancement that they have used for decades. Some critics see the movement along the lines of when tobacco firms claimed smoking cigarettes was not unhealthy, charging that cosmetic firms knowingly put harmful chemicals in cosmetics. Furthermore, they argue, the advertising of the beauty claims is deceptive without divulging the true components. Naturally(!), the Canadian Cosmetic, Toiletry and Fragrance Association challenges these claims, saying there are not harmful chemicals in the products.

And while accuracy is important, how it is presented is equally important, as shown in a court decision against *Time* magazine. To encourage subscriptions, a headline on the registration claimed the recipient had won a contest. Of course, the fine print made certain that this was in fact not true, but that the possibility existed with a subscription. However, one confused customer took issue with this approach and won $16,000 for damages from the ill-conceived come-on.

Source: Carly Weeks, "Bad. Good?" *The Globe and Mail,* October 17, 2011, p. L1; Michelle Warren, "Are Cosmetics the New Tobacco?" *Marketing Magazine,* February 6, 2012, pp. 10–11; Erin O'Toole, "Read This & Win," *Marketing Magazine,* April 9, 2012, p. 23; Tristin Hopper, "Detroit Takes Credit for Cars Made in Canada," *National Post,* October 12, 2011, p. A2; http://www.adstandards.com/en/ConsumerComplaints/2012adComplaintsReport.pdf.

Question:

1. Are these issues of accuracy in ads relevant for the products purchased by the average student?

Not everyone shares the positive view regarding the role of marketing communication in today's society that our text illustrates thus far. Our perspective looks at advertising and other promotional tools as marketing activities used to convey information to consumers and influence their behaviour in an appropriate manner to facilitate a mutually satisfying exchange. Advertising and promotion are the most visible of all business activities and face scrutiny from scholars, economists, politicians, sociologists, government agencies, social critics, special-interest groups, and consumers, who criticize advertising for its excessiveness, the way it influences society, the methods it uses, its exploitation of consumers, and its effect on our economic system.

Advertising is a very powerful force, and this text would not be complete without a look at the criticisms regarding its ethical, social, and economic effects as well as defences against these claims. Before we entertain this debate, we review the regulations affecting advertising in Canada. The perspectives presented in this chapter reflect judgments of people with different backgrounds, values, and interests. Some students may see nothing wrong with advertising while others may oppose some ads on moral and ethical grounds (Exhibit 18-1). We attempt to present the arguments on both sides of these controversial issues and allow individuals to draw their own conclusions.

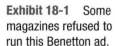 Advertising Regulation in Canada

Regulation of advertising in Canada occurs through both government regulation and self-regulation. In this section, we review both of these topics. With respect to government regulation, we focus on four prevalent domains. The Canadian Radio-television and Telecommunications Commission (CRTC) is responsible for laws and regulations concerning broadcasting and telecommunications, so its role in advertising is relevant. The *Competition Act* regulates misleading or deceptive ads. Finally, the Quebec government has strong regulations with respect to advertising to children. In the other direction, Advertising Standards Canada (ASC) acts as the self-regulation body for the advertising industry. Responsibility for many of the federal laws regarding the content of advertising messages for specific product categories has been transferred to ASC by the request of the federal government.

CANADIAN RADIO-TELEVISION AND TELECOMMUNICATIONS COMMISSION (CRTC)

The mandate of the CRTC is to ensure that the *Broadcasting Act of 1991* and the *Telecommunications Act of 1993* are upheld throughout Canada. The broad objective of both acts is to make

Exhibit 18-1   Some magazines refused to run this Benetton ad.

certain that all Canadians can receive broadcasting and telecommunications services. In attaining its mandate, the CRTC is required to delicately balance the needs of citizens, industries, and interest groups with respect to programming and costs. For purposes of advertising, we will concentrate on the broadcasting side.

The CRTC regulates more than 5,900 media organizations (i.e., television, cable distribution, AM and FM radio, pay and specialty television, direct-to-home satellite systems, multipoint distribution systems, subscription television, and pay audio). The CRTC is responsible for granting the licences for these media and ensuring that they comply with the *Broadcasting Act.* Within the context of the *Broadcasting Act,* the CRTC focuses on a number of relevant issues (i.e., content, competition, technology). There are three areas for broadcasting ads where the CRTC is involved significantly:

- *Signal substitution.* In an effort to keep advertising revenue in Canada, the CRTC allows television broadcasters to substitute Canadian-sponsored ads on programming originating from the United States when shows are delivered at the same time on both Canadian and American networks. While this appears acceptable to most Canadians most of the time, football viewers often feel left out when some U.S. ads are not part of the domestic feed for the Super Bowl.
- *Advertising limits.* The CRTC ensures that specialty services carry 12 minutes of advertising during the broadcast day, which lasts 18 hours beginning at 6:00 a.m. However, public service announcements or "ads" for Canadian TV shows are not counted in this total.
- *Infomercials.* An infomercial is a program lasting more than 12 minutes that combines the promotion of a product in an engaging, entertainment-like style. The CRTC approves all infomercials for any television station, network, or specialty service.

There are three areas where the CRTC is not involved significantly:

- *False or misleading ads.* The CRTC does not address complaints of these types of ads and refers complaints to the Competition Bureau of the federal government. The CRTC has left this for the ASC as well.
- *Alcohol and drugs.* There are regulations for advertising these products, but the CRTC has disbanded the screening process of the ads. This is now the responsibility of the ASC, and we will summarize this later in this section.
- *Internet.* The CRTC does not regulate content on the Internet or require licences for those that "broadcast" on this medium. It currently is investigating whether video content delivered via the Internet falls under the jurisdiction of the broadcast code since it is technically not a broadcast like original TV and radio signals.[1]

As a regulator, the CRTC evaluated a highly topical application that would have changed the advertising industry. A marketing firm with the support of the Canadian Association of Advertisers wanted to insert Canadian ads during feeds from U.S. specialty services (e.g., TBS, A&E). The Canadian Association of Broadcasters argued against this change suggesting that sufficient advertising capacity existed in Canada, and that increased capacity would reduce advertising revenue.[2] The CRTC denied the application.

COMPETITION ACT

The federal *Competition Act* prevents false or misleading advertising. Significantly revised in 1999, most of the act contains civil provisions to ensure compliance with the act rather than seeking punishment. In this situation, the goal is not so much to prove deliberate intent, but rather to remedy the situation with the most appropriate solution, such as cease and desist orders. Some criminal provisions still exist for the most serious offences, where false advertising occurred knowingly. Enforcement of the act falls under the jurisdiction of the Competition Bureau of Industry Canada. Some examples of what is not permissible are shown in Figure 18-1.[3] In 2009, the Act underwent revision with respect to deceptive marketing, items pertaining to pricing, and some other amendments. In particular, the fines for misleading representation in advertising increased substantially for non-criminal offences.[4] Industry people expect strong enforcement in the coming years, since Moores and the Brick have both received warnings for

Figure   18-1   Advertising and marketing law in Canada

Guideline	Advertising Claim	Misleading Content
Cannot make false claims	Buy this vacuum and get a year's supply of vacuum bags absolutely free	There is a $12 administration fee for the vacuum bags
Even if claim is true, do not give false impression	Drive away in a Corvette for just $39,000	The visual display is a version with a sport package and costs $50,000
Avoid double meanings	Number one in the category	Best in sale, but not in quality
Disclaimers should not contradict headlines or body copy	Don't pay a cent until 2014	Fine-print says except for taxes and $750 freight

Source: Adapted from *Advertising and Marketing Law In Canada*, Brenda Pritchard and Susan Vogt, LexisNexis, Butterworths, 2006.

inappropriate communication for their sales promotions. Some questioned whether the changes were constitutional or whether the expanded situations of misrepresentation were clearly identified; nevertheless, the laws are currently in place.[5]

REGULATIONS ON ADVERTISING TO CHILDREN

Although no federal laws specifically regulate advertising to children, the Broadcast Code for Advertising to Children acts as an important guide to ensure that children are not easily manipulated with exaggerated claims. In contrast, the province of Quebec provides strict regulations. According to the *Consumer Protection Act of Quebec*, it is illegal to direct commercial advertising messages to persons younger than 13 years of age. Provisions are in place to determine whether or not an ad is directed to children. Specifically, the provisions concern the product, the way the ad is presented, and the time and place the ad is shown. One exception to the law is a regularly published magazine that is for sale. These magazines, however, have 16 guidelines with respect to their advertising claims; the types of products; the portrayal of people's behaviour, motivation, or attitude reflected in the ad; and the source of the message (i.e., a person or character).

To apply the law, the Quebec government provides summary guidelines for advertisers to follow, and it also provides screening services for advertisers if they are uncertain whether an item contravenes the law. The purpose of the guidelines is to ensure that advertisers fully understand and correctly interpret the law. The guidelines pertain to precisely describing the types of advertising appeals that are not permitted, clearly defining what is meant by a children's TV program, and exactly stating the percentage of children in the audience that constitutes a children's TV program. The guidelines include the degree to which messages can be directed toward children depending upon whether the product is exclusively for children (i.e., candy), partially for children (i.e., cereal), or not for children. There are also specific guidelines for public service announcements directed to children, even though there is no commercial message. Ethical Perspective 18-1 identifies some new trends on this topic.

Even though Quebec's stringent guidelines regarding advertising to children should be a sufficient deterrent, some advertisers push the limit—as seen by Vachon, maker of the Jos Louis and Passion Flakie treats. Vachon created a cartoon character named Igor to represent its chocolate-filled, gorilla-shaped muffins. Vachon placed the imagery on CDs, DVDs, and other materials for daycare centres to use when entertaining the children.

In this situation Vachon tested the laws in three ways—the product, the message, and the time and place—and faced a $44,000 fine. It appears that the Quebec government is getting tougher with not-so-healthy products with the higher incidence of child obesity. However, there are indications that brands of healthier products, or a corporate initiative to encourage children to stay active, might not be as scrutinized. So while there are laws governing advertising to children in Quebec, the consistent application appears murky given the ethical implications.[6]

New Directions for Advertising to Children

Historically, advertising to children has been rife with challenges and controversy. It becomes even more so now—children use many digital media such that the issues are increasingly complex, with new ideas for protection and groups making suggestions on how marketers should abide by the spirit of the laws prescribed for existing media. Despite this positive trend, marketers remain intrusive within the everyday lives of children.

Currently, 90 percent of the most popular children's Internet sites contain advertising, and many are really advertising disguised as content in the form of games or activities associated with toys, TV characters, or some other kind of brand identification. It's no wonder we see children exposed to more advertising through their increased use of technology compared to even just a few years ago. It seems kids are using apps before they are even capable of tying their own shoes. And despite the concern for privacy exemplified in the *Personal Information Protection and Electronic Documents Act,* very little exists for guiding what is acceptable for advertising to children.

An interpretation guideline of federal laws by Advertising Standards Canada is a good start; however, it does not contain guidance for digital sources although the general message is certainly applicable. As well, the Canadian Children's Food and Beverage Advertising Initiative provides strong guidance that includes measures for digital communication, but adherence remains voluntary. Experts in the field expect direction and regulation soon in the aftermath of recent hearings by the Office of the Privacy Commissioner regarding online tracking and behavioural advertising. In the meantime, the following suggestions appear reasonable for marketers to consider.

One, even if there are no guidelines for online, advertisers should just use the broadcast code instructions and its interpretation guidelines for digital since they are readily adaptable. Two, advertisers should involve parents as much as possible. Three, advertisers should have an understanding from a moral perspective on blurring the lines between advertising and content since the receiver should always know and understand that advertising has occurred. Four, advertisers should be respecting children's privacy and treating data the same way it is done with adults. Five, advertisers should apply the standard found in other media for online communication. Six, advertisers should assess whether advertising to children is actually financially viable, as they have no income and do not make purchases. Echoing these thoughts is David Buckingham, director of the Centre for the Study of Children, Youth, and Media in the United Kingdom, who advocates the importance of distinguishing between content and advertising directed to children because they are unable to discern the difference for themselves as they cognitively develop.

Despite these suggestions for improvements, advertisers continue to look for ways of influencing children. Another attempt in this direction occurred with the placement of TVs in schools as a pilot project to keep students informed of schedules, events, activities, and student content. To support the cost, the TVs had messages for "good" products such as milk, government, and higher education institutions. With positive reactions initially, conflict arose when a planned expansion included a movement toward many more minutes of advertising per day, with some concerned it would be the start of messages that many would not welcome in schools. Further, some did question why even "good" advertising messages should be in the school in the first place.

Source: Kate Hammer, "Advertising on School TV Screens Raises Alarm?" *The Globe and Mail,* March 9, 2011, p. A14; Dakshana Bascaramurty, "The Fine Line between a Pokemon Ad and Entertainment," *The Globe and Mail,* November 15, 2011, p. L1; Joanna Pachner and Alicia Androich, "Kids in Play," *Marketing Magazine,* March 14, 2011, pp. 27–28, 30–31.

Question:

1. What limits or controls do you believe should be in place for children of varying ages?

Exhibit 18-2   Ad by ASC communicating its purpose.

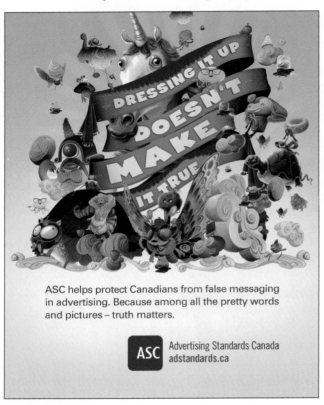

ASC helps protect Canadians from false messaging in advertising. Because among all the pretty words and pictures – truth matters.

ASC Advertising Standards Canada
adstandards.ca

ADVERTISING STANDARDS CANADA (ASC)

The ASC is a not-for-profit, self-regulatory industry body with a mandate to create and maintain community confidence in advertising. The ASC represents advertisers, media organizations, and advertising industry suppliers and has more than 200 corporate members. Its Standards Division administers the industry's self-regulatory codes (i.e., *Canadian Code of Advertising Standards, Gender Portrayal Guidelines*), handles complaints about advertising, and administers any disputes that arise between advertisers. Its Advertising Clearance Division previews advertisements in five industry categories, as well as ads directed toward children, ensuring that advertisers will follow applicable legislation, regulatory codes, and industry standards. An example of one of its public service ads is shown in Exhibit 18-2.

Canadian Code of Advertising Standards   The Code, as it is known, describes what is not acceptable advertising. According to the ASC, "Advertising is defined as any message (the content of which is controlled directly or indirectly by the advertiser) expressed in any language and communicated in any medium to Canadians with the intent to influence their choice, opinion or behaviour." The Code pertains to the content of ads only. It does not limit the promotion of legal products or the demonstration of products for their intended purpose. The intention of the Code is to provide standards so that responsible and effective advertising results without minimizing the right of firms to advertise. It does not supersede any laws or regulations.

The Code is used as the criteria to assess whether a complaint is legitimate or not, and the ASC is very clear in how it uses the Code to resolve complaints. "The context and content of the advertisement and the audience actually, or likely to be, or intended to be, reached by the advertisement, and the medium/media used to deliver the advertisement, are relevant factors in assessing its conformity with the Code."

The Code is supported by all member organizations as it sets the standard for advertising with respect to honesty, truth, accuracy, fairness, and propriety. Members are expected to follow the Code both in letter and in spirit and are expected to substantiate any advertised claims when requested. The Code contains 14 clauses:

1. Accuracy and Clarity
2. Disguised Advertising Techniques
3. Price Claims
4. Bait and Switch
5. Guarantees
6. Comparative Advertising
7. Testimonials
8. Professional or Scientific Claims
9. Imitation
10. Safety
11. Superstitions and Fears
12. Advertising to Children
13. Advertising to Minors
14. Unacceptable Depictions and Portrayals

In 2003, ASC updated clauses 6, 10, and 14 as part of its ongoing mandate to ensure that the Code reflects current practices and fairness. While on the surface the changes were just a few words for each clause, the meaning permitted a more reasonable and flexible interpretation. For the past decade, ASC has compiled "interpretation guidelines" so that members could understand how ASC will evaluate ads in terms of specific codes or advertising trends.[7] The first and fourth guidelines concern Clauses 10 or 14 and motor vehicle advertising. The second guideline provides extensive documentation on advertising to children pertaining to Clause 12. Environmental claims and how they are related to Clause 1, the Competition Bureau, and the Canadian Standards Association is the topic of the third guideline.

As part of the second guideline, ASC acts as the administrator for the Canadian Children's Food and Beverage Advertising Initiative (CAI).[8] Canada's largest food and beverage marketers have committed to not advertise directly to children under 12 years of age, although some committed to advertise only "better-for-you" products to children. The initiative is in response to the growing obesity problem among children. In doing so, the marketers agreed to five core principles for advertising directed to children under 12 years of age:

- Devote 100 percent of television, radio, print, and Internet advertising to further the goal of promoting healthy dietary choices and/or healthy active living.
- Incorporate only products that represent healthy dietary choices in interactive games primarily directed to children under 12 years of age.
- Reduce the use of third-party licensed characters in advertising for products that do not meet the CAI's product criteria.
- Not pay for or actively seek to place food and beverage products in program/editorial content of any medium.
- Not advertise food or beverage products in elementary schools.

The principles apply to other avenues of communication directed to children under 12 such as micro-sites, early childhood (EC) video/computer games, DVDs, mobile devices, and word-of-mouth. ASC monitored the performance of all 19 organizations committed to CAI in 2011 and concluded in its report that all companies complied with all guidelines in all media and promotional vehicles.[9]

Gender Portrayal Guidelines   The guidelines, based on a previous CRTC task force, attempt to ensure that women and men are portrayed appropriately and equally in advertising. The ASC presents the guidelines as the direction of areas or topics from which complaints or issues have arisen over the past 30 years. There are six overall clauses, pertaining to authority, decision making, sexuality, violence, diversity, and language. For example, some might find the passionate theme of Calvin Klein ads as conveying overt sexuality (Exhibit 18-3, Exhibit 18-4).

Exhibit 18-3   Calvin Klein ads depict women with sexual poses.

Exhibit 18-4   Calvin Klein ads depict men with sexual poses.

When interpreting the guidelines, the ASC has four suggestions that advertisers should consider. The overall impression of the ad should not violate the spirit of gender equality; there are clauses specifically addressed toward women, as men are at less risk of being negatively portrayed. History and art should not be used as an excuse for violating a clause. Finally, certain products and how they are advertised are amenable to more appropriate media.

Complaint Process   The Standards Division handles complaints in three streams. **Consumer complaints** are those from ordinary citizens who believe that an ad is unacceptable. The ASC receives these complaints directly as well as through government departments and agencies at all levels, such as the Better Business Bureau, the CRTC, and the Canadian Broadcast Standards Council. **Special interest group complaints** are those from a demonstrated organization that expresses a unified viewpoint. Complaints from other advertisers are known as **trade disputes**. While there is a distinct complaint process for consumers and special interest groups, the general procedures for each have a degree of similarity that we will touch upon. One difference, however, is that ASC first determines that the special interest group complaint is not a disguised trade dispute.

The initial complaint is authenticated to make sure that it is, in fact, a consumer or special interest group complaint and not a trade dispute. From there, the complaint is evaluated to determine whether it legitimately violates a Code provision or whether it is not a legitimate complaint. Reasons for a complaint not being legitimate include that the complaint did not identify a specific advertiser, that the ad was no longer current, and that the communication was not advertising. This initial assessment occurs at the national (i.e., Toronto) or regional (i.e., Alberta, Atlantic, British Columbia) Consumer Response Councils for English ads, and le Conseil des normes in Montreal for French ads. If the complaint is valid, the advertiser is contacted and has an opportunity to respond to the complaint before the Council makes a formal ruling. On the other hand, the advertiser can take an appropriate action to remedy the complaint as part of the response. In these cases, the advertiser would not be identified in the ASC complaints report. An advertiser who responds and does not remedy the situation can be identified in the report if the Council upholds the complaint.

The Council for Canadians filed a special interest group complaint against Nestlé for a claim that "most water bottles avoid landfill sites and are recycled" in a *Globe and Mail* ad. Its complaint cited a statement from Nestlé's annual report stating the contrary. And while this appeared to be a complaint with merit, ASC dismissed the case since the Council went public with its complaint thereby contravening the confidentiality requirement of the proceedings.[10] Sierra Club Canada filed a special interest complaint concerning a Canwest piece that stated, "in partnership with Shell Canada." The oil company put the advertorial series together as a public relations information source for the media, the government, and the general public. An editor with the media organization stated that the layout of the ad was not consistent with the editorial content and that "readers would realize the pages are advertisements for Shell." However, the executive director of Sierra Club concluded they appeared like neither advertising nor editorial.[11]

For trade disputes, there is a formal adjudication procedure where each party represents its point of view at a hearing if an initial first-stage resolution is unsuccessful. An appeal of the decision is possible, but eventually there is a resolution if an advertiser is found in violation. As members of the ASC, they follow the recommendations of ASC similar to the consumer and special interest process. However, a situation emerged where for the first time ever an advertiser did not follow ASC's decision. Rogers disputed a Bell advertising claim and ASC upheld the complaint, suggesting Bell amend the ad or stop showing it. Bell did not participate in the hearing or comply with the decision since it was not a member and continued running the ad. In turn, and for the first time, ASC asked media companies to refrain from airing the ad.[12]

Complaints Report   The ASC has published a more comprehensive annual report since 1997. This format includes the identification of advertisers and the details of all complaints. Previously, the annual report provided global statistics. Figure 18-2 shows a capsule summary of the past few years. For each statistic, the first data point is the number of complaints, while the second is the number of ads those ads represent. The ratio of the number of complaints

	2012	2011	2010
Number of Complaints (ads)			
Received	1,310 (1,057)	1,809 (1,153)	1,200 (743)
Pursued	854 (688)	1,210 (1,129)	1,059 (642)
Evaluated by Council	141 (112)	177 (109)	180 (122)
Upheld by Council	116 (87)	146 (83)	84 (58)
Upheld Complaints (ads)			
Received	9% (8%)	8% (7%)	7% (8%)
Pursued	14% (13%)	12% (7%)	8% (9%)
Evaluated by Council	82% (78%)	82% (76%)	47% (48%)

Sources: http://www.adstandards.com/en/ConsumerComplaints/2012adComplaintsReport.pdf; http://www.adstandards.com/en/ConsumerComplaints/2011adComplaintsReport.pdf; http://www.adstandards.com/en/ConsumerComplaints/2010adComplaintsReport.pdf

Figure 18-2

Summary of complaints from Advertising Standards Canada's annual Complaints Report

to the number of ads indicates that the number of complaints per ad is fewer than two. This underscores the fact that the content of the complaint is justification for investigating an ad. The percentage of complaints upheld has seen some modest movement, as expressed by the number of complaints received, pursued, and evaluated by the council.

In 2012, television, Internet, and out-of-home media generated 43 percent, 21 percent, and 7 percent of all complaints, respectively. With increased online advertising expenditure, we now see a greater number of complaints. A pattern on the source of the complaint occurs each year, with clause 1 (accuracy and clarity), clause 3 (price), clause 14 (unacceptable depictions and portrayals), and clause 10 (safety) consistently receiving the most complaints. We now briefly review ads that achieved notoriety over the past decade, summarized from past reports found at the ASC website.

Complaints for Debate   One of the most controversial rulings occurred in 2001. A Ford Motor Company TV ad showed a young female shoving a male store clerk into the hatchback of her car and driving away with him. This ad received nine complaints, and the Council upheld the complaints, citing clause 14 as the ad depicted an abduction, which is an unlawful activity. Ford appealed the decision; however, the Appeal Panel confirmed the original decision. Ford's post-appeal statement makes this example an interesting debate:

> Ford of Canada did not intend to offend any segment of the population in this particular advertisement; rather the aim of the ad was to show the attributes of the Focus. The identical advertisement shown in Quebec (both in English and in French) was determined not to contravene the *Code* by the Consumer Response Council and Appeal Panel in Quebec. Particulars of this complaint were provided to the press by a consumer complainant even though this process is intended to be confidential. Subsequent to the Appeal Decision, Margaret Wente, in a lengthy *Globe and Mail* article dated January 31, 2002, gave strong positive support for the ad. However, in light of the decision of the ASC Appeal Panel, Ford of Canada will withdraw the current English advertisement.[13]

In early 2004, a television ad for an alcohol beverage depicted two women engaging in a passionate kiss. The 113 complaints indicated that the scene was inappropriate for family viewing programming. Council upheld this complaint, stating, "the commercial displayed obvious indifference to conduct or attitudes that offended standard of public decency prevailing among a significant segment of the population." Council concluded that the ad in question did not contravene the code providing it was shown later than 9:30 in the evening.

A Kia Canada television commercial caused controversy during 2007 and received 77 complaints from individuals and those in the law-enforcement profession. The advertised vehicle contained two adults "making out," after which the woman returned to a police car wearing an officer's uniform. Council upheld the complaint citing clause 14(c) and concluded that the ad demeaned female officers in particular and all law-enforcement officials in general. Kia responded to the complaint with the following statement:

> As a responsible advertiser, Kia Canada Inc. [Kia] is aware of Advertising Standards Canada [ASC] guidelines, of which its media service agencies are members, and strives to adhere to the spirit of which they have been written. While not in agreement with the Council's final decision, Kia respects it and the process by which it was achieved. Kia believes it has responded to the subject of the complaints by making revisions to the commercial in question, and in adherence to the ASC's Advertising Standards Code.[14]

However, Kia's concern became more public when it ran an edited version of the ad that did not show the woman leaving the car. Instead, words on the screen announced a more suitable ending to the commercial for all audiences. The final scene featured a goat eating in a meadow for 10 seconds while light-hearted music played. We leave the interpretation of this revised ending for interested students to debate![15]

Also in 2007, the council determined certain Dairy Queen ads showed an unsafe act and reinforced bullying behaviour as the TV ad characters restrained others while eating Dairy Queen ice cream. The response from managers of the brand appears to suggest caution to advertisers with co-branding messages:

> Dairy Queen is all about creating smiles and stories for families and often uses irreverent, off-beat humour in its commercials. The Kit Kat commercial was meant to accentuate this in a humorous way how families interact in a playful manner. Although we are not in agreement with the Council's decision, we are respectful of the process.[16]

An ad from Auto Trader, part of an overall campaign that compared buying a used car online to meeting another person with an online dating service, received only six complaints. However, the complaint, the council decision, and the advertiser statement cover new ground:

> In a television commercial, a man and a woman met in a coffee shop for the first time. After exchanging names, the woman asked the man if she could "take a quick peek". The man obliged by lowering his pants so the woman could look at his private parts from various angles. In the audio portion of the commercial the announcer said that "You can do that on Auto Trader—where you can research your car before you buy it."[17]

The complaint alleged that the ad depicted a demeaning portrayal of men and offended standards of public decency. However, the council agreed with the latter point but concluded that the ad denigrated both men and women. Auto Trader's rebuttal statement takes into account the media time frame and media vehicle, two critical points that ASC highlighted in previous rulings for more acceptable adult messages. And its inclusion as part of a television show makes this case another one for debate:

> Trader Corporation is not condoning the behaviour in the commercial "Research". We believe it is clear to anyone viewing that the actions in the commercial are exaggerated and, via the copyline "You can do that on AutoTrader.ca", clearly portrayed as behaviour that is not socially acceptable. Rather these actions are used in a humourous and entertaining manner to support the campaign message—It is easier to find your perfect "match" (car) with Auto Trader. Our belief that most people understand the humour is supported not only by positive reviews by the advertising press for its empowering message to female car buyers but also by quantifiable market research that indicates that the commercial performed significantly above industry norms on scores such as 'enjoyable' and 'appropriate and fits my lifestyle'. We have also tried to put it into adult-oriented television programs which match the content of the ads realizing that the commercial is somewhat risque for Canadian standards. It is also interesting to note that the commercial was recently selected for the U.S.-based show World's Funniest TV Commercials.[18]

We included these cases as they represent milestones in the relationship between ASC and it members. They show disagreement between ASC administrators (i.e., Ford), one of the most complaints ever (i.e., alcohol beverage), the most unexpected reaction from a member (i.e., Kia), a difficulty with co-branding (i.e., Dairy Queen), and a substantial rebuttal (i.e., Auto Trader). Exhibit 18-5 shows an ad from ASC to encourage consumer awareness of truthfulness in advertising.

Clearance Process The ASC provides clearance services for ads for many product categories and ads directed toward children for all jurisdictions except Quebec.

- *Alcohol.* The ASC adheres to the CRTC *Code for Broadcast Advertising of Alcoholic Beverages.* The CRTC disbanded clearance services in 1997. This code gives 17 precise guidelines on what is not permitted in alcohol ads. Some of the guidelines pertain to not attracting underage drinkers, non-drinkers, or problem drinkers. Many other guidelines focus on the message with respect to the type of consumption motivation, consumption situation, source, and appeal. The ASC will review all TV and radio ads across the country as well as print and out-of-home ads in British Columbia.

- *Cosmetics.* Health Canada transferred the clearance for cosmetic products ads to the ASC in 1992, although clearance is not an absolute requirement. The ASC follows the *Guidelines for Cosmetic Advertising and Labelling Claims.* The most recent version is a joint publication of the ASC, Health Canada, and the Canadian Cosmetic, Toiletry and Fragrance Association, and was published in 2000. The guidelines list acceptable and unacceptable claims for two types of hair care products, nail products, and five types of skin care products. Another set of guidelines list unacceptable and acceptable claims for toothpaste, deodorant, mouthwash, perfumes/fragrances/colognes, sun-care products, vitamins, and aromatherapy products. Finally, the same is done for different benefit claims, such as anti-wrinkle, healthy ingredients, nourishment, relaxation, respiration, revitalization, therapy/treatment, and lifting.

- *Non-prescription drugs.* Health Canada also transferred the clearance of non-therapeutic aspects of non-prescription drug ads directed toward consumers to the ASC in 1992. The ASC ensures that broadcast and print copy comply with Health Canada's *Consumer Drug Advertising Guidelines* and the *Food and Drugs Act and Regulations.* Health Canada has also given to the ASC the responsibility for resolving any complaints of advertising for this category. To facilitate this change, Health Canada has published a document that describes its role, the ASC's role, and the claims that can be made in ads directed to consumers. Most of the guidelines in this document focus on the need for advertisers to provide factual information of the product's attributes and benefits and that the claims are scientifically valid.

- *Ads directed to children.* The ASC uses the *Broadcast Code for Advertising to Children (Children's Code),* published by the Canadian Association of Broadcasters in cooperation with the ASC, to assess whether ads directed toward children are appropriate. The code takes into account the unique characteristics of children to ensure adequate safety and has nine guidelines concerning factual presentation, product prohibitions, avoiding undue pressure, scheduling, source or endorser of the message, price, comparison claims, safety, and social values. The code also gives seven instructions on clearance procedures, such as when clearance is required or not, when ads can be directed to children, and during which programs ads can be directed to children.

- *Food.* The ASC evaluates broadcast ads with respect to the *Food and Drugs Act and Regulations* and the *Guide to Food Labelling and Advertising.* Its policy guidelines make a distinction between food claims that are exempt from clearance and those that require clearance in four categories: general advertising, occasion-greeting advertising (i.e.,

Exhibit 18-5 An ASC ad humorously shows how truth in advertising is important.

Christmas), promotional advertising, and sponsorship advertising. In addition, the ASC guidelines for the use of comparative advertising in food commercials outline six principles for appropriate executions of this presentation style. Finally, the ASC guidelines on claims based on research and survey data have requirements pertaining to all aspects of the research design (i.e., sample, data collection).

In conclusion, Advertising Standards Canada self-regulates advertising in Canada based on Canadian laws. However, as the name indicates, it is responsible only for advertising. Other brand messages arising from more innovative communication tools are not covered by these guidelines. For example, product reviews found on Internet sites or brand evaluations on blogs are not considered advertising, even though the actual effect may be quite similar in terms of awareness or influencing consumer opinion.

ⓛⓞ² Ethical Effects of Advertising

While many laws and regulations determine what advertisers can and cannot do, not every issue is covered by a rule. Marketers must often make decisions regarding appropriate and responsible actions on the basis of ethical considerations rather than on what is legal or within industry guidelines. **Ethics** are moral principles and values that govern the actions and decisions of an individual or group.[19] Advertising and promotion are areas where a lapse in ethical standards or judgment can result in actions that are highly visible and often very damaging to a company, so ethical considerations are imperative when planning IMC decisions. Much of the controversy over advertising stems from the ways companies use it as a selling tool and from its impact on society's tastes, values, and lifestyles. Specific techniques used by advertisers are criticized as deceptive or untruthful, offensive or in bad taste, and exploitative of certain groups, such as children. We discuss each of these criticisms, along with advertisers' responses.

ADVERTISING AS UNTRUTHFUL OR DECEPTIVE

One of the major complaints against advertising is that many ads are misleading or untruthful and deceive consumers. A number of studies have shown a general mistrust of advertising among consumers.[20] A study by Banwari Mittal found that consumers felt that less than one-quarter of TV commercials are honest and believable.[21] Sharon Shavitt, Pamela Lowery, and James Haefner conducted a major national survey of more than 1,000 adult consumers to determine the general public's current attitudes toward and confidence in advertising. They found that consumers generally do not trust advertising, although they tend to feel more confidence in advertising claims when focused on their actual purchase decisions.[22] Ethical Perspective 18-2 tells the story of deceptive advertising in Canada.

Advertisers should have a reasonable basis for making a claim about product performance and may be required to provide evidence to support their claims. However, deception can occur more subtly as a result of how consumers perceive the ad and its impact on their beliefs.[23] The difficulty of determining just what constitutes deception, along with the fact that advertisers have the right to use puffery and make subjective claims about their products, tends to complicate the issue. **Puffery** has been legally defined as "advertising or other sales presentations which praise the item to be sold with subjective opinions, superlatives, or exaggerations, vaguely and generally, stating no specific facts."[24] But a concern of many critics is the extent to which advertisers are *deliberately* untruthful or misleading.

Sometimes advertisers have made overtly false or misleading claims or failed to award prizes promoted in a contest or sweepstakes. However, these cases usually involve smaller companies and a tiny portion of the billions of dollars spent on advertising and promotion each year. Most advertisers do not design their messages with the intent to mislead or deceive consumers or run sweepstakes with no intention of awarding prizes. Not only are such practices unethical, but the culprits would damage their reputation and risk prosecution by regulatory groups or government agencies. National advertisers in particular invest large sums of money to develop

ETHICAL PERSPECTIVE 18-2

Deceptive Ad Practices Halted

Led by Melanie Aitken, the Competition Bureau levied a $10 million penalty on Bell for misleading advertising over the course of three and a half years. Rogers faced the same penalty of $10 million previously for claiming that it was a more reliable service than its competitor Wind Mobile. "The Competition Bureau determined that, since December 2007, Bell has charged higher prices than advertised for many of its services, including home phone, Internet, satellite TV and wireless. The advertised prices were not in fact available, as additional mandatory fees were hidden from consumers in fine-print disclaimers," announced Aitken.

As support for its ruling the Bureau cited one example of an ad that claimed $69.90/month, yet the price rose to $80.27 with the required mandatory fees, a 15 percent increase. Commented Aitken once again, "If you're going to be talking about something as important as the total cost to consumers, you had better make it sufficiently prominent and clear." In making the decision, Aitken identified the geographic scale and the length of time the marketing message occurred as critical factors in the size of the fine. She also hoped that the fine would be a signal regarding the importance of being open and honest with customers in advertising for all industries.

In response, a Bell spokesperson said, "While we totally disagree, we agreed to resolve the issue with the consent agreement and move forward rather than grinding through a lengthy and costly legal challenge." In contrast, Rogers planned to legally challenge the Competition Bureau's decision.

The impetus for the investigation stemmed from consumer complaints to the Bureau, and it appears the fines did not stem the tide as growing consumer complaints emerge with these two competitors and others. The Competition Bureau sought an additional $10 million from Bell, Rogers, and Telus for misleading wireless consumers about the cost of downloading trivia questions, ringtones, and other services, and sought $1 million from the Canadian Wireless Telecommunications Association. The Bureau also looked to stop ads that do not disclose the cost of premium-rate digital content and to ensure that consumers received a refund for the costs they did not expect to incur. In response, the wireless carriers claimed they only do the billing for third-party digital providers and are not responsible for the charges or the communication of the charges. It had previously sought guidance from the Competition Bureau on how to handle the situation and appeared at a loss as to why the Bureau deemed it necessary to pursue the charges.

And the telecommunications battle heated up beyond the Competition Bureau when Telus filed a lawsuit against Mobilicity for false advertising. The critter-loving phone firm alleged that its competitor's message of, "What you see isn't always what you get" caused "irreparable harm" to its business.

Sources: Scott Deveau, "Aitken Wages War on Pricing's Fine Print," *National Post,* June 30, 2011, p. FP3; Jamie Sturgeon, "Bell Hit for $10M over Misleading Advertising," *National Post,* June 29, 2011, p. FP1; Canadian Press, "Competition Bureau Sues Canada's 3 Wireless Giants over Texting Advertising," *Marketing Magazine,* September 14, 2012; Chris Koentges, "United by Telco Animosity," *Marketing Magazine,* January 15, 2013.

Question:

1. Do you think these fines will ensure that Canadians receive accurate price information in ads in the future?

---

loyalty to, and enhance the image of, their brands. These companies are not likely to risk hard-won consumer trust and confidence by intentionally deceiving consumers. Some companies test the limits of industry and government rules and regulations to make claims that will give their brands an advantage in highly competitive markets.

Periodically, we find advertising that some may claim to be deceptive on unethical. Labatt Breweries of Canada advertised its Hockey Playoff Payoff: Hockey Tickets for Life during the NHL playoffs. The prize featured tickets for 20 games per year over 50 years, with the fine print stating that the winner could take the money instead. The fine print also acknowledged that the brand, Budweiser, was not an official sponsor of the NHL as Labatt had lost that title a year previously. One sponsorship agency executive publicly criticized Labatt for crossing the ethical line since the promotion could damage the brand rights of Molson.[25]

While many critics of advertising would probably agree that most advertisers are not out to deceive consumers deliberately, they are still concerned that consumers may not be receiving enough information to make an informed choice. They say advertisers usually present only information that is favourable to their position and do not always tell consumers the whole truth about a product or service.

Many believe advertising should be primarily informative in nature and should not be permitted to use puffery or embellished messages. Others argue that advertisers have the right to present the most favourable case for their products and services and should not be restricted to just objective, verifiable information.[26] They note that consumers can protect themselves from being persuaded against their will and that the industry and government regulations suffice to keep advertisers from misleading consumers. Figure 18-3 shows the advertising principles of the Association of Canadian Advertisers, which advertisers may use as a guideline in preparing and evaluating their ads.

Figure   18-3

Advertising principles of the Association of Canadian Advertisers

1. *Advertisers must behave responsibly.* ACA believes:
   - Industry self-regulation is in the best interests of all Canadians. Self-regulatory policy exists to ensure that Canadians' fundamental rights and social values are not only acknowledged, but also protected.
   - Advertisers already demonstrate their responsibility by endorsing the Canadian Code of Advertising Standards—the principal instrument of self-regulation for the advertising industry in Canada.
   - The Code of Advertising Standards is only one of many industry codes and guidelines. For example, there are guidelines for gender portrayal, advertising to children, and food labelling, to name just a few.

2. *Advertisers have a right to freedom of speech.* Specifically:
   - The ACA does not believe it is reasonable for a government to allow companies to manufacture and sell legal products, and collect taxes, and then restrict them from telling anyone about it.
   - The ACA remains vigilant in ensuring advertisers' commercial freedom of speech.
   - Advertising, including advertising of products we may not like, is an aspect of free speech, and that free speech is one of society's highest values.

3. *Advertisers make an important contribution to the Canadian economy and culture.* Specifically:
   - Advertising is important to the economic and cultural life of Canadians.
   - In all its forms, advertising is estimated to represent an annual $10-billion investment in the Canadian economy.
   - Advertising revenues fuel the Canadian broadcasting system. Advertisers pay for the production and delivery into Canadian homes of programs that entertain, inform, and educate. It also funds newspapers, magazines, and even movies and Internet sites.
   - Commercials reflect our life. They are a powerful tool and means of passing along our values, traditions, and lifestyles to new citizens and the next generation.
   - Locally produced commercials contribute to our sense of identity and promote national unity.

4. *Advertisers support a vibrant, competitive economy.* The ACA believes:
   - An increased reliance on market forces does not mean that a strong and enriched local and Canadian identity cannot be maintained.
   - Our ability to protect culture by limiting access to communications vehicles is becoming increasingly difficult. A prime example is the Internet.
   - In the rapidly changing world of communications, market conditions, not protectionism, should prevail.

Source: The Association of Canadian Advertisers, www.aca-online.com.

ADVERTISING AS OFFENSIVE OR IN BAD TASTE

Another common criticism of advertising by consumers is that ads are offensive, tasteless, irritating, boring, or obnoxious. Studies have found that consumers sometimes feel offended by advertising or that advertising insults their intelligence and that many ads are in poor taste.[27] Consumers can be offended or irritated by advertising in a number of ways, such as product type, fear appeals, sexual appeals, and shock appeals.

Product Type   Consumers object when certain products—like personal hygiene products or contraceptives—are advertised at all; however, the objections vary over time. Historically, media did not accept ads for condoms, but they reconsidered with the emergence of AIDS; currently, these ads do not register the same level of concern as in the past. A study of prime-time TV commercials found a strong product class effect (i.e., some personal care products) with respect to the types of ads consumers perceived as distasteful or irritating.[28] Another study found that consumers are more likely to dislike ads for products they do not use and for brands they would not buy.[29] ASC's 2012 annual report identified a number of complaints pursued for product categories, with retail (247), service (157), and food products/supermarkets (126) leading the way and accounting for 62 percent of all complaints (534/854). These data suggest that some general categories are more concerning for consumers, although these groupings are very broad compared to individual personal care products. Some products, such as snack foods and sugared beverages, as shown in Exhibit 18-6, may experience consumer objection by encouraging consumption. However, the development of the Canadian Children's Food and Beverage Advertising Initiative, as noted earlier in this chapter, may reassure consumers that the advertising is more appropriate for healthy living.

One product came under fire when it planned a campaign featuring a streetcar's exterior wrapped with the slogan, "Life Is Short. Have an Affair." The slogan is used by Ashley Madison, a married dating service. The phrase would also be placed in all other advertising slots and extended to 10 streetcars, for total revenue of $200,000 for the TTC. A day after the Ashley Madison controversy hit the news, the TTC's advertising review committee decided not to run the ads. According to one voter, "When it's a core fundamental value around cheating or lying, we're not going to let those kinds of ads go on. It's not about sexuality, it's about cheating. We would not have accepted an ad that said 'Life is short, cheat on your exams.' It's frankly a no-brainer."[30]

Fear Appeals   Another way advertising can offend consumers is by the type of appeal or the manner of presentation. For example, many people object to appeals that exploit consumer anxieties. Fear appeal ads, especially for products such as deodorants, mouthwash, and dandruff shampoos, are criticized for attempting to create anxiety and using a fear of social rejection to sell these products. The idea of fear is embodied with suicide, which became the central message of a campaign. Toronto's Virgin Radio 99.9 created three ads showing a radio resting at the edge of a bridge, sitting beside a bathtub, and standing at the edge of subway platform—all with the impression of the radio about to commit suicide—with the copy "Give Your Radio a Reason to Live." Virgin Radio was stopped in its tracks when the Toronto Transit Commission (TTC) denied the "subway platform" ad to be placed on bus shelters, even though the first two ads had appeared on bus shelters for the previous six weeks. Interestingly, ownership of the

Exhibit 18-6   Advertisers for certain products may experience consumer objections.

Exhibit 18-7   This Airwalk ad was criticized for being suggestive and symbolizing sexual submission.

shelters and the placement of the ads is the domain of Astral Media, not the TTC; however, a contract stipulates that any TTC request for removal of ads must be honoured by Astral. Public reaction to this theme is consistent as ads depicting suicide have been previously rejected. In 2001, a potato impaled itself on a fork after discovering an empty Imperial margarine container, which required Unilever to pull the ad. In 2007, a robot jumped off a bridge after dropping a screw while assembling a GM vehicle, which required GM to revise the ad.[31]

Sexual Appeals   The advertising appeals that have received the most criticism for being in poor taste are those using sexual appeals and/or nudity. These techniques are often used to gain consumers' attention and may not even be appropriate to the product being advertised. Even if the sexual appeal relates to the product, people may be offended by the nudity or sexual suggestiveness in the advertising message.

Another common criticism of sexual appeals is that they can demean women or men by depicting them as sex objects. Some women's groups criticized the Airwalk ad shown in Exhibit 18-7, arguing that it showed a submissive and sexually available woman. One argued that the ad contains a number of symbolic cues that are sexually suggestive and combine to reinforce an image of the woman's sexual submission to the man.[32]

Attitudes toward the use of sex in advertising is a polarizing issue as opinions vary depending upon the individual's values and religious orientation, as well as across demographic groups including age, education, and gender. A study found major differences between men and women in their attitudes toward sex in advertising.[33] As shown in Figure 18-4, while almost half of men

Figure   18-4

Attitudes toward sex in advertising, men vs. women

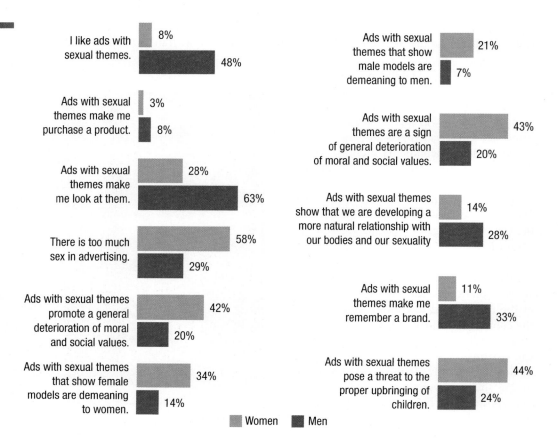

said they liked sexual ads, only 8 percent of women felt the same way. Most men (63 percent) indicated that sexual ads have high stopping power and get their attention, but fewer women thought the same (28 percent). Also, most women (58 percent) said there is too much sex in advertising, versus only 29 percent of the men. Women were also much more likely than men to say that sexual ads promote a deterioration of moral and social values and that they are demeaning of the models used in them.

Critics are particularly concerned about sexual appeals that glorify the image of alcohol consumption. Skyy Spirits used provocative, sexually oriented ads to promote its popular namesake vodka brand. Some of its ads using stylized images placing the brand's distinctive blue bottle in suggestive situations have received criticism (Exhibit 18-8). However, a company spokesperson has responded to the criticisms by noting, "Style is a maker of interpretation and like with all art we appreciate all points of view."[34]

Shock Appeals Because of advertising clutter, brands continue to use sexual appeals that may offend people but catch the attention of consumers and possibly generate publicity. Heighted emotional intensity occurs with a shock appeal in which marketers use startling or surprising images of nudity, sexual suggestiveness, or other unexpected aspects of society. A shock appeal is not new; Benetton (Exhibit 18-9) used this approach in ads for many years, yet it remains an interesting example and continues to intrigue students today. Advertising experts argue that what underlies the use of shock appeals is the pressure on marketers and their agencies to do anything to attract atten-

Exhibit 18-8 Ads are often criticized for being sexually suggestive.

tion. However, critics argue that the more advertisers use the appeal, the more shocking the ads have to be to achieve this objective. How far advertisers can go with this appeal will probably depend on the public's reaction. When advertisers have gone too far, they are likely to pressure the advertisers to change their ads and the media to stop accepting them. Exhibit 18-10 shows a more current Benetton ad. While marketers and ad agencies often acknowledge that their ads push the limits with regard to taste, they also complain about a double standard that exists for advertising versus editorial television program content. They argue that even the most suggestive commercials are bland compared with the content of many television programs.

ADVERTISING AND CHILDREN

A controversial topic is advertising to children. TV is a vehicle through which advertisers can reach children easily. Children between the ages of 2 and 11 watch an average of 15.5 hours of TV a week. Studies show that television is an important source of information for children about products.[35] Concern has also been expressed about marketers' use of point-of-purchase displays, premiums in packages, and commercial characters as the basis for TV shows.

Critics argue that children, particularly young ones, are especially vulnerable to advertising because they lack the experience and knowledge to understand and evaluate critically the purpose of persuasive advertising appeals. Research has shown that preschool children cannot differentiate

Exhibit 18-9 Benetton's "Death Row" ads created a major controversy.

Exhibit 18-10   Benetton's advertising continues to focus on socially relevant issues.

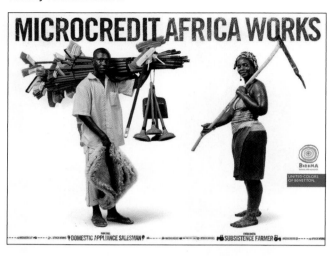

between commercials and programs, do not perceive the selling intent of commercials, and cannot distinguish between reality and fantasy.[36] Research has also shown that children need more than a skeptical attitude toward advertising; they must understand how advertising works in order to use their cognitive defences against it effectively.[37] Because of children's limited ability to interpret the selling intent of a message or identify a commercial, critics charge that advertising to them is inherently unfair and deceptive and should be banned or severely restricted.

At the other extreme are those who argue that advertising is a part of life and children must learn to deal with it in the **consumer socialization process** of acquiring the skills needed to function in the marketplace.[38] They say existing restrictions are adequate for controlling children's advertising. A study by Tamara Mangleburg and Terry Bristol provided support for the socialization argument. They found that adolescents developed skeptical attitudes toward advertising that were learned through interactions with socialization agents such as parents, peers, and television. They also found that marketplace knowledge plays an important role in adolescents' skepticism toward advertising. Greater knowledge of the marketplace appears to give teens a basis by which to evaluate ads and makes them more likely to recognize the persuasion techniques used by advertisers.[39]

The *Children's Code* and the Canadian Children's Food and Beverage Advertising Initiative discussed earlier recognize the above debate explicitly to find a balance between these two points of view. A study comparing the attitudes of business executives and consumers regarding children's advertising found that marketers of products targeted to children believe advertising to them provides useful information on new products and does not disrupt the parent–child relationship. However, the general public did not have such a favourable opinion. Older consumers and those from households with children had particularly negative attitudes toward children's advertising.[40] Clearly, companies communicating directly to children need to be sensitive to the naiveté of children as consumers to avoid potential conflict with those who believe children should be protected from advertising.

🗨️ L03 Social Effects of Advertising

Concern is expressed over the impact of advertising on society, particularly on values and lifestyles. While a number of factors influence the cultural values, lifestyles, and behaviour of a society, the overwhelming amount of advertising and its prevalence in the mass media lead many critics to argue that advertising plays a major role in influencing and transmitting social values. While there is general agreement that advertising is an important social influence agent, opinions as to the value of its contribution are often negative. Advertising is criticized for encouraging materialism, manipulating consumers to buy things they do not really need, perpetuating stereotypes, and controlling the media.

ADVERTISING ENCOURAGES MATERIALISM

Critics claim advertising has an adverse effect on consumer values by encouraging **materialism**, a preoccupation with material things rather than intellectual or spiritual concerns. Critics contend that an ad like the one shown in Exhibit 18-11 can promote materialistic values. In summary, they contend that advertising seeks to create needs rather than merely showing how a product or service fulfills them; surrounds consumers with images of the good life and suggests the acquisition of material possessions leads to contentment and happiness and adds to the joy of living; and suggests material possessions are symbols of status, success, and accomplishment and/or will lead to greater social acceptance, popularity, sex appeal, and so on.

This criticism of advertising assumes that materialism is undesirable and is sought at the expense of other goals, but some believe materialism is acceptable. For example, some consumers believe their hard work and individual effort and initiative allows for the accumulation of material possessions as evidence of success. Others argue that the acquisition of material possessions has positive economic impact by encouraging consumers to keep consuming after their basic needs are met. Many believe economic growth is essential and materialism is both a necessity and an inevitable part of this progress.

It has also been argued that an emphasis on material possessions does not rule out interest in intellectual, spiritual, or cultural values. Defenders of advertising say consumers can be more interested in higher-order goals when basic needs have been met. Raymond Bauer and Stephen Greyser point out that consumers may purchase material things in the pursuit of non-material goals.[41] For example, a person may buy an expensive stereo system to enjoy music rather than simply to impress someone or acquire a material possession.

Even if we assume materialism is undesirable, there is still the question of whether advertising is responsible for creating and encouraging it. While critics argue that advertising is a major contributing force to materialistic values, others say advertising merely reflects the values of society rather than shaping them.[42] They argue that consumers' values are defined by the society in which they live and are the results of extensive, long-term socialization or acculturation.

The argument that advertising is responsible for creating a materialistic and hedonistic society is addressed by Stephen Fox in his book *The Mirror Makers: A History of American Advertising and Its Creators*. Fox concludes advertising has become a prime scapegoat for our times and merely reflects society.[43] Advertising does contribute to our materialism by portraying products and services as symbols of status, success, and achievement and by encouraging consumption, but as Richard Pollay says, "While it may be true that advertising reflects cultural values, it does so on a very selective basis, echoing and reinforcing certain attitudes, behaviours, and values far more frequently than others."[44]

Exhibit 18-11 Critics argue that advertising contributes to materialistic values.

ADVERTISING AND PERSUASION

A common criticism of advertising is that it manipulates and exploits consumers by persuading them to buy things they do not need. Critics say advertising should just provide information useful in making purchase decisions and should not persuade. They view information advertising (which reports price, performance, and other objective criteria) as desirable but persuasive advertising (which plays on consumers' emotions, anxieties, and psychological needs and desires such as status, self-esteem, and attractiveness) as unacceptable. Persuasive advertising is criticized for fostering discontent among consumers and encouraging them to purchase products and services to solve deeper problems.

Defenders of advertising offer three rebuttals to these criticisms. First, they point out that a substantial amount of advertising is essentially informational in nature.[45] Also, it is difficult to separate desirable informational advertising from undesirable persuasive advertising. Shelby Hunt, in examining the *information–persuasion dichotomy,* points out that even advertising that most observers would categorize as very informative is often very persuasive.[46] Hunt says, "If advertising critics really believe that persuasive advertising should not be permitted, they are actually proposing that no advertising be allowed, since the purpose of all advertising is to persuade."[47]

Exhibit 18-12 Trojan expanded its product line to fulfill lower-level needs.

Second, defenders of advertising also take issue with the argument that it should be limited to dealing with basic functional needs. In our society, most lower-level needs recognized in Maslow's hierarchy, such as the need for food, clothing, and shelter, are satisfied for most people. It is natural to move from basic needs to higher-order ones such as self-esteem and status or self-actualization. Consumers are free to choose the degree to which they attempt to satisfy their desires, and wise advertisers associate their products and services with the satisfaction of higher-order needs. However, one element of lower-level needs may require enhancing and benefit from advertising (Exhibit 18-12).

Third, this criticism attributes too much power to advertising and assumes consumers have no ability to defend themselves since it ignores the fact that consumers have the freedom to make their own choices when confronted with persuasive advertising. While they readily admit the persuasive intent of their business, advertisers are quick to note it is extremely difficult to make consumers purchase a product they do not want or for which they do not see a personal benefit. If advertising were as powerful as the critics claim, we would not see products with multimillion-dollar advertising budgets failing in the marketplace. The reality is that consumers do have a choice, and they are not being forced to buy. Consumers ignore ads for products and services they do not really need or that fail to interest them.

ADVERTISING AND STEREOTYPING

Advertising is often accused of creating and perpetuating stereotypes through its portrayal of women and ethnic minorities.

Women   The portrayal of women in advertising is an issue that has received a great deal of attention through the years.[48] Advertising has received much criticism for stereotyping women and failing to recognize the changing role of women in our society. Critics have argued that advertising often depicts women as preoccupied with beauty, household duties, and motherhood, or shows them as decorative objects or sexually provocative figures. The research studies conducted through the years show a consistent picture of gender stereotyping that has varied little over time. Portrayals of adult women in American television and print advertising have emphasized passivity, deference, lack of intelligence and credibility, and punishment for high levels of effort. In contrast, men have been portrayed as constructive, powerful, autonomous, and achieving.[49]

Research on gender stereotyping in advertising targeted to children has found a pattern of results similar to that reported for adults. A study found sex-role stereotyping in television advertising targeted at children in the United States as well as in Australia.[50] Boys are generally shown as being more knowledgeable, active, aggressive, and instrumental than girls. Nonverbal behaviours involving dominance and control are associated more with boys than girls. Advertising directed toward children has also been shown to feature more boys than girls, to position boys in more dominant, active roles, and to use male voiceovers more frequently than female ones.[51]

While stereotyping still exists, advertising's portrayal of women is improving in many areas as advertisers now portray women realistically. Researchers argue that the transformed social positioning of women in North American society is perhaps the most important social development of this century.[52] They note that as women have crossed the boundary from the domestic sphere to the professional arena, expectations and representations of women have changed as well. For example, magazines incorporate and appeal to the sociocultural shifts in women's lives. Advertisers depict women in a diversity of roles that reflect their changing place in society. The stereotypic character traits attributed to women have shifted from weak and dependent to strong and autonomous.[53] The ad for Network Solutions shown in Exhibit 18-13 is an example of how advertisers portray women in their ads. However, brands like Axe continue to portray women in an entirely different manner, raising criticism toward the parent company Unilever, which portrayed women naturally in its famous Dove Campaign for Real Beauty. A Canadian advertising agency executive responsible for the Axe account claimed the ads reflected a "fun and cheeky" brand personality, and that the product helped in facilitating girls and guys to come together.[54]

This trend is seen in the 2012 annual report published by Advertising Standards Canada (ASC). It received a total of 297 complaints associated with clause 14 (unacceptable depictions and portrayals). However, most of these concerned personal taste or preference, and the council ultimately upheld 16 complaints for 5 ads. This represented 1.6 percent of all complaints for this clause (5/297). As Figure 18-2 indicated, ASC upheld complaints for 116 ads in 2012, so these 5 ads accounted for 4.3 percent of the total number of complaints (5/116). In contrast, ASC received 526 complaints for clause 1 (accuracy and clarity) and clause 3 (price claims) combined and upheld 95 complaints for 79 ads, which accounted for the clear majority at 68 percent (79/116).[55] Over the past decade, the percentage of complaints for clause 14 dropped from 56 percent to 23 percent, with a corresponding increase of 7 percent to 40 percent for clause 1. While the statistics are a positive indication, the issue of digitally altering

Exhibit 18-13   Many advertisers now portray women in powerful roles.

photographic images is a concern. An illustration of this occurred with a Polo Ralph Lauren ad, where one astute viewer commented, "Dude, her head's bigger than her pelvis." Upon investigation, Polo apologized and claimed the mistake would not occur in future.[56]

It should be noted that portrayal and depiction problems occurring in advertising are not necessarily reflected in the statistics, as advertising gets amended or withdrawn prior to anyone making a complaint to ASC. And if the ad is no longer running, then ASC does not investigate. In the case of a Loblaws flyer featuring Joe Fresh ads for women's underwear and night clothes, the retailer immediately pulled its flyers once a few consumers complained directly and a media story questioned whether the images should be displayed in such a public manner. One vice president for the brand noted, "We stand by the flyer. We think the photography is beautiful, and we have definitely seen a positive reflection in our sales since the flyer went out."[57]

Finally, the shoe is on the other foot, so to speak, as one advertising professional observed that some ads portray a stereotype of men as dumb, goofy, or inept. Deborah Adams, senior vice-president of Harbinger Communications, a consultancy firm that focuses on marketing to women, recounted a comment from a woman on their market research panel, "You know, if you want to make inroads with me, if you want to resonate with me, you really shouldn't be showing my husband as an idiot."[58] This is precisely the reason why the ASC guidelines on depictions and portrayal include both women and men. In addition, other criticism of ads focused on men and their role as fathers in unflatteringly portrayals. Huggies came under fire for an ad that showed fathers incapable of leaving the TV to tend to the diaper changing needs of their infants. Consumers' criticism resulted in the brand altering the ad to include a more palatable conclusion.[59]

Visible Minorities   Several U.S. academic studies in the late 1980s and early 1990s examined the incidence of visible minorities in advertising. A study conducted in 1987 found that

11 percent of the people appearing in commercials were African-Americans.[60] Another study conducted two years later found that African-Americans appeared in 26 percent of all ads on network TV that used live models but Hispanics appeared in only 6 percent of the commercials with live models. The researchers also found that TV ads in which blacks appeared were overwhelmingly integrated and that blacks were likely to have played either minor or background roles in the majority of the ads.[61] A study conducted in 1995 found that 17 percent of prime-time network TV ads featured African-Americans as dominant characters and the majority of commercials featured them in minor roles.[62] A study by Corliss L. Green found that ads targeting African-Americans through racially targeted media, especially with race-based products, benefit from featuring African-American models with a dominant presence in the ad.[63]

A study of U.S. prime-time TV commercials found that Asian male and female models are overrepresented in terms of their proportion of the U.S. population (3.6 percent), appearing in 8.4 percent of the commercials. However, Asian models were more likely than members of other minority groups to appear in background roles, and Asian women were rarely depicted in major roles. The study also found that portrayals of Asian-Americans put more emphasis on the work ethic and less on other aspects of their lives.[64]

It may be difficult to generalize these findings to Canada; however, we should keep in mind that Canadians are exposed to these ads when watching U.S. television programs that do not simulcast Canadian commercials or when reading American magazines. So to a degree, Canadian consumers will experience and perceive some amount of imbalance through this exposure. Walmart is an example of one leader that initiated multicultural ads. It began in 1997; with its agency's assistance, Walmart used Print Measurement Bureau and Census Canada data and identified a large and growing segment of the population that did not receive the existing advertising. Executives also truly believed that communicating to customers in a language of their choice was a sign of respect. In that first year, Walmart produced original TV creative for four ethnic groups: Italian, Portuguese, Cantonese, and South Asian, all but the latter in their own language. From then on, multicultural ads continued and the retailer remains one of a handful of companies producing original creative for ethnic TV.[65] The ad with an interracial couple in Exhibit 18-14 shows that the issues discussed in this section may move in a different direction within the multicultural milieu of Canada.

Exhibit 18-14   Interracial couples occur in ads more frequently than in the past.

ADVERTISING AND THE MEDIA

The fact that advertising plays such an important role in financing the media has led to concern that advertisers may influence or even control the media. It is well documented that *economic censorship* occurs, whereby the media avoid certain topics or even present biased news coverage in acquiescence to advertiser demands.[66] Having the media in Canada supported by advertising means we can enjoy them for free or for a fraction of what they would cost without advertising. The alternative to an advertiser-supported media system is support by users through higher subscription costs for the print media and a fee or pay-per-view system with TV. Although not perfect, our system of advertising-supported media provides the best option for receiving information and entertainment, however the points on both sides of the issue have merit.

Critics charge that the media's dependence on advertisers' support makes them susceptible to influence, including exerting control over the editorial content of magazines and newspapers; biasing editorial opinions to favour the position of an advertiser; limiting coverage of a controversial story that might reflect negatively on a company; and influencing the program content of television. A survey of 147 daily newspapers found that more than 90 percent of editors have been pressured by advertisers and more than one-third of them said advertisers had succeeded in influencing news at their papers.[67] Thus, a newspaper may be reluctant to print an unfavourable story about local business upon whose advertising it depends. For TV, programming decisions are made largely on the basis of what shows will attract the most viewers and thus be most desirable to advertisers. Critics say this results in lower-quality television as educational, cultural, and informative programming is sacrificed for shows that get high ratings and appeal to the mass markets.

Media executives cite two reasons why advertisers do not exert undue influence over the media. First, it is in the media's best interest to not to be influenced by advertisers. To retain public confidence, media must report the news fairly and accurately without showing bias or attempting to avoid controversial issues. The vast array of topics media cover and their investigative reporting is evidence of their objectivity. Second, media executives note that an advertiser needs the media more than they need any individual advertiser, particularly when the medium has a large audience or does a good job of reaching a specific market segment. Many publications and stations have a very broad base of advertising support and can afford to lose an advertiser that attempts to exert too much influence.

ADVERTISING AND SOCIAL BENEFIT

It is important to note that advertising and other IMC tools play an important role in many activities that provide tremendous social benefit in a number of ways. Companies use advertising in their sponsorship or cause-related activities that encourage participation to help raise money for important causes. For example, communicating to the thousands who participated in CIBC's Run for the Cure and Becel's Ride for Heart efforts would not be possible without advertising—and, more importantly, would not occur without the existing advertising industry and infrastructure.

Organizations dealing with social problems, such as alcohol-impaired driving, use advertising to influence attitudes and behaviour. Exhibit 18-15 identifies one organization that uses advertising and other marketing communication tools to achieve these objectives. Their messages try to persuade those at risk to not engage in the behaviour or to take precautions.

One study reviewing the effects of mass media campaigns found a 13 percent decline in alcohol-related crashes and concluded that the social benefit of the advertising clearly outweighed the cost of the advertising.[68] Furthermore, advertising attempts to influence social norms by giving friends and family the courage to intervene. A multimedia ad campaign from the provincial distributor of alcohol in Ontario supported this idea. Its research indicated that consumers often feel embarrassed or awkward when stopping someone from drinking and driving. An interactive website (deflatetheelephant.com) allowed users to practise, with the elephant shrinking as they achieved success.[69]

Non-profit organizations that raise funds for their worthy causes rely on advertising as well. The United Way campaigns are certainly successful, with thousands of volunteers; however, the whole campaign requires some assistance with advertising. To facilitate the delivery of government services or implementation of policy, advertising is used extensively. Transit systems, generally a part of most city governments, rely on advertising to communicate routes, and so on. Provincial governments encourage visitors from other provinces to plan a vacation. Advertising for health care service resulted in positive results. Flu shot advertising in Ontario contributed to raising the participation rate from 14 percent to 34 percent. Informing Ontario consumers about health-care options lowered the number of non-emergency visits to emergency rooms by 13 percent.[70]

Exhibit 18-15 MADD encourages people to take action against drinking and driving.

One interesting criticism is that agency creative specialists take pro bono work for charities that are seeking increased donations with ads that are emotionally involving and creative so that the agency can win awards beyond its roster of paying clients of established products who rely on more rational messages that have less creative latitude. This issue resulted in Cannes not permitting pro bono work to be submitted for its categories, allowing it to compete only in the "Grand Prix for Good" category. In fact, agencies arrive at creative ideas and actively seek out non-profit organizations and pitch the ideas for increased business.[71]

Ⓞ Economic Effects of Advertising

Advertising develops consumer awareness of products and services by providing them with information for decision making; however, it affects the functioning of our entire economic system. Advertising can encourage consumption and foster economic growth, facilitate entry into markets for a firm or a new product or brand; and lead to economies of scale in production, marketing, and distribution, thereby increasing the standard of living. In contrast, critics view advertising as detrimental since it fails to perform its basic function of information provision adequately, adds to the cost of goods and services, and discourages competition and market entry, leading to industrial concentration and higher prices for consumers. To resolve this debate we turn to economists who take a macro-economic perspective as they consider the economic impact of advertising on an industry or on the economy. Our examination focuses on advertising's effects on consumer choice, competition, and product costs and prices.

Exhibit 18-16   Head & Shoulders advertisements inform consumers of its uniqueness.

EFFECTS ON CONSUMER CHOICE

Critics say advertising hampers consumer choice, as large advertisers use their power to limit our options to a few well-advertised brands. Economists argue that advertising is used to achieve (1) **differentiation**, whereby the products or services of large advertisers are perceived as unique or better than competitors', and (2) brand loyalty, which enables large national advertisers to gain control of the market, usually at the expense of smaller brands. Larger companies often charge a higher price and achieve a more dominant position in the market than smaller firms that cannot compete against them and their large advertising budgets. When this occurs, advertising not only restricts the choice alternatives to a few well-known, heavily advertised brands but also becomes a substitute for competition based on price or product improvements.

Heavily advertised brands dominate the market in certain product categories (e.g., soft drinks).[72] But advertising defenders claim it generally does not create brand monopolies and reduce the opportunities for new products to be introduced to consumers. In most product categories, a number of different brands are on the store shelves and thousands of new products are introduced every year. The opportunity to advertise gives companies the incentive to develop new brands and improve their existing ones. When a successful new product such as a smartphone is introduced, competitors quickly follow and use advertising to inform consumers about their brand and attempt to convince them it is superior to the original. Brands like Head & Shoulders recognize that advertising has been an important part of their success (Exhibit 18-16).

EFFECTS ON COMPETITION

Critical economists argue that power in the hands of large firms with huge advertising budgets creates a **barrier to entry**, which makes it difficult for other firms to enter the market. This results in less competition and higher prices. Economists note that smaller firms already in the market find it difficult to compete against the large advertising budgets of the industry leaders and are often driven out of business. Large advertisers clearly enjoy certain a competitive advantage through **economies of scale** in advertising, particularly with respect to factors such as media costs. Firms such as Procter & Gamble, which spends millions of dollars per year on advertising and promotion, are able to make large media buys at a reduced rate and allocate them to their various products. Large advertisers usually sell more of a product or service, which means they may have lower production costs and can allocate more monies to advertising, so they can afford the costly but more efficient media like network television. Their large advertising outlays also give them more opportunity to differentiate their products and develop brand loyalty. To the extent that these factors occur, smaller competitors are at a disadvantage and new competitors are deterred from entering the market.

While advertising may have an anticompetitive effect on a market, there is no clear evidence that advertising alone reduces competition, creates barriers to entry, and thus increases market concentration. High levels of advertising are not always found in industries where firms have a large market share as there is an inverse relationship between intensity of product class advertising and stability of market share for the leading brands.[73] These findings run contrary to many economists' belief that industries controlled by a few firms have high advertising expenditures, resulting in stable brand shares for market leaders. Defenders of advertising say it is unrealistic to attribute a firm's market dominance and barriers to entry solely to advertising. Industry leaders often tend to dominate markets because they have superior product quality and the best management and competitive strategies, not simply the biggest advertising budgets.[74] While market entry against large, established competitors is difficult, companies with a quality product at a reasonable price often find a way to break in. Moreover, they usually find that advertising actually facilitates their market entry by making it possible to communicate the benefits and features of their new product or brand to consumers.

EFFECTS ON PRODUCT COSTS AND PRICES

Critics such as consumer advocates argue that advertising increases the prices consumers pay for products and services. First, they say the large sums of money spent advertising a brand constitute an expense that must be covered and the consumer ends up paying for it through higher prices. Several studies show that firms with higher relative prices advertise their products more intensely than do those with lower relative prices.[75]

A second way advertising can result in higher prices is by increasing product differentiation and adding to the perceived value of the product in consumers' minds. Paul Farris and Mark Albion note that product differentiation occupies a central position in theories of advertising's economic effects.[76] The fundamental premise is that advertising increases the perceived differences between physically homogeneous products and enables advertised brands to command a premium price without an increase in quality. Critics point to the differences in prices between national brands and private-label brands that are physically similar as evidence of the added value created by advertising. They see consumers' willingness to pay more for heavily advertised national brands rather than purchasing the lower-priced, non-advertised brand as wasteful and irrational.

Proponents of advertising acknowledge that advertising costs are at least partly paid for by consumers. But advertising may help lower the overall cost of a product more than enough to offset them. For example, advertising may help firms achieve economies of scale in production and distribution by providing information to and stimulating demand among mass markets. These economies of scale help cut the cost of producing and marketing the product, which can lead to lower prices—if the advertiser chooses to pass the cost savings on to the consumer.

Advertising can also lower prices by making a market more competitive, which usually leads to greater price competition. A study found that prices of eyeglasses were 25 to 30 percent higher in states that banned eyeglass advertising than in those that permitted it.[77] One researcher of the toy industry concluded that advertising resulted in lower consumer prices and that curtailment of TV advertising would drive up consumer prices for toys.[78] Economist James Ferguson argues that advertising cannot increase the cost per unit of quality to consumers because if it did consumers would not continue to respond positively to advertising.[79] He believes advertising lowers the costs of information about brand qualities, leads to increases in brand quality, and lowers the average price per unit of quality. Finally, advertising is a means to market entry rather than a deterrent and helps stimulate product innovation, which makes markets more competitive and helps keep prices down.

SUMMARIZING ECONOMIC EFFECTS

Albion and Farris suggest that economists' perspectives can be divided into two principal schools of thought that make different assumptions regarding the influence of advertising on the economy.[80] Figure 18-5 summarizes the main points of the "advertising equals market power" and "advertising equals information" perspectives.

Advertising Equals Market Power   The belief that advertising equals market power reflects traditional economic thinking and views advertising as a way to change consumers' tastes, lower their sensitivity to price, and build brand loyalty among buyers of advertised brands. This results in higher profits and market power for large advertisers, reduces competition in the market, and leads to higher prices and fewer choices for consumers. Proponents of this viewpoint generally have negative attitudes regarding the economic impact of advertising.

Figure   18-5   Two schools of thought on advertising's role in the economy

Advertising = Market Power		Advertising = Information
Advertising affects consumer preferences and tastes, changes product attributes, and differentiates the product from competitive offerings.	Advertising	Advertising informs consumers about product attributes but does not change the way they value those attributes.
Consumers become brand loyal and less price sensitive and perceive fewer substitutes for advertised brands.	Consumer buying behaviour	Consumers become more price sensitive and buy best "value." Only the relationship between price and quality affects elasticity for a given product.
Potential entrants must overcome established brand loyalty and spend relatively more on advertising.	Barriers to entry	Advertising makes entry possible for new brands because it can communicate product attributes to consumers.
Firms are insulated from market competition and potential rivals; concentration increases, leaving firms with more discretionary power.	Industry structure and market power	Consumers can compare competitive offerings easily and competitive rivalry increases. Efficient firms remain, and as the inefficient leave, new entrants appear; the effect on concentration is ambiguous.
Firms can charge higher prices and are not as likely to compete on quality or price dimensions. Innovation may be reduced.	Market conduct	More informed consumers pressure firms to lower prices and improve quality; new entrants facilitate innovation.
High prices and excessive profits accrue to advertisers and give them even more incentive to advertise their products. Output is restricted compared with conditions of perfect competition.	Market performance	Industry prices decrease. The effect on profits due to increased competition and increased efficiency is ambiguous

Advertising Equals Information The belief that advertising equals information takes a more positive view of advertising's economic effects. This model sees advertising as providing consumers with useful information, increasing their price sensitivity (which moves them toward lower-priced products), and increasing competition in the market. Advertising is viewed as a way to communicate with consumers and tell them about a product and its major features and attributes. More informed and knowledgeable consumers pressure companies to provide high-quality products at lower prices. Efficient firms remain in the market, whereas inefficient firms leave as new entrants appear. Proponents of this model believe the economic effects of advertising are favourable and think it contributes to more efficient and competitive markets. Exhibit 18-17 shows an ad from the International Advertising Association used to support this positive role of advertising.

A Final Thought The debate over the economic effects of advertising will likely continue; however, the point of view expressed by Leo Burnett many years ago seems relevant today with the growth of mobile devices and other innovations (Figure 18-6). While many advertising and marketing experts agree that advertising and promotion play an important role in helping to expand consumer demand for new products, not everyone would agree that this is desirable.

Exhibit 18-17 This ad promotes the value of advertising in building strong brands.

To me it means that if we believe to any degree whatsoever in the economic system under which we live, in a high standard of living and in high employment, advertising is the most efficient known way of moving goods in practically every product class.

My proof is that millions of businessmen have chosen advertising over and over again in the operations of their business. Some of their decisions may have been wrong, but they must have thought they were right or they wouldn't go back to be stung twice by the same kind of bee.

It's a pretty safe bet that in the next 10 years many Americans will be using products and devices that no one in this room has even heard of. Judging purely by past performance, American advertising can be relied on to make them known and accepted overnight at the lowest possible prices.

Advertising, of course, makes possible our unparalleled variety of magazines, newspapers, business publications, and radio and television stations.

It must be said that without advertising we would have a far different nation, and one that would be much the poorer—not merely in material commodities, but in the life of the spirit.

Leo Burnett

These excerpts are from a speech given by Leo Burnett on the American Association of Advertising Agencies' 50th anniversary, April 20, 1967.

Figure 18-6

This message describes the positive economic effects of advertising

Learning Objectives Summary

 Describe the advertising regulation system in Canada.

Various levels of government regulate different aspects of Canadian advertising; however, self-regulation of these laws is quite prominent in Canada. This self-regulation occurs through Advertising Standards Canada (ASC), a non-profit organization of advertising industry members. The ASC responds to all complaints with respect to advertising and publishes an annual report that summarizes the complaints it receives each year. The ASC is also responsible for clearing ads prior to their airing for a number of products. Some of the ASC's responsibilities have been given to it as the federal government has withdrawn services with the belief that industry is sufficiently responsible.

 Evaluate the ethical perspectives of advertising.

Even though there appears to be sufficient control of advertising, it is a very powerful institution that has been the target of considerable criticism regarding its ethical, social, and economic impact. The criticism of advertising concerns the specific techniques and methods used as well as its effect on societal values, tastes, lifestyles, and behaviour. Critics argue that advertising is deceptive and untruthful; that it is often offensive, irritating, or in poor taste; and that it exploits certain groups. Many people believe advertising should be informative only and advertisers should not use subjective claims, puffery, embellishment, or persuasive techniques.

Advertising often offends consumers by the type of appeal or manner of presentation used; sexually suggestive ads and nudity receive the most criticism. Advertisers say their ads are consistent with contemporary values and lifestyles and are appropriate for the target audiences they are attempting to reach. Advertising to children is an area of particular concern, since critics argue that children lack the experience, knowledge, and ability to process and evaluate persuasive advertising messages rationally.

 Explain the social effects of advertising.

The pervasiveness of advertising and its prevalence in the mass media have led critics to argue that it plays a major role in influencing and transmitting social values. Advertising has been charged with encouraging materialism, manipulating consumers to buy things they do not really want or need, and perpetuating stereotypes through its portrayal of certain groups such as women and visible minorities.

 Examine the economic role of advertising and its effects on consumer choice, competition, and product costs and prices.

Advertising has also been scrutinized with regard to its economic effects. The basic economic role of advertising is to give consumers information that helps them make consumption decisions. Some people view advertising as a detrimental force that has a negative effect on competition, product costs, and consumer prices. Economists' perspectives regarding the effects of advertising follow two basic schools of thought: the advertising equals market power model and the advertising equals information model. Arguments consistent with each perspective were considered in analyzing the economic effects of advertising.

Key Terms   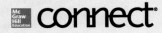

Review key terms and definitions on Connect.

Review Questions

1. Explain why you agree or disagree with the rulings of the ASC presented in this chapter regarding the Ford Focus and Kia automobile ads.

2. Evaluate the arguments for and against advertising to children. Do you feel restrictions are needed for advertising and other forms of promotion targeted to children?

3. Discuss how attitudes toward the use of sex in advertising differ between men and women. Discuss the implications of these attitudinal differences for marketers who are developing ads for each gender.

4. Describe the differences between the two major perspectives of the economic impact of advertising: "advertising equals market power" versus "advertising equals information."

Applied Questions

1. Why are the laws for advertising regulation not applied to sponsorship and some other IMC tools?

2. Find the most offensive ad possible and express why it is so offensive. Apply the ASC code to determine which guidelines it violates.

3. Explain which position you agree with and why: "Advertising determines Canadian consumers' tastes and values and is responsible for creating a materialistic society," or "Advertising is a reflection of society and mirrors its tastes and values."

4. Do you believe advertising power has ever restricted your personal choice in buying products?

Endnotes

CHAPTER ONE

1. "AMA Board Approves New Marketing Definition," *Marketing News,* March 1, 1985, p. 1.
2. Richard P. Bagozzi, "Marketing as Exchange," *Journal of Marketing, 39* (4), October 1975, pp. 32–39.
3. Kristin Laird, "Art Is Joyful for BMW," *Marketing Magazine,* May 8, 2009.
4. J. Paul Peter and Jerry C. Olson, *Consumer Behavior* (Burr Ridge, IL: Richard D. Irwin, 1987), p. 505.
5. Michael R. Solomon, "The Role of Products as Social Stimuli: A Symbolic Interactionism Perspective," *Journal of Consumer Research, 10* (3), December 1983, pp. 319–29.
6. Matt Semansky, "Labatt Defends Kokanee's Mountain Territory," *Marketing Magazine,* September 17, 2009.
7. Michelle Warren, "Flight of the Stinger," *Marketing Magazine,* May 1, 2006; Michelle Warren, "The Trouble with Tag Lines," *Marketing Magazine,* March 6, 2006.
8. Rebecca Harris, "Nice Package," *Marketing Magazine,* September 4, 2012.
9. Kevin Lane Keller, "Conceptualizing, Measuring, and Managing Customer Based Brand Equity," *Journal of Marketing, 57* (1), January 1993, pp. 1–22.
10. Sreedhar Madhavaram, Vishag Badrinarayanan, and Robert E. McDonald, "Integrated Marketing Communication (IMC) and Brand Identity as Critical Components of Brand Equity Strategy," *Journal of Advertising, 34* (4), Winter 2005, pp. 69–80.
11. Canada's Most Valuable Brands 2009, Brand Finance (http://www.level5.ca/pdf /Brand_Finance_Canada-Press%20Release -Most_Valuable_Brands_2009.pdf).
12. Rebecca Harris, "The Influencers," *Marketing Magazine,* February 6, 2012, pp. 12–13.
13. Peter and Olson, *Consumer Behavior,* p. 571.
14. Brent Jang, "Ottawa Forces Airlines to Advertise Full Ticket Price," *The Globe and Mail,* December 17, 2011; Scott Deveau, "Airlines Speed Up Full Ads," *National Post,* February 9, 2012.
15. Paul W. Farris and David J. Reibstein, "How Prices, Ad Expenditures, and Profits Are Linked," *Harvard Business Review,* November–December 1979, pp. 172–84.
16. Dhruv Grewal, Kent B. Monroe, & R. Krishnan, "The Effects of Price-Comparison Advertising on Buyers' Perceptions of Acquisition Value, Transaction Value, and Behavioral Intentions," *Journal of Marketing, 62* (2), April 1998, pp. 46–59; Daniel J. Howard & Roger A. Kerin, "Broadening the Scope of Reference Price Advertising Research: A Field Study of Consumer Shopping," *Journal of Marketing, 70* (4), October 2006, pp. 185–204.
17. Roger A. Kerin, Steven W. Hartley, Eric N. Berkowitz, and William Rudelius, *Marketing,* 8th ed. (Burr Ridge, IL: Irwin/McGraw-Hill, 2006).
18. Michael L. Ray, *Advertising and Communication Management* (Englewood Cliffs, NJ: Prentice Hall, 1982).
19. Ralph S. Alexander, ed., *Marketing Definitions* (Chicago: American Marketing Association, 1965), p. 9.
20. BBM.CA, Weekly Top 30 Programs.
21. "Analysis of the Economics of Canadian Television Programming." Study performed by Nodicity Group Ltd., March 2009.
22. Arjun Chaudhuri, "How Brand Reputation Affects the Advertising–Brand Equity Link," *Journal of Advertising Research, 42* (3), May–June 2002, pp. 33–43.
23. Kristin Laird, "Broil King Heats Up Advertising for Summer," *Marketing Magazine,* May 5, 2009.
24. Jeromy Lloyd, "Amex Invests in Major Brand Campaign," *Marketing Magazine,* October 6, 2009.
25. Megan Hayes, "Marketers of the Year: Sandra Sanderson Keeps Shoppers Fabulous," *Strategy,* December 7, 2012.
26. H. Frazier Moore and Bertrand R. Canfield, *Public Relations: Principles, Cases, and Problems,* 7th ed. (Burr Ridge, IL: Irwin, 1977), p. 5.
27. Karin Scott, "Beyond Press Coverage," *Marketing Magazine,* June 16, 2003.
28. Kristin Laird, "Tim Hortons Is Turning Green," *Marketing Magazine,* June 1, 2009.
29. Emily Wexler, "Driving Away a Winner," *Strategy,* February 1, 2011.
30. David Brown, "Rogers Media," *Marketing Magazine,* November 14, 2011.
31. Don E. Schultz, "Integrated Marketing Communications: Maybe Definition Is in the Point of View," *Marketing News,* January 18, 1993, p. 17.
32. Don Shultz and Philip Kitchen, "Integrated Marketing Communications in US Advertising Agencies: An Exploratory Study," *Journal of Advertising Research,* September–October 1997, pp. 7–18.
33. Tom Duncan and Sandra E. Moriarty, "A Communication-Based Model for Managing Relationships," *Journal of Marketing, 62* (2), April 1998, pp. 1–13.
34. Joep P. Cornelissen and Andrew R. Lock, "Theoretical Concept or Management Fashion? Examining the Significance of IMC," *Journal of Advertising Research, 37* (5), September–October 2000, pp. 7–15.
35. Philip J. Kitchen, Joanne Brignell, Tao Li, and Graham Spickett Jones, "The Emergence of IMC: A Theoretical Perspective," *Journal of Advertising Research, 44* (1), March 2004, pp. 19–30.
36. Don E. Schultz, "IMC Receives More Appropriate Definition," *Marketing News,* September 15, 2004, pp. 8–9.
37. Dong Hwan Lee and Chan Wook Park, "Conceptualization and Measurement of Multidimensionality of Integrated Marketing Communications," *Journal of Advertising Research, 47* (3), September 2007, pp. 222–36.
38. Mike Reid, Sandra Luxton, and Felix Mavondo, "The Relationship between Integrated Marketing Communication, Market Orientation, and Brand Orientation," *Journal of Advertising, 34* (4), Winter 2005, pp. 11–23.
39. George Low, "Correlates of Integrated Marketing Communications," *Journal of Advertising Research, 40* (3), January–February 2000, pp. 27–39.
40. Cornelissen and Lock, "Theoretical Concept or Management Fashion?"
41. Harlan E. Spotts, David R. Lambert, and Mary L. Joyce, "Marketing Déjà Vu: The Discovery of Integrated Marketing Communications," *Journal of Marketing Education, 20* (3), December 1998, pp. 210–18.
42. Lisa d'Innocenzo, "Inside P&G," *Strategy,* June 2006.
43. Kitchen, Brignell, Li, and Jones, "The Emergence of IMC: A Theoretical Perspective."
44. Jonathan Paul, "Nissan's Jeff Parent: No Guts, No Glory," *Strategy,* December 2009, p. 34; Jeromy Lloyd, "Nissan Gives Football Fans a Chance to Play with the CFL," *Marketing Magazine,* August 21, 2009; Jeromy Lloyd, "Nissan Canada Launches New Site to Make Car Buyers Smile," *Marketing Magazine,* August 21, 2009; Kristin Laird, "TV Ads Show How Nissan Spices Up the Mundane," *Marketing Magazine,* July 15, 2009; cassies.ca.
45. Calvin Leung, "Social Media," *Canadian Business Magazine,* June 15, 2009; Matt Semansky, "Montreal Filmmaker Achieves Doritos Guru Status," *Marketing Magazine,* May 4, 2009; Jeromy Lloyd, "Doritos Unveils Consumer-Generated Brand Launch," *Marketing Magazine,* February 13, 2009; Jonathan Paul, "The Doritos Guru Chips In," *Strategy,* April 2009, p. 30; Jennifer Wells, "It's Crunch Time," *The Globe and Mail,* February 13, 2009, p. B7.
46. Leonard L. Berry, "Relationship Marketing of Services—Growing Interest, Emerging Perspectives," *Journal of the Academy of Marketing Science, 23* (4), Fall 1995, pp. 236–45; Jonathan R. Capulsky and Michael J. Wolfe, "Relationship Marketing: Positioning for the Future," *Journal of Business Strategy, 11* (4), July–August 1991, pp. 16–26.
47. B. Joseph Pine II, Don Peppers, and Martha Rogers, "Do You Want to Keep Your Customers Forever?" *Harvard Business Review,* March–April 1995, pp. 103–14.
48. Lisa M. Keefe, "What Is the Meaning of 'Marketing'?" *Marketing News,* September 15, 2004, pp. 17–18.
49. Adrian Payne and Pennie Flow, "Strategic Framework for Customer Relationship Management," *Journal of Marketing, 69* (4), October 2005, pp. 167–76.
50. Michelle Halpern, "In Your Face," *Marketing Magazine,* July 16, 2007; Rob Gerlsbeck, "Socially Awkward," *Marketing Magazine,* November 20, 2006.

51. Anthony J. Tortorici, "Maximizing Marketing Communications through Horizontal and Vertical Orchestration," *Public Relations Quarterly,* 36 (1), 1991, pp. 20–22.

52. Mike Reid, "Performance Auditing of Integrated Marketing Communication (IMC) Actions and Outcome," *Journal of Advertising, 34* (4), Winter 2005, pp. 41–54.

53. Eve Lazarus, "Tourist Contraction," *Marketing Magazine,* November 28, 2011.

54. Cassies.ca.

55. Paul-Mark Rendon, "Where Above Meets Below," *Marketing Magazine,* May 8, 2006.

CHAPTER TWO

1. Sharon Horsky, Steven C. Michael, and Alvin J. Silk, "The Internalization of Advertising Services: An Inter-Industry Analysis," Working Paper, Harvard Business School, 2008.

2. Sharon Edelson, "Target Drops Wieden + Kennedy as Lead Ad Agency," *Women's Wear Daily,* January 9, 2012; http://target-creative.com/

3. Kristin Laird, "Joe Fresh," *Marketing Magazine,* November 28, 2011, p. 29.

4. M. Louise Ripley, "What Kind of Companies Take Their Advertising In-House?" *Journal of Advertising Research,* October/November 1991, pp. 73–80.

5. Rupal Parekh, "Thinking of Pulling a CareerBuilder? Pros and Cons of Bringing an Account In-house," *Advertising Age, 31* (5), May 18, 2009.

6. Horsky, Michael, and Silk, "The Internalization of Advertising Services: An Inter-Industry Analysis."

7. Jeromy Lloyd, "A New Kind of MARCOM," *Marketing Magazine,* August 31, 2009.

8. "*Marketing's* 2009 Agency Family Tree," *Marketing Magazine,* July 20, 2009, pp. 16–23.

9. Melinda Mattos, "Canadian Agencies Go Global," *Strategy,* June 3, 2011, p. 8.

10. Chris Powell, "NO, Canada," *Marketing Magazine,* June 13, 2011, pp. 31, 32, 34, 36, 37.

11. Eve Lazarus, "Rising in the West," *Marketing Magazine,* December 12, 2011, pp. 23–25, 27, 29.

12. Bill Currie, "Tiny Ad Agency Gains Tories' Favour," *The Globe and Mail,* January 21, 2012, p. A13.

13. Jeromy Lloyd, "Creativity Built Upon the Rock," *Marketing Magazine,* October 24, 2011, p. 12.

14. Jon Steel, *Truth, Lies & Advertising: The Art of Account Planning* (New York: Wiley, 1998).

15. Jeromy Lloyd, "Rumbles in the Jungles," *Marketing Magazine,* February 28, 2011, pp. 22–23, 25–26, 28–29. A video format of this material is on marketingmag.ca published in February 2011.

16. Susan Krashinsky, "Two Ad Agencies Become One," *The Globe and Mail,* July 16, 2012, p. B3.

17. Lloyd, "Rumbles in the Jungles."

18. Simon Houpt, "Beyond Advertising," *Strategy,* June 3, 2011, p. 39.

19. Jeffery Thibodeau, "Better Ways to Get Paid," *Marketing Magazine,* March 22, 2004.

20. www.aca-online.com

21. Paul-Mark Rendon, "Pay as You Play," *Marketing Magazine,* June 21, 2004.

22. "The Benefits of PBR," *Marketing Magazine,* July 9, 2001; "Executive Summary," *Marketing Magazine,* July 9, 2001; "Finding the Right PBR Performance Measures," *Marketing Magazine,* July 16, 2001.

23. Rob Gerlsbeck, "Creative Compensation," *Marketing Magazine,* April 17, 2006.

24. Chris Daniels, "Part-Time Partners," *Marketing Magazine,* June 23, 2003.

25. Michelle Warren, "Project Work," *Marketing Magazine,* April 19, 2004; Michelle Warren, "The Year of Treading Water," *Marketing Magazine,* November 24, 2003.

26. Fred Beard, "Marketing Client Role Ambiguity as a Source of Dissatisfaction in Client–Ad Agency Relationships," *Journal of Advertising Research,* 36 (5), September/October 1996, pp. 9–20; Paul Michell, Harold Cataquet, and Stephen Hague, "Establishing the Causes of Disaffection in Agency–Client Relations," *Journal of Advertising Research, 32* (2), March–April 1992, pp. 41–8; Peter Doyle, Marcel Corstiens, and Paul Michell, "Signals of Vulnerability in Agency–Client Relations," *Journal of Marketing, 44* (4), Fall 1980, pp. 18–23; Daniel B. Wackman, Charles Salmon, and Caryn C. Salmon, "Developing an Advertising Agency–Client Relationship," *Journal of Advertising Research, 26* (6), December 1986/January 1987, pp. 21–29.

27. Mukund S Kulkarni, Premal P. Vora, and Terence A. Brown, "Firing Advertising Agencies," *Journal of Advertising, 32* (3), Fall 2003, pp. 77–86.

28. Matt Semansky, "A Tighter Grip," *Marketing Magazine,* February 23, 2009.

29. "Whither the Full-Service Agencies?" *Marketing Magazine,* February 28, 2011, p. 9.

30. "Call in the Specialists," *Marketing Magazine,* June 4, 2001.

31. Prema Nakra, "The Changing Role of Public Relations in Marketing Communications," *Public Relations Quarterly, 36* (1), Spring 1991, pp. 42–45.

32. Hy Haberman, "Walking the Talk on Integration," *Marketing Magazine,* February 9, 2004.

33. Study cited in Michael Bush, "Memo to Marketers: It's Your Fault if Your Shops Flounder," *Advertising Age,* March 29, 2010.

34. Lloyd, "Rumbles in the Jungles."

35. Philip J. Kitchen and Don E. Schultz, "A Multi-Country Comparison of the Drive for IMC," *Journal of Advertising Research, 39* (1), January/February 1999, pp. 21–38; William N. Swain, "Perceptions of IMC after a Decade of Development: Who's at the Wheel and How Can We Measure Success?" *Journal of Advertising Research, 44* (1), March 2004, pp. 46–67.

36. David N. McArthur and Tom Griffin, "A Marketing Management View of Integrated Marketing Communications," *Journal of Advertising Research, 37* (5), September/October 1997, pp. 19–26.

37. Joan Voight, "Study: Clients Want Multiple Partners," *Adweek,* May 14, 2007, pp. 20–21.

38. Study cited in Bush, "Memo to Marketers: It's Your Fault if Your Shops Flounder."

39. Michelle Warren, "What Marketers Want," *Marketing Magazine,* November 24, 2003.

40. Kevin Astle, "The Shaky State of Marketer–Agency Relations," *Marketing Magazine,* November 24, 2003.

CHAPTER THREE

1. Leon G. Schiffman and Leslie Lazar Kannuk, *Consumer Behavior,* 4th ed. (Englewood Cliffs, NJ: Prentice Hall, 1991), p. 192.

2. Eric N. Berkowitz, Roger A. Kerin, Steven W. Hartley, and William Rudelius, *Marketing,* 6th ed. (Burr Ridge, IL: Irwin/McGraw-Hill, 2000), p. 14.

3. A. H. Maslow, "'Higher' and 'Lower' Needs," *Journal of Psychology, 25* (1948), pp. 433–36.

4. For an excellent discussion of memory and consumer behaviour, see James R. Bettman, "Memory Factors in Consumer Choice: A Review," *Journal of Marketing, 43* (2), Spring 1979, pp. 37–53.

5. Danny Kucharsky, "World Wide Vacations," *Marketing Magazine,* June 12, 2006.

6. Chris Powell, "iPhone Helping Change Canadian Wireless Attitudes," *Marketing Magazine,* April 9, 2009.

7. Gilbert Harrell, *Consumer Behavior* (San Diego: Harcourt Brace Jovanovich, 1986), p. 66.

8. Raymond A. Bauer and Stephen A. Greyser, *Advertising in America: The Consumer View* (Boston: Harvard Business School, 1968).

9. J. Paul Peter and Jerry C. Olson, *Consumer Behavior,* 2nd ed. (Burr Ridge, IL: Irwin/McGraw-Hill, 1990), p. 73.

10. Gordon W. Allport, "Attitudes," in *Handbook of Social Psychology,* ed. C. M. Murchison (Winchester, MA: Clark University Press, 1935), p. 810.

11. Robert B. Zajonc and Hazel Markus, "Affective and Cognitive Factors in Preferences," *Journal of Consumer Research, 9* (2), September 1982, pp. 123–31.

12. Alvin Achenbaum, "Advertising Doesn't Manipulate Consumers," *Journal of Advertising Research, 10* (2), April 1970, pp. 3–13.

13. William D. Wells, "Attitudes and Behavior: Lessons from the Needham Lifestyle Study," *Journal of Advertising Research, 25* (1), February–March 1985, pp. 40–44; and Icek Ajzen and Martin Fishbein, "Attitude–Behavior Relations: A Theoretical Analysis and Review of Empirical Research," *Psychological Bulletin, 84* (5), September 1977, pp. 888–918.

14. Joel B. Cohen, Paul W. Minniard, and Peter R. Dickson, "Information Integration: An Information Processing Perspective," in *Advances in Consumer Research,* vol. 7, ed. Jerry C. Olson (Ann Arbor, MI: Association for Consumer Research, 1980), pp. 161–70.

15. Peter and Olson, *Consumer Behavior,* p. 182.

16. Peter L. Wright and Fredric Barbour, "The Relevance of Decision Process Models in Structuring Persuasive Messages," *Communications Research, 2* (3), July 1975, pp. 246–59.

17. James F. Engel, "The Psychological Consequences of a Major Purchase Decision," in *Marketing in Transition,* ed. William S. Decker (Chicago: American Marketing Association, 1963), pp. 462–75.

18. Richard L. Oliver, *Satisfaction: A Behavioral Perspective on the Consumer* (New York: McGraw-Hill, 1997).

19. John A. Howard and Jagdish N. Sheth, *The Theory of Consumer Behavior* (New York: John Wiley & Sons, 1969).

20. Lyman E. Ostlund, *Role Theory and Group Dynamics in Consumer Behavior: Theoretical Sources*, ed. Scott Ward and Thomas S. Robertson (Englewood Cliffs, NJ: Prentice Hall, 1973), pp. 230–75.

21. James Stafford and Benton Cocanougher, "Reference Group Theory," in *Perspective in Consumer Behavior*, ed. H. H. Kassarjian and T. S. Robertson (Glenview, IL: Scott, Foresman, 1981), pp. 329–43.

22. Jagdish N. Sheth, "A Theory of Family Buying Decisions," in *Models of Buying Behavior*, ed. Jagdish N. Sheth (New York: Harper & Row, 1974), pp. 17–33.

23. Larry Percy and Richard Rosenbaum-Elliot, *Strategic Advertising Management*, 4th ed. (Oxford University Press, 2012). The first OUP edition (2001) included Rossiter as an author.

24. Eve Lazarus, "Tea's Time," *Marketing Magazine*, September 25, 2006.

25. Mary Maddever, "Media," *Strategy*, June 2009, p. 44.

26. Norma Ramage, "Educating the Young," *Marketing Magazine*, March 22, 2004.

27. David Booth, "The New Harley-Davidson: We Are Everyone," *National Post*, March 9, 2012, p. DT2.

28. Michael R. Solomon, *Consumer Behavior: Buying, Having, and Being*, 8th ed. (Pearson Prentice Hall, 2009).

29. Norma Ramage, "Chinese Theme Added to Bell Effort," *Marketing Magazine*, February 2, 2004.

30. Celine Wong, "Can't Knock the Hustle," *Marketing Magazine*, May 3, 2004.

31. For an excellent discussion of social class and consumer behaviour, see Richard P. Coleman, "The Continuing Significance of Social Class to Marketing," *Journal of Consumer Research, 10* (3), December 1983, pp. 265–80.

32. Chris Daniels, "Almost Rich," *Marketing Magazine*, April 26, 2004.

33. Russell Belk, "Situational Variables and Consumer Behavior," *Journal of Consumer Research, 2* (3), December 1975, pp. 157–64.

34. Norma Ramage, "Mark's Work Wearhouse Tries on New Women's Line," *Marketing Magazine*, September 2, 2009.

35. John Rossiter and Larry Percy, *Advertising Communications and Promotion Management* (New York: McGraw Hill, 1996). An updated version is Larry Percy and Richard Rosenbaum-Elliott, *Strategic Advertising Management*, 4th ed. (Oxford University Press, 2012). The first OUP edition (2001) included Rossiter as an author.

36. Chris Powell, "TMN Puts Spotlight on Subscribers," *Marketing Magazine*, February 23, 2004.

37. Stephen Beatty, "How to Win Back Your Customers, Toyota-Style," *Marketing Magazine*, May 16, 2011, pp. 22–23.

38. Susan Krashinsky, "RIM's Marketing Challenge: Revive the CrackBerry addiction," *The Globe and Mail*, January 25, 2012, p. B1.

39. Dave Scholz and Jean-Marc Leger, "The Fickle Beer Consumer," *Marketing Magazine*, May 10, 2004.

40. Thomas J. Reynolds and Carol B Phillips, "In Search of True Brand Equity Metrics: All Market Share Ain't Created Equal," *Journal of Advertising Research, 45* (2), June 2005, pp. 171–86.

41. Scholz and Leger, "The Fickle Beer Consumer."

42. Melita Kuburas, "Initiative's Meaghan Stafford: Savvy Hyper-Targeter Hits Her Mark," *Strategy*, June 2009, p. 25.

43. Theresa Wood, "Design," *Strategy*, June 2009, p. 48.

44. Sarah Dobson, "Coffee Crisp Targets Caffeine Crowd," *Marketing Magazine*, February 10, 2003.

45. Simon Houpt, "Trying on a Younger, Hipper Image," *The Globe and Mail*, August 5, 2011, p. B7.

46. Eve Lazarus, "Vancouver's Driving Force," *Marketing Magazine*, August 28, 2006.

47. "Interactive IMC: The Relational-Transactional Continuum and the Synergistic Use of Customer Data," *Journal of Advertising Research, 46* (2), June 2006, pp. 146–59.

48. Ace Alvarez, "How to Send Happiness," *Marketing Magazine*, August 28, 2006.

49. Lisa D'Innocenzo, "Is Your Target a Man's Man? Then Reach Out to Women," *Strategy*, February 2006.

CHAPTER FOUR

1. Wilbur Schram, *The Process and Effects of Mass Communications* (Urbana: University of Illinois Press, 1955).

2. Ibid.

3. David G. Mick, "Consumer Research and Semiotics: Exploring the Morphology of Signs, Symbols, and Significance," *Journal of Consumer Research, 13* (2), September 1986, pp. 196–213; Edward F. McQuarrie and David Glen Mick, "Figures of Rhetoric in Advertising Language," *Journal of Consumer Research, 22* (4), March 1996, pp. 424–38.

4. Barry L. Bayus, "Word of Mouth: The Indirect Effect of Marketing Efforts," *Journal of Advertising Research, 25* (3), June/July 1985, pp. 31–39; Robert E. Smith and Christine A. Vogt, "The Effects of Integrating Advertising and Negative Word-of-Mouth Communications on Message Processing and Response," *Journal of Consumer Psychology, 4* (2), 1995, pp. 133–51; Kate Niederhoffer, Rob Mooth, David Wiesenfeld, and Jonathon Gordon, "The Origin and Impact of CPG New-Product Buzz: Emerging Trends and Implications," *Journal of Advertising Research, 47* (4), December 2007, pp. 420–26.

5. Tralee Pearce, "Word of Mom: Publicity Money Can't Buy," *The Globe and Mail*, November 18, 2011, p. L2.

6. "Hollie Shaw, "He Exposes Insidious Marketing Ploys and Shines Light on How We React to Brands," *National Post*, November 25, 2011, p. FP12.

7. Emily Wexler, "Dove's Online Song and Dance," *Strategy*, April 1, 2011, p. 10.

8. Larry Yu, "How Companies Turn Buzz into Sales," *MIT Sloan Management Review*, Winter 2005, pp. 5–6.

9. John E. Hogan, Katherine N. Lemon, Barak Libai, "Quantifying the Ripple: Word-of-Mouth and Advertising Effectiveness," *Journal of Advertising Research, 44* (3), September 2004, pp. 271–80; Jeffrey Graham and William Havlena, "Finding the Missing Link: Advertising's Impact on Word of Mouth, Web Searches, and Site Visits," *Journal of Advertising Research, 47* (4), December 2007, pp. 427–35.

10. Ed Keller and Brad Fay, "The Role of Advertising in Word of Mouth," *Journal of Advertising Research, 49* (2), June 2009, pp. 154–63.

11. Niederhoffer, Mooth, Wiesenfeld, and Gordon, "The Origin and Impact of CPG New-Product Buzz."

12. Paul Brent, "From Broadcast to Broadband," *Marketing Magazine*, April 30, 2007.

13. Garine Tcholakian, "Volkswagen Webisodes to Air on Sympatico.ca," *Media in Canada*, October 5, 2009; Emily Wexler, "Volkswagen Canada: Defying Das Odds," *Strategy*, June 2009, p. 13.

14. Simon Houpt, "Budding Filmmakers Need Not Apply," *The Globe and Mail*, July 14, 2011.

15. Jonathan Paul, "Carrying the Torch for Coke," *Strategy*, February 2009, p. 19.

16. Emily Wexler, "Roundtable: Surviving the Social Revolution," *Strategy*, October 2009, p. 17.

17. E. K. Strong, *The Psychology of Selling* (New York: McGraw-Hill, 1925), p. 9.

18. Jonathan Paul, "Value Targeting: Top Youth Brands' Niche Connection Plans," *Strategy*, April 1, 2011, p. 34.

19. Robert J. Lavidge and Gary A. Steiner, "A Model for Predictive Measurements of Advertising Effectiveness," *Journal of Marketing, 24* (4), October 1961, pp. 59–62.

20. Jonathan Paul, "Value Targeting: Top Youth Brands' Niche Connection Plans," *Strategy*, April 1, 2011, p. 34.

21. William J. McGuire, "An Information Processing Model of Advertising Effectiveness," in *Behavioral and Management Science in Marketing*, ed. Harry J. Davis and Alvin J. Silk (New York: Ronald Press, 1978), pp. 156–80.

22. "Canada's Most Trusted Brands in 2011," *Marketing Magazine*, May 16, 2011, pp. 17–21.

23. Anthony G. Greenwald and Clark Leavitt, "Audience Involvement in Advertising: Four Levels," *Journal of Consumer Research, 11* (1), June 1984, pp. 581–92; Judith L. Zaichkowsky, "Conceptualizing Involvement," *Journal of Advertising, 15* (2), September 1986, pp. 4–14.

24. Michael L. Ray, "Communication and the Hierarchy of Effects," in *New Models for Mass Communication Research*, ed. P. Clarke (Beverly Hills, CA: Sage, 1973), pp. 147–75.

25. Robert E. Smith, "Integrating Information from Advertising and Trial: Processes and Effects on Consumer Response to Product Information," *Journal of Marketing Research, 30* (2), May 1993, pp. 204–19.

26. DeAnna S. Kempf and Russell N. Laczniak, "Advertising's Influence on Subsequent Product Trial Processing," *Journal of Advertising, 30* (2), Fall 2001, pp. 27–38.

27. Herbert E. Krugman, "The Impact of Television Advertising: Learning without Involvement," *Public Opinion Quarterly, 29* (3), Fall 1965, pp. 349–56.

28. Scott A. Hawkins and Stephen J. Hoch, "Low-Involvement Learning: Memory without Evaluation," *Journal of Consumer Research, 19* (2), September 1992, pp. 212–25.

29. Emily Wexler, "Fiona Stevenson: P&G's Cover Girl Blasts the Competition," *Strategy,* October 2009.

30. Jerry C. Olson, Daniel R. Toy, and Phillip A. Dover, "Mediating Effects of Cognitive Responses to Advertising on Cognitive Structure," in *Advances in Consumer Research,* ed. H. Keith Hunt (Ann Arbor, MI: Association for Consumer Research, 1978), pp. 72–78.

31. Anthony A. Greenwald, "Cognitive Learning, Cognitive Response to Persuasion and Attitude Change," in *Psychological Foundations of Attitudes,* ed. A. G. Greenwald, T. C. Brock, and T. W. Ostrom (New York: Academic Press, 1968); Peter L. Wright, "The Cognitive Processes Mediating Acceptance of Advertising," *Journal of Marketing Research, 10* (1), February 1973, pp. 53–62; Brian Wansink, Michael L. Ray, and Rajeev Batra, "Increasing Cognitive Response Sensitivity," *Journal of Advertising, 23* (2), June 1994, pp. 65–76.

32. Peter Wright, "Message Evoked Thoughts, Persuasion Research Using Thought Verbalizations," *Journal of Consumer Research, 7* (2), September 1980, pp. 151–75.

33. Morris Holbrook and Rajeev Batra, "Assessing the Role of Emotions as Mediators of Consumer Responses to Advertising," *Journal of Consumer Research, 14* (3), December 1987, pp. 404–20.

34. Raffi Chowdhury, Douglas Olson, John Pracejuc, "Affective Responses to Images in Print Advertising," *Journal of Advertising, 37* (3), Fall 2008, pp. 7–18.

35. Scott B. Mackenzie, Richard J. Lutz, and George E. Belch, "The Role of Attitude Toward the Ad as a Mediator of Advertising Effectiveness: A Test of Competing Explanations," *Journal of Marketing Research, 23* (1), May 1986, pp. 130–43; Rajeev Batra and Michael L. Ray, "Affective Responses Mediating Acceptance of Advertising," *Journal of Consumer Research, 13* (2), September 1986, pp. 234–49.

36. Tim Ambler and Tom Burne, "The Impact of Affect on Memory of Advertising," *Journal of Advertising Research, 29* (3), March/April 1999, pp. 25–34.

37. Abhilasha Mehta, "Advertising Attitudes and Advertising Effectiveness," *Journal of Advertising Research, 40* (3), May–June 2000, pp. 67–72.

38. David J. Moore and William D. Harris, "Affect Intensity and the Consumer's Attitude toward High Impact Emotional Advertising Appeals," *Journal of Advertising, 25* (1), Summer 1996, pp. 37–50; Andrew A. Mitchell and Jerry C. Olson, "Are Product Attribute Beliefs the Only Mediator of Advertising Effects on Brand Attitude?" *Journal of Marketing Research, 18* (3), August 1981, pp. 318–32.

39. David J. Moore, William D. Harris, and Hong C. Chen, "Affect Intensity: An Individual Difference Response to Advertising Appeals," *Journal of Consumer Research, 22* (2), September 1995, pp. 154–64; Julie Edell and Marian C. Burke, "The Power of Feelings in Understanding Advertising Effects," *Journal of Consumer Research, 14* (3), December 1987, pp. 421–33.

40. Richard E. Petty and John T. Cacioppo, "Central and Peripheral Routes to Persuasion: Application to Advertising," in *Advertising and Consumer Psychology,* ed. Larry Percy and Arch Woodside (Lexington, MA: Lexington Books, 1983), pp. 3–23.

41. David A. Aaker, Rajeev Batra, and John G. Myers, *Advertising Management,* 5th ed. (Upper Saddle River, NJ: Prentice Hall, 1996).

42. Gerald J. Gorn, "The Effects of Music in Advertising on Choice: A Classical Conditioning Approach," *Journal of Marketing, 46* (1), Winter 1982, pp. 94–101; James J. Kellaris, Anthony D. Cox, and Dena Cox, "The Effect of Background Music on Ad Processing: A Contingency Explanation," *Journal of Marketing, 57* (4), Fall 1993, p. 114.

43. Richard E. Petty, John T. Cacioppo, and David Schumann, "Central and Peripheral Routes to Advertising Effectiveness: The Moderating Role of Involvement," *Journal of Consumer Research, 10* (2), September 1983, pp. 135–46.

44. Demetrios Vakratsas and Tim Ambler, "How Advertising Works: What Do We Really Know?" *Journal of Marketing, 63* (1), January 1999, pp. 26–43.

45. John Rossiter and Larry Percy, *Advertising Communications and Promotion Management* (New York: McGraw Hill, 1996). An updated version is Larry Percy and Richard Rosenbaum-Elliott, *Strategic Advertising Management,* 4th ed. (Oxford University Press, 2012). The first OUP edition (2001) included Rossiter as an author.

46. William M. Weilbacher, "Point of View: Does Advertising Cause a 'Hierarchy of Effects'?" *Journal of Advertising Research, 41* (6), November/ December 2001, pp. 19–26; Thomas E. Barry, "In Defense of the Hierarchy of Effects: A Rejoinder to Weilbacher," *Journal of Advertising Research, 42* (3), May/June 2002, pp. 44–47; William M. Weilbacher , "Weilbacher Comments on 'In Defense of the Hierarchy of Effects'," *Journal of Advertising Research, 42* (3), May/June 2002, pp. 48–49; William M. Weilbacher, "How Advertising Affects Consumers," *Journal of Advertising Research, 43* (2), June 2003, pp. 231–34; Stephen D. Rappaport, "Lessons from Online Practice: New Advertising Models," *Journal of Advertising Research, 47* (2), June 2007, pp. 135–41.

47. Weilbacher, "How Advertising Affects Consumers."

48. Figure 4-8 is a shorter adaptation from William J. McGuire, "An Information Processing Model of Advertising Effectiveness," in *Behavioral and Management Science in Marketing,* ed. Harry J. Davis and Alvin J. Silk (New York: Ronald Press, 1978), pp. 156–80.

CHAPTER FIVE

1. Robert A. Kriegel, "How to Choose the Right Communications Objectives," *Business Marketing,* April 1986, pp. 94–106.

2. Hollie Shaw, "Data Overload: Marketers Not Ready for Digital Influx," *National Post,* October 28, 2011, p. FP7.

3. Donald S. Tull, "The Carry-Over Effect of Advertising," *Journal of Marketing, 29* (2), April 1965, pp. 46–53.

4. Darral G. Clarke, "Econometric Measurement of the Duration of Advertising Effect on Sales," *Journal of Marketing Research, 23* (4), November 1976, pp. 345–57.

5. Philip Kotler, *Marketing Decision Making: A Model Building Approach* (New York: Holt, Rinehart & Winston, 1971), ch. 5.

6. Russell H. Colley, *Defining Advertising Goals for Measured Advertising Results* (New York: Association of National Advertisers, 1961).

7. Stewart H. Britt, "Are So-Called Successful Advertising Campaigns Really Successful?" *Journal of Advertising Research, 9* (2), 1969, pp. 3–9.

8. Steven W. Hartley and Charles H. Patti, "Evaluating Business-to-Business Advertising: A Comparison of Objectives and Results," *Journal of Advertising Research, 28* (2), April/May 1988, pp. 21–27.

9. Study cited in Robert F. Lauterborn, "How to Know If Your Advertising Is Working," *Journal of Advertising Research, 25* (1), February/March 1985, pp. RC 9–11.

10. John Rossiter and Larry Percy, *Advertising Communications and Promotion Management* (New York: McGraw Hill, 1996). An updated version is Larry Percy and Richard Rosenbaum-Elliot, *Strategic Advertising Management,* 4th ed. (Oxford University Press, 2012). The first OUP edition (2001) included Rossiter as an author.

11. Jennifer Wells, "Cossette Duo's Tricks Are a Treat," *The Globe and Mail,* May 8, 2009, p. B8; Jonathan Paul, "McDonald's Big Bean Blitz," *Strategy,* June 2009, p. 21; Lesley Ciarula Taylor, "McD's Goes Free to Counter Tim Hortons," *Toronto Star,* March 2, 2010.

12. Kristin Laird, "Canadian Blood Services Gets Personal," *Marketing Magazine,* May 5, 2009.

13. Susan Krashinsky, "To Catch Coke, Pepsi Dusts Off an Old Trick," *The Globe and Mail,* May 17, 2012, p. B3.

14. Eric Lam, "Curtain Still Rises," *National Post,* June 4, 2011, p. FP6.

15. "Shopper Marketing," *Marketing Magazine,* October 24, 2011, p. 29.

16. Michelle Warren, "Engagement Marketing: The Back-to-School Edition," *Marketing Magazine,* September 12, 2011, pp. 40–43.

17. Brian Wansink and Michael Ray, "Estimating an Advertisement's Impact on One's Consumption of a Brand," *Journal of Advertising Research, 40* (6), November–December 2000.

18. Angela Scardillo, "Making Milk COOL," *Marketing Magazine,* August 11, 2003.

19. Nick Krewen, "Prairie Dairy Milks Teen Media," *Strategy,* December 2009, p. 9.

20. Susan Krashinsky, "Stalking the Elusive Millennial Male," *The Globe and Mail,* July 20, 2012, p. B5.

21. Susan Krashinsky, "A Fresh Twist on Tried-and-True Brews," *The Globe and Mail*, May 18, 2012, p. B6.
22. Frank Dennis, "Selling Hidden Brands," *Marketing Magazine*, May 10, 2004.
23. http://cassies.ca/entry/viewcase/7522
24. http://cassies.ca/entry/viewcase/7111
25. http://cassies.ca/content/caselibrary/winners/2011_Activia.pdf
26. Kristin Laird, "Everything You Want in a Drug Store," *Marketing Magazine*, December 2012.
27. Carly Weeks, "How Green Is Your Wallet?" *The Globe and Mail*, March 15, 2011, p. L1.
28. Jeremy Cato, "Mazda Needs the BMW Blueprint," *The Globe and Mail*, March 9, 2012, p. D10.
29. Melinda Mattos, "BC Hydro Regenerates," *Strategy*, April 1, 2011, p. 27.

CHAPTER SIX

1. *Ayer's Dictionary of Advertising Terms* (Philadelphia: Ayer Press, 1976).
2. Eve Lazarus, "Happy Planet Takes a Shot at Energy Drinks," *Marketing Magazine*, May 29, 2009.
3. Jonathan Paul, "Sobeys Takes a Fresh Approach," *Strategy*, March 1, 2011, p. 21.
4. Usage data observed from University of Ottawa subscription of Print Measurement Bureau. Data collection questions for brand and usage are publicly available at PMB.ca.
5. Charles Blankson, Stavros P. Kalafatis, Julian Ming-Sung, and Costas Hadjicharalambous, "Impact of Positioning Strategies on Corporate Performance," *Journal of Advertising Research, 48* (1), March 2008, pp. 106–22; Charles Blankson and Stavros P. Kalafatis, "Congruence between Positioning and Brand Advertising," *Journal of Advertising Research, 47* (1), March 2007, pp. 79–94.
6. Jack Trout, "Branding Can't Exist without Positioning," *Advertising Age*, March 14, 2005, p. 25.
7. Al Ries and Jack Trout, *Positioning: The Battle for Your Mind*, McGraw-Hill, 2001.
8. John Rossiter and Larry Percy, *Advertising Communications and Promotion Management* (New York: McGraw Hill, 1996).
9. David Aaaker, Rajeev Batra, and John Myers, *Advertising Management*, 4th ed. (Englewood Cliffs, NJ: Prentice Hall, 1992); Larry Percy and Richard Elliot, *Strategic Advertising Management*, 4th ed. (Oxford University Press, 2012).
10. Larry Percy and Richard Elliot, *Strategic Advertising Management*, 4th ed. (Oxford University Press, 2012); Orville Walker Jr., John Mullins, Harper Boyd Jr., and Jean-Claude Larreche, *Marketing Strategy: A Decision-Focused Approach*, 8th ed. (McGraw-Hill Irwin, 2006).
11. Jeremy Cato, "The Changing Face of Luxury Cars," *The Globe and Mail*, December 16, 2011.
12. Based on case study available at www.cassies.ca
13. Based on case study available at www.cassies.ca
14. Hollie Shaw, "Sinking Roots in Canada," *National Post*, June 10, 2011, p. FP12.

15. Chris Powell, "Reebok Gets Fired Up in New Hockey Campaign," *Marketing Magazine*, February 5, 2013.
16. http://cassies.ca/winners/2011/cassies.ca/winners/2011Winners/2011_winners_Activia.html
17. Jonathan Paul, "Dentsu's Min Ryuck: Driving Interactive Digital," *Strategy*, June 2009, p. 24.
18. Susan Krashinsky, "The Food Industry's Real Message," *The Globe and Mail*, February 24, 2012, p. B6.
19. Jonathan Paul, "Molson Paints It Black," *Strategy*, April 1, 2011, p. 14.
20. Russ Martin, "Nutella Launches Better Breakfast Challenge," *Marketing Magazine*, May 13, 2009.
21. Brian Wansink and Jennifer Marie Gilmore, "New Uses That Revitalize Old Brands," *Journal of Advertising Research, 39* (2), April 1999, pp. 90–98.
22. Paul Brent, "Craft Brewers Carve Out a Niche," *National Post*, June 29, 2011, p. AL7.
23. Kristin Laird, "Reitman's Beats Haute Couture Again," *Marketing Magazine*, May 5, 2009.
24. Matt Semansky, "Yves Rocher Plants New Brand, Store, Concept in Montreal," *Marketing Magazine*, May 22, 2009.
25. Theresa Wood, "Lay's Calls on Local Spuds," *Strategy*, March 2009, p. 17.
26. Russ Martin, "Concerts Kick Off Samsung Galaxy S4 Possibilities," *Marketing Magazine*, April 26, 2013.
27. Russ Martin, "Molson Brings Back 'I Am Canadian' for Canada Day," *Marketing Magazine*, June 24, 2013.
28. Jonathan Paul, "Wanna Talk About It?" *Strategy*, January 2009, p. 23.
29. Jennifer Wells, "Brock Offers a Lesson in Boldness," *The Globe and Mail*, April 17, 2009, p. B5.
30. For a review of multiattribute models, see William L. Wilkie and Edgar A. Pessemier, "Issues in Marketing's Use of Multiattribute Models," *Journal of Marketing Research, 10* (4), November 1983, pp. 428–41.
31. Joel Rubinson and Markus Pfeiffer, "Brand Key Performance Indicators as a Force for Brand Equity Management," *Journal of Advertising Research, 45* (3), June 2005, pp. 187–97.
32. Marc Stoiber, "The Death of Green Has Been Greatly Exaggerated," *Marketing Magazine*, September 12, 2011, p. 8.
33. Based on case study available at www.cassies.ca
34. Based on case study available at www.cassies.ca
35. Based on case study available at www.cassies.ca
36. Krashinsky, "The Food Industry's 'Real' Message."
37. Hollie Shaw, "Duelling Couches," *National Post*, July 24, 2009, p. FP10; Jonathan Paul, "Bell & Rogers: Couch Wars," *Strategy*, September 2009, p. 24; Scott Deveua, "Telus Sues Rogers Over 'Fast' Claims," *National Post*, November 19, 2009, p. FP1; Simon Houpt, "Telus, B.C. Judge on Same Wavelength," *The Globe and Mail*, November 25, 2009, p. B1; Simon Houpt, "B.C. Judge Tells Rogers: Tear Down Those Billboards," *The Globe and Mail*, December 1, 2009, p. B1; Simon Houpt, "Rogers Suit Turns the

Tables on Competition," *The Globe and Mail*, December 2, 2009, p. B1.
38. Chris Powell, "ING Adopts New Positioning, Unveils New Marketing," *Marketing Magazine*, April 24, 2013.
39. Chris Powell, "Mobilicity Targets Wireless Big 3 in New Campaign," *Marketing Magazine*, January 13, 2012; Simon Houpt, "Disconnecting from Discontent," *The Globe and Mail*, July 2011, p. B6.
40. Chris Powell, "Van Houtte Explores Coffee Culture in New Video Series," *Marketing Magazine*, March 21, 2013.
41. Jonathan Paul, "Mr. Lube Is a Homewrecker," *Strategy*, February 1, 2011, p. 14.
42. Kristin Laird, "Cassies Target Newfoundland Tourism Campaign," *Marketing Magazine*, January 24, 2012.
43. Hollie Shaw, "'Wellthy' Trending: Brands Such as Adidas Link Good Health to Status," *National Post Magazine*, April 27, 2012, p. FP6.
44. Stefania Moretti, "An Empire State of Mind," *Canadian Business*, March 12, 2013.
45. Based on case study available at www.cassies.ca

CHAPTER SEVEN

1. Mary Teresa Bitti, "Future Ad Execs?" *National Post*, April 14, 2009, p. FP14.
2. Jaafar El-Murad and Douglas C. West, "The Definition and Measurement of Creativity: What Do We Know?" *Journal of Advertising Research, 44* (2), June 2004, pp. 188–201.
3. Robert E. Smith, Scott B. MacKenzie, Xiaojing Yang, Laura Buchholz, William K. Darley, and Xiaojing Yang, "Modeling the Determinants and Effects of Creativity in Advertising," *Marketing Science, 26* (6), November–December 2007, pp. 819–33.
4. Robert E. Smith and Xiaojing Yang, "Toward a General Theory of Creativity in Advertising: Examining the Role of Divergence," *Marketing Theory, 4* (1/2), June 2004, pp. 29–55.
5. Jeff Cioletti, "In a Changing World, There's Only One Absolut," *Beverage World*, July 2007, pp. 20–25; Stuart Elliott, "In an 'Absolut World,' a Vodka Could Use the Same Ads for More Than 25 Years," *The New York Times*, April 27, 2007, p. C3.
6. Sheila L. Sasser and Scott Koslow, "Desperately Seeking Advertising Creativity," *Journal of Advertising, 37* (4), Winter 2008, pp. 5–19.
7. Leonard N. Reid, Karen Whitehall, and Denise E. DeLorme, "Top-Level Agency Creatives Look at Advertising Creativity Then and Now," *Journal of Advertising, 27* (2), Summer 1998, pp. 1–16.
8. Anonymous, "Envisioning the Future of Advertising Creativity Research," *Journal of Advertising, 37* (4), Winter 2008, pp. 131–149.
9. Daniel W. Baack, Rick T. Wilson, and Brian D. Till, "Creativity and Memory Effects," *Journal of Advertising, 37* (4), Winter 2008, pp. 85–94; Brian D. Till and Daniel Baack, "Recall and Persuasion," *Journal of Advertising, 34* (3), Fall 2005, pp. 47–57.
10. Elizabeth C. Hirschman, "Role-Based Models of Advertising Creation and Production,"

Journal of Advertising, 18 (4), 1989, pp. 42–53.

11. Edith G. Smit, Lex Van Meurs, and Peter C. Neijens, "Effects of Advertising Likeability: A-Year Perspective," *Journal of Advertising Research, 46* (1), March 2006, pp. 73–83.

12. Karolien Poel and Siegfried Dewitte, "Getting a Line on Print Ads," *Journal of Advertising, 37* (4), Winter 2008, pp. 63–74.

13. Micael Dahlen, Sara Rosengren, and Fredrick Torn, "Advertising Creativity Matters," *Journal of Advertising Research, 48* (3), September 2008, pp. 19–26.

14. Charles Young, "Creative Differences between Copywriters and Art Directors," *Journal of Advertising Research, 40* (3), May–June 2000, pp. 19–26.

15. Alisa White and Bruce L. Smith, "Assessing Advertising Creativity Using the Creative Product Semantic Scale," *Journal of Advertising Research, 41* (6), November–December 2001, pp. 27–34; Douglas C. West, Arthur J. Kover, and Alber Caruana, "Practitioner and Customer Views of Advertising Creativity," *Journal of Advertising, 37* (4), Winter 2008, pp. 35–45.

16. Robert E. Smith, Jiemiao Chen, and Xiaojing Yang, "The Impact of Advertising Creativity on the Hierarchy of Effects," *Journal of Advertising, 37* (4), Winter 2008, pp. 47–61.

17. Smith, MacKenzie, Yang, Buchholz, Darley, and Yang, "Modeling the Determinants and Effects of Creativity in Advertising."

18. Swee Hoon Ang, Yih Hwai Lee, and Siew Meng Leong, "The Ad Creativity Cube: Conceptualization and Initial Validation," *Journal of the Academy of Marketing Science, 35* (2), Summer 2007, pp. 220–32; Arthur J. Kover, Stephen M. Goldenberg, and William L. James, "Creativity vs. Effectiveness? An Integrative Classification for Advertising," *Journal of Advertising Research, 35* (6), November/December 1995, pp. 29–38.

19. Smith, MacKenzie, Yang, Buchholz, Darley, and Yang, "Modeling the Determinants and Effects of Creativity in Advertising."

20. For an interesting discussion on the embellishment of advertising messages, see William M. Weilbacher, *Advertising,* 2nd ed. (New York: Macmillan, 1984), pp. 180–82.

21. David Ogilvy, *Confessions of an Advertising Man* (New York: Atheneum, 1963); Hanley Norins, *The Compleat Copywriter* (New York: McGraw-Hill, 1966).

22. Hank Sneiden, *Advertising Pure and Simple* (New York: ANACOM, 1977).

23. Scott Koslow, Sheila L. Sasser, and Edward A. Riordan, "Do Marketers Get the Advertising They Need or the Advertising They Deserve?" *Journal of Advertising, 35* (3), Fall 2006, pp. 81–101.

24. "Residence Inn by Marriott Breaks Out of the Box with New Ad Campaign Featuring Exotic Acrobatic Performers," *PR Newswire,* July 19, 2007.

25. James Webb Young, *A Technique for Producing Ideas,* 3rd ed. (Chicago: Crain Books, 1975), p. 42.

26. W. Glenn Griffin, "From Performance to Mastery: Development Models of the Creative Process," *Journal of Advertising, 37* (4), Winter 2008, pp. 95–108.

27. Arthur J. Kover, "Copywriters' Implicit Theories of Communication: An Exploration," *Journal of Consumer Research, 21* (4), March 1995, pp. 596–611.

28. Sasser and Koslow, "Desperately Seeking Advertising Creativity."

29. Jon Steel, *Truth, Lies and Advertising: The Art of Account Planning* (Wiley, 1998).

30. Sandra E. Moriarty, *Creative Advertising: Theory and Practice* (Englewood Cliffs, NJ: Prentice Hall, 1986).

31. Bruce MacDonald, "The Art of the Brief," *Marketing Magazine,* October 27, 2003.

32. Susan Krashinsky, "For Tough Times, A Sobering Sell," *The Globe and Mail,* January 26, 2012, p. B3; Hollie Shaw, "Need Your Bank Say More?" *National Post,* February 10, 2012, p. FP12.

33. Simon Houpt, "A Singular Point of View," *The Globe and Mail,* October 7, 2011, p. B1.

34. John O'Toole, *The Trouble with Advertising,* 2nd ed. (New York: Random House, 1985), p. 131.

35. Rosser Reeves, *Reality in Advertising* (New York: Knopf, 1961), pp. 47, 48.

36. Susan E. Morgan and Tome Reichert, "The Message Is in the Metaphor: Assessing the Comprehension of Metaphors in Advertisements," *Journal of Advertising, 28* (4), Winter 1999, pp. 1–12; Barbara J. Phillips and Edward F. McQuarrie, "Impact of Advertising Metaphors on Consumer Belief," *Journal of Advertising, 38* (1), Spring 2009, pp. 49–61.

37. Martin Mayer, *Madison Avenue, U.S.A.* (New York: Pocket Books, 1958).

38. Al Ries and Jack Trout, *Positioning: The Battle for Your Mind* (McGraw-Hill, 2001).

39. Timothy R. V. Foster, "The Art & Science of the Advertising Slogan," 2001, www.adslogans.co.uk

40. Russ Martin, "Kobo Launches First John St. Campaign," *Marketing Magazine,* May 1, 2013; Carly Lewis, "Understanding the YOLO Generation," *Marketing Magazine,* April 22, 2013; Chris Powell, "Tassimo Touts Barcode Technology in New Campaign," *Marketing Magazine,* May 18, 2012; Rebecca Harris, "Hawaiian Punch Comes Back to Canada with a Smash," *Marketing Magazine,* March 14, 2013; David Brown, "Autotrader Refinances Brand Position," *Marketing Magazine,* March 4, 2013; Carly Lewis, "Corona Targets Adventurous Millennials in New Campaign," *Marketing Magazine,* March 20, 2013; Marina Straus, "Canadian Tire Waves the Flag in New Campaign," *The Globe and Mail,* March 17, 2011, p. B3.

41. Matt Semansky, "Koodo Ditches Spandex for New Language," *Marketing Magazine,* March 16, 2009.

42. Lara Mills, "Campaigns with Legs," *Marketing Magazine,* May 15, 2000.

43. Emily Wexler, "Labatt's Kristen Morrow: Beer Drinkers' Best Bud," *Strategy,* July 2009, p. 10.

44. Carey Toane, "Creating a New Connection," *Strategy,* January 2009, p. 30.

45. Michael Adams, *Fire and Ice* (Penguin, 2003).

46. Nancy Evans and Bruce MacLellan, "The Risk of Frost Bite," *Marketing Magazine,* June 30, 2003.

47. David MacDonald and Michael Adams, "We Are What We Drive," *Marketing Magazine,* March 15, 2004.

48. Stan Sutter, "Canada's Ad Renascence," *Marketing Magazine,* March 2004.

49. Stan Sutter, "Vive la Difference," *Marketing Magazine,* January 2004.

50. Susan Krashinsky, "Maytag Comes Up with a New Canadian Spin Cycle," *The Globe and Mail,* March 2012, p. B6.

51. Moriarty, *Creative Advertising,* p. 76.

52. William Wells, John Burnett, and Sandra Moriarty, *Advertising* (Englewood Cliffs, NJ: Prentice Hall, 1989), p. 330.

53. William M. Weilbacher, *Advertising,* 2nd ed. (New York: Macmillan, 1984), p. 197.

54. William L. Wilkie and Paul W. Farris, "Comparative Advertising: Problems and Potential," *Journal of Marketing, 39* (4), October 1975, pp. 7–15.

55. For a review of comparative advertising studies, see Cornelia Pechmann and David W. Stewart, "The Psychology of Comparative Advertising," in *Attention, Attitude and Affect in Response to Advertising,* eds. E. M. Clark, T. C. Brock, and D. W. Stewart (Hillsdale, NJ: Lawrence Erlbaum, 1994), pp. 79–96; Thomas S. Barry, "Comparative Advertising: What Have We Learned in Two Decades?" *Journal of Advertising Research, 33* (2), March–April 1993, pp. 19–29.

56. Stuart J. Agres, "Emotion in Advertising: An Agency Point of View," in *Emotion in Advertising: Theoretical and Practical Explanations,* eds. Stuart J. Agres, Julie A. Edell, and Tony M. Dubitsky (Westport, CT: Quorom Books, 1991).

57. Susan Krashinsky, "Google Puts Fizz Back in Classic Coke Ad," *The Globe and Mail,* April 13, 2012, p. B6.

58. Clair Cain Miller, "Google Advertising 'About Emotion' Love, Babies," *National Post,* January 3, 2012, p. FP2.

59. Hamish Pringle and Peter Field, *Brand Immortality, How Brands Can Live Long and Prosper* (London: Kogan Page Limited), 2009.

60. Kate Macarthur, "Big Mac's Back," *Advertising Age,* March 13, 2004, pp. S1–8.

61. Emily Bryson York, "McDonald's Unveils 'I'm Lovin' It' 2.0," *Advertising Age,* April 22, 2010.

62. Edward Kamp and Deborah J. MacInnis, "Characteristics of Portrayed Emotions in Commercials: When Does What Is Shown in Ads Affect Viewers?" *Journal of Advertising Research, 35* (6), November/December 1995, pp. 19–28.

63. For a review of research on the effect of mood states on consumer behaviour, see Meryl Paula Gardner, "Mood States and Consumer Behavior: A Critical Review," *Journal of Consumer Research, 12* (3), December 1985, pp. 281–300.

64. Kristin Laird, "Women Feel Good in Lusty Ads for Second Clothing," *Marketing Magazine,* November 2009.

65. Dacher Keltner and Jennifer S. Lerner, "Emotion," *Handbook of Social Psychology,* eds. Susan T. Fiske, Daniel T. Gilbert, and Gardner Lindzey (John Wiley & Sons, 2010).

66. Michael L. Ray and William L. Wilkie, "Fear: The Potential of an Appeal Neglected by Marketing," *Journal of Marketing, 34* (1), January 1970, pp. 54–62.

67. Brian Sternthal and C. Samuel Craig, "Fear Appeals Revisited and Revised," *Journal of Consumer Research, 1* (3), December 1974, pp. 22–34.

68. Punam Anand Keller and Lauren Goldberg Block, "Increasing the Persuasiveness of Fear Appeals: The Effect of Arousal and Elaboration," *Journal of Consumer Research, 22* (4), March 1996, pp. 448–60.

69. John F. Tanner, Jr., James B. Hunt, and David R. Eppright, "The Protection Motivation Model: A Normative Mode of Fear Appeals," *Journal of Marketing, 55* (3), July 1991, p. 45.

70. Ibid.

71. Herbert Jack Rotfeld, "The Textbook Effect: Conventional Wisdom, Myth and Error in Marketing," *Journal of Marketing, 64* (2), April 2000, pp. 122–27.

72. Hollie Shaw, "Sell It with a Laugh," *National Post,* March 2009, p. FP12.

73. For a discussion of the use of humour in advertising, see C. Samuel Craig and Brian Sternthal, "Humor in Advertising," *Journal of Marketing, 37* (2), October 1973, pp. 12–18.

74. Harlan E. Spotts, Marc G. Weinberger, and Amy L. Parsons, "Assessing the Use and Impact of Humour on Advertising Effectiveness: A Contingency Approach," *Journal of Advertising, 26* (3), Fall 1997, pp. 17–32.

75. Yong Zhang, "Response to Humorous Advertising: The Moderating Effect of Need for Cognition," *Journal of Advertising, 25* (1), Spring 1996, pp. 15–32; Marc G. Weinberger and Charles S. Gulas, "The Impact of Humor in Advertising: A Review," *Journal of Advertising, 21* (4), December 1992, pp. 35–59.

76. Marc G. Weinberger and Leland Campbell, "The Use of Humor in Radio Advertising," *Journal of Advertising Research, 30* (6), December 1990–January 1991, pp. 44–52.

77. Thomas J. Madden and Marc C. Weinberger, "Humor in Advertising: A Practitioner View," *Journal of Advertising Research, 24* (4), August/September 1984, pp. 23–26.

78. David Ogilvy and Joel Raphaelson, "Research on Advertising Techniques That Work and Don't Work," *Harvard Business Review,* July/August 1982, p. 18.

79. Garine Tcholakian, "Kia Gets Soul-ful," *Media in Canada,* February 9, 2009; Jonathan Paul, "Kia Incites Vehicular Voyeurism," *Strategy,* March 2009, p. 16; Kristin Laird, "Kia Bares Its Soul," *Marketing Magazine,* February 10, 2009.

80. Herbert C. Kelman, "Processes of Opinion Change," *Public Opinion Quarterly, 25* (1), Spring 1961, pp. 57–78.

81. William J. McGuire, "The Nature of Attitudes and Attitude Change," in *Handbook of Social Psychology,* 2nd ed., eds. G. Lindzey and E. Aronson (Cambridge, MA: Addison-Wesley, 1969), pp. 135–214; Daniel J. O'Keefe, "The Persuasive Effects of Delaying Identification of High- and Low-Credibility Communicators: A Meta-Analytic Review," *Central States Speech Journal, 38,* 1987, pp. 63–72.

82. Roobina Ohanian, "The Impact of Celebrity Spokespersons' Image on Consumers' Intention to Purchase," *Journal of Advertising*

Research, 31 (1), February/March 1991, pp. 46–54.

83. Erick Reidenback and Robert Pitts, "Not All CEOs Are Created Equal as Advertising Spokespersons: Evaluating the Effective CEO Spokesperson," *Journal of Advertising, 15* (1), (1986), pp. 35–50; Roger Kerin and Thomas E. Barry, "The CEO Spokesperson in Consumer Advertising: An Experimental Investigation," in *Current Issues in Research in Advertising,* eds. J. H. Leigh and C. R. Martin (Ann Arbor: University of Michigan, 1981), pp. 135–48.

84. A. Eagly and S. Chaiken, "An Attribution Analysis of the Effect of Communicator Characteristics on Opinion Change," *Journal of Personality and Social Psychology, 32* (1), 1975, pp. 136–44.

85. For a review of these studies, see Brian Sternthal, Lynn Phillips, and Ruby Dholakia, "The Persuasive Effect of Source Credibility: A Situational Analysis," *Public Opinion Quarterly, 43* (3), Fall 1978, pp. 285–314.

86. Brian Sternthal, Ruby Dholakia, and Clark Leavitt, "The Persuasive Effects of Source Credibility: Tests of Cognitive Response," *Journal of Consumer Research, 4* (4), March 1978, pp. 252–60; Robert R. Harmon and Kenneth A. Coney, "The Persuasive Effects of Source Credibility in Buy and Lease Situations," *Journal of Marketing Research, 19* (2), May 1982, pp. 255–60.

87. For a review, see Noel Capon and James Hulbert, "The Sleeper Effect: An Awakening," *Public Opinion Quarterly, 37* (3), 1973, pp. 333–58.

88. Darlene B. Hannah and Brian Sternthal, "Detecting and Explaining the Sleeper Effect," *Journal of Consumer Research, 11* (2), September 1984, pp. 632–42.

89. H. C. Triandis, *Attitudes and Attitude Change* (New York: Wiley, 1971).

90. J. Mills and J. Jellison, "Effect on Opinion Change Similarity between the Communicator and the Audience He Addresses," *Journal of Personality and Social Psychology, 9* (2), June 1968, pp. 153–56.

91. Ben Kaplan, "A&W Guys Are the New Apple Guys," *National Post,* November 19, 2009, p. AL1.

92. Matt Semansky, "Harry Rosen Keeps It Real," *Marketing Magazine,* February 2009.

93. For an excellent review of these studies, see Marilyn Y. Jones, Andrea J. S. Stanaland, and Betsy D. Gelb, "Beefcake and Cheesecake: Insights for Advertisers," *Journal of Advertising, 27* (2), Summer 1998, pp. 32–51; W. B. Joseph, "The Credibility of Physically Attractive Communicators," *Journal of Advertising, 11* (3), 1982, pp. 13–23.

94. Michael Solomon, Richard Ashmore, and Laura Longo, "The Beauty Match-Up Hypothesis: Congruence between Types of Beauty and Product Images in Advertising," *Journal of Advertising, 21* (4), December 1992, pp. 23–34; M. J. Baker and Gilbert A. Churchill, Jr., "The Impact of Physically Attractive Models on Advertising Evaluations," *Journal of Marketing Research, 14* (4), November 1977, pp. 538–55.

95. Robert W. Chestnut, C. C. La Chance, and A. Lubitz, "The Decorative Female Model:

Sexual Stimuli and the Recognition of the Advertisements," *Journal of Advertising, 6* (4), Fall 1977, pp. 11–14; Leonard N. Reid and Lawrence C. Soley, "Decorative Models and Readership of Magazine Ads," *Journal of Advertising Research, 23* (2), April/May 1983, pp. 27–32.

96. Amanda B. Bower, "Highly Attractive Models in Advertising and the Women Who Loathe Them: The Implications of Negative Affect for Spokesperson Effectiveness," *Journal of Advertising, 30* (3), Fall 2001, pp. 51–63; Amanda B. Bower and Stacy Landreth, "Is Beauty Best? Highly Versus Normally Attractive Models in Advertising," *Journal of Advertising, 30* (1), Spring 2001, pp. 1–12.

97. Jack Neff, "In Dove Ads, Normal Is the New Beautiful," *Advertising Age,* September 27, 2004, pp. 1, 80.

98. Michelle Jeffers, "Behind Dove's 'Real Beauty,'" *Adweek,* September 12, 2005, pp. 34–35.

99. B. Zafer Erdogan, Michael J. Baker, and Stephen Tagg, "Selecting Celebrity Endorsers: The Practitioner's Perspective," *Journal of Advertising Research, 41* (3), May–June 2001, pp. 39–48; B. Zafer Erdogan and Tanya Drollinger, "Endorsement Practice: How Agencies Select Spokespeople," *Journal of Advertising Research, 48* (4), December 2008, pp. 573–82.

100. Matt Semansky, "Brand Nash," *Marketing Magazine,* September 14, 2009.

101. Jason Stein, "Inside Chrysler's Celine Dion Advertising Disaster," www.adage.com, November 24, 2003.

102. Valerie Folkes, "Recent Attribution Research in Consumer Behavior: A Review and New Directions," *Journal of Consumer Research, 14* (4), March 1988, pp. 8–65; John C. Mowen and Stephen W. Brown, "On Explaining and Predicting the Effectiveness of Celebrity Endorsers," in *Advances in Consumer Research,* vol. 8 (Ann Arbor, MI: Association for Consumer Research, 1981), pp. 437–41.

103. Charles Atkin and M. Block, "Effectiveness of Celebrity Endorsers," *Journal of Advertising Research, 23* (1), February/March 1983, pp. 57–61.

104. Grant McCracken, "Who Is the Celebrity Endorser? Cultural Foundations of the Endorsement Process," *Journal of Consumer Research, 16* (3), December 1989, pp. 310–21.

105. Michael A. Kamins, "An Investigation into the 'Match-Up' Hypothesis in Celebrity Advertising," *Journal of Advertising, 19* (1), Spring 1990, pp. 4–13.

106. McCracken, "Who Is the Celebrity Endorser? Cultural Foundations of the Endorsement Process."

CHAPTER EIGHT

1. Gerald J. Gorn and Charles B. Weinberg, "The Impact of Comparative Advertising on Perception and Attitude: Some Positive Findings," *Journal of Consumer Research, 11* (2), September 1984, pp. 719–27.

2. "If You Don't Like This Ad, You're Simply Not Subaru Material," *National Post,* November 20, 2009, p. FP10.

3. Norma Ramage, "Toyota Owners Drive Prairie Effort," *Marketing Magazine,* March 17, 2003.

4. Bob Garfield, "Listerine Eschews 'Creativity' for an Ad That Actually Works," *Advertising Age,* September 20, 2004, p. 57.

5. Jennifer Wells, "So, How Does Microsoft Keep the Vision Alive? Ask 'Durf.'" *The Globe and Mail,* January 16, 2009, p. B5.

6. Judith A. Garretson and Scot Burton, "The Role of Spokescharacters as Advertisement and Package Cues in Integrated Marketing Communications," *Journal of Marketing, 69* (4), October 2005, pp. 118–32.

7. David Brown, "The Birth of a Freedom Farter," *Marketing Magazine,* May 16, 2011, p. 13.

8. Hollie Shaw, "Aliens 'Natural Fit' for Mobilicity," *National Post,* July 22, 2011, p. FP12.

9. Gail Powell, "Salad, Fries and Exercise," *Marketing Magazine,* June 27, 2005.

10. Angela Kryhul, "The Great Canadian Icon," *Marketing Magazine,* June 26, 2000.

11. Barbara B. Stern, "Classical and Vignette Television Advertising: Structural Models, Formal Analysis, and Consumer Effects," *Journal of Consumer Research, 20* (4), March 1994, pp. 601–15; John Deighton, Daniel Romer, and Josh McQueen, "Using Drama to Persuade," *Journal of Consumer Research, 15* (3), December 1989, pp. 335–43.

12. Karen Howe and Ian Mcintosh, "A Clever Parody," *Marketing Magazine,* January 12, 2004.

13. Susan Krashinsky, "We Interrupt This Ad to Bring You…Another Ad," *The Globe and Mail,* March 9, 2012, p. B7.

14. Susan Krashinsky, "Creative Ad Campaign Gives Boston Pizza a Boost," *The Globe and Mail,* April 9, 2012, p. B4.

15. Herbert E. Krugman, "On Application of Learning Theory to TV Copy Testing," *Public Opinion Quarterly, 26* (4), 1962, pp. 626–39.

16. William E. Baker, Heather Honea, and Cristel Antonia Russell, "Do Not Wait to Reveal the Brand Name: The Effect of Brand-Name Placement on Television Advertising Effectiveness," *Journal of Advertising, 33* (3), Fall 2004, pp. 77–85.

17. C. I. Hovland and W. Mandell, "An Experimental Comparison of Conclusion Drawing by the Communicator and by the Audience," *Journal of Abnormal and Social Psychology, 47,* July 1952, pp. 581–88.

18. Alan G. Sawyer and Daniel J. Howard, "Effects of Omitting Conclusions in Advertisements to Involved and Uninvolved Audiences," *Journal of Marketing Research, 28* (4), November 1991, pp. 467–74.

19. George E. Belch, "The Effects of Message Modality on One- and Two-Sided Advertising Messages," in *Advances in Consumer Research, 10,* eds. Richard P. Bagozzi and Alice M. Tybout (Ann Arbor, MI: Association for Consumer Research, 1983), pp. 21–26.

20. Robert E. Settle and Linda L. Golden, "Attribution Theory and Advertiser Credibility," *Journal of Marketing Research, 11* (2), May 1974, pp. 181–85; Edmund J. Faison, "Effectiveness of One-Sided and Two-Sided Mass Communications in Advertising," *Public Opinion Quarterly, 25* (3), Fall 1961, pp. 468–69.

21. Susan Krashinsky, "For Buckley's, It's All About Being Frank," *The Globe and Mail,* April 11, 2011, p. B7.

22. Alan G. Sawyer, "The Effects of Repetition of Refutational and Supportive Advertising Appeals," *Journal of Marketing Research, 10* (1), February 1973, pp. 23–37; George J. Szybillo and Richard Heslin, "Resistance to Persuasion: Inoculation Theory in a Marketing Context," *Journal of Marketing Research, 10* (4), November 1973, pp. 396–403.

23. Andrew A. Mitchell, "The Effect of Verbal and Visual Components of Advertisements on Brand Attitudes and Attitude toward the Advertisement," *Journal of Consumer Research, 13* (1), June 1986, pp. 12–24; Julie A. Edell and Richard Staelin, "The Information Processing of Pictures in Advertisements," *Journal of Consumer Research, 10* (1), June 1983, pp. 45–60; Elizabeth C. Hirschmann, "The Effects of Verbal and Pictorial Advertising Stimuli on Aesthetic, Utilitarian and Familiarity Perceptions," *Journal of Advertising, 15* (2), 1986, pp. 27–34.

24. Jolita Kisielius and Brian Sternthal, "Detecting and Explaining Vividness Effects in Attitudinal Judgments," *Journal of Marketing Research, 21* (1), 1984, pp. 54–64.

25. H. Rao Unnava and Robert E. Burnkrant, "An Imagery-Processing View of the Role of Pictures in Print Advertisements," *Journal of Marketing Research, 28* (2), May 1991, pp. 226–31.

26. Susan E. Heckler and Terry L. Childers, "The Role of Expectancy and Relevancy in Memory for Verbal and Visual Information: What Is Incongruency?" *Journal of Consumer Research, 18* (4), March 1992, pp. 475–92.

27. Michael J. Houston, Terry L. Childers, and Susan E. Heckler, "Picture–Word Consistency and the Elaborative Processing of Advertisements," *Journal of Marketing Research, 24* (4), November 1987, pp. 359–69.

28. Hollie Shaw, "The Elephant in the Room," *National Post,* December 18, 2009, p. FP10.

29. William F. Arens, *Contemporary Advertising,* 6th ed. (Burr Ridge, IL: Irwin/McGraw-Hill, 1998), p. 284.

30. W. Keith Hafer and Gordon E. White, *Advertising Writing,* 3rd ed. (St. Paul, MN: West Publishing, 1989), p. 98.

31. Michelle Warren, "Press and Poster," *Marketing Magazine,* March 24, 2003.

32. Surendra N. Singh, V. Parker Lessig, Dongwook Kim, Reetina Gupta, and Mary Ann Hocutt, "Does Your Ad Have Too Many Pictures?" *Journal of Advertising Research, 40* (1/2), January–April 2000, pp. 11–27.

33. Susan Krashinsky, "As Seen on TV, A Lot," *The Globe and Mail,* June 29, 2012, p. B5.

34. Matt Semansky, "2008 Marketer of the Year: Quality Kraft-Manship," *Marketing Magazine,* December 8, 2008.

35. Simon Houpt, "Building a Better World, One Cup at a Time," *The Globe and Mail,* July 8, 2011, p. B6.

36. Hollie Shaw, "It's a New Reality," *National Post,* May 15, 2009, p. FP10.

37. Matt Semansky, "Kokanee Says It's Time to Move Beyond Ranger," *Marketing Magazine,* May 28, 2009.

38. David Allan, "A Content Analysis of Music Placement in Prime-Time Advertising," *Journal of Advertising Research, 48* (3), September 2008, pp. 404–14.

39. Russell I. Haley, Jack Richardson, and Beth Baldwin, "The Effects of Nonverbal Communications in Television Advertising," *Journal of Advertising Research, 24* (4), August–September 1984, pp. 11–18.

40. Gerald J. Gorn, "The Effects of Music in Advertising on Choice Behavior: A Classical Conditioning Approach," *Journal of Marketing, 46* (1), Winter 1982, pp. 94–100.

41. Steve Oakes, "Evaluating Empirical Research into Music in Advertising: A Congruity Perspective," *Journal of Advertising Research, 47* (1), March 2007, pp. 38–50.

42. Matt Semansky, "Delissio Touts the Multiple Advantages of Garlic," *Marketing Magazine,* June 4, 2009.

43. Susan Krashinsky, "Changing Their Tune," *The Globe and Mail,* July 13, 2012, p. B6.

44. Angela Kryhul, "Name Your Tune," *Marketing Magazine,* October 14, 2002.

45. Linda M. Scott, "Understanding Jingles and Needledrop: A Rhetorical Approach to Music in Advertising," *Journal of Consumer Research, 17* (2), September 1990, pp. 223–36.

46. Jeromy Lloyd, "Swiss Chalet Blasts Back from the Past," *Marketing Magazine,* September 23, 2009.

47. Simon Houpt, "Poutine, Pussycats and Political Messages," *The Globe and Mail,* March 25, 2011, p. B6.

48. Chris Powell, "Astral Media Expands Its Audio Identity," *Marketing Magazine,* April 2009.

49. Richard Vaughn, "How Advertising Works: A Planning Model," *Journal of Advertising Research, 20* (5), October 1980, pp. 27–33.

50. Richard Vaughn, "How Advertising Works: A Planning Model Revisited," *Journal of Advertising Research, 26* (1), February/March 1986, pp. 57–66.

51. John Rossiter and Larry Percy, *Advertising Communications and Promotion Management* (New York: McGraw Hill, 1996).

52. Christopher P. Puto and William D. Wells, "Informational and Transformational Advertising: The Different Effects of Time," in *Advances in Consumer Research, 11,* eds. Thomas C. Kinnear (Ann Arbor, MI: Association for Consumer Research, 1984), p. 638.

53. www.cassies.ca

CHAPTER NINE

1. Spike Cramphorn, "What Advertising Testing Might Have Been, If We Had Only Known," *Journal of Advertising Research, 44* (2), June 2004, pp. 1–2.

2. John M. Caffyn, "Telepex Testing of TV Commercials," *Journal of Advertising Research, 5* (2), June 1965, pp. 29–37; Thomas J. Reynolds and Charles Gengler, "A Strategic Framework for Assessing Advertising: The Animatic vs. Finished Issue," *Journal of Advertising Research, 31* (5), October/November 1991, pp. 61–71; Nigel A. Brown and Ronald Gatty, "Rough vs. Finished TV Commercials in Telepex Tests," *Journal of*

Advertising Research, 7 (4), December 1967, p. 21.

3. Ye Hu, Leonard Lodish, Abba Krieger, and Babk Hayati, "An Update of Real-World TV Advertising Tests," *Journal of Advertising Research, 49* (2), June 2009, pp. 201–06.

4. Paul J. Watson and Robert J. Gatchel, "Autonomic Measures of Advertising," *Journal of Advertising Research, 19* (3), June 1979, pp. 15–26.

5. Priscilla A. LaBarbera and Joel D. Tucciarone, "GSR Reconsidered: A Behavior-based Approach to Evaluating and Improving the Sales Potency of Advertising," *Journal of Advertising Research, 35* (5), September/October 1995, pp. 33–40.

6. Flemming Hansen, "Hemispheric Lateralization: Implications for Understanding Consumer Behavior," *Journal of Consumer Research, 8* (1), June 1988, pp. 23–36.

7. Jan Stapel, "Recall and Recognition: A Very Close Relationship," *Journal of Advertising Research, 38* (4), July/August 1998, pp. 41–45.

8. Hubert A. Zielske, "Does Day-After Recall Penalize 'Feeling Ads'?" *Journal of Advertising Research, 22* (1), 1982, pp. 19–22.

9. Arthur J. Kover, "Why Copywriters Don't Like Advertising Research—And What Kind of Research Might They Accept," *Journal of Advertising Research, 36* (2), March/April 1996, pp. RC8–RC10; Gary Levin, "Emotion Guides BBDO's Ad Tests," *Advertising Age,* January 29, 1990, p. 12.

10. Dave Kruegel, "Television Advertising Effectiveness and Research Innovations," *Journal of Consumer Marketing, 5* (3), Summer 1988, pp. 43–52.

11. John Philip Jones, "Single-Source Research Begins to Fulfill Its Promise," *Journal of Advertising Research, 35* (3), May/June 1995, pp. 9–16.

12. James F. Donius, "Marketing Tracking: A Strategic Reassessment and Planning Tool," *Journal of Advertising Research, 25* (1), February/March 1985, pp. 15–19.

13. "Positioning Advertising Copy-Testing," *Journal of Advertising, 11,* no. 4 (1982), pp. 3–29.

14. Ibid.

15. Russell I. Haley and Allan L. Baldinger, "The ARF Copy Research Validity Project," *Journal of Advertising Research, 31* (2), April/May 1991, pp. 11–32.

CHAPTER TEN

1. William A. Cook and Vijay S. Talluri, "How the Pursuit of ROMI Is Changing Marketing Management," *Journal of Advertising Research, 44* (3), September 2004, pp. 244–54; Joan Fitzgerald, "Evaluating Return on Investment of Multimedia Advertising with a Single-Source Panel: A Retail Case Study," *Journal of Advertising Research, 44* (3), September 2004, pp. 262–70.

2. Bruce Grondin, "Building North–South Links," *Marketing Magazine,* March 15, 2004.

3. Chris Powell, "Talking Heads," *Marketing Magazine,* March 23, 2009.

4. Jennifer Wells, "Finding the There, There," *The Globe and Mail,* January 23, 2009, p. B6.

5. Carey Toane, "Integrated," *Strategy,* June 2009, p. 51.

6. Jonathan Paul, "Adidas Goes All In," *Strategy,* April 1, 2011, p. 12.

7. Mary Teresa Bitti, "Manage Your Message," *National Post,* July 7, 2009, FP7.

8. Jeromy Lloyd, "'Cough Sir' Redefined," *Marketing Magazine,* March 12, 2012.

9. Lesley Young, "Primus Takes Aim at Cable, Telcos," *Marketing Magazine,* January 19, 2004.

10. Chuck Ross, "Study Finds for Continuity vs. Flights," *Advertising Age,* April 19, 1999, p. 2.

11. Lesley Young, "Campbell Warms Up to Bad Weather," *Marketing Magazine,* February 16, 2004.

12. Kristin Laird, "Agencies Collaborate to Make Sport Chek More Inspiring," *Marketing Magazine,* August 29, 2012.

13. Marina Strauss, "Back-to-School Marketing Hits the Books Early," *The Globe and Mail,* August 10, 2009, p. B3.

14. Susan Krashinsky, "Advertisers Compete for the Online Podium," *The Globe and Mail,* July 2012, p. B6.

15. Michael J. Naples, *Effective Frequency: The Relationship between Frequency and Advertising Effectiveness* (New York: Association of National Advertisers, 1979).

16. Joseph W. Ostrow, "Setting Frequency Levels: An Art or a Science?" *Journal of Advertising Research, 24* (4), August/September 1984, pp. 9–11.

17. Joseph W. Ostrow, "What Level Frequency?" *Advertising Age,* November 1981, pp. 13–18.

18. Jack Myers, "More Is Indeed Better," *Media Week,* September 6, 1993, pp. 14–18; Jim Surmanek, "One-Hit or Miss: Is a Frequency of One Frequently Wrong?" *Advertising Age,* November 27, 1995, p. 46.

19. Ostrow, "What Level Frequency?"

20. Hugh M. Cannon, John D. Leckenby, and Avery Abernethy, "Beyond Effective Frequency: Evaluating Media Schedules Using Frequency Value Planning," *Journal of Advertising Research, 42* (6), November–December 2002, pp. 33–47.

21. William Havlena, Robert Cardarelli, and Michelle De Montigny, "Quantifying the Isolated and Synergistic Effects of Exposure Frequency for TV, Print, and Internet Advertising," *Journal of Advertising Research, 47* (3), September 2007, pp. 215–21.

22. David A. Aaker and Phillip K. Brown (1972), "Evaluating Vehicle Source Effects," *Journal of Advertising Research, 12* (August), pp. 11–16.

23. Joel N. Axelrod, "Induced Moods and Attitudes toward Products," *Journal of Advertising Research, 3,* June 1963, pp. 19–24; Lauren E. Crane, "How Product, Appeal, and Program Affect Attitudes toward Commercials," *Journal of Advertising Research, 4,* March 1964, p. 15.

24. Nick Allen, "Microsoft Wants Out of the Family," *National Post,* October 28, 2009, p. A1; "Microsoft Pulls Out of *Family Guy* Sponsorship," *Marketing Magazine,* October 28, 2009.

25. Max Kilger and Ellen Romer, "Do Measures of Media Engagement Correlate with Product Purchase Likelihood?" *Journal of Advertising Research, 47* (3), September 2007, pp. 313–25.

26. Kazuya Kusumot, "Affinity-based Media Selection: Magazine Selection for Brand Message Absorption," *Journal of Advertising Research, 42* (4), July–August 2002, pp. 54–65.

27. George S. Low and Jakki Mohr, "Setting Advertising and Promotion Budgets in Multi-Brand Companies," *Journal of Advertising Research, 39* (1), January/February 1999, pp. 667–78.

28. Jody Harri and Kimberly A. Taylor, "The Case for Greater Agency Involvement in Strategic Partnerships," *Journal of Advertising Research, 43* (4), December 2003, pp. 346–52.

29. Frank M. Bass, "A Simultaneous Equation Regression Study of Advertising and Sales of Cigarettes," *Journal of Marketing Research, 6* (3), August 1969, p. 291; David A. Aaker and James M. Carman, "Are You Overadvertising?" *Journal of Advertising Research, 22* (4), August/September 1982, pp. 57–70.

30. Julian A. Simon and Johan Arndt, "The Shape of the Advertising Response Function," *Journal of Advertising Research, 20* (4), 1980, pp. 11–28.

31. Boonghee Yoo and Rujirutana Mandhachitara, "Estimating Advertising Effects on Sales in a Competitive Setting," *Journal of Advertising Research, 43* (3), August 2003, pp. 310–20.

32. James O. Peckham, "Can We Relate Advertising Dollars to Market Share Objectives?" in *How Much to Spend for Advertising,* ed. M. A. McNiven (New York: Association of National Advertisers, 1969), p. 30.

33. http://cassies.ca/entry/viewcase/4468; http://cassies.ca/content/caselibrary/winners/2011_KNORR.pdf; http://cassies.ca/content/caselibrary/winners/2011_NISSAN.pdf

34. Demetrios Vakratsas and Zhenfeng Ma, "A Look at the Long-Run Effectiveness of Multimedia Advertising and Its Implications for Budget Allocation Decisions," *Journal of Advertising Research, 45* (2), June 2005, pp. 241–54.

35. David Berkowitz, Arthur Allaway, and Giles d'Souza, "The Impact of Differential Lag Effects on the Allocation of Advertising Budgets across Media," *Journal of Advertising Research, 41* (2), March/April 2001, pp. 27–36.

36. John P. Jones, "Ad Spending: Maintaining Market Share," *Harvard Business Review,* January/February 1990, pp. 38–42; James C. Schroer, "Ad Spending: Growing Market Share," *Harvard Business Review,* January/February 1990, pp. 44–48.

37. Randall S. Brown, "Estimating Advantages to Large-Scale Advertising," *Review of Economics and Statistics, 60* (3), August 1978, pp. 428–37.

38. Kent M. Lancaster, "Are There Scale Economies in Advertising?" *Journal of Business, 59* (3), 1986, pp. 509–26.

39. Johan Arndt and Julian Simon, "Advertising and Economics of Scale: Critical Comments on the Evidence," *Journal of Industrial Economics, 32* (2), December 1983, pp. 229–41; Aaker and Carman, "Are You Overadvertising?"

40. George S. Low and Jakki J. Mohr, "The Budget Allocation between Advertising and Sales Promotion: Understanding the Decision

Process," *1991 AMA Educators' Proceedings,* Chicago, Summer 1991, pp. 448–57.

CHAPTER ELEVEN

1. TV Basics 2012–2013, Television Bureau of Canada website (www.tvb.ca), p. 28.
2. Hollie Shaw, "Yum, Yum: Loblaw Cooks Up Some Branding Subtleties," *National Post,* December 2, 2011, p. FP12.
3. Steve Ladurantaye, "Rogers' New Reality Show: Canada's Next Broadcast Strategy," *The Globe and Mail,* April 6, 2012, p. B1.
4. TV Basics 2012–2013, Television Bureau of Canada website (www.tvb.ca), p. 29.
5. Ibid.
6. TV Basics 2012–2013, Television Bureau of Canada website (www.tvb.ca), p. 13.
7. Kristin Laird, "Shaw Across the Bow," *Marketing Magazine,* March 14, 2011, p. 12.
8. Media Digest 2012–2013, Canadian Media Director's Council, p. 8.
9. Kristin Laird, "Brick Puts Red Baron on TV for First Time," *Marketing Magazine,* January 5, 2010.
10. Simon Houpt, "Where Did the Kids Go?" *The Globe and Mail,* June 16, 2012, p. R12.
11. Kristin Laird, "Not So, Much," *Marketing Magazine,* January 24, 2011, p. 10.
12. Robert J. Kent, "Second-by-Second Looks at the Television Commercial Audience," *Journal of Advertising Research, 42* (1), January–February 2002, pp. 71–78.
13. Stephen Stanley and Carey Toane, "NFLD Tourism: Target Truly Transports You," *Marketing Magazine,* June 2009, p. 50.
14. http://www.tvb.ca/page_files/pdf/RTSA/RTS12.pdf
15. Susan Krashinsky, "Why Most Super Bowl Ads Get Stopped at the Border," *The Globe and Mail,* February 3, 2012, p. B8.
16. Ibid.
17. Kate Lynch and Horst Stipp, "Examination of Qualitative Viewing Factors of Optimal Advertising Strategies," *Journal of Advertising Research, 39* (3), May–June 1999, pp. 7–16.
18. TV Basics 2012–2013, Television Bureau of Canada website (www.tvb.ca), p. 28.
19. Stephen Stanley and Carey Toane, "Subaru: DDB's Sumos Get Sexy," *Marketing Magazine,* June 2009, p. 50.
20. John J. Cronin, "In-Home Observations of Commercial Zapping Behavior," *Journal of Current Issues and Research in Advertising, 17* (2), Fall 1995, pp. 69–75.
21. Paul Surgi Speck and Michael T. Elliot, "Predictors of Advertising Avoidance in Print and Broadcast Media," *Journal of Advertising, 26* (3), Fall 1997, pp. 61–76.
22. Carrie Heeter and Bradley S. Greenberg, "Profiling the Zappers," *Journal of Advertising Research, 25* (2), April/May 1985, pp. 9–12; Fred S. Zufryden, James H. Pedrick, and Avu Sandaralingham, "Zapping and Its Impact on Brand Purchase Behavior," *Journal of Advertising Research, 33* (1), January/February 1993, pp. 58–66.
23. Lex van Meurs, "Zapp! A Study on Switching Behavior during Commercial Breaks," *Journal of Advertising Research, 38* (1), January/February 1998, pp. 43–53.
24. Alan Ching Biu Tse and Rub P w. Lee, "Zapping Behaviour during Commercial Breaks," *Journal of Advertising Research, 41* (3), May/June 2001, pp. 25–29.
25. TV Basics 2012–2013, Television Bureau of Canada website (www.tvb.ca), p. 13.
26. Kirsten Chase, "Confessions of a PVR User," *Marketing Magazine,* March 26, 2007; Chris Powell, "PVRs: Canadians vs. Americans," *Marketing Magazine,* March 26, 2007; Pierre Delagrave, "Dawn of the Ad Zapper," *Marketing Magazine,* February 20, 2006.
27. TV Basics 2012–2013, Television Bureau of Canada website (www.tvb.ca), p. 21.
28. Kenneth C. Wilbur, "How the Digital Video Recorder (DVR) Changes Traditional Television Advertising," *Journal of Advertising, 37* (1), Spring 2008, pp. 143–49.
29. Cristel Antonia Russell and Christopher P. Puto, "Rethinking Television Audience Measures: An Exploration into the Construct of Audience Connectedness," *Marketing Letters, 10* (4), August 1999, pp. 393–407.
30. Kristin Laird, "Corus Begins Simple Pleasures Campaign for Dare," *Marketing Magazine,* July 20, 2009.
31. Linda F. Alwitt and Parul R. Prabhaker, "Identifying Who Dislikes Television Advertising: Not by Demographics Alone," *Journal of Advertising Research, 32* (5), September–October 1992, pp. 30–42.
32. Banwari Mittal, "Public Assessment of TV Advertising: Faint Praise and Harsh Criticism," *Journal of Advertising Research, 34* (1), January–February 1994, pp. 35–53; Ernest F. Larkin, "Consumer Perceptions of the Media and Their Advertising Content," *Journal of Advertising, 8* (2), Spring 1979, pp. 5–7.
33. Lucy L. Henke, "Young Children's Perceptions of Cigarette Brand Advertising Symbols: Awareness, Affect, and Target Market Identification," *Journal of Advertising, 24* (4), Winter 1995, pp. 13–28.
34. Media Digest 2012–2013, Canadian Media Director's Council, p. 8.
35. Ibid.
36. Ibid.
37. Media Digest 2012–2013, Canadian Media Director's Council, p. 33.
38. Radio Engagement in Canada, October 2012, Vision Critical, radioahead.ca
39. Emily Wexler, "Radio," *Strategy,* June 2009, p. 46.
40. Verne Gay, "Image Transfer: Radio Ads Make Aural History," *Advertising Age,* January 24, 1985, p. 1.
41. Carey Toane, "James Ready Shares the Radio Waves," *Strategy,* June 2009, p. 8.
42. Brian Dunn, "Boston Pizza Promotes Specials with Radio Spots," *Marketing Magazine,* April 13, 2009.
43. Avery Abernethy, "Differences between Advertising and Program Exposure for Car Radio Listening," *Journal of Advertising Research, 31* (2), April/May 1991, pp. 33–42.
44. Foundation Research Study 2007–2009 accessed on RMB website (rmb.ca)
45. Ibid.

CHAPTER TWELVE

1. Herbert E. Krugman, "The Measurement of Advertising Involvement," *Public Opinion Quarterly, 30* (4), Winter 1966–67, pp. 583–96.
2. Magazinescanada.ca.
3. Maureen Cavan, "Building Our Own," *Marketing Magazine,* April 14, 2003.
4. Consumer Magazine Fact Book 2012, Magazines Canada, p. 33.
5. Ibid.
6. Consumer Magazine Fact Book 2012, Magazines Canada, p. 31
7. http://cardonline.ca/listings/14345.jsf.
8. Chris Powell, "*Hello!*'s Rising Star," *Marketing Magazine,* April 6, 2009.
9. http://cardonline.ca/listings/13639.jsf; Media Digest, Canadian Media Director's Council, 2012–2013, p. 70.
10. Chris Powell, "La Difference," *Marketing Magazine,* May 10, 2004.
11. Doug Bennet, "How Many City Magazines Does Toronto Actually Need?" *Marketing Magazine,* May 16, 2011.
12. Consumer Magazine Fact Book 2012, Magazines Canada, p. 26.
13. Consumer Magazine Fact Book 2012, Magazines Canada, p. 48.
14. Consumer Magazine Fact Book 2012, Magazines Canada, p. 45.
15. Chris Powell, "*Maclean's* Opens Up for Audi," *Marketing Magazine,* April 1, 2009.
16. Jonathan Paul, "Cundari's Camo *Vice* Cover Ad," *Strategy,* June 2009, p. 47.
17. Consumer Magazine Fact Book 2012, Magazines Canada, page 24.
18. "Crunch," *Marketing Magazine,* May 16, 2011, p. 46.
19. Tom Gierasimczuk, "Where the Young Readers Are," *Marketing Magazine,* May 16, 2011, p. 30.
20. Consumer Magazine Fact Book 2012, Magazines Canada, p. 38.
21. Consumer Magazine Fact Book 2012, Magazines Canada, p. 39.
22. Mary Pompili and Janet Eger, "Power Tools," *Marketing Magazine,* April 19, 2004.
23. Media Digest, Canadian Media Director's Council, 2012–2013, p. 53.
24. Val Maloney, "*Globe and Mail* Tops in Paid Circulation," *Media in Canada,* April 30, 2013.
25. Steve Ladurantaye, "Slow Online Ad Sales Hurt Publishers," *The Globe and Mail,* May 10, 2012, p. B6.
26. Chris Powell, "Custom Takes Off," *Marketing Magazine,* June 4, 2012.
27. Kristin Laird, "Molson Is in the Fridge for Christmas Promo," *Marketing Magazine,* December 11, 2009.
28. Media Digest, Canadian Media Director's Council, 2012–2013, p. 55.
29. Media Digest, Canadian Media Director's Council, 2012–2013, p. 62.
30. Chris Powell, "When Push Comes to Shove It," *Marketing Magazine,* March 15, 2004.
31. Chris Powell, "Cheery of Evolution," *Marketing Magazine,* November 20, 2006.
32. Consumer Magazine Fact Book 2012, Magazines Canada, pp. 59, 60.
33. Consumer Magazine Fact Book 2012, Magazines Canada, pp. 73, 74.

CHAPTER THIRTEEN

1. Mukesh Bhargava and Naveen Donthu, "Sales Response to Outdoor Advertising," *Journal of Advertising Research, 39* (4), August 1999, pp. 7–18.

2. Theras Wood, "Milk Coats Quebec with Cheer," *Strategy,* March 2009, p. 6.

3. Charles R. Taylor, George R. Franke, and Hae-Kyong Bang, "Use and Effectiveness of Billboards," *Journal of Advertising, 35* (4), Winter 2006, pp. 21–34.

4. Lex Van Meurs and Mandy Aristoff, "Split-Second Recognition: What Makes Outdoor Advertising Work?" *Journal of Advertising Research, 49* (1), March 2009, pp. 82–92.

5. Chris Powell, "Dundas Square to Get Creamed by Cadbury," *Marketing Magazine,* February 25, 2009.

6. Jonathan Paul, "Media Merchants Ninja," *Strategy,* July 2009, p. 7.

7. Hollie Shaw, "Driving the Message," *National Post,* March 20, 2009, p. FP12.

8. Tom Shepansky, "The Exotic Tuna," *Marketing Magazine,* March 10, 2003.

9. Day in the Life Study accessed at omaccanada.ca

10. Danny Kucharsky, "Outdoor's Measurement Challenge," *Marketing Magazine,* May 17, 2004.

11. David Chilton, "Eying Outdoors," *Marketing Magazine,* October 26, 2006.

12. Jeromy Lloyd, "Next Stop," *Marketing Magazine,* August 1, 2011, p. 7.

13. Emily Wexler, "Getting Cadbury More Face Time," *Strategy,* March 1, 2009, p. 20.

14. Susan Krashinsky, "An Advertising Concept Takes Viewers for a Ride," *The Globe and Mail,* July 3, 2012, p. B3.

15. Emily Wexler, "Travel Alberta's Subway Slopes," *Strategy,* January 2009, p. 8.

16. Jeromy Lloyd, "In-Flight Magazine Smack-Down," *Marketing Magazine,* November 28, 2011, p. 15.

17. "Cinema Advertising Comes of Age," *Marketing Magazine,* May 6, 2002.

18. Joanna Phillips and Stephanie M. Noble, "Simply Captivating: Understanding Consumers' Attitudes toward the Cinema as an Advertising Medium," *Journal of Advertising, 36* (10), Spring 2007, pp. 81–94.

19. Jeromy Lloyd, "Toyota's Cinema Spot 20 Years in the Making," *Marketing Magazine,* December 22, 2009.

20. Rick T. Wilson and Brian D. Till, "Airport Advertising Effectiveness," *Journal of Advertising, 37* (1), Spring 2008, pp. 59–72.

21. Jonathan Paul, "Lexus RX's Touch Screen Touchdown at Airport," *Strategy,* June 2009, p. 22.

22. Tim Shepherd, "West Valley Market's Lilliputian Strategy," *Strategy,* September 2009, p. 10.

23. Hollie Shaw, "With the West Coast in the Grip of Hot Weather, Things Can Get a Little Hairy," *National Post,* July 31, p. FP10; Jonathan Paul, "Parissa Brings Sexy Back-Vertising," *Strategy,* September 2009, p. 10.

24. Michael A. Belch and Don Sciglimpaglia, "Viewers' Evaluations of Cinema Advertising," Proceedings of the American Institute for Decision Sciences, March 1979, pp. 39–43.

25. "Catch a Commercial at the Movies," *Center for Media Research,* October 29, 2007.

26. Phillips and Noble, "Simply Captivating."

27. Promotional Products Association International (Irving, TX), 1996.

28. Kristin Laird, "Sweet-ish," *Marketing Magazine,* September 12, 2011, p. 14.

29. 2009 Promotional Products Industry Sales Volume Study, Promotional Products Association of Canada, May 2009.

30. Mark Freed, "Trinkets to Treasure," *Marketing Magazine,* May 8, 2006; Norma Range, "Treasured Trinkets," *Marketing Magazine,* August 28, 2006.

31. http://www.ppai.org/inside-ppai/research/research-summaries

32. http://www.pqmedia.com/about-press-201212.html

33. Michael Belch and Cristel A. Russell, "A Managerial Investigation into the Product Placement Industry," *Journal of Advertising Research, 45* (1), March 2005, pp. 73–92.

34. Carrie La Ferle and Steven M. Edwards, "Product Placement," *Journal of Advertising, 35* (4), Winter 2006, pp. 65–89.

35. Simon Houpt, "Why Timbits Aren't Likely to Drive the Plot of *The Border*," *The Globe and Mail,* August 21, 2009, p. B4.

36. Susan Krashinsky, "*Mad Men* Serves Canadian Club a Bracer," *The Globe and Mail,* April 20, 2012, p. B7.

37. Siva K. Balasubramanian, James A. Karrh, and Hemant Patwardhan, "Audience Response to Product Placements," *Journal of Advertising, 35* (3), Fall 2006, pp. 115–41.

38. Carrie La Ferle and Steven M. Edwards, "Product Placement," *Journal of Advertising, 35* (4), Winter 2006, pp. 65–89.

39. Susan Krashinsky, "He Shoots–and the Advertisers Score!" *The Globe and Mail,* April 21, 2011.

40. John Intini, "*Will & Grace* Loved Their *Maclean's*," *Maclean's,* June 26, 2006.

41. La Ferle and Edwards, "Product Placement."

42. Ibid.

43. Kristin Laird, "Beam Me Up, Bombardier," *Marketing Magazine,* December 12, 2011, p. 11.

44. Jennifer Wells, "The Right Breaks at the Right Time," *The Globe and Mail,* May 29, 2009, p. B5.

45. Pola Gupta and Kenneth Lord, "Product Placement in Movies: The Effect of Prominence and Mode on Audience Recall," *Journal of Current Issues and Research in Advertising, 20* (1), Spring 1998, pp. 1–29.

46. Pola B. Gupta and Stephen J. Gould, "Consumers' Perceptions of the Ethics and Acceptability of Product Placements in Movies: Product Category and Individual Differences," *Journal of Current Issues and Research in Advertising, 19* (1), Spring 1997, pp. 40–49.

CHAPTER FOURTEEN

1. Louis J. Haugh, "Defining and Redefining," *Advertising Age,* February 1983, p. M44.

2. Pierre Chandon, Brian Wansik, and Gilles Laurent, "A Benefit Congruency Framework of Sales Promotion Effectiveness," *Journal of Marketing, 64* (4), October 2000, pp. 65–81.

3. Judith A. Garretson and Scot Burton, "Highly Coupon and Sales Prone Consumers: Benefits Beyond Price Savings," *Journal of Advertising Research, 43* (3), June 2003, pp. 162–72.

4. Scott A. Nielsen, John Quelch, and Caroline Henderson, "Consumer Promotions and the Acceleration of Product Purchases," in *Research on Sales Promotion: Collected Papers,* ed. Katherine E. Jocz (Cambridge, MA: Marketing Science Institute, 1984).

5. J. Jeffrey Inman and Leigh McAlister, "Do Coupon Expiration Dates Affect Consumer Behavior?" *Journal of Marketing Research, 31* (3), August 1994, pp. 423–28.

6. Wayne Karl, "The Cup Runneth Over," *Marketing Magazine,* August 27, 2007.

7. Leonard M. Lodish and Carl F. Mela, "If Brands Are Built over Years, Why Are They Managed over Quarters?" *Harvard Business Review,* July–August 2007, pp. 104–12.

8. Annette Bourdea, "Rocket Launcher—Unilever's Jillian McLaughlin Prepped for the Massive Sunsilk Launch by Immersing Her Team in the Demo's World—and the Method Paid Off," *Strategy,* August 2006, p. 16.

9. R. M. Prentice, "How to Split Your Marketing Funds Between Advertising and Promotion Dollars," *Advertising Age,* January 10, 1977, pp. 41–42, 44.

10. Adapted from Terrence A. Shimp, *Advertising, Promotion, and Supplemental Aspect of Integrated Marketing Communication,* 4th ed. (Fort Worth, TX: Dryden Press, 1997), p. 487.

11. Brian C. Deslauries and Peter B. Everett, "The Effects of Intermittent and Continuous Token Reinforcement on Bus Ridership," *Journal of Applied Psychology, 62* (4), August 1977, pp. 9–75.

12. Michael L. Rothschild and William C. Gaidis, "Behavioural Learning Theory: Its Relevance to Marketing and Promotions," *Journal of Marketing Research, 45* (2), Spring 1981, pp. 70–78.

13. "Hostess's Heroes," *Marketing Magazine,* August 6, 2001.

14. Kristin Laird, "McDonald's Serves Up Fresh, Free Coffee for All," *Marketing Magazine,* April 20, 2009.

15. Jonathan Paul, "HarperCollins Opens Eyes and Ears," *Strategy,* November 2009, p. 80.

16. "Trial and Conversion VI: Consumers' Reactions to Samples and Demonstrations," Promotional Marketing Association, Inc. 2002.

17. Jerry Langton, "Economics of the Humble Coupon," *Toronto Star,* July 7, 2008.

18. "Fine Print: Extreme Couponing as a Canadian Sport," Sympatico, November 12, 2011.

19. Inman and McAlister, "Do Coupon Expiration Dates Affect Consumer Behavior?"

20. Wayne Mouland, "Choosing the Right Face Value," *Marketing Magazine,* May 10, 2004.

21. Kristin Laird, "Promopost Launching New Click-and-Save-Service," *Marketing Magazine,* June 4, 2009; Andrew Lavallee, "Unilever Begins 'Holy Grail' Test of Mobile Coupons," *The Globe and Mail,* May 29, 2009, p. B7; Anne D'Innocenzio, "Come On, Cough Up the Coupons," *The Globe and Mail,* June 4, 2009, p. L6.

22. Ibid.

23. Gerard P. Prendergast, Derek T. Y. Poon, Alex S. L. Tsang, and Ting Yan Fan, "Predicting Deal Proneness," *Journal of Advertising Research, 48* (2), June 2008, pp. 287–96.

24. Michelle Halpern, "Labatt's Big PROMO! Score," *Marketing Magazine,* October 6, 2003.

25. "Doughboy Promo Pops Off the Shelf," *Marketing Magazine,* January 14, 2002.

26. Wayne Mouland, "Sweeping Up Additional Sales," *Marketing Magazine,* October 6, 2003.

27. Garine Tcholakina, "Honda Drives Civic Nation Mix-Off," *Strategy,* November 2009, p. 40.

28. Jonathan Paul, "Life's Good, But LG Thinks It's Better in HD," *Strategy,* September 2009, p. 8.

29. Denise Ryan, "Can You Brand the West Coast?" *National Post,* November 16, 2009, p. B16.

30. Brenda Pritchard and Susan Vogt, *Advertising and Marketing Law in Canada* (LexisNexis, Butterworths, 2006).

31. Peter Tat, William A. Cunningham III, and Emin Babakus, "Consumer Perceptions of Rebates," *Journal of Advertising Research, 28* (4), August/September 1988, pp. 45–50.

32. Edward A. Blair and E. Lair Landon, "The Effects of Reference Prices in Retail Advertisements," *Journal of Marketing, 45* (2), Spring 1981, pp. 61–69.

33. Kristin Laird, "Milestones Wants to Make Dates," *Marketing Magazine,* April 28, 2009.

34. James Adams, "Who Gets the Biggest Piece of the Digital Pie?" *The Globe and Mail,* February 28, 2009.

35. Greg Keenan, "Saving the Civic," *The Globe and Mail,* February 15, 2011, p. B1.

36. Kristin Laird, "Perrier Goes Clubbing in Toronto," *Marketing Magazine,* November 27, 2009.

37. Jonathan Paul, "Adidas's Hipster House Party: 60 Is the New 20-Something," *Strategy,* April 2009, p. 28.

38. Jonathan Paul, "Promotion," *Strategy,* June 2009, p. 443.

39. Paul N. Bloom, Gregory T. Gundlach, and Joseph P. Cannon, "Slotting Allowances and Fees: Schools of Thought and Views of Practicing Managers," *Journal of Marketing, 64* (2), April 2000, pp. 92–108.

40. http://www.popai.com/engage/docs /Media-Topline-Final.pdf

41. Scot Burton, Donald R. Lichtenstein, and Richard G. Netemeyer, "Exposure to Sales Flyers and Increased Purchases in Retail Supermarkets," *Journal of Advertising Research, 39* (5), September–October 1999, pp. 7–14.

42. Srinath Gopalakrishna, Gary L. Lilien, Jerome D. Williams, and Ian K. Sequeria, "Do Trade Shows Pay Off?" *Journal of Marketing, 38* (3), July 1995, pp. 75–83.

43. Priya Raghubir and Kim Corfman, "When Do Price Promotions Affect Pretrial Brand Evaluations?" *Journal of Marketing Research, 36* (2), May 1999, pp. 211–22.

44. Elizabeth Gardener and Minakshi Trivedi, "A Communications Framework to Evaluate Sales Promotion Strategies," *Journal of Advertising Research, 38* (3), May/June 1998, pp. 67–71.

CHAPTER FIFTEEN

1. Raymond Simon, *Public Relations, Concept and Practices,* 2nd ed. (Columbus, OH: Grid Publishing, 1980), p. 8.

2. John Heinzl, "Tims v. Mickey D's," *The Globe and Mail,* November 30, 2011, p. B15.

3. Scott M. Cutlip, Allen H. Center, and Glen M. Broom, *Effective Public Relations,* 10th ed. (Upper Saddle River, N.J.: Prentice Hall, 2009).

4. William N. Curry, "PR Isn't Marketing," *Advertising Age,* December 18, 1991, p. 18.

5. Martha M. Lauzen, "Imperialism and Encroachment in Public Relations," *Public Relations Review, 17* (3), Fall 1991, pp. 245–55.

6. Cutlip, Center, and Broom, *Effective Public Relations.*

7. Carol Neshevich, "Royal Bank of Canada," *Marketing Magazine,* November 28, 2011, pp. 35, 40.

8. Carey Toane, "Overall Winner: Cisco's One Million Acts of Green," *Strategy,* May 2009, p. 30.

9. Susan Krashinsky, "Fantasy Cars for Real-Life Drivers," *The Globe and Mail,* February 17, 2012, p. B6.

10. Thomas L. Harris, "How MPR Adds Value to Integrated Marketing Communications," *Public Relations Quarterly, 38* (2), Summer 1993, pp. 13–18.

11. http://www.ikea.com/ms/en_CA/about_ikea /press_room/press_release/national/sleep _newsrelease.html

12. Hollie Shaw, "GM Reinvented," *National Post,* June 26, 2009, p. FP10.

13. Jonathan Paul, "Childlike Fascination Insightful for Honda," *Strategy,* May 2009, p. 19.

14. "Toyota Launches Ad Blitz to Reassure Customers," *Marketing Magazine,* February 1, 2010; "*Marketing*'s Q&A: Toyota Boss Talks Brand Re-Building After Massive Recall," *Marketing Magazine,* February 2, 2010; "Toyota Canada Launches Campaign to Distance Itself from U.S. Problems," *Marketing Magazine,* February 23, 2010.

15. Mark Weiner, "Marketing PR Revolution," *Communication World,* January/February 2005, pp. 1–5.

16. Walter K. Lindenmann, "An Effectiveness Yardstick to Measure Public Relations Success," *Public Relations Quarterly, 38* (1), Spring 1993, pp. 7–10.

17. Linda Smith, "When the Trust Begins to Rust," *Marketing Magazine,* March 1, 2004.

18. Rebecca Harris, "Best Brand Reputations 2012," *Marketing Magazine,* May 20, 2012.

19. Ibid.

20. Siri Agrell, "Ads Aim to Win Hearts, Change Minds," *The Globe and Mail,* June 22, 2011, p. A6.

21. Kristin Laird, "IBM's Smart Conversation with CBC, CANWEST," *Marketing Magazine,* September 15, 2009.

22. Claudia Cattaneo, "Gas Industry on Fracking Offensive," *National Post,* May 28, 2011, p. FP3; Mark Hume, Enbridge Ads Intensify Pipeline Battle," *The Globe and Mail,* May 30, 2012, p. S1.

23. Harvey Meyer, "When the Cause Is Just," *Journal of Business Strategy, 20* (6), November/December 1999, pp. 27–31.

24. Katie Bailey, "Becel to Debut *The Heart* at Oscars," *Strategy,* February 25, 2010; Emily Wexler, "Becel's Margaret McKellar: Marketing with Heart," *Strategy,* June 2009, p. 18; Carey Toane, "Top Health Awareness Program: Becel's Heart Truth," *Strategy,* May 2009, p. 37.

25. Emily Wexler, "Virgin Re*Generates," *Strategy,* January 2009, p. 8.

26. Kristin Laird, "Kraft Has a Recipe for Joy," *Marketing Magazine,* December 18, 2009.

27. Emily Wexler, "Indigo Fights Illiteracy with Squirrel Power," *Strategy,* November 2009, p. 90.

28. Kristin Laird, "Cadbury Builds Bikes for Africa," *Marketing Magazine,* April 17, 2009; Emily Wexler, "Cadbury Bikes to Africa," *Strategy,* May 2009, p. 6.

29. T. Bettina Cornwall, Donald P. Roy, and Edward A. Steinard II, "Exploring Manager's Perceptions of the Impact of Sponsorship on Brand Equity," *Journal of Advertising, 30* (2), Summer 2001, pp. 41–51.

30. Kirk L. Wakefield, Karen Becker-Olsen, and T. Bettina Cornwell, "I Spy a Sponsor," *Journal of Advertising, 36* (4), Winter 2007, pp. 61–74.

31. Julie A. Ruth and Bernard L. Simonin, "Brought to You by Brand A and Brand B," *Journal of Advertising, 32* (3), Fall 2003, pp. 19–30; Julie A. Ruth and Bernard L. Simonin, "The Power of Numbers," *Journal of Advertising, 35* (4), Winter 2006, pp. 7–20.

32. Simon Houpt and David Shoalts, "For Molson, Hockey's a Springboard to U.S." *The Globe and Mail,* July 13, 2011, p. B1.

33. Sarah Dobson, "The Hucksters Are Gone," *Marketing Magazine,* April 5, 2004.

34. www.sponsorshipmarketing.ca press release.

35. Hollie Shaw, "Carpetbragging," *National Post,* September 18, 2009, p. FP12.

36. Michelle Warren, "The Sporting Life," *Marketing Magazine,* February 23, 2004.

37. Mark Harrison, "Own Alone," *Marketing Magazine,* February 23, 2004.

38. Dan Cimoroni, "Don't Just Wish Upon a Star," *Marketing Magazine,* February 23, 2004.

39. Sarah Dobson, "The Measurement Question," *Marketing Magazine,* December 4, 2006.

40. Chris Daniels, "Show Time," *Marketing Magazine,* January 16, 2006.

41. Chris Daniels, "Take It Down a Notch," *Marketing Magazine,* December 4, 2006.

42. Bettina Cornwell and Isabelle Maignan, "An International Review of Sponsorship Research," *Journal of Advertising, 27* (1), March 1998, pp. 1–21.

43. Michel Tuan Pham, "The Evaluation of Sponsorship Effectiveness: A Model and Some Methodological Considerations," *Gestion 2000, 8* (4), July–August 1991, pp. 47–65.

44. Sandra Iacobelli, "Harder-Working Sponsorships," *Marketing Magazine,* October 6, 2003.

45. Ian Malcolm, "Made to Measure," *Marketing Magazine,* February 23, 2004.

46. Dobson, "The Measurement Question."

47. Bill Harvey, Stu Gray, and Gerald Despain, "Measuring the Effectiveness of True Sponsorship," *Journal of Advertising Research, 46* (4), December 2006, pp. 398–409.

48. Arlene Lebovic, "A Eureka Moment," *Marketing Magazine,* September 18, 2006.

CHAPTER SIXTEEN

1. Bob Stone and Ron Jacobs, *Successful Direct Marketing Methods* (New York, McGraw-Hill, 2010).

2. Sarah Dobson, "Knorr Says 'Frozen' Doesn't Have to be a Bad Word," *Marketing Magazine,* April 11, 2006; Canadian Marketing Association Awards Magazine, November 16, 2007.

3. Susan Krashinsky, "AMEX, Pearson Team Up on Perks," *The Globe and Mail,* June 18, 2012, p. B3.

4. Stan Maklan, Simon Knox, and Joe Peppard, "Why CRM Fails—and How to Fix it," *National Post,* October 25, 2011, p. FE7.

5. Jeromy Lloyd, "Target Nets Top ICE Award for Turtle Campaign," *Marketing Magazine,* October 29, 2009.

6. The Goldstein Group, "Acquisition Marketing in a Multi-Channel World: The Resiliant Principles of Successful Direct Mail." Report on Canada Post Website.

7. Ibid.

8. Marketing Research Fact Sheet, from Canada Post website, based on their Canada Facts study done every two years (approx).

9. Emily Wexler, "Cannes Lions: Grey Canada Wins Direct Gold," *Strategy,* June 21, 2010; www.canneslions.com

10. Goldstein Group, "Acquisition Marketing in a Multi-Channel World."

11. Chris Powell, "Canadian Tire Launches 'The Canadian Way' Catalogue Online," *Marketing Magazine,* April 10, 2013.

12. Michelle Warren, "Counting on Catalogues," *Marketing Magazine,* March 6, 2006; Kristin Laird, "IKEA's Mobile-Enabled Catalogue Goes Live in Canada," *Marketing Magazine,* August 13, 2012.

13. Basil Katz, "Email Newsletters Aim for Men's Inbox, Wallet," *National Post,* September 2009, p. FP10.

14. Brett A.S. Martin, Joel Van Durme, Mika Raulas, and Marko Merisavo, "E-mail Advertising: Exploratory Insights From Finland," *Journal of Advertising Research, 43* (3), September 2003, pp. 293–300.

15. David Chilton, "Spreading the Message," *Marketing Magazine,* March 6, 2006.

16. Joseph E. Phelps, Regina Lewis, Lynne Mobilio, David Perry, and Niranjan Raman, "Viral Marketing or Electronic Word-of-Mouth Advertising: Examining Consumer Responses and Motivations to Pass Along Email," *Journal of Advertising Research, 44* (4), December 2004, pp. 333–48.

17. Alexandra Lopez-Pacheco, "Nirvana Is the Exception," *National Post,* July 14, 2009, p. FP7.

18. Ibid.

19. Media Digest 2012–2013.

20. Mandeep Singh, Siva K. Balasubramanian, and Goutan Chakraborty, "A Comparative Analysis of Three Communication Formats: Advertising, Infomercial, and Direct Experience," *Journal of Advertising, 29* (4), Winter 2000, pp. 59–75.

21. Simon Houpt, "Call Now to Take Advantage of this Special TV Advertising Offer," *The Globe and Mail,* December 16, 2011, p. B5; http://www.thaneinc.com

22. www.theshoppingchannel.com

23. Canadian Marketing Association 2005 Fact Book, 2005.

24. Tammo Bijmolt, Matilda Dorotic, and Peter Verhoef, "Loyalty Programs: Generalizations on Their Adoption, Effectiveness and

Design," *Foundations and Trends in Marketing, 5* (4), 2010, pp. 197–258.

25. Yuping Liu, "The Long-Term Impact of Loyalty Programs on Consumer Purchase Behavior and Loyalty," *Journal of Marketing, 71* (4), October 2007, pp. 19–35.

26. Bijmolt, Dorotic, and Verhoef, "Loyalty Programs: Generalizations on Their Adoption, Effectiveness and Design."

27. Ibid.

28. www.airmiles.ca

29. Eve Lazarus, "Gap Turns Upside Down for New Loyalty Program," *Marketing Magazine,* November 6, 2009.

30. Kristin Laird, "Canadian Tire Putting New Money into Loyalty Program," *Marketing Magazine,* December 2, 2009; Emily Wexler, "Club Sobeys Hits a Million," *Strategy,* January 2009, p. 6.

31. Matt Semansky, "Canadian Tire Pilots New Loyalty Program in Nova Scotia," *Marketing Magazine,* February 15, 2012.

32. Matthew Chung, "Shoppers Takes Personalized Deals National," *Strategy,* April 22, 2013; Val Maloney, "Shoppers Drug Mart Launches Summer Campaign," *Strategy,* May 15, 2013.

33. Matt Semansky, "Threats and Opportunities in the Loyalty Game," *Marketing Magazine,* March 28, 2011, pp. 26–27.

34. Matt Semansky, "Jack Astor's Triples the V in VIP," *Marketing Magazine,* August 26, 2011.

35. Semansky, "Threats and Opportunities in the Loyalty Game."

36. Alicia Androcih, "Get in the Game," *Marketing Magazine,* August 29, 2011, pp. 54–56.

37. Goldstein Group, "Acquisition Marketing in a Multi-Channel World."

CHAPTER SEVENTEEN

1. Chang Hoan Cho and Hyoung Koo Khang, "The State of Internet-Related Research in Communications, Marketing, and Advertising: 1994–2003," *Journal of Advertising, 35* (3), Fall 2006, p. 143–63.

2. Juran Kim and Sally J. McMillan, "Evaluation of Internet Advertising Research," *Journal of Advertising, 37* (1), Spring 2008, pp. 99–112.

3. http://www.ipsos.ca/common/dl/pdf/Ipsos _InteractiveReidReport_FactGuide_2012.pdf

4. "Canadians Getting More News from the Web: Survey," *Marketing Magazine,* May 20, 2009.

5. Cate Riegner, "Word of Mouth on the Web: The Impact of Web 2.0 on Consumer Purchase Decisions," *Journal of Advertising Research, 47* (4), December 2007, 436–47.

6. Statistics Canada, "Canadian Internet Use Survey," CANSIM 358-0153.

7. Jonathan Paul, "What's Next: Molson Dry Pioneers a New Media Twist," *Strategy,* September 2009, p. 9.

8. Nigel Hollis, "Ten Years of Learning on How Online Advertising Builds Brands," *Journal of Advertising Research, 45* (2), June 2005, pp. 255–68.

9. Mathew Ingram, "Catering to Web-Savvy Moms," *The Globe and Mail,* January 18, 2007; Stuart Elliott, "Online, P&G Gets a Little Crazy," *The New York Times,* December 14, 2006; Diane Francis, "P&G's Army of 'Moms,'" *National Post,* July 7, 2006.

10. Jeromy Lloyd, "Nissan Decides to Augment Reality," *Marketing Magazine,* April 2009.

11. "Molson Puts Social Media at Centre of Legendary Promotion," *Marketing Magazine,* June 4, 2009.

12. Simon Houpt, "Wind Finally Gets Its Moment in the Sun," *The Globe and Mail,* December 18, 2009, p. B7.

13. Grace J. Johnson, Gordon C. Bruner II, and Anand Kumar, "Interactivity and Its Facets Revisited," *Journal of Advertising, 35* (4), Winter 2006, pp. 35–52.

14. Ibid.

15. Maria Sicilia, Salvador Ruiz, and Jose L. Munuera, "Effects of Interactivity in a Web Site," *Journal of Advertising, 34* (3), Fall 2005, pp. 31–45; Alex Wang, "Advertising Engagement: A Driver of Message Involvement on Message Effects," *Journal of Advertising Research, 46* (4), December 2006, pp. 355–68.

16. Qimei Chen and William Wells, "Attitude toward the Site," *Journal of Advertising Research, 39* (5), September–October 1999, pp. 27–38; Qimei Chen, Sandra J. Clifford, and William Wells, "Attitude toward the Site II: New Information," *Journal of Advertising Research, 42* (2), March–April 2002, pp. 33–45.

17. Gary L. Geissler, George M. Zinkhan, and Richard T. Watson, "The Influence of Home Page Complexity on Consumer Attention, Attitudes, and Purchase Intent," *Journal of Advertising, 3* (2), Summer 2006, pp. 69–80.

18. Micael Dahlen, Alexandra Rasch, and Sara Rosengren, "Love at First Site? A Study of Website Advertising Effectiveness," *Journal of Advertising Research, 43* (1), March 2003, pp. 25–33.

19. Julie S. Stevenson, Gordon Bruner II, and Anand Kumar, "Webpage Background and Viewer Attitudes," *Journal of Advertising Research, 40* (1/2), January–April 2000, pp. 29–34; Gordon Bruner II and Anand Kumar, "Web Commercials and Advertising Hierarchy-of-Effects," *Journal of Advertising Research, 40* (1/2), January–April 2000, pp. 35–42.

20. Jeromy Lloyd, "Bolder Man Is Bull's Eye for Kraft," *Marketing Magazine,* June 1, 2009.

21. Interactive Advertising Bureau of Canada, 2011 Canadian Advertising Revenue Survey, www.iabcanada.com

22. http://www.iab.net/media/file/IAB_Internet _Advertising_Revenue_Report_FY_2012 _rev.pdf

23. http://www.comscore.com/Insights /Presentations_and_Whitepapers/2013/2013 _Canada_Digital_Future_in_Focuscomscore

24. Simon Houpt, "Wind Finally Gets Its Moment in the Sun," *The Globe and Mail,* December 18, 2009, p. B7.

25. comScore.

26. www.mediamind.com, MediaMind Global Benchmarks 2011.

27. Chang-Hoan Cho, Jung-Gyo Lee, and Marye Tharp, "Different Forced-Exposure Levels to Banner Advertisements," *Journal of Advertising Research, 41* (4), July–August 2001, pp. 45–56.

28. Prem N. Shamdasani, Andrea J. S. Stanaland, Juliana Tan, "Location, Location, Location: Insights for Advertising Placement on the Web," *Journal of Advertising Research, 41* (4),

July–August 2001, pp. 7–21; Wenyu Dou, Randy Lim, and Sixian Yang, "How Smart Are 'Smart Banners'?" *41* (4), July–August 2001, pp. 31–43.

29. Micael Dahlen, "Banner Advertisement through a New Lens," *Journal of Advertising Research, 41* (4), July–August 2001, pp. 21–30.

30. Kelli S. Burns and Richard J. Lutz, "The Function of Format: Consumer Responses to Six On-line Advertising Formats," *Journal of Advertising, 35* (1) Spring 2006, pp. 53–63; Robert S. Moore, Claire Allison Stammerjohan, and Robin A. Coulter, "Banner Advertiser—Web Site Context Congruity and Color Effects on Attention and Attitudes," *Journal of Advertising, 34* (2) Summer 2005, pp. 71–84; Ritu Lohtia, Naveen Donthu, and Edmund K. Hershberger, "The Impact of Content and Design Elements on Banner Advertising Click-through Rates," *Journal of Advertising, 43* (4), December 2003, pp. 410–18.

31. Peter J. Danaher and Guy W. Mullarkey, "Factors Affecting Online Advertising Recall: A study of Students," *Journal of Advertising Research, 43* (3), September 2003, pp. 252–267; Idil Yaveroglu and Naveen Donthu, "Advertising Repetition and Placement Issues in On-Line Environment," *Journal of Advertising, 37* (2), Summer 2008, pp. 31–43.

32. Jonathan Paul, "ICE Widget Activates Ads," *Strategy*, February 2009, p. 26.

33. Kanter Media—Canadian Online Advertising Trends Analysis, March 2012.

34. IAB Internet Advertising Revenue Report, 2012 Full Year Results.

35. http://www.iab.net/about_the_iab/recent _press_releases/press_release_archive /press_release/pr-020226_adportfolio

36. Tessa Wegert, "Consumers Unhappy with Web Site Simply Go Away," www.Center forMediaResearch.com, August 23, 2005, pp. 1–2.

37. Steven M. Edwards, Hairong Li, and Joo-Hyun Lee, "Forced Exposure and Psychological Reactance: Antecedents and Consequences of the Perceived Intrusiveness of Pop-Up Ads," *Journal of Advertising, 31* (3), Fall 2002, pp. 83–95.

38. http://www.google.com/adwords; http:// www.google.com/adsense

39. Jessica E. Vascellaro, "Yahoo Set to Aid Marketers with New Online Ad Tools," *The Globe and Mail*, February 2009, p. B12.

40. "Getting Search Right," *Marketing Magazine*, March 1, 2010.

41. Carey Toane, "Cyber," *Strategy*, June 2009, p. 49.

42. Chris Powell, "Broadband or Bust," *Marketing Magazine*, June 19, 2006.

43. Chris Powell, "Online TV Accounts for 1.6% of Canadian TV Ad Spend: Study," *Marketing Magazine*, April 8, 2009.

44. Alicia Androich, "The Future is Data," *Marketing Magazine*, August 13, 2012, p. 14.

45. Daniel M. Haygood, "A Status Report on Podcast Advertising," *Journal of Advertising Research, 47* (4), December 2007, pp. 518–23.

46. http://www.comscore.com/Insights /Presentations_and_Whitepapers/2013/2013 _Canada_Digital_Future_in_Focuscomscore

47. IAB Internet Advertising Revenue Report, 2012 Full Year Results.

48. Gary Schwartz, "Mobile Marketing," *Marketing Magazine*, July 14, 2003.

49. Ibid.

50. Chris Daniels, "Rewards for the Mobile Masses," *Marketing Magazine*, August 29, 2011, pp. 51–53.

51. Grant Buckler, "From Your Smartphone to the Big Screen," *The Globe and Mail*, November 23, 2011, p. B18.

52. Daniels, "Rewards for the Mobile Masses."

53. Jeromy Lloyd, "Txting Out an SOS," *Marketing Magazine*, May 18, 2009.

54. Jacque Natel and Yasha Sekhavat, "The Impact of SMS Advertising on Members of a Virtual Community," *Journal of Advertising Research, 48* (3), September 2008, pp. 363–74.

55. Simon Houpt, "Why Click When You Can Scan Your Way to Ad Messages?" *The Globe and Mail*, October 2009, p. B8.

56. Ivor Tossell, "Wave of the Future, or Just Annoying?" *The Globe and Mail*, August 16, 2011, p. L2.

57. Hollie Shaw, "Wind Mobile–MyScreen Partnership Gives Customers Rewards and Discounts," *National Post*, January 7, 2011, p. FP12.

58. http://cwta.ca/wordpress/wp-content /uploads/2011/08/CWTA-2012Consumer Attitudes1.pdf

59. Jeromy Lloyd, "Gone Mobile," *Marketing Magazine*, March 1, 2010.

60. "Mobile Applications: The Next Big Thing in Mobile Marketing?" http://www.mobi adnews.com/?p=3172

61. http://cwta.ca/wordpress/wp-content /uploads/2011/08/CWTA-2012Consumer Attitudes1.pdf

62. Jonathan Paul, "It's Still All About Location, Location, Location," *Strategy*, February 1, 2011, p. 20.

63. Simon Houpt, "It's All Fun and Games— Until Someone Bonds with a Brand," *The Globe and Mail*, January 2, 2011, p. B1.

64. Matt Semansky, "Location-based Marketing for the Rest of Us," *Marketing Magazine*, August 1, 2011, pp. 16–21.

65. Alicia Androich, "Ready to Get More Social with Your TV?" *Marketing Magazine*, April 12, 2013.

66. Chris Daniels, "Tiny Screen, Huge Potential," *Marketing Magazine*, May 2006.

67. Joe Plummer, Steve Rappaport, Taddy Hall, Robert Barocci, *The Online Advertising Playbook, 2007* (John Wiley & Sons, Hoboken, NJ).

68. Andreas M. Kaplan and Michael Haenlein, "Users of the World, Unite! The Challenges and Opportunities of Social Media," *Business Horizons*, 2010, 53, pp. 59–68.

69. Daniel G. Muntinga, Marjolein Moorman, and Edith G. Smit, "Introducing COBRAs: Exploring Motivations for Brand-Related Social Media Use," *International Journal of Advertising, 30* (1), 2011, pp. 13–46.

70. Simon Houpt, "The Tweet Taste of Success," *The Globe and Mail*, September 6, 2012, p. B9.

71. https://www.mtm-otm.ca/files/Reports /Social%20Networking%20-%20 Anglophones-cli.pdf

72. Kaplan and Haenlein, "Users of the World, Unite!"

73. http://fbrep.com//SMB/Pages_Product _Guide.pdf

74. David Ebner, "EA Makes Bet on Social Media Game," *The Globe and Mail*, November 2009, p. B6.

75. https://business.twitter.com

76. Alicia Androich, "Twitter Canada Talks Targeting, Engagement at Official Launch," *Marketing Magazine*, June 14, 2013.

77. https://business.twitter.com

78. http://searchenginewatch.com/article /2190651/Twitter-Advertising-Guide

79. Matt Hartley, "The Revolution Will Be Monetized," *National Post*, March 19, 2011, p. FP1; Christina Rexrode, "How Twitter Changed #endorsements," *The Globe and Mail*, November 4, 2009, p. L2.

80. "Where the Party?" *Marketing Magazine*, October 10, 2011, p. 31.

81. Kristin Laird, "The Very Necessary Twitter Guide for Canadian Marketers," *Marketing Magazine*, October 10, 2011, pp. 24–27.

82. Kristin Laird, "Accelerating Social Media," *Marketing Magazine*, October 10, 2011, pp. 28–29.

83. "Who Should Own a Client's Social Media Duties?" *Marketing Magazine*, February 28, 2011, pp. 30–31.

84. Kristin Laird, "Chasing Koodo's Gingerbread Man," *Marketing Magazine*, December 10, 2009.

85. Simon Houpt, "What Makes a Video Go Viral?" *The Globe and Mail*, May 26, 2011.

86. Melita Kuburas, "Updating Molson's Social Media Status," *Strategy*, May 1, 2009, p. 25.

87. Susan Krashinsky, "Lululemon Ad Pokes Fun at Own Customers—and Goes Viral," *The Globe and Mail*, January 13, 2012, p. B5.

88. Ibid.

89. Houpt, "What Makes a Video Go Viral?"

90. http://www.blogto.com/blogto-mediakit.pdf

91. Chris Koentges, "The Hypest of the Hyperlocal," *Marketing Magazine*, June 4, 2012, pp. 21–22.

92. Michelle Warren, "Blogger Knows Best," *Marketing Magazine*, April 6, 2009.

93. Simon Houpt, "For Popular Bloggers, Some Things Come for Free," *The Globe and Mail*, October 9, 2009, p. B5.

94. Sara Perry, "Opinions Are My Own and the Sponsoring Brand's," *Marketing Magazine*, August 29, 2012, p. 19.

95. Angela Hickman, "In Blogs They Trust," *National Post*, August 20, 2011, p. WP5.

96. http://en.wikipedia.org/wiki/Wikipedia :Advertisements

97. https://s3.amazonaws.com/answ-img /AnswersMediaKit_20130201.pdf

98. Kristin Laird, "Pinterest Rate," *Marketing Magazine*, April 9, 2012, pp. 8–10.

99. http://business.pinterest.com/case-study -sephora/

100. Houpt, "It's All Fun and Games—Until Someone Bonds with a Brand."

101. Paul, "It's Still All about Location, Location, Location."

102. Subdh Bhat, Michael Bevans, and Sanjit Sengupta, "Measuring Users' Web Activity to Evaluate and Enhance Advertising Effectiveness," *Journal of Advertising, 31* (3), Fall 2002, pp. 97–106.

103. Alexa Bezjian-Avery, "New Media Interactive Advertising vs. Traditional Advertising," *Journal of Advertising Research, 38* (4), August 1998, pp. 23–32; Qimel Chen and William D. Wells, "Attitude toward the Site," *Journal of Advertising Research, 39* (5), September–October 1999, pp. 27–38; Kim Bartel Sheehan and Sally J. McMillan, "Response Variation in E-Mail Surveys," *Journal of Advertising Research, 39* (4), July–August 1999, pp. 45–54; John Eighmey, "Profiling User Responses to Commercial Websites," *Journal of Advertising Research, 37* (3), May–June 1997, p. 66.

104. "Measurement Guidelines and Measurement Certification," www.iab.net, 2006.

105. Kanter Media-Canadian Online Advertising Trends Analysis, March 2012.

106. Melita Kuburas and Carey Toane, "Ben & Jerry's," *Strategy,* June 8, 2009, p. 7.

107. Katie Bailey, "Banff Goes Nuts with Crasher Squirrel," *Strategy,* October 2009, p. 9.

108. Matt Semansky, "Silk Seeks Smiles for New Campaign," *Marketing Magazine,* April 21, 2009.

109. Hollie Shaw, "Doing Digital Right," *National Post,* May 8, 2009, p. FP9.

110. Anonymous, "Internet Marketing: Daunting," *National Post,* November 11, 2009, p. FP3.

111. Sung-Joon Yoon and Joo-Ho Kim, "Is the Internet More Effective Than Traditional Media? Factors Affecting the Choice of Media," *Journal of Advertising Research, 41* (6), November–December 2001, pp. 53–60.

112. Katherine Gallagher, K. Dale Foster, and Jeffrey Parsons, "The Medium Is Not the Message: Advertising Effectiveness and Content Evaluation in Print and on the Web," *Journal of Advertising Research, 41* (4), July–August 2001, pp. 57–70; Katherine Gallagher, Jeffrey Parsons, and K. Dale Foster, "A Tale of Two Studies: Replicating 'Advertising Effectiveness and Content Evaluation in Print and on the Web,'" *Journal of Advertising Research, 41* (4), July–August 2001, pp. 71–81.

113. Johanna S. Ilfeld and Russell S. Winer, "Generating Website Traffic," *Journal of Advertising Research, 42* (5), September–October 2002, pp. 49–61.

114. Yumiin Chang and Esther Thorson, "Television and Web Advertising Synergies," *Journal of Advertising, 33* (2), Summer 2004, pp. 75–84.

115. Ali M. Kanso and Richard Alan Nelson, "Internet and Magazine Advertising: Integrated Partnerships or Not?" *Journal of Advertising Research, 44* (4), December 2004, pp. 317–26.

116. Jonathan Paul, "*The Score* Draft Pick: Gillette," *Strategy,* October 2009, p. 8.

117. Robert Davis and Laszlo Sajtos, "Measuring Consumer Interactivity in Response to Campaigns Coupling Mobile and Television Media," *Journal of Advertising Research, 48* (3), September 2008; Randolph J. Trappey III and Arch G. Woodside, "Consumer Responses to Interactive Advertising Campaigns Coupling Short-Message-Service Direct Marketing and TV Commercials," *Journal of Advertising Research, 45* (4), December 2005, pp. 382–401.

CHAPTER EIGHTEEN

1. "CRTC Keeps Hands Off New Media," *Calgary Sun,* June 5, 2009.

2. Chris Powell, "The Inventory Debate," *Marketing Magazine,* January 26, 2004.

3. Brenda Pritchard and Susan Vogt, *Advertising and Marketing Law in Canada* (LexisNexis, Butterworths, 2006).

4. A Guide to the Amendments of the *Competition Act,* Competition Bureau Canada, April 22, 2009.

5. Hollie Shaw, "Bogus Ads," *National Post,* May 22, 2009, p. FP12.

6. Jean-Francois Ouellet, "Vachon's Igor Crossed the Line in Quebec," *National Post,* March 10, 2009, p. FP13.

7. Canadian Code of Advertising Standards Interpretation Guidelines, http://www .adstandards.com/en/ASCLibrary /interpretationGuidelines.pdf

8. http://www.adstandards.com/en/childrens initiative

9. http://www.adstandards.com/en/childrens initiative/2011ComplianceReport.pdf

10. Jeremy Lloyd, "Hot Water," *Marketing Magazine,* April 20, 2009.

11. Jeremy Lloyd, "Shell Advertorials Spurn Complaint to Ad Standards Council," *Marketing Magazine,* February 11, 2010.

12. Matt Semansky, "Bell Ignores ASC Ruling," *Marketing Magazine,* February 23, 2009.

13. http://adstandards.com/en/standards /complaints_report/2001ascReportEn.pdf, accessed December 12, 2007.

14. http://www.adstandards.com/en/-standards /adComplaintsReports.asp?periodquarter =1&periodyear=2007, accessed December 12, 2007.

15. David Brown, "Kia Gets the Goat," *Marketing Magazine,* February 27, 2007.

16. http://www.adstandards.com/en/Standards /adComplaintsReports.asp?periodquarter =2&periodyear=2007

17. http://www.adstandards.com/en/standards /adComplaintsReports.asp?periodquarter =2&periodyear=2008

18. Ibid.

19. Eric N. Berkowitz, Roger A. Kerin, Steven W. Hartley, William Rudedius, et al., *Marketing,* 5th ed. (Burr Ridge, IL: Irwin/McGraw-Hill, 1997), p. 102.

20. Stephanie O'Donohoe, "Attitudes to Advertising: A Review of British and American Research," *International Journal of Advertising, 14* (3), 1995, pp. 245–61.

21. Banwari Mittal, "Public Assessment of TV Advertising: Faint Praise and Harsh Criticism," *Journal of Advertising Research, 34* (1), January–February 1994, pp. 35–53.

22. Sharon Shavitt, Pamela Lowery, and James Haefner, "Public Attitudes toward Advertising; More Favorable Than You Might Think," *Journal of Advertising Research, 38* (4), July/August 1998, pp. 7–22.

23. Gita Venkataramini Johar, "Consumer Involvement and Deception from Implied Advertising Claims," *Journal of Marketing Research, 32* (3), August 1995, pp. 267–79; J. Edward Russo, Barbara L. Metcalf, and Debra Stephens, "Identifying Misleading Advertising," *Journal of Consumer Research, 8* (2), September 1981, pp. 119–31.

24. Ivan L. Preston, *The Great American Blow-Up: Puffery in Advertising and Selling* (Madison: University of Wisconsin Press, 1975), p. 3.

25. Bruce Dowbiggin, "TV Beer Battle Comes to a Head," *The Globe and Mail,* May 18, 2012, p. S5.

26. Shelby D. Hunt, "Informational vs. Persuasive Advertising: An Appraisal," *Journal of Advertising, 5* (3), Summer 1976, pp. 5–8.

27. Mittal, "Public Assessment of TV Advertising: Faint Praise and Harsh Criticism"; J. C. Andrews, "The Dimensionality of Beliefs toward Advertising in General," *Journal of Advertising, 18* (1), 1989, pp. 26–35; Shavitt, Lowery, and Haefner, "Public Attitudes toward Advertising; More Favorable Than You Might Think."

28. David A. Aaker and Donald E. Bruzzone, "Causes of Irritation in Advertising," *Journal of Marketing, 13* (1), Spring 1985, pp. 47–57.

29. Stephen A. Greyser, "Irritation in Advertising," *Journal of Advertising Research, 13* (1), February 1973, pp. 3–10.

30. Kenyon Wallace, "TTC Flirts with Online Adulterers," *National Post,* December 11, 2009, p. A1; Kenyon Wallace, "Pro-adultery Agency Loses TTC Ad Bid," *National Post,* December 12, 2009, p. A21.

31. Chris Powell, "Astral Campaign Gives Radio Hope," *Marketing Magazine,* March 5, 2009; "Toronto Unhappy About Virgin Suicides," *Marketing Magazine,* April 17, 2009; Jeff Gray, "Suicide Ad Irks Transit Authority," *The Globe and Mail,* April 17, 2009, p. A3.

32. For an interesting analysis of an interpretation of this ad from a literary theory perspective see Aaron C. Ahuvia, "Social Criticism of Advertising: On the Role of Literary Theory and the Use of Data," *Journal of Advertising, 27* (1), Spring 1998, pp. 143–62.

33. Tim Nudd, "Does Sex Really Sell?" *Adweek,* October 17, 2005, pp. 14–17.

34. James B. Arndorfer, "Skyy Hit the Limit with Racy Ad: Critics," *Advertising Age,* February 7, 2005, p. 6.

35. Scott Ward, Daniel B. Wackman, and Ellen Wartella, *How Children Learn to Buy: The Development of Consumer Information Processing Skills* (Beverly Hills, CA: Sage, 1979).

36. Thomas S. Robertson and John R. Rossiter, "Children and Commercial Persuasion: An Attribution Theory Analysis," *Journal of Consumer Research, 1* (1), June 1974, pp. 13–20; Scott Ward and Daniel B. Wackman, "Children's Information Processing of Television Advertising," in *New Models for Communications Research,* eds. G. Kline and P. Clark (Beverly Hills, CA: Sage, 1974), pp. 81–119.

37. Merrie Brucks, Gary M. Armstrong, and Marvin E. Goldberg, "Children's Use of Cognitive Defenses against Television Advertising: A Cognitive Response Approach," *Journal of Consumer Research, 14* (4), March 1988, pp. 471–82.

38. For a discussion on consumer socialization, see Scott Ward, "Consumer Socialization," *Journal of Consumer Research, 1* (2), September 1974, pp. 1–14.

39. Tamara F. Mangleburg and Terry Bristol, "Socialization and Adolescents' Skepticism

toward Advertising," *Journal of Advertising, 27* (3), Fall 1998, pp. 11–21.

40. Robert E. Hite and Randy Eck, "Advertising to Children: Attitudes of Business vs. Consumers," *Journal of Advertising Research, 27* (5), October/ November 1987, pp. 40–53; Ann D. Walsh, Russell N. Laczniak, and Les Carlson, "Mother's Preferences for Regulating Children's Television," *Journal of Advertising, 27* (3), Fall 1998, pp. 23–36.

41. Raymond A. Bauer and Stephen A. Greyser, "The Dialogue That Never Happens," *Harvard Business Review,* January/February 1969, pp. 122–28.

42. Morris B. Holbrook, "Mirror Mirror On the Wall, What's Unfair in the Reflections on Advertising," *Journal of Marketing, 5* (3), July 1987, pp. 95–103; Theodore Levitt, "The Morality of Advertising," *Harvard Business Review,* July/August 1970, pp. 84–92.

43. Stephen Fox, *The Mirror Makers: A History of American Advertising and Its Creators* (New York: Morrow, 1984), p. 330.

44. Richard W. Pollay, "The Distorted Mirror: Reflections on the Unintended Consequences of Advertising," *Journal of Marketing, 50* (2), April 1986, p. 33.

45. Jules Backman, "Is Advertising Wasteful?" *Journal of Marketing, 32* (1), January 1968, pp. 2–8.

46. Hunt, "Informational vs. Persuasive Advertising."

47. Ibid., p. 6.

48. Alice E. Courtney and Thomas W. Whipple, *Sex Stereotyping in Advertising* (Lexington, MA: Lexington Books, 1984).

49. Daniel J. Brett and Joanne Cantor, "The Portrayal of Men and Women in U.S. Television Commercials: A Recent Content Analysis and Trends of 15 Years," *Sex Roles, 18* (9/10), 1998, pp. 595–608; John B. Ford and Michael La Tour, "Contemporary Perspectives of Female Role Portrayals in Advertising," *Journal of Current Issues and Research in Advertising, 28* (1), Spring 1996, pp. 81–93.

50. Beverly A. Browne, "Gender Stereotypes in Advertising on Children's Television in the 1990s: A Cross-National Analysis," *Journal of Advertising, 27* (1), Spring 1998, pp. 83–96.

51. Richard H. Kolbe, "Gender Roles in Children's Advertising: A Longitudinal Content Analysis," in *Current Issues and Research in Advertising,* ed. James H. Leigh and Claude R. Martin, Jr. (Ann Arbor: University of Michigan, 1990), pp. 197–206.

52. Steven M. Kates and Glenda Shaw-Garlock, "The Ever Entangling Web: A Study of Ideologies and Discourses in Advertising

to Women," *Journal of Advertising, 28* (2), Summer 1999, pp. 33–49.

53. Basil Englis, Michael Solomon, and Richard Ashmore, "Beauty before the Eyes of Beholders: The Cultural Encoding of Beauty Types in Magazine Advertising and Music Television," *Journal of Advertising, 23* (2), June 1994, pp. 49–64.

54. Hollie Shaw, "Axe Kicks It Up a Notch," *National Post,* September 9, 2011, p. FP12.

55. www.adstandards.com/en/consumer complaints/2012adcomplaintsreport.pdf

56. Nathalie Atkinson, "Picture-Perfect Manipulation," *National Post,* October 10, 2009, p. A3.

57. Kristin Laird, "Loblaw Stands by Sexy Joe Fresh Underwear Flyer," *Marketing Magazine,* April 7, 2009; Kelly Egan, "Sexualized Ads Signal Disturbing Trend," *Ottawa Citizen,* April 3, 2009.

58. Jeromy Lloyd, "Shell Advertorials Spurn Complaint to Ad Standards Canada," *Marketing Magazine,* February 11, 2010.

59. Susan Krashinsky, "You've Come a Long Way, Dad," *The Globe and Mail,* May 4, 2012, p. B7; Seth Stevenson, "The Reign of The Doltish Dad," *National Post,* March 29, 2012, p. A18.

60. James Stearns, Lynette S. Unger, and Steven G. Luebkeman, "The Portrayal of Blacks in Magazine and Television Advertising," in *AMA Educator's Proceedings,* eds. Susan P. Douglas and Michael R. Solomon (Chicago: American Marketing Association, 1987).

61. Robert E. Wilkes and Humberto Valencia, "Hispanics and Blacks in Television Commercials," *Journal of Advertising, 18* (1), 1989, pp. 19–26.

62. Julia Bristor, Renee Gravois Lee, and Michelle Hunt, "Race and Ideology: African American Images in Television Advertising," *Journal of Public Policy and Marketing, 14* (1), Spring 1995, pp. 48–59.

63. Corliss Green, "Ethnic Evaluations of Advertising: Interaction Effects of Strength of Ethnic Identification, Media Placement, and Degree of Racial Composition," *Journal of Advertising, 28* (1), Spring 1999, pp. 49–64.

64. Charles R. Taylor and Barbara B. Stern, "Asian-Americans: Television Advertising and the 'Model Minority' Stereotype," *Journal of Advertising, 26* (2), Summer 1997, pp. 47–61.

65. Lou Puim, "How Wal-Mart Learned Diversity," *Marketing Magazine,* January 23, 2006.

66. Jef I. Richards and John H. Murphy, II, "Economic Censorship and Free Speech: The Circle of Communication between Advertisers, Media and Consumers," *Journal*

of Current Issues and Research in Advertising, *18* (1), Spring 1996, pp. 21–33.

67. Lawrence C. Soley and Robert L. Craig, "Advertising Pressure on Newspapers: A Survey," *Journal of Advertising,* December 1992, pp. 1–10.

68. Randy W. Elder, Ruth A. Shults, David A. Sleet, James L. Nichols, Robert S. Thompson, and Warda Rajab, "Effectiveness of Mass Media Campaigns for Reducing Drinking and Driving and Alcohol-Involved Crashes," *American Journal of Preventative Medicine, 27* (1), July 2004, pp. 57–65.

69. Kristin Laird, "LCBO Is Deflating Elephants," *Marketing Magazine,* December 9, 2009.

70. Hollie Shaw, "Campaign Brings Home Hard Reality about Health Care," *National Post,* January 28, 2011, p. FP6.

71. Jeromy Lloyd, "A Prize at What Price?" *Marketing Magazine,* September 12, 2011, pp. 38–39; David Brown, "The Ethics Talk," *Marketing Magazine,* September 12, 2011, p. 27.

72. For a discussion of monopolies in the cereal industry, see Paul N. Bloom, "The Cereal Industry: Monopolists or Super Marketers?" *MSU Business Topics,* Summer 1978, pp. 41–49.

73. Lester G. Telser, "Advertising and Competition," *Journal of Political Economy,* December 1964, pp. 537–62.

74. Robert D. Buzzell, Bradley T. Gale, and Ralph G. M. Sultan, "Market Share—A Key to Profitability," *Harvard Business Review,* January/February 1975, pp. 97–106.

75. Robert D. Buzzell and Paul W. Farris, *Advertising Cost in Consumer Goods Industries,* Marketing Science Institute, Report No. 76, August 1976, p. 111; Paul W. Farris and David J. Reibstein, "How Prices, Ad Expenditures, and Profits Are Linked," *Harvard Business Review,* November/ December 1979, pp. 173–84.

76. Paul W. Farris and Mark S. Albion, "The Impact of Advertising on the Price of Consumer Products," *Journal of Marketing, 44* (3), Summer 1980, pp. 17–35.

77. Lee Benham, "The Effect of Advertising on the Price of Eyeglasses," *Journal of Law and Economics, 15* (October 1972), pp. 337–52.

78. Robert L. Steiner, "Does Advertising Lower Consumer Price?" *Journal of Marketing, 37* (4), October 1973, pp. 19–26.

79. James M. Ferguson, "Comments On 'The Impact of Advertising on the Price of Consumer Products'," *Journal of Marketing, 46* (1), Winter 1982, pp. 102–05.

80. Farris and Albion, "The Impact of Advertising."

Credits and Acknowledgements

CHAPTER 1

p. 2: © Streetka2004/Dreamstime.com/ GetStock.com; p. 4: Used with permission of AB World Foods; p. 5: Courtesy of the Movado Group; p. 6: Courtesy of Joe's Jeans; p. 7 (top): AP/Wide World Photos/PR Newswire; p. 7 (bottom): Courtesy of Maserati North America and Ross Design; p. 8: Used by permission of Rogers Media; p. 10: Courtesy of GE and AMV BBDO; p. 11: Used with permission of Dole Foods of Canada Limited; p. 12: Used with permission of Jackson Triggs Estate Wines and Vincor; p. 13 (top): Courtesy of Under Armour Inc.; p. 13 (bottom): Courtesy of Naked Juice; p. 14: Courtesy of National Geographic Society; p. 16: © John Hryniuk; p. 20: Used with permission of Maple Lodge Farms Ltd. Created by Riddoch Communications, Toronto, ON; p. 23: © Nathan Danette/The Canadian Press; p. 25 (top): Starbucks Coffee Company; p. 25 (bottom): www.tourismkelowna.com; p. 26: Copyright © 2010 Heart and Stroke Foundation.

CHAPTER 2

p. 32: © Deborah Baic/Globe and Mail/The Canadian Press; p. 35: © Copyright Mentus; p. 36 (top): Courtesy of TAG Heuer; p. 36 (bottom): Courtesy of the Procter & Gamble Company; p. 38: © Hupeng/Dreamstime.com/ GetStock.com; p. 46: Used with permission of Rethink Canada; p. 47: © Initiative; p. 48: © Roberto Herrett/Alamy; p. 49: Courtesy of Protocol Integrated Direct Marketing; p. 50: Courtesy of AvenueSocial.

CHAPTER 3

p. 54: © Stefanolunardi/Dreamstime.com/ GetStock.com; p. 57 (top): Courtesy of Tommy Bahama; p. 57 (bottom left): Used with permission of The Gillette Company; p. 57 (bottom right): © Moen Incorporated; p. 58 (left): © Columbia Sportswear Company; p. 58 (right): The PORSCHE CREST, PORSCHE 911 and the distinctive shape of the PORSCHE 911 automobile are registered trademarks in the United States of America. Dr. Ing. H.c.F. Porsche AG. Used with permission of Porsche Cars North America, Inc. Copyrighted by Porsche Cars North America, Inc. Photographer: Erik Chmil; p. 60: Courtesy of Tropicana; p. 61: Used with permission of Procter & Gamble; p. 62: Used by permission of photographer Angus MacPherson and Kruger Products L.P.; p. 63: The adidas word mark, "The Globe," the NEO logo, and the "3-stripes" are registered marks of the adidas Group used with permission; p. 64: © PRNewsFoto/Levi Strauss & Co/ AP Photos; p. 66 (top): © Sun-Rype Products Ltd.; p. 66 (bottom): Used by permission of Plan Canada; p. 67: Used by permission of Ferrero; p. 69: © Arne9001/Dreamstime.com/

GetStock.com; p. 71: © Maybelline Canada. © All rights reserved. Any reproduction, even partial, is forbidden without the express written authorization of Maybelline Canada; p. 73: © PRNewsFoto/Jaguar/AP Photos; p. 74: © New York Fries; p. 75 (left): Courtesy of P&G; p. 75 (right): Courtesy of P&G; p. 76: NICODERM®, CQ®, COMMITTED QUITTERS® and design, SmartControl TM, Shield Trade Dress/Designs are trademarks owned by and/or licensed to GlaxoSmithKline; p. 77 (top): Courtesy of Grolsch Canada; p. 77 (bottom): Canadian Tourism Commission.

CHAPTER 4

p. 82: Used by permission of Subaru Canada; p. 85: © Nestlé Canada Inc.; p. 86: Courtesy of Coach, Inc.; p. 87 (top): Courtesy of Rolex; p. 87 (bottom): © Yield Branding; p. 88: Used with permission of HMWV Advertising; p. 89: Photo courtesy of Molson Coors Canada; p. 91: Vistakon ®, Division of Johnson & Johnson Vision Care, Inc. Used by permission of copyright owner; p. 92: Courtesy of Sony Corporation of America; p. 93 (top): Courtesy of Acura; p. 93 (bottom): Used with permission of VISA, USA. Photography © Karen Moscowitz/Getty Images; p. 94: Courtesy H.J. Heinz Company LLP. Used with permission; p. 95: © Google/Rex Features/The Canadian Press; p. 97 (top): Used with permission of The Procter & Gamble Company; p. 97 (bottom): Courtesy of Alberto-Culver Company; p. 99: © McCormick & Company, Inc.; p. 100 (top): © PRNewsFoto/Elizabeth Arden, Inc./AP Photos; p. 100 (bottom): © Eveready Battery Company, Inc. Printed with permission.

CHAPTER 5

p. 108: © Justaman/Dreamstime.com/GetStock. com; p. 110: © Copyright Royal Bank of Canada; p. 111: Courtesy of Michelin North America, Inc.; p. 113: © Markhunt/Dreamstime. com/GetStock.com; p. 114: Used with permission of Unilever Canada Inc.; p. 115: © Photog2112/Dreamstime.com/GetStock.com; p. 116: Used with permission of Procter & Gamble Company; p. 117: © Westend61 GmbH/Alamy; p. 119: Used by permission of Chocolaterie Guylian NV; p. 120: Used with permission from Labatt's Canada; p. 121: Used by permission of Air Transat; p. 122 (top): © 2008 Kimberly-Clark Worldwide, Inc.; p. 122 (bottom): Used with permission of Unilever Canada Inc.; p. 123 (top): Used with permission of Procter & Gamble Company; p. 123 (bottom): Used with permission of Nestlé Waters Canada; p. 124: Courtesy of LG Electronics; p. 125 (top): © Combat Sports Group; p. 125 (bottom): Used with permission from the Almond Board of California; p. 127 (top): Courtesy AP Photo/PR

Newswire; p. 127 (bottom): Saputo Cheese G.P.; p. 128 (top): PR Newswire/Nike/AP Photos; p. 128 (bottom): Courtesy of Roots Canada; p. 129 (top): © 2011 Hyundai Sonata; p. 129 (bottom): With permission from The Beef Information Centre; p. 130: © Nestlé Canada Inc.

CHAPTER 6

p. 134: © Subbotina/Dreamstime.com/GetStock. com; p. 137 (top): PRNewsFoto/Mercedes-Benz USA/AP Photos; p. 137 (bottom): Used with permission of Porter Airlines Inc.; p. 139: The Coca-Cola Company; p. 142: Courtesy of Campbell Soup Company; p. 143: Photo courtesy of Molson Coors Canada; p. 144: Used with permission of Unilever Canada Inc.; p. 145 (top): Courtesy of Pepsi-Cola Company; p. 145 (bottom): Courtesy of Intuit ®; p. 146 (top): Used with permission of VIA Rail Canada Inc.; p. 146 (bottom): Courtesy of Pepsi-Cola Company; p. 147 (top): © Newscom Photos; p. 147 (bottom left): Used with permission of Unilever; p. 147 (bottom right): © PRNewsFoto/ Burt's Bees/AP Photos; p. 148 (top): Courtesy of DC Shoes; p. 148 (bottom): Courtesy of Unilever; p. 149: © AugustSnow/Alamy; p. 150: Used by permission of Kruger Products L.P.; p. 151 (top): Mott's Fruitsations is a trademark of Mott's LLP., used with permission. All rights reserved; p. 151 (bottom): Courtesy of Kyocera; p. 153 (top): Courtesy of WD-40 Company; p. 153 (bottom): Used with permission of Nestlé Canada; p. 154: Courtesy of Verticle Marketing; p. 156 (top): © Goldenkb/Dreamstime.com/ GetStock.com; p. 156 (bottom): Used by permission of Kruger Products L.P.; p. 157 (top): Photo courtesy of Molson Coors Canada; p. 157 (bottom): © Sam D'Cruz, www.samd cruzphotography.com; p. 158 (top): Used with permission of Unilever Canada Inc.; p. 158 (bottom): Used by permission of Subaru Canada; p. 159 (top): © Chris Young/The Canadian Press; p. 159 (bottom): © Zbigniew Tomaszewski/ Alamy; p. 160 (top): © Ivansabo/Dreamstime. com; p. 160 (bottom left): Canadian Tourism Commission; p. 160 (bottom right): Courtesy of McNeil Consumer Healthcare, division of Johnson & Johnson Inc.; p. 161 (top): Used with permission from Tata Global Beverages; p. 161 (bottom): Used with permission of Canadian Tire Corporation.

CHAPTER 7

p. 166: Red Urban Canada. Newspaper double page spread; p. 169: Courtesy of BMW of North America; p. 170 (top): Courtesy of V & S Vin and Spirit AB. Imported by the Absolut Spirits Co., New York, NY; p. 170 (bottom): Used by permission of Knowledge Adventure; p. 172: Used by permission of Telus Communications Company; p. 173: PR Newswire/AP Photos;

Name and Company Index

Subject Index